JAMES STOKES LECTURESHIP ON POLITICS

EW YORK UNIVERSITY · STOKES FOUNDATION

THE PRESIDENT: OFFICE
AND POWERS

1787-1948

THE PRESIDENT
OFFICE AND POWERS
1787-1948

History and Analysis of
Practice and Opinion

BY

EDWARD S. CORWIN

4th ed. 1957 also in stock.

"*We elect a king for four years, and give him absolute power within certain limits, which after all he can interpret for himself.*"
— *Secretary of State Seward*

NEW YORK UNIVERSITY PRESS
WASHINGTON SQUARE · NEW YORK

London: Geoffrey Cumberlege · Oxford University Press

FIRST EDITION, 1940
SECOND EDITION (REVISED), 1941
THIRD EDITION (REVISED), 1948

131925

c

Printed in the United States of America
George Grady Press · New York

TO

M. S. C.

MY MOST ENCOURAGING
AND
CONSTRUCTIVE CRITIC

PREFACE

THE original edition of this treatise appeared in 1940. In a second edition the following year some errors of the previous printing were corrected and note was taken of a few more recent happenings, but the pagination was not disturbed. The purpose of the present edition is to bring the subject up to date, and in view of all that has happened to and through the Presidency since 1940, this has been no light task. Much of the text has been rewritten. In some instances matter has been shifted from one chapter to another, and in the case of Chapters V and VI the order of treatment has been reversed. Chapters III to VI inclusive contain considerable new matter, the last being almost entirely new. The note material has also been carefully revised; out-of-date material has been cast aside, and much fresh material introduced. Altogether, the new edition is about 80 pages longer than the original.

The general character of the work remains nevertheless the same. It is primarily a study in American public law. The approach is partly historical, partly analytical and critical. The central theme is the development and contemporary status of presidential power and of the presidential office under the Constitution. At the same time, the personal and political aspects of the subject have not been ignored. For American constitutional law, far from being a closed system, often bristles with alternatives; and especially is this true of the segment of it with which these pages are concerned. Consequently, it often becomes pertinent to raise the question as to which of two or more available theories of the Constitution is to be preferred on grounds of policy. Indeed, for reasons which the reader will discover for himself, it is only rarely that previous practice or agreed doctrine, either one, can be dogmatically asserted to have foreclosed all choice between the logical alternatives which the record of discussion concerning the constitutional position and powers of the President discloses. Likewise, I have felt free to comment on the personal traits of individual Presidents when they seemed to me to have materially affected the development of the office and its powers. For the Presidency unfolds a daily drama of the reciprocal interplay of human character and legal concepts which no other office on earth can quite emulate.

For the convenience of my readers, I list here some of the topics which events since 1940 have thrust into these pages for the first time or have given increased prominence. I confine my references to the text, trusting the reader to look up the accompanying notes.

In Chapter II, consideration is given the Joint Resolution of March 24, 1947, proposing an amendment to the Constitution to restrict reëligibility to the Presidency (pp. 46–49); also the Act of July 18, 1947, establishing a new order of succession to the Presidency when both President and Vice-President shall have disappeared from the scene (pp. 67–71).

In Chapter III, President Truman's "Loyalty Order" of March 21, 1947, and the controversy, still unsettled, between the President and the House over the question of the immunity of executive personnel from congressional inquiry as to their loyalty are treated (pp. 121–145).

In Chapter IV, presidential intervention in industrial disputes and certain novel aspects of the use of injunctions in such disputes are dealt with (pp. 186–192).

In Chapter V, attention is given, in the light of events between 1938 and Pearl Harbor, to the President's initiative in the field of foreign relations vis à vis Congress's "power to declare war"; to the declension of the role of formal treaty-making in face of the "executive agreement" device; and to the enlarged role of Congress in the foreign-relations field under the United Nations

Participation Act of December 20, 1945 (pp. 235–272). Some of
these paragraphs are taken, with the kind permission of Princeton
University Press, from my chapter in *The Second Chance, America and the Peace* (1944).

Chapter VI, which deals with the vastly expanded role of
the President as "Commander-in-Chief in time of war," as illustrated by the late President Roosevelt's exercise of the office in
World War II, is almost completely new matter so far as the
theme of this volume is concerned. Much of this new matter is
drawn from my *Total War and the Constitution* (1947), with
the obliging consent of the University of Michigan and Alfred
A. Knopf, Inc.

Finally in Chapter VII, I deal with some recent phases of the
veto power (pp. 339–345); and pose the question whether the
Presidency is today a potential matrix of dictatorship, and discuss
in that connection ways and means of bringing about closer and
more harmonious relations between President and Congress (pp.
353–364). For I agree heartily with Professor Laski's dictum in
his *The American Presidency* that the relationship between the
two departments is one that "cries to heaven for readjustment."
To this end I suggested in the original edition of this work a new
type of Cabinet, and I offer a variation of that suggestion in the
present edition, one which, by facilitating the legislative process,
seems to me calculated to minimize the need for autocratic
courses under the pressure of emergency conditions.

While this work is based throughout upon a direct examination of firsthand materials, the debates of the Philadelphia Convention, debates in Congress, acts of Congress, presidential
messages and papers, controversial writings, and press despatches,
yet I have often profited by the guidance afforded by other writers
in the field, Thach, Binkley, Horwill, Berdahl, Randall, Small,
Warren, Laski, Herring. Professor Caleb Perry Patterson's in-

teresting volume on *Presidential Government in the United States* came out too late to be of use to me except on one or two minor points. I wish, however, to draw the attention of my readers to the persuasive argument advanced by Professor Patterson for a Cabinet proposal akin to my own.

Both originally and subsequently my work with graduate students has been a source of constant stimulation and benefit in the preparation of this treatise. I think particularly in this connection of Professor Arnold J. Zurcher, Dr. Turner C. Cameron, and Dr. Clinton L. Rossiter, all of whom did their doctoral theses in the general field of this volume under my supervision. I wish also to note my continued endebtedness to *The New York Times* both as a chronicle of current events and as a repository of public documents.

Some more special acknowledgments in connection with the preparation of this revision are the following: to Sarah Livingston Davis, Robert Dishman, Harold Chase, and William A. Mitchell, all former graduate students of mine, the Honorable Hugh B. Cox, Professor Everett S. Brown, and Dr. Louis Brownlow for bringing to my attention certain materials of special interest and value; to Jean B. Barr, Editor of New York University Press, for her skill and unflagging interest in bringing the revision about, to Anne Koreny for her intelligent editorial work, and to Alma Fell for her unfailing proficiency as transcriber and copyist.

Lastly, I wish to thank Mr. Arthur Krock for taking time out of a very busy season to prepare the Foreword to this volume. Because of his interest in the repercussion of events on our governing institutions, I have long found his column in *The New York Times* a frequent source of stimulation, even when I disagreed with his views.

EDWARD S. CORWIN

Princeton, N. J.
August 1, 1948

FOREWORD

THE struggle between President and Congress for domination of the government of the United States grows out of the compromise in the Constitution as to their respective powers and has recurred throughout American history. But the perils to our security which the twentieth century has evoked, and the vast burdens which world leadership have imposed on the American system of divided authorities (neither of them envisaged by the Framers of the Constitution and the Bill of Rights), have intensified this struggle and produced a major threat to the progress of the nation and the world.

It is to this vast and menacing aspect of implicit rivalry that Professor Corwin has addressed in part this revision of a book which first appeared in 1940. Events of that year and the preceding decade required that this calm and objective study should be laid before the public. Events since 1940 have invested the unsolved problem with dangers which no previous experience of the United States suggested. The fact that, in the presence of a war-breeding crisis with the Soviet Union in Berlin, President Truman based his claim for election on the righteousness of his differences with Congress vividly demonstrated the nature and effect of the problem.

Many scholars and thinkers have proposed solutions of the ancient competition, and in his 1940 text Professor Corwin offered one—a Legislative Council to replace the Cabinet. This he now repeats with added detail, and supports it from the history of the presidential office since 1932. For this section alone the revised version would be a major contribution to the literature on this essential subject.

But Professor Corwin's study is not only the most comprehensive. It is truly a *study,* unlike the work of many others who were more intent on giving their views of what ought to be the functions and scope of the Presidency than on explaining what various Presidents have in fact made, or attempted to make, of them; and what have been, and can be, the conflicts and the consequences.

Happily combined with the recent and the current, Professor Corwin's treatment lends impressiveness and persuasion to the solution he proposes. As he points out, a Cabinet composed of the legislative leaders of both major parties would not, as now, be dependent on the President for the places these members occupy. It could in advance assure the passage of legislation agreed on and the contrary fate of programs which the leaders of the majority in Congress disapproved. It is a constitutional solution because it could be arranged by statute: the Cabinet as such does not exist through the national Charter. And it reflects the idea of the Founders that, in Professor Corwin's phrase, the people are *"re-presented* in the legislature and *embodied* in the Executive."

Basic to the problem which he states in this book are these factors: "The cyclical character" of presidential powers, which wax and wane in proportion to the popular appeal of a chief executive's personality and methods. The circumstance that a President's responsibility to the people, either for excess or neglect in duty, is not judicially enforceable; only by impeachment, which disparages and undermines the office. The dispute, that still persists despite Franklin Roosevelt's unilateral decision upon it, over whether as Commander-in-Chief the President, without congressional sanction, can order the Navy to convoy against the interest of one belligerent in behalf of another. The fiction that only Congress can declare war in contrast to the fact that a President can make that declaration an inevitable formality. The uneasy balance between the power of the purse in Congress and the power of the sword in the White House. The repeated demonstrations that, as in Lincoln's time, the courts do not get around to a redress of executive dictatorship until it is over (the decision in *ex parte Milligan*); and that congressional correctives, too, usually come long after the fact (the quarrel of the Capitol with Andrew Johnson).

Asking the question, "Is Presidential leadership as good an instrument as it should be to meet the popular demand that produced it?", Professor Corwin answers in the negative for many reasons, among them the highly personalized power of the office, the "haphazard" system of choosing Presidents (which the conventions of 1948 have exposed with unusual vividness), and the present constitution of the Cabinet, by reason of which there is no body which a President is *obliged* to consult in advance of decision and which can give him truly independent advice.

The Legislative Council would remedy all this. And it would not require the constitutional change which nearly all other solutions would make necessary. The best of these proposes an interim election after an executive-legislative stalemate or a succession of presidential defeats in Congress—the President to ask the country to return him, the Cabinet, and the members of Congress that stand with him; his congressional opponents and their leaders to do the same.

But, even if Professor Corwin made no attempt to level this greatest systemic obstacle to coherent domestic government and effective foreign policy, his revised edition would still acknowledge only his earlier work as rival for first honors in the field. For this book is a thorough review of the presidential power, and its scope is as broad as the subject. My emphasis on the proposal Professor Corwin has advanced is not intended to obscure this more important aspect. He has labored successfully to produce, not a tract for the times, not a campaign history of the executive office—to be read with the rivalries and personalities of

1948 in mind—but one of those rare historical treatises that open the past to the enlightened scrutiny of the wide future.

ARTHUR KROCK

Washington, D. C.
July 20, 1948

TABLE OF CONTENTS

THE PRESIDENT: OFFICE AND POWERS

1787–1948

CHAPTER I

CONCEPTIONS OF THE OFFICE

SPECULATIVE writers have sometimes traced the origins of government to a monarch in the forest who gathered in his person all power. At length wearying of his responsibilities, the hypothetical potentate delegated some of them to followers who eventually became "courts," and shared others with a more numerous body of subjects who in due time organized themselves into a "legislature." The indefinite residuum, called "executive power," he kept for himself.

Thus it happens that, whereas "legislative power" and "judicial power" today denote fairly definable *functions* of government as well as fairly constant *methods* for their discharge, "executive power" is still indefinite as to *function* and retains, particularly when it is exercised by a single individual, much of its original plasticity as regards *method*. It is consequently the power of government which is most spontaneously responsive to emergency conditions; conditions, that is, which have not attained enough of stability or recurrency to admit of their being dealt with according to rule. The reversion of certain democracies within recent years in the presence of social crisis to more primitive types of government presents therefore no cause for astonishment.

Indeed, agreement is general among technical students of government that the retention of democratic institutions depends today largely upon the capacity of these to afford a matrix for strong executive leadership. What resources does our own Constitution offer in this respect? The answer brings under survey our practice and discussion for 160 years.

The Notes to this chapter begin on page three hundred seventy-four

"EXECUTIVE POWER"—A TERM OF UNCERTAIN CONTENT

Article II is the most loosely drawn chapter of the Constitution. To those who think that a constitution ought to settle everything beforehand it should be a nightmare; by the same token, to those who think that constitution makers ought to leave considerable leeway for the future play of political forces, it should be a vision realized.

We encounter this characteristic of Article II in its opening words: "The executive power shall be vested in a President of the United States of America." Do these words comprise a grant of power or are they a mere designation of office? If the former is the case, then how are we to explain the more specific clauses of grant in the ensuing sections of the same article? Some of these no doubt may be accounted for by the provision which they make for the participation of the Senate in the "executive power"; but several of them are not to be disposed of in this expeditious fashion. In the famous Oregon Postmaster Case of 1926 the difficulty is met by Chief Justice Taft with the statement that such clauses of specific grant lend "emphasis where emphasis is appropriate."[1] Not only is this an entirely novel canon of constitutional interpretation, it is one which, if it were applied to the "general welfare" clause of Article I of the Constitution, would pave the way for a complete revolution in our system by converting the National Government from one of "enumerated" powers into one of plenary power. Yet if there *is* "executive power" which has been found essential in other systems of government and which is not granted the President in the more specific clauses of Article II, how is it to be brought within the four corners of the Constitution except by means of the "executive power" clause?

And is the President's executive power the *only* executive power known to the Constitution? This same clause seems to make an affirmative answer to this question logically imperative; but, if this is so, then what kind of power is that which Congress bestows by virtue of its power to make "all laws which shall be necessary and proper for carrying into execution" the powers of the National Government;[2] and what of the assumption that the President shall "take care that the laws be faithfully executed"[3]— executed, that is, by *others?* Again, is "executive power" the only kind of power which the President is capable of exercising? For, if that is the case, how can he receive power from the legislature, which, by the same course of reasoning, has only "legislative power" to confer?

Then to complicate matters further is the fact that the diverse powers of the President are by no means of uniform quality either as to scope or authoritativeness when laid alongside the powers of Congress. By virtue of his power of veto and his duty to inform Congress as to the state of the Union the President himself participates in the legislative power. On the other hand, certain specifically granted "executive" powers, or "prerogatives," such as his power to pardon "offenses against the United States," his power to receive ambassadors, and so forth, are, when properly defined, theoretically autonomous and hence not subject to the legislative power. In the words of Chief Justice Marshall, the President in their exercise is "responsible only to the country in his political capacity and to his own conscience."[4] But the question remains, in what terms are they properly defined? Other, "implied" powers which are logically deducible from the above are even less definite of contour and are proportionately less secure against legislative restriction—the power to recognize new governments, to remove appointees from office, and so on. Finally the President is charged with the duty to "take care that the laws be faithfully executed." What powers are properly inferable from this duty? Can the duty confer power to override otherwise constitutional acts of Congress? Or suppose a situation in which enforcement of the law would be aided if the President exercised one of his autonomous powers in the furtherance of ends of which he disapproved. Would he be nonetheless obliged to exercise such autonomous power for this purpose? How are such paradoxes to be resolved; how in practice have they been resolved?

SOURCES OF THE FRAMERS' IDEAS OF EXECUTIVE POWER

The earliest American repositories of an executive power that was at all distinguishable as something other than a mere legislative agency were the governors of the royal provinces. This functionary, acting independently or with a council, was customarily entrusted with the powers of appointment, military command, expenditure, and—within limitations—that of pardon, as well as with large powers in connection with the process of lawmaking.[5] At the same time, however, he was also the point of tangency with the British Crown, and so the point of friction between the imperial interest and the local interest, the latter being represented by the colonial assembly. Gradually the assemblies in most of the royal provinces, thanks especially to their control over supplies, were able to bring the governor under a large degree of legislative control and direction; and during the French and Indian War, when the governors were in constant need of money and of men for the forces, this development went forward by strides. The colonial period ended with the belief prevalent that "the executive magistracy" was the natural enemy, the legislative assembly the natural friend of liberty, a sentiment strengthened by the contemporary spectacle of George III's domination of Parliament.

In most of the early state constitutions accordingly we find the gubernatorial office reduced almost to the dimensions of a symbol. In these instruments the governors were for the most part elective annually by the legislature, were stripped of every prerogative of their predecessors in relation to legislation—the right to convene the assembly, to prorogue it, to dissolve it, to veto its acts—and were forced to exercise even their more strictly executive functions subject to the advice of a council of state which was also elective by the legislature and, if the latter so desired, from its members.[6] Several of these constitutions, to be sure, enunciate Montesquieu's doctrine of the separation of powers with considerable emphasis; but their actual application of the principle, when it was anything more than a caution against the same persons being entrusted with office in more than one department at a time, was directed especially against the executive. In the language of Madison in *The Federalist:*

"The founders of our republics . . . seem never for a moment to have turned their eyes from the overgrown and all-grasping prerogative of an hereditary magistrate, supported and fortified by an hereditary branch of the legislative authority. They seem never to have recollected the danger from legislative usurpations, which, by assembling all power in the same hands, must lead to the same tyranny as is threatened by executive usurpations."[7]

Finally, in the Virginia constitution of 1776 it was stipulated, as if out of abundant caution, that "the executive powers of government" were to be exercised "according to the laws" of the commonwealth, and that no power or prerogative was ever to be claimed "by virtue of any law, statute, or custom of England."[8] "Executive power," in short, was left to legislative definition and was cut off entirely from the resources of the common law and of English constitutional usage.

But while the above is a just characterization of the majority of the Revolutionary state constitutions, there were exceptions in which a more generous conception of the executive office is at least foreshadowed. Thus in the famous report of the Pennsylvania Council of Censors of 1784 the Pennsylvania constitution of 1776 is interpreted as entrusting all power not otherwise specifically provided for either to "the legislative or the executive *according to its nature*";[9] and as is pointed out by Hamilton in *The Federalist*, the New York constitution of 1777 suggested not a few of the outstanding features of the Presidency. The New York governor was not a creature of the legislature but was directly elective by the people; his term was three years and he was indefinitely reëligible; except in the matter of appointments and vetoes, he was untroubled by a council; he bore the designation of "Commander-in-Chief," possessed the pardoning power, and was charged with the duty of "taking care that the laws are faithfully executed to the best of his ability."[10] The first effective gubernatorial veto, however, was that set up in the Massachusetts constitution of 1780, and the designation "President" occurred in several of the state constitutions of that date.

Furthermore, the early state constitutions were by no means the only source, or even the chief source, upon which the Framers of the Constitution were able to draw in shaping their ideas of executive power. Locke, Montesquieu, and Blackstone were the common reading of them all, and in the pages of these writers executive power is delineated in no suspicious or grudging terms. Especially illuminating in this connection is Locke's description of "Prerogative" in the Fourteenth Chapter of his famous *Treatise*:[11]

"Where the legislative and executive power [the passage reads] are in distinct hands, as they are in all moderated monarchies and well-framed governments, there the good of the society requires that several things should be left to the discretion of him that has the executive power. For the legislators not being able to foresee and provide by laws for all that may be useful to the community, the executor of the laws, having the power in his hands, has by the common law of Nature a right to make use of it for the good of the society, in many cases where the municipal law has given no direction, till the legislative can conveniently be assembled to provide for it; nay, many things there are which the law can by no means provide for, and those must necessarily be left to the discretion of him that has the executive power in his hands, to be ordered by him as the public good and advantage shall require; nay, it is fit that the laws themselves should in some cases give way to the executive power, or rather to this fundamental law of Nature and government—viz., that as much as may be all the members of the society are to be preserved. . . . "

Designating then "this power to act according to discretion for the public good, without the prescription of the law and sometimes even against it," as "prerogative," Locke continues:

"This power, whilst employed for the benefit of the community and suitably to the trust and ends of the government, . . . never is questioned. For the people are very seldom or never scrupulous or nice in the point or questioning of prerogative whilst it is in any tolerable degree employed for the use it was meant—that is, the good of the people, and not manifestly against it. . . .

"And therefore he that will look into the history of England will find that prerogative was always largest in the hands of our wisest and best princes, because the people observing the whole tendency of their actions to be the public good, or if any human frailty or mistake (for princes are but men, made as others) appeared in some small declinations from that end; yet it was visible the main of their conduct tended to nothing but the care of the public. The people, therefore, finding reason to be satisfied with these princes, whenever they acted without, or contrary to the letter of the law, acquiesced in what they did, and without the least complaint, let them enlarge their prerogative as they pleased, judging rightly that they did nothing herein to the prejudice of their laws, since they acted conformable to the foundation and end of all laws—the public good. . . ."

Most readers come upon these passages for the first time with considerable astonishment, and wonder how the views which they express are to be harmonized with the doctrine advanced in the same pages that in a free commonwealth the "legislative is not only the supreme power," but is "sacred and unalterable in the hands where the community have once placed it."[12] The probability is that Locke himself was quite untroubled by the inconsistency both because he had a special talent for inconsistencies, and because this particular inconsistency was not of his contrivance. For while the Glorious Revolution, which Locke wrote primarily to justify, had settled it that the King would be henceforth dependent on Parliament for supplies, it had at the same time left him an unlimited veto wherewith to protect his other prerogatives against Parliament. So what Locke gives us in the final analysis is *not* legislative supremacy really, but—as his Whig commentators pointed out—"a balanced constitution."

And a "balanced constitution" is also what "the celebrated Montesquieu" had in mind when, following a hint of Locke's, he revived Aristotle's doctrine that government comprised three intrinsically distinct elements,[13] and reshaped it for the uses of eighteenth-century libertarianism. In a passage which the Framers of the Constitution regarded as embodying the greatest discovery of "political science" since the time of Adam, Montesquieu wrote:

"In every government there are three sorts of power: the legislative; the executive in respect of things dependent on the law of nations; and the executive in regard to matters that depend on the civil law. . . .

"When the legislative and executive powers are united in the same person, or in the same body of magistrates, there can be no liberty; because apprehensions may arise, lest the same monarch or senate should enact tyrannical laws, and execute them in a tyrannical manner. Again, there is no liberty, if the judiciary power be not separated from the legislative and executive. Were it joined with the legislative, the life and liberty of the subject would be exposed to arbitrary control; for the judge would be then the legislator. Were it joined to the executive power, the judge might behave with violence and oppression. There would be an end of everything, were the same man or the same body, whether of the nobles or of the people, to exercise those three powers, that of enacting laws, that of executing the public resolutions, and of trying the causes of individuals."[14]

The doctrine of the Separation of Powers comprises, along with the doctrine of Dual Federalism, one of the two great structural principles of the American constitutional system; and from it certain other ideas follow logically, even though not inevitably: first, that the three functions of government are reciprocally limiting; secondly, that each department should be able to defend its characteristic functions from intrusion by either of the other departments; thirdly, that none of the departments may abdicate its powers to either of the others. The first two of these ideas reënforce executive power, particularly as against the principle of legislative supremacy; the last one operates the other way, and— significantly—it has today almost completely disappeared as a viable principle of American constitutional law.

Lastly, many of the Framers had also read Blackstone, another exponent of the "balanced constitution."[15] In the *Commentaries* Parliament's power is depicted in terms most sweeping:

"It can . . . do everything that is not naturally impossible; and therefore some have not scrupled to call its power, by a figure rather too bold, the omnipotence of Parliament. True it is, that what Parliament doth, no authority upon earth can undo."[16]

Likewise the subordination of the King to the law is constantly insisted upon. That, nevertheless, the *law* in question comprises a good deal more than acts of Parliament is amply apparent from the description given of the royal prerogative, especially in the joint fields of diplomacy and military command.[17]

In a word, the blended picture of executive power which is derivable from the pages of Locke, Montesquieu, and Blackstone is of a broadly discretionary, residual power which is available when other governmental powers fail; which is capable of setting bounds to some indefinite extent even to the supreme legislative power; and which, in defense of these bounds, embraces an absolute veto on legislation. How far did this picture prevail with the Framers?[18]

THE PHILADELPHIA CONVENTION AND *THE FEDERALIST*

In the problem of "a national executive"—the phrase used by the authors of the Virginia Plan—the Philadelphia Convention was faced with a difficult dilemma. The majority of the Framers ardently desired to provide an executive power which should be capable of penetrating to the remotest parts of the Union, not only for the purpose of enforcing the national laws, but also—a lesson from Shays' Rebellion—for the purpose of bringing assistance to the states in grave emergencies of domestic disorder. At the same time, most of them recognized that it was absolutely indispensable that the Convention should avoid stirring up the widespread popular fear of monarchy. Nor did the vast size of the country and the difficulties of travel and transportation make the problem any easier of solution. How could a political force be provided that would be sufficient to overcome these natural obstacles and yet be safe—or at least *thought* safe—from the point of view of popular liberty?

Of those who would fain have carried over into the projected national constitution the conception of executive power which predominated in the state constitutions the outstanding representative was Sherman of Connecticut. In the words of Madison's *Notes:*

"Mr. Sherman said he considered the Executive magistracy as nothing more than an institution for carrying the will of the legislature into effect, and that the person or persons ought to be appointed by and accountable to the legislature only, which was the depository of the supreme will of the Society. They were the best judges of the business which ought to be done by the Executive department, and consequently of the number necessary from time to time for doing it. He wished that the number might not be fixed, but that the legislature should be at liberty to appoint one or more as experience might dictate."[19]

Had this conception prevailed the Convention would have anticipated the collegiate executive of the present Swiss Federation.

The leader of the "strong executive" party was James Wilson of Pennsylvania. He "preferred," Madison records, "a single magistrate, as giving most energy, dispatch, and responsibility to the office." He was also for rendering the executive "independent of the legislature," and to this end proposed that he be elected by the people at large and be vested with an absolute negative upon acts of the legislature. "Without such a defense," said he of the latter proposal, "the legislature can at any moment sink it [the executive] into non-existence."[20]

As chairman of the Committee of Detail, Wilson had the opportunity to incorporate his conception of the executive office in the preliminary draft of the Constitution. In Articles VI and X of the committee's report of August 6, the issue between a single and a plural executive was settled in favor of the former alternative; the idea was adopted of assuring the executive his principal powers by definite constitutional grant instead of leaving them contingent upon legislation; and the executive was armed, in protection of the powers thus committed him, with a qualified veto upon all legislation.[21] Not, however, till the close of the Convention was the last of a persistent and constantly renewed series of efforts to load the President with a council finally defeated;[22] and it was also at this late date that he was made a party to the treaty-making power and the power to appoint justices of the Supreme Court and ambassadors, both of which functions had been at first lodged in the Senate alone.[23]

Lastly, from the Committee of Style, of which Gouverneur Morris, another exponent of strong executive power, was chairman, came the present form of the opening clause of Article II. The corresponding clause from the Committee of Detail had read as follows: "The executive power shall be vested in a single person. His style shall be 'the President of the United States' and his title shall be 'His Excellency'"—phraseology which designates the presidential office, but is less readily interpretable as a grant of power.[24] Curiously enough, the present form of the clause was never separately acted upon by the Convention as a whole.

But the problem of "executive independence" also involved, it was generally conceded, the problem of providing a mode for the President's election which would not bring him under the domination of the legislature, and on no other problem did the Convention expend more time and effort. In the Virginia Plan it was proposed that Congress should elect the executive, and that he, or they, should be ineligible for a second term. The New Jersey Plan likewise provided for election by Congress. Another proposal, which first appeared in Hamilton's Plan, was of indirect election by Electors chosen *ad hoc,* and without stipulation regarding reëligibility. A third suggestion was Wilson's for popular election, and again without restriction as to reëligibility.[25]

When the question was taken up in committee of the whole on

July 17, popular election received the vote of only Pennsylvania; and shortly afterward choice by Electors was also rejected. Thereupon election by the legislature was voted unanimously, only to be upset two days later in favor of election by Electors, who were to be chosen by the state legislatures. What were the considerations which brought about this *volte-face?* Some of them at least were set forth at the time by Gouverneur Morris in a characteristic speech worth quoting for its own sake.

"It is necessary [said Morris] to take into one view all that relates to the establishment of the executive; on the due formation of which must depend the efficacy and utility of the Union among the present and future States. It has been a maxim in political science that Republican Government is not adapted to a large extent of Country, because the energy of the Executive Magistracy can not reach the extreme parts of it. Our Country is an extensive one. We must either then renounce the blessings of the Union, or provide an Executive with sufficient vigor to pervade every part of it. . . . One great object of the Executive is to control the Legislature. The Legislature will continually seek to aggrandise & perpetuate themselves; and will seize those critical moments produced by war, invasion or convulsion for that purpose. It is necessary then that the Executive Magistrate should be the guardian of the people, even of the lower classes, agst Legislative tyranny, against the Great & the wealthy who in the course of things will necessarily compose the Legislative body. . . . If he is to be the Guardian of the people let him be appointed by the people. If he is to be a check on the Legislature let him not be impeachable. Let him be of short duration, that he may with propriety be re-eligible. . . . He suggested a biennial election of the Executive at the time of electing the 1st. branch, and the Executive to hold over, so as to prevent any interregnum in the Administration. An election by the people at large throughout so great an extent of country could not be influenced by those little combinations and those momentary lies which often decide popular elections within a narrow sphere. . . . He saw no alternative for making the Executive independent of the Legislature but either to give him his office for life, or make him eligible by the people. . . ."[26]

Five days later (July 24) election by the legislature was voted again, a vote which was adhered to on July 26. And so matters stood till almost the end of the Convention, when the question was handed over to a committee on unfinished business which, with Morris as chairman, recommended the substance of the present method of election. There can be no doubt that the motive which chiefly influenced the Convention to make this important change at the last moment was to secure the President's reëligibility, and apparently his indefinite reëligibility, without at the same time subjecting him to the temptation of courting legislative favor. To be sure, popular election too would have done this; but the electoral method had the additional advantage that it left each state free to determine its own rule of suffrage without sacrificing its due weight in the choice of a President. It was this consideration, urged particularly by Madison, which turned the scale against the more democratic method, but it was not the only one offered against it.

The people were liable to deceptions; the people in large areas were too ignorant of the characters of men; elective monarchies were turbulent and unhappy; the people would vote for their state candidates; the people would be led by a few active and designing men and would not be better able to judge than the legislature; "it were as unnatural to refer the choice of a proper character for chief magistrate to the people, as it would be to refer a trial of colours to a blind man"—so it was argued from various quarters.[27] Electors, on the contrary, would be men of special discernment into the qualities demanded by the office of President, and be capable of viewing the national scene as a whole, while being both a numerous and a transitory body, their choice would not excite the community in the way that the direct election of "the final object of the public wishes" would.[28]

Suppose election by the houses had been finally adopted, would "the Cabinet System" have resulted, with the President finally settling into the neutral—and largely nugatory—role of the British monarch of today? It seems extremely unlikely. The method by which the President is elected is about the least formidable barrier which the Constitution sets up to the development under it of a system like the British. Nor does the provision that "no person holding any office under the United States shall be a member of either house during his continuance in office"[29] present an insuperable difficulty although it is often cited as doing so. In the face of this provision the President might still constitute a cabinet council out of the chairmen of the principal congressional committees and then put his own powers and those of the heads of departments at the disposal of this council. A more formidable obstacle is the great power of the Senate as compared with the British House of Lords, although the equality of the French legislative chambers did not prevent the rise in that country of a modified cabinet system. Probably the greatest constitutional obstacle to the development of the cabinet system in the National Government consists in the fact that the two houses of Congress are elected for set terms which are different for the two bodies, and the further fact that the President lacks the power of dissolution. The cabinet system pivots upon the substantial agreement at all times of the executive and the legislative branches on important questions of policy, and the Constitution makes it fairly certain that such agreement will at times be lacking.

The fact is that what the Framers had in mind was not the cabinet system, as yet nonexistent even in Great Britain, but the "balanced constitution" of Locke, Montesquieu, and Blackstone, which carried with it the idea of a *divided initiative in the matter of legislation and a broad range of autonomous executive power or "prerogative."* Sir Henry Maine's dictum, that "the American constitution is the British constitution with the monarchy left out," is, from the point of view of 1789, almost the exact reverse of the truth, for the Presidency was designed in great measure to reproduce the monarchy of George III with the corruption left out, and also of course the hereditary feature. And the opponents of the Constitution pounced upon this likeness to the former "despicable tyrant," which they greatly exaggerated, as offering them one of their best arguments.

As Hamilton wrote in *The Federalist:*

"Here the writers against the Constitution seem to have taken pains to signalize their talent of misrepresentation. Calculating upon the aversion of the people to monarchy, they have endeavored to enlist all their jealousies and misapprehensions in opposition to the intended President of the United States. . . . He has been decorated with attributes superior in dignity and splendor to those of the King of Great Britain. He has been shown to us with the diadem sparkling on his brow and the imperial purple flowing in his train. He has been seated on a throne surrounded with minions and mistresses, giving audience to the envoys of foreign potentates, in all the supercilious pomp of majesty. The images of Asiatic despotism and voluptuousness have scarcely been wanting to crowd the exaggerated scene. We have been taught to tremble at the terrific visages of murdering janizaries and to blush at the unveiled mysteries of a seraglio."[30]

Hamilton endeavored to allay these terrors, real or pretended, by pointing out how much the country had suffered under the Articles of Confederation, as well as under the state constitutions, from lack of adequate executive power. "Energy in the executive," he wrote, "is a leading character in the definition of good government"; and of "the ingredients which constitute energy in the executive" the first is "unity,"[31] as it is also of responsibility; and he expressed entire agreement with Delolme's contention that,

"'the executive power is more easily confined when it is ONE'; that it is far more safe there should be a single object for the jealousy and watchfulness of the people, and, in a word, that all multiplication of the Executive is rather dangerous than friendly to liberty."[32]

For the rest, Hamilton discharged the duties of advocacy by pointing out that if the President was beyond the menaces of Congress, so also was Congress beyond the President's power to corrupt; by emphasizing the participation of the Senate in some of the most important powers of the President, among which he included the removal power in the case of officers appointed with the Senate's consent; by emphasizing Congress's control of the purse; and, lastly, by dwelling upon the mode of election by a temporary agency called into existence for the occasion and therefore not under presidential influence.[33] The role of the President as the leader of a national party was still beyond the vaticinations of either Hamilton or the opponents of the Constitution. Having disposed of corruption, they had, forsooth, forestalled parties!

THE PRESIDENCY FROM WASHINGTON TO THE 2ND ADAMS

Of the three departments of the National Government the Supreme Court, as representing the Judiciary, has been most uniformly successful, at least until recent years, in establishing its own conception of its authority and functions, the President next, and Congress the least successful. Judicial review has been, in fact, of somewhat minor importance in determining the scope of presidential powers. While the Court has sometimes rebuffed presidential pretensions, it has more often labored to rationalize them; but most of all it has sought on one pretext or other to keep its sickle out of this "dread field." This policy may be owing partly to the fact that the President has "the power of the sword," that is, immediate command of the physical forces of government; partly to the related fact that while the Court can usually assert itself successfully against Congress by merely "disallowing" its acts, presidential exercises of power will generally have produced some change in the external world beyond ordinary judicial competence to efface. Nor should it be overlooked that the same course of reasoning upon which "executive power" as conferred by the opening clause of Article II has thriven is equally favorable to the pretensions of the bearers of "judicial power" under Article III. In supporting "executive power" against Congress the Court is often fighting its own battle for "judicial power."[34]

The two earliest contests over the "executive power" of the President, indeed, were fought anywhere else than in the judicial forum. The first was the debate in 1789 in the first Congress over the location of the power of removal in relation to "executive officers" appointed "by and with the advice and consent of the Senate."[35] The second concerned the validity of the so-called "Proclamation of Neutrality" which President Washington issued in 1793 at the outbreak of war between France and Great Britain.[36] Both episodes are dealt with at some length later on in this volume; at this point all that is required is reference to the principal issue, which was the same on both occasions, namely, whether the opening clause of Article II was a grant of power or not. In the 1789 controversy Madison said that it was; four years later he took the opposite view, while Hamilton supported the affirmative thesis, and *practically* it was this thesis which prevailed in both instances.

But this confrontation of Hamilton and Madison in 1793 is of importance for a second reason; it signalized the early differentiation of what may be termed the quasi-monarchical and the ultra-Whig conceptions of the Presidency.[37] Under the first two Presidents the former conception prevailed as of course. The Presidency at once furnished what Walter Bagehot would have termed the "dignified element of government" and also directed the legislative process to a notable extent, although without diminishing in the least the spontaneous legislative initiative of the houses themselves; exactly as in contemporary Britain before the younger Pitt, the legislative initiative was divided. The famous Judiciary Act of 1789 was elaborated in the Senate; the acts creating the great executive departments came from the House; Hamilton's financial measures exemplified the legislative leadership of the executive. This leadership Hamilton was encouraged to assume by the very terms of the act of Congress by which the Department of the Treasury was established. "The Secretary of the Treasury," this act read, in fact still reads,

"shall from time to time ... make report and give information to either branch of the legislature in person or in writing, as may be required, respecting all matters referred to him by the Senate or House of Representatives, or which shall appertain to his office; and generally shall perform all services relative to finances as he shall be directed to perform. ... "[38]

Indeed, had it not been for the pedantry of Madison and the jealousy of Jefferson, Hamilton would probably have been asked to report to the House in person—a precedent which might in time have blossomed into something approximating the cabinet system. As it was, the ever alert suspicion of Jefferson discovered that Hamilton's connection with Congress, whereby "the whole action of the Legislature was . . . under the direction of the Treasury," tended definitely toward the overthrow of republican institutions; and it was on this fundamental ground, according to his own later account in his famed *Anas,* that he erected against

Hamilton's measures the opposition from which the Jeffersonian party in due course took its rise. In his words:

"Its [the oppositions's] object was to preserve the Legislature pure and independent of the Executive, to restrain the administration to republican forms and principles, and not permit the Constitution to be construed into a monarchy, and to be warped in practice into all the principles and pollutions of their [the Hamiltonian Federalists'] favorite English model."[39]

For the rest the relations of the two departments were featured by considerable ceremony. The President gave his annual "address" in person, and it was answered by formal "addresses" from the two houses, and to each of these was returned in due course an equally formal "reply"—all of which "trappings of monarchy" were incontinently consigned to the trash basket by "the Revolution of 1800."[40]

Jefferson's conception of executive power, on the other hand, was more Whig than that of the British Whigs themselves in subordinating it to "the supreme legislative power." At the time when the presidential election of 1800 was pending in the House, John Marshall predicted that if Jefferson was chosen he would "embody himself in the House of Representatives, and by weakening the office of President" would "increase his personal power. He will ... become the leader of that party which is about to constitute the majority of the legislature."[41] Confined to the President's legislative role, this was uncommonly good prophecy.[42] What we encounter in Jefferson for the first time is a President who is primarily a party leader, only secondarily Chief Executive. The tone of his messages is uniformly deferential to Congress. His first one closes with these words: "Nothing shall be wanting on my part to inform, as far as in my power, the legislative judgment, nor to carry that judgment into faithful execution."[43] His actual guidance of Congress's judgment was nonetheless constant and unremitting even while often secret and sometimes furtive.[44] The chief instruments of his leadership were the party caucus, which enabled the party membership to present on the floor a united front and over which he himself is alleged to have presided now and then, and his Secretary of the Treasury, Albert Gallatin, whose own influence with Congress was also enormous.[45]

Nor can there be any doubt that, despite its later repercussions upon the Presidency, Jefferson's technique, as administered by himself, was remarkably productive in terms of legislative accomplishment. Comparing in this respect Jefferson's record with Woodrow Wilson's, Dr. Small remarks:

"In according him [Wilson] a primacy in this field of Presidential activity, one ought not to underestimate the significance of Jefferson's achievement. If allowance is made for the fact that, in 1800, the Federal Government was not subjected to any centralizing influence, that, consequently, it legislated upon a smaller number of problems immediately affected with a public interest, and finally, that its legislative machinery was not capable of churning out laws with the rapidity characteristic of the present day, the disparity between the accomplishment of these two Executives is readily explainable; and, when compared on the basis of the success with which they carried out their legislative programs, the leadership of these two Presidents approaches an equality."[46]

What, then, of Marshall's prophecy that Jefferson would weaken the office of President? This, too, was justified by events when the Ulysses bow of party leadership passed to feebler hands. With the practical disappearance of the Federalist party the Republican caucus became "the Congressional Caucus," by which Madison and Monroe were successively put in nomination for the Presidency, while the younger Adams, although not its nominee, was virtually elected by it through the election being thrown into the House. So, for twenty years the plan rejected by the Framers, of having the President chosen by Congress, was substantially in operation. During this period the practice grew up of each succeeding President continuing a considerable part of his predecessor's Cabinet in office; and when he convened them in council the Chief Executive counted the votes of the heads of departments as of equal weight with his own. Hardly more than *primus inter pares* in his own sight, he was glad if Congress accorded him that degree of deference. In short, the Presidency was in commission.[47]

FROM JACKSON'S REVOLUTION TO LINCOLN'S "DICTATORSHIP"

With Jackson's accession this enfeebling tendency was checked as decisively as it was abruptly. Jackson's Presidency was, in truth, no mere revival of the office—it was a remaking of it. The credit, however, should not go to Jackson alone. He contributed an imperious temper, a military reputation, and a striking personality; and he had the good luck to have an admiring public in the shape of a new and ignorant electorate. But the lasting impact of the Jacksonian Presidency upon American constitutional practice also owed much to the constructive skill of his political lieutenants, and particularly to their success in engrafting the Spoils System to the National Government and their invention of the National Nominating Convention. The precise significance of the latter institution is, to be sure, frequently misapprehended, as when it is said to have made the President "the Elect of the People at Large." Jackson himself did not owe his being "the People's Choice" to the National Convention, which was not yet in existence when he became President; nor did the nomination of Mr. Harding by a coterie of bosses in "a smoke-filled room" at two o'clock in the morning, nearly a century later, make him the elect of the people at large in any genuine sense. The National Convention is the periodic reminder of the party's entity. It dramatizes and climaxes the procedures by which a party sustains the consciousness of its nation-wide character and mission. Its primary business—almost its only business— is to select somebody to carry the party standard in an approaching presidential election. If the person chosen is successful, is elected President, then, ordinarily, he remains party leader throughout his official term, and is able in that capacity to summon the party to the support of his policies, as well as to renominate himself or name his successor as party champion. When Jefferson retired in 1809 his party began at once to dissolve into local or personal followings. That the same thing did not happen on Jackson's retirement was due to the rise of the National Convention and the political devices which cluster about it.[48]

And backed by a party organization which reached far beyond the halls of Congress, indeed eventually penetrated the remotest corners of the Union, Jackson became the first President in our history to appeal to the people over the heads of their legislative representatives. At the same time the office itself was thrust forward as one of three *equal* departments of government and to each and every of its powers was imparted new scope, new vitality. The Presidency became tridimensional, and all of the dimensions underwent more or less enlargement. Jackson was a more dominant party leader than Jefferson; his claim to represent the American people as a whole went to the extent of claiming to embody them; his claim to be one of three *equal* departments implied the further claim that *all* his powers were autonomous, even his purely executive powers.

The classic statement of this tenet of his creed occurs in his famous message of July 10, 1832, vetoing Clay's bill for recharter-ing the second Bank of the United States. The salient passage of the message reads:

"The Congress, the Executive, and the Court must each for itself be guided by its own opinion of the Constitution. Each public officer who takes an oath to support the Constitution swears that he will support it as he understands it, and not as it is understood by others. It is as much the duty of the House of Representatives, of the Senate, and of the President to decide upon the constitutionality of any bill or resolution which may be presented to them for passage or approval as it is of the supreme judges when it may be brought before them for judicial deci-sion. The opinion of the judges has no more authority over Congress than the opinion of Congress has over the judges, and on that point the President is independent of both. The authority of the Supreme Court must not, therefore, be permitted to control the Congress or the Executive when acting in their legislative capacities, but to have only such influence as the force of their reasoning may deserve."[49]

The Supreme Court's ratification of this doctrine so far as it bears on the President's duty to the law is dealt with on a later page.

The logical implications of Jackson's position were not exag-gerated by his Whig critics, although its practical effects were. "I look upon Jackson," Kent wrote Story early in 1834, "as a detestable, ignorant, reckless, vain and malignant tyrant. . . . This American elective monarchy frightens me. The experiment, with its foundations laid on universal suffrage and our unfettered press, is of too violent a nature for our excitable people." "The President," thundered Webster in the Senate, "carries on the government; all the rest are sub-contractors. . . . A Briareus sits in the centre of our system, and with his hundred hands touches everything, controls everything." "We are in the midst of a revo-lution," lamented Clay, "hitherto bloodless, but tending rapidly towards a total change of the pure republican character of the

Government, and to the concentration of all power in the hands of one man."[50]

Indeed, the Framers of the Constitution themselves did not escape censure for their responsibility for this state of things, as we discover when we turn to Abel Upshur's essay on *Federal Government,* which appeared in 1840. Dealing with the Presidency, Upshur wrote:

"The most defective part of the Constitution beyond all question, is that which relates to the Executive Department. It is impossible to read that instrument, without being struck with the loose and unguarded terms in which the powers and duties of the President are pointed out. So far as the legislature is concerned, the limitations of the Constitution, are, perhaps, as precise and strict as they could safely have been made; but in regard to the Executive, the Convention appears to have studiously selected such loose and general expressions, as would enable the President, by implication and construction either to neglect his duties or to enlarge his powers. We have heard it gravely asserted in Congress that whatever power is neither legislative nor judiciary, is of course executive, and, as such, belongs to the President under the Constitution. . . ."[51]

Eight years later so sober and generally well balanced a critic as Reverdy Johnson of Maryland spoke in the Senate "of the overshadowing influence of power of a President," and added:

"So great a latitude of construction has not of late prevailed in relation to the power of the other departments as to the power of the President. If he adheres to the letter of the Constitution, he is to be sustained, whatever departure there might be from the spirit of the instrument, while charges of usurpation of power are constantly made against Congress. . . . It may yet be that a diadem may sparkle on the brow of an American President."[52]

This same year, 1848, the Swiss people framed a new constitution;

but although imitating our national Constitution in several other respects, they steered conspicuously clear of the Presidency, because they felt it to be favorable to dictatorship.

Actually, prior to the Civil War, the menace was more apparent than real. For this there were several reasons. In the first place, while magnifying the powers of the Presidency, Jackson subscribed to the States Rights doctrine of strict construction of Congress's powers. His legislative role consequently was chiefly negative, being confined for the most part to a vigorous use of the veto power.[53] In the second place, the further development in the houses after Jefferson's day of the committee system interposed obstacles in the way of presidential participation in legislation which had not existed at first. But the circumstance which contributed most to the temporary declension of the Jacksonian Presidency was the emergence after 1846 of the issue of slavery in the territories. For the handling of this highly charged question by the devices of negotiation and compromise, Congress, and especially the Senate, offered a far better theater than the Presidency. So the forces making for compromise systematically depressed the Presidency by taking care that only secondary and manageable personalities should be elevated to it. From the close of the Mexican War to 1861 the Presidency was in the doldrums, definitely.[54]

The last important contribution to the theory of the Presidency until recent decades was Lincoln's, whose ultimate conception of the office was as much an expression of temperament as was Jackson's. A solitary genius who valued the opportunity for reflection above that for counsel, Lincoln came to regard Congress as a more or less necessary nuisance and the Cabinet as a usually unnecessary one.[55] Nor could it have escaped Lincoln's intuition—especially after Buchanan's message of December 3, 1860[56]—that, if the Union was to be saved, recourse must be had to some still untested source of national power, one which had not become entangled, as had Congress's, in the strangulating sophistries of States Rights. So, for a double reason, Lincoln turned to the "Commander-in-Chief" clause, from which, read in conjunction with the "shall take care" clause, he drew the conclusion that "the war power" was his.[57] Originally, it is true, he appears to have assumed that his power was a simple emergency power whose *ad interim* decisions Congress must ratify if they were to be permanently valid. But, as the problems of Emancipation and then of Reconstruction loomed, he shifted ground, and his final position was, as Professor Randall phrases it, "that as President he had extraordinary legal resources which Congress lacked."[58] The practical fruitage of this theory is treated at length in a later chapter.

But, while Lincoln's invocation of "the war power" added a new dimension to the Presidency in the presence of national emergency, his incumbency was in certain other respects a calamity for the office. A frontiersman, his conceptions of the requirements of sound administration were no less naïve than Jackson's, whose record as a spoilsman he far surpassed;[59] while except for an ineffectual endeavor to interest Congress in the subject of compensated emancipation, he left the task of procuring necessary legislation to his Cabinet secretaries, and especially to Chase and Stanton, theirs being the departments most concerned.[60] The outcome in the latter case was the creation of a direct relationship between the War Department and the congressional Committee on the Conduct of the War which under Johnson brought the Presidency to the verge of disaster.

THE PRESIDENCY OCCULTED — CONGRESS DOMINANT

The schism between the President and Congress which nearly cost Johnson his official life was, in fact, well under way before

Johnson became President. The subject of controversy was the right to determine the conditions on which the seceding states should be restored to their normal position in the Union. Lincoln professed to regard "the war power," supplemented by the pardoning power, as the constitutionally designated agency for this important task, while the Republican leadership in Congress proclaimed the paramountcy of the national legislative power, their reliance being on the guarantee by "the United States," in Article IV, section 4, of "a republican form of government" to the states.[61] The President's duty, Lincoln was warned in the Wade-Davis Manifesto of August 5, 1864, was "to obey and execute, not to make the laws . . . to suppress by arms armed rebellion and leave political organization to Congress";[62] and two years later the same warning was addressed to Johnson by Thaddeus Stevens in still stronger terms:

"He [the President] is the servant of the people as they shall speak through Congress. . . . Andrew Johnson must learn that he is your servant and that as Congress shall order he must obey. There is no escape from it. God forbid that he should have one tittle of power except what he derives through Congress and the Constitution."[63]

Johnson spurned the admonition. An obstinate, ill-educated man, he took his constitutional beliefs with fearful seriousness, and points which his predecessor would have yielded with little compunction for a workable plan, he defended as if they had been transmitted to him from Sinai. Few Presidents have surpassed Johnson in the exorbitance of his pretensions for the office, none in his inability to make them good.

Final appraisement of Johnson's incumbency for the theory of the Presidency is, nevertheless, not easy. Johnson escaped dismissal from office by the High Court of Impeachment by a single vote, but he *escaped!* What is more, it was during his administration that the Supreme Court confessed its inability, in *Mississippi v. Johnson,*[64] to enjoin a President from exceeding his constitutional powers or to order him to perform his constitutional duties. The principle that Marshall had stated as applicable to the President's "important political powers," that "in their exercise he is to use his own discretion, and is accountable only to his country in his political character, and to his own conscience," was thus extended even to the President's duty to enforce the law. Furthermore, whatever of popular glamour the office had lost under Johnson was promptly restored to it when "the man from Appomattox and its famous apple tree" became President.

Reflecting upon all of which, Henry C. Lockwood, in his *The Abolition of the Presidency,* which appeared in 1884, advanced the thesis that only by replacing the President with an executive council after the Swiss model could American liberty be preserved. He wrote:

"The tendency of all people is to elevate a single person to the position of ruler. The idea is simple. It appeals to all orders of intellects. It can be understood by all. Around this centre all nationality and patriotism are grouped. A nation comes to know the characteristics and nature of an individual. It learns to believe in the man. Certain contingencies are likely to take place. It does not require a great amount of political knowledge to form an opinion as to the course of their favorite statesman, whose character they have studied. Under these circumstances, let a person be chosen to an office, with power conferred upon it equal to that of the Presidency of the United States, and it will make but little difference whether the law actually gives him the right to act in a particular direction or not. He determines a policy. He acts. No argument that the law has been violated will avail. He is the chief officer of the nation. He stands alone. He is a separate power in himself. The lines with which we attempt to mark the limits of his power are shadowy and ill-defined. A party, real or imaginary, stands back of him demanding action. In either event, the President acts. The sentiment of hero worship, which to a great extent prevails among the American people, will endorse him. Under our form of government, we do not think so much of what Congress may do. A great multitude declared: 'Give us President Grant! We know him. He is strong! He will rule!' "[65]

Lockwood's re-echo of Locke was an anachronism, coming at once too late and too early. This appears most strikingly when we set against it Woodrow Wilson's *Congressional Government*, which issued from the press the year following. In this famous volume we encounter the pioneer attempt to give a nonlegalistic, factual description of the reciprocal roles of Congress and the President, and it is evident that Wilson regarded Congress as decidedly the dominant member in the partnership. I quote some characteristic passages from the "Introduction":

"The noble charter of fundamental law given us by the Convention of 1787 is still our Constitution; but it is now our *form of government* rather in name than in reality, the form of the Constitution being one of nicely adjusted, ideal balances, whilst the actual form of our present government is simply a scheme of congressional supremacy. . . .

"It is said that there is no single or central force in our federal scheme . . . but only a balance of powers and a nice adjustment of interactive checks, as all the books say. How is it, however, in the practical conduct of the federal government? In that, unquestionably, the predominant and controlling force, the center and source of all motive and of all regulative power, is Congress. . . .

"Congress [is] the dominant, nay, the irresistible, power of the federal system, relegating some of the chief balances of the Constitution to an insignificant role in the 'literary theory' of our institutions. . . ."

And then by way of "Conclusion":

"Congress is fast becoming the governing body of the nation, and yet the only power which it possesses in perfection is the power which is but a part of government, the power of legislation."[66]

Contrast with this the picture which Wilson draws of the Presidency at this period:

"Independently of experience, however, it might reasonably have been expected that the prerogatives of the President would have been one of the most effectual restraints upon the power of Congress. He was constituted one of the three great coordinate branches of the government; his functions were made of the highest dignity; his privileges many and substantial—so great, indeed, that it has pleased the fancy of some writers to parade little doubt that, had the presidential chair always been filled by men of commanding character, of acknowledged ability, and of thorough political training, it would have continued to be a seat of the highest authority and consideration, the true center of the federal structure, the real throne of administration, and the frequent source of policies.

"But the prestige of the presidential office has declined with the character of the Presidents. And the character of the Presidents has declined as the perfection of selfish party tactics has advanced. . . .

"I am disposed to think, however, that the decline in the character of the Presidents is not the cause, but only the accompanying manifestation, of the declining prestige of the presidential office. That high office has fallen from its first estate of dignity because its power has waned; and its power has waned because the power of Congress has become predominant. . . ."[67]

Searching for an explanation for this outcome of the struggle for power between the President and Congress, Wilson finds one ready at hand in a passage of Bagehot's famous work on the Eng-

lish Constitution, which he paraphrases, substituting "Congress" for "Parliament":

"Congress is 'nothing less than a big meeting of more or less idle people. In proportion as you give it power it will inquire into everything, settle everything, meddle in everything. In an ordinary despotism the powers of the despot are limited by his bodily capacity, and by the calls of pleasure; he is but one man; there are but twelve hours in his day, and he is not disposed to employ more than a small part in dull business; he keeps the rest for the court, or the harem, or for society.' But Congress 'is a despot who has unlimited time,—who has unlimited vanity,—who has, or believes he has, unlimited comprehension, —whose pleasure is in action, whose life is work.' Accordingly it has entered more and more into the details of administration, until it has virtually taken into its own hands all the substantial powers of government. It does not domineer over the President himself, but it makes the Secretaries its humble servants. Not that it would hesitate, upon occasion, to deal directly with the chief magistrate himself; but it has few calls to do so, because our latter-day Presidents live by proxy; they are the executive in theory, but the Secretaries are the executive in fact." [68]

Wilson had an axe to grind—two axes in fact. For himself he desired to emulate Bagehot's attack on "the literary theory" of the British Constitution; from a broader point of view he wished to see the British cabinet system adapted to the American Constitution; and this twofold bias led him to exaggerate the phenomenon which he recorded. Yet when James Bryce brought out his *American Commonwealth* some three years later, he did little more than retouch Wilson's picture. He wrote:

"In quiet times the power of the President is not great. He is hampered at every turn by the necessity of humouring his party. He is so much engrossed by the trivial and mechanical parts of his work as to have little leisure for framing large schemes of policy, while in carrying them out he needs the cooperation of Congress, which may be jealous, or indifferent, or hostile. He has less influence on legislation,— that is to say, his individual volition makes less difference to the course legislation takes—than the Speaker of the House of Representatives."[69]

Virtually without initiative in legislation, what strength the President possessed in that field, Bryce held, lay in his veto power. And why had the President lost ground? In the first instance Bryce answered this question as follows:

"Men come and go, but an assembly goes on forever; it is immortal, because while the members change, the policy, the passion for extending its authority, the tenacity in clinging to what has once been gained, remain persistent. A weak magistrate comes after a strong magistrate, and yields what his predecessor had fought for; but an assembly holds all it has ever won. Its pressure is steady and continuous; it is always, by a sort of natural process, expanding its own powers and devising new methods for fettering its rival. Thus Congress, though it is no more respected or loved by the people now than it was seventy years ago, though it has developed no higher capacity for promoting the best interests of the State, has succeeded in occupying nearly all the ground which the Constitution left debatable between the President and itself; and would, did it possess a better internal organization, be even more plainly than it now is the supreme power in the government."[70]

Yet Bryce is not altogether satisfied with this dismissal of the subject; and when at the very end of his work he recurs to it, he ventures a word of prophecy:

"One is sometimes inclined to think that Congress might lose its hold on the respect and confidence of the nation, and sink into a subordinate position, were there any other authority which could be substituted for it. There is, however, no such authority, for lawmaking cannot be given to a person or to a court, while the State legislatures have the same faults as Congress in a greater degree. We may accordingly surmise that Congress will retain its present place;

but so far as can be gathered from present phenomena, it will retain this place in respect not of the satisfaction of the people with its services, but of their inability to provide a better servant.

"The weakness of Congress is the strength of the President. Though it cannot be said that his office has risen in power or dignity since 1789, there are reasons for believing that it may reach a higher point than it has occupied at any time since the Civil War. The tendency everywhere in America to concentrate power and responsibility in one man is unmistakable. There is no danger that the President should become a despot, that is, should attempt to make his will prevail against the will of the majority. But he may have a great part to play as the leader of the majority and the exponent of its will. He is in some respects better fitted both to represent and to influence public opinion than Congress is. . . .

"A vigorous personality attracts the multitude, and attracts it the more the huger it grows; while a chief magistrate's influence excites little alarm when exerted in leading a majority which acts through the constitutional organs of government. There may therefore be still undeveloped possibilities of greatness in store for the Presidents of the future. But as these possibilities depend, like the possibilities of the British and German Crowns, perhaps one may add of the Papacy, on the wholly unpredictable element of personal capacity in the men who may fill the office, we need speculate on them no further."[71]

EMERGENCE OF THE TWENTIETH-CENTURY PRESIDENCY

Congressional Government and *The American Commonwealth* were written in a period of declension of the presidential office in all its phases. Henry Jones Ford, in his *Rise and Growth of American Politics,* which appeared in 1898, was encouraged by more recent developments, and especially the two Cleveland administrations, to spotlight the office in the tradition of its successes rather than its failures. In this discerning volume one reads:

"The agency of the presidential office has been such a master force in shaping public policy that to give a detailed account of it would be equivalent to writing the political history of the United States. From Jackson's time to the present day it may be said that political issues have been decided by executive policy. . . .

"While all that a President can certainly accomplish is to force a submission of an issue to the people, yet such is the strength of the office that, if he makes a sincere and resolute use of its resources, at the same time cherishing his party connection, he can as a rule carry his party with him, because of the powerful interests which impel it to occupy ground taken for it by the administration. . . .

"On the other hand, unless a measure is made an administrative issue, Congress is unable to make it a party issue. . . .

"The rise of presidential authority cannot be accounted for by the intention of presidents; it is the product of political conditions which dominate all the departments of government, so that Congress itself shows an unconscious disposition to aggrandize the presidential office. . . .

"The truth is that in the presidential office, as it has been constituted since Jackson's time, American democracy has revived the oldest political institution of the race, the elective kingship. It is all there: the precognition of the notables and the tumultuous choice of the freemen, only conformed to modern conditions. That the people have been able to accomplish this with such defective apparatus, and have been able to make good a principle which no other people have been able to reconcile with the safety of the state, indicates the highest degree of constitutional morality yet attained by any race."[72]

There is considerable exaggeration here. It was quite untrue that after Jackson's day "political issues" had been "settled by executive policy." The issue of slavery in the territories first arose in Congress and was "settled"—temporarily, to be sure—by the Supreme Court, eventually by war; and the issue of Reconstruction, as well as that of the Tariff, was settled in Congress. But Ford's brilliant volume was really oriented toward the future, and the future came to its rescue. The same year it appeared occurred the Spanish-American War, and the Presidency was, as is always the case, lifted by emergency into a new high relief. Contributing a new preface to the fifteenth impression of *Congressional Government,* Woodrow Wilson noted the fact in these words:

"Much the most important change to be noticed [*i.e.,* since 1885] is the result of the war with Spain upon the lodgment and exercise of power within our federal system: the greatly increased power and opportunity for constructive statesmanship given the President, by the plunge into international politics and into the administration of distant dependencies, which has been that war's most striking and momentous consequence. When foreign affairs play a prominent part in the politics and policy of a nation, its Executive must of necessity be its guide: must utter every initial judgment, take every first step of action, supply the information upon which it is to act, suggest and in large measure control its conduct. The President of the United States is now, as of course, at the front of affairs, as no president, except Lincoln, has been since the first quarter of the nineteenth century, when the foreign relations of the new nation had first to be adjusted. There is no trouble now about getting the President's speeches printed and read, every word. Upon his choice, his character, his experience hang some of the most weighty issues of the future. The government of dependencies must be largely in his hands. Interesting things may come out of the singular change."[73]

An assassin's bullet soon put this prophecy on the way to fulfillment. In his *Constitutional Government in the United States,* comprising lectures delivered at Columbia in 1908, Wilson reassessed the Presidency in the light of the first Roosevelt's performance, and in words which offer a striking contrast to his disparaging evaluation twenty-three years earlier. Here are some of the more exuberant sentences from the third chapter of the book:

"He cannot escape being the leader of his party except by incapacity and lack of personal force, because he is at once the choice of the party and of the nation."

"He can dominate his party by being spokesman for the real sentiment and purpose of the country, by giving direction to opinion, by giving the country at once the information and the statements of policy which will enable it to form its judgments alike of parties and of men."

"His is the only national voice in affairs. Let him once win the admiration and confidence of the country, and no other single force can withstand him, no combination of forces will easily overpower him. His position takes the imagination of the country. He is the representative of no constituency, but of the whole people."

"He may be both the leader of his party and the leader of the nation, or he may be one or the other. If he lead the nation, his party can hardly resist him. His office is anything he has the sagacity and force to make it."

"Some of our Presidents have deliberately held themselves off from using the full power they might legitimately have used, because of conscientious scruples, because they were more theorists than statesmen. . . . The President is at liberty, both in law and conscience, to be as big a man as he can."

"His is the vital place of action in the system, whether he accept it as such or not, and the office is the measure of the man,—of his wisdom as well as of his force."[74]

Further details of the revival under Wilson himself and the two Roosevelts of presidential initiative in the legislative field are given later in this volume. Nor is it only in this field that presidential power has expanded since the turn of the century. This is evidenced by the first Roosevelt's so-called "stewardship theory" of the Presidency; and on a much enlarged scale by the second Roosevelt's conception of the President's power as "Commander-in-Chief in time of war." Both these developments also, as well as other lesser ones of like tendency, are dealt with at later points in appropriate contexts.

Taken by and large, the history of the Presidency is a history of aggrandizement, but the story is a highly discontinuous one. Of the thirty-two individuals who have filled the office only about one in three has contributed to the development of its powers;[75] under other incumbents things have either stood still or gone backward. That is to say, what the Presidency is at any particular moment depends in important measure upon who is President, as indeed Wilson had insisted in 1908, four years before he was given the opportunity to animate by his own practice the figure which he had wrought in the academic atelier. Yet the accumulated tradition of the office is also of great importance. Precedents established by a forceful or politically successful personality in the office are available to less gifted successors, and permanently so because of the difficulty with which the Constitution is amended. Hence the rise and spread from the Jacksonian period onward of the doctrine of popular sovereignty operated very differently upon the Presidency than it did upon the governorship in the states. In the case of the latter there was for years a progressive splitting up of the executive power, accompanied by the transference of its component parts to elective officials over whose tenure and conduct the governor had no control. In the National Government, on the contrary, the dogma of popular sovereignty had to adapt itself to the comparative rigidity of the national Constitution, which it did by exalting and consolidating the power of the one national official who is—in a sense—elective by the people as a whole. The claim set up by Jackson to be the "People's Choice" has been reiterated, in effect, by his successors many times, and with decisive results for the presidential office.[76]

CHAPTER II

ELECTION, TENURE, IMPEACHMENT, ETC.

THE one hundred and fiftieth anniversary of the Constitution naturally evoked many encomiums of it. Especially was Gladstone's famous eulogy of the document of 1787 as the "most wonderful work ever struck off at a given time by the brain and purpose of man" repeated many times. The provisions of the Constitution which are to be considered in this chapter would certainly blush to hear such words, had they ears and a proper moral sensibility. For this portion of the Framers' work the only thing to be said is that it no doubt represented their conscientious belief that they had done the best they could in the circumstances. To it applies emphatically the astringent estimate voiced by Gladstone's contemporary Bagehot of the entire instrument: "The men of Massachusetts could work any Constitution"; and William Penn's equally sceptical estimate of constitutions in general:

"When all is said, there is hardly any frame of government so ill designed by its founders that in good hands would not do well enough; and story tells us the best, in ill ones, can do nothing that is great or good .... Governments, like clocks, go from the motion men give them; and as governments are made and moved by men, so by them they are ruined too. Therefore governments rather depend upon men than men upon governments."

The business of this chapter will be to show how "the men of Massachusetts"—and, incidentally, of the other states—have "worked" the first section of Article II of the Constitution.

WHO MAY BE PRESIDENT; THE BAN ON THIRD TERMS

Paragraph 5 of this section reads as follows:

"No person except a natural-born citizen, or a citizen of the United

The Notes to this chapter begin on page three hundred eighty-six

States at the time of the adoption of this Constitution, shall be eligible to the office of President; neither shall any person be eligible to that office who shall not have attained to the age of thirty-five years, and been fourteen years a resident within the United States."

Do the qualifications here specified need to be possessed at the time of a person's being chosen President, or is it sufficient if he possesses them at the time of entering upon the office? Etymologically "eligible" means *choosable*; but state courts, in interpreting analogous provisions of the state constitutions,[1] have often defined the word as meaning *qualified,* and following this reading of it the provision just quoted is satisfied when a President-elect possesses the qualifications stipulated for at the time of taking office.

The words "a citizen of the United States at the time of the adoption of this Constitution" are today of historical interest only. It has been conjectured that it was the purpose of this clause to render Wilson, Hamilton, Robert Morris, and a few others, who had been born abroad, eligible to the Presidency. Wilson, a member of the Committee of Detail, seems to have felt the need of such a clause in his own behalf especially keenly. But the fact is that nobody old enough to become President in 1787, or for a long time afterward, was a "natural-born citizen of the United States"; all, like the men just mentioned, had been *born* British subjects, and had become American citizens in consequence of the casting off of allegiance to the British monarch by the Declaration of Independence. The clause may very well have been inserted with that entire generation of Americans in mind, and not merely a half-dozen representatives of it.[2]

But who are "natural-born citizens"? By the so-called *jus soli,* which comes from the common law, the term is confined to persons born on the *soil* of a country; and this rule is recognized by the opening clause of the Fourteenth Amendment, which declares to be citizens of the United States "all persons born or naturalized within the United States and subject to the jurisdiction thereof." On the other hand, by the so-called *jus sanguinis,* which underlay early Germanic law and today prevails on the continent of Europe, nationality is based on *parentage,* a principle which was recognized by the first Congress under the Constitution in the following words:

"The children of citizens of the United States that may be born beyond sea, or outside the limits of the United States, shall be considered as natural-born citizens of the United States; provided that the right of citizenship shall not descend to persons whose fathers have never been resident in the United States."[3]

By succeeding legislation the general sense of this provision has been continued in force to this day.[4] The question arises, whence did Congress obtain the power to enact such a measure? By the Constitution Congress is authorized to pass "an uniform rule of naturalization,"[5] that is, a uniform rule whereby *aliens* may be admitted to citizenship; while the provision under discussion purports to recognize a certain category of persons as citizens from and because of *birth.* The provision must undoubtedly be referred to the proposition that, as the legislative body of a nation which is sovereign at international law, Congress is entitled to determine who shall and who shall not be admitted to the body politic.[6]

Should, then, the American people ever choose for President a person born abroad of American parents, it is highly improbable that any other constitutional agency would venture to challenge their decision—a belief which is supported by the fact that Mr. Hoover's title to the Presidency was not challenged although he had not been fourteen years a resident of the United States immediately preceding his assumption of office.[7]

The question arises whether the above stated qualifications may be added to by act of Congress. Actually Congress has never enacted legislation for this specific purpose, but that fact does not warrant the dogmatic assertion that anybody who possesses the constitutionally stipulated qualifications of a President is under all circumstances qualified in the contemplation of the Constitution to be President. Thus a number of sections of the national Criminal Code contain the provision that any one who is convicted under them shall, in addition to other penalties, "be incapable of holding office under the United States." One convicted of treason finds himself in this situation; likewise one convicted of inciting rebellion or insurrection against the United States; likewise any officer of the United States convicted of taking a bribe; and so on.[8] It can hardly be questioned that such provisions are capable of excluding an otherwise qualified person from the Presidency.

Rather different was the issue which presented itself when, in 1920, the Socialist party nominated Mr. Debs, while he was residing in a federal penitentiary for violating the Espionage Act. As his supporters pointed out, this act did not contain the disqualifying clause among its penalties, from which it was a fair deduction that Mr. Debs was still in full possession of his civil rights, including eligibility to the Presidency. To be sure, his place of abode would not have been the most convenient one from which to administer the presidential office; but the situation would not have been irremediable, for once Mr. Debs had taken office, he would have possessed the pardoning power, and I see no reason why he should not have exercised it in his own behalf, supposing his predecessor had lacked the magnanimity to spare him this embarrassment.

The term of four years during which the President "shall hold office" was, prior to the adoption of the Twentieth Amendment, reckoned from March 4 of the alternate odd years beginning with 1789. This came about from the circumstance that under the Act of September 13, 1788, of "the Old Congress," "the first Wednesday in March," which was March 4, 1789, was fixed as the time "for commencing proceedings under the said Constitution." Although as a matter of fact Washington was not inaugurated until April 30 of that year, by an act approved March 1, 1792, it was provided that the presidential term should be reckoned from "the fourth day of March next succeeding" the date of election.[9] And so things stood until the adoption of the Twentieth Amendment by which the terms of the President and Vice-President end at noon on the 20th of January.

As was pointed out in the preceding chapter, the prevailing sentiment of the Convention of 1787 favored the indefinite reëligibility of the President, a sentiment which was owing in considerable part to the universal expectation that Washington would be the first person to be chosen President, and would be willing to serve indefinitely. The custom which limits any individual's tenure of the presidential office to two terms was initiated by Washington himself, although purely on grounds of personal preference and without seeming thought of creating a precedent; but that did not prevent Jefferson, when making public his own decision in 1807 to withdraw at the end of his second term, from stressing Washington's example. Indefinite reëligibility, Jefferson argued, would so undermine the elective system that, while the office would remain "nominally elective," it would "in fact be for life" and "degenerate into an inheritance." Considering how universal monarchy was at that date—to say nothing of the common law concept of property in office which had just received countenance from the Supreme Court's decision in *Marbury v. Madison*—the argument possessed contemporaneously a good deal of force, and would have doubtless possessed more if either Washington or Jefferson had had a son.[10]

Sanctioned by the examples of Washington, Jefferson, Madison, Monroe, and Jackson, the "no-third-term" tradition had become by the Civil War a generally accepted tenet of the American constitutional credo. Indeed, Jackson while President had called repeatedly for a constitutional amendment which should render the President directly elective for a single term of four or six years. Although his crusade failed of its immediate purpose, yet following his retirement no other President was reëlected till 1864— the ban on third terms had become in effect one on second terms as well, a point which was strenuously urged by his party opponents against Lincoln's renomination that year.[11]

The "no-third-term" taboo was first definitely challenged in 1876, when a coterie of Republican politicians broached the idea of running President Grant again. The popular reaction was strongly adverse; and when four years later a similar movement was launched, Grant being now in retirement, its sponsors professed the greatest deference to the principle but contended that it applied only to a third consecutive term.

Within more recent years the scope of the tradition became involved in uncertainty repeatedly, and this circumstance no doubt contributed to loosening its hold on the popular regard. The prestige of the tradition was never higher than when the first Roosevelt, following his election in 1904, construed it as covering the term which he was then completing in consequence of McKinley's assassination and death in September 1901. "The wise custom," said he, "which limits the President to two terms regards the substance and not the form." "Under no circumstances will I be a candidate for or accept another nomination." And, when later a strong "third-term" movement developed in his behalf, he declared himself to be still of the same determination. All of which, nevertheless, did not hinder his running for President in 1912, and justifying himself for doing so by the argument that if at some time he had declined "a third cup of coffee" nobody would suppose that he had meant never to take another cup. "I meant, of course," said he, "a third consecutive term." Nor, apparently, would Mr. Wilson have been averse, had health permitted, to seeking a third term in 1920,[12] a course which would have been quite in harmony with his conception of the Presidency as the American equivalent of the British premiership.[13]

Roosevelt's succession to McKinley was matched in August 1922 by Coolidge's succession to Harding; but there was the difference that the segment of term which remained to Mr. Coolidge was considerably less than that which had fallen to his predecessor. The question was thus sharply provoked, when is a President to be regarded as having had a "term" in the sense of the custom which condemns a third term for the same individual? Does a third "term" mean a third period of full four years, or a third time? This question Mr. Coolidge coyly side-stepped by not choosing "to run for President in 1928." Whether he would choose to run at some other date was a question left open, as was also the question whether he might not be run even in 1928 without his choosing to. At least we have Mr. "Ike" Hoover's word for it that those who indicated to Mr. Coolidge an opinion that his statement was really no obstacle to his being "drafted" in 1928 were generally invited to the White House again while those who took the other view were apt not to be.[14] That Mr. Coolidge, had he chosen to run, would have been re-elected, seems altogether probable.

Meantime, alongside the doctrine that a President shall have no more than two terms had arisen the inverse doctrine that he is entitled to a renomination at the hands of his party. This, to be sure, is less the consequence of the taboo upon a third term than of the position of the President as party leader. If a President in power is a failure, then the party which is responsible for having put him there is a failure too, and for it to refuse him a nomination is to confess both failures. Nor is a President on completing his second term forbidden by the tradition to name his successor. Jefferson did this, so did Madison with Jefferson's assistance, so did Jackson, so did the first Roosevelt, and so might Woodrow Wilson have done in 1920 had he desired.

Today the anti-third-term tradition qua tradition is no more, having succumbed to the late President's successful defiance of it in 1940, which was repeated in 1944.[15] But where tradition finally failed, partly on account of its vagueness, a more precisely formulated constitutional amendment may perhaps still rescue the general conception and establish it permanently. At any rate, some such calculation may be imputed to the authors of the congressional Resolution of March 24, 1947, the first section of which provides:

"No person shall be elected to the office of the President more than twice, and no person who has held the office of President, or acted as President, for more than two years of a term to which some other person was elected President shall be elected to the office of the President more than once. But this Article shall not apply to any person holding the office of President when this Article was proposed by the Congress, and shall not prevent any person who may be holding the office of President, or acting as President, during the term within which this Article becomes operative from holding the office of President or acting as President during the remainder of such term."

To be effective the amendment must be ratified within seven years.[16]

What are the merits of this question? To begin with, it is as-

serted that the apparent indifference of the people toward the
tradition in 1940 and 1944 was not a passing opinion induced by
temporary crisis but represented their matured judgment, and in
this connection it is pointed out that of all the hundred or more
proposals which have been brought forward in Congress within
the last fifty years to limit the presidential term, not one has ever
reached first base.[17] Yet it is just possible that this outcome is to be
explained not by popular indifference toward the tradition, but
by popular reliance on it—why amend the Constitution when
custom had already done the job satisfactorily? Again, it is contended that eight years may be too short a time to permit a President to establish a needed program. This, obviously, is but the
"indispensable man" argument, to accept which, some one has
wittily said, is next door to despairing of the country. Indeed, the
logic of the argument is that not only should the indispensable
man be renominated as long as he remains indispensable, but that
no one should be nominated to oppose him; in short, that when
the "indispensable man" is in office, presidential elections should
be abolished.[18] Still, this reasoning cannot be conceded for all circumstances, for it is also obvious that political talent is not at all
times equally plentiful, nor necessarily most plentiful just when
there is most need for it. On the other hand, the failure of a President to develop talent capable of carrying on is certainly not an
argument for continuing him in office; to make such provision
is of the business of an executive, of its very essence. And an
untried President may be better than a tired one; a fresh approach
better than a stale one.

Again, it is argued that any such attempt to curtail popular
judgment, to put it in leading strings, is "undemocratic"; "a vote
of lack of confidence in the people"; and contrary to the underlying genius of American institutions, which, while it admits of the
idea of putting restraints on the *government,* does not tolerate

the idea of putting restraints upon the *people* themselves.[19]

But who, it may be asked in answer, *are* "the people"? Does the expression designate an authority more ultimate than that whereby the Constitution is amended? If so, then the entire Constitution curtails their judgment. If not, then ratification of the amendment by the prescribed process will represent the judgment of the people, and the argument against the proposed amendment turned against itself. In fact, of course, the Constitution already curtails the judgment of the people in the matter of the choice of President, who must be among other things "a natural-born citizen of the United States."

Finally, it is urged that the proposal was "politically motivated." No doubt it was, and no doubt opposition to it is politically motivated. Most things that reach us by the political route have a political coloration; that is the way we do things in this country—that is *democracy*. Standing by itself, therefore, this argument is without force. If, however, the political motive which stimulated the promoters of the proposal caused them to scamp the job, then the objection does have force, and to my mind this is exactly what happened. In their haste to register disapproval of the late President for seeking a third and then a fourth term, these gentlemen neglected or ignored the really critical issue, which is *whether a President should be permitted to succeed himself at all*. Inasmuch as the Presidency is a "killing job," to which few men come until they have passed the peak of their physical vigor, few Presidents will be likely to seek a third term, and certainly not a fourth, remembering the penalty which Mr. Roosevelt paid for doing so.

The chief objection to presidential reëligibility, to my mind, is just as valid against a *second* successive term as it would be against a *third* one. It consists in the fact that a President who is looking forward to reëlection will evaluate all programs and policies primarily for their probable effect on his political fortunes and will, in fact, be expected and required by his party to do so. In failing to discuss this, the really fundamental element of the question of presidential reëligibility under modern conditions, the authors of the proposed amendment are, in my opinion, self-convicted of frivolity.[20]

THE ELECTORAL COLLEGE—DANGEROUS BREAKDOWNS

The so-called "Electoral College"—actually a congeries of "colleges"—is provided for in the Constitution in the following terms:

"Each State shall appoint, in such manner as the legislature thereof may direct, a number of electors, equal to the whole number of Senators and Representatives to which the State may be entitled in the Congress; but no Senator or Representative, or person holding an office of trust or profit under the United States, shall be appointed an elector."[21]

The power to determine the manner in which the Electors from any state shall be chosen is thus delegated to the legislature thereof for its exclusive determination, and the most diverse methods have been at various times resorted to. The history of practice in this matter is extensively reviewed in the Court's opinion in *McPherson v. Blacker,* decided in 1892.[22] In summary, the Court says, Electors have been chosen

"by the legislature itself on joint ballot; by the legislature through a concurrent vote of the two houses; by vote of the people for a general ticket; by vote of the people in districts; by choice partly by the people voting in districts and partly by the legislature; by choice by the legislature; by choice by the legislature from candidates voted for by the people in districts; and in other ways, as, notably, by North Carolina in 1792, and Tennessee in 1796 and 1800."[23]

Lot, it is true, seems not to have been resorted to so far, although this method of choosing Electors from Congress itself was actually proposed in the Philadelphia Convention.²⁴ Nor has any state legislature as yet delegated to a President the right to cast the state's vote for his successor.

In the first three presidential elections choice by the legislature itself was the usual method. In the election of 1824, when the choice fell eventually to the House, Electors were chosen by popular vote, either by districts or by general ticket in all but six states; and from 1832 till the Civil War they were chosen by popular vote and by *general ticket* in all states except South Carolina, where the legislature still chose. Since the Civil War there have been but two departures from the general ticket system. In 1876 in Colorado, which had been recently admitted into the Union, choice was by the legislature; and in 1892 Michigan, whose legislature was then in the hands of the Democrats, who however had no hope of retaining their hold on the state as an entirety in the approaching presidential election, choice was by districts, some of which went Democratic.²⁵ There have also been cases in which individual Electors have, on account of personal popularity, been chosen by the minority party.

It was the belief of the Framers of the Constitution that the Electors would exercise their individual judgments in the choice of a President, a belief which the universal understanding that Washington would be the first President, and probably for an indefinite number of terms, went to sustain. But the requirement that the Electors meet "in their respective states," which reflected the poor condition of travel in those days, destroyed the possibility of a deliberative body from the outset; and with the first avowed appearance of party organizations on a national scale, in consequence of Washington's announcement in 1796 that he would not stand for a third term, the Electors became promptly transmuted into party dummies, a character they have retained ever since. Probably the last independent Elector was William Plumer, Sr., whose vote for John Quincy Adams in 1821 prevented Monroe's unanimous reëlection. It has been customary to explain this apparently eccentric conduct of the New Hampshire Elector as arising from his unwillingness to see Monroe honored as only the great Washington had ever been thus far. But Plumer himself asserted at the time that it was his desire to bring the younger Adams to the notice of the country, which he did to such good purpose that four years later Adams became Monroe's successor.[26]

A half century later occurred the disputed election of 1876, and James Russell Lowell, who had been chosen by the Republicans as an Elector from Massachusetts, was besought to save the country from threatened civil war by casting his vote for Tilden. Lowell refused on the ground that he had been elected not as an individual but solely as a party representative.

"I was nominated [said he] and elected by my fellow-citizens of the Republican party to give effect to their political wishes as expressed at the polls, and not to express my own personal views. I am a delegate carrying a definite message, a trustee to carry out definite instructions; I am not a free agent to act upon my own volition; in accepting a place on the Republican ticket I accepted all its limitations and moral obligations. . . . My individual sympathies and preferences are beside the matter; to refuse to comply with the mandate I received when I accepted my party's nomination would be treacherous, dishonorable, and immoral."[27]

Indeed, it was a former President's considered opinion that "an Elector who failed to vote for the nominee of his party would be the object of execration, and in times of very high excitement might be the subject of a lynching."[28] Theoretically, to be sure, the Electors retain their *constitutional* discretion as against any outside *legal* control. But what a totally hollow sham that is, is shown by the fact that in many of the states nowadays the names of the party choices for Elector do not appear on the ballot at all, and the voters vote only for their party.[29]

But, although composed of anonymous mammets, the intervention of the Electoral College in the choice of a President remains a matter of importance—at times, of decisive importance. Because of the state-wide ticket system, each state's representation in the College is ordinarily a party unit; yet because of the intervention of the College the plurality by which it is chosen is, however large or small, operative only within the state's boundaries. The result is that the discrepancy between the size of a candidate's vote in the Electoral College and that of his so-called "popular vote" is often enormous; and particularly is this apt to be so when more than two considerable parties take the field. Thus in 1860 Lincoln and Hamlin received 180 of the 303 electoral votes, but only about two fifths of the total popular vote; and in 1912 Mr. Wilson, while receiving 435 of the 531 electoral votes, was the choice of but few more than six million of the sixteen million voters voting; and in both cases the discrepancy might conceivably have been increased, for many thousands of the votes cast for Lincoln in 1860 and for Wilson in 1912 were cast in states which went for their opponents, and so did not contribute to the choice of members of the Electoral College. Nor should it be overlooked that every state has two Electors who correspond to its representation in the Senate and so are assigned to it without reference to popular voting strength.[30]

The manner in which the Electors originally exercised their function is described in paragraph 3 of section 1 of Article II. The failure of the Electors, however, under this method to distinguish their choice for Vice-President from that of President having produced a tie in the election of 1800 between Jefferson and Burr, this part of the Constitution was presently superseded by Amendment XII, which reads as follows:[31]

"The Electors shall meet in their respective States, and vote by ballot for President and Vice-President, one of whom at least shall not be an inhabitant of the same State with themselves; they shall name in their ballots the person voted for as President, and in distinct ballots the person voted for as Vice-President and they shall make distinct lists of all persons voted for as President, and of all persons voted for as Vice-President, and of the number of votes for each, which lists they shall sign and certify, and transmit sealed to the seat of the government of the United States, directed to the President of the Senate; the President of the Senate shall, in the presence of the Senate and House of Representatives, open all the certificates and the votes shall then be counted; the person having the greatest number of votes for President shall be the President, if such number be a majority of the whole number of Electors appointed; and if no person have such majority, then from the persons having the highest numbers not exceeding three on the list of those voted for as President, the House of Representatives shall choose immediately, by ballot, the President. But in choosing the President, the votes shall be taken by States, the representation from each State having one vote; a quorum for this purpose shall consist of a member or members from two-thirds of the States, and a majority of all the States shall be necessary to a choice. And if the House of Representatives shall not choose a President whenever the right of choice shall devolve upon them, before the fourth day of March next following, then the Vice-President shall act as President, as in the case of the death or other constitutional disability of the President.

"The person having the greatest number of votes as Vice-President shall be the Vice-President, if such number be a majority of the whole number of Electors appointed; and if no person have a majority, then, from the two highest numbers on the list the Senate shall choose the Vice-President; a quorum for the purpose shall consist of two-thirds of the whole number of Senators, and a majority of the whole number shall be necessary to a choice. But no person constitutionally ineligible to the office of President shall be eligible to that of Vice-President of the United States."

But the Twelfth Amendment was itself far from settling all dangerous questions. Thus, who was to count the electoral vote; what powers did this function carry with it; and when was an Elector to be considered as definitely "appointed"? All these questions were involved in the famous Hayes-Tilden election dispute of 1876.[32]

It was conceded by everybody that Mr. Hayes had 165 votes in the Electoral College and that Mr. Tilden had 184 votes, or one vote less than a majority of the College and so of the number necessary for a choice. The House at this time was in the control of the Democrats, the Senate of the Republicans. Although the latter set up the claim that the counting was to be done by the President of the Senate, that functionary discreetly declined to assume a power which none of his predecessors in office had ventured to assert. Custom at least had settled that the counting was to be done by the houses, and by the houses as separate entities and not as composing one joint assembly.[33] Furthermore, under the so-called "Twenty-second Joint Rule," which had been followed in the counting of the electoral vote since 1864, the consent of both houses was necessary to count the vote of any state. That is to say, under this rule either house was in position to exclude the electoral vote of any state from being taken into account in determining "the whole number of Electors appointed." In the existing situation the rule was obviously favorable to the Democrats; but, not having been reënacted by the houses in 1876, it was binding only by acquiescence, and the Republicans, although they were the original authors of the rule, naturally refused acquiescence.

The really vital question in 1876, however, concerned the scope of the power of the houses in *counting* the vote in relation to power of the states to *appoint* Electors. By one theory the two powers were exclusive and coterminous, and the function of the houses was the purely ministerial one of counting the votes of persons who were formally authenticated to them as Electors of a state by the state's election officials. By the other theory the function of the houses overlapped that of the state in some measure, and involved the right on their part to enter into the question whether the appointment of the Electors of a state was tainted with fraud or violence. Again we note a curious reversal of constitutional creeds in the respective attitudes of the two parties. Controlling as they did the election boards of the states involved, the Republicans were all for States Rights in this matter, while the Democrats took the diametrically opposed position.

The dispute was eventually put in the way of settlement by what is undoubtedly the most extraordinary measure in American legislative history. The two houses being hopelessly at loggerheads in the matter of counting the electoral vote, Congress, by an act approved by the President January 29, 1877, created an Electoral Commission, to which, in practical effect, it delegated the power of the houses, as well as power to determine what that power was.[34]

As constituted under the act the Electoral Commission consisted of five members of the House chosen thereby; five Senators chosen by the Senate; and five Justices of the Supreme Court, four of whom were designated in the act itself by reference to their circuits, while the fifth was to be chosen by these four. The House contingent comprised, naturally, three Democrats and two Republicans; the Senate contingent comprised three Republicans and two Democrats; while the four Justices designated by the act were divided equally as to earlier party affiliations. The fifth Justice would therefore presumably be the pivotal member of the commission; and it was originally supposed that this post would be filled by Justice David Davis from Illinois, whose political record was sufficiently ambiguous to suggest a fair possibility of impartiality, or at least the appearance of it. Justice Davis, however, "loved his ease" and was little disposed to assume so arduous a role. When, accordingly, the Democrats of the Illinois legislature, with singular maladroitness from the point of view of party advantage, elected him to a seat in the Senate, he quickly resigned his justiceship and took the proffered post. Thereupon, the judicial members turned to Justice Joseph P. Bradley of New Jersey as the remaining member of the Bench most likely to pursue an unbiased course. In fact Bradley, a Republican, voted with his party throughout on all crucial issues before the commission, though this is not to say that partisan bias was the only consideration determining his decision. The line of reasoning which Justice Bradley developed in his opinions was, save in one instance, consistently adhered to, and was furthermore supported by a practical consideration of the greatest weight. What the Democrats had wanted the houses, and now the commission, to do was to institute an inquiry into the circumstances surrounding the choice of Electors in Florida, South Carolina, and Louisiana. To have done so would have been to postpone any possibility of electing a President far beyond March 4.

Bradley's attitude on the crucial issue before the commission is given in the following passage from his opinion on the reception of the Louisiana vote as attested by the board of canvassers of that state:

"I cannot bring my mind to believe that fraud and misconduct on the part of the State authorities, constituted for the very purpose of declaring the final will of the State, is a subject over which the two Houses of Congress have jurisdiction to institute an examination. The question is not whether frauds ought to be tolerated, or whether they ought not to be circumvented; but whether the Houses of Congress, in exercising their power of counting the electoral votes, are entrusted by the Constitution with authority to investigate them. . . . Evidently no such proceeding was in the minds of the framers of the Constitution. The short and explicit directions there given, that the votes should first be produced before the Houses when met for that purpose, and that 'the votes shall then be counted,' is at variance with any such idea. An investigation beforehand is not authorized and was not contemplated, and would be repugnant to the limited and special power given. What jurisdiction have the Houses on the subject until they have met under the Constitution, except to provide by law for facilitating the performance of their duties? An investigation afterwards, such as the question raised might and frequently would lead to, would be utterly incompatible with the performance of the duty imposed."[35]

In short, the houses, and hence the commission, were unauthorized to go behind the returns as authenticated by the state election officials. In a later paragraph Bradley added, nevertheless: "Whether the legislative power of the government might not, by law, make provision for an investigation into frauds and illegalities, I do not undertake to decide. It cannot be done, in my judgment, by any agency of the Federal Government without legislative regulation."[36]

Thus were nineteen of the disputed electoral votes disposed of. The twentieth was that of an Oregon Elector. That the three Republican Electors of that state had received a majority of the votes cast was not questioned. But one of them, named Watts, had unfortunately at the time of his appointment held "an office of trust and profit under the United States," to wit, that of postmaster. Having resigned his postmastership, however, he had been promptly rechosen by the two remaining Republican Electors under a provision of the Oregon law for the filling of "vacancies" in the post of Elector. But had there been a vacancy? The highest Democratic Elector, one Cronin, claimed not, his contention being that he was the third Elector. Furthermore, Cronin had been able to convince the secretary of state and the governor of the correctness of his view, and they had issued him a certificate of election. Notwithstanding their previous emphasis upon the sanctity of the election certificate, the Republican members of the commission rejected Cronin and recognized Watts.

The act establishing the Electoral Commission contained a proviso reserving any right existing under the Constitution to question before the national courts the titles of the persons who should be declared elected President and Vice-President. Despite the intensity of feeling which the contest had produced no action of the sort was brought, although Justice Field expressed the hope that one would be.[37]

By the Act of February 3, 1887, passed to prevent a recurrence of the episode of 1876 but not until eleven years later, it is provided that if a contest arises in any state over the appointment of any of its Electors, the state itself is authorized to determine such contest, provided it does so at least six days before the time for the meeting of the Electors; and all determinations of such contests made pursuant to state law shall be "conclusive, and shall govern the counting of the electoral votes as provided in the Constitution" when duly certified to the houses by the executive of the state under the seal thereof. But if a state neglects to provide machinery for this purpose, in other words, fails to comply with the act, then the electoral vote of such state is not to be received unless both houses of Congress are favorable.[38] In short, the act adopts and gives statutory form to the principle which was followed by the Electoral Commission.

Paragraph 4 of section 1 of Article II of the Constitution empowers Congress to "determine the time of choosing the Electors and the day on which they shall give their votes, which day shall be the same throughout the United States." Under the Act of March 1, 1792, previously mentioned, the Electors are chosen on the Tuesday following the first Monday in November of every fourth year; while by the Act of June 5, 1934, enacted to give effect to the Twentieth Amendment, the Electors of each state meet and give their votes the first Monday after the second Wednesday in December following the November election, and the two houses meet to count the votes in the hall of the House of Representatives on the ensuing January 6 at one p.m.[39]

Has Congress any further powers with respect to the choice and functioning of the presidential Electors? On first consideration it might seem not, inasmuch as the Court has more than once characterized Electors as "state officers." But, to begin with, the accuracy of this designation is open to serious challenge. Certainly the mode of choice does not determine the question— United States Senators were not state officers even when they were chosen by state legislatures. The office of Elector is created by the Constitution of the United States and the function which Electors perform is a national function. In the face, therefore, of the proposition that Electors are "state officers," the Court held shortly after the Civil War that Congress had power to protect the right of all citizens who were entitled to vote to lend aid and support "in any legal manner" to the election of any lawfully qualified person as a presidential Elector, and latterly it held that Congress may enact legislation calculated to protect the choice of President and Vice-President from corruption. "That a government," the Court declared in the earlier of these cases,

"whose essential character is republican, whose executive head and legislative body are both elective, whose most numerous and powerful branch of the legislature is elected by the people directly, has no power by appropriate laws to secure this election from the influence of violence, of corruption, and of fraud, is a proposition so startling as to arrest attention and demand the gravest consideration.

"If this government is anything more than a mere aggregation of delegated agents of other States and governments, each of which is superior to the general government, it must have the power to protect the elections on which its existence depends from violence and corruption.

"If it has not this power it is left helpless before the two great natural and historical enemies of all republics, open violence and insidious corruption."[40]

The Court then quoted with approval the following words from Chancellor Kent's *Commentaries:*

"The government of the United States was created by the free voice and joint will of the people of America for their common defence and general welfare. Its powers apply to those great interests which relate to this country in its national capacity, and which depend for their protection on the consolidation of the Union. It is clothed with the principal attributes of political sovereignty, and it is justly deemed the guardian of our best rights, the source of our highest civil and political duties and the sure means of national greatness."

And the decision in *Burroughs v. United States,*[41] referred to above, is grounded on like doctrine. Indeed, it would seem that this reasoning should be given still wider application. Why, for instance, should not Congress, taking account of the fact that presidential Electors are today mere party dummies, turn its attention to the political activities which *really* determine the choice of Presidents, and regulate such activities to the extent which it deems necessary for the purpose of keeping them open and aboveboard and free from corrupt manipulation?[42]

Again, by virtue of its power to implement the Fifteenth Amendment, Congress has enacted penalties against persons who, under color of state authority, deprive any person on account of race, color, or previous condition of servitude, of the right to vote for members of Congress or presidential Electors, a right which under recent decisions includes the right to participate in party primaries in states where nomination to office is equivalent to election.[43] Also, during the recent war Congress laid claim in the Act of September 16, 1942, to the power "in time of war" to secure to every member of the armed services the right to vote for members of Congress and presidential Electors "notwithstanding any provision of State law relating to the registration of qualified voters," or any poll-tax requirement under state law. By the Act of April 1, 1944, however, these pretensions were substantially abandoned. The latter act established a United States War Ballot Commission which was directed to prepare "an adequate number of official Federal war ballots" whereby the servicemen would be enabled in certain contingencies to vote for members of Congress and presidential Electors; but the validity of such ballots was left to be determined by state election officials under state laws.[44]

The constitutional validity of the Act of September 16, 1942, was open to serious question, to say the least. Undoubtedly Congress has the right to pass legislation for the purpose of protecting the rights of servicemen. But the "right" in this case is one that springs in the first instance from state law, and is defined by it, subject only to the provisions of the Fifteenth and Nineteenth Amendments. Besides, there is nothing in the Constitution to prevent a state from adopting some other method of "appointing" presidential Electors than by popular vote, as by relegating the business once more to the state legislature.

On no problem did the Convention of 1787 expend more time and effort than that of devising a suitable method of choosing a President. With no other feature of the Constitution did they express greater satisfaction than on the method finally devised. It is, Hamilton declared in *The Federalist,* "the only part of the Constitution not condemned by its opponents."[45] Actually, no feature of the Constitution has raised more difficulties in the past, or remains at this moment a graver menace to our domestic peace. Based on the theory that George Washington was going to live practically forever, the scheme has remained workable since his demise only in consequence of the rise of national parties, a development which the Convention did not foresee and would have deplored. And even with the national party organizations to supplement it the system was confronted with serious breakdown in 1800, 1824, 1860, and 1876. The same sort of breakdown may easily occur again, with results that are unpredictable. Imagine the capture of a substantial electoral vote by a "third party"; either the Electoral College would be forced to choose a minority President as in 1860 and 1912, or the election would be thrown into the House, and Nevada would have equal voice with New York in the final choice of a President. One feature of this preposterous arrangement is mitigated by the Twentieth Amendment—a new House of Representatives would do the electing instead of one possibly under the control of a defeated party. But this reform is only a short first step in the revision which must be effected sooner or later of this vital feature of our constitutional system.

Serious consideration ought, therefore, be given a proposal which had the support of the late Senator Norris. By this plan, while the Electoral College would be abolished, each state would remain an electoral unit with the same relative strength as at present in the choice of a President, which, however, would be divided among the contesting parties in proportion to their popular vote in the state. Also, a plurality of electoral votes would elect. Thus, the danger would be obviated of the election ever being thrown into the House of Representatives, which is the outstanding peril of the present arrangement.[46]

ANOTHER DANGER SPOT—PRESIDENTIAL DISABILITY

Article II, section 1, paragraph 6, of the Constitution reads as follows:

"In case of the removal of the President from office, or of his death, resignation, or inability to discharge the powers and duties of the said office, the same shall devolve on the Vice President, and the Congress may by law provide for the case of removal, death, resignation, or inability, both of the President and Vice President, declaring what officer shall then act as President, and such officer shall act accordingly until the disability be removed or a President shall be elected."

Who is authorized to say whether a President is unable to discharge the powers and duties of his office? When he is unable to do so, does the said office become vacant? What is it to which the Vice-President succeeds when the President is disabled, or is removed, or has died—to the "powers and duties of the said office," or to the office itself? Or does he succeed to the former when the President is disabled, and to the latter when the President has vanished permanently from the scene? And what is the election referred to in the last clause of the above provision—is it the next regular presidential election or a special election to be called by Congress? Finally, suppose a vacancy were to exist in the Presidency for some reason not mentioned above, as it would if the Electoral College, and then the House and Senate, respectively, failed to elect either a President or Vice-President or if both President-elect and the Vice-President-elect died before their assumption of office—what provision does the Constitution make for such a situation?

Twice in the history of the country Presidents have been unable to discharge their official duties for extended periods. President Garfield was thus disabled from July 2, 1881, when he was shot by Guiteau, till his death the following September 19; and President Wilson was disabled for many weeks following his collapse September 26, 1919.

Out of each of these episodes an extended discussion arose as to how such a situation was to be dealt with constitutionally. Apparently the most widely held view was that it was the duty of the Vice-President alone to decide the issue of "inability," since if inability existed it was he who must act; but the case must be a clear one, otherwise the Vice-President would be a mere usurper and punishable as such. Another theory conceded that the *initial* responsibility lay with the Vice-President, but urged that his action must receive the ratification of Congress, as in effect it had in the case of both Tyler and Fillmore; and until such ratification was forthcoming a succeeding Vice-President was, it was contended, only "acting President *de facto*," while following it he became "acting President *de jure*." A third view put the initial responsibility on Congress to provide beforehand for the determination, on the basis of evidence, of a President's alleged "inability" by the Supreme Court, or the President's own Cabinet, or by the houses of Congress themselves, acting by concurrent resolution. And of course there were variants of these views, some people urging that the Vice-President could be compelled by mandamus to take action, others that any action he took would be subject to judicial review, and yet others that Congress was entitled to define "inability," and so on.[47]

In point of fact, in the case of neither Garfield nor Wilson did either Congress or the Vice-President act. In both cases alike the official powers and duties of the disabled President were left to be discharged in such manner and by such devices as his immediate family and personal entourage had a mind to contrive. To all intents and purposes it was they who determined the issue of disability, and determined it contrary to apparent fact.[48]

All Vice-Presidents—seven of them—who have succeeded to
the Presidency have done so in consequence of the death of the
President, and this fact has made easy the establishment of the
idea that they were entitled to succeed to the presidential *office*
rather than merely to "the powers and duties of the said office."
But the question still remains whether this result, sanctioned
though it now is by repeated usage, is harmonious with the
original intention of the Constitution; and also the more important question practically, whether the usage established for
the only kind of case that has hitherto arisen should be considered as applying to all possible occasions of vice-presidential
succession.

The first instance of a Vice-President succeeding was that of
Tyler to the elder Harrison, in 1841. Certain circumstances in
connection with the event are worth recounting. Harrison died
April 4 and two days later Tyler took the oath prescribed by the
Constitution for the President, but only, as he explained at the
time, for "greater caution," his own conviction being that he was
fully "qualified to perform the duties and exercise the powers and
offices of President . . . without any other oath than that which
he" had taken as Vice-President. In other words, it was clearly
Tyler's original belief that he was Vice-President acting as President, and not President. But as was apt to be the case with Tyler,
reflection enhanced his self-assurance and stiffened his attitude,
and in the "inaugural address" which he published on April 5
he boldly proclaimed that he had been called to "the high office
of President of this Confederacy," though by whom called he
did not say. In other quarters, nevertheless, some doubt seems
still to have lingered. For when, with the convening of Congress
nearly two months later, the customary resolutions were introduced into the two houses to inform "the President" that they
were in session, amendments were promptly offered to substitute

the term "Vice-President," but were with equal promptitude voted down, that in the Senate by a vote of thirty-eight to eight.[49]

And unquestionably it was malice pure and simple which a quarter of a century later would fain have seen Andrew Johnson impeached as "Vice President discharging the powers and duties of the office of President of the United States"; and the move was ineffectual, for the impeachment ultimately voted was of "Andrew Johnson, President of the United States."[50] Nor was the question again mooted outside of books till 1927, when a Republican advocate of a third term for Mr. Coolidge informed the latter that it would not be a third term, inasmuch as following Mr. Harding's death he had been only "acting President."[51]

But is the outcome of usage regarding this matter harmonious with the original intention of the Constitution? In his *Usages of the American Constitution,* Mr. Henry W. Horwill asserts confidently that it is not, but his argument is not altogether persuasive.[52] The constitutional provision on which Mr. Horwill most relies is the provision quoted above, in which, he contends, "the powers and duties of the said office" is "grammatically" the antecedent of "the same." To the contrary, as it seems to me, the requirements of *grammar* are better met by making "the office" the antecedent, this alone being mentioned in the opening clause of the paragraph. Also, we may note the care which the Twelfth Amendment manifests to require the same qualifications for the Vice-Presidency as for the Presidency, although the original Constitution did not. That the Vice-President succeeds permanently when the President dies, resigns, or is removed is not disputed; and this being so, he may well be held to succeed to the office of President, for what is the difference between an "office" and "the powers and duties" thereof when to the latter is joined a guaranteed tenure? What is more, when the Vice-President succeeds he also succeeds, by uncontroverted practice, to the salary of "the

President"—a circumstance which President Coolidge regarded with obvious approval.[53]

On one point, nevertheless, Mr. Horwill's argument is conclusive. The existing precedents do not, and should not, apply in the case of a temporary disability of the President; and this also seems to be the theory of Amendment XX.[54]

If the President leaves the country, does his absence disable him from exercising the powers and duties of his office? The question was raised by critics of President Wilson when he went abroad following the war with Germany. President Washington, the critics pointed out, had refused even to enter Rhode Island until that stiff-necked little commonwealth had joined the Union; and while President Taft had visited the Canal Zone in 1910, being absent from November 9 to November 23, he had been scrupulous to travel on an American war vessel and to remain on soil subject to American jurisdiction. But then, President Wilson also traveled on a government vessel; and if such technicalities avail it would seem that wherever an American President treads is for the moment American soil.[55]

Even more extreme was the implication of a resolution adopted by the Democratic House of Representatives in 1876 that the President must perform his official acts at the "seat of government established by law." President Grant, who was the target of the resolution, had the satisfaction of demonstrating to his Democratic critics that of all Presidents Thomas Jefferson was the one who had been most persistently absent from the Capitol, his record of absenteeism being 796 days, or more than one fourth of his eight years in office;[56] and any significance that the issue thus raised may have had in the past has been pretty well eliminated by modern ease and speed of travel.

In enforcement of its power to provide for the lack of "both a President and a Vice-President," Congress has passed three "Presidential Succession Acts" so-called. The Act of 1792 provided for the succession first of the President *pro tempore* of the Senate and then of the Speaker, who however were to hold office only until a new President could be chosen for another four years. The act thus violated the principle of the separation of powers by investing an officer of the national legislature in his quality as such with the full executive power; while by the provisions which it made for an intermediate election for a full term it set at naught the synchrony evidently demanded by the Constitution in the choice of President with that of a new House of Representatives and one third of the Senate. Furthermore, it failed to deal with the possibility of there being no President *pro tempore* or Speaker, which would be the case if the Congress in office had not yet organized; and it boldly flouted the probability that neither the Speaker nor the President *pro tempore* is an "officer" in the sense of this paragraph of the Constitution.[57]

The Act of January 19, 1886, recently repealed,[58] provided for the succession of members of the Cabinet in the order of the establishment of their respective offices, provided the incumbent possessed the constitutional qualifications for the Presidency. On the plausible theory that the officer "acted as President" by virtue of his post in the Cabinet, he continued in the latter—a member of his own Cabinet. The statute also required that if Congress was not already in session when such a contingency arose or was not scheduled to meet within twenty days, it should be convened in extraordinary session; but it made no reference, as had the earlier act, to the possibility of a special, intermediate election.

Recent consideration of the subject by Congress dates from President Roosevelt's death, April 12, 1945. A few days later Mr. James A. Farley attacked as "undemocratic" the power vested by the Act of 1886 in a Vice-President, once he has succeeded to the Presidency, to name his own successor. The criticism was widely echoed by the press, and this, together with the wish to be able to effect certain Cabinet changes without being embarrassed by the "succession" question, caused President Truman to send to Congress, June 19, a message urging a new Presidential Succession Act. The President based his demand on the contention that in a democracy the President should not have the power to appoint his successor if the office could be filled by an elective officer; and of all elective officers, he argued, "the Speaker is the official in the federal government whose election next to that of the President and Vice President can be most accurately said to stem from the people themselves." But if a Speaker was lacking, then the President suggested that the President *pro tempore* of the Senate be put next in the line of succession, and after him the Cabinet officers, as under the Act of 1886. Finally, however, an election ought to be held as soon as possible "to fill out the unexpired term." [59]

For a time popular interest continued keen, and numerous proposals were forthcoming both from members of Congress and from outsiders, some of them highly original. [60] But when Mr. Byrnes, who as head of OWMR (Office of War Mobilization and Reconversion) had served acceptably as a sort of assistant President, became Secretary of State, interest fell off rapidly, and remained at a low ebb until after the November 1946 election. With it certain that the House of Representatives in the Eightieth Congress would be Republican, members of that body challenged the President to stand by his proposal, which Mr. Truman sportingly declared that he was prepared to do. [61]

The consequence is that Congress has recently enacted a measure which embodies all of Mr. Truman's proposals except the one for an interim election, and adds two improvements. The first is that it provides for vacancies by reason not only "of death, resignation, removal from office, inability," but also by reason of "failure to qualify," an addition which is meant to implement Amendment XX. In the second place it provides that whoever succeeds to "act as President" under the act must straightway resign the post by virtue of which he succeeded, and if it is the Speaker he must also resign "as Representative in Congress."[62]

The argument for the measure, aside from its relation to Amendment XX, was not impressive. The Speaker may "stem from the people" but it is only from the people of one out of four hundred and thirty-five congressional districts. And when we put the names of the men who have filled the Speaker's office in the past alongside those who have filled the office of Secretary of State, the comparison is decidedly to the advantage of the latter. As Professor Rankin has put the matter, "As a whole the Secretaries of State have, throughout our history, been more nearly of the calibre that Americans desire for a President than have Speakers of the House." Nor is this surprising, for the latter is usually a man who represents a "sure district—which is less likely than a close district to produce a superior man." On the other hand, it has happened more than once since the days of Monroe and John Quincy Adams that Secretaries of State have cast their official superiors somewhat in the shade.

What Congress might and should have done in this matter is fairly clear. For cases of vacancy occurring in the second half of a presidential term the Act of 1886 was quite sufficient and easily workable. For cases of vacancy occurring in the first half of the term Congress ought to provide for a regular presidential election at the time of the mid-term congressional election. Such a measure would not only preserve intact the assumption of the Constitution that the terms of a new President, a new House of Representatives, and one third of the Senate shall start together; it would at the same time reduce to its proper dimensions the question what "officer shall act as President" when both President and Vice-President are lacking,[63] and that such a measure would be constitutional seems to be evident, there being no restriction upon the power of Congress to set the date of a presidential election other than that such date shall be the same "throughout the United States"; but, of course, Congress cannot shorten the presidential term, which is definitely stipulated to be "four years."

It is the purpose also of the Twentieth Amendment to prevent certain types of vacancy arising in the presidential office. The relevant provisions are the following:

Section III

"If, at the time fixed for the beginning of the term of the President, the President elect shall have died, the Vice-President elect shall become President. If a President shall not have been chosen before the time fixed for the beginning of his term, or if the President elect shall have failed to qualify, then the Vice-President elect shall act as President until a President shall have qualified; and the Congress may by law provide for the case wherein neither a President elect nor a Vice-President elect shall have qualified, declaring who shall then act as President or the manner in which one who is to act shall be selected, and such person shall act accordingly until a President or Vice-President shall have qualified."

Section IV

"The Congress may by law provide for the case of the death of any of the persons from whom the House of Representatives may choose a President whenever the right of choice shall have devolved upon them, and for the case of the death of any of the persons from whom the Senate may choose a Vice-President whenever the right of choice shall have devolved upon them."

Without supplementary legislation by Congress these provisions were only partially efficacious for their purpose, but the new Succession Act fills the gaps. This much, at any rate, is to be said for it.[64]

OATH OF OFFICE; COMPENSATION; THE VICE-PRESIDENT

Paragraph 8 of section 1 of Article II of the Constitution reads:

"Before he enter on the execution of his office he shall take the following oath or affirmation:

"'I do solemnly swear (or affirm) that I will faithfully execute the office of President of the United States, and will, to the best of my ability, preserve, protect, and defend the Constitution of the United States.'"

Is the President already in office when he takes the above oath, or is taking it a necessary step in his assumption of office? The former would seem to be the correct theory. It is "the President" who is required to take the oath; the Act of March 1, 1792, referred to on an earlier page, assumed that President Washington became President on March 4, 1789, although he did not take the oath till the following April 30; and in the parallel case of the coronation oath, the royal succession is not dependent on the heir's taking it. The ceremony is, in fact, sometimes deferred for years.[65] In short, the President's first official duty is to take the above prescribed oath, and his refusal to do so would be a violation of the Constitution.

The question whether the oath confers upon the President powers which he would not otherwise possess, especially in connection with interpreting the Constitution, is dealt with in the following section.

Paragraph 7 of section 1 of Article II reads as follows:

"The President shall, at stated times, receive for his services a compensation, which shall neither be increased nor diminished during the period for which he shall have been elected, and he shall not receive within that period any other emolument from the United States or any of them."[66]

A decision of the Supreme Court, rendered in 1920, held that the salary of a judge of the United States would be "diminished" contrary to Article III, section 1, by the application to it of a general income tax which was levied after the judge took office; and a later case held the same as to an income tax which was in force when he took office.[67] Clearly, the same rule would apply to the President's salary; and furthermore, since this may not be "increased" during his term, and he may receive no "other emolument from the United States," a general income tax in force when he took office would have to be maintained at the same rate during such term, and not only as to his salary but also as to his income from private sources, even though repealed as to everybody else's income! Awareness of these absurdities was probably one of the reasons why the Court recently overruled the second of the decisions referred to and laid the ax to the roots of the other.[68]

A further word or two should be added regarding the Vice-President.[69] In the first Senate a debate sprang up over how the President should be addressed. "His High Mightiness" was one proposal, "His Excellency" another. Thereupon, the further question arose of how the Vice-President should be addressed, and some one suggested "His Superfluous Excellency." From that date to this the Vice-Presidency has been a theme for disparagement even by its incumbents. "My country," wrote the first Vice-President to his wife, "has in its wisdom contrived for me the most insignificant office that ever the invention of man contrived or his imagination conceived";[70] and a century and a quarter later Vice-President Marshall compared his official condition to that of "a man in a cataleptic fit. He is conscious of all that goes on but has no part in it."

Actually the first Vice-President played no inconsiderable role. As president of the Senate he exerted a control over its proceedings which its later rules were to make impossible. He also had occasion to exercise his constitutional prerogative of giving the casting vote to break a tie no less than twenty times—a record which no successor has approached. President Washington, too, frequently consulted with him, as he did with the Chief Justice and many others in the interval before the definite appearance of the Cabinet. Besides, prior to the Twelfth Amendment, the Vice-President was in a sense—a fact not overlooked by Adams—"the constitutional equal of the President," having been voted for by the Electors, not for "Vice-President," but for "President."[71] He was, in other words, the second political figure in the country, and due as such to succeed the existing incumbent of the Presidency, as in fact the first two Vice-Presidents did.

Following the retirement of Washington, however, the office received a succession of blows. President and Vice-President were now of opposed parties, with the result that official intimacy ceased. Then came the Twelfth Amendment, and along with it the practice of "the Virginia School of Presidents" of making their Secretaries of State their successors-designate. Thereafter the Vice-Presidency was ordinarily a somewhat secondary pawn in the game of choosing a President. Lastly, Calhoun, who had aimed for higher things, had his revenge on the office by his famous ruling in 1826 that as presiding officer of the Senate he was not entitled to call a Senator to order—those proud ambassadors of the Sovereign States—thereby pointing senatorial procedure toward its present individualism.

The inherent feebleness of the office was never better exemplified than in the negligible role which it played in 1881 and again in 1919. Yet this is not without its element of compensation; at least we have never seen the country plunged into civil war by a scheming Vice-President; and latterly the office has shown some signs of revival—not dangerous, yet promising. The succession of the first Roosevelt and of Coolidge, occurring as they did within a few years of each other, conveyed a warning of the potentialities of the office which has not gone altogether unheeded by the party Warwicks. At the same time Presidents have also given thought to making the Vice-Presidency an instrument of presidential leadership, though thus far with varying success. Mr. Coolidge by Mr. Harding's invitation sat in the latter's Cabinet, but could not persuade Mr. Dawes to follow suit. Mr. Garner sat in Mr. Roosevelt's Cabinet, not always to the entire satisfaction of either, it may be suspected. Perhaps Gouverneur Morris had the right of the matter in the Philadelphia Convention. Objecting to the proposal to make the Vice-President president of the Senate, Elbridge Gerry had said: "We might as well put the President himself at the head of the Legislature. The close intimacy that must subsist between the President and the Vice President makes it absolutely improper," to which Morris retorted: "The Vice President then will be the first heir apparent that ever loved his father!"[72]

THE OATH AGAIN; JOHNSON'S IMPEACHMENT

We return to the President's oath to "preserve, protect and defend the Constitution" "to the best of my [his] ability." Two questions arise: (1) Does the oath add anything to the President's powers? (2) Does it add anything to his reading of these powers?

Logically, there is obvious difficulty in claiming for the President powers which the Constitution otherwise withholds from him simply on the score of his obligation to protect and preserve it. Nor does history prior to the establishment of the Constitution aid the case for treating the oath as an independent source of power. The Philadelphia Convention in elaborating the oath drew upon the constitutions of Pennsylvania, Georgia, and South

Carolina in which the oaths required of the governors of these states were certainly not regarded as augmenting their powers. Nor was a word spoken in the Convention, or afterwards while ratification of the Constitution was pending, so far as I have discovered, which lends any countenance to the idea that the oath would increase presidential powers. And even more clearly, if possible, does the coronation oath of the English King, from which the President's oath is lineally descended, refuse to lend itself to any such interpretation. By it the King swore to "confirm to the people of England the laws and customs granted to them by the ancient kings of England," and to "hold and keep the righteous customs which the community" of the realm should have chosen and to "defend and strengthen the same."[73] Its purpose, definitely, was to put the King's conscience in bonds to the law.

The notion that the President's oath adds indeterminate cubits to his constitutional stature is a phase of the Jacksonian conception of the powers of the office as autonomous, and the *locus classicus* of the idea is Jackson's Bank Veto Message of July 10, 1832.[74] Jackson's primary intention was to assert his right to veto, on the ground that it was unconstitutional, a measure which by existing decisions of the Court was clearly constitutional; but he used language, or Taney—the real author of the message—used language which was construable as claiming for the President the right to refuse to enforce both statutes and judicial decisions on his own independent finding that they were not warranted by the Constitution. Many years later Taney, now Chief Justice, in a letter to Van Buren, vigorously repudiated this reading of the message. "General Jackson," said he, "never expressed a doubt as to the duty and obligation upon him in his executive character to carry into execution any act of Congress regularly passed, whatever his own opinion might be of the constitutional question."[75]

The legend that Jackson declared of the Supreme Court's decision in *Worcester v. Georgia,* "Well, John Marshall has made his decision, now let him enforce it!" may be *only* legend.[76]

The outstanding precedent, however, for treating the oath as a source of power is not of Jacksonian but—ironically enough—of Whig provenience. I mean Lincoln's invocation of it in his message of July 4, 1861, in partial defense of his suspension of the writ of habeas corpus without obtaining congressional authorization, "Are all the laws *but one,*" he inquired, "to go unexecuted, and the Government itself go to pieces lest that one be violated? Even in such a case, would not the official oath be broken if the Government should be overthrown when it was believed that disregarding the single law would tend to preserve it?"[77] He straightway added, it is true, that he did not believe the question he had put "was presented" or that "any law was violated"; but if anything can be certain it is that by previously established tests of constitutionality the law *was* violated, and not alone with respect to the suspension of habeas corpus. Furthermore, Lincoln's apology is immensely weakened by his failure to summon Congress long prior to this date, for it is this which made necessary most of the acts that the apology was intended to justify. Nor can there be any doubt that in proceeding as he did Lincoln permanently recruited power for the President—recruited it, that is, from the presidential oath.

The question raised by Jackson in 1832—perhaps inadvertently —was brought forward deliberately, albeit with some caution, by Johnson's counsel in his impeachment trial in 1868. The main charge against Johnson was that in removing Stanton from office as Secretary of War he had deliberately violated the Tenure of Office Act of 1867. Conceding for the sake of argument that the act had been violated, Evarts contended for Johnson that the latter's course was justifiable as a bona fide attempt to bring before the Supreme Court the question whether the act did not unconstitutionally invade the powers of his office; and he pointed out that in no other way and by no other person could this question have been submitted to judicial determination.[78] Another of the President's counsel, Groesbeck, seems indeed to have gone even further. "Shall he [the President]," Groesbeck queried, "execute all laws?" and answered:

"No. If a law be declared by the Supreme Court unconstitutional he should not execute it. If the law be upon its very face in flat contradiction to plain express provisions of the Constitution, as if a law should forbid the President to grant a pardon in any case, or if a law should declare that he should not be Commander-in-chief, or if a law should declare that he should take no part in the making of a treaty, I say the President, without going to the Supreme Court of the United States, maintaining the integrity of his department, which for the time being is intrusted to him, is bound to execute no such legislation; and he is cowardly and untrue to the responsibilities of his position if he should execute it."[79]

The position of Johnson's impeachers was stated by one of them in the following uncompromising terms:

"If a law be in fact unconstitutional it may be repealed by Congress, or it may, possibly, when a case duly arises, be annulled in its unconstitutional features by the Supreme Court of the United States. The repeal of the law is a legislative act; the declaration by the court that it is unconstitutional is a judicial act; but the power to repeal, or to annul, or to set aside a law of the United States, is in no aspect of the case an executive power. It is made the duty of the Executive to take care that the laws be faithfully executed—an injunction wholly inconsistent with the theory that it is in the power of the Executive to repeal, or annul, or dispense with the laws of the land. To the President in the performance of his executive duties all laws are alike. He can enter into no inquiry as to their expediency or constitutionality. All laws are presumed to be constitutional, and whether in fact constitutional or not, it is the duty of the Executive so to regard them while they have the form of law."[80]

And another of the impeachers answered Groesbeck thus: "It is not a supposable contingency that two-thirds of both houses of Congress will flatly violate their oaths in a clear case."[81] That is, it is not "a supposable contingency" that the President should be more conscientious than two thirds of both houses. The argument from the "clear case" did not apply.

The outcome of Johnson's trial, his acquittal by a single vote—not to mention the political maneuvers which account for this outcome—make the episode of slight value as a precedent. But viewing the question from the angle of the actual record of practice under the Constitution, it seems clear that the impeachers had the better of the argument for all but the most urgent situations. No one doubts that the President possesses prerogatives which Congress may not constitutionally invade; but neither does any one doubt that he is under obligation to "take care that the laws be faithfully executed." And, he was endowed by the Constitution with a qualified veto upon acts of Congress with the idea among others in mind that he might thus protect his prerogatives from legislative curtailment. But this power being exercised, this power of self-defense is at an end; and once a statute has been duly enacted, whether over his protest or with his approval, he must promote its enforcement by all the powers which are constitutionally at his disposal unless and until enforcement is prevented by regular judicial process. And his oath, far from diminishing this obligation, on the contrary reënforces it.[82] These conclusions apply, however, only to his executive capacity; in his legislative capacity the President stands in all respects on a constitutional level with Congress.[83]

While the foregoing pages hardly require summarization, it may be appropriate to recur to one or two matters of topical interest and importance. The Framers devised the Electoral College with the intention of rendering the President indefinitely reëligible. Conversely, they assumed that the College would prove workable because they believed the President would be indefinitely reëligible, and that when one retired the incumbent Vice-President would usually succeed him. Granted these assumptions, and the adoption of the Electoral College becomes understandable. However, the Jeffersonian ban on indefinite reëligibility must soon have put matters in a different light, had not Jefferson been able to offset his work of destruction with one of construction; I mean his creation of a national party. For a quarter of a century following his election a single political party dominated the country and hence the College, and by so doing kept the latter workable. Nor, thanks to the rise of the Jacksonian Democracy, did the breakdown which occurred in 1825 long continue.

The verdict of actual practice is that the Electoral College provides a feasible method of choosing a President so long as there is a continuously dominant party in the country, as was the case from 1801 to 1825, and again with two interruptions from 1829 to 1861, and again from 1861 to 1873. Moreover, it remains a more or less feasible method in the presence of two fairly equal, alternating parties, despite the fact that the majority party in the College may be the minority party at the polls—even overwhelmingly so. But should a strong third party ever spring up the scheme would be confronted with the dangerous possibility of entire collapse. Although just such a danger has impended several times already, the lesson of the situation has been obscured each time by a fortuitously fortunate dénouement. But we should not continue to rely solely on the intervention of that Providence which is said to have fools and the American people in its special care. Hence serious attention ought to be given the proposed constitutional amendment, sponsored by the late Senator Norris, to which reference was made early in this chapter. Nor should another case of presidential disability be permitted to occur without some procedure for handling such situations having been enacted. In a word, Congress should wake up to its responsibility for keeping the Constitution a workable instrument of government. Unfortunately, its recent exploits having that apparent end in view are not highly encouraging as to its capacity for such work.

Finally, as to the presidential oath, it is still "a bridle" and not "a spur," but the impeaching power holds the reins of that bridle very loosely.

CHAPTER III

ADMINISTRATIVE CHIEF

LOGICALLY, in some measure chronologically, the President's first duty is to constitute an "administration," that is to say, a more or less integrated body of officials whose chief duty is the enforcement of the acts of Congress. The President's own duty in connection with the enforcement of the laws is phrased by the Constitution as follows: "He shall take care that the laws be faithfully executed." What precisely is the scope of the *power* which this *duty* implies? The Constitution is ambiguous regarding this most interesting matter. The opening clause of Article II carries the implication that the sum total of executive power which is known to or recognized by the Constitution belongs to the President. The clause just quoted suggests, on the contrary, that there is, or can be, in connection with the enforcement of the laws, an executive power which does not belong to the President, although he must supervise it.

What, then, is the scope of the President's supervisory powers over his "subordinates," and is it subject to any extent to determination by Congress? And what is the scope of the President's power to appoint to office; and of his power to remove therefrom? Obviously, all these questions are more or less related; and particularly is the question of the scope of the President's removal power closely connected with that of the scope of his supervisory power—whom the President may remove he may dominate.

It is the purpose of the first three sections of this chapter to deal with the above questions in relation to the upper levels of federal administrative personnel, those whose members are clothed with "discretionary" powers. Then will follow a section devoted to

The Notes to this chapter begin on page four hundred fourteen

consideration of Executive Order 9835, which in dealing with the problem of disloyalty in the civil service represents the projection of presidential disciplinary power into all levels of the service. A final section will treat of the kindred powers of the President to stop the mouths of his subordinates even when one of the other branches is trying to force them to talk.

"OFFICE" AND APPOINTMENT THERETO

It was formerly, and within limits is still, an element of the royal prerogative in England to create offices as well as to appoint to them.[1] At the outset, in fact, the two things were indistinguishable. Etymologically, an "office" is an *officium,* a duty; and an "officer" was simply one whom the King had charged with a duty. In the course of time certain frequently recurrent and naturally coherent duties came to be assigned more or less permanently, and hence emerged the concept of "office" as an *institution* distinct from the person holding it and capable of persisting beyond his incumbency.

The Constitution, however, by the "necessary and proper" clause assigns the power to *create* offices to Congress, while it deals with the *appointing power* in the following words of Article II, section 2, paragraph 2:

"And he [the President] shall nominate, and by and with the advice and consent of the Senate shall appoint ambassadors, other public ministers and consuls, judges of the Supreme Court, and all other officers of the United States, whose appointments are not herein otherwise provided for and which shall be established by law; but the Congress may by law vest the appointment of such inferior officers as they think proper in the President alone, in the courts of law, or in the heads of departments."

An appointment is, therefore, ordinarily to an *existing* office, and one which owes its existence to an act of Congress.[2] The contention has, nevertheless, been advanced at times that certain offices are the creation of the Constitution itself. This is obviously so as to the two great elective offices of President and Vice-President. How, then, is it as regards membership on the Supreme Court, which is an appointive office? The Court has voiced the theory more than once that it derives its existence directly from the Constitution,[3] an idea which logically implies that membership on it arises from the same source, it being rather difficult to imagine a court without members. The size of the Court would then be for the appointing power—the President acting with the advice and consent of the Senate—to determine, although in point of fact Congress has always done this. On the other hand, until 1855 Congress left it entirely with the President, subject to the advice and consent of the Senate, to appoint such "public ministers and consuls" as in his judgment the national interests required, the theory being, as stated by Attorney General Cushing, that the designations of such officers were "derived from the law of nations and the authority to appoint from the Constitution."[4]

Furthermore, beginning with Washington, Presidents have, practically at discretion, despatched "secret" agents on diplomatic or semi-diplomatic missions without nominating them to the Senate;[5] while at other times they have, with or without the consent of the Senate, designated members of that body or of the House to represent the United States on international commissions and at diplomatic conferences; and this in face of Article I, section 6, paragraph 2, of the Constitution, which reads:

"No Senator or Representative shall, during the time for which he was elected, be appointed to any civil office under the authority of the United States, which shall have been created, or the emoluments whereof shall have been increased, during such time; and no person holding any office under the United States shall be a member of either house during his continuance in office."

How are the above mentioned practices, which have long since become established usage under the Constitution, to be reconciled with these provisions? Only on the theory, apparently, that such diplomatic assignments are not "offices" in the sense of the Constitution, being summoned into existence only for specific, temporary purposes and carrying with them, in the case of Senators and Representatives, no extra compensation, whereas the constitutional term connotes "tenure, duration, emolument and duties."[6]

And a like explanation is probably available to vindicate a practice, first resorted to on any scale by President Theodore Roosevelt, of constituting "volunteer unpaid commissions" for the purpose of investigating certain factual situations and reporting their findings to the President.[7] Eventually Mr. Roosevelt's enthusiasm for this method of informing himself concerning "the state of the nation" came to be denounced in Congress as "unconstitutional," and an amendment to the Sundry Civil Act of 1909 undertook to forbid the practice.[8] Mr. Roosevelt signed the measure but proclaimed his intention of ignoring the restriction. "Congress," he argued, "cannot prevent the President from seeking advice," nor disinterested men from giving their service to the people,[9] and that this view of the subject had won out by the time of Mr. Hoover appears from the fact that as President he appointed literally dozens of fact-finding commissions, most of them without statutory basis.[10]

Finally, Congress has on a few occasions endowed the President with its own power to establish offices and has merged therewith the full power to appoint to such offices, that is, without consulting the Senate. Thus Title II of the National Recovery Act of June 16, 1933, authorized President Roosevelt to create the post of Federal Administrator of Public Works and to "establish such agencies . . . to appoint, without regard to the civil service laws, such officers and employees, and to utilize such Federal officers and employees...as he may find necessary"; and a similar provision occurred earlier in the Lever Food and Fuel Control Act, passed early in World War I.[11] President Wilson's creation during World War I of the War Industries Board, the Committee on Public Information, and the first War Labor Board, all bodies that exercised vast powers in the President's name, must be credited to the general expansion that presidential authority always undergoes in wartime; and President Roosevelt's enlargement upon his predecessor's practice in this matter, not only during but prior to World War II, may be explained more or less the same way. The topic is dealt with in a later chapter.[12]

The Constitution distinguishes three stages in appointments by the President with the advice and consent of the Senate. The first is the "nomination," which is by the President alone; the second is the assent of the Senate to the "appointment"; the third is the final appointment and commissioning of the appointee by the President.[13] The only limitation which is imposed by the Constitution itself on the President's freedom of choice in nominating or appointing to office is the one, already noted, which results from the disqualification of Senators and Representatives in certain instances. This restriction came under scrutiny in connection with the appointment in 1937 of Senator Hugo L. Black of Alabama to the Supreme Court shortly following the passage by Congress of an act improving the financial position of Justices retiring from the Court at the age of seventy. Although Mr. Black's term had still some months to run, his appointment was defended by the argument that, inasmuch as he was only fifty-one years old and so would be ineligible for the "increased emolument" for nineteen years, it was not *as to him* an increased emolument.[14] Similarly, when in 1909 Senator Knox of Pennsylvania wished to become Secretary of State in President Taft's

Cabinet, the salary of which office had been recently increased, Congress accommodatingly repealed the increase for the period which still remained of Mr. Knox's senatorial term.[15] In other words, a Senator or Representative—and especially a Senator— may, "during the time for which he was elected, be appointed to any civil office under the authority of the United States, . . . the emoluments whereof shall have been increased during such time," *provided* that the increase in emolument is not available to the appointee "during such time."

Much more extensive is the control which is exerted over the President's freedom of choice by a set of usages which go by the name of "senatorial courtesy." If the President in nominating to an office within a state fails to consult the preferences of the Senator or Senators of his own party from that state, he is very likely to see the appointment defeated upon an appeal to the Senate by the slighted member or members. Reciprocally, the Senate will ordinarily interpose no objection to the President's nominees for Cabinet or diplomatic posts. While any attempt to find basis in the written Constitution for this interesting understanding would be disappointing, since it is the advice and consent of the Senate which the Constitution requires and not that of individual Senators,[16] yet there is no usage of the Constitution affecting the powers of the President which is more venerable. As early as August 6, 1789, we find President Washington addressing to the Senate the following message:

"My nomination of Benjamin Fishbourn for the place of naval officer of the port of Savannah not having met with your concurrence, I now nominate Lachlan McIntosh for that office. Whatever may have been the reasons which induced your dissent, I am persuaded they were such as you deemed sufficient. . . ."[17]

It is barely possible that these words were, as Josh Billings would have said, "wrote sarcastic," for in fact the reason which induced the Senate's dissent was the dissent in the first instance of the Senator from Georgia, and this apparently had nothing to do with the question of Fishbourn's fitness.

The practical importance, nevertheless, of this interesting institution in curtailing the President's power over appointments has often been a good deal exaggerated. The number of nominations for a given vacancy rejected by the Senate on this score has never apparently exceeded two, while the talent from which a President bent on making a sound appointment may choose is by no means ordinarily so limited. Thus the recent classic battle between the Truman administration and Senator McKellar over the appointment of Mr. David Lilienthal as Chairman of the Atomic Energy Commission and the unconscionable delay thereby occasioned to an urgent appointment must be chalked up against the Senate's antiquated methods of doing business rather than against "senatorial courtesy" per se, which in fact was not involved. If Hamilton's prediction in *The Federalist* that the Senate would concern itself only with the merits of suggested appointees has not been realized, neither on the other hand has James Wilson's prediction that the President would be "but the minion of the Senate."[18]

But by far the most important limitation upon presidential autonomy in this field of power is that which results from the fact that, in creating an office, Congress may stipulate the qualifications of appointees thereto. First and last, legislation of this character has laid down a vast variety of qualifications, depending on citizenship, residence, professional attainments, occupational experience, age, race, property, sound habits, political, industrial, or regional affiliations, and so on and so forth. It has even confined the President's selection to a small number of persons to be named by others.[19] Indeed, it has contrived at times, by particularity of description, to designate a definite eligible, thereby, to all intents and purposes, usurping the appointing power.[20]

For the proposition is universally conceded that some choice, however small, must be left the appointing authority.[21] Thus the Civil Service Act of 1883 leaves the appointing officer the right to select from *"among* those graded highest as the result of" the competitive examinations for which the act provides,[22] and supplementary executive orders have customarily further restricted choice to the *three highest*. The Foreign Service Act of 1924 is notable in that it extended for the first time the principle of competitive examinations to certain offices appointment to which was formerly made with the advice and consent of the Senate,[23] although logically there would seem to be no reason why this should not be done in all cases, the appointive power being the same power whether it is exercised by the President with the Senate or by the President alone. Likewise, by the Act of June 25, 1938, first-, second-, and third-class postmasters are brought under the Civil Service Act and rules, although their initial appointment continues to be by the President and Senate.[24]

Another power of Congress which must be distinguished from the appointing power is that of determining the powers and duties of officers of the United States. In the case of an existing office Congress may increase these to an indefinite extent without necessitating a reappointment to the office;[25] but it appears to be the Court's opinion, and is certainly a logical one, that new duties should be "germane" to the existing office, at least to the extent that their assignment shall not transgress the principle of the separation of powers.[26]

Another characteristic of the President's power of appointment is that while the power connotes a choice among eligibles, it involves ordinarily no choice whether there shall be an appointment. This results from the fact that the vast majority of civil offices under the National Government are instrumentalities for carrying into effect one or more of Congress's delegated powers and represent its views of what is "necessary and proper" to that end. The President's duty therefore to make an appointment to such an office flows from his duty to "take care that the laws be faithfully executed." But if the President fails to make an appointment there is, of course, no legal remedy, any more than there is when he fails to exercise any other of his powers. The late President Roosevelt's success therefore in keeping the office of Comptroller General unfilled for many months following Mr. McCarl's retirement in 1937 was of some interest at the time as suggesting the possibility of a usage which would transfer the question of the need for continuing an existing office to the final discretion of the President.

Except the President and Vice-President, all members of the civil service of the National Government are appointive and fall into one of three categories, those who are appointed by the President "by and with the advice and consent of the Senate"; "inferior officers" whose appointment Congress has vested by law "in the President alone, in the courts of law, or in the heads of departments"; and *employees*.

As here used, the term "employee" bears a very special meaning. Ordinarily the term denotes one who stands in a contractual relationship to his "employer," but here it comprises all subordinate officials of the National Government receiving appointment at the hands of officials who are not specifically recognized by the Constitution as capable of being vested by Congress with the appointing power.[27] The concept thus affords a way of circumventing the apparent purpose of the Constitution to confine the power to appoint "inferior officers," by the authorization of Congress, to the President alone, the courts of law, and the heads of departments. As used in the statutes the term "officers" is frequently construed to cover "employees" in the above sense.

What officers are "inferior" in the sense of the constitutional provision? Thanks to the jealous vigilance of the Senate, Congress has exercised its power in the vesting of appointments quite sparingly, and so the question just put has never been adjudicated by the Supreme Court. The term seems to suggest in this particular context officers intended to be subordinate to those in whom their appointment is vested, and at the same time to exclude the courts of law and heads of departments.[28]

The sole case in which the Supreme Court has had occasion to pass directly upon the participation of the Senate in the appointing power is that of *United States v. Smith*,[29] which grew out of an attempt by the Senate early in 1931 to recall its consent to certain nominations by President Hoover to the Federal Power Commission. In support of its course the Senate invoked a long-standing rule which permits a motion to reconsider a resolution of confirmation and to recall the notification thereof within "the next two days of actual executive session of the Senate." Inasmuch as the nominees involved had meantime taken the oath of office and entered upon the discharge of their duties, President Hoover denied the request, which he stigmatized as an attempt "to encroach upon the executive function by removal of a duly appointed executive officer under the guise of reconsideration of his nomination."[30] The Senate thereupon voted to reconsider the nominations in question, again approving two of the nominees but rejecting the third, against whom by the Senate's order the district attorney of the District of Columbia forthwith instituted *quo warranto* proceedings. From an extensive review of previous occurrences of the same general nature the Court, speaking by Justice Brandeis, concluded that the Senate's rule as heretofore applied did not reach the case of an appointee who had already been installed in office on the faith of the Senate's initial consent and notification to the President, and that this interpretation bound the Senate in the instant case.

Just how the Court became entitled to construe the Senate's rules, which it conceded were subject to change by the Senate without notice, does not appear from Justice Brandeis's opinion; but at any rate the expedient enabled the Court to evade the question whether the rule governing the reconsideration of nominations is *constitutionally* valid once notification has gone forward to the President. Jefferson in his *Manual* asserted unqualifiedly that "If, after the vote, the paper on which it [the Senate] passed has been parted with, there can be no reconsideration." But, as already indicated, practice has been far from supporting this sweeping assertion; nor is its logic inescapable, for it may with equal logic be contended that the senatorial consent is only "a warrant of attorney, valid until revoked," or that it is akin to a proffer and hence may be withdrawn at any time before acceptance. In Smith's case the revocation or withdrawal—depending on the analogy adopted—clearly came too late.

The most recent bearing on this subject is that furnished by the late President Roosevelt's refusal in 1939 to honor the request of the Senate that he return its resolution consenting to the appointment of Elmer D. Davies to be United States judge for the Middle District of Tennessee. "I regret," the President wrote, "that I cannot accede to this request as before its receipt I had signed and sent out a commission appointing Judge Davies, by and with the advice and consent of the Senate." [31] It is not impossible that Mr. Roosevelt's action was influenced by the reflection that if Mr. Davies was in office he would be irremovable, but that fact hardly lessens its value as a precedent—and a sound one.

May the Senate attach conditions to its approval of an appointment, as it frequently does to its approval of a treaty? The entire record of practice under the Constitution negatives the suggestion, as also does that of opinion. Madison, Hamilton, Jefferson, and Story all expressed themselves to the effect that the Senate's role in relation to appointments is only that of rejecting or confirming nominations without condition.[32] Moreover, the conditions which the Senate would attempt to attach would be apt either to invade the powers of the office, which come from the law, or to limit the officer's tenure, which also comes from the law or is subject to determination by the removal power. And in principle at least the Senate's pretensions would extend to judicial no less than to executive appointees.

Although the Constitution says that the President *"shall* commission all officers,"* etc., this, as applied in practice, does not appear to mean that he is under constitutional or legal obligation to commission those whose appointments have reached that stage, but merely that it is he and no one else who has the power to commission them. The sealing and delivery of the commission is, on the other hand, in the case both of appointees by the President and Senate and by the President alone, a purely ministerial act which has been lodged by statute with the Secretary of State, and the performance of which may be compelled by mandamus unless the appointee has been in the meantime validly removed.[33]

A further element of the appointing power is contained in the following provision of Article II, section 2, paragraph 3:

"The President shall have power to fill up all vacancies that may happen during the recess of the Senate, by granting commissions which shall expire at the end of their next session."

The significant word is "happen." Setting out from the proposition that the very nature of the executive power requires that it shall always be "in capacity for action," Attorneys General came early to interpret this to mean "happen to exist," and long-continued practice securely establishes this construction.[34] It follows that whenever a vacancy may have occurred in the first instance or for whatever reason, if it still continues after the Senate has ceased to sit and hence cannot be consulted, the President may fill it in the way described. But a Senate "recess" does not include holiday or temporary adjournments,[35] while by an act of Congress, if the vacancy existed when the Senate was in session, the *ad interim* appointee may receive no salary until he has been confirmed by the Senate.[36] Also, there appears to be an informal understanding, although it is not always observed, that the President will not extend a recess appointment to a rejected nominee.[37]

To be distinguished from the power to make recess appointments is the power of the President to make temporary assignments of officials to the duties of other absent or incapacitated officials. Usually a situation of this nature is provided for in advance by a statute which designates the inferior officer who is to act in place of his immediate superior, but, in the lack of such provision, theory and practice alike concede the President the power to make a designation.[38]

THE PRESIDENT AS SUPERVISOR OF LAW ENFORCEMENT; THE CABINET

The acts of the British monarch are judicially noticeable only as the acts of his agents. "The King can do no wrong" because, in strict law, he can do nothing. In the case of the President, on the contrary, there are many acts which to be done constitutionally must presumably have been done by him personally or in the exercise of his personal judgment.[39] In the words of an opinion rendered by Attorney General Cushing in 1855:

"It may be presumed that he, the *man* discharging the Presidential office, *and he alone,* grants reprieves and pardons for offenses against the United States."

And again:

"No act of Congress, no act even of the President himself, can, by constitutional possibility authorize or create any military officer not subordinate to the President."[40]

May this type of obligation be created by statute? Dealing with this question in a case before the Civil War, which grew out of a statutory provision expressly prohibiting the advancing of public money to the disbursing officers of the government except under "the special direction of the President," the Court said:

"The President's duty in general requires his superintendence of the administration; yet this duty cannot require of him to become the administrative officer to every department and bureau, or to perform in person the numerous details incident to services which, nevertheless, he is, in a correct sense, by the Constitution and laws required and expected to perform. This cannot be, 1st, Because if it were practicable, it would be to absorb the duties and responsibilities of the various departments of the government in the personal action of one chief executive officer. It cannot be, for the stronger reason, that it is impracticable —nay, impossible."[41]

It is true that the Court once held a certain decree of a court-martial void because, although it had been confirmed by the Secretary of War, it was not specifically stated to have received the sanction of the President as required by the 65th Article of War; but later decisions call this holding into question.[42] Such legislation is at any rate quite exceptional. The general rule is stated by the Court to be that when any duty is cast by law upon the President it may be exercised by him "through the head of the appropriate department," whose acts, if performed within the law, become the President's acts; and, in point of fact, most orders and instructions emanating from the heads of the departments, even when in pursuance of powers conferred by statute on the President, do not mention him.[43]

Suppose, on the other hand, that the law casts a duty upon a subordinate executive agency *eo nomine,* does the President thereupon become entitled, by virtue of his "executive power" or of his duty to "take care that the laws be faithfully executed," to substitute his own judgment for that of the agency regarding the discharge of such duty? An unqualified answer to this question would invite startling results. An affirmative answer would make all questions of law enforcement questions of discretion, the discretion moreover of an independent and legally uncontrollable branch of the government. By the same token, it would render it impossible for Congress, notwithstanding its broad powers under the "necessary and proper" clause, to leave anything to the specially trained judgment of a subordinate executive official with any assurance that his discretion would not be perverted to political ends for the advantage of the administration in power. At the same time, a flatly negative answer would hold out consequences equally unwelcome. It would, as Attorney General Cushing quaintly phrased it, leave it open to Congress so to divide and transfer "the executive power" by statute as to change the government "into a parliamentary despotism like that of Venezuela or Great Britain, with a *nominal* executive chief or president, who, however, would remain without a shred of actual power." [44] Or, in different words, it would leave it open to Congress to destroy unity of administration in the National Government, as it has long since been destroyed in the state governments. There are some critics, indeed, who profess to believe that this has already occurred. The subject is dealt with later in this chapter.

The earliest discussion of this crucial issue is to be found in the argument which was made by Madison in the first Congress in behalf of attributing the removal power to the President. It was "the intention of the Constitution," Madison contended, expressed especially in the "take care" clause, that the first magistrate should be responsible for the executive departments, and this responsibility, he urged, carried with it power to "inspect and *control*" the conduct of all subordinate executive officers.[45]

Yet when in the same year it organized the first executive departments, Congress itself adopted a radically different principle. The acts creating the Departments of State and of War specifically recognize the responsibility of the heads of those departments to the President, but not so with the act organizing the Department of the Treasury, the head of which is required to "perform all services relative to finances as he shall be directed to perform—" directed, that is, by Congress.[46] Nor is the reason underlying this difference far to seek. The State and War Departments are principally, although not exclusively, organs of the President in the exercise of functions which are assigned him by the Constitution itself, while the Treasury Department is primarily an instrument for carrying into effect Congress's constitutional powers in the field of finance. For like reasons, when in 1794, the Post Office was established on a permanent foundation, it was not placed under the control of the President, nor was the Interior Department when it was formed in 1849; although the Navy Department, established in 1798, was so placed.[47]

Meanwhile, in *Marbury v. Madison,* Chief Justice Marshall had suggested a parallel distinction between the duties of the Secretary of State under the original act which had created a "Department of Foreign Affairs," and those which had been added by the later act changing the designation of the department to its present one. The former were, he pointed out, entirely in the "political field," and hence for their discharge the secretary was left responsible absolutely to the President. The latter, on the other hand, were exclusively of statutory origin and sprang from the powers of Congress. For these, therefore, the secretary was "an officer of the law" and "amenable to the law for his conduct."[48]

Nor is the doctrine which was advanced by Attorney General Wirt in 1823 of substantially different import when it is confined to the field of Congress's delegated powers, which is evidently what Wirt was thinking of. It is that the President's duty under the "take care" clause requires of him scarcely more than that he should bring a *criminally negligent* official to book for his derelictions, either by removing him or by setting in motion against him the processes of impeachment or of criminal prosecution,[49] an opinion which voiced the point of view of "the Virginia School of Presidents," including the later Madison. The doctrine, on the other hand, that Congress is unable to vest any executive agency even within the field of its own specifically delegated powers with any legal discretion which the President is not entitled to appropriate to himself is, of course, the very hallmark of the Jacksonian conception of the Presidency, although the groundwork for it was prepared much earlier, first, by "the decision of 1789," which is treated below; secondly, by the rise of the President's Cabinet.

Like its British namesake, the American Cabinet is entirely extra-constitutional.[50] The President, the Constitution states, "may require the opinion, in writing, of the principal officer in each of the executive departments, upon any subject relating to the duties of their respective offices."[51] The consultative relationship thus suggested is an entirely one-sided affair, is to be conducted in writing with the "principal officers" separately and individually, and is to relate only "to the duties of their respective offices." If an executive council was needed, it was the general idea in 1789 that the Senate would serve the purpose.[52]

The Cabinet may be said to have emerged as a definite institution of the National Government from the diplomatic crisis of 1793. Washington had previously called the three Secretaries and the Attorney General into assembled consultation, but now such meetings became frequent. "The most notable of these was the meeting of April 19 of that year, at which the issuance of the so-called 'Neutrality Proclamation' was agreed upon. Writing at this time, Jefferson refers to the meetings as occurring 'almost every day'"; and so matters continued more or less till the close of the year.[53] Two years later "the Cabinet," as it was now generally termed, underwent another notable stage in its evolution when Washington, as a result of Secretary of State Randolph's equivocal attitude in the fight over the Jay Treaty, proceeded to reconstruct his Cabinet on the avowed basis of loyalty to his own policies, and in so doing created a precedent which, with negligible exceptions, has guided Presidents in their choice of departmental heads ever since then. Meantime, by "the decision of 1789," the President had been endowed with an unqualified power of removal over the heads of the executive departments.

Thus from the first the heads of these departments have occupied, when exercising powers delegated them by statute, a dual role and have been subject to a dual responsibility. The inevitable clash between these two roles came in 1833 as an incident of Jackson's "War on the Bank." Convincing himself by a characteristic process of self-hypnosis that the Bank was an unsafe depository for the national funds, Jackson ordered Secretary of the Treasury Duane to transfer them, which Duane had power under the law to do. As it happened, however, the House of Representatives had recently expressed its confidence in the Bank by formal resolution, and Duane's own instructed judgment was to the same effect. He accordingly refused to comply with Jackson's demand, was promptly removed, and his successor Taney at once gave the desired order.[54]

Although in commenting on this episode writers are apt to treat it as the outcome solely of the President's possession of the removal power,[55] this was far from Jackson's own theory of the matter. This, as it was stated in his Protest Message of April 15, 1834, was "that the entire executive power is vested in the President"; that the power to remove "those officers who are to aid him in the execution of the laws" is an incident of that power; that the Secretary of the Treasury is such an officer; that "the custody of the public property and money is an executive function" exercised through the Secretary of the Treasury and his subordinates; that "in the performance of these duties he [the Secretary] is subject to the supervision and control of the President"; and finally that the act establishing the Bank "did not and could not change the relation between the President and Secretary—did not release the former from his obligation to see the law faithfully executed nor the latter from the President's supervision and control."[56]

In short, *the Constitution knows only one "executive power," that of the President, whose duty to "take care that the laws be faithfully executed" thus becomes the equivalent of the duty and power to execute them himself according to his own construction of them.* The removal of Duane was, therefore, the constitutionally ordained result of that officer's attempt to usurp the President's constitutional prerogative; or, in broader terms, the President's removal power, in this case unqualified, was the *sanction provided by the Constitution for his power and duty to control all his subordinates in all their official actions of public consequence.*

Five years later the case of *Kendall v. United States*[57] arose. The United States owed one Stokes a sum of money, and, when Postmaster General Kendall at Jackson's instigation refused to pay it, Congress passed a special act ordering payment. But Kendall still proving noncompliant, Stokes sought and obtained a mandamus in the United States circuit court for the District of Columbia, and on appeal this decision was affirmed by the Supreme Court.

While *Kendall v. United States,* like *Marbury v. Madison,* involved the question of the responsibility of a head of department for the performance of a ministerial duty, the discussion by counsel before the Court and the Court's own opinion covered the entire subject of the relation of the President to his subordinates in the performance by them of statutory duties. The lower court had asserted that the duty of the President under the "faithfully executed" clause gave him "no other control over the officer than to see that he acts honestly, with proper motives," but "no power to construe the law and see that the executive action conforms to it."[58] Counsel for Kendall attacked this position vigorously, relying largely upon statements by Hamilton, Marshall, Wilson, and Story having to do with the President's power in the field of foreign relations.[59]

This argument the Court rejected with calculated emphasis. "There are," it pointed out,

"certain political duties imposed upon many officers in the executive departments, the discharge of which is under the direction of the President. But it would be an alarming doctrine that Congress cannot impose upon any executive officer any duty they may think proper, which is not repugnant to any rights secured and protected by the Constitution; and in such cases, the duty and responsibility grow out of and are subject to the control of the law, and not to the direction of the President."[60]

In short, the Court recognized that the underlying question of the case was whether the President's "executive power," coupled with his duty to "take care that the laws be faithfully executed," made it constitutionally impossible for Congress ever to entrust the construction of its statutes to anybody but the President; and it answered this question with an emphatic "no."

How does this exceedingly important issue stand today?

THE REMOVAL POWER—THE MYERS AND HUMPHREY CASES

Except for the provision which it makes for a power of impeachment of "civil officers of the United States,"[61] the Constitution contains no reference to a power to remove from office, a situation in which early resort to the judicial divining rod would seem on first consideration to have been highly likely and necessary. Actually, until its decision in *Myers v. United States*,[62] October 25, 1926, the Supreme Court had contrived to side-step every occasion for a decisive pronouncement regarding the removal power, its extent and location.

How explain this strange hesitancy on the Court's part to advance the cause of judicial review? Two reasons suggest themselves. The first is the strong course taken by the first Congress under the Constitution in undertaking to settle the removal issue by legislation. Throughout the ensuing one hundred and forty years the initiative thus asserted, at first in favor of the power of the President and later against it, was respected by the Court.

But in the second place, it may be surmised, the Court has always been uneasily distrustful of its ability to intervene effectively in this primarily political field. So long as Congress chooses to permit it to do so the Court is free to decree that an official who has been ousted contrary to its view of the constitutional proprieties shall be paid his salary, but as the statutes stand today that is ordinarily the full extent of its competence in such situations.[63] Curiously enough, in the two principal cases which are reviewed below—the first being the Myers Case—the ousted official died while his suit for salary was pending, with the result that the inherent inadequacy of the Court's remedial powers in such cases was conveniently obscured.

The point immediately at issue in the Myers Case was the effectiveness of an order of the Postmaster General, acting by direction of the President, to remove from office a first-class postmaster, in view of the following provision of an act of Congress passed in 1876:

"Postmasters of the first, second and third classes shall be appointed and may be removed by the President with the advice and consent of the Senate, and shall hold their offices for four years unless sooner removed or suspended according to law."[64]

A divided court, speaking by Chief Justice Taft, held the order of removal valid, and the statutory provision just quoted void. Standing by itself this disallowance does not necessarily imply more than that so long as Congress chooses to leave the appointment of an inferior officer with the President, acting with the advice and consent of the Senate, it may not make the officer's removal dependent also on such consent. But with this comparatively narrow holding the Court was not content, and in the Chief Justice's elaborate opinion the sweeping doctrine was advanced that the President is endowed by Article II of the Constitution with a power of removal which, so far as "executive officers of the United States appointed by him" are concerned, is not susceptible constitutionally of any restraint or limitation by Congress, and that all such officers are intended by the Constitution to be left removable at the President's will.

The Chief Justice's main reliance was upon "the decision of 1789" previously alluded to. The incident may be briefly described.[65] On June 16 of that year the first House of Representatives under the Constitution went into committee of the whole to consider a bill proposed by Madison for establishing a Department of Foreign Affairs, the opening clause of which provided that the principal officer of the new department was "to be removable from office by the President of the United States." In the debate which ensued three fairly equal groups disclosed themselves: first, those who, headed by Madison, argued that the power of removal was an inherent element both of "executive power" and of the duty to "take care that the laws be faithfully executed"; secondly, those who, headed by Sherman—also a former member of the Philadelphia Convention—contended that the power of removal was conferred as an incident of the power of appointment jointly on the President and Senate; and, thirdly, those who held that the Constitution had left it with Congress, by virtue of the "necessary and proper" clause, to locate the power of removal where it thought fit. A fourth group, comprising only three or four members, urged that unless removed for misbehavior in office by the power of impeachment, or by judicial process known to the common law, an officer had a vested right in his office for the term of his appointment as fixed by law.

The mode in which the theoretical issue thus raised was disposed of is somewhat confusing. The objection having been raised to the clause "to be removable by the President" that it represented an attempt by Congress to confer power on the President which was not otherwise provided for in the Constitution, the clause was stricken out, and in its place were inserted the words "whenever the said principal officer shall be removed from office by the President of the United States," which were thought to infer that the President already had the power of removal, in certain cases at least, without grant from Congress. Subsequently the Senate ratified the action of the House by the casting vote of Vice-President Adams, and like action was later taken with regard to the Secretary of the Treasury and the Secretary of War.

Was the "decision of 1789" capable of sustaining the sweeping conclusions of the Chief Justice's opinion? It seems very questionable. While the decision undoubtedly avoids the direct implication that the President owed the power of removal to a grant by

Congress, yet this outcome was brought about by the indispensable aid of those who throughout the debate had championed the doctrine that Congress could determine the question of the scope and location of the removal power in any way it saw fit. What is more, the question related, as was repeatedly emphasized in the debate by the champions of presidential power, to a high political office, one which was to be the instrument of the President in the principal field of executive prerogative and whose tenure was, for this very reason, being left *indeterminate*. While, therefore, the decision may be fairly considered as ascribing to the President alone the power to remove executive officers appointed with the consent of the Senate whom Congress chooses to leave removable *by not fixing their terms,* it certainly did not establish the proposition of the Myers Case that Congress is without power to *fix the terms* of any executive officers whatever as against the President's power of removal.

Nor does the record of opinion respecting the power of removal under the Constitution, prior at least to the Civil War, generally support the results arrived at in the Myers Case. In *The Federalist* Hamilton had stated explicitly that the Senate would be associated with the President in the removal of officers, although he seems later to have retracted this opinion.[66] Neither Marshall, Kent, Story, nor Webster regarded the decision of 1789 as reaching officers of determinate tenure; and all but Marshall were quite clearly of the opinion that the correct reading of the Constitution located the power of removal in both the President and Senate in the case of officers appointed with the Senate's consent, although they were willing to concede the binding effect of the decision of 1789 as "a practical construction of the Constitution" till Congress should choose to revise it.[67] That the Supreme Court of the period shared these views is indicated by its opinion in *ex parte* Hennen[68] in 1839.

The literary source of the Chief Justice's opinion is Jackson's famous Message of Protest, which was dealt with in the previous section.[69] There all the essential elements of the Chief Justice's doctrine were assembled for the first time, and, it may be added, for the *last* time until the Myers Case was decided. Other partial sources are certain opinions of Attorneys General, although the real preponderance of opinion from this source by no means supports the sweeping propositions advanced by the Chief Justice. Still another source is the debate stirred by the Tenure of Office Act of 1867, while a fourth source is to be discovered in the arguments developed by President Johnson's counsel at the time of his impeachment trial. Yet even these gentlemen, it is worth noting, generally contented themselves with asserting that Johnson, assuming that he had violated the Tenure of Office Act, had acted in good faith, not that he had beyond peradventure acted constitutionally.[70]

But apart from the verdict of past opinion, the Chief Justice also urged the theory that the power of removal was inherently "executive" on its own merits. His contention was based on the two grounds of history and of necessity; and in assertion of the former he instanced the power of "the British Crown" in the appointment and removal of officers. The argument proves too much. The power of the British Crown in the appointment and removal of officers, as we saw earlier, is an historical outgrowth of and is still intimately involved with a much wider prerogative in the creation of offices, while the only offices known to the Constitution of the United States in normal times are, with the possible exception of Justices of the Supreme Court and diplomatic officers, those "which shall be established by law."[71]

The ultimate basis of the decision in the Myers Case is undoubtedly to be sought far less in constitutional history and legal theory than in certain practical considerations which naturally loomed large in the mind of a Chief Justice who had once been President himself. That this is so is clearly indicated in the following salient passage of the opinion:

"There is nothing in the Constitution which permits a distinction between the removal of the head of a department or a bureau, when he discharges a political duty of the President or exercises his discretion, and the removal of executive officers engaged in the discharge of their other normal duties. The imperative reasons requiring an unrestricted power to remove the most important of his subordinates in their most important duties must, therefore, control the interpretation of the Constitution as to all appointed by him."[72]

That the President ought to be able to remove at will all subordinates whose discretion he is entitled by the Constitution or by the laws of Congress to control, and for whose policies he is hence responsible, must be granted, as we have seen. But the Chief Justice's conclusion that this fact "must control interpretation of the Constitution as to all appointed by him" was much too drastic and resulted in the paradox, conceded by the Chief Justice himself, that, while the Constitution permitted Congress to vest "duties of a quasi-judicial character" in executive officers in the performance of which they were to exercise their own independent judgment, it at the same time permitted the President to guillotine such officers for exercising the very discretion which Congress had the right to require!

Nor was the menace of this paradox a merely theoretical one. For, as was pointed out earlier, recent decades have witnessed the establishment of a number of "administrative tribunals" outside and independent of any department. The Interstate Commerce Commission was thus established in 1887, the Federal Trade Commission in 1914, the Federal Tariff Commission in 1916, the Federal Power Commission in 1920 (revamped in 1930), the Federal Communications Commission (succeeding the Federal Radio Commission) in 1934, and the Securities and Exchange Commission in 1934. The members of all these bodies are appointed by the President and Senate *for fixed terms,* while the members of the first three are removable by the President for "inefficiency, neglect of duty or malfeasance in office"—a provision which is not repeated as to the last three, possibly because of the influence of the Myers Case.

And meantime, in the Act of 1920 creating the Railroad Labor Board, Congress had taken a further step. In an endeavor to confer upon the members of this body a quasi-judicial status, it provided that they should be removable by the President "for neglect of duty or malfeasance in office, but for no other cause"; and a similar tenure was bestowed upon the members of the Board of General Appraisers and the Board of Tax Appeals by the Acts of 1922 and 1924, respectively.[73] Nor should the enactment in 1921 of the Budget and Accounting Act, whereby Congress inaugurated an almost revolutionary reform in methods of national financial legislation, be overlooked in this connection. The act sets up the office of Comptroller General of the United States and endows this functionary with a fifteen-year term during which, save upon impeachment, he is removable only by joint resolution of Congress and then only after a hearing which shall establish to Congress's satisfaction his incapacity, inefficiency, neglect of duty or malfeasance, or "conduct involving moral turpitude."[74] Finally, by the Wagner National Labor Relations Act of July 5, 1935, a National Labor Relations Board was created, to consist of three members appointed by the President and Senate for five-year staggered terms, and to be removable by the President for neglect of duty or malfeasance in office, after notice and hearing.[75]

There can be little doubt that all these measures, so far as they purported to restrict the President's power of removal, were by the Chief Justice's opinion in the Myers Case constitutionally ineffective, and that the Court would have been compelled sooner or later, had it adhered to that opinion, either to set aside the restrictive provisions or to have interpreted them away. In point of fact, it has since recanted much of the Taft opinion in its decision in 1935 in *Humphrey v. United States.*[76]

The material facts of this case were as follows: Humphrey, a member of the Federal Trade Commission, was reappointed to his post by President Hoover, by and with the advice and consent of the Senate, on December 10, 1931, for a term of seven years. On July 25, 1933, and again on August 31, President Roosevelt wrote the commissioner requesting his resignation on the ground that the two entertained divergent views of public policy, but at the same time disclaiming any reflection on Mr. Humphrey personally or on his official conduct. Said the President:

"You will, I know, realize that I do not feel that your mind and my mind go along together on either the policies or the administering of the Federal Trade Commission, and, frankly, I think it is best for the people of this country that I should have a full confidence."

Humphrey having declined to resign, the President on October 7 notified him that he was from that date "removed" from office; and in due course Humphrey brought suit for salary.[77]

The principal basis of the Court's unanimous decision sustaining Humphrey's claim that he was wrongfully removed from office is indicated in the following paragraphs of Justice Sutherland's opinion. Distinguishing the Myers Case, the Justice says:

"A postmaster is an executive officer restricted to the performance of executive functions. He is charged with no duty at all related to either the legislative or judicial power. The actual decision in the Myers Case finds support in the theory that such an office is merely one of the units in the executive department and hence inherently subject to the exclusive and illimitable power of removal by the chief executive, whose subordinate and aid he is. . . . It goes no farther;—much less does it include an officer who occupies no place in the executive department and who exercises no part of the executive power vested by the Constitution in the President.

"The Federal Trade Commission is an administrative body created by Congress to carry into effect legislative policies embodied in the statute. . . . Its duties are performed without executive leave and in the contemplation of the statute must be free from executive control. . . .

"We think it plain under the Constitution that illimitable power of removal is not possessed by the President in respect of officers of the character of those just named [the Interstate Commerce Commission, the Federal Trade Commission, the Court of Claims]. The authority of Congress, in creating quasi-legislative or quasi-judicial agencies, to require them to act in discharge of their duties independently of executive control, cannot be well doubted; and that authority includes, as an appropriate incident, power to fix the period during which they shall continue, and to forbid their removal except for cause in the meantime. For it is quite evident that one who holds his office only during the pleasure of another cannot be depended upon to maintain an attitude of independence against the latter's will."[78]

Elsewhere in his opinion Justice Sutherland takes pains to point out that "the decision of 1789" concerned an office which "was not only purely executive" but an officer "who was responsible to the President and to him alone, in a very definite sense.[79]

That this holding, considered in the light of this opinion, goes a long way toward scrapping the Myers decision is fairly clear. Not only does the opinion entirely ignore Chief Justice Taft's invocation of the opening clause of Article II, but it employs the term "executive power" throughout either in the sense of the President's constitutional prerogatives or in the narrow sense of

non-discretionary duties. All other official functions which grow
out of or succeed to legislation by Congress within the field of its
delegated powers are comprised, when they do not fall to the
regular courts, under the captions of "quasi-legislative" and
"quasi-judicial." It seems to follow that the President's constitutionally illimitable power of removal reaches only two classes of
officials: (1) those whose statutory powers are ministerial merely;
(2) those who exercise the President's own powers, whether of
statutory or constitutional origin.[80]

In thus getting rid of a constitutional limitation upon Congress's power in a field which is essentially political in nature—in
which, properly speaking, no vested rights except the right of an
officer to salary earned are or can be involved—this decision is
undoubtedly to be applauded. But that does not mean that the
doctrine of the case is invariably sound. The truth is that some of
Justice Sutherland's dicta are quite as extreme in one direction as
some of Chief Justice Taft's dicta were in the opposite direction;
and especially does he provoke wonderment by his assertion that
a member of the Federal Trade Commission *"occupies no place
in the executive department."* Taken literally, this statement
would mean that the Court was ready to scrap the principle
of separation of powers as the formal principle of classification of
governmental functions under the Constitution. I say *"formal*
principle," since I see no reason for supposing that Justice Sutherland had any intention of challenging the power of Congress to
vest the functions of the Federal Trade Commission in a departmental officer if it chose to do so, functions of like nature having
been so vested again and again. The dictum seems to have been
the product of hasty composition, for certainly it is not to be
squared by any verbal legerdemain with more deliberate utterances of the same Justice, as, for example, his statement in
Springer v. Philippine Islands that "legislative power, as distin-

guished from executive power, is the authority to make laws but not to enforce them or appoint the agents charged with the duty of such enforcement. The latter are executive functions."[81] Moreover, if a Federal Trade Commissioner is not in the executive department, where is he? In the legislative department; or is he, forsooth, in the uncomfortable halfway condition of Mahomet's coffin, suspended 'twixt Heaven and Earth? The latter is, I should say, just about the condition of the Comptroller General, but the anomaly is based on historical grounds which do not hold for Federal Trade Commissioners and the like.[82] Nor is Justice Sutherland's endeavor to make out that the latter are any more "agents of Congress" than is a postmaster at all persuasive. Both officials get their powers—such as they are—from an exercise by Congress of its constitutionally delegated powers—there is no other possible source.[83]

Still another phase of the general question of the constitutional basis and scope of presidential removal power emerged in 1938 in connection with Mr. Roosevelt's removal of Dr. A. E. Morgan from the chairmanship of the Tennessee Valley Authority for the latter's refusal to produce evidence in support of statements which he had made to the detriment of his fellow directors. The act of Congress creating TVA contains two provisions regarding removal,[84] the first of which says that "any member of the board may be removed at any time by a concurrent resolution of the Senate and House of Representatives"; while the other provides that any member of said board found to be guilty of applying "political tests in the selection or promotion of the corporation's employees and officials" "shall be removed from office by the President of the United States." The question raised by Morgan's dismissal is whether the latter provision should be given an exclusive construction. The answer is both "yes" and "no." Inasmuch as it was the obvious intention of Congress that the board of directors of TVA should be an independent body, the President has no right to construe their legal duties for them, and hence no right to remove them for a refusal on their part to permit him to do so. But the President was not attempting to construe Dr. Morgan's legal duties for him. He was merely requiring his coöperation in attempting to clear up charges which had called into question the honesty of the other directors and which had virtually brought the activities of the board to a standstill. To deny the President the power of removal in such a case would be to make it impossible for him to discharge his duty to "take care that the laws be faithfully executed" under the most modest interpretation of that duty,[85] an observation which is further illustrated by the President's recent "Loyalty Order." I deal with the subject later in this chapter.

The provision of the TVA Act which makes the directors of TVA removable by a concurrent resolution of the houses also challenges a moment's attention. Since a concurrent resolution is not submitted to the President for his approval, and hence can effect no legal change under the terms of Article I, section 7, of the Constitution, the question arises, on what theory can such a resolution remove from office one who was appointed thereto by legal or constitutional authority? Only on the theory, I should say, that Congress's power to create suitable agencies for carrying into effect its delegated powers embraces the power—as the dictum in the Humphrey Case suggests—of locating them in the legislative department; and, secondly, that Congress acting in its legislative capacity—as, of course, it was doing when it created TVA—may delegate this power to the two houses.

To consider the second proposition first—it is undoubtedly true, as the history of practice under the Constitution amply demonstrates, that Congress may delegate to the houses powers which it might have exercised itself. That, however, it had power in this instance to delegate seems to me highly questionable. Certainly the holding in the Myers Case, that when the law permits the removal of an officer in whose appointment the President has participated, the power of making such removal belongs to the President alone, has never been overruled.

One further point—What has been said above boils down to this: (1) as to agents of his own powers, the President's removal power is illimitable; (2) as to agents of Congress's constitutional powers, Congress may confine it to removal for cause, which implies the further right to require a hearing as a part of the procedure of removal.[86] Does the maintenance of the distinction between the two kinds of removal power have to be left exclusively with the President's unaided sense of duty to the law? Personally I can see no constitutional reason why it should not be stimulated, if Congress wishes to make provision to that end, by authorizing *quo warranto* proceedings to test the title to office of successors to officers who claim to have been wrongfully removed.[87] And, of course, in the case of officers appointed with its consent, the Senate is always in position to uphold the distinction when it is minded to do so.[88]

THE PROBLEM OF ADMINISTRATIVE REORGANIZATION

A final implication of the Humphrey Case remains to be noticed. This is that, in the last analysis, it is for Congress itself to say what degree of freedom from presidential control such bodies as the ICC, the FTC, etc., shall enjoy. Thus Congress may at any time it chooses make officials in like case with Mr. Humphrey removable by the President on the same terms and with the same facility as purely "executive officers"—to use Justice Sutherland's terminology. Why, then, should not Congress be persuaded to do this very thing? And doubtless it was with the purpose of effecting such persuasion that the President, early in 1936, created a

Committee on Administrative Management to report a plan for the systematic overhauling of the national administrative machine, which that body did January 8, 1937.[89] Inasmuch as "reorganization of the Executive Branch" is a problem which is still undergoing study, much of what was said and done—and not done—in 1937 remains of practical, as well as of historical, interest.

In the report which accompanied its recommendations the Committee set forth a point of view that was thoroughgoingly Jacksonian.[90] The Constitution, it declared, "places in the President, and the President alone, the whole executive power of the Government of the United States," a thought which Mr. Roosevelt took occasion to emphasize in his message transmitting the Committee's report to Congress, in the following words: "The Presidency as established in the Constitution of the United States has all the powers that are required. In spite of timid souls in 1787 who feared effective government the Presidency was established as a single strong Chief Executive office in which was vested the entire executive power of the National Government, even as the legislative power was placed in the Congress, and the judicial in the Supreme Court." And surveying the independent commissions from this angle, the Committee viewed them as constituting "a headless 'fourth branch' of the government, a haphazard deposit of irresponsible agencies and uncoordinated powers," a constant obstruction to "effective over-all management of national administration." The report then continued:

"The commissions produce confusion, conflict, and incoherence in the formulation and in the execution of the President's policies. Not only by constitutional theory, but by the steady and mounting insistence of public opinion, the President is held responsible for the wise and efficient management of the Executive Branch of the Government. The people look to him for leadership. And yet we whittle away the effective control essential to that leadership by parceling out to a dozen or more irresponsible agencies important powers of policy and administration."

Moreover, the worst was yet to come, since

"Congress is always tempted to turn each new regulatory function over to a new independent commission. This is not only following the line of least resistance; it is also following a 50-year-old tradition. The multiplication of these agencies cannot fail to obstruct the effective over-all management of the Executive Branch of the Government almost in geometric ratio to their number. At the present rate we shall have 40 to 50 of them within a decade. Every bit of executive and administrative authority which they enjoy means a relative weakening of the President, in whom, according to the Constitution, 'the executive Power shall be vested.' As they grow in number his stature is bound to diminish. He will no longer be in reality *the Executive,* but only one of many executives, threading his way around obstacles which he has no power to overcome."

What, then, did the Committee propose should be done about the matter? "Any program," it asserted, "to restore our constitutional ideal of a fully coordinated Executive Branch responsible to the President must bring within the reach of that responsible control all work done by these independent commissions which is not judicial in nature." More definitely, the Committee proposed to replace the independent commissions with two sorts of agencies, both to be organized within one or other of the departments, whose heads are subject to the President's discretionary power of removal. In one of the agencies would be lodged the "quasi-judicial" functions of the present commissions, and it would exercise these just as the commissions do, without being responsible to any higher authority in the administrative hierarchy. The other agency, however, would be accountable for all its acts to the head of department, and through him to the President. Thus any discretion not classifiable as "quasi-judicial" which Congress chose at any time to repose in any administrative agency of the National Government would be at the ultimate disposal of the President.

So far as the Committee's case rested on historical grounds it was far from impregnable. From data assembled in earlier pages of this volume it appears extremely probable that most people qualified to pass on the matter would have said, whether in 1787 or forty years later, that Congress was entitled, by virtue of its power "to make all laws which shall be necessary and proper for carrying into execution the foregoing [that is, its own constitutional] powers," to create executive agencies *ad libitum,* and to vest in them powers not controllable by the President. While Madison anticipated the later Jacksonian thesis when the office of Secretary of State was under discussion in the first Congress, yet he shortly afterward abandoned it as to the Comptroller of the Treasury, and indeed in implication as to the Secretary of the Treasury as well; and Hamilton's arguments in support of Washington's "Neutrality Proclamation" of 1793 had only to do with presidential prerogative in the "political field." Neither Madison nor Hamilton appears at any time to have had clearly in mind that executive power which results from an exercise by Congress of its own delegated powers. Still less if possible would the Committee have been able to draw support from acts or words of "the Virginia School of Presidents," including the later Madison. Nor is the very development stigmatized by the Committee without evidential value for the historical issue. This began with the creation of the Civil Service Commission in 1883, that is to say, some sixty-five years ago—and sixty-five years is two fifths of our national existence. We are compelled, therefore, to conclude that when it is viewed simply in the perspective of American constitutional history, the establishment by Congress of the independent commissions within the field of its granted powers does not represent, as the Committee alleged it to do, "a relative weakening of the President"; but that, on the contrary, it may only represent a disinclination on the part of Congress to let the increased use of its own powers always serve as a source for further aggrandizement of presidential power.

And in this connection it is pertinent to comment briefly upon the Committee's use of the words "responsibility," "irresponsible," and the like. The independent commissions are said to be "irresponsible agencies," and to "enjoy power without responsibility." But this can mean only that they are not responsible to the President. It is not shown, nor could it be, that they are less responsible to the law, or less disposed to observe it according to their own conscientious interpretation of it than is the President himself, or that their acts are less readily subject to judicial review. The President is, to be sure, "responsible" to the electorate in a general way, while the commissions are not, but this kind of responsibility is certainly a frail reliance when private rights are concerned. What the Committee really meant undoubtedly by "responsibility" is *capacity for effective action,* not accountability to the law; and it is the former, not the latter, which its proposals were intended to promote.[91]

Is, then, centralized administration necessarily the best administration for so vast an area as the United States? The Committee itself professed to look forward to the regional decentralization of administration; but argued that, before this could take place, the principle of "over-all management" centering in the President must be securely established. Its prima facie case is no doubt a strong one. The principle of hierarchy appeals to one's demand for symmetry, one's sense of order. Why is it, moreover, that the National Government has come to fill the vast role that it does today in the economic field if not for the very purpose of mitigating the conflicting policies of Big Business on the one hand and of the local governments on the other? And how is this purpose to be realized if the translation of the legislative policy of the government into terms of administration is to be the work of multiple independent agencies?

Yet, there are powerful considerations on the other side too. From the very nature of things a considerable part of the administrative tasks of government will always have to be performed by the functionaries who are immediately charged with them, without there being any opportunity for "over-all management" to be consulted or, in fact, intelligently applied. In other words, the world of administration is a *pluralistic* rather than a *monistic* world, and reposes in great measure on the loyalty and competence of individual bureaucrats, qualities which thrive best in conditions making for independence of judgment and pride in a job well done.[92] Certainly, to conceive of the President as a potential "boss of the works" save in situations raising broad issues of policy would be both absurd and calamitous; and for such issues the legislative process is still available, a field in which presidential leadership is today a more vital factor than ever before. At the same time, it is not even today the only factor; and the committee's complaint that the commissions produce "confusion" and "conflict" "in the execution of the President's policies" is, consequently, only partly valid. Indeed, an authoritative writer on this subject has recently shown that presidential supervision and coördination of policy in the very departments which the Committee would fain see aggrandized is today extremely haphazard and fragmentary.[93] Why clamor for other worlds to conquer when those at hand are still out of control? Nor should we overlook the fact that the broader policies which the independent commissions were created to carry out are laid down in the law itself, in the making of which Congress also still shares.

Thus far Congress has declined to put into the President's hands the means of sundering at one fell blow the "Gordian knot" of the problem of administrative organization. The Reorganization Act of April 3, 1939, specifically excepted the great independent agencies from its provisions, and the Act of December 20, 1945, followed suit.[94] In the case of the vast welter of lesser executive agencies, however, the President was empowered in the interest of economy and efficiency to regroup and transfer them or to reassign their functions at discretion, although no "plan" of reorganization was to take effect till the expiration of sixty calendar days following its transmission to Congress, and then "only if during such sixty-day period there has not been passed by the two Houses a concurrent resolution stating in substance that the Congress does not favor it." The act also created the Executive Office of the President, to which by Reorganization Plan No. 1, effective July 1, 1939, the Bureau of the Budget was transferred from the Treasury Department, thus dramatizing the power of the President under the Budget and Accounting Act of 1921 in preparation of the budget and the formulation of the fiscal program of the government. Later the Executive Office became a convenient façade behind which the various executive war agencies were ostensibly assembled.

To return for a moment to the more general problem: Congress does appear to have overlooked one method of promoting administrative collaboration without materially aggrandizing presidential power, and that is to require the independent commissions and similar agencies to report to the President periodically or at his request. Exaction of such a duty would work beneficially in two ways: (1) it would bring divergent tendencies in administration to the light of day and put them on justification; (2) it would inform the legislative judgment of the President.

The hierarchical principle, it has been acutely suggested, may be less important for its authoritative than for its communicative aspects.[95]

A NEW PROBLEM IN AMERICAN GOVERNMENT— DISLOYALTY IN THE BUREAUS

Whatever may be the ultimate fate of President Truman's "Loyalty Order" of March 21 last—Executive Order 9835[96]—its issuance marked the close of an epoch, the Age of Innocency of a democratic faith still untainted by European revolutionary nihilism and its mordant class hatreds. In the early days of the Civil War, it is true, the problem existed of ridding some of the bureaus of suspected "spies," but it soon yielded to the forthright methods of those days, when "the native hue of resolution" was not yet "sicklied over with a pale cast of thought."[97]

How much at variance, indeed, the set of conditions on which Order 9835 is postulated is from those which obtained two generations ago is revealed by Rule I, which was issued in 1884 by the still dewy Civil Service Commission, and which had for its purpose the maintenance of the service on a nonpartisan basis. The rule, still unrepealed, reads as follows:

"No question in any form or application in any examination shall be so framed as to elicit information concerning the political or religious opinions or affiliations of any applicant, nor shall any inquiry be made concerning such opinions, or affiliations, and all disclosures thereof shall be discountenanced."[98]

The American people were first alerted to "Communism" as a menace in World War I by strikes of the IWW (International Workers of the World, alias "Wobblies") in the forests of the Pacific Northwest and by Russian sympathizers in munitions factories in the East. Congress's reaction was shown by the passage of the Espionage Act of May 16, 1918, under which the famous Abrams Case was decided three years later,[99] and meantime on April 7, 1917, the day after our declaration of war upon Germany, President Wilson issued an unnumbered executive order, authorizing any "head of department or independent office to remove" forthwith "any employee" whose retention "he had ground for believing" would be "inimical to the public welfare." The order, which has reposed since then in government files, is given, with companion documents, in the notes.[100] The war being over, however, quiet again settled down upon the fluttered dovecotes of bureaucracy. For the antecedents of Order 9835 we need to turn to congressional action and opinion of the last nine years.

By section 9A of the Hatch Act of August 2, 1939, it was made

". . . unlawful for any person employed in any capacity by any agency of the Federal Government, whose compensation, or any part thereof, is paid from funds authorized or appropriated by any Act of Congress, to have membership in any political party or organization which advocates the overthrow of our constitutional form of government in the United States."[101]

This measure is, of course, still on the statute books. Further legislative concern over the problem was evidenced when the following June the 76th Congress authorized the Secretaries of the War and Navy Departments to remove summarily any employee in the interest of the national security, "any legal provisions, rules, or regulations governing the removal of employees to the contrary notwithstanding"—authority which the 77th Congress renewed. Meantime, by section 15 of the Emergency Relief Act of 1941 it was provided that "no Alien, no Communist, and no member of any Nazi Bund Organization shall be given employment . . . on any work project" to be prosecuted under the act. At the same session of Congress the practice was initiated of embodying in appropriation acts riders barring the use of any of the funds appropriated for the payment of salary or wages to "any person who advocates or belongs to an organization which advocates, the overthrow of the Government by force," a practice since repeated and extended.[102]

And at this point Mr. Dies and his Committee on Un-American Activities entered the picture, when in 1942 it requested the FBI to investigate a list of 1,100 allegedly "disloyal" employees, of whom two were ultimately found to deserve dismissal.[103] Despite this meager grist, the Attorney General now felt it to be incumbent upon him to set up an advisory Interdepartmental Committee to regularize and coördinate the handling of FBI reports. The committee failed of its purpose, as likewise did the committee of presidential creation which replaced it early in 1943.[104] Nevertheless, it was not until three years later, on November 25, 1946, to be precise, that the President decided on further action. On that date, following the urging of a subcommittee of the Civil Service Commission, the President's Temporary Commission was created by Executive Order 9806 to make a full investigation of the disloyalty problem and to propose an adequate program; and it is from the report of this body, which comprised representatives of the Civil Service Commission and of the State, War, Navy, Treasury, and Justice Departments, that Order 9835 directly stems.

Meantime, Congress had begun to manifest a renewed and more urgent interest in the question of employee loyalty. This was evidenced by its adoption early in July 1946 of the "McCarran Rider" to the State Department appropriation whereby the Secretary was empowered, in his "absolute discretion," to "terminate the employment of any officer or employee of the Department of State or of the Foreign Service of the United States whenever he shall deem such termination necessary or advisable in interests of the United States"—a provision repeated the following year[105] —and by the passage by the House July 15, 1947, of the so-called Rees bill, providing an expeditious procedure for the separation of "disloyal" employees from all branches of the civil service.[106] A year earlier had occurred the Canadian spy exposé, the central figures in which, officials of the Dominion government with university background, were shown to have communicated "defense secrets" to a member of the USSR legation at Ottawa simply from the motive, it appeared, of forwarding the cause of world-wide revolution.[107] The episode produced an immense and prolonged sensation on this side of the line, and especially on Capitol Hill. When it was promulgated Order 9835 was not improbably designed in part to head off more drastic action by Congress itself.

Order 9835 falls into six "parts," of which Part I provides for the investigation of applicants for posts in the executive branch, and Part II for the removal of disloyal incumbents. The former business is assigned, in the case of persons handling the competitive service, to the Civil Service Commission; in the case of others, it falls to the employing department or agency itself. Provision for an effective program to assure that disloyal civilian officers or employees are separated from the public service is, on the other hand, made the personal responsibility of the head of "each department and agency in the executive branch of the government," in discharge of which each head is required to set up one or more "loyalty boards" of not less than three representatives of the department or agency, to inquire into the loyalty of existing personnel and "make recommendations" respecting removal "on grounds relating to disloyalty." It is further ordered (Part III) that the Civil Service Commission shall establish from its membership "a Loyalty Review Board of not less than three impartial persons with authority to review cases of persons recommended for dismissal on grounds of disloyalty by any loyalty board."

In Part V of the order is defined the standard for refusal of employment and for dismissal from employment in an executive department or agency, which is stated to be that *"on all the evidence, reasonable grounds exist for belief that the person involved is disloyal to the Government of the United States"*; and in this connection it is provided that certain activities and associations of an applicant or incumbent "may be considered," to wit: "sabotage, espionage," "treason or sedition," "advocacy of revolution or force or violence to alter the constitutional form of government of the United States," "intentional, unauthorized disclosure . . . under circumstances which may indicate disloyalty to the United States," of official documents or information of a confidential character, "serving the interests of another government in preference to the interests of the United States," and, finally,

"membership in . . . or sympathetic association with any foreign or domestic organization, association, movement, group or combination of persons, designated by the Attorney General as totalitarian, Fascist, Communist, or subversive, or as . . . seeking to alter the form of government of the United States by unconstitutional means."

The first constitutional question to arise on the order concerns the source of the President's power to issue it. This, perhaps, is not quite so obvious as might appear on first consideration, since it is Congress who brings the civil service into being, who determines the powers and duties of its members, their pay, tenure, terms of promotion, and so forth. That, on the other hand, the President had, in the absence of any conflicting expression of policy by Congress, the power to issue the order seems to me indubitable, in view of his duty to "take care that the laws be faithfully executed," which embraces not only such legislative provisions as those reviewed above, which voice Congress's apprehensions of disloyalty, but any and all laws for the enforcement of which loyalty may be reasonably deemed a necessary prerequisite—in short, *the laws in general.* That the President is entitled to claim broad powers under his duty to take care "that the laws be faithfully executed" has been demonstrated many times in our history.[108] In the case of the heads of departments, moreover, the order is assured effective sanction from the President's unqualified power of removal over them; while by the precedent of Arthur E. Morgan's removal from TVA a recalcitrant head of an independent agency who flouted the order would be subject to disciplinary removal for the good of the service. Whether a specific incumbent shall be removed for disloyalty is, to be sure, left by the order itself with the head of the department or agency affected; yet even in such a case it is plausible doctrine that the President enjoys an overriding power of removal.[109]

A more serious constitutional question is whether the order infringes constitutional rights of federal officers and employees. Such curtailment as may result from it to an incumbent's liberty of political action certainly would not condemn the order. Chief Justice Holmes's epigram, when he was required nearly sixty years ago to pass upon the dismissal of a policeman under a Massachusetts statute which forbade political activity on the part of policemen, that "the petitioner may have a constitutional right to talk politics, but he has no constitutional right to be a policeman"[110] would perhaps, standing by itself, be regarded nowadays as a rather too summary dismissal of the issue. But in fact it does not stand by itself, for earlier in his opinion Holmes had used these, possibly "consolatory," words:

"There are few employments for hire in which the servant does not agree to suspend his constitutional right of free speech, as well as idleness, by the implied terms of his contract. The servant cannot complain, as he takes the employment on the terms which are offered him. On the same principle the city may impose any reasonable condition upon holding offices within its control. The condition that a policeman shall not engage in political activity seems to us reasonable."[111]

And it was precisely on this ground that the Supreme Court recently sustained the restrictions which the Hatch Act of 1939 imposes upon the political activities of certain categories of federal functionaries. The activities banned, a majority of the seven Justices sitting in the case held, could be "reasonably" thought to interfere with the efficient discharge by the persons affected of their official duties.[112] Moreover, the Court recently declined to review a lower court decision refusing to enjoin the Secretary of Labor from carrying out an order of the Civil Service Commission which directed the dismissal of an employee whose attitude toward American participation in the recent war had undergone a remarkable change at the time of Hitler's invasion of Russia. Such suspicious loyalty, the lower court held, was ample ground for the removal of a government employee "in wartime."[113] I doubt very much if the Court would boggle over the phrase "in wartime" in another case presenting similar facts, especially in view of the present state of our relations with the USSR and the latter's known aptitude in the field of espionage. And that it is "reasonable" for the government to require loyalty of its employees and to exact an oath of loyalty from them, nobody seems to question.

But do these considerations dispose of the subject? Professor Chafee and three of his colleagues in Harvard Law School contend not. They say:[114]

"It is imperative to keep clearly in mind what a dismissal under the order means. Far more is involved than the loss of job. It means that:

"(1) The person dismissed will be denied all opportunity for employment anywhere in the Federal Government.

"(2) As a practical consequence, he will also lose almost all possibility of finding employment within any State or Municipal Government.

"(3) Also, he will encounter special difficulties in obtaining employment in private organizations.

"Consider the case of one who, for twenty or thirty years—his entire mature life—has worked in the Forestry Service, or the Bureau of Animal Industry of the Department of Agriculture, or the Postal Service, or the Bureau of Standards, or the Tennessee Valley Authority. To deny him all opportunity for employment in governmental service, federal, state or municipal, is to deprive him of the only means of livelihood for which he has any training or experience.

"The tested wisdom of our tradition and national experience dictate that no sanction so drastic should be applied save after adjudication of wrongdoing based upon a full hearing before responsible and impartial public officers, who are not themselves in fear of losing their own jobs."

Reciting then the procedure outlined by the order, its critics continue:

"There is no provision that the accused shall be confronted by such evidence as there may be to support the charges against him, so that he may undertake to rebut it. Indeed, there is no requirement that the evidence against him shall be introduced at the hearing at all.

"No provision is made for a detailed record of the hearings or, for that matter, for a record of any kind. There is no requirement that the findings of the loyalty board must be supported by the evidence. In fact, there is no requirement that the loyalty board make any findings whatever. After the 'hearing,' the loyalty board makes its recommendation to the head of the department or agency. If the recommendation is for removal and is accepted by the departmental head, his decision is subject to an 'appeal' to the Loyalty Review Board of the Civil Service Commission, which, after review, makes an 'advisory recommendation.'"

They also criticize the role of the Attorney General:

"Here we swim in a sea of ambiguity. Is the Attorney General's designation [of organizations as "subversive," etc.] to be taken as final? May the defendant undertake to show that a group with which he is sympathetically associated is not subversive, or must he limit his defense to an attempt to show that he has no connection with the organization? If he concedes his membership, and is foreclosed by the Attorney General's characterization of the organization, will this be taken as 'proof' that he, as an individual, is likewise subversive, or at least as 'reasonable grounds for belief' that he is disloyal? Where is the burden of proof? Is it on the accused?"

The substance of this criticism has been repeated by many others.[115] How are such criticisms to be met; how, to date, have they been met?

Despite a faint suggestion to the contrary in the Harvard statement, recourse to the courts to correct the faults of the President's order from the point of view of the employee's interest would in all probability prove futile, and certainly would in the face of the opposition to be anticipated from Congress and the President. For while it is true that the Court took jurisdiction under the Declaratory Judgments Act of the case above mentioned involving the Hatch Act, yet had it decided in favor of the plaintiff employee it would have been entirely powerless to award him a remedy. Its opinion would have had the force of a homily in constitutional ethics, and no more.[116] Likewise it is true, as we saw in an earlier section of this chapter, that the Court has reviewed decisions by the Court of Claims in suits for unpaid salary which rested on the proposition that the plaintiff functionary had been dismissed from his post by some one not possessing the power of removal over him.[117] But all such actions are brought with the consent of the government, which could at any time be withdrawn. And I know of no case in which the Court has ever held that, unaided by an act of Congress, it possessed power to restore a wrongfully dismissed functionary to his former post.[118]

But the matter of jurisdiction and remedial powers of the courts quite aside, the further question arises whether the judicial power is authorized to pass upon otherwise valid measures of the government on account of their collateral or "consequential" detriment to private interests. Generally speaking, the answer is no. The country goes dry, but the producers of alcoholic beverages are not compensated for their ruined businesses; the tariff is lowered, and the law cannot save from bankruptcy those who built in reliance on it; Congress declares war, and scores of enterprises great and little are sunk without trace and without expectation of restitution.[119] Conceding, therefore, that the government has the constitutional power to dismiss officers or employees on the charge of disloyalty by a certain procedure, the fact that the stigma of "disloyalty" was in consequence affixed to the dismissed employee would not affect the case.

What is more, the Court has never thus far manifested the least interest in the procedures by which government employees have been put out of their jobs, far less any intention of squaring them with those conceptions of "due process of law" which apply in penal cases, and upon which the critics of the order have mainly based their objection to it. For more than thirty-five years there has been on the statute books a provision which confines the power to remove persons in the classified civil service to "such cause as will promote the efficiency of the said service and for reasons given in writing." The provision then continues:

"The person whose removal is sought shall have notice of the same and of any charges preferred against him, and be furnished with a copy thereof, and also be allowed a reasonable time for personally answering the same in writing; and affidavits in support thereof; but no examination of witnesses nor any trial or hearing shall be required except in the discretion of the officer making the removal; and copies of charges, notice of hearing, answer, reasons for removal, and of the order of removal shall be made a part of the records of the proper department or office."[120]

The safeguards here thrown about the employee are, if anything, less liberal than those which Order 9835 lays down for the removal of employees for disloyalty. Yet I know of no instance in which this procedure has been successfully attacked, or even challenged, in court as constitutionally inadequate. Furthermore, as its phrasing clearly indicates, the above quoted statutory provision was enacted as a *concession* to federal employees. Prior to that time no official power was more arbitrarily exercised than the removal power. It was a law unto itself.

We are forced to the conclusion that any effort to meet criticism of Executive Order 9835 must come from Congress or the President or from those whose business it will be to carry the order into effect. Confining attention to the third possibility, I wish to review the outstanding features of the statement which was made public December 28 last by Mr. Seth W. Richardson, Chairman of the Civil Service Commission's recently created Loyalty Review Board.[121] The powers of this body are, to be sure, merely advisory, but there is good reason to believe that its advice will usually be followed, and that it will be able to lend effective guidance to the development of the policy which is represented by the order.

The legal theory on which the statement is based is phrased by Mr. Richardson as follows:

"The Board is of the opinion, that, legally, the Government is entitled to discharge any employee for reasons which seem sufficient to the Government, and without extending to such employee any hearing whatsoever. We believe that the rights of the Government in that respect are at least equal to those possessed by private employers. We also think that the Government, if necessary, may conclude that any suspicion of disloyalty whatsoever, however remote, might, in view of the dangerous possibilities involved, suffice to warrant employee dismissal without hearing."

By this view any concession made to persons charged with "disloyalty" under the order is a voluntary one on the part of the agencies exercising the removal power. For reasons already canvassed, the position is not open to serious attack, but obviously it does not settle the question of what concessions *ought* to be made from the point of view of justice and sound administrative policy.

The principal objection urged against the order is stated by Mr. Richardson as follows:

"The point has been vigorously presented to us as follows, 'Every employee accused of disloyalty should be given the right to confront his accusers, and subject them to cross examinations.' This contention has obvious force, and presents grave considerations to us. Why have we been unable to accept it?"

The answer which Mr. Richardson returns to this question is a forthright adoption of the FBI's position that it cannot afford to dry up its sources of confidential information by revealing them. Inasmuch as the FBI has many other tasks to perform than the investigation of federal employees as to their loyalty, the position seems to me sound, and as is pointed out in the succeeding section was advanced in another connection some years ago. At the same time, it was hardly necessary for Mr. Richardson to out-Herod Herod, as he appears to do in the following sentence of his statement:

"We recognize that the use of such a report as evidence by the various Loyalty Boards, without disclosure of the contents to the employee, does subject the employee to non-confrontation of witnesses against him, and does deprive him of the right of cross-examination of such witnesses,—a situation which ought to, and does, give rise to most serious questions in the minds of the general public."

But in the November 16 issue of the *New York Herald Tribune* Mr. Hoover, in answer to a question put to him by Mr. Bert Andrews, said:

". . . While the F.B.I. does not approve its reports being made public, nevertheless, it expects the contents of its reports to be used, and it has no objection to a loyalty hearing board confronting an individual with charges based upon the contents of its report. The President's executive order provides that 'the investigating agency may refuse to disclose the names of confidential informants.' "

In short, while Mr. Hoover bars disclosure "of the names of confidential *informants*," Mr. Richardson appears to ban disclosure of their *information* as well. At the same time, he in part at least compensates for this with the following pledge:

"Moreover, we shall specifically require the Loyalty Board to give careful consideration in its final determination as to whether, in the opinion of the Board, the employee has been actually handicapped in his defense because of the non-confrontation and lack of opportunity to cross-examine source witnesses."

Turning, then, to the second main objection urged by critics of the order, what they term its "doctrine of guilt by association," Mr. Richardson writes:

"We are not at all oblivious to the difficulties involved in the determination of questions sounding in personal loyalty. We intend to point out to all persons charged with the carrying out of our proposed program, that the probative value of evidence of past or present membership in, affiliation with or sympathetic association with, any one or more of the organizations now or hereafter designated by the Attorney General can be fairly evaluated only after determining, so far as possible, the character of the organization, the period, nature and duration of the association, whether the employee or applicant was aware of the subversive character of the organization at the time of such association, and the nature of his activities in connection with such organization."

This, it seems to me, goes far to meet the criticism leveled by the Harvard group against the vagueness of the Attorney General's role under the order. Pertinent, too, is Mr. Richardson's reminder that under the order itself "a specific rule of decision is established, to wit:

"'. . . whether on all the evidence in the record, reasonable grounds exist for belief that the person involved is disloyal.'"

And, as he further points out, no person can be ousted from the government service under the order until his case has been passed upon by three bodies, the Loyalty Board of his own agency, the head of the agency, and a panel of the Loyalty Review Board.

Altogether, therefore, it seems to me that the statement does go a considerable way toward meeting objections to the order which have been based on concern for justice to those who are subject to removal under it. Even the implication that an employee under charges might be denied confrontation with the evidence against him may have been the product of hasty composition, of which the statement does not lack other indications.

But *what* categories of federal employees precisely are covered by the statement? Some six weeks prior to the publication of the Richardson statement the President himself had issued a statement assuring the country that, while "disloyal and subversive elements must be removed from the employ of the government," there would be no "witch hunt." Although the statement sketched a procedure that was apparently intended for all cases, yet when the specific question was put to him the President answered that it would not govern the Department of State or the Atomic Energy Commission.[122] On December 10, moreover, a release from the State Department made it clear that the Department intended to retain the right to discharge or transfer an employee as "a bad security risk" even though he might have been cleared by the Loyalty Review Board. To quote:

"'The State Department will accept the recommendation of the Loyalty Review Board in so far as the employee's loyalty is concerned, but reserves the right to determine for itself whether or not, for security reasons, the employee is to continue in his old job.'"[123]

The Department of State intends, in short, to retain the "absolute discretion" which existing legislation accords it until June 30, 1948. And it is highly probable that the Department of Defense, as residuary legatee of the old Army and Navy Departments, will assert similar powers.

This difference in relationship to Order 9835 and to Chairman Richardson's gloss upon it between the so-called "sensitive" agencies and the others seems to me, in view of present perils, to be entirely reasonable.[124] The "sensitive" agencies constitute our first line of defense. In them the most complete loyalty is a value overtopping all others from the point of view of the national security which, as Adam Smith conceded, is the first and highest responsibility of government. To adopt and adapt a brocard from our constitutional law, disloyalty in the "sensitive" agencies presents "a clear and present danger" that authorizes procedures not otherwise justifiable. At the same time, the "sensitive" agencies, like all the others, are bound to bear in mind that sound administration will not flout the importance of *esprit de corps* in the service and keeping it attractive to young persons of talent, or overlook the undesirability of infecting the service with fear, hysteria, mutual suspicion, chauvinism, and fascism.

EXECUTIVE IMMUNITY VERSUS LEGISLATIVE PREROGATIVE

And so much for the President as disciplinarian. He is not always such; sometimes he appears in the gracious capacity of defender of the men and women through whom the law is carried into execution. Yet even in such cases he ordinarily has an axe of his own to grind, and a potent one.

President Monroe, in the last days of his Presidency, declined a call for papers from the House of Representatives on the ground that their publication might do a naval officer still at sea an injustice.

It is important [said he] that the public servants in every station should perform their duty with fidelity, according to the injunctions of the law and the orders of the Executive in fulfillment thereof. . . . It is due to their rights and to the character of the Government that they be not censured without just cause, which can not be ascertained until, on a view of the charges, they are heard in their defense, and after a thorough and impartial investigation of their conduct.[125]

A generation later the Attorney General informed President Pierce that the President of the United States "in the discharge of his constitutional duty to take care that the laws be faithfully executed, may, in his discretion, well assume, in certain cases the defense of ministerial officers."[126]

It was also in this tradition for the late President Roosevelt, when Congress attempted in 1943 to remove from the government pay roll three officials whom it charged with radicalism, to come to their defense both by a special message to Congress assailing the "rider" as a "bill of attainder" and "an unwarranted encroachment upon the authority of both the executive and judicial branches." And later the Supreme Court endorsed the first of these criticisms in a case in which the Department of Justice appeared by the President's order on behalf of the assailed officials.[127]

The occasion for most presidential interventions between Congress and executive personnel has been of the type illustrated by President Monroe's in 1825. The point at issue, however, has generally been not justice to the official involved but the right of the Executive Department to keep its own secrets. In the famous case of *Marbury v. Madison* the question arose early in the proceedings whether Attorney General Lincoln was obliged to answer certain questions put to him in support of Marbury's application for an injunction to Secretary of State Madison. In Cranch's report of the case we read:

"Mr. Lincoln, attorney general, having been summoned, and now called, objected to answering. . . . On the one hand he respected the jurisdiction of this court, and on the other he felt himself bound to maintain the rights of the executive. He was acting as secretary of state at the time when this transaction happened. He was of opinion, and his opinion was supported by that of others whom he highly respected, that he was not bound, and ought not to answer, as to any facts which came officially to his knowledge while acting as secretary of state. . . .

"Mr. Lee stated that the duties of a secretary of state were two-fold. In discharging one part of those duties he acted as a public ministerial officer of the United States, totally independent of the President, and that as to any facts which came officially to his knowledge, while acting in this capacity, he was as much bound to answer as a marshal, a collector, or any other ministerial officer. But that in the discharge of the other part of his duties, he did not act as a public ministerial officer, but in the capacity of an agent of the President, bound to obey his orders, and accountable to him for his conduct. And that as to any facts which came officially to his knowledge in the discharge of this part of his duties, he was not bound to answer.

"The court said, that if Mr. Lincoln wished time to consider what answers he should make, they would give him time; but they had no doubt he ought to answer. There was nothing confidential required to be disclosed. If there had been he was not obliged to answer it; and if he thought that any thing was communicated to him in confidence he was not bound to disclose it."[128]

Here, of course, the question at issue was whether the Supreme Court could require an official to answer, but the doctrine stated is equally applicable to the case of an investigation by a congressional committee. This doctrine is that a high executive official is not bound to divulge matters regarding which he is a confidant of the President. At the same time the Court impliedly claims the right to say finally whether such a plea on the part of an official is a valid one. In both these respects subsequent practice has broadened the scope of the immunity which the President can throw about a subordinate member of the executive department from judicial and legislative investigatory processes.

In addition to his duty to the laws, a supplementary basis of the President's power to do this is the principle of his own immunity from judicial process. The question whether there was such a principle was discussed at the very beginning of the government by Vice-President Adams, Representative Fisher Ames, and Senator William Maclay. The first two stated the conclusion that a President in office was answerable to no judicial process except impeachment. The President, they argued, was above "all judges, justices, etc.," and, secondly, that judicial interposition involving the President personally was liable to interfere with the operation of the governmental machinery. This, too, seems to have been future Chief Justice Oliver Ellsworth's opinion; Maclay thought decidedly otherwise.[129]

A decade later Jefferson's followers made it one of the grounds of their attack upon Justice Samuel Chase that he had refused to subpoena President Adams during the trial of Dr. Cooper for sedition, but this did not prevent Jefferson when President from refusing to respond to Chief Justice Marshall's subpoena in Aaron Burr's Trial for Treason, nor from casting the robe of his immunity over three members of his Cabinet and three clerks in the State Department whose testimony was desired by the defense in another trial. Being summoned to appear in court, these officials refused, writing the trial judges that the President "has especially signified to us that our official duties cannot . . . be at this juncture dispensed with."[130]

In the many years that have rolled by since Jefferson's Presidency there have been hundreds of congressional investigations. But I know of no instance in which a head of department has testified before a congressional committee in response to a subpoena, nor been held for contempt for refusal to testify. All appearances by these high officials seem to have been voluntary. The rule of immunity is, however, regarded with special deference in the case of the Secretary of State. When recently a green Congressman, whose head had possibly been turned by his finding himself a member of a subcommittee of the House on the Merchant Marine, issued a subpoena to Secretary Marshall, his embarrassed associates promptly recalled the document and gave their brash colleague a little lecture on the "protocol" obtaining in such matters.[131] Likewise, while other heads of departments may be "directed" by Congress or one of its committees to furnish needed documents, the Secretary of State is invariably "requested" to furnish them; and in both instances the call is usually qualified by the softening phrase "if the public interest permits."

Certain recent episodes relate the immunity principle to the double problem of national security and employee loyalty. In a letter addressed to Attorney General Jackson under date of April

23, 1941, Representative Carl Vinson of Georgia, writing in the capacity of Chairman of the House Committee on Naval Affairs, requested that the Committee be furnished with "all" FBI reports since June 1939, "together with all future reports," etc., from the same source in connection with "investigations made by the Department of Justice arising out of strikes, subversive activities," and so forth. The Attorney General refused the request, saying:

"It is the position of this Department, restated now with the approval of and at the direction of the President, that all investigative reports are confidential documents of the executive department of the Government, to aid in the duty laid upon the President by the Constitution to 'take care that the laws be faithfully executed,' and that congressional or public access to them would not be in the public interest.

"Disclosure of the reports could not do otherwise than seriously prejudice law enforcement. Counsel for a defendant or prospective defendant, could have no greater help than to know how much or how little information the Government has, and what witnesses or sources of information it can rely upon. This is exactly what these reports are intended to contain.

"Disclosure of the reports at this particular time would also prejudice the national defense and be of aid and comfort to the very subversive elements against which you wish to protect the country. For this reason we have made extraordinary efforts to see that the results of counter-espionage activities and intelligence activities of this Department involving those elements are kept within the fewest possible hands. A catalogue of persons under investigation or suspicion, and what we know about them, would be of inestimable service to foreign agencies; and information which could be so used cannot be too closely guarded.

"Moreover, disclosure of the reports would be of serious prejudice to the future usefulness of the Federal Bureau of Investigation. As you probably know, much of this information is given in confidence and can only be obtained upon pledge not to disclose its sources. A disclosure of the sources would embarrass informants—sometimes in their employment, sometimes in their social relations, and in extreme cases might even endanger their lives. We regard the keeping of faith with confidential informants as an indispensable condition of future efficiency.

"Disclosure of information contained in the reports might also be the grossest kind of injustice to innocent individuals. Investigative reports include leads and suspicions, and sometimes even the statements of malicious or misinformed people. Even though later and more complete reports exonerate the individuals, the use of particular or selected reports might constitute the grossest injustice, and we all know that a correction never catches up with an accusation."[132]

The bearing of some of Mr. Jackson's observations on matters discussed in the preceding section is evident.

Other occurrences of like character are the following: In July 1943 the War and Navy Departments, acting on the order of President Roosevelt, refused certain information to a House committee investigating the Federal Communications Commission, on the ground that to do so would be "contrary to the public interest." Early in 1944 the head of FBI refused to testify before the same committee, and was supported by Attorney General Biddle in doing so. The latter also refused to produce the President's "directive" on which Mr. Hoover had based his refusal, saying:

"It is my view that, as a matter of law and of long-established constitutional practice, communications between the President and the Attorney General are confidential and privileged, and not subject to inquiry by a committee of one of the houses of Congress. In this instance it seems to me that the privilege should not be waived; to do so would be to establish an unfortunate precedent, inconsistent with the position taken by my predecessors. I must, therefore, respectfully decline to produce before your committee the President's communications."

A few months later Mr. Byron Price, Director of CO (Office of Censorship), declined to transmit to a Senate committee, without first being subpoenaed by it, a file of intercepts, and no subpoena was issued. Then in May 1947 President Truman refused to let the Senate War Investigating Committee comb the late President Roosevelt's files bearing on its Arabian oil inquiry, but at the same time requested executors of the Roosevelt estate to produce any such documents which it might uncover.[133]

The *cause célèbre* to date, however, in this matter is one involving the present director of the Bureau of Standards, Dr. Edward U. Condon. As a physicist of note, Dr. Condon has had an important part in the development of the atomic bomb. Recently the House Committee on Un-American Activities, in rummaging through the files of the Department of Commerce, came upon one in which Dr. Condon was absolved by the department's loyalty board of being "one of the weakest links in our atomic security" and an associate of "alleged Soviet agents." The basis of the board's finding, it transpired, was an FBI report, and this the Un-American Activities Committee decided that it must see. On March 3, 1948, consequently, after less formal approaches, the committee adopted the extraordinary course of subpoenaing Secretary Harriman to produce the file, which, by order of the President, Mr. Harriman refused to do. Logically this recalcitrance on the Secretary's part should have been followed by an order of the House citing him for "contempt," and then his trial under the Act of 1857 in the District Court on the charge of "misdemeanor," unless meantime the President had pardoned him, as he would have been entitled to do. The committee, however, being at this stage in the position of seeking an appropriation from the House for the coming year, decided to proceed more conservatively. The result was that not only did the committee get a handsome appropriation, but on April 22 the House itself adopted a resolution peremptorily ordering the administration to surrender the desired data. Meantime, on March 15, the President had issued a general order forbidding all executive departments and agencies to furnish information concerning the loyalty of their employees to any court or committee of Congress. And so matters stand as this book goes to press.[134]

The constitutional merits of the quarrel between the House and the administration are easily assessed. No one questions, or can question, the constitutional right of the House to inform itself through committees of inquiry on subjects which fall within its legislative competence and to hold for contempt recalcitrant witnesses before such committees, and undoubtedly the question of employee loyalty is such a subject. On the other hand, this prerogative of Congress has always been regarded as limited by the right of the President to have his subordinates refuse to testify either in court or before a committee of Congress concerning matters of confidence between them and himself. Are, then, communications to the President or to officials who are authorized by him to receive them concerning the loyalty of federal executive personnel such matters of confidence? The question must certainly be answered in the affirmative. The President's "freeze order" of March 15, 1948, is the logical corollary of his "Loyalty Order" of March 11, 1947, and a necessary expedient to prevent the demoralization of the Civil Service.

To sum up briefly: From the outset the relation of the President to the remainder of the executive establishment of the government has been influenced by two more or less conflicting ideas. Originally the notion of legislative supremacy enjoyed a preponderating influence, but under Jackson the notion of presidential domination underwent a great accession of power. *En revanche,* to escape the operation of an uncontrolled presidential removal power—the result for constitutional doctrine of the Duane ouster in 1833—Congress fifty years later set up the Civil Service Commission outside the executive departments, although not outside the Executive Department, unless we reject the principle of the separation of powers as an underlying doctrine of our constitutional system; and thus was inaugurated an experiment from which have latterly issued a considerable number of executive agencies not subject to presidential direction in the performance of their functions.

The Myers Case was decided by a former President under the influence of Jacksonian concepts, and went to such lengths that Congress was stripped of all power to protect the independence of these bodies even when exercising their "quasi-judicial" functions. This result, however, was soon perceived by the Court to clash with the doctrines which it had been building up since about 1890 with regard to "a fair hearing" in connection especially with rate regulation; and in the Humphrey Case it beat a precipitate retreat from the ideology of the Myers decision.

Yet, despite their contradictions, one common purpose can be perceived in both these decisions; namely, to make presidential removal power and presidential supervisory power march abreast. How extensive, then, ought the latter be? The President's Committee on Administrative Management urged in 1937 that it ought to be complete as to all "non-judicial" duties of administrative agents; but so far Congress has not accepted the suggestion; nor ought it, save in full recognition of the dangers of political interference with tasks which often require a trained judgment for their satisfactory performance. Nor should it be forgotten that the national legislative power, in which the President's part is very important these days, is always available to correct the more serious aberrations of its administrative agents.

For all that, recent developments have forced a partial return to the ideology of the Myers Case. Since 1939 both Congress and the President have become increasingly aware that the subversive methods of contemporary totalitarian governments have given rise to a novel problem in administration, that of making sure of the loyalty to the United States of the men and women employed in its service. Executive Order 9835 accordingly claims for the President, as an offshoot of his duty to "take care that the laws be faithfully executed," the power to sift incoming and existing personnel as to "loyalty." The power itself is not open to serious challenge, nor is its exercise open to challenge in court. Reliance must therefor be had on the willingness of the political branches to do the fair thing by government employees, bearing in mind that, while the national security is indeed a primary interest, yet sound administration will not neglect the claims of justice or ignore the probable demands of those who contemplate staking a career in the public service.

As the converse of his power to discipline unfit personnel, the President, aided by his pardoning power, is able to spread over them to some uncertain extent the mantle of his own immunity from judicial process and from legislative inquiry, except of course in impeachment proceedings against himself. This, however, should not be done for the protection of the persons thus immunized, but only for that of state secrets, or what purport to be such; and among these today may ordinarily be classified information bearing on the loyalty of federal executive personnel. That the power is capable of colliding head on with Congress's inherent power to investigate all matters as to which it may legislate is obvious. Thus far the adjustment of the two powers to one another has been effected by the give-and-take of the political process and presumably it must continue to be.

CHAPTER IV

CHIEF EXECUTIVE

THE President's role of Chief Executive is a varied one. It stems immediately from his duty to "take care that the laws be faithfully executed," but it also draws sustenance from the opening clause of Article II, from his role as "Commander-in-Chief," from his prerogative to pardon "offenses against the United States," and from certain theories outside the Constitution. Many questions of constitutional interpretation arise in consequence. As was shown in the preceding chapter, the President's duty to the law often puts upon him the duty to interpret it for the Executive Department. While this has always been the case, thanks to the broad terms in which congressional legislation has in recent years come to be couched even in times of peace, executive interpretation of statutes frequently amounts today to a species of subordinate legislation. The question naturally arises whether there are statable limits to this kind of thing, or available safeguards against the indefinite accumulation of power by this method in the hands of the President.

Again, the President has in certain contingencies employed the armed services in the enforcement of the law, has even proclaimed martial law and suspended the privilege of the writ of habeas corpus. What constitutional limitations exist to the utilization of these procedures; what constitutional machinery exists to make any such limitations effective? Then there are those "emergencies" short of war, more frequent nowadays than of yore, emergencies for which either no legislative provision has been made or for which the provision made is, in the judgment of the President, inadequate. What in such situations are his power and

The Notes to this chapter begin on page four hundred thirty-seven

duty? All these and others are matters to be discussed under the above caption.

THE PRESIDENT AS LAW INTERPRETER; DELEGATED LEGISLATIVE POWER — APPROPRIATION ACTS — CONCURRENT RESOLUTIONS

There is no doctrine of American constitutional law which is more securely established than that when the courts are employed in the enforcement of the law their interpretation of it is final for the situation submitted to them. All executive readings of the laws are, therefore, when they give rise to litigation, subject to review by the courts, and so ultimately by the Supreme Court.[1] Yet even in such instances the Court is free to retire behind the maxim, which also goes back to an early date, that great weight ought to be accorded an executive interpretation, particularly if it has been uniform and is of long standing.[2]

Certain acts of the first Roosevelt in promotion of his "conservation policy" are illustrative in this connection. As the statutes then stood the President was specifically authorized to withdraw from private entry all lands in which "mineral deposits" had been found, and so inferentially *only* such lands. In the teeth of this provision Mr. Roosevelt withdrew, "pending legislation," many parcels of land for forest and bird reserves, or because they were supposed to contain oil, coal, or phosphate, or for other reasons.[3] Later with the advent of the Taft administration many of the above orders were canceled as being invalid, but eventually President Taft himself withdrew a large tract in California in which oil had been discovered, asking Congress at the same time to ratify his action. The Act of June 25, 1910, however, which Congress presently passed, while it gave the President *carte blanche* as to future temporary withdrawals, made no reference to past withdrawals.[4] In *United States v. Midwest Oil Co.*[5] the Taft order was nevertheless upheld on the ground that it was supported by long-continued usage which Congress had had ample opportunity to correct but never had. Prior to 1910, the Court pointed out, there had been scores of executive orders establishing or enlarging governmental reservations of various sorts, and all without definite statutory warrant. Indeed, the Court itself had nearly fifty years previously justified this very practice on the ground of its having existed from "an early period in the history of the Government."[6] In short, the President was recognized as being able to acquire authority from the silences of Congress as well as from its positive enactments, provided only the silences were sufficiently prolonged.

Furthermore, whenever executive constructions of a statute assume a negative shape every possibility of their coming under judicial scrutiny is obviated automatically. Indeed, the very kernel of the power to interpret a statute preparatory to its enforcement is the power to determine whether a prosecution or other positive act shall be attempted under it. While at the outset of the government this power was apparently regarded as being dispersed among the various United States district attorneys, it was another of Jackson's achievements, facilitated by the ever compliant Taney, to make good the right of the President to the final voice in all such matters when he chooses to assert it. The point arose in connection with some jewels which had been stolen from the Princess of Orange and seized by officers of the United States Customs in the hands of the thief. A request was thereupon filed by the minister of the Netherlands for the restoration of the booty, but not before the local United States district attorney had begun condemnation proceedings on behalf of the United States which, as he soon indicated, he was indisposed to discontinue. In this dilemma Attorney General Taney informed the President that since the district attorney had the option under the law to discontinue the suit, the President had the constitutional right to compel him to exercise that option or to effect his removal and appoint a more responsive successor.[7] Subsequent legislation has, in effect, ratified this doctrine. By the Act of August 2, 1861, the Attorney General, a member of the President's Cabinet, was endowed with power of supervision and direction of all marshals and district attorneys of the United States, while by the Act of March 3, 1887, he was authorized to determine in all cases whether appeal should be taken from decisions adverse to the United States;[8] that is to say, in effect the President was so authorized.

Theoretically, to be sure, the decision of the designated agents of national law enforcement, at whose head stands the Chief Executive, whether or not to enforce a statute in a given situation or situations, may not be based on mere grounds of expediency but must be required by the statute in question, or at least have its sanction. Actually, any particular statute is but a single strand of a vast fabric of laws demanding enforcement; nor—simply from the nature of the case—can all these be enforced with equal vigor, or with the same vigor at all times. So the President's duty to "take care that the laws be faithfully executed" has come to embrace a broad power of selection among the laws for this purpose; and that this power is today without statable limits the history of the Sherman Act alone is sufficient proof. In a word, the President's very *obligation to* the law becomes at times an authorization to *dispense with* the law.[9]

Nor is it alone in prosecutions that executive interpretations of statutes may flower. Nowadays they give rise to proclamations, orders, ordinances, rules, regulations, "directives"—what have you?—to supplement the law as it comes from the hands of Congress, and to give it definiteness—in a word, to *executive lawmaking*.[10] We are thus brought face to face with the maxim, derived immediately from John Locke's *Treatise on Civil Gov-*

ernment, more remotely from a passage of Justinian's *Digest* having nothing to do with legislative power, that "the legislature may not delegate its power."[11]

By the strict logic of the principle of the separation of powers, the only power which the legislature possesses to delegate is legislative power; yet by the maxim just quoted it is this power precisely which the legislature cannot delegate. Conversely, by the principle of the separation of powers the executive should be incapable of receiving or exercising anything but executive power, from which it must follow either that the executive can never receive any power from the legislature or that when power passes it is automatically transmuted from legislative into executive power. But the former alternative is obviously contrary to fact, and the latter opens the way to delegation by the legislature of all its power to the executive. Nor is it sufficient to urge that executive power is a mere capacity to act within limits set by the legislature. For the obvious answer is that, on this assumption too, the maxim against delegation loses all its virtue unless there is some intrinsic limitation to the capacity of the executive thus to act, which again would render the maxim superfluous.[12]

First and last, we find it to be the fact that the legislature has always been acknowledged to have the right to pass three kinds of laws, every one of which represents a delegation of powers which the legislature itself might exercise. These are: (1) laws delegating to local units powers of local self-government; (2) laws to go into effect upon the happening of some future event to be ascertained by some other authority; (3) laws delegating a considerable measure of choice or discretion as to the actual content and application of the law. The first category has always been recognized by American courts as furnishing an exception to the maxim, and as being justified by the fact that local self-government is "fundamental" to the American constitutional system.[13] All the cases accordingly which have arisen under the maxim touching the relation of legislative to executive power represent an endeavor to set limits either to the practice of "contingent" legislation—category (2); or to the not always distinguishable practice of vesting executive discretion regarding the application of the law to a situation deemed to be already in existence—that is, category (3).[14]

The earliest case bearing upon the relation of the legislative power of Congress to national executive power was that of *United States v. Brig Aurora*,[15] which arose out of the Non-Intercourse Act of 1809. This act, in forbidding trade with Great Britain and France, authorized the President to suspend its provisions when in his judgment certain events had taken place, and likewise to revive them upon the occurrence of certain other events, of which also he was to be the judge. The *Aurora* was seized for attempting to trade contrary to the provisions of the act after it had been revived by presidential proclamation. Counsel for claimant argued: "To make the revival of a law dependent upon the presidential proclamation is to give that proclamation the force of a law." "Congress cannot transfer the legislative power to the President." The Court, nevertheless, upheld the government, saying, "We see no sufficient reason why the legislature should not exercise its discretion in reviving the act of 1809, either expressly or conditionally as its judgment should direct."

The precedent thus established was followed in 1891 in the case of *Field v. Clark*,[16] in which the point at issue was the validity of a provision of the Tariff Act of 1890 empowering the President to suspend certain other provisions of the act in described contingencies to be ascertained by him. The Court cited an imposing list of similar provisions from earlier statutes and of presidential proclamations in pursuance thereof, and concluded that both on the basis of precedent and of principle the provision in question was unassailable. "That Congress cannot delegate legislative power to the President," Justice Harlan asserted,

"is a principle universally recognized as vital to the integrity and maintenance of the system of government ordained by the Constitution. The act of October 1, 1890 ... is not inconsistent with that principle. ... Nothing involving *the expediency or just operation* of such legislation was left to the determination of the President. . . . Legislative power was exercised when Congress declared that the suspension should take effect upon a named contingency. What the President was required to do was simply in execution of the act of Congress."[17]

The stress of the argument, it will be observed, is on the alleged *definiteness* of the "fact" to be ascertained by the President, for it was this which precluded the executive power from varying the application of the will of Congress in accordance with considerations of expediency, and so kept it strictly *"executive."* Evaluated by this test, subsequent acts of Congress in the same field have gone much further. By the Tariff Act of 1922 the duty was imposed upon the President of determining, with the aid of advisers, differences in costs of production here and abroad, and of making increases and decreases in the customs rates in order to equalize such costs; and by the Tariff Act of 1930 he was authorized to raise or lower the rates set by the statute as much as fifty per cent. In *Hampton v. United States*[18] the former provision was attacked on the ground that "the difference in cost of production at home and abroad cannot be found as a fact without using ... *choice* between results at every stage, thus expressing the exercise of the legislative will." The Court overruled the contention, but in doing so found it necessary to supplement the reasoning in *Field v. Clark* with precedents and arguments of a radically different tendency—which brings us to the final and most significant of the three categories distinguished above.[19]

From its very beginning railway rate regulation was character-ized by the courts as a "legislative" function. How then could it be denied that, in delegating the same function to commissions, legislatures were delegating "legislative power"? The question first emerged in certain of the state courts in the early 80's, and was met with a significant modification of the maxim against delegated legislation. Instead of saying flatly that the acts creating these commissions did not constitute delegations of legislative power, they said that they did not constitute *invalid* delegations thereof, the power involved being of such a nature that the legis-lature could not itself "satisfactorily" exercise it.[20] Subsequently the Supreme Court came to adopt closely similar language in sustaining delegations of authority to certain of the departmental heads to make regulations of a statutory character, and later still it advanced an even more elastic test.

Three cases of special relevance are *Buttfield v. Stranahan, United States v. Grimaud,* and *Clark Distilling Co. v. West Mary-land Railway Co.,* which were decided respectively in 1904, 1911, and 1917.[21] The first mentioned involved an act which authorized the Secretary of the Treasury to fix "uniform standards of purity, quality and fitness for consumption of all" teas to be imported into the United States. Said the Court, speaking by Justice White:

"Congress legislated on the subject as far as was *reasonably practica-ble,* and from the necessities of the case was compelled to leave to executive officials the duty of bringing about the result pointed out by the statute. To deny the power of Congress to delegate such a duty would, in effect, amount but to declaring that the plenary power vested in Congress to regulate foreign commerce could not be efficaciously exercised."[22]

In short, Congress may delegate its powers when it is necessary to do so in order to achieve the results which it desires.

To the same effect is the lesson of the Grimaud Case. Here defendants had been indicted for grazing sheep in the national forest reserves in violation of regulations which the Secretary of Agriculture had promulgated under authority conferred by Congress. The trial court held the statute in question to be an unconstitutional delegation of legislative power; and on appeal the Supreme Court originally sustained this holding by a divided vote,[23] but a rehearing convinced it of its error and its final decision sustaining the government was unanimous. Speaking for the Court, Justice Lamar relied in part upon a distinction between "legislative power to make laws" and "administrative authority to make regulations." When allowance is made for the fact that the latter must always conform to the former, the distinction is obviously only verbal, a begging of the question. The real basis of the decision is to be found in the Justice's recognition that "in the nature of things *it was impracticable for Congress to provide general regulations*" for the "various and varying details" of the situation which had called for its intervention. For, quoting again:

"What might be harmless in one forest might be harmful in another. What might be injurious in one stage of timber growth, or at one season of the year, might not be so at another.... Each reservation had its peculiar and special features...."[24]

The mental image conjured up by these words is symbolic of the ever present complexity of the conditions with which governments have to deal today and in the presence of which the Lockian aphorism has fought a losing rear-guard action.

Indeed, in the Clark Distilling Company Case the Court seemed to be on the verge of chucking the maxim entirely. The statute involved was the Webb-Kenyon Act of 1913 which subjected interstate commerce in intoxicants to the police powers of the states. To the argument that this amounted to an unconstitutional delegation by Congress of its legislative power, Chief Justice White answered simply that Congress could at any time recover the power which it had delegated.[25] By this reading the maxim does little more than reword the truism that legislative power is not diminished by exercise, and what it forbids is outright and complete abdication.[26] It may be added that, in all probability, this was precisely the sense which Locke intended to give the maxim.

During World War I and again in World War II congressional delegations of power to the President exceeded all previous patterns, as will be shown in due course. Meantime, in a period of "emergency greater than war," as the late President characterized it, the Court undertook to revise its previous latitudinarian doctrines, but with very indifferent success. I have in mind its decisions in 1935 in the "Hot Oil" and Poultry Cases,[27] in which for the first time in our history legislation by Congress was disallowed as contravening the Lockian maxim. Neither of these precedents materially influenced congressional policy even at the time, and both have been subsequently relegated by the Court to its increasingly crowded cabinet of juridical curiosities.

Fairly typical of later New Deal legislation in the matter of delegation is the Agricultural Marketing Agreement Act of 1937, by which the Secretary of Agriculture is authorized to set the prices of certain agricultural products, including milk, with the end in view of restoring their purchasing power to what it had been during a previous "base period."[28] Furthermore, in the particular case of milk, the Secretary was ordered to take into account the price and supply of feed in the "marketing area" for which the price was fixed, as well as "other pertinent economic conditions"; but in any event was empowered to set a price that would "provide adequate quantities of wholesome milk and be in the public interest." And along with this delegation of power to the Secretary went supplementary delegations of power to producers to approve a marketing order without an agreement by handlers and to coöperatives to cast the votes of producer patrons. In *United States v. Rock Royal Cooperative,* this entire scheme of legislation was sustained against all objections to its delegative features, and at the same time a price-fixing order of the Secretary of Agriculture was upheld as tending to "effectuate the declared policy of the act."[29]

And so much for the Lockian axiom as it operates in peacetime and in those fields of power in which it is recognized as applying in full force. But there are other fields in which there is even less application, if indeed any at all; the fields, namely, in which congressional power and presidential prerogative merge into each other. One such field is that of foreign relations, to be dealt with later; another is that of expenditure. The pertinent provision of the Constitution in the latter connection reads thus: "No money shall be drawn from the Treasury, but in consequence of appropriations made by law. . . . "[30] Inasmuch as this provision could have been intended to operate only on the executive branch, it assumes that expenditure is primarily an executive function, and conversely that the participation of the legislative branch is essentially for the purpose simply of setting bounds to executive discretion—a theory which is confirmed by early practice under the Constitution. Thus the first appropriation act under the Constitution, which received Washington's approval September 29, 1789, read as follows:

"An act making appropriations for the present year; Section I. Be it enacted by the Senate and House of Representatives of the United States of America in Congress assembled, That there be appropriated for the service of the present year, to be paid out of the monies which arise, either from the requisitions heretofore made upon the several states, or from the duties on impost and tonnage, the following sums, viz. A sum not exceeding two hundred and sixteen thousand dollars for defraying the expenses of the civil list, under the late and present government; a sum not exceeding one hundred and thirty-seven thousand dollars for defraying the expenses of the department of war; a sum not exceeding one hundred and ninety thousand dollars for discharging the warrants issued by the late board of treasury, and remaining unsatisfied; and a sum not exceeding ninety-six thousand dollars for paying the pensions to invalids."

And the second appropriation act (March 26, 1790) proceeded in the same general categories as the first, although it also contained some more specific items. The third act (February 11, 1791) contained only the same general categories as the first, and the grant for "the civil list" was stated to be based on estimates from the Secretary of the Treasury. The entire act fills about two thirds of a page.[31]

Beginning with the second Congress, however, the annual appropriation acts became more and more detailed; those voted by the twenty-fourth Congress (May 9 and 14, 1836) filling more than fourteen pages of minute specifications.[32] Even so, there were still certain fields in which Congress long left executive discretion a nearly free hand in this matter. Thus the provision made in the annual appropriation acts during Jefferson's two administrations and during Madison's first administration "for the expenses of intercourse with foreign nations" was voted in lump sums. In the words of Attorney General Cushing, "Just those words, and nothing more, disposed of the whole question during the time of Mr. Jefferson."[33] Indeed it was not until 1855 that Congress began to assign definite diplomatic grades to named countries with a specified annual compensation for each.

The latest chapter in this history is supplied by the Budget and Accounting Act of 1921,[34] which, following similar reforms in municipal government in various cities of the United States, represents an effort to restore to the national executive the function of planning expenditure, while leaving to Congress its proper function of consent and grant. In the words of Professor Willoughby, the act makes the President "the working head of the administration in fact as well as in name. The budget serves as his plan of operations."[35]

Of course, I am not suggesting that Congress may not stipulate any terms it chooses as the condition of making an appropriation and thereby limit the effective scope of the inherently executive prerogative of planning and directing expenditure. But, if the above argument is correct—and it is supplemented by best modern practice—Congress is not *required* to stipulate *any* terms beyond directing that its grants be applied in promotion of the "general welfare."[36]

The most recent development of the delegation problem suggests the possibility of its permanent solution in a way that promises to satisfy the historical sense of the Lockian formula and at the same time assure both Congress and the President needed elbowroom in dealing with the complexities of modern industrial life. As was noted in the preceding chapter, the Reorganization Acts of 1939 and 1945, in authorizing the President to regroup certain executive agencies and functions, stipulated that no "plan" of reorganization was to go into effect until after sixty days, during which it might be killed at any time by the two houses passing a "concurrent resolution" disapproving it. Between these two dates this procedure was repeatedly copied, when in the Lend-Lease Act, the First War Powers Act, the Emergency Price Control Act, and other war measures provisions were incorporated that rendered the powers which these measures delegated subject to repeal at any time by "concurrent resolution"— that is to say, by a "vote" or "resolution" which, since it is not laid before the President, is not subject to his power of veto.[37]

It is argued, to be sure, that the use of the "concurrent resolution" device is unconstitutional, in view of the language of Article I, section 7, of the Constitution, which reads:

"Every order, resolution or vote to which the concurrence of the Senate and House of Representatives may be necessary (except on a question of adjournment) shall be presented to the President of the United States; and before the same shall take effect shall be approved by him, or being disapproved by him, shall be repassed by two-thirds of the Senate and House of Representatives, according to the rules and limitations prescribed in the case of a bill."

The fact is, nevertheless, that concurrent resolutions have been employed for a great variety of purposes from the very beginning —for expressing the opinion of the two houses on this, that, or the other matter, for devising a common program of action, for creating joint committees, for directing the expenditure of funds appropriated to the use of the two houses, and even for proposing amendments to the Constitution—a practice that the Supreme Court has sanctioned from the beginning.[38] It is generally agreed that Congress, being free not to delegate power, is free to do so on certain stipulated conditions, as, for example, that the delegation shall terminate by a certain date or upon the occurrence of a specified event, the end of a war, for instance. Why, then, should not one condition be that the delegation shall continue only as long as the two houses are of opinion that it is working beneficially? Furthermore, if the national legislative authority is free to delegate powers to the President, then why not to the two houses, either jointly or singly? And if the Secretary of Agriculture may be delegated powers the exercise of which is subject to a referendum vote of producers from time to time, as he may be,[39] then why may not the two houses of Congress be similarly authorized to hold a referendum now and then as to the desirability of the President's continuing to exercise certain legislatively delegated powers?

As we have seen, moreover, it is generally agreed that the maxim that the legislature may not *delegate* its powers signifies at the very least that the legislature may not *abdicate* its powers. Yet how, in view of the scope that legislative delegations take nowadays, is the line between *delegation* and *abdication* to be maintained? Only, I urge, by rendering the delegated powers recoverable without the consent of the delegate; and for this purpose the concurrent resolution seems to be an available mechanism, and the only one.[40]

MILITARY POWER IN LAW ENFORCEMENT—
PRESIDENT VERSUS CONGRESS

We turn now to the physical aspects of the President's duty to the law. The discussion focuses initially upon the twofold question: What are the respective powers of the President and Congress in the face of situations of widespread disorder in determining (1) the employment of the national forces in the enforcement within the United States of the national laws and treaties; (2) their employment in fulfillment of the guarantee of Article IV, section 4, to the several states against "domestic violence"?

The earliest piece of legislation that is relevant to the subject is the Act of May 2, 1792, under which the famous "Whiskey Rebellion" was put down.[41] The act dealt only with the "calling forth" of the state militias, but this circumstance is probably without interpretative significance, inasmuch as the small Regular Army of that day was fully employed in manning the seacoast and frontier fortifications. The notable feature of the measure is its formulation of the contingency in which the powers it conferred were to be exercised: "Whenever the laws of the United States shall be opposed or the execution thereof obstructed, in any state by combinations too powerful to be suppressed by the ordinary course of judicial proceedings or by the power vested in the marshals." Upon such a situation being "notified" to him by an associate Justice or district judge of the United States, it was made "lawful for the President" to call forth the militia of the state involved in the disturbance, and, if necessary, the militias of other states; but before despatching them against "the insurgents" the President must first issue a proclamation commanding the latter "to disperse and retire peaceably to their respective abodes."

In the Act of February 28, 1795,[42] the above measure underwent revision in two important respects. The requirement that a situation bringing its provisions into operation must be first judicially "notified to the President" was eliminated, with the result of making him, in the language of the Court, "the sole and exclusive judge" of the facts justifying a use of his powers under the act.[43] At the same time he was authorized to call forth the militia to aid a state in suppressing "domestic violence," a provision which evidently assumes a close identity between "domestic violence" and "insurrection," and in so doing enlarges the possible realm of martial law.

Twelve years later, by the Act of March 8, 1807,[44] Congress extended the provisions of the Act of 1795 to the national forces in the following terms:

"That in all cases of insurrection or obstruction to the laws, either of the United States or of any individual State or Territory, where it is lawful for the President of the United States to call forth the militia for the purpose of suppressing such insurrection or of causing the laws to be duly executed, it shall be lawful for him to employ, for the same purposes, such part of the land or naval force of the United States as shall be judged necessary, having first observed all the prerequisites of the law in that respect."

Presumably this measure testifies to Jefferson's conception of the proper relation both of the legislative to the executive power and of the civil to the military power. All the more, therefore, ought it be observed that, in availing himself of the resources which the act put at his disposal, Jefferson by no means confined himself to its precise terms. Thus in his proclamation of April 19, 1808, addressed to "sundry persons" in the region of Lake Champlain who were found to be "combining and confederating" against the enforcement of the Embargo Act, Jefferson supplemented the customary warning to "the insurgents" that they disperse, with a sweeping command to "all officers having authority, civil or military, and all other persons, civil or military, who shall be found in the vicinity" to aid and assist "by all means in their power, by force of arms and otherwise" the suppression of the unruly combinations.[45]

Manifestly, this comes very near asserting that all citizens of the United States whose services may be needed in that connection may be called upon by the President to act as a *posse comitatus* to aid in the enforcement of "the laws of the Union." The idea thus set going lay dormant until 1851, when it was revived by President Fillmore in an effort to overcome resistance in Boston to the Fugitive Slave Act. On the same occasion Fillmore urged Congress to modify the proclamation requirement of the Acts of 1795 and 1807 on the ground that it seriously diminished the availability of military aid to the civil authority by putting unruly elements on notice. Indeed, so far as the requirement purported to restrain the President's employment of the Army and Navy in enforcing "the laws of the Union," Fillmore challenged its constitutional validity. By the Constitution, said he, "The Army and Navy are ... placed under the control of the Executive; and probably no legislation by Congress could add to or diminish the power thus given but by increasing or diminishing or abolishing altogether the Army and Navy."[46]

Though Congress did not amend the Act of 1807 to meet Fillmore's ideas, the virtual elimination of the proclamation requirement was accomplished three years later by an ingenious opinion of Pierce's Attorney General, Caleb Cushing, which attributed to *marshals* of the United States, when opposed in the execution of their duties by unlawful combinations, the authority to summon to their aid not only bystanders and citizens generally, but armed forces within their precincts, both state militia and United States officers, soldiers, sailors, and marines.[47] Then early in 1856 Pierce himself, pursuing the logic of this opinion a step farther, announced the doctrine, apropos of the civil war then raging in Kansas, that it lay within his obligation to "take care that the laws be faithfully executed" to place the forces of the United States in Kansas at the disposal of the marshal there, "to be used as a portion of the *posse comitatus.*"[48] Lincoln's call of April 15, 1861, for 75,000 volunteers was, on the other hand, a fresh invocation, though of course on a vastly magnified scale, of Jefferson's conception of a *posse comitatus* subject to presidential call; and the Act of July 29, 1861, ratified this conception so far as the state militias and the national forces were concerned. By this measure, still on the statute books, "whenever by reason of unlawful obstructions, combinations," etc., "it shall become impracticable, in the judgment of the President, to enforce, by the ordinary course of judicial proceedings, the laws of the United States," "it shall be lawful" for him "to call forth the militia of any or all the States, and to employ such parts of the land and naval forces of the United States as he may deem necessary to enforce the faithful execution of the laws of the United States...."[49] Nor is the earlier requirement of a preliminary proclamation repeated. Finally, in 1903 the President was authorized, when calling a state militia into the national service, to issue his orders for that purpose, via the governor, to the militia officers.[50] Previously the call had gone simply to the governor.

In short, the President's power to employ military force in the enforcement of the laws of the United States has undergone enlargement from the first, thanks in part to presidential initiative, in part to congressional legislation. How has it been with the discharge by the "United States" of its guarantee to the states against "domestic violence"? Although it is clearly assumed by the Acts of 1795 and 1807 that the term "United States" here means *Congress* primarily—a theory which Chief Justice Taney's opinion in *Luther v. Borden*[51] ratifies—yet in the great railway strikes of 1877, which came finally to involve some ten states, President Hayes broke through the trammels of these acts, as well as those of Article IV itself, again and again. Upon quite informal requests of governors, and without awaiting their assurance that the legislatures of their states could not be convened, Hayes repeatedly furnished the state authorities with arms from the national arsenals. Exercising, too, his indubitable right to dispose the national forces, or professing the purpose of aiding in the enforcement of "the laws of the Union," and "to protect the property of the United States," he transferred troops from remote posts to posts adjacent to the scenes of trouble, where as he explained to Congress "the influence of their presence" contributed "to preserve the peace and restore order."[52]

The tactics thus inaugurated by Hayes were adopted and extended by President Cleveland in the Pullman strike of 1894, when, in the face of the vehement protests of Governor Altgeld, the President despatched troops to Chicago to protect the property of the United States and to "remove obstructions to the United States mails"[53]; and in the Debs Case, decided a few months later, the Supreme Court not only underwrote Cleveland's course, but it improved upon his plea in justification, in a dictum which enlarges indefinitely the basis for such action. I refer to Justice Brewer's statement in his opinion for the unani-

mous Court that "the entire strength of the nation may be used to
enforce in any part of the land the full and free exercise of all
national powers and the security of all rights entrusted by the
Constitution to its care." [54] Read in the context of the contemporaneous situation, these words could only have meant that the
national forces were thus available, at least in the absence of restrictive legislation, at the President's discretion. In other words,
they reverse the assumption of the Act of 1807 that such employment of the national forces must first be authorized by Congress.

   Nor, with the exception to be noted in a moment, has Congress ever enacted such restrictive legislation. On the contrary,
by the Act of April 20, 1871, it imparted to presidential authority
a new extension. This measure, passed in the presumed exercise
by Congress of its power to enforce the opening section of the
Fourteenth Amendment, makes it the right and the duty of the
President, whenever unlawful combinations in a state hinder
the execution of the laws, state or national, with the result that
any class is denied the equal protection of its constitutional rights,
or "the due course of justice" is obstructed,

"to take such measures, by the employment of the militia or the land
and naval forces of the United States, or of either, or by other means,
as he may deem necessary, for the suppression of such insurrection,
domestic violence, or combinations." [55]

While no President since Reconstruction days has ever invoked
the vague powers conferred by this measure, it still remains on
the statute books a potential threat to lynchers and their ilk.

   Finally, in the course of the years 1917–1922, we discover the
most complete, sustained, and altogether deliberate neglect of
the formalities required by Article IV and the supplementary acts
of Congress that has thus far occurred. The controlling factor at
the outset of this period was the circumstance that the National

Guard had been drafted under the National Defense Act of 1916 into the national service, thus leaving the states practically stripped of armed forces. In view of this condition of affairs, Secretary of War Baker as early as May 29, 1917, requested General Bliss

"to direct the commanders of the several departments to maintain relations of cordial cooperation with the Governors of the several States in their respective departments, and to respond to any call for military assistance from such Governors for the purpose of maintaining the domestic peace within the State, by the use of any troops under the command of the department commander as are available for the duty."[56]

The following November 20 the extremely expeditious procedure here outlined was modified by the requirement that commanders of the national forces should, "except in cases of unforeseen emergency," refer all requests of the kind indicated above to the Adjutant General of the Army at Washington. And so matters stood until September 29, 1919, when, following President Wilson's collapse, a telegram was sent to all department commanders ordering them henceforth to furnish troops directly on the request of state authorities without consulting Washington. First and last, between 1917 and 1922 soldiers were sent into states under the procedures sketched above more than thirty times, the majority of the instances being occasioned by labor troubles.

Fifty years ago the Court proclaimed, in the Neagle Case, that "there is a peace of the United States." Today we have to go further and recognize that the line which Article IV impliedly draws between this general peace and the domestic peace of the individual states has become an extremely tenuous one. That is the moral to be drawn from the record of legislation and practice just reviewed, and it is confirmed by many other trends in our contemporary constitutional development.

There is, to be sure, another side to the story—not a vastly impressive one perhaps, yet one requiring passing notice. What it amounts to is for the most part simply this: that from time to time members of Congress have arisen in their places, and others have echoed them, to proclaim that Congress, and Congress alone, is entitled, by virtue of its creative powers over the national forces and its control of the purse, to say for what purposes these forces may be employed, whether at home or abroad; or, at least, is entitled to say for what purposes they shall *not* be employed.

Certainly this is an arguable position on both logical and historical grounds, and particularly as respects control of the purse. Throughout the centuries lying between the first convocation of the Mother of Parliaments down to the formation of the Constitution of the United States the right to withhold supplies was the unrestricted right which accompanies all largess. It has been urged, to be sure, that under the Constitution this unrestricted right becomes clipped to the dimensions of a constitutional right and must accommodate itself to the entire constitutional structure.[57] But, although the principle be conceded, the question still remains as to who possesses final authority in applying it; and the verdict of practice under the Constitution is that this authority lies with Congress itself except so far as its determinations may be upset by presidential veto.

Unfortunately, a power or control claimable in theory may be unavailable in fact, or at best be so only with considerable difficulty. When Congress appropriates several billions of dollars for the support of the Army it unavoidably leaves many loopholes to executive discretion in their expenditure. Indeed, under the Budget and Accounting Act of 1921 appropriation bills are virtually drawn by the executive in the first instance. Furthermore, a military or naval unit can often be maintained quite as inexpensively at one station as at another, and whether it is active in enforcing "the laws of the Union" or protecting American interests abroad, or is merely engaged in the daily routine of camp or ship life. Besides, even lack of funds will not necessarily deter a sufficiently enterprising President, who has been duly instructed by his Attorney General in his prerogatives as Commander-in-Chief, from an occasional dramatic and popular stroke, as when the first Roosevelt started the fleet off around the world and left it to Congress to provide the wherewithal to bring it back home.[58] The statutes, it is true, say:

"All sums appropriated for the various branches of expenditure in the public service shall be applied solely to the objects for which they are respectively made, and for no others."[59]

The principle, indeed, is axiomatic, and hardly required formal statement. The difficulty is to give "the objects" a definition which is capable of restricting presidential discretion without at the same time nullifying "the objects" for which an army or a fleet is maintained at all.

The one legislative result from the attempts which have been made in Congress on various occasions to restrict the power of the President in the use of the national forces is to be found in section 15 of the Army Appropriation Act of June 18, 1878, which was the meager result of a protracted struggle between a Republican President and a Democratic Congress over federal interference in elections in the South. The provision is still on the statute books, and reads as follows:

"From and after the passage of this act it shall not be lawful to employ any part of the Army of the United States, as a *posse comitatus* or otherwise, for the purpose of executing the laws, except in such cases and under such circumstances as such employment of said force may be expressly authorized by the Constitution or by act of Congress; and no money appropriated by this act shall be used to pay any of the expenses incurred in the employment of any troops in violation of this section; and any person wilfully violating the provisions of this section shall be deemed guilty of a misdemeanor, and on conviction thereof shall be punished by fine not exceeding $10,000 or imprisonment not exceeding two years, or by both such fine and imprisonment."[60]

This measure was hailed by its sponsors at the time as a tremendous victory for the cause of "government by the laws." Said one of these gentlemen:

"Thus have we this day secured to the people of this country the same great protection against a standing army which cost a struggle of two hundred years for the Commons of England to secure for the British people."[61]

Actually, what the provision does, and all that it does, is to repeal the Cushing-Pierce device for getting around the proclamation requirement. Nor does it necessarily operate beneficially for "government of the laws," since in minor emergencies it may easily provoke resort to martial law when, but for the restriction, the forces employed would have been put at the disposal of a federal court and marshal.

In fact, the comparative ineffectiveness of the measure led the year following to a further attempt in Congress to curtail presidential prerogative. In his veto of the main effort of this sort Hayes stated the issue as follows:

"[The] principle is [asserted] that the House of Representatives has the sole right to originate bills for raising revenue, and therefore has the right to withhold appropriations upon which the existence of the Government may depend unless the Senate and the President shall give their assent to any legislation which the House may see fit to attach to appropriation bills. To establish this principle is to make a radical, dangerous, and unconstitutional change in the character of our institutions. The various departments of the Government and the Army and Navy are established by the Constitution or by laws passed in pursuance thereof. Their duties are clearly defined and their support is carefully provided for by law. . . . It was not the intention of the framers of the Constitution that any single branch of the Government should have the power to dictate conditions upon which [the public funds] should be applied to the purpose for which [they were] collected. Any such intention, if it had been entertained, would have been plainly expressed in the Constitution."[62]

While the abstract merits of this argument are open to serious question on grounds already indicated, it prevailed at the time, and the appropriations were voted without the objectionable riders.[63]

In short, it still rests with the President, as it has ever since the Act of 1807, to say when the national forces shall be employed "against combinations too powerful to be dealt with in the ordinary course of judicial proceedings," and hence to say whether such combinations exist. The formula, vague as it is, yet lays a restraining hand upon the presidential conscience, or at least provides a plausible pretext for presidential inaction;[64] and when the use of force goes to the length of involving "martial law" it may at times afford basis for some measure of judicial review.[65]

MARTIAL LAW UNDER THE CONSTITUTION; HABEAS CORPUS

A regime of martial law may be compendiously, if not altogether accurately, defined as one in which the ordinary law, as administered by the ordinary courts, is superseded for the time being by the will of a military commander. It follows that, when martial law is instituted under national authority, it rests ultimately on the will of the President of the United States in his capacity as Commander-in-Chief. It should be added at once, nevertheless, that the subject is one in which the record of actual practice fails often to support the niceties of theory. Thus, the employment of the military arm in the enforcement of the civil law does not invariably, or even usually, involve martial law in the strict sense, for, as was noted in the preceding section, soldiers are often placed simply at the disposal and direction of the civil authorities as a kind of supplementary police, or *posse comitatus;*[66] on the other hand, due to the discretion which the civil authorities themselves are apt to vest in the military in any emergency requiring its assistance, the line between such an employment of the military and a regime of martial law is frequently anything but a hard and fast one. And partly because of these ambiguities the conception itself of martial law today bifurcates into two conceptions, one of which shades off into *military government*[67] and the other into the situation just described, in which the civil authority remains theoretically in control although it is dependent on military aid. Finally, there is the situation which obtained throughout the North during the Civil War, when the privilege of the writ of habeas corpus was suspended as to certain classes of suspects, although other characteristics of martial law were generally absent.

The Petition of Right of 1628 forbade "commissions of martial law," which is perhaps the first use of the term. The immediate occasion for this provision was furnished by the fact that Charles I, following a bad example set by several of his predecessors, had haled certain of his subjects before military courts for offenses against the ordinary law. But, whether with design or not, the sweeping terms of the prohibition gave countenance to the claim, soon advanced by the King's enemies, that it forbade *courts-martial* even for the trial of soldiers charged with breaches of discipline. By this view a standing army became impossible, and James II's endeavor to maintain one in the face of it was a principal cause contributing to his forced abdication. From 1690 on a standing army was rendered possible in England only by the annual enactment by Parliament of the Mutiny Act, authorizing courts-martial for the maintenance of discipline in the army but for no other purpose. Meanwhile, out of the facts just recited arose the dogma that "the common law knows nothing of martial law." Numerous English authorities, reaching far down into the nineteenth century, ring the changes on this theme: martial law has "no place whatsoever in this realm"; it can never be resorted to without parliamentary authorization; since the time of the Stuarts it has been "a totally exploded thing"; "it is the most unconstitutional procedure conceivable"; "no authority for anything of the sort can be found"—a chorus which an American writer swells with the assertion that martial law "is a threat . . . a mere bluff. There is under the Constitution [of the United States] no such thing." [68]

How seriously are these asseverations to be taken? To say the least, they befog the issue, for that there is such a thing as "martial law" in some sense of the term is today recognized by the most conservative authorities. An outstanding illustration is Professor Albert Venn Dicey's *Introduction to the Law of the Constitution,* where martial law is depicted, like the British constitution itself, as an outgrowth of principles of the common law. More in detail, Dicey's conception sums up in the following propositions: (1) Aside from the Crown's right to put down breaches of the peace, martial law does not depend upon any official prerogative, but only on a right and duty shared by all. (2) Martial law is not *established* by the customary official declaration of its existence, but arises "from the nature of things"—it is, in fact, "the law of paramount necessity." (3) The necessity of martial law, therefore, as well as of whatever measures are resorted to in its name, is a matter to be "ultimately determined by a judge and jury." Lastly, the measures thus taken must be purely of a *"preventive"* nature—martial law cannot *punish.*[69]

"Martial law," in other words, is hardly anything more than a general term for the operation in situations of public emergency of certain well-known principles of the common law—the right of self-defense of the individual, his right, attended by the correlative liability, to abate a nuisance, his right and duty to arrest one whom he knows to have committed a felony or whom he observes in the act of committing a breach of the peace. But if the individual, official or otherwise, exceeds the rights of "self-help" just enumerated, then he himself becomes subject to the penalties of the law notwithstanding the excellence of his motives, and only an omnipotent Parliament can save him from the unpleasant consequences of his zeal by an act of indemnity."[70]

The judicial history of martial law under the Constitution opens with the case of *Luther v. Borden,* which grew out of Dorr's insurrection in Rhode Island in the year 1842. In meeting the situation caused by the insurrection, the *legislature* of Rhode Island, which in those days exercised at will any and all of the powers of government in that commonwealth, had declared martial law, and under the authority thereby created Luther's house had been invaded and Luther himself put under arrest. The majority of the Court held that the questions raised by the case were "political" and so not within the judicial province to decide; but Justice Woodbury, in a dissenting opinion, argued at length that in thus declaring martial law the Rhode Island legislature had exceeded its powers under the Constitution of the United States. "By it [martial law]," said he, "every citizen, instead of reposing under the shield of known and fixed laws as to liberty, property, and life, exists with a rope round his neck, subject to be hung up by a military despot at the next lamp-post under the sentence of some drum-head court-martial." Such a regime, he insisted, could exist under the Constitution only as an incident of the rights of war, which belonged only to the National Government; for not only could Congress alone declare war but the states were forbidden to engage in it without the consent of Congress. "All other conditions of violence," he continued, within the states "are regarded by the Constitution as but cases of private outrage, to be punished by prosecutions in the courts; or as insurrections, rebellions, or domestic violence to be put down by the civil authorities, aided by the militia; or, when these prove incompetent, by the general government, when appealed to by a state for aid"; and it was only in the last instance that, following a declaration of war by Congress, martial law might be resorted to."[71]

The majority of the Court, however, while conceding that "military government" unduly prolonged would not be "a republican form of government" in the sense of the Constitution, was of the opinion that the situation in Rhode Island had been "a state of war" and that the local government had been within its rights in resorting "to the rights and usages of war." It added, nevertheless, that in such a situation "no more force . . . can be used than is necessary to accomplish the object. And if power is exercised for purposes of oppression, or any injury wilfully done to person or property, the party by whom, or by whose order, it is committed would undoubtedly be answerable." Just how this accountability was at that date supported by the Constitution of the United States the opinion does not indicate.

The President's powers in relation to martial law were first dealt with by the Court during the Civil War, in the famous Prize Cases.[72] It was there held that the President, by virtue of his power as chief executive and his power as Commander-in-Chief, was entitled to treat a region known to be in insurrection as enemy country and thereby strip all of its inhabitants of their constitutional rights. The case thus ascribes to the *President alone* the power which in *Luther v. Borden* is attributed to government as a whole; and it builds upon the proposition in *Luther v. Borden* that *an insurrection may be treated as constituting a state of war,* which it pursues to its logical conclusion. For if insurrection is war, then the scene of it is *a seat of war,* and the difference between *martial law* and *military government* becomes merely one of probable duration and objective. Such being the case, the possibility of a judicial remedy for acts performed by presidential authorization in the suppression of insurrection at the seat of it, except possibly in the extremest cases of outrage, becomes negligible.

The authority of the Prize Cases as a definition of the President's power in the employment of martial law was, however, soon seriously qualified by the decision in *ex parte* Milligan, in which the conception of martial law as resting on the war power and as measured by its rights was superseded by the British conception of it as a law of necessity to be determined ultimately by the ordinary courts. In the words of the Court:

"If, in foreign invasion or civil war, the courts are actually closed, and it is impossible to administer criminal justice according to law, then, on the theatre of active military operations, where war really prevails, there is a necessity to furnish a substitute for the civil authority, thus overthrown, to preserve the safety of the army and society; and as no power is left but the military, it is allowed to govern by martial rule until the laws can have their free course. As necessity creates the rule, so it limits its duration; for, if this government is continued after the courts are reinstated, it is a gross usurpation of power. Martial rule can never exist where the courts are open, and in proper and unobstructed exercise of their jurisdiction. It is also confined to the locality of actual war."[73]

The holding thus turns the doctrine of *Luther v. Borden* and the Prize Cases against itself. What the Court says in effect is that, *unless* a situation of disorder amounts to "war," a question impliedly reserved to the Court, then there can be no martial law. Even Dicey's summarization of the British conception of martial law as a law of "necessity," to be judged ultimately by the courts, is exceeded in rigor.

A generation later, however, the limiting force of the Milligan Case on executive power was in turn materially modified in the presence of industrial disorder. The leading case is that of *Moyer v. Peabody*[74] in which plaintiff, a labor leader, brought suit against Peabody, a former governor of Colorado, for ordering his imprisonment in the course of a labor dispute which arose during Peabody's incumbency. Speaking for the Court, Justice Holmes conceded that the state courts were open at the time; also, "as it must be, that the governor's declaration that a state of insurrection existed is conclusive on the courts"; and, lastly, "that the governor, without sufficient reason but in good faith, in the course of putting the insurrection down, held the plaintiff until he thought that he safely could release him." In the face of these admissions—or rather on the basis of them—the Court held that Moyer had no action. Quoting the constitution and statutes of the state to the effect that the governor was empowered to employ the National Guard to suppress insurrection, the opinion proceeds:

"This means that he shall make the ordinary use of the soldiers to that end; that he may kill persons who resist, and of course, that he may use the milder measure of seizing the bodies of those whom he considers to stand in the way of restoring peace. . . . So long as such arrests are made in good faith and in the honest belief that they are needed in order to head the insurrection off, the Governor is the final judge and cannot be subjected to an action after he is out of office on the ground that he had not reasonable ground for his belief. . . . When it comes to a decision by the head of the State upon a matter involving its life, the ordinary rights of individuals must yield to what he deems the necessities of the moment. Public danger warrants the substitution of executive process for judicial process."[75]

The opinion thus brushed aside as immaterial the fact which the majority opinion in the Milligan Case treats as absolutely crucial. In spite of that fact, the governor's finding that an insurrection existed and that the arrest and detention of Moyer was a necessary measure toward putting it down was accepted as conclusive because, although it was "without sufficient reason," it was "in good faith." The one handle, in short, which the case offers for judicial review of executive proceedings to *put down* private violence, in distinction to *punishing* it, is the question of the executive's "good faith."

And it is this handle which the Court seizes upon in the case of *Sterling v. Constantin*,[76] which grew out of an attempt by the governor of Texas to enforce the law of the state limiting the production of petroleum, by declaring martial law in certain counties. A federal three-judge court received testimony flatly contradicting the allegations of the governor's proclamation that the region involved was in "a state of insurrection, riot, and a breach of the peace." It found, on the contrary, that the evidence showed "no insurrection nor riot in fact . . . no closure of the courts, no failure of the civil authorities," and on this ground enjoined the governor from proceeding with his military measures; and on appeal it was sustained by the Supreme Court in so doing.

The most recent utterance of the Court on the subject of martial law is its decision in the Hawaiian Martial Law Cases,[77] which will be considered in Chapter VI. The holding of the cases as stated in the headnote amounts substantially to a reiteration of the Milligan decision, but Justice Black's controlling opinion for the Court advances the thesis that the only employment of the military in the enforcement of the civil law which the Constitution contemplates is its use as adjunct police taking its orders from the civil authorities. Any implication, however, that the Court wished to call *Moyer v. Peabody* into question is diligently avoided.

We turn now to the President's power in relation to the writ of habeas corpus, that greatest of all muniments of Anglo-American liberty, whereby is guaranteed, so long as it is available, prompt judicial inquiry into all cases of physical restraint and, where the restraint is found to be without legal justification, the release of the party. The relevant constitutional provision reads as follows: "The privilege of the writ of habeas corpus shall not be suspended, unless when in cases of rebellion or invasion the public safety may require it."[78] It is a significant fact that this is the only mention of the writ in the entire Constitution. Its existence as part and parcel of the law of the land is taken for granted.

The first question to arise on the above clause was as to the location of the power to suspend. In the once famous Merryman Case,[79] which arose early in the Civil War out of Lincoln's suspension of the writ along "any military line" between New York and Washington, Chief Justice Taney, then on circuit, argued that only Congress possessed this power. The clause occurs, he pointed out, among the restraints on the powers of Congress, and in Article I which deals primarily with the legislative power. Furthermore, in England only Parliament may suspend the writ. Also, it was universally assumed at the time of the Burr Conspiracy that the power was Congress's, a view in which Story later concurred in his *Commentaries*.[80] The only power of the President where the rights of the citizen are concerned, said the Chief Justice, "is to take care that they [the laws] be faithfully carried into execution as they are expounded and adjudged by the coordinate branch of the government to which that duty is assigned by the Constitution," in other words, the judicial department.

Taney's views were sharply challenged from many quarters, and of course remained practically ineffective, their intended beneficiary continuing to languish in Fort McHenry. Attorney General Bates answered Chief Justice Taney's conception of executive power as subject to judicial guidance by reiterating the very different theory of Attorney General Taney. The executive was not subordinate to the judicial power, but one of three coördinate departments of government. It was, moreover, "the most active of all," "the most constantly in action"; and, while the other departments were sworn to support the Constitution, the President was sworn to "preserve, protect and defend it." Furthermore, under the legislation of Congress the President was explicitly empowered to use the military forces of the country to suppress insurrection, which meant that he must be free to judge what measures this exigency required. He had, therefore, the right to "arrest and imprison persons guilty of holding criminal intercourse" with the authors of insurrection, and of this right the power to suspend the writ of habeas corpus was a necessary and logical ingredient.[81]

The President's action was also endorsed by a number of publicists. One of these urged the ingenious argument that the constitutional clause itself stood "in the place of an act of Parliament," with the result that the President did not need congressional authorization. Others held that the President's power was an emergency power, and action under it was subject to congressional review. A third view was that "in case of invasion from abroad or rebellion at home, the President may declare, or exercise, or authorize, martial law at his discretion," and in so doing suspend the writ.[82]

Lincoln's own views, it is evident, underwent a gradual stiffening. In his message of July 4, 1861, he had asked for congressional ratification, but fifteen months later he proclaimed a far more sweeping suspension of the privilege without apparent thought of Congress. And Congress was also uncertain of its ground. Not until March 3, 1863, did it finally authorize a suspension of the habeas corpus privilege, and then in terms which still left the constitutional issue open. Nor is the verdict of judicial opinion free from doubt. The controlling opinion in the Prize Cases squints one way, that in *ex parte* Milligan the other. Indeed, even the minority in the latter case would apparently have required congressional ratification for a suspension of the habeas corpus privilege in areas not subject to martial law or to military government.

Nowadays, the consensus of learned opinion seems to favor Taney's doctrine that Congress has the *exclusive* suspending power, though it is not clear whether those who take this view would also accept what Taney himself undoubtedly regarded as the corollary principle—that a presidential suspension was in any circumstances mere usurpation which even ratification by Congress could not legalize. For my own part, I am inclined to think that Professor Randall has the nub of the matter when he says:

"In a future crisis the Presidential power to suspend would probably be just as much an open question as during the Civil War. As to the actual precedent of that war, the outstanding fact is that the Chief Executive 'suspended the writ,' and that, so far as legal consequences were concerned, he was not restrained in so doing by Congress nor by the Courts."[83]

The further question presents itself, whether, "when the writ is suspended, the executive is authorized to arrest as well as to detain." The majority opinion in *ex parte* Milligan implies a negative answer to this question, to which the minority demurs; and certainly the latter is the logical view. How can there be detention if there is not an arrest in the first place; and if the arrest was not for justifiable cause, how can the resulting detention be?

But conceding that a justifiable cause exists, does suspension of the writ relieve the executive from the necessity of complying with the requirements of the Fourth Amendment and the common law regarding arrests? As a matter of fact, summary arrests were frequent throughout the Civil War, and made without any pretense of complying with either the forms of the common law or the Fourth Amendment; and because of this Congress eventually passed an act to indemnify the authors of such arrests against "any action or prosecution, civil or criminal," which of course is tantamount to a claim of power to have authorized the questioned procedures in the first place.[84] So again, the weight of authority is undoubtedly in favor of the more conservative view of executive power, the verdict of practice under a suspension of the writ distinctly otherwise.

The question arises, lastly, whether a suspension of the writ is subject to judicial review on the complaint that the disorders pleaded in its justification did not amount to "rebellion" and that "the public safety" did not "require" it. To answer on the basis of the cases already reviewed, the first part of the question is subject to judicial review, the second part is not, being "political" in nature; and in fact judicial intervention will not take place at all until the emergency is safely past. The Court will see to that.[85]

But the paucity of judicial restraints upon presidential action which is based on the plea of necessity does not mean that such action is subject to *no* restraint. On the contrary, the final evaluation of such a plea would seem theoretically to rest with the national *legislative* authority under the "necessary and proper" clause. At the same time, the practical efficacy of even this limitation upon a resolute President who felt he had the backing of public opinion may well be questioned. A statutory rule definitive of occasions requiring martial law would have to be in such broad terms as to leave it at the mercy of interpretation. This, in fact, is proved, as we have seen, by the existing statutes which have to do with the employment by the President of the national forces and of the state militias. On the other hand, for Congress to interfere with an executive declaration of necessity would require, in the face of certain veto, a two-thirds vote in each house. *We thus see illustrated in this instance, as we shall later again and again, the critical importance of any course of reasoning whereby the initiative is attributed to the President in the presence of emergency conditions, whether at home or abroad.*

EMERGENCY POWERS OF THE PRESIDENT—
THE "STEWARDSHIP THEORY"

While he was a preëminent exponent of the idea of "a government of laws and not of men" and hence of the supremacy in the English constitution of the lawmaking organ, this fact did not, as we have seen, deter John Locke from claiming for the executive in its own right a broad discretion capable even of setting aside the ordinary law in the meeting of special exigencies for which the legislative power had not provided. Nor did he regard this prerogative as limited to wartime, nor even to situations of great urgency. It was sufficient if the "public good" might be advanced by its exercise.[86] To what extent has this doctrine received recognition in constitutional law and theory appertaining to the President's power?

The most important utterance of the Court which is relevant

in this connection is to be found in the opinion of Justice Miller delivered in 1890 in the case of *in re* Neagle.[87] The material facts of the case were as follows: Because of threats against the life of Justice Field by one Terry, a resident of California, the Attorney General had detailed Neagle, a United States marshal, to act as Field's bodyguard while the latter was traveling on circuit in that state. In the discharge of his duty Neagle shot and killed Terry and was taken into custody by the California authorities for so doing. The question before the Supreme Court was whether Neagle was entitled to his release on a writ of habeas corpus under section 753 of the Revised Statutes, which authorizes the writ to issue in the case of a prisoner in jail "for an act done or committed in pursuance of *a law* of the United States."

The difficulty of the case arose from the fact that Neagle's assignment was not traceable to any definite statutory provision. The Court held, nonetheless, that the order of the Attorney General, given with the presumed consent of the President, had adequate basis in the duty of the latter to "take care that the laws be faithfully executed" and hence should be treated as "a law" in the sense of section 753. The broad doctrine was stated by Justice Miller that the President's duty is not limited "to the enforcement of the acts of Congress or of treaties of the United States according to their express terms," but embraces also "the rights, duties and obligations growing out of the Constitution itself, our international relations, and all the protection implied by the nature of the government under the Constitution."[88] He further cited the act of Congress which clothes marshals of the United States with the same powers in each state "in executing the laws of the United States" as its sheriffs have in executing the laws of the state; and asserting that "there is a peace of the United States" which was violated by an assault on one of its judges, he held that

Neagle was as much entitled to protect this peace as a California sheriff would have been in analogous circumstances to protect the local peace.[89]

The Neagle Case brings to focus the implications of executive actions and of opinion in confirmance thereof in a variety of fields. As early as 1818 it had been recognized by the Court that the United States had, in the absence of statutory provision to the contrary, a common-law right to sue on a bill of exchange which had been endorsed to the Treasurer of the United States;[90] and a few years later the broad general doctrine had been laid down "that the United States, being a body politic, as an incident to their general sovereignty, have a capacity to enter into contracts" "within the general sphere of their constitutional powers" through the instrumentality of the appropriate executive department "whenever such contracts . . . are not forbidden by law."[91] In the latter case, moreover, the Court had listened to argument by the Attorney General that in the performance of the trust enjoined upon him by the "take care" clause, the President "not only may, but . . . is bound to avail himself of every appropriate means not forbidden by law";[92] and, while the Court does not advert to this contention, the immediate and inevitable result of its holding was the location in the executive department of the power which it ascribed to the United States Government in its corporate capacity.[93]

A series of opinions handed down by Attorney General Cushing in the years 1853 and 1854 are also significant in this connection. One of these claimed for the President the power, as growing out of his duty, to "take care that the laws be faithfully executed," to institute investigations and incur expenditures therefor which it became the moral obligation of Congress to meet.[94] Another held that although no statute made it the duty of the United States to assume the legal defense by counsel of

marshals and other ministerial officers of the law when they were
sued for their official acts, yet it was within the discretion of the
President to do so if he was persuaded that such officers were
being harassed by suits on this account.[95] Pertinent too was Cushing's holding a little later that a marshal of the United States,
when opposed in the execution of his duty by unlawful combinations, had authority to summon the entire able-bodied force of
his precinct as a *posse comitatus,* comprehending not only bystanders and citizens generally but any and all organized armed
forces, whether militia of the state, or officers, soldiers, sailors, and
marines of the United States.[96] Lincoln's invocation of the same
theory in justification of his call for volunteers of April 15, 1861,
has already been adverted to.[97] I shall return to this phase of the
subject in Chapter VI.

In 1895, five years after the Neagle Case, *in re* Debs[98] was de-
cided along closely parallel lines. The case arose out of the same
Pullman strike which had caused the despatch of troops to
Chicago the year before. Coincidently with this move, the United
States district attorney stationed there, acting upon orders from
Washington, obtained an injunction from the United States circuit court forbidding the strike on account of its interference with
the mails and with interstate commerce. The question before the
Supreme Court was whether this injunction, for violation of
which Debs had been jailed for contempt of court, had been
granted with jurisdiction.

The Court conceded, in effect, that there was no statutory basis
for the injunction, but sustained it on the ground that the government was entitled thus to protect its property in the mails,
and on a much broader ground which is stated in the following
passage from the Court's opinion:

"Every government, entrusted, by the very terms of its being, with
powers and duties to be exercised and discharged for the general wel-

fare, has a right to apply to its own courts for any proper assistance in the exercise of the one and the discharge of the other.... While it is not the province of the Government to interfere in any mere matter of private controversy between individuals, or to use its granted powers to enforce the rights of one against another, yet, whenever wrongs complained of are such as affect the public at large, and are in respect of matters which by the Constitution are entrusted to the care of the Nation and concerning which the Nation owes the duty to all the citizens of securing to them their common rights, then the mere fact that the Government has no pecuniary interest in the controversy is not sufficient to exclude it from the courts, or prevent it from taking measures therein to fully discharge those constitutional duties."[99]

Taken in conjunction with the doctrine of the Neagle Case that "there is a peace of the United States," this later ruling embraces possibilities which ex-President Taft did not exaggerate when he interpreted it as signifying that the national executive may seek an injunction in the national courts in any case "involving a wide-spread public interest." A century earlier the Court had refused to concede that the Attorney General had a right *ex officio* to move for a writ of mandamus.[100]

The question arises, however, whether the Debs Case is still law of the land in this respect in view of the limitations which were imposed in 1932 by the Norris-La Guardia Act on the issuance of injunctions by the national courts in "any case involving or growing out of any labor dispute."[101] The Court's decision in the recent case of *United States v. United Mine Workers*,[102] while not decisive, appeared at the time of its rendition to have important bearing on this question. The point at issue was whether, in view of the terms of the Norris-La Guardia Act, the district court for the District of Columbia had jurisdiction to enjoin a strike against the National Government, which at the time was operating a large proportion of the nation's soft-coal mines under the War Labor

Disputes Act of June 25, 1943. Answering the defendant's argument in denial of the district court's jurisdiction, the Chief Justice said:

"There is an old and well-known rule that statutes which in general terms divest pre-existing rights or privileges will not be applied to the sovereign without express words to that effect. It has been stated, in cases in which there were extraneous and affirmative reasons for believing that the sovereign should also be deemed subject to a restrictive statute, that this rule was a rule of construction only. Though that may be true, the rule has been invoked successfully in cases so closely similar to the present one, and the statement of the rule in those cases has been so explicit, that we are inclined to give it much weight here. Congress was not ignorant of the rule which those cases reiterated; and, with knowledge of that rule, Congress would not, in writing the Norris-LaGuardia Act, omit to use 'clear and specific [language] to that effect' if it actually intended to reach the Government in all cases."

Yet when he came to apply "this exclusionary rule," the Chief Justice "agreed" that it took from under the Norris-La Guardia Act only cases in which the government itself appeared as "employer," and that "Congress, in passing the Act, did not intend to permit the United States to continue to intervene by injunction in purely private labor disputes" "where some public interest was thought to have become involved." He straightway added, nevertheless, "Whether Congress so intended or not is a question different from the one now before us. Here we are concerned only with the Government's right to injunctive relief in a dispute with its own employees"—which right, as we have just seen, was conceded.

The Court's reasoning, so far as it affects the Debs Case, is unsatisfactory and confused. The "exclusionary rule" that statutes which deal in general terms will not be applied to the diminution of the powers of the enacting sovereign would be involved most directly in a case in which the government asked for an injunction in the protection of the public interest. Indeed, in the case before the Court "the United States acted," as the Chief Justice states, "in the exercise of a sovereign and not a private function." This being so, it is difficult to see how it could have been advantaged by the fact that it appeared before the Court also in the role of a party in interest. This adventitious role would seem rather to cloud its right to plead its sovereignty. Nor does it appear that the question was argued whether Congress could constitutionally abandon a power which was held to spring, and obviously does spring, from the responsibilities of the National Government under the Constitution.[103]

The latest, and at present writing still controlling, answer to our question as to the status today of the Debs Case is supplied by the recently enacted Taft-Hartley Act,[104] which, among other things, provides that whenever in his opinion a threatened or actual strike or lockout affecting the whole or a substantial part of an industry engaged in interstate commerce will, "if permitted to occur or continue, imperil the national health or safety," the President may appoint a board of inquiry and upon its reporting "may direct the Attorney General to petition any district court of the United States having jurisdiction of the parties to enjoin such strike or lock-out or the continuing thereof . . . ," and the Court shall have jurisdiction to do so, provided it shares the President's view of the situation, the Norris-La Guardia Act to the contrary notwithstanding. In short, the act builds on the doctrine of the Debs Case without necessarily limiting it.

As in the Neagle Case, so also in the Debs Case the Court attributes powers to the President in his executive capacity on the score of their belonging to the United States; i.e., to the National Government as a whole. The translation of the imputation into the vernacular fell, however, to a former President of the United

States. The allusion is to Theodore Roosevelt's so-called "Steward-ship Theory" of the Presidency as set forth in T. R.'s *Autobiography*. I quote:

"The most important factor in getting the right spirit in my Administration, next to the insistence upon courage, honesty, and a genuine democracy of desire to serve the plain people was my insistence upon the theory that the executive power was limited only by specific restrictions and prohibitions appearing in the Constitution or imposed by the Congress under its Constitutional powers. My view was that every executive officer, and above all every executive officer in high position, was a steward of the people, and not to content himself with the negative merit of keeping his talents undamaged in a napkin. I declined to adopt the view that what was imperatively necessary for the Nation could not be done by the President unless he could find some specific authorization to do it. My belief was that it was not only his right but his duty to do anything that the needs of the Nation demanded unless such action was forbidden by the Constitution or by the laws. Under this interpretation of executive power I did and caused to be done many things not previously done by the President and the heads of the Departments. I did not usurp power, but I did greatly broaden the use of executive power. In other words, I acted for the public welfare, I acted for the common well-being of all our people, whenever and in whatever manner was necessary, unless prevented by direct constitutional or legislative prohibition. I did not care a rap for the mere form and show of power; I cared immensely for the use that could be made of the substance." [105]

A vigorous critic of the "Stewardship Theory" was the late President Taft, who, in his book *Our Chief Magistrate and His Powers,* warmly protested against the notion that the President had any constitutional warrant to attempt the role of "a Universal Providence." Later, to be sure, as Chief Justice, Mr. Taft was to appeal in his opinion in the Myers Case to the opening clause of

Article II as a grant of power; but in 1916 his view was substantially different. "The true view of the executive functions," he then wrote, "is, as I conceive it, that the President can exercise no power which cannot be fairly and reasonably traced to some specific grant of power or justly implied and included within such express grant as proper and necessary." Mr. Roosevelt's theory of "a residual executive power" he thought thoroughly "unsafe."[106]

Whether "safe" or not, the "Stewardship Theory" has been proved by events to have been prophetic of developments, and in a field which T.R. himself staked out for its application—that of industrial relations. The anthracite coal strike of 1902 was the first in the nation's history to paralyze a vital, although geographically localized, industry. It was also the first which a President attempted to mediate personally. In the five months that the strike continued, the President took four successive steps intended to hasten or influence its settlement. At the end of the third week he directed his Commissioner of Labor to investigate the strike and make recommendations, which, however, when they were made neither side would accept. In the strike's fifth month he endeavored unsuccessfully, in conferences with representatives of both sides, to persuade them to compromise their differences. He next sent Secretary of War Root to New York City to confer with J. P. Morgan, with whose assistance an agreement was drafted to submit the dispute to an arbitration commission. Finally, having induced the operators to accept the proposal, the President made sure that the award would not go too decidedly against the miners by appointing to the board a Catholic bishop and a union official, the latter of whom he palmed off as an "eminent sociologist." Even more significant, perhaps, is the action he says he *intended* to take if his other efforts had failed; namely, to "get" the Governor of Pennsylvania to ask him to keep order, then "put in" the army under the command of some "first-rate" general with orders to preserve order, and to "dispossess the operators and run the mines as a receiver" until the arbitration board could make its report. Such is the story told in the *Autobiography*. One fact "T.R." omits to mention, and that is that Attorney General Knox advised him that his "intended" step would be illegal and unconstitutional. For some reason the opinion is still buried among similar arcana of the Department of Justice.[107]

Subsequently, down to the present moment, Presidents have intervened without specific legal authorization, or even to the derogation of the law in some instances, in no fewer than twenty-five major industrial disputes. President Wilson intervened eight times, President Harding twice, President F. D. Roosevelt eleven times (twice during the war), and to date President Truman has intervened no fewer than three times. The first of Mr. Truman's interventions occurred early in 1946 when, apprehending that his whole reconversion program was at stake, being already shaken by strikes in the automobile, meat-packing, and electrical-equipment industries, he moved to head off the strike which was threatened for mid-January by the United Steel Workers. His initial move was to appoint a fact-finding body, but when, two days before the scheduled stoppage, it had failed to report, he took it upon himself to mediate the dispute by proposing that the companies agree to a wage increase of 18 cents an hour, on the understanding that OPA would permit them to raise the price of steel $4 per ton. The companies rejected the proposal, and the strike began on January 21 at the scheduled hour. The final settlement twenty-six days later embraced the 18-cent wage increase and an increase in the price of steel of $5 per ton.[108]

The story illustrates graphically the enormous potentialities for the nation's economy of this use of presidential power and prestige. And matching its importance in this respect is its political significance. The great unions claim to be able to swing 15 million votes, a fact which is inevitably a heavy makeweight in their favor in any political mediation in which their interests are importantly involved.

Finally, and by way of linking this section with the preceding one, a moment's attention must be given certain acts of Congress which—to use a phrase coined by the "Hot Oil" Cases—supplement the "cognate" presidential prerogative in situations of emergency. By the Alien Act of 1798, Congress delegated to the President virtually unlimited power to "direct the conduct" of nationals of hostile countries whenever the United States should be engaged in a declared war or its territory threatened with invasion, and this enactment, somewhat amended, still remains on the statute books. Indeed, for nearly one hundred and twenty years it was almost the only provision of its kind. The approach of war with Germany, however, the war itself, and finally the economic situation which confronted the country in 1933 and the years immediately following produced a considerable crop of statutory provisions delegating powers to the President to be exercised by him "in cases of emergency," of "extreme emergency," "sufficient emergency," "in time of war or similar emergency," in "a state of public peril," and so on. In the presence of any such contingency, of which he is of course the sole judge, the President may today increase the Army and Navy beyond their authorized enlisted strength; prohibit transactions in foreign exchange; forbid the Federal Reserve banks to transact business except under regulations to be made by the Secretary of the Treasury with his approval; take over powerhouses, reservoirs, and so forth, for the purpose of manufacturing munitions of war, "or any other purpose involving the safety of the United States"; alter the monthly apportionments of appropriations among the various departments and agencies of the government; suspend or amend the rules and regulations governing the transmission of communications by radio or wire—not to mention any number of lesser delegations of power.[109] All these measures were on the statute books when the crisis developed that led to our entry into World War II, and still are.

PARDONS, AMNESTIES, REPRIEVES

In a peculiarly complacent passage of the *Commentaries,* Blackstone asserts it to be "one of the great advantages of monarchy in general, above any other form of government, that there is a magistrate who has it in his power to extend mercy wherever he thinks it is deserved," adding that "in democracies ... this power of pardon can never subsist, for there nothing higher is acknowledged than the magistrate who administers the laws."[110] In the very face of this warning the Framers provided that "he [the President] shall have power to grant reprieves and pardons for offenses against the United States, except in cases of impeachment"![111] Their temerity was due partly to the fact that whereas Blackstone was thinking of pardon as an instrument only of clemency, and so more or less opposed to the law, the Framers regarded it as also an instrument of law enforcement. This is shown by the fact that when it was moved in the Convention to confine the power by inserting in the clause the words "after conviction" objection was at once offered that "pardon before conviction might be necessary in order to obtain the testimony of accomplices," and the motion was withdrawn. Likewise, an effort to transfer the power to the legislature in "cases of treason" failed.[112] As Hamilton explains in *The Federalist,* "in seasons of insurrection or rebellion there are critical moments when a well-timed offer of pardon to the insurgents or rebels may restore the tranquillity of the commonwealth," and "the dilatory process of convening the legislature," if it was not in session, would mean the sacrifice of a golden opportunity.[113] The development of the power by usage and adjudication has been influenced by similar considerations.

By the theory of the common law, as summed up by Chief Justice Marshall in the early case of *United States v. Wilson*,[114] a pardon is like a deed, to the validity of which delivery and acceptance are essential; nor may it be known judicially, being "the private though official act of the President," unless it be pleaded by its intended beneficiary.[115]

In short, the granting of a pardon is an essentially man-to-man transaction, from which it would seem to follow that the power of granting it does not embrace the power to issue a general amnesty, of which the courts would be obliged to take notice. From the first, nevertheless, the contrary was assumed. General amnesties were issued by Washington in 1795, by Adams in 1800, by Madison in 1815, by Lincoln in 1863, by Johnson in 1865, 1867, and 1868, and by the first Roosevelt—to Aguinaldo's followers— in 1902. It is true that Johnson's enemies in Congress made a half-hearted effort to challenge his power in this respect, but without avail. In cases decided in 1871 the Court declared that "pardon includes amnesty," and that a proclamation of amnesty by the President was a public act of which "all courts in the United States are held to take notice and to which all courts are bound to give effect."[116]

Other limitations on the pardoning power arising from the conception of it as "private though official" were slower to be removed. The starting point is the Burdick Case,[117] the circumstances of which reduced the doctrine of the Wilson Case to palpable absurdity. Burdick, having declined to testify before a federal grand jury on the ground that his testimony would tend to incriminate him, was proffered by President Wilson "a full and unconditional pardon for all offenses against the United States" which he might have committed or participated in in connection with the matter he had been questioned about. Burdick, nevertheless, refused to accept the pardon and persisted in his contumacy with the unanimous support of the Supreme Court. "The grace of a pardon," remarked Justice McKenna sententiously,

"may be only a pretense involving consequences of even greater disgrace than those it purports to relieve. Circumstances may be made to bring innocence under the penalties of the law. If so brought, escape by confession of guilt implied in the acceptance of a pardon may be rejected."[118]

And this, in face of the fact that it was Burdick himself who first suggested the idea that he was guilty of a crime! Nor did the Court give any attention to the fact that the President had accompanied his proffer to Burdick with a proclamation, although a similar procedure had been held to bring Johnson's amnesties to the Court's notice.[119]

For rescuing the Court from the entanglements of this pedantical nonsense principal credit should go to President Coolidge. In 1923 Coolidge "remitted" the sentence which had been imposed for contempt upon one Craig by the United States district court for the southern district of New York. Craig, evidently bent on martyrdom, had already given notice that he would refuse a pardon if it was tendered him, but the President's action, which merely closed the jail against him, left him nothing to reject.[120] In other words, the pardoning power was found to embrace a previously undiscovered attribute, the power to *remit* sentences—at least jail sentences—without consultation of the other party.

Two years later occurred a similar episode involving the poet-gunman, Gerald Chapman, who had escaped from the federal penitentiary at Atlanta. On his recapture Chapman found himself confronted with a Connecticut indictment charging him with murder, and an order by President Coolidge "commuting" his federal sentence to the portion of it which he had already served and handing him over to the Connecticut authorities, who promptly tried and convicted him and sentenced him to hang. Again a discriminating choice of phraseology proved decisive. In an application for a writ of habeas corpus in the United States district court for Connecticut, Chapman's counsel vainly urged that the alleged commutation of sentence was a pardon which, to be valid, must be accepted by their client.

"To speak of a 'right' [said Judge Thomas] to be imprisoned is to invest that word with a significance not to be found in common parlance nor in legal definition. If there is such a thing as a 'right' to incarceration, it is certain that it is not one of the rights guaranteed by the Fourteenth Amendment to the Constitution of the United States nor by any other provision of that document." [121]

An appeal to the Supreme Court only evoked an order declining review.

This long-standing issue was finally disposed of in 1927 in the case of one Perovich, [122] who in 1909 had a sentence of death "commuted" by President Taft to one of life imprisonment. Repenting now nearly twenty years later his choice of life, Perovich assailed the Taft order on the ground that it was the equivalent of a pardon and that he had never accepted it. That he—and Chapman as well—had a pretty solid argument on the basis of the Burdick Case can hardly be gainsaid, nor in fact did the Court attempt to gainsay it. It simply discarded outright the common law theory of pardon. Said Justice Holmes speaking for the Court:

"A pardon in our days is not a private act of grace from an individual happening to possess power. It is a part of the constitutional scheme.

When granted it is a determination of the ultimate authority that the public welfare will be better served by inflicting less than what the judgment fixed. . . . The only question is whether the substituted punishment was authorized by law—here, whether the change is within the scope of the words of the Constitution, Article II, Section 2. . . . By common understanding imprisonment for life is a less penalty than death." [123]

In short, the Constitution knows nothing of "*private* official acts" done in exercise of the powers granted by it. From this it follows that not only need a pardon not be accepted to be valid, but it need not be pleaded to be known judicially, being the official act of a coördinate department of government. But the President is not authorized to *add* to sentences imposed by the courts— he may only *mitigate* them, such being the common understanding of a pardon. And the question whether an alleged pardon does the one thing or the other, and so is a pardon or not, is a question ultimately for the Court.

But while the common law has been largely abandoned as a disabling factor of presidential pardoning power, in other respects it remains in full force, as we discover when we turn to certain questions concerning the *scope* of the power and of its *effect*. The leading case dealing with the first of these aspects is *ex parte* Grossman,[124] which was decided in 1925. Grossman had been enjoined under the National Prohibition Act from further violations thereof and had violated the injunction, for which he had been sentenced to a year's imprisonment and a fine for contempt of court. President Coolidge, seeing an opportunity to save the government Grossman's board bill, commuted the latter's sentence to the payment of the fine; and Grossman with reasonable promptitude paid up, despite which he was committed by the offended tribunal to the Chicago house of correction. The question before the Supreme Court was whether he was entitled, in view of the President's order, to his release on a writ of habeas corpus.

The argument most stressed in support of the district court's action is that set forth in the following passage from Judge Wilkerson's opinion:

"The power to punish for contempt is inherent in and essential to, the very existence of the judiciary. If the President is allowed to substitute his discretion for that of the courts in this vital matter, then truly the President becomes the ultimate source of judicial authority. Such a holding would be a distortion of that cardinal principle of American institutions that the executive, legislative and judicial branches of government are coordinate and proudly independent."[125]

But it was also argued that the only "offenses against the United States" known to the Constitution were offenses in violation of some definite statute of the United States, that the term was interchangeable with "crimes" and "criminal prosecutions" in the Constitution, and that a contempt of court was not such an offense but *sui generis*—all which assertions had considerable support in judicial dicta.[126]

The Court ordered Grossman's release on the basis of the twofold proposition that the President's pardoning power extends to "criminal" contempts, as above defined, but "may not interfere with the use of coercive measures to enforce a suitor's rights." Chief Justice Taft's opinion deals largely in historical data. The pardoning power, it urges, having been conferred upon the President in the light of English practice, must be defined by common law standards. "The King of England, before our Revolution, had always exercised the power to pardon contempts of court, just as he did ordinary crimes and misdemeanors."[127] "Moreover, criminal contempts of a federal court had been pardoned for eighty-five years. In that time the power had been exercised twenty-seven times" and with repeated approval by Attorneys General.[128] Nor was any new or special danger to be apprehended from this view of the pardoning power. "If," says the Chief Justice, "we could conjure up in our minds a President willing to paralyze the courts by pardoning all criminal contempts, why not a President ordering a general jail delivery?"[129] Indeed, he queries further, in view of the peculiarities of procedure in contempt cases,

"may it not be fairly said that in order to avoid possible mistake, undue prejudice, or needless severity, the chance of pardon should exist at least as much in favor of a person convicted by a judge without a jury as in favor of one convicted in a jury trial?"[130]

On the other hand, the opinion continues, the President's prerogative does not reach "civil contempts," that is to say, noncompliance with orders issued in support of the rights of private litigants. The distinction is vaguely supported by Blackstone but hardly, if at all, by the opinions of Attorneys General which the Chief Justice cites in behalf of his main proposition.[131] Indeed, the terms "criminal" and "civil" contempts are set in opposition to each other for the first time in an opinion of the Supreme Court in 1904.[132]

The practical significance of the Grossman Case is that it clearly recognizes a pardoning power which is able to cope with "government by injunction." The recognition is important not only in the field of labor law, but in that of the ordinary criminal law, whose sanctions are nowadays—as in the Grossman Case itself—frequently supplemented by the injunctive process. Furthermore, the holding arms the President with a power which might conceivably become of great importance in enabling him to protect his official subordinates against judicial interference.

Finally, the case has a certain theoretical interest, for, contrasted with the Perovich Case, which was decided only two years later, it illustrates the variety and diversity of the materials which are often available to the Court in its highly selective work of constitutional interpretation.[133]

The third dimension of the pardoning power is supplied by the doctrines of the Court concerning the *effect* of a pardon. Under this heading the leading case is still *ex parte* Garland,[134] decided in 1867, although not everything said on that occasion is still good law. By an act passed in 1865 Congress had prescribed that before any person should be permitted to practise in a federal court he must take oath asserting that he had never voluntarily borne arms against the United States, had never given aid or comfort to enemies of the United States, and so on. Garland, who had been a Confederate sympathizer and so was unable to take the oath, had however received from President Johnson the same year "a full pardon for all offences committed by his participation, direct or implied, in the Rebellion." The question before the Court was whether, armed with this pardon, Garland was entitled to practise in the federal courts despite the act of Congress just mentioned.

A closely divided Court held with Garland. The position of the majority, speaking through Justice Field, was that the act of Congress was intended to punish past acts, that it was therefore *ex post facto,* and that, furthermore, to give it operation in Garland's case would be to deny his pardon by the President its constitutional efficacy. "The inquiry arises," the opinion runs,

"as to the effect and operation of a pardon, and on this point all the authorities concur. A pardon reaches both the punishment prescribed for the offence and the guilt of the offender; and when the pardon is full, it releases the punishment and blots out of existence the guilt, so that in the eye of the law the offender is as innocent as if he had never committed the offence. If granted before conviction, it prevents any of the penalties and disabilities consequent upon conviction from attaching thereto; if granted after conviction, it removes the penalties and disabilities, and restores him all his civil rights; it makes him, as it were, a new man, and gives him a new credit and capacity."[135]

The minority, speaking by Justice Miller, challenged both the majority's view of the intention of the act of Congress and its view of the efficacy of a pardon. As to the former point he said: "Attorneys are often deprived of this right [to practise in court] upon evidence of bad moral character, or specific acts of immorality or dishonesty, which show that they no longer possess the requisite qualifications"; and he asked what qualification could more properly be demanded of an attorney than fidelity to the government in whose tribunals he sought to practise. The oath prescribed by the act of Congress being, therefore, no more than a test of professional fitness was in no wise affected by Garland's pardon. That relieved him "from all the penalties . . . which the law inflicted for his offense," but it could not relieve him from meeting appropriate tests of fitness laid down by the law for the pursuit of his profession. This, Justice Miller continued,

"is not only the plain rule as between the legislative and executive departments of government, but it is the declaration of common sense. The man who, by counterfeiting, by theft, by murder, or by treason, is rendered unfit to exercise the functions of an attorney or counsellor at law, may be saved by the executive pardon from the penitentiary or the gallows, but he is not thereby restored to the qualifications which are essential for admission to the bar."[136]

The merits of the question are somewhat divided as regards both earlier law and later.[137] Justice Field's latitudinarian view of the effect of a pardon undoubtedly still applies ordinarily where the pardon is issued *before conviction*. He is also correct in saying that a pardon restores a *convict* to his "civil rights"; and this is so even though simple completion of the convict's sentence would not have had that effect. One such right is the right to testify in court, and in *Boyd v. United States*[138] the Court held that "the disability to testify being a consequence, according to principles of the common law, of the judgment of conviction, the pardon obliterated that effect."

Indeed, this discrepancy between the effect of a pardon on the one hand and a completion of sentence on the other has given rise to frequent applications to the President for pardons by one-time offenders under the national statutes who have discharged the penalties laid upon them by the national courts, but still find themselves denied their civil rights in the states of their residence on account of their former conviction. So common, in fact, have such applications become in recent times that the Department of Justice has adopted a regular procedure for sifting them before bringing them to the President's attention. And while the immediate source of the disabilities which are thus removed is state law, state courts never fail to give full effect to such presidential pardons, a fact which testifies to the continued influence of Justice Field's opinion.[139]

Notwithstanding which, Justice Field's unqualified assertion that a pardon "blots out of existence the guilt, so that in the eyes of the law the offender is as innocent as if he had never committed the offense," must today be set down as much too sweeping. A case immediately in point is *Carlesi v. New York*,[140] decided in 1914. Carlesi was convicted in the New York courts and sentenced as a "second offender," his prior offense having been one against the United States for which he had been pardoned by the President. His contention in the later case was that, in thus taking account of this prior conviction, the New York courts were unconstitutionally denying the presidential pardon its full operation. The Court rejected the argument. The New York statute, it said, did not purport to authorize additional punishment for the act pardoned, but only prescribed such penalties as were appropriate "in view of the nature of the [later] offense and the character of the offender, taking in view his past conduct"; and it intimated that Congress could validly do the same thing without infringing in any way upon the President's power of pardon.

That is to say, a pardon does not necessarily blot out the fact of guilt *if it has been established by previous conviction.* That fact thus established may be validly treated as evidence of habitual criminality whether it was the occasion of an exercise of the pardoning power or not. But, if this is true, it is difficult to see how a pardon can qualify a man for a pursuit from which those convicted of crime are validly excluded. In the one case as in the other the pardoned man would appear to stand in the same situation as the man who has served his sentence—the holding in the Garland Case to the contrary notwithstanding. The ultimate question, therefore, regarding the effect of a pardon in the case of a convicted offender is this: what line will the courts draw between the "civil rights" of which his conviction deprived him and the power of the legislature—national or state—to lay down suitable qualifications for certain pursuits?[141]

Other phases of the subject may be dismissed rather briefly. It is only "offenses against the *United States*" that the President may pardon; and the offense must have been already committed, that is, it may not be anticipated, otherwise the power to pardon would be a power to dispense with observance of the law. On the other hand, pardon may precede trial, and so dispense with it. Also, pardons may be absolute or they may be conditional, and may cancel the entire sentence or may commute to a lesser sentence.[142] Where the penalty takes the form of a fine or forfeiture a pardon by the President restores to the offender so much of his property as has not become vested in third parties or covered into the Treasury, whence no money may be paid out "but in consequence of appropriations by law."[143] While Congress may not restrict the pardoning power, it may itself, under the "necessary and proper" clause, enact amnesty laws remitting penalties incurred under the national statutes, and may stipulate that witnesses before the courts or other bodies qualified to take testimony shall not be prosecuted by the National Government for any offenses disclosed by their testimony.[144] It may also authorize judges of the United States to suspend sentences, action which without such authorization is an invasion of the President's prerogative.[145]

Finally, by the words of the Constitution itself, the pardoning power does not extend to "cases of impeachment." What does this mean? As it stood in the Report of the Committee of Detail of the Convention which framed the Constitution, the original of this clause read "his [the President's] pardon shall not be pleadable in bar of an impeachment," which is taken from the English Act of Settlement of 1701, although the principle it states had been asserted by the Commons as early as 1679.[146] The evident purpose in the form finally adopted is not only to prevent a presidential pardon from constituting a bar to impeachment proceedings, but also to prevent it from relieving one thus convicted of the penalties imposed by the court of impeachment, it being elsewhere provided that these "shall not extend further than to removal from office, and disqualification to hold and enjoy an office of honor, trust, or profit under the United States."[147]

Thus the development of the President's power to pardon has proceeded along two different, even conflicting, lines: (1) the power has been augmented by drawing into it certain positive elements of what Blackstone terms "the most amiable prerogative" of the British Crown; (2) it has been released from certain cramping restrictions upon that prerogative. And both these developments are in harmony with the undoubted outlook of the

Framers, who regarded the pardoning power as a very positive adjunct of the law-enforcing machinery of government.

To summarize: The President's power as Chief Executive is multidimensional, and has expanded along almost every dimension. His role as interpreter of the law has become, with the watering down in recent times of the Lockian maxim against the delegation of legislative power, a power of quasi legislation, and in times of emergency, power of legislation unqualified by "the softening word quasi." His power as Commander-in-Chief to employ the armed forces to put down "combinations too powerful to be dealt with by ordinary judicial processes" is, in the absence of definitely restrictive legislation, almost plenary, as is also his power to employ *preventive* (as against *punitive*) martial law. Furthermore, the line which today separates the "peace of the United States" from the domestic peace of the states severally has been since World War I a tenuous one. The third source of presidential power as Chief Executive is the theory which attributes to him the responsibility of "stewardship" to act for the public good so far at least as the laws do not inhibit. Following in the track of this theory the Presidency has in recent years come to take on some of the aspects of primitive monarchy in the settlement of the industrial disputes of a far from primitive society. The monarchical quality of his pardoning power has, on the other hand, fallen by the wayside, but with the result nevertheless of augmenting that power also.

In his opinion in the Myers Case, written in 1926, Justice Holmes said:

"The duty of the President to see that the laws be executed is a duty that does not go beyond the laws or require him to achieve more than Congress sees fit to leave within his power."

It is interesting to lay these words alongside those of Justice Miller, quoted earlier in this chapter, from his opinion in the Neagle Case, which was decided in 1890. Whatever may have been the case in 1926, there can be no doubt whatsoever that in this year of grace 1948 the earlier statement comes vastly nearer to stating the truth.

CHAPTER V

ORGAN OF FOREIGN RELATIONS

WHERE does the Constitution lodge the power to determine the foreign relations of the United States?[1] Before this question can be profitably considered a distinction or two must be noted. The most centralized government on earth is, simply from the nature of things, incapable of determining beforehand the actual conditions with which it will have to deal in its intercourse with other governments. The humblest subject of the most thoroughpaced autocrat may plunge his sovereign into war, as did a Spanish *gardacosta* early in the eighteenth century, when he struck off the famous Jenkins' gory ear.[2] Nor is our Constitution at all superior in this respect to those of other governments—rather, owing especially to the large powers which it leaves with local authorities, it is sometimes inferior. Certainly it contains no guarantee that a mob, a petty magistrate, a city council, or a state legislature may not at any time do something calculated to cast a shadow upon our relations with a friendly power. Friendly relations with friendly governments have been jeopardized more than once in just these ways.[3]

Indeed, a nation's relations with another nation may be determined by the latter's decisions rather than by its own. The United States may proclaim its intention of rendering all possible aid falling "short of war" against "aggressor nations"; but if the latter choose to regard the aid rendered under this formula as amounting to war upon themselves and proceed accordingly, then such aid will not, in fact, have fallen short of war. Likewise an announced policy of keeping out of war would not necessarily produce that outcome, but might lead to the exactly opposite result.

The Notes to this chapter begin on page four hundred fifty-nine

The question in which we are interested demands, therefore, a somewhat precise statement. It may be put thus: *Where does the Constitution vest authority to determine the course of the United States as a sovereign entity at international law with respect to matters in which other similar entities may choose to take an interest?* Many people are inclined to answer offhand, in the President; but they would be hard put, if challenged, to point out any definite statement to this effect in the Constitution itself. What the Constitution does, *and all that it does,* is to confer upon the President certain powers capable of affecting our foreign relations, and certain other powers of the same general nature upon the Senate, and still other such powers upon Congress; but which of these organs shall have the decisive and final voice in determining the course of the American nation is left for events to resolve.

All of which amounts to saying that the Constitution, considered only for its affirmative grants of powers which are capable of affecting the issue, is an invitation to struggle for the privilege of directing American foreign policy. In such a struggle the President has, it is true, certain great advantages, which are pointed out by Jay in *The Federalist;* the *unity* of the office, its capacity for *secrecy* and *despatch,* and its superior sources of *information;* to which should be added the fact that it is always on hand and ready for action, whereas the houses of Congress are in adjournment much of the time.[4] But despite all this, actual *practice* under the Constitution has shown that while the President is usually in a position to *propose,* the Senate and Congress are often in a technical position at least to *dispose.* The verdict of history, in short, is that the power to determine the substantive content of American foreign policy is a *divided* power, with the lion's share falling usually to the President, though by no means always.

NATIONAL SOVEREIGNTY IN THE FOREIGN FIELD;
CONGRESSIONAL INDEPENDENCE AND JUDICIAL
ABSTENTION

It will be of referential value later if, before undertaking to describe the powers which the President exercises in the foreign field, and the relation of these powers to the impinging powers of the Senate and of Congress, I discuss briefly some of the principles which delimit the field itself, and so supply the setting in which presidential prerogative operates. The most important of these, indeed the controlling one, is that the power of the National Government in respect to external affairs is as broad, as complete as that of any other nation. Indeed, as Hamilton pointed out in *The Federalist,* it could not safely be otherwise;[5] and another member of the Convention, James Wilson, implied the same conclusion in his assertion that:

"When the United States declared their independence, they were bound to receive the Law of Nations in its modern state of purity and refinement."[6]

Whether from the angle of self-interest or that of international obligation the powers of the new government were assumed to match those of other civilized states.[7]

But whence comes this plenary power? Is it the summation of constitutionally delegated powers, or does it come from some source external to the Constitution? That the Constitution assigns to the President, to the Senate, and to Congress many powers in the exercise of which these bodies are respectively able to influence the conduct of the nation's foreign relations is unquestionable. To assume, however, that these powers are sufficient, either separately or together, to meet all the requirements of an expedient and just foreign policy would be entirely gratuitous; and, as a matter of fact, many powers have been asserted both by the President and by Congress in the field of foreign relations as to which the Constitution is completely silent.

It must follow, then, that the Constitution, instead of being the *immediate* source of the external powers of the National Government, is only their *mediate* source, and confers them simply in consequence of having established a nation which is truly sovereign in relation to other nations. Or in other words, the power of the National Government in the diplomatic sphere, while susceptible of limitation by the Constitution when the restrictions which it imposes upon all power apply, is an *inherent* power, *one which owes its existence to the fact that the American People are a sovereign entity at international law.*

And not only is this power of the National Government an *inherent* power, it is also an *inherited* power, though as to whence inherited there has always been some disagreement. In his opinion in the early case of *Penhallow v. Doane,*[8] Justice Iredell advanced the theory that sovereignty originally belonged to the states in the external as well as the internal field, but that upon the establishment of the Constitution their sovereignty in the former field passed to the National Government. Justice Paterson, on the other hand, took the position that external sovereignty never did belong to the states and that the sovereignty of the National Government as to foreign relations was an inheritance from the Continental Congress; and this latter theory is adopted by the Court in 1936 in the case of *United States v. Curtiss-Wright Export Corporation.* Said Justice Sutherland on that occasion:

"As a result of the separation from Great Britain by the colonies, acting as a unit, the powers of external sovereignty passed from the Crown not to the colonies severally, but to the colonies in their collective and corporate capacity as the United States of America. Even before the Declaration, the colonies were a unit in foreign affairs, acting through a common agency—namely the Continental Congress, composed of delegates from the thirteen colonies. That agency exercised the powers of war and peace, raised an army, created a navy, and finally adopted the Declaration of Independence. Rulers come and go; governments end and forms of government change; but sovereignty survives. A political society cannot endure without a supreme will somewhere. Sovereignty is never held in suspense. When, therefore, the external sovereignty of Great Britain in respect of the colonies ceased, it immediately passed to the Union."[9]

But the other theory, too, is perfectly adequate logically if we assume that the states are today devoid of capacity to sustain foreign relationship, inasmuch as, unless it has dropped entirely out of existence, their former sovereignty in this respect must have passed to the National Government, and hence be as complete in the latter as by hypothesis it originally was in the former.[10]

That national power is *exclusive* in the realm of foreign relations is, in fact, an obvious corollary of its being *plenary,* even though the deduction is not entirely sustained by the language of the Constitution itself. Thus section 10 of Article I quite clearly recognizes the states as retaining a certain rudimentary capacity in this field, upon the exercise of which it lays certain restraints. No state, the section reads, may enter into "any treaty, alliance or confederation," or grant "letters of marque and reprisal," nor, *"without the consent of Congress,"* enter "into any agreement or compact with a foreign state." The capacity thus implied must, nevertheless, be today regarded as atrophied, no such consent having ever been sought or granted.

Curiously enough, the notion of the complete incapacity of the states for foreign relationship first achieved judicial recognition during the very period when States Rights were most dominant in the Court's thinking. I refer to the case of *Holmes v. Jennison,*[11] which was decided in 1841. The matter at issue was whether

Jennison, governor of Vermont, was constitutionally entitled to surrender Holmes to the government of Lower Canada from whose justice the latter was alleged to be fugitive. On account of the equal division of the Justices respecting the Court's jurisdiction no judgment was handed down in the case, but the opinion of Chief Justice Taney for himself and three associates denied the power of the Vermont governor in unqualified terms. "All the powers which relate to our foreign intercourse," the Chief Justice asserted, "are confided to the general government." "The framers of the Constitution manifestly believed that any intercourse between a state and a foreign nation was dangerous to the Union"; and one of their main objects was "to make us, so far as regarded our foreign relations, one people and one nation; and to cut off all communications between foreign governments and the several state authorities." [12]

Later utterances of the Court unite assertion of the principle of the exclusiveness to that of the completeness and inherency of the national power. In the words of the opinion by Justice Sutherland which was quoted from above:

"The investment of the Federal government with the powers of external sovereignty did not depend upon the affirmative grants of the Constitution. The powers to declare and wage war, to conclude peace, to make treaties, to maintain diplomatic relations with other sovereignties, if they had never been mentioned in the Constitution, would have vested in the Federal government as necessary concomitants of nationality." [13]

Lastly, the plenary character of national power in the foreign field involves the consequence that it is not affected by the principle of "dual federalism"; that is, is not limited by the so-called "reserved powers" of the states. This obvious corollary was first recognized and applied with regard to the treaty-making power

in 1796, in the case of *Ware v. Hylton*,[14] and during Marshall's
Chief Justiceship the same or equivalent doctrine was reiterated
many times. During Chief Justice Taney's presidency of the
Court, it is true, the theory was repeatedly broached, although it
never became the basis of a decision, that the treaty-making power
was restricted to some indefinite extent by state power; but the
latest utterances of the Court go straight back to the original conception of the subject.[15] In sustaining in *Missouri v. Holland*[16] the
right of the National Government to treat with another nation
with regard to birds which were seasonally migratory between
them, the Court disparaged the idea that some "invisible radia-
tion from the Tenth Amendment" limited the treaty-making
power, and hinted that the fact that treaties do not have to be "in
pursuance of the Constitution" but only "under the authority of
the United States" was not without significance.[17] And more
recently still, in sustaining the right of the National Government
to levy customs duties upon apparatus imported by a state university, Chief Justice Hughes, speaking for the Court, remarked
generally:

"In international relations and with respect to foreign intercourse
and trade the people of the United States act through a single government with unified and adequate power . . . there is no encroachment
[here] on the power of the state, as none exists with respect to the subject over which the federal power has been exerted."[18]

Such are the general contours of this field of national power;
but there are also one or two matters of internal arrangement, as
it were, which need to be mentioned at this point. The first of
these—an aspect of the principle of departmental autonomy[19]—is
the doctrine that neither Congress nor the Senate can be *constitutionally* bound—however ineffective *practically* their freedom
may be—by anything done previously by the President in his

capacity as organ of foreign relations. Sometimes termed the doctrine of "concurrent" or "coördinate powers," this principle first assumed importance in the controversy over Congress's duty to appropriate certain monies needed to carry the highly unpopular Jay Treaty into effect. Spokesmen for the administration, notably Hamilton, argued that in making treaties "supreme law of the land" the Constitution converted the obligation of a treaty at international law into complete *constitutional* obligation, and hence left Congress no discretion in such a situation.[20] Madison and Gallatin answered that the very purpose of the Constitution in forbidding any money to be paid out of the Treasury except in consequence of "an appropriation made by law" was to leave Congress a free agent in voting such appropriations.[21] Although few if any treaty provisions have ever failed for lack of funds to carry them out, the latter view has in principle prevailed. Today it is well established that Congress may even repeal treaties in their quality as law of the land; and, more generally, that whatever any department does in the exercise of its powers is frequently at the mercy of what another department may do—or refuse to do—in the exercise of its powers.[22] Thus the argument which was advanced in 1919, both in the Senate and elsewhere, against our entering the League of Nations, that to do so would deprive Congress "unconstitutionally" of its discretion in the matter of declaring war, was valid only in the loose general sense which enjoins Congress always to observe good faith toward other nations in the exercise of all its powers. Almost any treaty whatsoever would be open to the same criticism.[23]

The second matter of "internal arrangement" is the doctrine of Political Questions which was first formulated by Chief Justice Marshall in the early case of *Foster v. Neilson*.[24] The question at issue was the validity of a grant made by the Spanish government in 1804 of land lying to the east of the Mississippi River, but underlying this question was the broader one whether the region between the Perdido and Mississippi Rivers belonged in 1804 to Spain or to the United States; and on this point the Court held that its judgment was concluded by the action of "the political departments," the President and Congress, in claiming the land for the United States. The Chief Justice said:

"If those departments which are entrusted with the foreign inter-course of the nation, which assert and maintain its interests against foreign powers, have unequivocally asserted its rights of dominion over a country of which it is in possession, and which it claims under a treaty; if the legislature has acted on the construction thus asserted, it is not in its own courts that this construction is to be denied. A ques-tion like this respecting the boundaries of nations is, as has been truly said, more a political than a legal question, and in its discussion, the courts of every country must respect the pronounced will of the legislature."[25]

On the basis of this principle the Court has subsequently held at one time or another that it must accept as final and binding on itself the determinations of one or other, or both, of "the political departments," with respect to all such questions as, whether a certain newly constituted community was a qualified belligerent at international law; what was the correct boundary of a certain country; what country was the sovereign of a particular region; whether a certain community was entitled to be considered as a "belligerent" or as an independent state; who was the *de jure,* who was the *de facto* ruler of a certain country; whether a par-ticular person was a duly accredited diplomatic agent to the United States; how long a military occupation of a certain region should continue in order to fulfill the terms of a treaty; whether a certain treaty was in effect; and so on.[26]

The reader will quickly perceive that it is the tendency of both the doctrines just considered to keep the powers of the National Government in the field of foreign relations continually fluid and easily available. By the same token, both doctrines also invite a constant struggle for power in this field on the part of the political branches of the government—President, Congress, and Senate.

"SOLE ORGAN OF EXTERNAL RELATIONS"—
HAMILTON VERSUS MADISON

"The President is the sole organ of the nation in its external relations, and its sole representative with foreign nations." These words of John Marshall, spoken in 1799, state what has today become a commonplace, which is the reason perhaps why their precise significance has been so rarely considered. The fact is that the statement is susceptible of two widely divergent interpretations.

Marshall's remark was made in his capacity as a member of the House of Representatives to uphold President John Adams in having ordered the extradition under the Jay Treaty of one Jonathan Robbins, who was alleged to be a fugitive from British justice. The President's critics contended that the situation was one which required judicial action, an argument which Marshall answered by pointing out that "the case was in its nature a national demand made upon the nation." The parties were two nations. "They cannot come into court to litigate their claims, nor can a court decide them." Then follow the words quoted above, which conclude with the statement, "of consequence, the demand of a foreign nation can only be made on him." [27]

Clearly, what Marshall had foremost in mind was simply the President's role as *instrument of communication* with other governments. And the same is true of Jefferson when, some years before, he answered Genêt's request for an exequatur for a consul whose commission was addressed to "the Congress of the United States." Jefferson's reply was that:

"As the President is the only channel of communication between the United States and foreign nations, it is from him alone that foreign nations or their agents are to learn what is or has been the will of the nation, and whatever he communicates as such they have a right and are bound to consider as the expression of the nation, and no foreign agent can be allowed to question it."[28]

That is to say, while the President alone may address foreign governments and be addressed by them, yet in fulfilling these functions he is, or at least may be, the mouthpiece of a power of decision which resides elsewhere. Nor do statements made in Congress in 1789 in the course of the debate on the removal power—which, it will be remembered, dealt with the official relationship between the President and the Secretary of State—necessarily imply a broader conception of the President's diplomatic role save in connection with the negotiation of treaties, an exception which both Marshall and Jefferson would unquestionably have allowed.

Elaboration of the conception of the President's external role as essentially dynamic and positive was the work in the first instance of Alexander Hamilton. The opportunity was furnished by the issuance of Washington's so-called "Proclamation of Neutrality" upon the outbreak early in 1793 of war between France and Great Britain. This document declared the intention of the United States to "pursue a course friendly and impartial to both belligerent powers" and enjoined upon all citizens its observance under pain of prosecution. While its author, Attorney General Randolph,[29] had industriously avoided the word "neutrality," the proclamation was immediately challenged by French sympathizers as having been outside the President's constitutional competence. Its defense was thereupon undertaken by Hamilton, writing over the pseudonym "Pacificus,"[30] in a series of articles in *The Gazette of the United States,* the first of which deals with the constitutional issue. In brief, Hamilton's argument comprises the following contentions: first, that the opening clause of Article II is a grant of power; secondly, that the succeeding more specific grants of the article, except when "coupled with express restrictions or limitations," "specify the principal articles" implied in the general grant and hence serve to interpret it; thirdly —by inference—that the direction of foreign policy is inherently an *"executive"* function.[31]

By way of illustrating his position Hamilton cites certain powers which he regards as exercisable by the President in conjunction with or in the interstices of the specific grants of the Constitution. One of these is the power of "recognition" of new governments; another the power to judge for the United States "what rights the law of nature and nations gives"; another the power to determine "virtually upon the operation of national treaties," for while "treaties can only be made by the President and Senate jointly; . . . their activity may be continued or suspended by the President alone." He then adds:

"This serves as an example of the right of the executive, in certain cases, to determine the condition of the nation, though it may, in its consequences, affect the exercise of the power of the legislature to declare war. Nevertheless, the executive cannot thereby control the exercise of that power. The legislature is still free to perform its duties, according to its own sense of them; though the executive, in the exercise of its constitutional powers, may establish an antecedent state of things, which ought to weigh in the legislative decision.

"The division of the executive power in the Constitution creates a *concurrent* authority in the cases to which it relates."[32]

In short, the President has all powers which the facts of international intercourse may at any time make conveniently applicable and which the Constitution does not vest elsewhere in clear terms; ordinarily this means that the *initiative* in the foreign field rests with him. He is consequently able to confront the other departments, and Congress in particular, with *faits accomplis* at will; although on the other hand Congress is under no *constitu-*

tional obligation to back up such *faits accomplis* or to support the policies giving rise to them.

Although he had approved of the proclamation Jefferson was so disturbed by Hamilton's constitutional views in support of it that he appealed to Madison to refute the latter. "Nobody," he wrote, "answers him and his doctrines are taken for confessed. For God's sake, my dear Sir, take up your pen, select the most striking heresies and cut him to pieces in face of the public."[33] Madison complied in the letters of "Helvidius," which also appeared in the *Gazette* and are devoted solely to the constitutional issue.[34] Endeavoring first to explain away his own argument four years before regarding the location of the removal power—an effort more adroit than convincing—he proceeds to charge Hamilton with seeking to annex to the Presidency the prerogative of the British Crown. His words are:

"Thus it appears that by whatever standard we try this doctrine, it must be condemned as no less vicious in theory than it would be dangerous in practice. It is countenanced neither by the writers on law; nor by the nature of the powers themselves; nor by any general arrangements, or particular expressions, or plausible analogies, to be found in the constitution.

"Whence then can the writer have borrowed it?

"There is but one answer to this question.

"The power of making treaties and the power of declaring war, are *royal prerogatives* in the *British government,* and are accordingly treated as *executive prerogatives* by British *commentators....*"[35]

Madison's own theory is that the right to determine the foreign policy of the United States devolves upon Congress by virtue of its power to declare war, and that the powers of the President in the diplomatic sphere are *instrumental* only, or involve at most no greater range of discretion than the determination of "matters of fact." Nor has he any patience with Hamilton's doctrine of *concurrent* powers, although two years later, when the Jay Treaty was under discussion in the House of Representatives, a close approximation to this theory was to furnish his main reliance—a *volte-face* which was matched by one on Hamilton's part in the opposite direction. But in 1793 the duties of advocacy required of Madison that he show that, if a power was claimable for the President on sound constitutional grounds, Congress was constitutionally obligated by the President's exercise thereof, for it would then follow that, *if* the President's proclamation was valid, it took from Congress the power to decide as between war and peace, a conclusion manifestly at variance with Congress's possession of the war-declaring power. The proclamation, therefore, was not valid, nor the conception of presidential power on which it was based a constitutionally tenable one.

However the palm for argumentation be awarded in this famous disputation, the practical fruits of victory were divided between the parties to it. In 1794 Congress passed our first Neutrality Act, and ever since then the subject of neutrality has been conceded to lie within its jurisdiction.[36] But to make up for this—indeed, much more than make up for it—were the two tendencies in constitutional interpretation to which Hamilton's argument gave rise: (1) that of regarding the "executive power" clause as an always available peg on which to hang any and all unassigned powers in respect to foreign intercourse; and (2) that of treating these and all other presidential powers in the diplomatic field as potentially *policy-forming powers,* and constitutionally independent of direction by Congress, though capable of being checked by it.

Both tendencies find ample illustration in the further proceedings of Washington's administration. Let us consider, for instance, what happened at this period to the President's power to "receive" ambassadors and other public ministers. As the above colloquy between Jefferson and Genêt suffices to show, this power was considered as embracing also the power to receive consuls; and sixty years later Attorney General Cushing was to assert sweepingly that it extended to "all possible diplomatic agents which any power may accredit to the United States"—doctrine which the record of practice amply confirms.[37]

Furthermore, the reception of Genêt himself involved consequences of the greatest moment. "Helvidius" had professed to consider exercise of the power of reception as a mere "ceremony," comprising only the examination and authentication of the credentials of the foreign representative, which "it would be highly improper to magnify . . . into an important prerogative." Such questions, he continued, "belong of necessity to the executive"; but they involve no cognizance of the question whether those exercising the government "which despatched the representative have the right along with the possession." That question could arise only on "great and extraordinary" occasions, "by no means submitted to so limited an organ of the national will as the executive of the United States."[38] Actually, the reception of Genêt involved this very issue, and yet it was decided by Washington without consulting Congress. Nor did Washington consult Congress when some months later he demanded Genêt's recall, thereby establishing a precedent which has been followed by later Presidents again and again, and more than once in the face of impending war.[39]

Another precedent of great significance from Washington's administration was the first President's refusal in 1796 to comply with a call from the House of Representatives for papers relative to the negotiation of the Jay Treaty. The demand was originally fathered by Madison, and presumably reflected the theory of "Helvidius" that the President's diplomatic role is chiefly instrumental of the national legislative power in the realm of foreign relationship. Washington's declination, nevertheless, he now conceded to be proper so far as it represented the President's deliberate judgment that the papers were "of a nature that did not permit of disclosure at this time."⁴⁰ The concession so broadened the force of the precedent that nowadays a President feels free by the same formula to decline information even to his constitutional partner in treaty making, whereas Washington's refusal rested primarily on his denial that the House was entitled to discuss the merits of a treaty. In 1906 a debate arose in the Senate over the adventurous foreign policy of the first Roosevelt, in the course of which the entire ground that had been covered by "Pacificus" and "Helvidius" more than a century before was retraveled, Senator Spooner assuming the Hamiltonian part, Senator Bacon the Madisonian. In the face of his general position Bacon conceded that "the question of the President's sending or refusing to send any communication to the Senate is not to be judged by legal right, but [is] . . . one of courtesy between the President and that body."⁴¹ The record of practice amply bears out this statement.

Washington's success in foreshadowing "the shape of things to come" is seen also when we turn again to presidential monopolization of the right to communicate with foreign governments. The process envisaged is, it should be noted, a two-way process, depending on whether the President is its *terminus ad quem* or is its *terminus a quo*; or, in other words, is functioning as the nation's earpiece or its mouthpiece. The latter, obviously, is the vastly more important capacity since, as was pointed out earlier, it involves potentially *formation,* as well as *formulation,* of the policy communicated; while the role of being earpiece is an essentially passive one. Even so, a Secretary of State found it necessary as late as 1833 to apprise foreign chancelleries that when they wished to inform the United States of royal births, deaths, marriages, and the like, they should address their communications to "the President of the United States of America" and leave Congress out of the business. As to ordinary diplomatic intercourse, he added, it should be "carried on as usual" through the State Department.[42]

And meantime Congress had itself come to the aid and protection of the President's prerogative to speak for the nation. This occurred in 1799, when one Logan, a Philadelphia Quaker, thought to avert war between the United States and France by undertaking a private negotiation with the latter. Manifesting perhaps some lack of humor, Congress passed a law to penalize such enterprises, entitling the measure "an Act to Prevent Usurpation of Executive Functions."[43] In later years, although presidential spokesmen frequently assumed strange disguises which might easily have caused confusion, "the Logan Act," while still on the statute books, dropped out of common ken till the period of World War I. Then from 1920 on for several years excited patriots were constantly arising to demand that its penalties be visited, now upon ex-President Taft and his League to Enforce Peace, now upon Senator France for his philandering with "the Genoa Economic Conference," and at various times upon Senator Borah who, having become Chairman of the Foreign Relations Committee about that time, had set up as a sort of State Department of his own.[44]

Indeed, World War I proved generally relaxing of the established etiquette of international intercourse, more or less permanently so. Early in 1920 Viscount Grey came to this country on an informal mission, but being unable to see the President, who was ill, held conversations with certain Senators respecting the League of Nations fight, following which he published a letter in the London *Times* stating that the Lodge reservations were "satisfactory" to the Allies. President Wilson, apparently missing the subtle flattery of this imitation of his own prior exploit in taking the Fiume question to the Italian people over the heads of their government, professed to be greatly angered at this "grossest possible breach of courtesy." Likewise, when Candidate Harding, who was then campaigning for the Presidency from his own front porch in Marion, Ohio, was quoted in the papers to the effect that a French representative had approached him "informally" with the hope that he would "lead the way to a world fraternity," Mr. Wilson sharply questioned the Republican leader, who replied with elaborate irony, "Official France would never seek to go over your high office as our Chief Executive to appeal to the American people or any portion thereof." By way of contrast, President Hoover, following his defeat at the polls in November 1932, actually invited his successful rival to discuss with him certain proposals of the British Ambassador with regard to the war-debt situation; and while Mr. Roosevelt declined the suggestion, he later on his own initiative invited the Ambassador to come to Warm Springs for a conference, thereby, as Mr. Krock of *The New York Times* commented, virtually taking over "this function of the Presidency a month before his inauguration."[45]

All such episodes to the contrary notwithstanding, there is no more securely established principle of constitutional practice than the exclusive right of the President to be the nation's intermediary in its dealing with other nations.[46]

CONGRESSIONAL COLLABORATION AND CONTROL—
RECOGNITION

But whatever emphasis be given the President's role as "sole organ of foreign relations" and the initiative thereby conferred upon him in this field, the fact remains that no presidentially devised diplomatic policy can long survive without the support of Congress, the body to which belongs the power to lay and collect taxes for the common defense, to regulate foreign commerce, to create armies and maintain navies, to pledge the credit of the

United States, to declare war, to define offenses against the law of nations, and to make "all laws which shall be necessary and proper" for carrying into execution not only its own powers, but all the powers "of the government of the United States and of any department or officer thereof." Hence the only question that can arise is as to the character which the relationship with Congress thus imposed upon the President by the Constitution shall assume at the latter's hands—shall it be the relationship of coöperation between constitutionally equal partners, or shall it be the relationship of principal and instrument; a relationship resting upon jointly held convictions as to what the interests of the United States require, or upon the calculation that when Congress is presented with a sufficiently imperative *fait accompli* it can be counted on to come to heel? Actually, while now coöperation, now subservience, has characterized the relations of Congress to the President at different times, yet down to the Mexican War the former was the prevailing pattern, while since then—and owing in part to that fateful precedent—it is the President who has more and more called the tunes. From the viewpoint of the present moment, it is not extravagant to say that *immensely the most important single factor in the determination of American foreign policy has been presidential guidance of it.*

Returning now to the subject of recognition, we again encounter Congress—that is, the national legislative power—as an influential factor in both the initiation and development of American foreign policy in its early days. The breakup of the Spanish Empire in America during the first quarter of the nineteenth century raised questions which Washingtonian precedents answered very imperfectly. When Louis XVI was dethroned by the French people he was at the same time "liquidated," so that recognition by our government that the French people had an inherent right to determine their own forms of government incurred slight if any risks. But when the South Americans revolted from the Spanish monarchy the latter still remained in existence with some power to resent and resist outside interference. The question whether the new governments should be recognized by the United States involved therefore the further question of the extent to which the danger of war should be taken into account, and consequently the attitude of the war-declaring organ.[47]

Moreover, this was the period when, as we saw in an earlier chapter, Congress, and especially the House of Representatives, was at the top of the governmental heap. This had been definitely shown in 1812 when James Madison had as President enjoyed the dubious satisfaction of seeing the theories of "Helvidius" realized, through being forced by Henry Clay and his swashbuckling followers into war with Great Britain. And six years later, when the South American issue first loomed on the horizon, though Monroe was now President, the House of Representatives was still dominant and Clay was still dominant in the House.

We learn from John Quincy Adams's *Memoirs* that as early as December 1817 Clay had in hand "a motion to acknowledge the Government of Buenos Ayres and perhaps Chile." The motion, in fact, was never offered. Instead, on March 24, 1818, Clay proposed in committee of the whole, as an amendment to the then pending appropriation bill, a motion to appropriate $18,000 for the outfit and one year's salary of a minister to "the independent provinces of the River Plata in South America." But this proposal, too, proved abortive, being replaced the day following by one which omitted the word "independent" and was to go into effect only "whenever the President shall deem it expedient to send a minister," etc.[48]

But even in this attenuated form Clay's amendment stirred up much opposition as invading presidential prerogative. Recalling the Washington administration's recognition of the French Republic, Smith of Maryland queried: "Did Congress on that occasion direct the conduct of General Washington? ... No, sir; they left him to exercise the powers vested in him by the Constitution—to the exercise of his own judgment."[49] And Adams recorded in his *Memoirs* the fact that in a Cabinet meeting he urged a like objection against such proceedings in Congress:

"Instead of admitting the Senate or House of Representatives to any share in the act of recognition, I would expressly avoid that form of doing it which would require the concurrence of those bodies. It was, I had no doubt, by our Constitution an act of the Executive authority. General Washington had exercised it in recognizing the French Republic by the reception of Mr. Genest. Mr. Madison had exercised it by declining several years to receive, and by finally receiving, Mr. Onis; and in this instance I thought the Executive ought carefully to preserve entire the authority given him by the Constitution, and not weaken it by setting the precedent of making either House of Congress a party to an act which it was his exclusive right and duty to perform."[50]

Nor did Clay in defending his measure suggest that Congress had power to compel presidential action; rather, his object, he declared, was to aid executive deliberations, a thought which was further elaborated by Tucker of Virginia in the following words:

"But gentlemen seem to consider this an interference with the constitutional powers of the Executive. I do not think so. This House has at all times, and on all subjects, a right to declare its opinions, leaving it to the Executive to act upon them or not, according to its pleasure. Nay, it has often done more. Whenever the act to be done by the Executive has been intimately connected with the constitutional powers of this body, it has always deemed itself competent to act. Thus, before the treaty for the purchase of Louisiana was made, $2,000,000 were put at the disposal of the Government for the purchase of Southern territory. Here there was an act perfectly analogous. This body had no right to make a purchase, or to command the President to do so; but, as the purchase, if made, would have called upon the legislative body for an appropriation, it was thought advisable to make it beforehand, and thus indicate a correspondence of views on the subject, where correspondence was necessary.... It would appear to me indeed of the utmost importance, that this correspondence of views should be preserved between these two branches of the Government. How embarrassing to the Executive must it be, if, after a treaty has been made calling for a large appropriation this body should refuse to make it, and to sanction a contract entered into with a foreign State. How much more embarrassing if, in the exercise of its constitutional powers, the Executive should involve the nation in a war against the wishes of its Representatives. The jarring and confusion and inefficiency that would result might have the most fatal influence on the national success. No, sir, frankness and candor, and a free and unreserved communication of the feelings and opinions of each by the other, can never have any other than the happiest influence upon the National Councils."[51]

Clay's motion failed, nevertheless, and recognition was postponed some four years. Yet when it did come the course which was followed by the administration vindicated his and Tucker's theory of executive-congressional coöperation most strikingly. On January 30, 1822, the House requested the President to lay before it such documents bearing on the South American question "as it may be consistent with the public interest to communicate," to which the President responded on March 8 following with a message stating that the time had come to recognize the new republics and inviting Congress, if it concurred in that view, to make "the necessary appropriations for carrying it into effect," and in due course Congress appropriated $100,000 for "such missions to the independent nations of the American continent as the President of the United States may deem proper."[52]

This entire story seems to me highly instructive. It reaffirms the President's monopoly of the function of international intercourse and his constitutional independence in the performance of that function. Not even Clay seems to have supposed either that Congress could "recognize" the new republics without executive approval and collaboration or that these were constitutionally required. At the same time Monroe, while fully advised as to his constitutional rights, seems not to have resented Congress's efforts to get its "views" on record; indeed, in the end he carefully invited congressional coöperation. It is thus borne in upon one that the principle of departmental autonomy does not necessarily spell departmental conflict, but that mutual consultation and collaboration are quite as logical deductions from it. Nor should it be overlooked that throughout this episode it was Congress who forced the pace, not the President.

The lessons deducible from our recognition of Texan independence in 1837 are similar.[53] Cuban recognition sixty years later suggests, to be sure, a somewhat different pattern.[54] In the spring of 1896, more than a year after the outbreak of revolution in the island, the two houses adopted a concurrent resolution expressing the opinion that the situation there called for the recognition of a state of belligerency. President Cleveland ignored the suggestion; but meantime congressional opinion of a more extreme brand was rapidly developing, with the result that early in 1897 two joint resolutions made their appearance in the Senate, one of which purported to acknowledge "the independence of the Republic of Cuba" and the other of which proffered "the friendly offices" of the United States "with the government of Spain to bring to a close the war between Spain and the Republic of Cuba." The two resolutions were referred to the Committee on Foreign Relations which, after an extensive survey of the precedents, rendered an adverse report on constitutional grounds. The tenor of the report is indicated in the following extracts from it:

"The executive branch is the sole mouthpiece of the nation in communication with foreign sovereignties. Foreign nations communicate only through their respective executive departments. Resolutions of their legislative departments upon diplomatic matters have no status in international law. In the department of international law, therefore, properly speaking, a Congressional recognition of belligerency or independence would be a nullity. . . .

"Congress can help the Cuban insurgents by legislation in many ways, but it can not help them legitimately by mere declarations, or by attempts to engage in diplomatic negotiations, if our interpretation of the Constitution is correct. That it is correct will be shown by the opinions of jurists and statesmen of the past."[55]

Notwithstanding the flavor of finality which attaches to this statement, a few months later when President McKinley proposed intervention in Cuba the whole question was reopened. The President was opposed to recognizing the Cuban insurgent government, as was also a strong majority of the Foreign Relations Committee. A minority of the committee on the other hand favored "the immediate recognition of the Republic of Cuba, as a free, independent and sovereign power"; and this view prevailed to the extent that the opening resolution of the measure which "authorized and directed" the President to employ the land and naval forces of the United States to expel Spain from Cuba declared that the "people of Cuba are and of right ought to be free and independent." So, by incorporating it in what was tantamount to a declaration of war, Congress contrived to perform an act of recognition of which a foreign government was entitled by international law to take direct notice.[56]

Throughout the entire course of our national history the President has performed dozens of acts of recognition of new *governments* without consulting, or being expected to consult, Congress. At times, indeed, this prerogative has proved a most potent instrument of foreign policy, a remark which applies as well to its nonuse as to its use. President Wilson encompassed the downfall of

Huerta's regime in Mexico in 1915 by refusing to recognize it as even a government *de facto,* and the pivotal feature of our relations with both Mexico and Russia for some years was the refusal of successive administrations at Washington to recognize as *de jure* the governments of those countries.

The general subject of congressional collaboration has, however, many other facets besides recognition. The principle that the National Government is as to external affairs a completely sovereign government being conceded, it logically follows that Congress's legislative power in the same field is also plenary. Except indeed for its inability to require the President to exercise his concurrent powers in the same field, Congress has approximately as broad powers over such matters as has the British Parliament. And of course once Congress has legislated, the President becomes constitutionally obligated to take care that its laws be "faithfully executed." Where—how—is a line to be drawn between these logical incompatibles? The answer seems to be, "that depends." For example, section 34 of the Jones Merchant Marine Act of 1920 "authorized and directed" the President within ninety days to give notice to the other parties to certain treaties, which the act infracted, of the termination thereof. President Wilson refused to comply, asserting that he "did not deem the direction contained in section 34 ... an exercise of any constitutional power possessed by Congress." His action was roundly denounced by Senator Harding from the front porch earlier mentioned, despite which one of the first things Mr. Harding did upon becoming President was to announce—presumably with the concurrence of his Secretary of State, Mr. Hughes—that he proposed to follow precisely the same course. And yet had Congress contented itself with enacting the material portions of the statute it would unquestionably have become the President's constitutional duty to enforce these, regardless of their operation upon existing treaties, and at least it would have been only common sense and common courtesy on his part, as the national organ of foreign relations, to have given the other parties to the treaties advance notice. In fact, Mr. Wilson did so proceed in 1915 in connection with the La Follette Act—despite the fact that that act "requested and directed" him to do so.[57]

Of course, when it comes to legislation which would be capable of tying his hands because of his constitutional obligation in respect to law enforcement, a President has usually an effective weapon of defense for his policies in his veto power. The trouble is that an act which was put on the statute books with the approval of a predecessor, or even with his own approval, may later turn out to be seriously cramping. Thus it was that President Wilson found it necessary early in 1914, when he was being subjected to strong pressure from Great Britain on account of his Mexican policy, to go before Congress and urge repeal of the Panama Tolls Act of 1911:

"I ask this of you in support of the foreign policy of the Administration. I shall not know how to deal with other matters of even greater delicacy and nearer consequence if you do not grant it to me in ungrudging measure."[58]

No more striking acknowledgment has ever been made by a President of the actual power of Congress in the foreign-relations field.

Some other measures which represent attempts by Congress to guide and control foreign policy warrant mention. Thus a rider to the Appropriation Act of March 4, 1913, forbids the President to "extend or accept any invitation to participate in any international congress, conference, or like event without specific authorization to do so."[59] Shades of Cairo, Teheran, Yalta, Potsdam! The Act of May 26, 1924, on the other hand, by which Japanese immigration to this country was brought to an abrupt halt, while it signalized a particularly wild romp of the congressional bull in the diplomatic porcelain shop, was a type of legislation which Congress has always had conceded power to enact.[60] Equally would it be impossible to challenge Congress's power to pass the Johnson Debt Default Act of April 13, 1934, which forbade the sale or purchase within American jurisdiction of any securities of a government in debt to the United States; and the same remark applies to the various neutrality acts of recent years. As was pointed out above, Congress turned its attention to the subject of neutrality as early as 1794. Earlier acts, to be sure, merely purported to declare and sanction the existing usages of international law, but the Act of 1939 cast off these trammels entirely.[61]

Congress has, to repeat, vast powers to determine the bounds within which a President may be left to work out a foreign policy. Indeed, it may effectively block presidential policy by simply declining to pass implementing legislation—appropriations for instance. What is more, in proportion as the prosecution of a foreign policy—"The Marshall Plan," for instance—requires lavish expenditure, so is the insistence of the body which controls the nation's purse strings that it be accepted as a partner in the determination of the objectives of our diplomacy likely to increase. Conflict and antagonism, nevertheless, are not inevitable; to the contrary, there may be—and should be—mutual consultation, coöperation, collaboration. In point of fact, congressional legislation has operated to augment presidential powers in the foreign field much more frequently than it has to curtail them. The Lend-Lease Act of March 11, 1941, the elaboration of which is sketched in the succeeding chapter, is a classic example, although it only brought to culmination a whole series of enactments with which Congress had aided and abetted the administration's foreign policy in the years between 1934 and 1941.[62]

234 PRESIDENT: OFFICE AND POWERS

But not only is Congress a legislative body, its houses are also forums of public opinion, and their right to act as such has been asserted by their members over and over again. In the debate in the House in 1826 on the proposed mission to the Panama Congress, a Kentucky member said:

"It is its duty upon all fit occasions to pronounce the judgment of the people upon measures perfected or contemplated touching the foreign relations of the United States."

This statement Webster endorsed in the following words:

"It has expressed its opinions, when it deemed proper to express them at all, on great leading questions, by resolution, and in a general form. These general opinions being thus made known have, doubtless, always had and such expressions of opinion doubtless always will have, their effect. This is the practice of the Government. It is a salutary practice."[63]

Almost one hundred years later resolutions were introduced in the House expressing "its cordial approval" of the World Court and its "earnest desire that the United States give early adherence to the protocol establishing the same with the reservations recommended by President Harding and President Coolidge." The resolutions were referred to the Committee on Foreign Affairs, which in reporting them favorably listed more than thirty "precedents relating to action by the House of Representatives upon treaties and foreign affairs." Some of the actions mentioned were based upon exaggerated, or otherwise mistaken, notions as to the consequences that ought to be expected to flow from them, but considered solely as expressions of opinion it is difficult to see what constitutional objection they were open to. Sometimes Presidents have found such resolutions embarrassing, and sometimes no doubt they were intended by their proponents to be precisely that. Yet even at such times Presidents would occasionally have done better to heed them for the indication they gave of the trend of public opinion. At any rate, there seems to be no constitutional way in which a President can stop Congress's mouth whether it is saying encouraging things or the reverse.[64]

Finally, the two houses, both separately and conjointly, are able to create committees and endow them with ample powers of investigation into matters of public interest.[65] In the realm of domestic legislation such bodies have frequently done work of great importance, and there is no *a priori* reason why they should not prove of comparable value when questions affecting the conduct of foreign relations are the subject of investigation. Actually, they have frequently accomplished very little in the latter field, for the reason principally that they have usually been brought about at the insistence of a special group which was much more bent on publicizing a special point of view than it was on getting sound information. Well-planned, properly staffed inquiries could be very different affairs.[66] It may very well be, however, that with the emergence upon the American scene of such sounding boards of opinion—not merely American, but international opinion—as the Security Council and the Assembly of the United Nations, the importance of the congressional investigating committee as a device—and a not very successful one—for keeping presidential foreign policy open and aboveboard has passed, for the time being at least.

EXECUTIVE OF THE LAW OF NATIONS—PRESIDENTIAL WARMAKING

We now resume consideration of the constitutional factors of presidential aggrandizement in the sphere of foreign relations. Two of these I have dealt with already—the natural advantages of his office as stressed by Jay in *The Federalist,* and the Hamiltonian conception of "executive power." But the President is also Com-mander-in-Chief of the Army and Navy, while upon him rests the duty to "take care that the laws be faithfully executed," a part of which law is international law. So from the first it has devolved upon him to protect American rights and to discharge American duties under the law of nations; and, as commonly happens, the path of duty became in time a road to power. Finally, the leader-ship which the President has achieved since the turn of the cen-tury in the field of legislation has proved at times of the very greatest value in bringing Congress into line in the field of foreign policy.

In a famous passage quoted on an earlier page, Justice Miller had in 1890 put the question with regard to the President's duty to "take care that the laws be faithfully executed":

"Is this duty limited to the enforcement of acts of Congress or of treaties of the United States according to their *express terms,* or does it include the rights, duties and obligations growing out of the Consti-tution itself, our international relations, and all the protection implied by the nature of the government under the Constitution?"[67]

The answer evidently intended is no. Indeed, nearly eighty years earlier Attorney General William Wirt had advanced precisely this answer. The "laws" to which the "faithfully executed" clause referred, said he, comprised not only the Constitution, statutes, and treaties, but also "those general laws of nations which govern the intercourse between the United States and foreign nations." The United States, having become a member of the Society of Nations, was obliged to respect the rights of other nations under that code of laws and the President, as the chief executive officer of the laws and the agency charged with the superintendence of the nation's foreign intercourse, was bound to rectify injury and preserve peace.[68]

And nearly thirty years before that "Pacificus" had written to like effect:

"The President is the Constitutional EXECUTOR of the laws. Our treaties, and the laws of nations, form a part of the law of the land. He, who is to execute the laws, must first judge for himself of their meaning. In order to the observance of that conduct which the laws of nations, combined with our treaties, prescribed to this country, in reference to the present war in Europe, it was necessary for the President to judge for himself, whether there was anything in our treaties, incompatible with an adherence to neutrality." [69]

With this duality of the executive role in mind, let us consider "Pacificus' " contention, mentioned earlier in this chapter, that the President has the "power of determining virtually upon the operation of national treaties." The question raised is a twofold one: that of the President's power in relation to treaties as "law of the land"; and that of his power in relation to treaties as international obligations.

Treaty provisions are sometimes addressed *exclusively* to the President, as for instance were certain articles of the treaties which resulted from the Washington Conference of 1921, and which provided for conference among the high contracting parties in named contingencies. The duty of communication thus cast upon the President was, obviously, well within his diplomatic prerogative. Other treaty provisions, however, are addressed primarily to Congress. Indeed, it is a strongly held view, and one that has usually prevailed in practice, that if a treaty provision would operate within the field of Congress's enumerated powers—as would, for instance, a commercial treaty—it can be put into effect as "law of the land" only by sanctioning legislation;[70] and, as we have seen, Congress is free in enacting such sanctioning legislation to vest the President with large discretionary powers.

Lastly, the doctrine was early established that treaty provisions which reciprocally accord privileges to the nationals of each of the contracting states within the other's jurisdiction were susceptible in the United States of direct application and enforcement through the ordinary courts.[71] In relation to such provisions, which are regarded as being addressed primarily to the judiciary, the President's power is simply that of Chief Executive, constitutionally bound to carry out the decisions of the courts.

But now suppose that it becomes desirable for the United States to cast off a treaty—whether justly or unjustly by the standards of international law—what is the constitutional procedure for accomplishing this end? The cases are clear in establishing the power of Congress to strike down in its quality as "law of the land" any treaty or treaty provision to which the United States is party;[72] while as a matter of fact treaties of the United States have been terminated on several occasions by the President, now on his own authority, now in accordance with a resolution of Congress, at other times with the sanction simply of the Senate.[73] I assume, I may add, that when a treaty or treaty provision has been discarded in any one of the ways just mentioned, it ceases to be "law of the land" for any purpose whatsoever—*ceases*, that is, *to be a source of authority* either for supplementary legislation by Congress, for action by the President, or for adjudication by the courts.

The question remains whether the *international* obligation of a treaty continues after it has ceased to exist as "law of the land" and the performance of the duties of the United States under it has accordingly come to an end. In general, the answer must be that the United States is no more entitled to determine finally its duties toward other nations than are the latter to determine finally their duties toward the United States.[74] At the same time, in the absence of an international tribunal with authority to pass ultimately upon such questions, each sovereign government is an organ of the international society, and in the case of the United States government the immediate bearer of this capacity is, by Hamiltonian doctrine, the President.

But the President may also make himself the direct administrator of the international rights and duties of the United States, or of what are adjudged by him to be such, without awaiting action either by the treaty-making power or by Congress, or by the courts. Significant in this connection is the course laid down by various Presidents with regard to the landing of foreign submarine cables.[75] President Grant established the germinal precedent in 1869, when he was approached with a request from a French company which desired to connect Duxbury, Massachusetts, with Brest, France, via the Island of St. Pierre in the Gulf of St. Lawrence. "In the absence of legislation by Congress" the President conceded the request upon certain stipulated conditions, and in 1879 and again in 1884 his successors followed suit. In 1893, however, President Cleveland refused a request of this sort on the ground of lack of statutory authority, with the result that the company proceeded to make a landing anyway. In the subsequent proceedings which the administration—quite inconsistently—brought to enjoin the intruder, the federal court hinted its opinion that the President's legal scruples had been misconceived. The question was finally disposed of by an opinion of Solicitor General Richards in 1898. Citing the Neagle Case, Mr. Richards placed power to act on the twofold basis of "the fundamental rights which ... grow out of the jurisdiction of this nation over its own territory" and the President's constitutional position as the organ of American foreign relations.[76]

And it was with these precedents back of him that President Wilson in August 1913 granted permission for the introduction of electrical current from Canada,[77] and thirteen months later closed the Marconi wireless station at Siasconset, when the company refused assurance that it would comply with naval censorship regulations. The former action was admittedly without statutory basis; and while the Act of August 19, 1912,[78] probably supported the later drastic invasion of private rights, justification for it was based by Attorney General Gregory largely on the President's powers as Commander-in-Chief and as organ of foreign relations:

"The President of the United States is at the head of one of the three great coordinate departments of the Government. He is Commander-in-Chief of the Army and Navy. . . . If the President is of the opinion that the relations of this country with foreign nations are, or are likely to be, endangered by action deemed by him inconsistent with a due neutrality, it is his right and duty to protect such relations; and in doing so, in the absence of any statutory restrictions, he may act through such executive office or department as appears best adapted to effectuate the desired end. . . . I do not hesitate, in view of the extraordinary conditions existing, to advise that the President, through the Secretary of the Navy, or any other appropriate department, close down or take charge of, and operate, the plant . . . should he deem it necessary to secure obedience to his proclamation of neutrality."[79]

And it was on comparable grounds that the President met the renewal by Germany of unrestricted submarine warfare by ordering on March 12, 1917, an armed guard to be placed on all American merchant vessels, action which followed hard upon the heels of failure by Congress, owing to the opposition of "a little group of willful men" in the Senate, to authorize it.[80]

But this is no more than the beginning of the story. Thanks to the same capacity to base action directly on his own reading of international law—a capacity which the Court recognized in terms in the Neagle Case—the President has been able to gather to himself powers with respect to warmaking which ill accord with the specific delegation in the Constitution of the war-declaring power to Congress.

The first question to be answered in this connection is whether the President may, without authorization by Congress, ever use force abroad. First and last, scores and dozens of episodes have occurred in our history in which Presidents have done this very thing, and have been defended by their champions with the argument that when action of this character is in defense of what international law itself recognizes as *rights of person and property*, and is not excessive, it is not an *act of war* nor a legitimate cause for warlike retort by the country suffering from it.[81] This principle was recognized, for example, by the United States itself when it condoned the action of Great Britain, in connection with the Canadian Rebellion of 1837, in invading American waters and destroying the *Caroline*, a vessel which was being employed by American sympathizers with the rebels to convey arms to them.[82] And the benefit of the same principle was accorded the United States by the Chinese Imperial Government in 1901, when it formally conceded that President McKinley's action in joining the powers in defense of the legations in Peking against the Boxers had not constituted an act of war.[83]

Furthermore, such action has received the highest judicial sanction. Thus one of the precedents relied upon by Justice Miller in the Neagle Case was the outgrowth of the bombardment in 1854 by Lieutenant Hollins of the U.S.S. *Cyane*, of Greytown, Nicaragua, in default of reparation from the local authorities for an attack by a mob on the United States Consul stationed at that place.[84] Upon his return to the United States Hollins was sued in a federal court by one Durand for the value of certain property which was alleged to have been destroyed in the bombardment.

His defense was based upon the orders of the President and Secretary of Navy, and was sustained by Justice Nelson in the following words:

"As the Executive head of the nation, the President is made the only legitimate organ of the General Government, to open and carry on correspondence or negotiations with foreign nations, in matters concerning the interests of the country or of its citizens. It is to him, also, that citizens abroad must look for protection of person and of property, and for the faithful execution of the laws existing and intended for their protection. For this purpose, the whole Executive power of the country is placed in his hands, under the Constitution, and the laws passed in pursuance thereof; and different Departments of government have been organized, through which this power may be most conveniently executed, whether by negotiation or by force—a Department of State and a Department of the Navy.

"Now, as respects the interposition of the Executive abroad, for the protection of the lives or property of the citizen, the duty must, of necessity, rest in the discretion of the President. Acts of lawless violence, or of threatened violence to the citizen or his property, cannot be anticipated and provided for; and the protection, to be effectual or of any avail, may, not unfrequently, require the most prompt and decided action. Under our system of Government, the citizen abroad is as much entitled to protection as the citizen at home. The great object and duty of Government is the protection of the lives, liberty, and property of the people composing it, whether abroad or at home; and any Government failing in the accomplishment of the object, or the performance of the duty, is not worth preserving."[85]

But is the President confined to "acts of defense"? Indeed, is the distinction between such acts and "acts of war" a sustainable one? And is the distinction between rights and "interests" sustainable —*any* interests which a President may choose to press by the use of force? The first question arose even earlier than the one just discussed. Writing in 1801 as "Lucius Crassus," Hamilton heaped scorn upon Jefferson's view that unless and until Congress formally declared war American naval vessels had the rights only of self-defense against vessels of the Bey of Tripoli. The plain meaning of the Constitution, Hamilton asserted, was

"That it is the peculiar and exclusive province of Congress, *when the nation is at peace* to change that state into a state of war; whether from calculations of policy or from provocations, or injuries received; in other words, it belongs to Congress only, *to go to war*. But when a foreign nation declares, or openly and avowedly makes war upon the United States, they are then by the very fact *already at war,* and any declaration on the part of Congress is nugatory; it is at least unnecessary."[86]

The same question came up again forty-five years later, when President Polk, in his message of May 11, 1846, wrote:

"After reiterated menaces, Mexico has passed the boundary of the United States, has invaded our territory and shed American blood upon the American soil. She has proclaimed that hostilities have commenced, and that the two nations are now at war.

"As war exists, and notwithstanding all our efforts to avoid it, exists by the act of Mexico herself, we are called upon by every consideration of duty and patriotism to vindicate with decision the honor, the rights, and the interests of our country.

"In further vindication of our rights and defense of our territory, I invoke the prompt action of Congress to recognize the existence of the war, and to place at the disposition of the Executive the means of prosecuting the war with vigor, and thus hastening the restoration of peace."[87]

When this message reached the Senate the portion of it just quoted was at once assailed by Calhoun, on the ground that "In the sense of the Constitution war could be declared only by Congress,"[88]—a contention with which Cass of Michigan joined issue in the following words:

"There can be no hostilities undertaken by a government which do not constitute a state of war. War is a fact, sir, created by an effort made by one nation to injure another. One party may make a war, though it requires two parties to make a peace. The Senator from South Carolina contends that as Congress alone have a right, by the Constitution, to declare a war, therefore there can be no war till it is thus declared. There is here a very obvious error. It is certain that Congress alone has the right to declare war. That is, there is no other authority in the United States, which, on our part, can change the relations of peace with another country into those of war. No authority but Congress can commence an aggressive war. But another country can commence a war against us without the co-operation of Congress. Another country can, at its pleasure, terminate the relations of peace with us, and substitute for these the relations of war, with their legitimate consequences. War may be commenced with or without a previous declaration. . . . All these facts prove conclusively that it is a state of hostilities that produces war, and not any formal declaration. Any other construction would lead to this practical absurdity. England, for instance, by an act of hostility or by a public declaration, announces that she is at war with us. If the view, presented by the honorable Senator from South Carolina, is correct, we are not at war with her till Congress has acted upon the subject. One party, then, is at war, while the other is at peace; or, at any rate, in this new intermediate state of hostilities, before unknown to the world. Now, sir, it is very clear that Mexico is at war with us, we at war with her. If she terminates the peaceful relations between two countries, they are terminated whether we consent or not. The new state of things thus created, does not depend upon the will of Congress. The two nations are at war, because one of them has chosen to place them both in that attitude."[89]

Sixteen years later the Cass-Hamilton argument was renewed by Richard Henry Dana in the Prize Cases, and was ratified by the Court for situations involving insurrection and actual invasion.[90] As to foreign wars, on the other hand, congressional declarations of war have always taken the form of merely recognizing a state of war begun by the hostile acts of the other party, and so have never exceeded the power which Hamilton and Dana claimed for the President acting alone.

Passing then from "rights" to "interests," the leading precedent was furnished by Tyler's action in 1844 in so disposing the naval and military forces of the United States as to protect Texas against Mexican wrath on account of the then pending treaty for the annexation of Texas to the United States. In answer to a resolution of inquiry by the Senate, Tyler defended his course as follows:

"It is due to myself that I should declare it as my opinion that the United States, having by the treaty of annexation acquired a title to Texas which requires only the action of the Senate to perfect it, no other power could be permitted to invade and by force of arms to possess itself of any portion of the territory of Texas pending your deliberations upon the treaty without placing itself in an hostile attitude to the United States and justifying the employment of any military means at our disposal to drive back the invasion."[91]

Tyler's efforts to annex Texas had their counterpart a quarter of a century later in Grant's efforts to annex Santo Domingo, and the question arose on the latter occasion as to the right of the President to protect what were termed "inchoate interests" of the United States in Santo Domingo until the final disposition of the main question. Drawing a sharp distinction between such "interests" and "rights," Grant's critics endeavored to confine existing precedents to the latter. But, notwithstanding their triumph, later events in the Caribbean, especially after 1916, went far to discredit this distinction for that particular region, where American interests have always been peculiarly sensitive.[92]

Presidents have, to be sure, performed again and again gestures of obeisance to Congress's "power to declare war." Jefferson, Madison, Jackson, Buchanan, Lincoln, Grant, McKinley, Wilson, and Franklin D. Roosevelt are all on record with words of deference, as are also several Secretaries of State.[93] Thus the late President was careful to qualify the promises of aid in his "utmost sympathy" message to France of June 14, 1940, with the warning: "These statements carry with them no implication of military commitments. Only Congress can make such commitments."[94] Three months later Mr. Roosevelt by his own unaided, unheralded act in effecting the "Fifty Destroyer Deal" converted, as it were at the blast of a trumpet, the international status of the United States as a neutral to that of a quasi belligerent in the war then raging in Europe.

The later steps by which the country passed gradually into actual "shooting" war underscore the same moral.

March 11, 1941, H.R. 1776 became the Lend-Lease Act, thereby marking congressional endorsement of the quasi-belligerent status of this country.

March 30, the Government seized sixty-five Axis-controlled ships in American ports.

April 9, the State Department entered into an executive agreement with the Danish Minister giving the United States the right to occupy Greenland during the emergency for defensive purposes. Protests by the Nazi-controlled regime at Copenhagen went unheeded.

April 10, the President proclaimed the Red Sea no longer "a combat area," thereby making it permissible under the Neutrality Act of 1939 for American ships to carry supplies to the British forces in that region.

May 15, the President appealed to the French people not to support the Vichy government, which, it charged, was collaborating with the Nazis.

May 21, the American steamer *Robin Moor* was torpedoed and shelled in the South Atlantic.

May 22, the President gave Admiral Stark, Chief of Naval Operations, "an overall limit of thirty days to prepare for an expedition to sail for and take the Azores," a project which was not, however, carried out.

May 27, the President, after declaring over the radio that the current developments of the war menaced the security of the Western Hemisphere, proclaimed an "unlimited emergency," and ordered American naval craft to "sink on sight" any foreign submarine discovered in our "defensive waters."

June 15, the President froze all previously unfrozen assets of Germany, Italy, and Axis-controlled countries.

June 20, the President sent a message to Congress denouncing the sinking of the *Robin Moor* as "piracy." The German chargé at Washington refused to transmit the message to Berlin.

July 7, the President announced to Congress that he had secured an agreement with the Icelandic government whereby the United States would take over from Great Britain the defense of that island during the emergency.

August 14, F. D. R. and Churchill announced that they had met at sea, "discussed lend-lease and other problems of common defense," and agreed upon a postwar "peace program," termed the Atlantic Charter. Thus, without consulting either the Senate or Congress, the President virtually committed the United States to a postwar alliance with Great Britain.

Meantime, though just when is not clear, the President had issued orders to the Navy to convoy supplies being sent to Great Britain under lend-lease as far as Iceland, a fact that he divulged in a message to Congress July 7, and four days later Secretary Knox confided to a Senate committee that "American warships were dropping depth charges in self-defense against Axis submarines."

September 4, Washington reported that a German submarine had fired two torpedoes in Icelandic waters at the United States destroyer *Greer,* but without effect. More than a month later the Navy Department revealed that the *Greer* had been trailing the U-boat for three and a half hours and broadcasting the latter's position when the submarine turned and attacked.

September 11, the President announced over the air that "henceforth American patrols would defend the freedom of the seas by striking first at all Axis raiders ('rattlesnakes of the Atlantic') operating within American defensive areas." Isolationists in Congress charged the President with usurping Congress's power to declare war.

October 8, shooting orders were issued to United States warships in the Atlantic to destroy any German or Italian sea or air forces encountered. Indeed, at times American vessels operated under British command.

October 17, it was announced that the American destroyer *Kearney* had been torpedoed off Iceland in what was later revealed to have been "a pitched battle" with German undersea craft.

October 27, "Navy Day," the President proclaimed that "the shooting has started."

October 30, the American destroyer *Reuben James,* engaged in convoying off Iceland, was torpedoed and sunk with the loss of about one hundred officers and men.

November 6, the President, finding the defense of Russia essential to that of the United States, pledged that country lend-lease aid to the amount of one billion dollars.

November 13, the House of Representatives, following the example set by the Senate six days earlier, voted 212 to 194 to repeal all restrictive provisions of the Neutrality Act of 1939.[95]

The story of the administration's policy with regard to Japan during these same years is of like import.[96] Throughout, the initiative was unremittingly with the President.

A summary history of the wars in which the United States has engaged since the adoption of the Constitution will concede to Congress that policies and views which were advanced within its walls were primarily responsible for two of these wars—the War of 1812 and the war with Spain. But our four great wars—all great for their results, three of them great for the effort they required of the country—were the outcome of presidential policies in the making of which Congress played a distinctly secondary role. I mean, of course, the war with Mexico, the Civil War, and our participation in World War I and World War II. "Helvidius'" contention that "Pacificus'" reading of the "executive power" clause contravened the intention of the Constitution that the war-making power should lodge with the legislative authority has been amply vindicated.

PRESIDENT VERSUS SENATE — "PERSONAL AGENTS"— "EXECUTIVE AGREEMENTS"

In the case of a document like the Constitution of the United States which lays down in distinct terms the method by which it is to be amended, a sort of scandalous interest attaches to those instances in which it has been in fact amended or even set aside by the less formal processes of life under it. The stock example of the Constitution's amendment by practice is, of course, furnished by the declension as early as 1796 of the "College of Electors" into a political side show of party marionettes.[27] But equally remarkable, though the fact has not attracted the same attention, is the transformation of the Senate's role in the conduct of foreign relations. This, too, began very early—earlier, in fact, than the transformation of the role of the "College of Electors"—but unlike the latter has been in more or less continuous process ever since.

"He [the President]," reads Article II, section 2, paragraph 2, "shall nominate, and, by and with the advice and consent of the Senate, shall appoint ambassadors, other public ministers and consuls. . . ." The earliest important controversy to arise on this language was provoked by Madison's action in appointing during a recess of the Senate the commission which negotiated for the United States the Treaty of Ghent.[98] The President's critics urged that the office to which the pretended appointment had been made, having never been authorized by Congress, did not exist, and that consequently no vacancy existed to which an appointment could be made during a recess of the Senate. The answer returned was that the office of ambassador or public minister exists by the Constitution itself whenever an international exigency arises which such office is calculated to serve, and that of such exigency the President is the sole judge; also that a vacancy *happens* during a recess of the Senate if for any reason it happens then to exist.

Subsequent developments have ratified the last of these propositions,[99] but have rejected the first though this too seems clearly to have the support of early practice and opinion under the Constitution. As I mentioned in another connection, early Congresses passed no act purporting to create any diplomatic office or rank, but merely appropriated lump sums "for the expenses of foreign intercourse" to be expended at the discretion of the President.[100] Not until March 1, 1855, in fact, was the practice that obtains today introduced. By this measure it was enacted that from a stated date the President should "by and with the advice and consent of the Senate" appoint representatives of specified grades to specified countries, which representatives must be citizens of the United States, etc.[101] Attorney General Cushing, with his accustomed zeal for executive power, endeavored to explain the act as merely a kind of notification by Congress as to the sort of diplomatic and consular representatives it would be willing to appropriate salaries for, and hence as recommendatory rather than mandatory;[102] but a series of enactments exemplified by that of August 18, 1924, are hardly susceptible of this mitigated construction. Today new posts of ministerial rank are dependent upon congressional authorization, and no new ambassadorships may be created for existing posts "unless the same shall be provided for by act of Congress"; while, in general, the entire regular diplomatic and consular establishment is organized in detail as to grades, salaries, appointments, promotions, and in part as to duties, by statute.[103]

But what the President has lost in one way he has more than made good in another. I refer to his long since conceded right to employ in the discharge of his diplomatic function so-called "special," "personal," or "secret" agents in whose designation the Senate has no voice.[104] Indeed, as was pointed out in the Senate itself in 1831, when Jackson without consulting that body sent a special commission to Turkey, a similar practice was "coeval with our existence as a nation." "All those great men," the speaker of these words continued,

"who have figured in the history of our diplomacy, began their career, and performed some of their most important services in the capacity of secret agents, with full powers. Franklin, Adams, Lee, were only commissioners; and in negotiating a treaty with the Emperor of Morocco, the selection of the secret agent was left to the Ministers appointed to make the treaty; and, accordingly, in the year 1785, Mr. Adams and Mr. Jefferson appointed Thomas Barclay, who went to Morocco and made a treaty, which was ratified by the Ministers at Paris."[105]

Under the Constitution the practice was resumed—or continued—by Washington. On February 14, 1791, the President informed the Senate that he had "employed Mr. Gouverneur Morris, who was on the spot," to confer with the British government concerning their further carrying out of the Treaty of Peace, "considering that in the possible event of a refusal of justice" on their part "we shall stand less committed should it be made to a private rather than a public person"; and four days later he reported having sent his friend Colonel David Humphreys to Madrid and Lisbon on a similar mission.[106] These precedents have since been multiplied many times, a peculiarly extreme example being President Cleveland's despatch of J. H. Blount to Hawaii in 1893. Blount was appointed while the Senate was in session, was given "paramount authority" over the American resident minister at Honolulu, and was further empowered to employ the military and naval forces of the United States if it was necessary to do so in order to protect American lives and property. Nevertheless a special committee of the Senate which was created to canvass the constitutional issue gave the President a clean bill of health.[107] For recent decades the continued vitality of the practice is sufficiently attested by the mere mention of President Wilson's *éminence grise,* Colonel House,[108] and the late Norman H. Davis, who filled the role of ambassador at large for a succession of recent administrations of both parties. And latterly President Truman has shown his strong liking for this type of diplomacy.

The convenience of employing such agents as "unofficial observers" of conditions abroad or to effect contact with communities or groups devoid of standing at international law is manifest. Manifest too is the fact that the practice, considering the dimensions which it has attained, is to be reconciled with the Constitution only by invoking the Hamiltonian conception of residual executive power. Though such agents are sometimes termed "secret," yet neither their existence nor their mission is invariably such. While they are sometimes called "private" or "personal" agents of the President, they have at times been appointed under the great seal. They have been justified as organs of negotiation and so as springing from the executive's power in negotiating treaties, yet this is also a normal function of our regular representatives. They have been considered as agents appointed for special occasions, although the term "public ministers" of the Constitution is broad enough to include all categories of diplomatic agents.[109] Theoretically, perhaps, they could not claim full diplomatic status abroad, yet when their identity is known it will in fact be accorded them.[110] Frequently, in short, the only test which is available for distinguishing this kind of agents from the other kind is to be found in the method of their appointment and in the fact that they are usually paid out of the "contingent fund."

But even more striking is the way in which, especially in recent years, presidential prerogative has sapped the Senate's role in treaty making. Paragraph 2 of section 2 of Article II reads: "He [the President] shall have power, by and with the advice and consent of the Senate, to make treaties, provided two-thirds of the Senators present concur." The significant thing about this phraseology is that it associates the President with the Senate *throughout the entire process of treaty making*. Commenting on this fact in *Federalist* 64, Jay mentions but one exception to the rule. Occasions may arise, he explains, when the initiation of a negotiation may require great secrecy and dispatch, and at such times the President must undoubtedly start the ball rolling; but otherwise all negotiations of treaties will be the joint concern of President and Senate. "Thus we see," he concludes, "that the Constitution provides that our negotiations for treaties shall have every advantage which can be derived from talents, information, integrity, and deliberate investigation on the one hand, and from secrecy and dispatch on the other." [111]

Some thirty years later Rufus King, who had been a member of the Philadelphia Convention, advanced in the Senate itself closely similar views concerning the relations of that body and the President so far as treaty making was concerned. I quote:

"In these concerns the Senate are the Constitutional and the only responsible counsellors of the President. And in this capacity the Senate may, and ought to, look into and watch over every branch of the foreign affairs of the nation; they may, therefore, at any time call for full and exact information respecting the foreign affairs, and express their opinion and advice to the President respecting the same, when, and under whatever other circumstances, they may think such advice expedient. . . .

"To make a treaty includes all the proceedings by which it is made; and the advice and consent of the Senate being necessary in the making of treaties, must necessarily be so touching the measures employed in making the same. The Constitution does not say that treaties shall be concluded, but that they shall be made, by and with the advice and consent of the Senate; none therefore can be made without such advice and consent; and the objections against the agency of the Senate in making treaties, or in advising the President to make the same, cannot be sustained, but by giving to the Constitution an interpretation different from its obvious and most salutary meaning." [112]

Indeed, even as late as 1908 Woodrow Wilson, having noted in his *Constitutional Government* that there could be little doubt that the Convention of 1787 intended that the Senate should advise the President as to appointments and treaties "in the spirit of an executive council associated with him upon terms of confidential cooperation," declared that on this premise it was still not only the President's privilege, but his best policy and plain duty to deal with the upper chamber on that footing. He thereupon added: "If he have character, modesty, devotion, and insight as well as force, he can bring the contending elements of the system together into a great and efficient body of common counsel." [113]

How far Mr. Wilson came himself from realizing this ideal eleven years later is a matter of recorded history.

The somber truth is that the conception of the Senate as a presidential council in the diplomatic field broke down the first time it was put to the test. The episode, the importance of which for American institutions and for the development of American foreign policy has been rarely if ever sufficiently appreciated, is narrated from the point of view of the Senate by Senator William Maclay of Pennsylvania in his celebrated *Journal*. I quote:[114]

"August 22d, Saturday [1789].— Senate met, and went on the Coasting bill. The doorkeeper soon told us of the arrival of the President. The President was introduced, and took our Vice-President's chair. He rose and told us bluntly that he had called on us for our advice and consent to some propositions respecting the treaty to be held with the Southern Indians. . . . Seven heads . . . were stated at the end of the paper which the Senate were to give their advice and consent to. They were so framed that this could be done by aye or no."

It speedily transpired, however, that the Senate was not inclined to stand and deliver forthwith, and presently Robert Morris, also of Pennsylvania, rose and moved that the papers communicated by the President be referred to a committee of five, a motion which was promptly seconded by another member. To continue Maclay's narrative:

"Several members grumbled some objections. Mr. Butler rose; made a lengthy speech against commitment; said we were acting as a council. No council ever committed anything. Committees were an improper mode of doing business; it threw business out of the hands of the many into the hands of the few, etc."

Maclay himself now spoke at length in favor of commitment "in a low tone of voice." "Peevishness itself," he asserts, "could not have taken offense at anything I said." Nevertheless, he continues:

". . . the President of the United States started up in a violent fret. *'This defeats every purpose of my coming here,'* were the first words that he said. He then went on that he had brought his Secretary of War with him to give every necessary information; that the Secretary knew all about the business, and yet he was delayed and could not go on with the matter. He cooled, however, by degrees. . . . He rose a second time, and said he had no objection to postponement until Monday at ten o'clock. By the looks of the Senate this seemed agreed to. A pause for some time ensued. We waited for him to withdraw. He did so with a discontented air. Had it been any other man than the man whom I wish to regard as the first character in the world, I would have said, with sullen dignity."

Maclay then adds his own interpretation of the event in these words:

"I can not now be mistaken. The President wishes to tread on the necks of the Senate. Commitment will bring the matter to discussion, at least in the committee, where he is not present. He wishes us to see with the eyes and hear with the ears of his Secretary only. The Secretary to advance the premises, the President to draw the conclusions, and to bear down our deliberations with his personal authority and presence. Form only will be left to us. This will not do with Americans. But let the matter work; it will soon cure itself."

The prophecy of these last five words has been amply verified by history. Washington went back to the Senate the following Monday for its answers to his questions, and while the ensuing colloquy seems to have moved along without any of the earlier jars, no President of the United States has since that day ever darkened the doors of the Senate for the purpose of personal consultation with it concerning the advisability of a desired negotiation.

From that time forth, in fact, the relations of President and Senate in the realm of diplomacy came rapidly to assume a close approach to their present form. The history of the famous Jay Treaty five years later is a prime illustration. The treaty was negotiated in London under instructions in the framing of which the Senate had no hand, and when it was laid before that body the latter, instead of rejecting or accepting it outright, as it would have done in dealing with a nomination to office, proceeded in effect to amend it as if it had been a legislative project; nor did the administration challenge the Senate's right to pursue this course, although the British government was at first disposed to do so.[115] In a word, the Senate's *character as an executive council was from the very beginning put, and largely by its own election, on the way to absorption into its more usual character as a legislative chamber,* and subsequent developments soon placed its decision in this respect beyond all possibility of recall.

One such development was mentioned earlier in this volume. I refer to the creation by Washington, early in 1793, of what soon came to be called "the Cabinet" out of the heads of the chief executive departments, to advise him as to the diplomatic crisis occasioned by the outbreak of war between France and Great Britain.[116] Another was Hamilton's formulation as "Pacificus" of his sweeping theory of presidential prerogative in the realm of foreign relations. Still another was the increase in the membership of the Senate between 1789 and 1795 from twenty-two to thirty-two members, thus foreshadowing a body too numerous to trust safely with some kinds of state secrets and too unwieldy for intimate consultation. Yet not until 1816 did the Senate, by setting up the standing Committee on Foreign Relations, formally recognize the realities of the situation which both its increasing size and its predominantly legislative role created;[117] and even then it still clung to the "executive session" in the consideration of treaties until the fight over the Treaty of Versailles, when this last vestige of its character as a council was ruthlessly sacrificed to its character as a chamber of unlimited debate.

In short, the Senate's role in treaty making is nowadays simply the power of saying whether a proposed treaty shall be ratified or not, the act of ratification being the President's. Its power is that of *veto*, which may be exercised outright, or conditionally upon the nonacceptance by the President or the other government or governments concerned of such amendments or reservations as it chooses to stipulate, the difference between the two being that while an amendment alters the content of the treaty itself, a reservation merely qualifies the obligations assumed thereunder by the United States.[118] There have been, it is true, occasions when the President has sought to share a specially heavy responsibility with the Senate by reverting to earlier practice, the most notable instance being Polk's successful effort in 1846 to obtain the Senate's promise in advance to ratify a convention with Great Britain for the settlement of the Oregon boundary question, thus enabling him to start his contemplated war with Mexico.[119] But such episodes only emphasize the general sway of the contrary rule. So far as practice and weight of opinion can settle the meaning of the Constitution, it is today established that the President alone has the power to negotiate treaties with foreign governments;[120] that he is free to ignore any advice tendered him by the Senate as to a negotiation; and that he is final judge of what information he shall entrust to the Senate as to our relations with other governments. More than that, however, constitutional devices today exist by which even the Senate's unquestioned power of veto can be side-stepped by a resolute President who is able to count on the support of legislative majorities in the houses for his policies.

The relevant precedents in this connection fall into three categories:[121] (1) those which have rootage in the President's powers as organ of foreign relations and as Commander-in-Chief, whereof the "executive agreement" properly so-called is the outstanding illustration; (2) those which stem for the most part from Congress's enumerated powers, although they, too, frequently assume the shape of "executive agreements" in a looser sense of the term, in consequence of a delegation of power by Congress to the President; (3) finally, there is a closely related group in which congressional action takes on all the characteristics of sovereign action.

An early instance of "treaty making" by the President without the aid or consent of either Congress or the Senate was the exchange of notes in 1817 between the British Minister Bagot and Acting Secretary of State Rush for the limitation of naval forces on the Great Lakes. Not till a year afterward was it submitted to the Senate, by which it was promptly approved. Nearly ninety years later occurred the parallel case, with appropriate deviations from the original model, of the first Roosevelt's treaty with Santo Domingo for putting the customs-houses of that bankrupt nation under American control in order to forestall an attempt by its European creditors to seize them. When the Senate failed to ratify the treaty with what he thought reasonable promptitude the President proceeded to put it into force as an "executive agreement," whereupon the Senate, following one or two face-saving gestures, capitulated.[122] And some years earlier, in 1900, President McKinley had on his own sole authority as Commander-in-Chief covenanted to contribute a land force of 5,000 men and a naval force to coöperate with similar contingents from other powers to rescue the legations in Peking from the Boxers; and a year later had, again without consulting either Congress or the Senate, accepted for the United States the Boxer Indemnity Protocol between China and the intervening powers.[123]

Writers on the subject sometimes assume that "executive agreements" are sufficiently differentiated from "treaties," in the making of which the Senate participates, whenever the former can be explained as issuing from the President's prerogative as Commander-in-Chief or his power as organ of foreign relations. But obviously this mode of reasoning ignores the essential question, which is not whether the President can constitutionally enter into executive agreements with other governments—a point universally conceded—but what *scope* these may today validly take.

It is apparent that if an executive agreement is a convenient instrument for carrying out a conceded executive power—or if an executive agreement, in the broader sense of the term, is a convenient instrument for effectuating a power of Congress, or merged powers of President and Congress—then the employment of this method of reaching an understanding with another government cannot be warrantably characterized as an "evasion" of the treaty-making power in which the Senate participates. It is true that executive agreements of both sorts are resorted to nowadays much more freely than formerly, but ordinarily this is simply from the plain necessities of the case. Even the most convinced critic of the executive-agreement device would scarcely contend that the late President ought to have gone to the Senate every time he found it desirable to arrive at a common understanding with one of our allies regarding matters of military policy. Yet if the President was not required by the Constitution to do this it was only because the subject matter of the agreement, being within his power as Commander-in-Chief, was not extruded from it by the circumstance that he was called upon, in order to exercise it most effectively, to covenant with the representatives of another government or other governments.[124]

From another angle it has been argued at times that executive agreements, in contradistinction to treaties, are not, unless they were initially authorized or have been subsequently approved by Congress, "law of the land," and hence are not noticeable by the courts. But if this was ever sound doctrine, it is no longer so in view of the explicit holding of the Court in 1937 in *United States v. Belmont.*[125] The point at issue in the Belmont Case was whether a district court of the United States was free to dismiss an action by the United States, as assignee of the Soviet government, for certain moneys which were once the property of a Russian corporation whose assets had been appropriated by the Soviet government. The Court, speaking by Justice Sutherland, held not. The President's act in recognizing the Soviet government, and the accompanying agreements, constituted, said the Justice, an international compact which the President, "as the sole organ" of international relations for the United States, was authorized to enter upon without consulting the Senate. Nor did state laws and policies make any difference in such a situation; for while the supremacy of treaties is established by the Constitution in express terms, yet the same rule holds "in the case of all international compacts and agreements from the very fact that complete power over international affairs is in the National Government and is not and cannot be subject to any curtailment or interference on the part of the several states."

Nor, again, can it be admitted on the basis of either principle or practice that, as some have contended, the *international* obligation of the United States under an executive agreement resting on presidential power alone terminates with the administration which entered into it. Conceding that the agreement was within the power of the President as the recognized constitutional organ of foreign relations, there is no reason why the nation should not be regarded as bound by it according to its plain terms just as truly as it would be by a treaty. And as for the precedents— it took the Washington Conference and at least two solemn treaties to rid us of the incubus of the Lansing-Ishii agreement of 1917; while the "Gentlemen's Agreement," first drawn in 1907, by which Japanese immigration to this country was regulated for some seventeen years, was finally put an end to only by an act of Congress. Moreover, the actual effect of an executive agreement on the foreign policy of the country, and thereby on its future welfare, may be quite as extensive as if the agreement had been a full-panoplied treaty. Thus the "Fifty Destroyer Deal," although its immediate and inducing purpose was accomplished with the end of the fighting phase of World War II, creates nonetheless a relationship between the United States and Great Britain of the nature of a regional defensive alliance which has presumably outlived the war, inasmuch as our leases of the British bases are for ninety-nine years.

We turn next to those precedents which stem primarily from Congress's powers. Some of these, as was noted above, spring immediately from a delegation of power by Congress to the President and so take the form of "executive agreements" in the broader sense of the term, outstanding illustrations being the so-called "foreign trade pacts," of which Secretary Hull was such a convinced exponent. The McKinley Tariff Act of 1890 furnished an ambiguous authorization for the earliest of this type of agreement, the constitutionality of which was attacked on the ground both that it represented a delegation of legislative power to the President and that it invaded the treaty-making power; but in the leading case of *Field v. Clark*[126] both contentions were overruled, the latter without further comment by the Court than its general observation that the challenged provision was a "necessary and proper" law for carrying Congress's power to regulate foreign commerce into effect. The precedent and supporting doctrine then established have since been gradually expanded until by the Act of 1934, which was renewed in 1937, 1940, and again in 1943, the President was authorized to lower customs rates as much as 50 per cent on imports from other countries in order to obtain equivalent concessions from them. Nor is the validity of the agreements by which such legislation is implemented longer open to serious question in view of the decisions.[127]

Yet that the same results could be obtained by treaty is certain. Indeed, in 1787 and for long afterward, that is exactly the way in which comparable results were obtained. So what this line of precedents establishes is that, *if the subject matter to be regulated falls within the powers of Congress, the latter may constitutionally authorize the President to deal with it by negotiation and agreement with other governments, the treaty-making power to the contrary notwithstanding.*

And the lesson afforded by the Act of February 9, 1922, by which a commission was created to effect agreements covering the debts owed this country by certain other governments, is the same. Since these agreements were to be laid before Congress, not before the Senate in its treaty-making capacity, Senator Walsh of Montana protested the measure as unconstitutional, a contention which Senator McCumber of North Dakota answered with the sweeping assertion that "anything done by treaty could be done by statute."[128] The fact is that on occasions like this the treaty-making power is a fifth wheel to the coach. For even had it been resorted to, the resulting agreements would still have had to receive the approval of Congress, to which the Constitution assigns the power to "dispose of property of the United States," which is what these debts undoubtedly were.

Similarly the Lend-Lease Act of March 11, 1941, was the fountainhead of the numerous Mutual Aid Agreements under which our government furnished our allies in the recent war more than forty billions worth of munitions of war and other supplies. In the case, on the other hand, of the United Nations Relief and Rehabilitation Convention, which was drawn up by a conference of United Nations representatives at Hot Springs, Virginia, in 1943, a different course was adopted. It was originally the intention of the State Department to treat the convention as an executive agreement, but protests from certain Senators against this procedure led to a series of conferences between representatives of the Department and a subcommittee of the Foreign Relations Committee. These conferences, in turn, led to a revision of the convention in certain particulars and a pledge by the subcommittee to recommend its validation by an act of Congress authorizing appropriations to carry it out, and this plan was followed.[129] It is interesting to note in passing that Senator Vandenberg, who was a member of the Senate subcommittee and approved the compromise plan just mentioned, had taken the position earlier that the convention was in every respect a treaty. In fact, the representatives of several of the signatory states signed *ad referendum* on the same assumption.[130]

But the most striking instances of the treaty-making process being superseded by the legislative process are those which have occurred in direct consequence of a breakdown of the former, either actual or prospective. Thus it was by simple congressional resolution that Texas was annexed in 1845 after the upper chamber had defeated a treaty for the same purpose. It was thus that Hawaii was annexed in 1898 after a treaty for the purpose had been blocked by a group of Cleveland Democrats; and it is altogether probable that the Philippines would have been annexed in the same manner the following year had the Senate eliminated, as it seemed likely for a time to do, the applicable provision of the

Treaty of Paris. Likewise, it was by a joint resolution that war with the Central Powers was finally terminated July 2, 1921, following the defeat of the Treaty of Versailles. Also, it was by a joint resolution, passed June 19, 1934, that Congress authorized the President to accede to Part XIII of the Treaty of Versailles, establishing the International Labor Office.[131]

And the significant thing about this third group of precedents is that they all exemplify Congress's power as the legislative organ of a nation which is sovereign at international law, *a power which is therefore measured by the external requirements of the nation.*

In a word, not only the President, but Congress too has in the course of years acquired power in the field of foreign relations at the expense of the Senate. It will be seen in the following section how certain developments in connection with our entry into the United Nations have still further strengthened the national legislative power at the expense of both Senate and President. Whether Congress is organized to maintain its advantage, whether the facts of life in the diplomatic arena make this possible is, however, still a question.

AMERICAN PARTICIPATION IN THE UNITED NATIONS

Any student of American constitutional law and theory must have been especially struck by one great difference between the reception given at Washington, and more particularly in the Senate, to the United Nations Charter and that which was extended a quarter of a century ago to the League of Nations Covenant. The Covenant instantly stirred up in many bosoms all kinds of doubts as to the constitutional competence of the treaty-making authority to put the United States into such an organization. The Charter provoked very few such reactions even in the Senate. One explanation of the difference is probably to be found in those enlarged conceptions of the constitutional powers of the National Government which are one result of the New Deal, and even more in an enlarged conception of the adaptability of the Constitution to problems of government in the modern era, all of which had been confirmed and reinforced by the developments of World War II.

Moreover, in the quarter of a century and more that had elapsed between the final defeat in the Senate of the League of Nations Covenant and the submission to that body of the United Nations Charter, the Supreme Court had on two occasions given its sanction to the most expansive views of the incompetence of the National Government in the field of foreign relations. I refer to its decision in *Missouri v. Holland,* which occurred precisely one month after the final destroying vote of the Senate on the Covenant; and the even more sweeping holding in the Curtiss-Wright Case sixteen years later.[132]

Furthermore, there can be no reasonable doubt that the Senate to which the Charter was submitted for approval was far less confident of the security of its own position in the constitutional system than was the Senate that rejected the Covenant. The Senate's triumph in 1919 was the most spectacular in its history; but indeed that was its fatal defeat. For as the years wore on and the world seemed to be getting into worse and worse shape, and the incompetence of the League to deal with the situation became more and more evident, people—who always look about for a devil to blame—began pointing the finger of reproach at the body that had so lightheartedly assumed responsibility for keeping the United States out of the League, the one great nation with a comparatively detached outlook and hence the one whose participation, it was said, was absolutely indispensable.

Finally, thanks to the expanded use of the executive-agreement device in recent decades, an alternative route into the United

Nations beckoned, provided the President and legislative majorities in the two houses concurred in favoring it. So, for one reason or another, the debate which occurred in government circles over the United Nations Charter scarcely touched upon the question of the constitutional power of the United States to enter such an arrangement, but dealt almost altogether with the constitutional problems affecting its implementation.

The principal objectives of the United Nations, as recited in Article I of the Charter, are

"To maintain international peace and security, and to that end: to take effective collective measures for the prevention and removal of threats to the peace, and for the suppression of acts of aggression or other breaches of the peace, and to bring about by peaceful means, and in conformity with the principles of justice and international law, adjustment or settlement of international disputes or situations which might lead to a breach of the peace."

The primary responsibility for realizing these ends is placed in a Security Council, consisting of eleven members, of which the United States, China, France, Great Britain, and the USSR are permanent members. Upon the occurrence of threats to international peace, of breaches of the peace, or of acts of aggression by one state upon another, it becomes the duty of the Council to make a finding of facts, and then, if peaceful measures of settlement fail, it has the further duty of deciding what coercive measures are necessary. "These may include," in the words of Article 41 of the Charter, "complete or partial interruption of economic relations and of rail, sea, air, postal, telegraphic, radio, and other means of communication, and the severance of diplomatic relations." The Charter then continues (Article 43):

"All Members of the United Nations, in order to contribute to the maintenance of international peace and security, undertake to make available to the Security Council, on its call and in accordance with a special agreement or agreements, armed forces, assistance, and facilities, including rights of passage, necessary for the purpose of maintaining international peace and security.

"Such agreement or agreements shall govern the numbers and types of forces, their degree of readiness and general location, and the nature of the facilities and assistance to be provided."

Out of these provisions three constitutional questions arose: first, by what means were they to be implemented on the part of the United States; secondly, which branch of the National Government was the American representative on the Council to speak for, the President or Congress; thirdly, which of these branches was to determine for the United States what armed forces it should put at the disposal of the Council? On the first point, there was initially a good deal of talk, especially by certain Senators, in favor of a supplementary treaty or treaties.[133] On the second point, the suggestion was advanced, on one occasion by the late President himself, that the American representative on the Council should be his own master.[134] In other words, the direction of American foreign policy was henceforth to be divided between the President and the American representative on the Security Council, with the lion's share, if United Nations proved successful, passing gradually to the latter. On the third point, three suggestions were offered: One was that the President alone should, by virtue of his power as Commander-in-Chief, determine what forces the United States should put at the disposal of the Council;[135] a second was that the matter should be determined by treaty; the third was that the question should be determined by Congress, "the war-declaring power."

By the United Nations Participation Act,[136] which President Truman approved December 20, 1945, the first question was settled, by the very fact of the enactment of the measure, in favor of Congress. The question of the constitutional status and powers of the American representative was settled by the same act in the following terms:

"The President, by and with the advice and consent of the Senate, shall appoint a representative of the United States at the seat of the United Nations who shall have the rank and status of envoy extraordinary and ambassador plenipotentiary, shall receive annual compensation of $20,000, and shall hold office at the pleasure of the President. Such representative shall represent the United States in the Security Council of the United Nations and shall perform such other functions in connection with the participation of the United States in the United Nations as the President may from time to time direct. . . .

"Nothing contained in this section shall preclude the President or the Secretary of State, at the direction of the President, from representing the United States at any meeting or session of any organ or agency of the United Nations. . . . The President shall, from time to time as occasion may require, but not less than once each year, make reports to the Congress of the activities of the United Nations and of the participation of the United States therein. He shall make current reports on decisions of the Security Council to take enforcement measures under the provisions of the Charter of the United Nations, and on the participation therein under his instructions, of the representative of the United States."

In short, the President was to retain his direction of American foreign policy.

Finally, the important question as to who should determine the extent of the American contribution in terms of military power to the United Nations is answered by the Participation Act in the following terms:

"The President is authorized to negotiate a special agreement or agreements with the Security Council which shall be subject to the approval of the Congress by appropriate Act or joint resolution, providing for the numbers and types of armed forces, their degree of readiness and general location, and the nature of facilities and assistance, including rights of passage, to be made available to the Security Council on its call for the purpose of maintaining international peace and security in accordance with article 43 of said Charter.... *Provided,* That nothing herein contained shall be construed as an authorization to the President by the Congress to make available to the Security Council for such purpose armed forces, facilities, or assistance in addition to the forces, facilities, and assistance provided for in such special agreement or agreements."

There are several significant things about this legislation. First and foremost is the fact of its having been enacted at all, for the consequence of this is that American implementation of the Charter, and hence its ultimately binding interpretation for the United States, is based *on the national legislative power,* not on the treaty-making power, nor on presidential prerogative. The second significant feature of the measure is its assertion of the right of Congress to be kept informed regarding both the activities of United Nations and American participation therein. The assertion follows logically from the premise of legislative implementation. The third feature of significance is the act's requirement that the special agreement or agreements that it authorizes the President to enter into with the Security Council respecting "the number and type of armed forces," etc., shall be submitted for approval by Congress; the authorization is strictly *ad referendum.* Finally, the act, without venturing any categorical statement regarding the extent of presidential prerogative over the armed forces, specifically withholds its approval of any suggestion that this prerogative would be an available recourse beyond the terms of the authorized agreement.

In brief, the *controlling theory of the act is that American participation in United Nations shall rest on the principle of departmental collaboration, and not on an exclusive presidential pre-*

rogative in the diplomatic field. Not only is this a sound constitutional principle in that it can claim a great deal of support from the history of the conduct of American foreign relations, especially in the period prior to the war with Mexico, it is the *only* practicable principle unless we wish to establish outright presidential dictatorship. The point is that the sort of foreign policy which present-day conditions require can never be kept going by attributing to the President, as in the past, the simple power to order the Navy around without consulting Congress. Far otherwise; Congress must be constantly asked to exercise powers which no President has ever ventured to exercise on any scale—the power to tax, to pledge the credit of the United States, to raise armies, to regulate commerce, and so forth and so forth. And if Congress cannot be persuaded to back presidential policy by bringing these powers to its support, then—the idea of a presidential *coup d'état* being dismissed—the policy fails, and that is all there is to it.[137]

But while the possibility of a presidential *coup d'état* may be counted out, two other possibilities remain, the Participation Act to the contrary notwithstanding—possibilities which have been realized in the past again and again. I refer to *faits accomplis* whereby Congress's hand may be forced and to secret executive agreements. Indeed, it would seem that as the condition of the world steadily worsens something closely akin to *faits accomplis* become almost unavoidable adjuncts of presidential direction of foreign policy. This is not because of presidential devising to that end, but because of the frightening risks which are inevitably incurred whenever our government takes a hand in, and thereby assumes a measure of responsibility for, events in Europe and the Near East—in those regions especially.[138]

How, then, is presidential direction of foreign policy to be reconciled at the present time with the degree of congressional collaboration which the Participation Act presupposes and with the democratic assumptions of such collaboration? Any answer to this question must, it seems to me, comprise the following requirements: first, the minimization of the principle of "hush-hush" in the conduct of foreign relations; secondly, the fullest disclosure on the part of the executive branch to the leadership of both parties in Congress prior to the announcement of important *démarches* in foreign policy; thirdly, a sufficiently seasonable application by the President to Congress for needed action to permit the parliamentary process to operate properly; fourth, an improved coördination between the two houses in the handling of this type of business; fifth, and last, parliamentary guarantees that when debate has ceased in either house to illuminate the issue further, it will be brought to an end, and a definite decision taken one way or the other.[139]

And the same procedures will make secret diplomacy difficult to carry on. It is, moreover, one great argument for United Nations that it affords pretty good assurance that any skeletons in the closet of this kind will be brought to light sooner or later. United Nations is a distinct asset on the side of "open covenants openly arrived at."[140]

By way of summary: The powers which under the Constitution are capable of determining the policy of the National Government toward other governments are divided. The states, to be sure, have no share in these powers—today there are no States Rights in the foreign field, and few private rights. The prime division is between the President—sometimes acting with the Senate, more often alone—and Congress, that is, the national legislative power; a secondary division is that between President and Senate.

Not only is a struggle for power in this field thus invited; in the absence of a coöperative disposition all around it is well-nigh inevitable. Nor do the applicable principles of constitutional law help much in resolving such a quarrel. By the doctrine of political questions the Court refrains from thrusting its oar into the troubled waters; by the principle of concurrent powers neither Congress nor the Senate is constitutionally concluded by anything done by the President, while he—because of his obligation to the law—*is* usually concluded by what Congress has done. Even so, if our diplomacy was to have a reasonable chance of success in the world at large it had to have unity of direction from an organ of government which was "always in session," which could act swiftly and secretly, and which commanded the widest information; and these requirements the Presidency met.

Definite clauses of the Constitution make the President the organ of communication with foreign governments; and since Hamilton's "Letters of Pacificus," written in 1793 in defense of Washington's Neutrality Proclamation, few have ever ventured to contend that when acting in this capacity the President is the mere mouthpiece of policies determined upon elsewhere. What is more, Hamilton's contention that the "executive power" clause of the Constitution embraces a prerogative in the diplomatic field which is plenary except as it is curtailed by more specific clauses of the Constitution has consistently prospered. The President today is not only the organ of communication of the United States with foreign governments—he is the *only* organ of communication herewith; and as such he is entitled to shape the foreign policies of the United States so far as he is actually able to do so within the conditions which are imposed by the acts of Congress; and more often than not Congress chooses to follow the leadership which his conspicuous advantages of position serve to confer upon him.

Moreover, it is necessary to remember that the President is not only the organ of foreign relations but also Chief Executive and Commander-in-Chief, since on the basis of these blended powers he has been able to lay claim successfully to a kind of international capacity as executive of the Law of Nations, especially when American interests abroad are menaced by other countries. He has thus come to exercise at times the war-making power without prior consultation of Congress, especially in the region of the Caribbean. What is of vastly greater importance, however, is the ability of the President simply by his day-to-day conduct of our foreign relations to create situations from which escape except by the route of war is difficult or impossible. And because of its primitive organization, executive power has an ever available capacity for putting forth new methods, new instruments of policy, in a way not open to the more complex and cumbrous agencies of government, a fact well illustrated by the expedients which were employed in carrying out prior to Pearl Harbor the policy of furnishing aid against aggressors "short of war."

And while the President's power in this field has waxed, that of his constitutional partner in treaty making has waned, recently in consequence of the expanded use of the "executive agreement" device. Nor is the President the sole beneficiary of this development—Congress too has benefited. An enlarged role for the national legislative power, which also controls the government's purse strings, is contemplated by the United Nations Participation Act. Whether this expectation will be realized depends in part, however, on whether the United Nations itself can supply a new basis for foreign policy. Unless and until it can the *fait accompli* is a serpent scotched, not killed, and the relationship between Congress and the President in the determination of our foreign policy will follow the pattern of the past.[141]

CHAPTER VI

COMMANDER–IN–CHIEF IN WARTIME

THE United States has fought three more or less "total wars." The first was the Civil War, and partly because it was a civil war, in which the President's duty to "take care that the laws be faithfully executed" was immediately involved, the principal result of the war for constitutional interpretation was a complete transformation in the President's role as Commander-in-Chief. The constitutional result, on the other hand, of our participation in World War I, thanks to the demands made upon the nation's industrial resources in support of both our forces in the field and those of our "associates," is to be seen in a vastly enlarged conception of legislative power. Finally in World War II we were confronted with a vastly enlarged replica of World War I. In consequence, all resources of constitutional power which had ever been previously uncovered were brought into requisition on a scale hitherto unparalleled, by a President who was happily free of any mistrust of power when it was wielded by himself.

But besides his power and duty to bring the energies of the nation to bear upon an enemy, the President has as Commander-in-Chief the powers of a supreme military commander in the establishment of military rule over areas found by him to be "theaters of war," in the enforcement of martial law, in the enforcement of the laws of war, and in still other respects. What scope have these powers today attained under the stimulation of modern warfare? These, too, are questions requiring to be answered.

LINCOLN AND THE "COMMANDER-IN-CHIEF" CLAUSE

The "Commander-in-Chief" clause reads: "The President shall

be the Commander-in-Chief of the Army and Navy of the United States, and of the Militia of the several States, when called into the actual service of the United States." Commenting in *Federalist* 69 on this provision, Hamilton wrote:

"In this respect his authority would be nominally the same with that of the King of Great Britain, but in substance much inferior to it. It would amount to nothing more than the supreme command and direction of the military and naval forces, as first General and Admiral of the Confederacy; while that of the British King extends to the *declaring* of war and to the *raising* and *regulating* of fleets and armies,—all which, by the Constitution under consideration, would appertain to the legislature."[1]

Rendered freely, this appears to mean that in any war in which the United States becomes involved—one presumably declared by Congress—the President will be top general and top admiral of the forces provided by Congress, so that no one can be put over him or be authorized to give him orders in the direction of the said forces. But otherwise he will have no powers that any high military or naval commander who was not also President might not have. Additional testimony as to the purely military significance originally attached to the clause is afforded by Story's statement in his *Commentaries,* written nearly half a century later, that the only objection leveled against it in the states' ratifying conventions was that "it would be dangerous to let him [the President] command in person." "The propriety," Story adds, "of admitting the President to be Commander-in-Chief, so far as to give orders and have a general superintendency, was admitted."[2]

And that the clause was still in 1850 the forgotten clause of the Constitution is shown by Chief Justice Taney's opinion in *Fleming v. Page,*[3] in which, in holding that the military occupancy of the port of Tampico in the course of the Mexican War by the order of the President did not annex that place to the United States, the Chief Justice, speaking for the unanimous Court, said:

"His [the President's] duty and his power are purely military. As commander-in-chief, he is authorized to direct the movements of the naval and military forces placed by law at his command, and to employ them in the manner he may deem most effectual to harass and conquer and subdue the enemy. He may invade the hostile country, and subject it to the sovereignty and authority of the United States. But his conquests do not enlarge the boundaries of this Union, nor extend the operation of our institutions and laws beyond the limits before assigned to them by the legislative power. . . .

"In the distribution of political power between the great departments of government, there is such a wide difference between the power conferred on the President of the United States, and the authority and sovereignty which belong to the English crown, that it would be altogether unsafe to reason from any supposed resemblance between them, either as regards conquest in war, or any other subject where the rights and powers of the executive arm of the government are brought into question."

The sudden emergence of the "Commander-in-Chief" clause as one of the most highly charged provisions of the Constitution occurred almost overnight in consequence of Lincoln's wedding it to the clause which makes it the duty of the President "to take care that the laws be faithfully executed." From these two clauses thus united Lincoln proceeded to derive what he termed the "war power," to justify the series of extraordinary measures which he took in the interval between the fall of Fort Sumter and the convening of Congress in special session on July 4, 1861. During this period of ten weeks Lincoln embodied the available state militias into a ninety days' volunteer force, called 40,000 volunteers for three years' service, added 23,000 men to the Regular Army and 18,000 to the Navy, paid out two millions from unappropriated funds in the Treasury to persons unauthorized to receive it, closed the Post Office to "treasonable correspondence," subjected passengers to and from foreign countries to new passport regulations, proclaimed a blockade of the Southern ports, suspended the writ of habeas corpus in various places, caused the arrest and military detention of persons "who were represented to him" as being engaged in or contemplating "treasonable practices"—and all this for the most part without the least statutory authorization.[4]

In his message of July 4 Lincoln expressed the opinion that his blockade declaration and his call for militia had been "strictly legal"; also the hope that Congress would "readily ratify" his enlargement of the Army and Navy, which Congress did a month later. As to his action respecting habeas corpus the President advanced two lines of reasoning. One of these, including his famous question: "Are all the laws *but one* to go unexecuted, and the Government itself go to pieces lest that one be violated?" logically implies that the President may, in an emergency thought by him to require it, partially suspend the Constitution. In the second place, he argued, the Framers could not have intended to leave the power of suspending the habeas corpus privilege solely to Congress, since that would mean "that in every case the danger should run its course until Congress could be called together, the very assembling of which might be prevented, as was intended in this case." But he was content, he added, to leave "the subject entirely to the better judgment of Congress," which by doing nothing left the President's action undisturbed and so in effect conceded his power to take it; and this inference was confirmed eighteen months later by the terms of the Act of March 3, 1863, which simply declared that "the President *is* authorized" to suspend the writ, without committing itself as to how or by whom authorized. His remaining extraordinary acts Lincoln did not report to Congress till nearly a year later, and by that time they had become history.

The secession crisis, however, was only the first, although the most urgent, of the crises with which Lincoln was called upon to deal. On August 4, 1862, confronted with an imminent break-down of voluntary recruiting, the President instituted a militia draft.[5] On September 24, in order to implement this measure and at the same time strike at the disloyalty that was rampant in certain of the Northern states, he proclaimed a nation-wide suspension of the habeas corpus privilege as to all persons "guilty of any disloyal practice" and pronounced such persons to be subject to trial and punishment by courts-martial and military commissions.[6] And meantime he had issued the first draft of his Emancipation Proclamation, in which he declared that on the following January 1 "all persons held as slaves within any State or designated part of a State, the people whereof shall then be in rebellion against the United States, shall be then, henceforth and forever free," and pledged "the Executive Government of the United States, including the military and naval authority thereof," to recognize and maintain the freedom thus conferred.[7]

What significance should we attribute to these extraordinary acts of Lincoln, undertaken in an era of *civil* war, as precedents for presidential action in relation to a national *foreign* war? The question can be answered more precisely if we group the measures in question in four categories. The first comprises those of which the domestic enemy was the immediate target, the blockade of the Southern ports and the Emancipation Proclamation being the outstanding instances.[8] While abounding in dramatic values, this category has no significance for our inquiry. Although the Court held in the Prize Cases in 1863 that the President was entitled to treat the blockaded states as enemy territory and their inhabitants as "enemies" of the United States, and thereby put them out of their constitutional rights, the holding adds nothing to the President's conceded powers as Commander-in-Chief against a *foreign* foe.[9]

The second category consists of measures which treated parts of the North itself as being in some sort a *theater of war,* the trial of civilians by military commissions affording the principal illustration. This category comes down to us seriously discredited by the decision in 1866 in the famous Milligan Case.[10] Indeed, even adopting the far more realistic opinion of the minority Justices in that case, we still find that the only power it attributes to the President to supersede the ordinary courts by military procedures is in direct connection with his power in "command of the forces and the conduct of campaigns." Any broader power of this nature, it is clearly stated, must come from Congress. And both wings of the Court were in agreement that the military commission which had tried Milligan was contrary to the Act of Congress of March 3, 1863, governing such cases.

This leaves, then, the third and fourth categories as comprising significant precedents for foreign war, those acts which were designed by the President to meet a temporary emergency until Congress had time to act, the enlargement of the Army and Navy in 1861 and the militia draft of 1862 being the principal examples; and those acts which were of like character except for the fact that the President never laid them before Congress for its sanction inasmuch as they had had their full intended effect before Congress could be consulted, the closing of the Post Office to treasonable correspondence and the paying out of two millions of unappropriated funds from the Treasury being illustrations. These two categories, taken together, *assert for the President, for the first time in our history, an initiative of indefinite scope and legislative in effect in meeting the domestic aspects of a war emergency.*

They represent a reversion for the time being to primitive conceptions of executive power.

Nor, if we are to rely upon counsel's summary of the government's argument in the Prize Cases, was this fact left to inarticulate inference at the time. The argument rested, said they,

"upon a figure of speech which is repugnant to the genius of republican institutions, and, above all, to our written Constitution. It makes the President, in some sort, the impersonation of the country, and invokes for him the power and right to use all the forces he can command to *save the life of the nation.* The principle of self-defense is asserted, and all power is claimed for the President. This is to assert that the Constitution contemplated and tacitly provided that the President should be dictator, and all constitutional government be at an end whenever he should think that 'the life of the nation' is in danger."[11]

Naturally, such highflying views did not escape contemporary challenge. In his notable *Trial of the Constitution,* published in 1862, Sidney George Fisher urged that by English law "executive power, even in its primary and essential attributes, is subjected to legislative power," and that this principle was incorporated and even expanded in the Constitution of the United States.[12] And on the floor of the Senate Charles Sumner early sounded a similar note:

"There are Senators [said Sumner] who claim these vast War Powers for the President, and deny them to Congress. The President, it is said, as Commander-in-Chief, may seize, confiscate and liberate under the Rights of War, but Congress cannot direct these things to be done. Pray, Sir, where is the limitation upon Congress? Read the text of the Constitution, and you will find its powers vast as all the requirements of war. There is nothing that may be done anywhere under the Rights of War, which may not be done by Congress. I do not mean to question the powers of the President in his sphere, or of any military commander within his department; but I claim for Congress all that belongs to any Government in the exercise of the Rights of War. . . . The government of the United States appears most completely in an Act of Congress. Therefore war is declared, armies are raised, rules concerning captures are made, and all articles of war regulating the conduct of war are established by Act of Congress. It is by Act of Congress that the War Powers are all put in motion. When once put in motion, the President must execute them. But he is only the instrument of Congress, under the Constitution."[13]

Sumner was right in contending that the prosecution of the war required the full exertion of the powers of Congress as well as those of the President. He was right, technically, in describing the President's powers as those simply of military command; so the constitutional law of the day described them even as late as the Milligan Case. He was deliberately wrong-headed in ignoring the cogent fact that Lincoln had laid hold upon vast emergency powers that were not describable in the usual terms of military command, the results of which, nevertheless, Congress had accepted, willy-nilly; and in these regards the Civil War was the prototype of both World War I and World War II.

In another respect the pattern of the Civil War was widely different from those of the two world wars. Because the former was fought at the national threshold, the President as Commander-in-Chief devoted great attention till 1864 to the war front, which, as we have seen, he regarded as embracing regions where disloyalty was rampant. For this reason, as well as because of his temperamental indifference to problems of administration, Lincoln left the leaders of Congress to take counsel respecting needed legislation from the individual members of his Cabinet whose departments were most immediately concerned, and especially from Chase and Stanton. It was thus that the two completely unprecedented measures, the Legal Tender Act of 1862 and the Draft Act of 1863, came about. The war was fought, in short, by a kind of diarchy. Only in the Act of January 31, 1862, which empowered the President, whenever "in his judgment the public safety shall require it," to take over any or all telegraph and railroad lines in the United States, together with their equipment and personnel, do we encounter a measure prophetic of the legislative phase of World War I and World War II, and a precedent for the collaboration of the two departments under presidential leadership which was an outstanding feature of those two wars on the domestic front.[14]

In short, while conventional constitutional law even as late as 1866 still described the President's power as Commander-in-Chief in Hamilton's terms in *The Federalist,* as the power simply to direct the operation of the national forces, yet the facts of the Civil War had shown conclusively that in meeting the domestic problems which a great war inevitably throws up an indefinite power must be attributed to the President to take emergency measures, even though Congress is thus confronted with irremediable *faits accomplis* and a permanent set given to policy touching matters of vital importance to the nation.

DELEGATED WAR POWER—THE TWO WORLD WARS

Prior to World War I it was customary for writers on the subject to treat war as an affair of governments, not of populations, and to draw a hard and fast line between "combatants" and "noncombatants." Both conceptions hail from the eighteenth century and are reflected in the Constitution. Even while insisting in *The Federalist* upon the unlimited character of the power of the proposed government for "the common defense," Hamilton described those powers as embracing simply "the formation, direction, and support of the National Forces."[15] Nor—unless the country was invaded—was any of these activities apt at that date to be of much concern to the great mass of citizens. Armies were still volunteer or mercenary. Supplies, when forthcoming from domestic sources, were usually purchased in the open market. Taxes were indirect. Some governmental propaganda there was no doubt, yet not on a scale demanding a name; and morale was something which pertained only to the forces in the field. The contrast which the two world wars present to this picture hardly requires elaboration. Both were struggles that came gradually to involve every energy, material and moral, of the populations concerned. They were accompanied by the most thoroughgoing social and industrial regimentation in each of the warring states; and in the endeavors put forth to this end small heed was paid to hitherto prevailing doctrines and principles which were designed to soften the impact of governmental powers on personal and property rights.

First and foremost of the constitutional problems which confronted the President and Congress in 1917 in the face of approaching war and thereafter during it was that of adapting legislative power to the needs of "total war." Congress was suddenly called upon to extend its powers to a vast new range of complex subject matter that had hitherto existed outside the national orbit, and at the same time to give its legislation a form capable of keeping it easily responsive to the ever changing requirements of a fluid war situation. The problem was solved by the delegation to the President of the broadest discretion in dealing with a broadly defined subject matter in the furtherance of objectives equally broad.

Of the multitudinous delegations of power to the President which followed our declaration of war, the most striking were those effected by the Lever Food and Fuel Control Act of August 17, 1917. These embraced the power to regulate by license the importation, manufacture, storage, mining, or distribution of necessaries; the power to requisition foods, feeds, fuels, and other necessaries; the power to purchase, store, and sell certain foods; the power to take over factories, packing houses, pipe lines, mines, or other plants, and operate the same; the power to fix a minimum price for wheat; the power to limit, regulate, or prohibit the use of food materials in the production of alcoholic beverages; the power to fix the price of coal and coke and to regulate the production, sale, and distribution thereof. Similarly, the Selective Service Act vested the President with authority to raise an army by conscription; the Espionage Act with power to declare certain exports unlawful; the Priority Shipment Act with power to determine priority in car service; the Trading with the Enemy Act with power to license trade with the enemy and his allies, and to censor all communications by mail, cable, radio, or otherwise with foreign countries. Still other statutes clothed him with authority to regulate the foreign-language press of the country, to regulate the conduct of enemy aliens resident in the country and its possessions, to take over and operate the rail and water transportation systems of the country, to take over and operate the telegraph and telephone systems, and to redistribute functions among the executive agencies of the National Government.[16]

Ordinarily the President's first step in exercise of the powers thus conferred was to redelegate them in whole or in part to a designated agent or agents, while first and last their exercise involved the issuance in the name of the President, or with his implied sanction, of a vast mass of administrative regulations outbulking many hundreds of times the statutory provisions upon which they were ultimately grounded. In its governmental aspect the war was fought by means of the administrative ordinance, or, in more recent parlance, the administrative "directive."[17]

What attitude did the Supreme Court assume toward this altogether revolutionary legislation—revolutionary both as to substance and as to method? The fact is that the Court had the opportunity to pass upon very little of it except the Selective Service Act during the period of the war; the legislation had accomplished its purpose before the formalities of appeal could be got through—something that with a little contriving would happen in any war. Still, it is satisfactory to know that sooner or later the major features of the above legislation were endorsed by the Court as to their constitutionality.

In the War Prohibition Cases[18] it was recognized that war endows Congress with an indefinite legislative competence in the promotion of "war efficiency" which is closely comparable with the power of the states at all times in the promotion of public welfare. In the Espionage Act Cases[19] it was held that freedom of speech and press may be abridged in wartime substantially at the discretion of the national legislative power. In the Selective Draft Cases[20] the power to raise armies was given previously unheard of extension, when the government was conceded the power to conscript men for service abroad.[21] In the Emergency Rent Cases[22] the "just compensation" clause of Amendment V was held to be less restrictive of governmental power in "a public exigency" and to "tide over a passing trouble" than in normal times. Nor did the Court at any time so much as hint that any of the war legislation was invalid as transgressing the maxim against delegation of legislative power.

In short, it is the lesson of these cases that in the war crucible the more general principles of constitutional law and theory, those which ordinarily govern the delegation of legislative power, the scope of national power over the ordinary life of the citizen, and the interpretation of the "due process" clause as a restraint on substantive legislative power, become highly malleable, and that even the more specific provisions of the Bill of Rights take on an unaccustomed flexibility.[23]

The contrast, therefore, between the Lincolnian "dictatorship" and the Wilsonian is not one of tenderness for customary constitutional restraints; it is one of method. The immediate basis of the former was the "Commander-in-Chief" clause and insistence upon the separation of powers principle; the immediate basis of the latter was the national legislative power and minimization of that principle. At the same time, Wilson did not by any means overlook his constitutional prerogatives as Commander-in-Chief. His creation of the Committee on Public Information, of the War Industries Board, and a War Labor Board rested exclusively on this basis, as did many of the vast powers exercised by these bodies in enforcing a so-called "voluntary censorship" of the press and in "coördinating" private industry.[24] And his action at the outbreak of the war in closing German wireless stations, and somewhat later with respect to German insurance companies and patent rights, invoked the same principle, as likewise did his subjection of all telephone, telegraph, and cable companies to regulation with respect to all messages received from or going abroad.[25] Conversely, Lincoln's "dictatorship" had been amplified by occasional delegations of power from Congress.[26]

The relation, on the other hand, of World War I to World War II as regards constitutional interpretation is that of prologue and rehearsal. In two respects, to be sure, the later struggle exceeds the pattern set by the earlier one. Not only did the vastly greater scope of the national effort in World War II throw its results for constitutional law into higher relief, but the concept of "emergency" underwent correlative enlargement. In World War I, as in the Civil War, the emergency which constitutional interpretation set itself to meet was a *war* emergency in the narrow, palpable sense.

In World War II the emergency preceded the war and has continued beyond it— a fact of special significance when it is considered in relation to the effect of wartime practices upon the constitutional law of peacetime.

No more sweeping delegation of legislative power has ever been made to an American President that that which was represented in the enactment of H. R. 1776 as the Lend-Lease Act of March 11, 1941,[27] and so occurred nearly nine months before our actual entry into a "shooting war." Indeed, the complete story commences three years earlier, when an executive order directed the Army to turn back older weapons to private contractors, who would then be free to dispose of them abroad, while replacing them with newer weapons for the Army. Nearly two years later, a liaison committee was established under the Secretary of the Treasury "to coordinate foreign military purchases with our domestic program." Then, on June 15, 1940, Public Resolution 83 was approved, which empowered the President to authorize the Secretary of War to manufacture "or otherwise procure" munitions and implements of war on behalf of any American republic, and to "sell or deliver" the same, to test and repair such armament, and to communicate any relevant information to the recipient government.[28]

At this moment occurred the fall of France, and a like fate for Great Britain seemed only a matter of weeks. The startled administration turned again to the above mentioned executive order of 1938, and through private concerns as intermediaries more than half a million Lee-Enfield rifles and large stocks of heavier guns, as well as of ammunition, soon found their way to the hard-pressed British.[29] Then on September 3 it was announced that the United States had entered into an agreement under which, in return for the lease of certain sites for naval bases in the British west Atlantic, our government had handed over to Britain fifty overage destroyers which had been recently reconditioned and recommissioned. Although the transaction was directly violative of at least two statutes and represented an exercise by the President of a power which by the Constitution is specifically assigned to Congress, it was defended by Attorney General, now Justice, Jackson as resting on the power of the President as Commander-in-Chief to "dispose" the armed forces of the United States, which was ingeniously, if not quite ingenuously, construed as the power to *"dispose of"* them!"[30]

Nor did the President ask Congress to ratify this extraordinary act as Lincoln had done when he increased the Navy in 1861; but when Congress appropriated money to build the bases the sites for which had been thus acquired, it in effect did ratify the agreement, and even more directly when it enacted the Lend-Lease Act. The "Fifty Destroyer Deal" was, moreover, only a temporary makeshift. If Britain was to remain in the war she needed many other things besides destroyers, to her acquisition of which in the United States there were two formidable legal obstacles. As a belligerent she must, under the Neutrality Act of 1939, pay for them "on the barrel head"; while as a defaulting debtor from World War I she was barred by the Johnson Act of 1934 from borrowing the needed dollars for purchases in the American market. What was to be done?

The Lend-Lease Act was designed to furnish the answer.[31] By it the President was empowered for something over two years— the measure was later twice extended—whenever he deemed it in the interest of national defense, to authorize "the Secretary of War, the Secretary of the Navy, or the head of any other department or agency of the Government" to manufacture in the government arsenals, factories, and shipyards, or "otherwise procure" to the extent which available funds made possible, "defense articles"—meaning thereby anything from butter to battleships

—and "sell, transfer title to, exchange, lease, lend, or otherwise dispose of" the same to the "government of any country whose defense the President deems vital to the defense of the United States," and on any terms that he "deems satisfactory." In brief, the act delegated to the President the power to fight wars by deputy; to all intents and purposes, it was a qualified declaration of war.[32]

Illustrative of the powers that were at presidential disposal during World War II from congressional legislation were those which were exercised principally through the War Production Board (WPB). A section of the National Defense Act of June 3, 1916, still on the statute books, already authorized the President, "in time of war or when war is imminent,"

"to place an order with any individual, firm . . . or organized manufacturing industry for such product or material as may be required, and which is of the nature and kind usually produced or capable of being produced by such individual, firm . . . or organized manufacturing industry."

The act then continues: "compliance with all such orders for products or materials shall be obligatory . . . "; and any firm failing in compliance "shall be deemed guilty of a felony. . . . "[33] The Act of March 4, 1917, extended the above powers to the procurement of "such ships and war material as the necessities of the government, to be determined by the President, may require." Coincidently the President was empowered "to modify or cancel any existing contract" for the production or purchase of ships or war material; "to require the owner or occupier of any factory" for the production of ships or war material "to place at the disposal of the United States the whole or any part of the output of such factory"; "to requisition and take over for use or operation by the government any factory, or any part thereof . . . "; all which powers were to be exercised subject to the requirements of the Fifth Amendment respecting "just compensation."[34]

Then by Section 9 of the Selective Training and Service Act of September 16, 1940, the above powers were reënacted and further reinforced by the penalty of plant seizure;[35] and meantime by the Act of June 28, 1940, it was provided, in effect, that deliveries under all contracts and orders of the Army and Navy for war equipment should, "in the discretion of the President, take priority over all deliveries for private account or export."[36] The idea thus set going was presently extended to implement Lend-Lease. By the Priorities Statute of May 31, 1941, it was enacted that the priority principle should reach, "in addition to deliveries under contracts of the Army or Navy, deliveries of material under":

"(A) contracts or orders for the Government of any country whose defense the President deems vital to the defense of the United States under the terms of the Act of March 11, 1941, entitled 'An Act to promote the defense of the United States';

"(B) contracts or orders which the President shall deem necessary or appropriate to promote the defense of the United States; and

"(C) subcontracts or suborders which the President shall deem necessary or appropriate to the fulfillment of any contract or order as specified in this section."[37]

Furthermore, the President was authorized, "whenever . . . satisfied that the fulfillment of requirements for the defense of the United States will result in a shortage in the supply of any material for defense or for private account or for export," to "allocate such material in such manner or to such extent as he shall deem necessary or appropriate in the public interest and to promote the national defense," which meant, it should be noted, "that the total demand, including defense, civilian, and export must exceed the supply," or the President might order the total available supply rationed.[38] Nor is this the whole story, for by the Second War Powers Act of March 27, 1942, authority to allocate "materials" was extended to "facilities," while disobedience of directives for carrying out the above powers, previously enjoinable, were made punishable as criminal offenses as well.[39] Yet, of all these measures, only this last one was enacted after Pearl Harbor!

Thanks, in part at least, to the intelligent and intensive campaign of education that WPB conducted among businessmen, its directives produced no important litigation requiring a judicial appraisal of the legislation recited above. With the Emergency Price Control Act of January 30, 1942,[40] it was otherwise. This act created the Office of Price Administration (OPA), headed by an Administrator to be appointed by the President with the advice and consent of the Senate, and conferred upon him authority to promulgate regulations fixing prices of commodities and rentals which "in his judgment will be duly fair and equitable and will effectuate the purposes of this Act." These were stated to be: "to stabilize prices and to prevent speculative, unwarranted, and abnormal increases in prices and rents; to eliminate and prevent profiteering, hoarding," etc.; to assure that defense appropriations are not dissipated by excessive prices; to protect persons with relatively fixed and limited incomes, consumers, wage earners from undue impairment of their standard of living," and so on.

In *Yakus v. the United States*[41] a defendant who had been convicted of violating orders of the Administrator contended that the act's declaration of purposes and the pretended limitations on the Administrator's powers were mere empty verbiage, a suggestion which the Court repelled. "The directions that the prices shall be fair and equitable," said the Chief Justice, "and that in addition they shall tend to promote the purposes of the Act ... confers no greater reach for Administrative determination than the power to fix just and reasonable rates," so often sustained by the Court. The answer is yes, often sustained, but often disallowed too. Justice Roberts dissented. "After showing," said he, "what needs no argument, that . . . [the] powers of Congress are very different from those exercised in peace, the Court then—without a sign that it realizes the great gap in the process—assumes that one of Congress's war powers is the power to transfer its legislative function to a delegate. By the same reasoning it could close this court or take away the constitutional prerogatives of the President as 'war measures.' " And, he continued, while there were references in the opinion to the war emergency, "yet the reasoning of the authorities there cited seems to indicate that the delegation would be good in peacetime in respect of peacetime administration."[42]

The sober truth is that the powers wielded by WPB in the theoretical capacity of adviser to the President, and by OPA in its own right theoretically, but actually subject to presidential control through the Director of Economic Stabilization, exceed any previous pattern of delegated legislation touching private rights directly.

PRESIDENTIAL LAWMAKING—THE WAR AGENCIES—LABOR —"INDIRECT SANCTIONS"

From delegated legislation we turn again to the "Commander-in-Chief" clause. President Wilson's invocation of the clause in World War I as enabling him to create what in effect were "offices" was dealt with previously.[43] Both before and during World War II these precedents were copied by President Roosevelt on a lavish scale. In a statement from the Executive Office of the President in April 1942, forty-two "executive agencies" were listed, of which thirty-five were of purely presidential creation. Eight of these, including the Combined Chiefs of Staff and the Combined

Raw Materials Board, were the joint creations of our own and certain other governments, out of, so far as our government was concerned, existing official personnel; nor was their role intended to be more than advisory. The remaining twenty-seven, however, were designed to operate and did operate, during their existence, on the home front, and of most of them the principal membership was nonofficial. Oldest of all was the Office for Emergency Management (OEM), which was created by an executive order dated May 25, 1940. I shall speak of it again in a moment. Others were the Board of Economic Warfare (BEW), the National Housing Agency (NHA), the National War Labor Board (NWLB, or more shortly WLB), the Office of Censorship (OC), the Office of Civilian Defense (OCD), the Office of Defense Transportation (ODT), the Office of Facts and Figures (OFF), presently absorbed into the Office of War Information (OWI), the War Production Board (WPB), which superseded the earlier Office of Production Management (OPM), the War Manpower Commission (WMC), and so on. Earlier there had been the Office of Price Administration and Civilian Supply (OPACS), but it had been replaced, as we have seen, under the Emergency Price Control Act of January 30, 1942, by OPA. Later OWI, mentioned above, was created by executive order, as was also the Office of Economic Stabilization (OES). The Office of War Mobilization and Reconversion (OWMR), the last of the war agencies to appear, was established by the War Mobilization and Reconversion Act of October 3, 1944.[44]

What was the constitutional and legal status of these various "offices," "administrations," "authorities," "committees"? In creating such an agency it was generally Mr. Roosevelt's practice to invoke his powers as "Commander-in-Chief in time of war" and the First War Powers Act. The latter reliance may be ruled out at once, both because several of the above listed agencies antedated

its enactment and also because the act does not purport to authorize the President to create new offices but only to "make such
redistribution of functions among executive agencies as he may
deem necessary."[45] That the administration was clearly aware of
these constitutional difficulties is shown by its endeavor to evade
them through the device of grouping its various creations under
the rooftree of the oldest of them, the Office of Emergency Management, which was in turn installed in the "Executive Office of
the President." The process is one that might have been dragged
out to even greater length without impairing the force of the
axiom that zero plus zero is zero still.

The question of the legal status of the presidential agencies was
dealt with judicially but once. This was in the decision, in June
1944, of the United States Court of Appeals of the District of
Columbia in a case styled *Employers Group of Motor Freight
Carriers v. NWLB*,[46] which was a suit to annul and enjoin a
"directive order" of WLB. The Court refused the injunction on
the ground that at the time when the directive was issued any
action of the Board was "informatory," "at most advisory." In
support of this view the Court quoted approvingly a statement by
the chairman of the Board itself:

"These orders are in reality mere declarations of the equities of each
industrial dispute, as determined by a tripartite body in which industry,
labor, and the public share equal responsibility; and the appeal of the
Board is to the moral obligation of employers and workers to abide by
the non-strike, no-lock-out agreement and . . . to carry out the directives
of the tribunal created under that agreement by the Commander-in-
Chief."

Nor, the Court continued, had the later War Labor Disputes Act[47]
vested WLB's "orders" with any greater authority, with the result
that they were still "judicially unenforceable and unreviewable."

Pursuing this theory, WLB was not an "office" wielding power, but a purely advisory body, such as Presidents have frequently created in the past without the aid or consent of Congress. Yet *actually* the Board generally proceeded independently of dictation from above and its "advice" was almost invariably "taken" —was not, in fact, even reviewed by the President. Indeed, this had to be the case if the Board was to realize the purpose for which it was created, which was to provide a *"tribunal"* to effect settlements of labor disputes in which the three interests, the public, management, and labor, should have equal voice.[48] And while WPB served a different purpose, it too exercised governing power which it would be purest fiction to characterize as "advisory." There were, to be sure, certain important differences between the two bodies. The powers that WLB exercised prior to the War Labor Disputes Act, being theoretically direct emanations from the President's constitutional prerogative in time of war, were not supported by legal penalties or judicial process in any way, while the powers exercised by WPB, being powers that the President had received from Congress, were supported by both legal penalties and equity process. Yet in both cases the advisory character of the agency was for the most part a sham and pretense, its *governing capacity* the substantial reality. In this respect neither board differed materially from OPA, whose head was appointed by the President with the advice and consent of the Senate and received his powers by direct delegation from Congress. Indeed, Congress itself both in its appropriation acts and in other legislation treated the presidential agencies as in all respects "offices."[49] Only Senator McKellar waged a protracted, albeit futile, war on them as "unconstitutional," and even he indicated that he could be appeased by subjecting appointments to them to Senate ratification, a requirement that would still have left them *not* "offices established by law."[50]

But the creation of "offices," while it is assigned by the Constitution to Congress, is after all an essentially *executive* function even in time of peace; indeed, under the British constitution it belongs to the Crown. Far otherwise is it with the power to govern industrial relations. If any power can be said to be *legislative* in character, it is surely this. Nevertheless, Mr. Roosevelt also laid claim to this power in the name of the "Commander-in-Chief" clause and on still vaguer grounds; nor did he wait upon our actual entry into war to assert it. On June 7, 1941, precisely six months before the Japanese descended upon Pearl Harbor, the late President, citing his proclamation thirteen days earlier of an "unlimited national emergency," issued an executive order seizing the North American Aviation plant at Inglewood, California, where, on account of a strike, production was at a standstill. Attorney General Jackson justified the seizure, the forerunner of many similar assertions of presidential prerogative, as growing out of the "duty constitutionally and inherently resting upon the President to exert his civil and military as well as his moral authority to keep the defense efforts of the United States a going concern," as well as "to obtain supplies for which Congress has appropriated money, and which it has directed the President to obtain."[51] On a like justification the Federal Shipbuilding and Dry Dock Company at Kearney, New Jersey, was taken over and operated by the Navy from August 23, 1941, to January 5, 1942, and the plant of the Air Associates, Incorporated, at Bendix, New Jersey, placed under Army control from October 30, 1941, to December 27, 1941.[52] Then from the creation of WLB on January 12, 1942, to the enactment of the War Labor Disputes Act, June 25, 1943, Mr. Roosevelt ordered the taking over of the plants of four other concerns, one of them the Brewster Aeronautical Corporation, the seizure of which was put on the ground of its "inefficient management"; another, the Toledo, Peoria and Western Railroad, which was destined to remain under the control of the Office of Defense Transportation (ODT) nearly three years and a half.[53]

Again, however, Wilsonian precedents from World War I led the way, except that Mr. Wilson confined his similar activities to the period of hostilities.[54] Also it was from Wilsonian precedents that the Roosevelt administration borrowed the idea of what have been variously termed "administrative sanctions," "indirect sanctions," or simply "sanctions." The following episode involving the Remington Arms Company of Bridgeport, Connecticut, in the fall of 1918 will serve to illustrate the subject. The narrative is by a member of President Wilson's WLB:

"After a prolonged strike and the War Labor Board had rendered a decision against the strikers they refused to return to work. The President of the United States then wrote to the strikers upholding the authority of the Board, pointing out that an appeal from it should be made through the regular channels and not by strike. He closed with the statement that if the strikers did not return to work they would be barred from any war work in Bridgeport for a year, that the United States Employment Service would not obtain positions for them elsewhere, and that the draft boards would be instructed to reject any claim for exemptions based upon their alleged usefulness in war production. This ended the strike."[55]

Indeed, according to Mr. Baruch, chairman of the War Industries Board, that agency carried the indirect sanctions idea even farther at times. Violators of its orders, "when detected, were induced or coerced into forfeiting materials or making 'voluntary' cash payments to philanthropic organizations, to the United States Treasury, etc." That is to say, forfeitures and payments that were in essence legal penalties "were imposed and acquiesced in," although, as Mr. Baruch concedes, they were utterly devoid of legal authority. They were in fact little short of blackmail.[56] In World War II the presidential agencies that were especially dependent on indirect sanctions were those which exercised the President's "prerogative" powers, in contrast to his "delegated" powers. As was indicated earlier, this was originally the situation of WLB; and it remained the situation with WMC throughout. Certain of the details are particularly instructive.[57]

The business of this agency was to bring about and maintain the most effective mobilization of the man power of the country that was available for war work after the armed services had taken their toll. Indeed, by Executive Order 9279, issued December 5, 1942, the President transferred the Selective Service System itself to WMC and thereby vested complete control of the man power of the country not yet enrolled in the armed services in Chairman McNutt. By the same order, "Each Executive department and agency" was ordered so to "utilize" its facilities, services, personnel, and powers as the chairman of WMC, "after consultation with such department or agency, determines necessary to promote compliance with . . . the policies, directions and regulations" of WMC.[58]

Two months later—on February 3, 1943, to be precise—Mr. McNutt issued his famous "work or fight" order requiring all workers designated as "non-deferrable"—that is, as nonessential —to choose between induction into the armed services and transferring to essential jobs. The order, the purpose of which was to remedy a labor scarcity in thirty-two specified areas, carried, for those subject to draft, the penalty for disobedience on the face of it. At the same time, draft requirements were significantly lowered.[59] Then on February 9 a presidential order decreed a fortyeight-hour week, for the duration, and instructed all departments and agencies to take any action within their authority which the chairman of WMC deemed necessary to effectuate the purposes of the order.[60]

A year and a half later WMC, now in control of eighty-five per cent of the working forces of the nation, decreed that henceforth all male workers in the United States were to be hired exclusively through USES (United States Employment Service), another presidential agency that acted subject to WMC's directives. To effectuate this turn of policy the support of employers was of course necessary, and this was guaranteed in a variety of ways. As the *Labor Relations Reporter* explained it, for employers who do not string along with the program, "psychological pressure" will be used at first, publicity to stir up community reaction, and then pressure from local management labor committees. In addition, they can have their power, lighting, and heat turned off and be deprived of shipping facilities and materials.

"The WMC stated [the *Reporter* continues] that government contracts might be withheld from employers found to be in willful and substantial noncompliance with the ceiling program. Since violators would have all their labor referrals and other manpower services cancelled, government procurement officers would be unable to renew or place contracts with such firms on the ground that they might be unable to manufacture the products specified for lack of available manpower."[61]

Sanctions so stringent, functioning mainly through employment ceilings and priority referrals, obviously approached the drastic character of a labor draft. If an employer had more workers than his ceiling, he was forced to give them up; if certain workers of a particular firm were needed elsewhere, the firm had to terminate their services and the workers had to transfer to the employment to which they were referred.[61a]

Two agencies there were whose orders were backed by legal sanctions, OPA and WPB. Yet OPA occasionally and WPB frequently resorted to "indirect sanctions," in the shape of "suspension orders," which, while they sent nobody to jail, were much more expeditious than criminal prosecutions, or even than suits in equity. So when a congressional committee proposed to forbid "any federal official the right to inflict or impose penalties, sanctions, or suspension orders of any kind" except as he was specifically authorized by statute to do, WPB protested vehemently. The proposal, said the Board's spokesman, "would destroy our control completely. We might as well close up the Compliance Division" of WPB; and the protest prevailed for the most part.[62] First and last, WPB issued over seven hundred suspension orders, many times the number of prosecutions that the Department of Justice undertook at its behest.[63]

The problem of accommodating indirect sanctions to the Constitution arose out of the accepted doctrine that Congress alone may enact penalties and that no one may be subjected to a penalty that was not duly enacted by Congress prior to his alleged offense.[64] Not, however, till 1944 did the Supreme Court finally become seized of the opportunity to reduce "sanctions" to some kind of constitutional regularity capable of differentiating the allowable type from straight-out administrative blackjacking. This was in the case of *Steuart and Bro., Inc. v. Bowles,*[65] in which a retail dealer in fuel oil in the District of Columbia was charged with having violated a rationing order of OPA by obtaining large quantities of oil from its supplier without surrendering ration coupons, by delivering many thousands of gallons of fuel oil without requiring ration coupons, and so on, and was prohibited by the agency from receiving oil for resale or transfer for the ensuing year. The offender conceded the validity of the rationing order in support of which the suspension order was issued, but challenged the validity of the latter as imposing a penalty that Congress had not enacted, and asked the district court to enjoin it. The court refused to do so and was sustained by the Supreme

Court in its position. Said Justice Douglas, speaking for the Court:

"Without rationing, the fuel tanks of a few would be full; the fuel tanks of many would be empty. Some localities would have plenty; communities less favorably situated would suffer. Allocation or rationing is designed to eliminate such inequalities and to treat all alike who are similarly situated. But middlemen—wholesalers and retailers—bent on defying the rationing system could raise havoc with it. . . . These middlemen are the chief if not the only conduits between the source of limited supplies and the consumers. From the viewpoint of a rationing system a middleman who distributes the product in violation and disregard of the prescribed quotas is an inefficient and wasteful conduit. . . . Certainly we could not say that the President would lack the power under this Act to take away from a wasteful factory and route to an efficient one a previous supply of material needed for the manufacture of articles of war. From the point of view of the factory owner from whom the materials were diverted the action would be harsh. . . . But in times of war the national *interest* cannot wait on individual claims to preference. . . . Yet if the President has the power to channel raw materials into the most efficient industrial units and thus save scarce materials from wastage it is difficult to see why the same principle is not applicable to the distribution of fuel oil."[66]

More briefly, indirect sanctions were constitutional when the deprivations they wrought were a reasonably implied amplification of the substantive power which they supported and were directly conservative of the interests which this power was created to protect and advance. Subjecting Mr. McNutt's "work or fight" order to this test, it does not come off well. To deprive an employer of his rights to certain priorities because he refused to pay a certain wage had no discernible tendency to forward the purposes for which the priorities system was instituted; and to send recalcitrant workers to the fighting front did not remedy the labor situation on the home front, but in the first instance actually impaired it by reducing the available stock of labor.

The fact of the matter is that Justice Douglas's language does not begin to envisage the administration's conception of permissible sanctions. By the latter the President was entitled to require any department or agency subject to presidential direction to do anything within its legal powers for the purpose of making life unpleasant for anybody who failed to obey an executive order within whose terms he fell. So when Montgomery Ward refused to write a "maintenance of membership" clause in its labor contracts as it had been ordered to do by WLB, it discovered that the United States Post Office had removed its seventy employees from the company's mail-order house, a service the Post Office had maintained for thirty years for handling parcel-post shipments to Ward's customers. Likewise, when OPA found that large numbers of dealers were violating its price "ceilings," it turned the names of more than 3,000 of the suspects over to the Bureau of Internal Revenue for an investigation into their income-tax returns. And when 16,700 rubber workers at Akron, Ohio, failed to heed an order by WLB to end a two-week-old strike, they were warned that the Goodyear Company might be released from its obligations with respect to "maintenance of membership," "check-off," "shift premium," vacations, sick leave, and the like.[67]

THE "STEWARDSHIP THEORY" IN TOTAL WAR

Presidential government on the basis of the supposed powers of the President as "Commander-in-Chief in time of war" attained its supreme exemplification in the "indirect sanction"; but the theory itself, as voiced by Mr. Roosevelt in his peremptory demand upon Congress on September 7, 1942, that it repeal forthwith a certain provision of the Emergency Price Control Act, went considerably further. I quote the salient passage from the President's remarkable address on that occasion:

"I ask the Congress to take this action by the first of October. Inaction on your part by that date will leave me with an inescapable responsibility to the people of this country to see to it that the war effort is no longer imperiled by threat of economic chaos.

"In the event that the Congress should fail to act, and act adequately, I shall accept the responsibility, and I will act.

"At the same time that fair prices are stabilized, wages can and will be stabilized also. This I will do.

"The President has the powers, under the Constitution and under Congressional acts, to take measures necessary to avert a disaster which would interfere with the winning of the war.

"I have given the most thoughtful consideration to meeting this issue without further reference to the Congress. I have determined, however, on this vital matter to consult with the Congress. . . .

"The American people can be sure that I will use my powers with a full sense of my responsibility to the Constitution and to my country. The American people can also be sure that I shall not hesitate to use every power vested in me to accomplish the defeat of our enemies in any part of the world where our own safety demands such defeat.

"When the war is won, the powers under which I act automatically revert to the people—to whom they belong."[68]

In a word, the President said to Congress: "Unless you repeal a certain statutory provision forthwith, I shall nevertheless treat it as repealed." On what grounds did Mr. Roosevelt rest his case for power of so transcendent a nature? Although he made a vague gesture toward "congressional acts," it is obvious that his principal reliance was, and could only have been, on his "powers under the Constitution"—that is to say, his conception of these. Presidents have before this in a few instances announced that they did not consider themselves constitutionally obligated by something which Congress had enacted but which, as they contended, trenched on presidential prerogatives. This, for example, was Johnson's position in 1867. But the position advanced by Mr. Roosevelt in the above quoted passage goes far beyond this, claiming as it does for the President the power and right to disregard a statutory provision which he did not venture to deny, and indeed could not possibly have denied, which Congress had complete constitutional authority to enact, and which, therefore, he was obligated by express words of the Constitution to "take care" should be "faithfully executed."

Nor did the first Roosevelt's celebrated "Stewardship Theory" of the Presidency furnish basis for the pretension advanced in the message of September 7, since it stopped short with claiming for the President the right to do anything that he thought would be in the public interest, *provided he was not prohibited by the Constitution or an act of Congress from doing it.*[69] The message of September 7 strikes this vital reservation out, at least so far as acts of Congress are concerned. The doctrine of the message answers, indeed, to John Locke's definition of "prerogative," which we had before us on an earlier page, "as the power to act according to discretion for the public good, without the prescription of the law and *sometimes even against it*"—a notion derived from Stuart practice, and one against which most of the Framers unquestionably thought they had provided by the "faithfully executed" clause.[70]

The message of September 7 can only be interpreted as a claim of power on the part of the President to suspend the Constitution in a situation deemed by him to make such a step necessary. The claim was not a totally unprecedented one, for Lincoln implied as much when in his message of July 4, 1861, he asked, with reference to his suspension of the writ of habeas corpus: "Are all the laws *but one* to go unexecuted, and the Government itself go to

pieces lest that one be violated?" But Mr. Roosevelt was proposing to set aside, not a particular clause of the Constitution, but its
most fundamental characteristic, its division of power between
Congress and President, and thereby gather into his own hands
the combined power of both. He was suggesting, if not threatening, a virtually complete suspension of the Constitution. No
doubt any candid person must admit that the circumstances of
total war may render such a measure necessary, but surely Congress, if on hand at the time, ought to be associated in so grave a
responsibility, the need for which would presumably be evident
to it also.

And certainly Mr. Roosevelt did not improve his case when he
said: "When the war is won, the powers under which I act automatically revert to the people—to whom they belong." The implication seemed to be that the President owed the transcendent
powers he was claiming to some peculiar relationship between
himself and the people—a doctrine with a strong family resemblance to the Leadership principle against which the war was
supposedly being fought.[71] A third world war—one ushered in
by an atomic bomb attack on our principal cities—might, nevertheless, vindicate even this feature of the message of September
7, or an equivalent thereof.

MARTIAL LAW, MILITARY GOVERNMENT, LAWS OF WAR

The presidential powers which we have just been considering,
while constitutionally justified as powers calculated to forward a
war effort, are nonetheless powers of *civil government,* and are
carried into effect through the civil official personnel and the civil
courts. The powers now to be dealt with are exercised subject to
direction by the President by *military men,* and are confined to
specified areas which are deemed by the President to be, for one
reason or another, virtually a *"theater of military operations."* If

we are to judge from the past, moreover, a presidential decision of this nature, while subject to judicial review after war is over, will not be disturbed by the Court so long as hostilities rage. In other words, in the making of such decisions in time of war the Commander-in-Chief is "accountable only by his own conscience."

When President Lincoln, in April 1861, suspended the writ of habeas corpus "in the vicinity of any military line" along which troops were being transported from Boston, New York, and other points to Washington, he was treating such vicinities, even though he did not say so, as theaters of military operations. Again, when he authorized the trial of Milligan in Indiana, a state which had been repeatedly threatened with invasion by Confederate forces and in which disloyalty was widespread, he was employing the same technique as counsel for government in *ex parte* Milligan were quick to recognize. Indiana, they contended, though unavailingly, had been "a seat of war."[72]

And in the late war, hardly had the Japanese planes left the skies over Pearl Harbor, December 7, 1941, when the governor of the Territory of Hawaii, invoking Section 67 of the Hawaiian Organic Act of April 30, 1900, proclaimed "martial law" throughout the Territory, action which the President confirmed two days later; and the regime of "martial law" thus set up remained in force with certain abatements from time to time till October 24, 1944.

By Section 5 of the Organic Act the Constitution of the United States is declared to "have the same effect within said Territory as elsewhere in the United States." Citing this twofold warrant the Supreme Court early in 1946 held the course of the President and the governor to have been both "illegal" and "unconstitutional."[73] The opinions which support the decision are not persuasive. As I pointed out in Chapter IV above, the conception of "martial law" on which they advance is even narrower than that set forth

by the majority of the Court in *ex parte* Milligan. At the same
time they completely ignore the primary issue presented by the
case. Martial law was not set up in Hawaii because of an existing
or anticipated breakdown in the processes of civil government
in the Islands, but because, as the attack which led to the governor's declaration of it would seem to have demonstrated with
satisfactory conclusiveness, the facts of geography and of modern
warfare rendered the Territory a theater of war. In the words of
Justice Burton, speaking for himself and Justice Frankfurter in
dissent:

"Once the Islands are visualized as a battle field under actual invasion, threatened with further invasion, and invaluable to the enemy as
a base from which to attack the continental United States, the situation
is completely changed from that of an ordinary civilian community.
Under conditions likely to disregard even the laws of civilized warfare, the island population was threatened with immediate destruction. It thus became necessary to organize and protect that population
against imminent danger from bombing, fire, disruption of water and
food supply, disease and all the other incidents of modern warfare.
The limited area, limited garrison and great isolation of the Islands
put a premium on the efficiency of its civilian defense and on the integration of it with the military defense. All activity was subordinated to
executive control as the best constitutional safeguard of the civilian as
well as the military life."[74]

"One way [the Justice later adds] to test the soundness of a decision
today that the trial of petitioner White on August 25, 1942, before a
provost court on a charge of embezzlement and the trial of petitioner
Duncan on March 2, 1944, before a similar court on a charge of mali-
ciously assaulting marine sentries were unconstitutional procedures, is
to ask ourselves whether or not on those dates, with the war against
Japan in full swing, this Court would have, or should have, granted a
writ of habeas corpus, an injunction or a writ of prohibition to release
the petitioners or otherwise to oust the provost courts of their claimed

jurisdiction. Such a test emphasizes the issue. I believe that this Court would not have been justified in granting the relief suggested at such times. Also I believe that this Court might well have found itself embarrassed had it ordered such relief and then had attempted to enforce its order in the theater of military operations, at a time when the area was under martial law and the writ of habeas corpus will still be [sic] suspended, all in accordance with the orders of the President of the United States and the Governor of Hawaii issued under their interpretation of the discretion and responsibility vested in them by the Constitution of the United States and by the Organic Act of Hawaii enacted by Congress."[75]

That this criticism of the Court's wisdom after the event was sound is strongly confirmed by the circumstance that while the Court granted certiorari in these cases on February 12, 1945, it did not get around to decide them till more than a year later. Can there be any real doubt that its hesitation was a cautionary one? The question inevitably arises whether the Court ought not to have conceded the military authorities, who were on the spot and on whose shoulders the responsibility for preventing fresh military disaster rested, at least an equal right to proceed cautiously?

But by far the most extreme exemplification of presidential power to designate a theater of military operations in furtherance of a war effort is furnished by President Roosevelt's order of February 19, 1942, which was intended to deal with the supposed danger of Japanese sabotage on the West Coast. The essential paragraphs of the document read:

"Whereas the successful prosecution of the war requires every possible protection against espionage and against sabotage to national-defense material, national-defense premises, and national-defense utilities. . . .

"Now, therefore, by virtue of the authority vested in me as President of the United States, and Commander-in-Chief of the Army and Navy,

I hereby authorize and direct the Secretary of War, and the military commanders whom he may from time to time designate, whenever he or any designated commander deems such action necessary or desirable, to prescribe military areas in such places and of such extent as he or the appropriate military commander may determine, from which any or all persons may be excluded, and with respect to which, the right of any person to enter, remain in, or leave shall be subject to whatever restrictions the Secretary of War or the appropriate military commander may impose in his discretion.

"The Secretary of War is hereby authorized to provide for residents of any such area who are excluded therefrom, such transportation, food, shelter, and other accommodations as may be necessary, in the judgment of the Secretary of War or the said military commander, and until other arrangements are made, to accomplish the purpose of this order. . . .

"I hereby further authorize and direct all executive departments, independent establishments and other Federal agencies, to assist the Secretary of War or the said military commanders in carrying out this Executive order, including the furnishing of medical aid, hospitalization, food, clothing, transportation, use of land, shelter, and other supplies, equipment, utilities, facilities and services."[76]

Before, however, anything was done by the West Coast command under this authorization, Congress, on March 21, 1942, passed a brief resolution making it a misdemeanor against the United States "to knowingly enter, remain in, or leave prescribed military areas" contrary to the orders of the Secretary of War or of the commanding officer of the area."[77] That is to say, Congress, in a dozen lines, adopted by anticipation any order which might be issued in pursuance of the order of February 19. Under this dual authorization some 112,000 Japanese residents of western states, the great majority of them native-born citizens of the United States, were removed from their homes and farms, first to temporary concentration camps, later to ten so-called "relocation centers" in the desert country of California, Arizona, Idaho, Utah, Colorado, Wyoming, and in the delta areas of Arkansas, where they were put in charge of a presidentially created civilian agency called the War Relocation Authority (WRA).

The validity of Executive Order 9066 and the supporting legislation of Congress was challenged in two cases, which were decided in June 1943 and December 1944, respectively.[78] In the earlier litigation the Court ingeniously pruned the issue immediately before it down to the right of the West Coast commander to subject citizens of Japanese ancestry to a special curfew order. Considering the order in the light of "the facts and circumstances of the particular war setting in which it was adopted," one which was still favorable to Japan, the Court unanimously sustained it as within the powers of President and Congress "acting in cooperation." In the second case, *Korematsu v. United States,* which came up a year and a half later, the Court, repeating its earlier tactic, pared down an order for detention in a particular area to one of exclusion from another, and—by a vote of 6 to 3—sustained it on the basis of the opinion in the earlier case, although in fact Japan was now in full retreat throughout the Pacific. Indeed, had the Court permitted itself the same scope in taking notice of current war developments in this case as in the earlier, or had it indulged the same measure of scepticism of official justification of our Japanese segregation policy as it later manifested of official justification of military government in Hawaii, the Korematsu Case must have been decided far otherwise. The Court's failure to do either of these things is, however, quite simply explicable. When the Korematsu Case was decided the war was still waging; when the Hawaiian Martial Law Cases were decided, fighting had ceased.[79]

We turn now to the Case of the Saboteurs,[80] which was decided by the Supreme Court at a special term called for the purpose in July 1942. The case illustrates the Commander-in-Chief's role as executive of the laws of war. Being a branch of international law, the laws of war are subject to the power of Congress to define the obligation of the United States under them, and Congress has done this in certain of the Articles of War, which also authorize the establishment of courts-martial and military commissions as agencies for enforcing them.[81]

The saboteurs were eight youths, seven Germans and one an American, who, following a course of training in sabotage in Berlin, were brought to this country in June 1942 aboard two German submarines and put ashore, one group on the Florida coast, the other on Long Island, with the idea that they would proceed forthwith to practise their art on American factories, military equipment, and installations. Making their way inland, the saboteurs were soon picked up by the FBI, some in New York, others in Chicago, and turned over to the Provost Marshall of the District of Columbia. On July 2, the President appointed a military commission to try them for violation of the laws of war, to wit: for not wearing fixed emblems to indicate their combatant status. In the midst of the trial, the accused petitioned the Supreme Court and the United States District Court for the District of Columbia for leave to bring habeas corpus proceedings.

Their argument embraced the contentions: (1) that the offense charged against them was not known to the laws of the United States; (2) that it was not one "arising in the land and naval forces"; and (3) that the tribunal trying them had not been constituted in accordance with the requirements of the Articles of War. The last contention the Court disposed of by declining to draw a line between the powers of Congress and the President in the premises, which means in effect that the latter is free to amend the Articles of War *ad libitum* in this kind of case. The other arguments, although it ultimately rejected them, the Court weighed with care on the evident assumption that the accused were entitled to the benefit of constitutional limitations. This assumption is open to rather serious challenge. These saboteurs were invaders; their penetration of the boundary of the country, projected from units of a hostile fleet, was essentially a military operation; their capture, followed by their surrender to the military arm of the government, was but a continuation of that operation. Punishment of the saboteurs was therefore within the President's power as Commander-in-Chief in the most elementary, the purely martial, sense of that power. Moreover, seven of the petitioners were enemy aliens, and so, strictly speaking, without constitutional status. Even had they been civilians properly domiciled in the United States at the outbreak of the war they would have been subject under the statutes to restraint and other disciplinary action by the President without appeal to the courts.[82]

What we have in this case, in fact, is yet another instance to which, in view of the characteristics of modern warfare, the concept of a theater of war could very properly have been applied. Later when General Yamashita's Case reached the Court it was disposed of on the proposition that the only part of the Constitution which had any relevance to it was the clause which makes the President Commander-in-Chief of the Army and Navy.[83] The case, in short, presented a situation as to which the military power of the President was recognized as being a constitutional absolute.

And the adherence of the United States to the Charter of London in August 1945, under which the Nazi leaders were brought to trial, is explicable the same way. These individuals were charged with the "crime" of instigating aggressive war, which at the time of its commission was not a crime either under international law or under the laws of the prosecuting governments.

Fortunately, the President is not in his capacity as Supreme Commander bound by the prohibition in the Constitution of ex post facto laws;[84] neither does international law forbid ex post facto laws.[85]

THE PRESIDENT AS SUPREME COMMANDER
OF THE FORCES

Certain other features of the Commander-in-Chiefship can be disposed of quite briefly. While the President usually delegates his power of supreme command over the national forces in active service, there is no constitutional reason why he should do so. At the time of the Whiskey Rebellion, Washington accompanied the forces as far as Bedford, Pennsylvania, but after reviewing them there returned to Philadelphia.[86] The early days of 1862 were signalized by orders from the White House for a general advance of the Union armies, the motivating purpose of which was to get the dilatory McClellan under motion;[87] and in the ensuing months Lincoln visited the Army of the Potomac repeatedly to advise with its commanders concerning plans of operation. Attorney General Bates contended, indeed, that "no general in chief should be selected, but that Lincoln should exercise his constitutional prerogative as Commander-in-Chief and assume personal direction of military operations."[88] However, once Grant assumed the command before Richmond the President's usually ill-advised interferences in military matters ceased; nor did President Wilson —some three thousand miles from the battle front—seek to emulate them during World War I. As a matter of fact, Mr. Wilson finally agreed to the American forces in France being placed under a command which was not subject to his ultimate control, although no doubt he could at any time have revoked his consent.[89]

As against an enemy in the field the President possesses the powers which are conceded by international law to any supreme commander, though the final interpretation of these appears theoretically to rest with Congress; as well as the power to requisition property and compel services from citizens of the United States and friendly aliens when necessity requires, thereby incurring for the United States the obligation to render adequate compensation. Actually Congress has never adopted any legislation that would seriously cramp the style of a President who was attempting to break the resistance of an enemy or seeking to assure the safety of the national forces.[90]

The President has also the power of any supreme commander to terminate hostilities by arranging an armistice, a power which has at times blended into and merged with his theoretically distinct power as the sole organ of diplomatic relations to negotiate the final peace. Thus the protocol which President McKinley authorized on August 12, 1898, with the Spanish government largely foreshadowed the ensuing Peace of Paris.[91] With a similar purpose in mind President Wilson obtained the incorporation of his Fourteen Points in the armistice which was imposed upon the Central Powers in November 1918; but this later endeavor to determine peace terms was somewhat less successful. Similarly, in the course of World War II the late President participated in a succession of conferences with the heads of state of our three principal Allies, and from these issued a series of agreements the effects of which seem likely to be felt by our diplomacy for some years to come.[92] The President was also empowered by many of the war statutes enacted during World War II in effect to repeal them by proclaiming "the end of hostilities," which President Truman did by his Proclamation of December 31, 1946.[92a]

Can the President as supreme military commander acquire territory for the United States? So far as international law is concerned the rule is generally stated to be that a conquest, to be valid, must be succeeded either by an act of cession on the part of the former sovereign of the conquered region or by continued occupancy on the part of the conquering nation, and this rule has been recognized by the Supreme Court.[93] So far as municipal law is concerned the final status of conquered territory is subject to determination by the treaty-making power or by Congress.[94] But whatever its status otherwise, recently acquired territory may be governed by the President until Congress steps in and provides a more permanent regime.[95] The Canal Zone was governed under presidential authorization for seven years, from 1905 to 1912.

Again, the President is chief executive of the rules and regulations which Congress adopts for the internal government of the land and naval forces and for their safety and welfare. Also, in the absence of conflicting legislation he has powers of his own which he may exercise for the same ends. Prior to 1830 courts-martial were convoked solely on the authority of the President as Commander-in-Chief.[96] At the outset of the Civil War, Lieber's Instructions for the Government of the Armies in the Field were promulgated on the same authority.[97] During World War I legislative provisions for the health of the forces were supplemented by executive orders.[98]

The action of the first Roosevelt in summarily dismissing on November 5, 1906, three companies of Negro soldiers for alleged disorderly behavior at Brownsville, Texas, is a further illustration of the President's residual power over the forces, and also of its limits. In the debate which developed in the Senate on the subject Senator Spooner's contention "that where Congress has failed to make rules for the discipline of the Army the power of command lodged in the President carries with it authority in him to issue an order absolutely necessary to the discipline of the Army" was not challenged. The President's critics contended only that Congress had laid down rules for such situations and that the President had violated them. Ultimately Mr. Roosevelt asked Congress to give him authority to reinstate the discharged men.[99]

One power of supreme military command the President curiously lacks—that of choosing his subordinates. Not only does Congress determine the grades to which appointments may be made and lay down the qualifications of appointees, but it has always been assumed that the Senate shares the appointing power in the case of military as well as of civil officers. Without doubt Congress could transfer the power to "the President alone," but has never done so.[100] Indeed, it has at times attempted to usurp the appointing power itself.[101]

Also, the President's power to dismiss an officer from the service, once unlimited, is today confined by statute in time of peace to dismissal "in pursuance of the sentence of a general court-martial or in mitigation thereof."[102] But the provision is not regarded by the Court as preventing the President from displacing an officer of the Army or Navy by appointing with the advice and consent of the Senate another person in his place.[103] The President's power of dismissal in time of war Congress has never attempted to limit and it remains absolute.

The war power of the United States has undergone a threefold development. In the first place, its constitutional basis has been shifted from the doctrine of delegated powers to the doctrine of inherent powers, thus guaranteeing that the full actual power of the nation is constitutionally available. In the second place, the President's power as Commander-in-Chief has been transformed from a simple power of military command to a vast reservoir of indeterminate powers in time of emergency—"an aggregate of powers," in the words of Attorney General Biddle. In the third place, the indefinite legislative powers which are claimable by Congress in wartime in consequence of the development first mentioned may today be delegated by Congress to the President to any extent, that is to say, may be merged to any extent with the indefinite powers of the Commander-in-Chief.

In other words, the principal canons of constitutional interpretation are in wartime set aside so far as concerns both the scope of national power and the capacity of the President to gather unto himself all constitutionally available powers in order the more effectively to focus them upon the task of the hour. And this is not all, for today the concept of "war" as a special type of emergency warranting the relaxation of constitutional limitations tends to spread, as it were, in both directions, so that there is not only "the war before the war," but the "war after the war." Indeed, in the economic crisis from which the New Deal may be said to have issued the nation was confronted in the opinion of the late President with "an emergency greater than war"; and in sustaining certain of the New Deal measures the Court invoked the justification of "emergency." In the final result the constitutional practices of wartime have moulded the Constitution to a greater or less extent for peacetime as well, and seem likely to do so still more pronouncedly under fresh conditions of crisis. For if we are to judge from the past, in each successive crisis the constitutional results of earlier crises reappear cumulatively and in magnified form.

CHAPTER VII

LEGISLATIVE LEADER

THE revival of presidential leadership in legislation is one phase of the revival of legislation of national scope. Sir Henry Maine's assertion that "the energy of legislatures is the prime characteristic of modern societies" is now more than three quarters of a century old, but it is only within the last sixty years that the activities of Congress have brought it notable confirmation. The Reconstruction Era was marked by an outpouring of legislation which was volcanic in volume and violence as well as in the suddenness with which it came to an end. The succeeding period was dominated by the gospel of *laissez faire,* that, except when it has favors to confer, government had best refrain from meddling in the economic field—doctrine which was reinforced in the case of the National Government by a rigidly conceptualistic constitutional law.

But gradually a new point of view emerged, the increasing influence of which appears especially in the history of congressional legislation touching interstate commerce. I quote from Professor Ribble's volume on *State and National Power Over Commerce.*

"Before 1887 there were but few statutes of material importance regulating the conduct of the inland commerce of the United States. Such statutes as existed dealt chiefly with bridges, the improvement of rivers and harbors, and general admiralty regulations. . . .

"This record is in sharp contrast with Congressional activity in succeeding years. To show an awakened Congress, it is sufficient to recite some of the more important statutes following the Interstate Commerce Act of 1887. Thus mention may be made of the following pieces of federal legislation dealing with commerce; Labor Arbitration Act

---

The Notes to this chapter begin on page four hundred ninety-seven

of 1888; Sherman Anti-Trust Act of 1890; Federal Safety Appliance Acts, beginning with that of 1893; Erdman Act of 1898; Elkins Act of 1903; Federal Employers' Liability Law of 1906; Hepburn Act of 1906; Federal Hours of Labor Law of 1907; Federal Employers' Liability Act of 1908; Mann-Elkins Act of 1910; Panama Canal Act of 1912; Newlands Act of 1913; Cotton Futures Act of 1914; Federal Trade Commission Act of 1914; Clayton Act of 1914; Adamson Act of 1916; the Transportation Act of 1920; Packers and Stockyards Act of 1921; Grain Futures Act of 1922; Air Commerce Act of 1926; Railway Labor Act of 1926; Radio Act of 1927; Longshoremen's and Harbor Workers' Compensation Act of 1927; Hawes-Cooper Act, 1929; Perishable Agricultural Commodities Act of 1930; Emergency Railroad Transportation Act of 1933; Agricultural Adjustment Act of 1933; National Industrial Recovery Act, 1933; Communications Act of 1934; Cotton Marketing Act of 1934; Act of 1934, prohibiting the moving in interstate commerce after the commission of certain specified crimes; National Stolen Property Act of 1934; Securities Exchange Act of 1934; National Labor Relations Act of 1935; Interstate Transportation of Petroleum Act of 1935; the Guffey-Snyder Coal Act of 1935; the Railroad Reorganization Act of 1935."[1]

This list was compiled in 1937. Today, without sticking too closely to the "commerce" clause, I should wish to add mention of the act establishing TVA in 1933, the Social Security Act of 1935, the Agricultural Adjustment Act of 1938, and the Fair Labor Standards Act of the latter year, to say nothing of the host of emergency acts which the great international crises leading to and involving our participation in the two world wars evoked.

The nationalization of American industry, the necessity of curbing monopolistic practices resulting from this development, the conservation movement of the first Roosevelt, the rise and consolidation of the labor movement, the altered outlook upon the proper scope of governmental function which the Great Depression produced, and finally two great wars and their aftermath have all conspired to thrust into the foreground of our constitutional system the dual role of the President as catalyst of public opinion and as legislative leader.

THE CONSTITUTIONAL BASIS AND *MODUS OPERANDI* OF PRESIDENTIAL LEADERSHIP — FROM ROOSEVELT I TO ROOSEVELT II

The formal taking-off ground of presidential leadership in legislation is furnished by the opening clause of Article II, section 3, of the Constitution: "He shall from time to time give to the Congress information of the state of the Union, and recommend to their consideration such measures as he shall judge necessary and expedient. . . ."[2] Although this language imposes a *duty* rather than confers a *power,* Presidents are apt to be like other people who feel they have a duty to perform; they can make themselves extremely importunate at times. Is there any constitutional reason why they should not do so in the present instance? Many people, including several Presidents, have argued at times that there is an excellent reason; namely, that the Constitution vests the legislative power in *Congress,* and that therefore performance by the President of the above duty ought to stop well short of invading Congress's "autonomy," an argument usually bolstered by an invocation of the principle of the separation of powers.

The relations of earlier Presidents with Congress were treated sufficiently for our purposes in Chapter I of this volume.[3] The present-day role of the President as policy determiner in the legislative field is largely the creation of the two Roosevelts and Woodrow Wilson, each of whom came to the Presidency following a notable and successful experience as governor of his home state. Discussing his governorship of New York in his *Autobiography,* the first Roosevelt remarks:

"In theory the Executive has nothing to do with legislation. In practice as things now are, the Executive is or ought to be peculiarly representative of the people as a whole. As often as not the action of the Executive offers the only means by which the people can get the legislation they demand and ought to have. Therefore a good executive under the present conditions of American political life must take a very active interest in getting the right kind of legislation, in addition to performing his executive duties with an eye single to the public welfare."[4]

As these words indicate, Roosevelt I's approach to the problem of executive leadership, while positive, was otherwise Jacksonian rather than Jeffersonian; but he enjoyed advantages which were not available to his predecessor, certainly not in the same measure. One of these was a quite personal gift. No more convinced preacher of the platitudes, none more adept at translating his preferences into moralistic axioms and attitudes, ever attained the Presidency. In his own words, "The White House is a bully pulpit"; and not only the White House, but the country-wide press as well. Not only had "T. R." access to the news columns of those hundreds of papers which supported him editorially, but also of those other hundreds which opposed him editorially. In part this was the result of clever contriving. The Sunday news release, it was early found, was always sure of making the first page in Monday's otherwise usually drab issue.[5] More largely it was the general result of good all-round showmanship. What "T. R." did was always interesting, or at least the correspondents came to think it was.[6]

The difficulties which Roosevelt I encountered in building up the legislative role of the President were, nevertheless, formidable. Foremost of these was the internal organization of the houses of Congress. The committee system was vastly more extended and more closely knit than in Jackson's time, and its governing principle was that of seniority. So, although Congress was in the hands of Roosevelt's own party, its immediate direction was in the hands of the older and more conservative members thereof, men who on the score of experience alone were disposed to regard the temporary occupant of the White House with a certain condescension. And aggravating this situation were the defects of "T. R.'s" personal qualities of combative assertiveness, impulsiveness, and habit of drastic criticism of any who opposed his purposes at the moment.[7] Commenting in his *Autobiography* on his relations with the principal congressional leaders of the period —Senators Aldrich and Hale and Speaker Cannon—Roosevelt wrote:

"I made a resolute effort to get on with all three and with their followers, and I have no question that they made an equally resolute effort to get on with me. We succeeded in working together, although with increasing friction, for some years, I pushing forward and they hanging back. Gradually, however, I was forced to abandon the effort to persuade them to come my way, and then I achieved results only by appealing over the heads of the Senate and House leaders to the people, who were the masters of both of us."[8]

These words are at once an avowal and a confession. For while resort to Jacksonian methods undoubtedly suited Roosevelt's boisterous temperament, yet the drawbacks to such methods are serious. As Dr. Small puts it:

"Unless an Executive be willing to jeopardize his chances of securing the adoption of his remaining recommendations, it is inadvisable to risk an appeal on a single issue; for though he may be successful in his attempt, his conduct is likely to rekindle even more intensely a spirit of resentment in Congress and to confirm it in its resolve to combat his leadership. Moreover, if the public fail to honor his petition . . . the President has thus by his own hand prematurely terminated his ascendancy. . . . An harmonious cooperation between Executive and Legislature in which the former aspires to the role of an uncompromising leader is unusually [usually ?] tenuous; and, when congressional leaders subsequently rebel against the abridgment of their freedom of discretion, the President has no alternative other than to revert to certain threats of coercion in order to achieve the acceptance of his program."⁹

While written with Wilson's abortive appeal in October 1918 for a Democratic Congress in mind, these words are more appropriately applicable to the closing chapter of "T. R.'s" dealings with Congress. They are also descriptive of more recent happenings.¹⁰

Although destined to be cast somewhat in the shade by subsequent achievements in the same field, the first Roosevelt's legislative performance was notable; while his contributions to the technique of presidential leadership were not only contemporaneously impressive but durable. Detailing the "arts of management" by which "Roosevelt, Taft and Wilson," Roosevelt leading the way, "pushed their suggestions to a legislative conclusion," Professor Finer writes:

"They sent messages to the Houses, and letters to party friends; held conferences and breakfasts in their room adjoining the Senate, and invited the Chairmen of Committees and the 'floor leaders' to the White House. Their most trusted and astute Cabinet officers were often sent to the Congressional lobbies to whip up support, and to exert the influence of personal representation of the President. Heads of departments attended caucus meetings; information was poured into Congress; party friends were provided with drafts of bills and the vindicating briefs."¹¹

It is the last of these devices which is of special interest from the constitutional point of view. Bills were not yet sent openly from the White House to the Capitol in those days, but Mr. Roosevelt's congressional spokesmen nevertheless admitted the practice occasionally. Said Senator Dolliver of Iowa at the time when the Senate was debating the Hepburn bill for amending the Interstate Commerce Act: "There are at least five acts of legislation, all of them referring to this and similar questions, that were put through both Houses of Congress in the last five years practically without change, as they came from the office of the Attorney General of the United States"; and a few weeks later it was admitted on the floor of the House that the then pending Pure Food and Drug bill was of similar provenience.[12]

One trick "T.R." missed, probably to his own considerable chagrin later. He retained the outworn and overgrown "annual message," even greatly distending it. It is true that he made the message a vehicle to Congress and the country of his legislative demands in a way not previously surpassed. Yet interlarded in a scissors and paste compilation from departmental reports which ran at times to nearly thirty thousand words, these naturally failed of full effectiveness. Woodrow Wilson was to demonstrate how much better the thing could be done.

Adding his observation of Roosevelt's successes and failures to his studies of British constitutional practice, Wilson had conceived the idea by 1908 that it was possible to remodel the Presidency somewhat after the pattern of the British Premiership.[13] For the first time in its history the United States had a President who knew something about the functioning of political institutions abroad, and who had the intellect and skill to apply his knowledge to the stimulation and enrichment of the political process in this country. A Jeffersonian in his acceptance of the legislative power as the supreme directing power in a popular government, Wilson rejected unconditionally Jefferson's conception of the separation of powers doctrine, and boldly proclaimed his constitutional right and duty as executive to guide the legislative process. The similar pretensions of Roosevelt I were divested of their accidental association with the latter's picturesque traits of personality and endowed with the authority of constitutional principle.

Nor was this the only advantage which "the Schoolmaster

President" enjoyed over his more "practical" forerunner. For one thing Wilson's party had been out of power for two decades. Consequently he was not compelled as Roosevelt had been to combat 'or else come to terms with an experienced and sophisticated leadership in the houses of Congress. On the contrary, Wilson's party associates were almost naïvely ready to concede his intellectual eminence, just as Jefferson's had been more than a century earlier. Best of all, Wilson had the inspiration to dramatize his conception of legislative leadership in a fashion which henceforth put all potential critics of it on the defensive.

This noteworthy event in the history of American governmental usages occurred on April 8, 1913, when the new President appeared before a special session of the 63rd Congress to demand a new tariff act. A memorable passage of his address on this occasion reads:

"I am very glad indeed to have this opportunity to address the two houses directly, and to verify for myself the impression that the president of the United States is a person, not a mere department of the government hailing Congress from some isolated island of jealous power, sending messages, and not speaking naturally and with his own voice, that he is a human being trying to coöperate with other human beings in a common service. After this first experience I shall feel quite normal in all our dealings with one another."[14]

On June 23 Wilson appeared a second time before the special session to urge it to attack the problem of currency reform. The closing words of this address too are noteworthy for their statement of Wilson's President-Prime Minister conception: "I have come to you as the head of the government and the responsible leader of the party in power to urge action now, while there is time to serve the country deliberately, and as we should, in a clear air of common counsel." The measure which was finally passed in response to this call to duty, the Federal Reserve Act of December 23, 1913, was largely drafted in conferences at the White House between the President and representatives of all shades of opinion, some quite sharply antagonistic to Mr. Wilson's views.[15] It was then ratified by the Democratic caucus, and so made an obligatory party measure. Its later progress through Congress was greatly aided by Mr. Bryan, whom Mr. Wilson had made a member of his Cabinet with just such services in contemplation.

When the European war loomed on the horizon in the summer of 1914 Mr. Wilson is reported to have remarked that it would be "the irony of fate" if his energies as President were to be diverted to problems of foreign relationship, whereas his training had been intended for a very different purpose. In point of fact, not only did the legislative output of Congress during the ensuing two years continue to testify to his strong guidance of its activities, but our own entrance into war in 1917 enabled him to rivet the principle of presidential leadership to the working Constitution of the United States in a way that the demands of domestic reform could hardly have done at that date.

The clash with the Senate mentioned on an earlier page, shortly before our entrance into World War I, over the question of arming American merchant vessels, afforded the President an opportunity to display to Congress the advantage over that body that would be his during a war emergency. For having failed to get Congress's consent to the proposed step, he took it anyway, in exercise, as he declared, of his "constitutional powers and duties." At the same time he denounced "the Senate of the United States" as "the only legislative body in the world which cannot act when the majority is ready for action." He continued:

"... A little group of willful men, representing no opinion but their own, have rendered the great Government of the United States helpless and contemptible.

"The remedy? There is but one remedy. The only remedy is that the rules of the Senate shall be so altered that it can act. The country can be relied upon to draw the moral. I believe that the Senate can be relied on to supply the means of action and save the country from disaster."[16]

Early in the first session of the 65th Congress the Senate for the first time in its history adopted a cloture rule—not a tremendously effective one, but still a rule.

Most, if not all, of the principal war statutes, from the Selective Service Act of June 5, 1917, to the Overman Act which, after being before the Senate eighty-three days, was finally passed by that body April 29, 1918, were drafted in the first instance—at times none too skillfully—in an executive department, and a head of department was generally told off to facilitate the passage of the bill through the purifying flames of the congressional purgatory.[17] From the very nature of the case, moreover, the houses were compelled to devote a goodly portion of their working hours and energies to the consideration of "administration measures," as they were termed. The situation was summed up at the time by a writer in *The New Republic* in these words:

"The private individual of Congress is dead, and it is surely important that there is none to sing his requiem. The traditional separation of powers has broken down for the simple reason that it results only in confounding them. Congress may delay presidential action; but there is evidence enough, even apart from the fact of war, that it is finding it increasingly difficult ultimately to thwart it. For congressional debate has largely ceased to influence the character of public opinion.... Nor is the individual member of Congress alone in his eclipse. The congressional committees have become less the moulders of legislation than the recipients who may alter its details. Even on the committees themselves the administration now has its avowed spokesmen. They seem to act very much as a British minister in charge of a measure in the House of Commons. They interpret the executive will; and we have seen recalcitrant members interviewed on policy by the President himself. The key to the whole, in fact, has come to lie in the President's hands. The pathway of decision is his own, influenced above all by his personal cast of mind and by the few who can obtain direct access to him. This is not, it is clear, the government envisaged by the Constitution. Equally certain it is not a government which meets with the approval of Congress. But outside of Washington, the old suspicion of executive power is dead, and popular sentiment has become so entirely uninterested in the processes of politics as to ask only for substantial results. In such an aspect, executive action is far more valuably dramatic than the action of Congress."[18]

The picture is somewhat exaggerated; but the thing itself was exaggerated by all previous standards, and the war being ended, some degree of reaction to earlier, conventional views of the relations of President and Congress was to be expected. The really surprising thing is that the reaction was so slight. Candidate Harding announced that while as President he would recommend a program, as the Constitution required him to do, legislation would be the work of Congress; but there is good reason to believe that he later regretted the promise thus implied. His ultimate failure to lead was apparently due much less to lack of willingness than of will. Although to Mr. Coolidge's ingrained conservatism legislation was in itself thoroughly distasteful, he nevertheless asserted it to be "the business of the President as party leader to do the best he can to see that the declared party platform purposes are translated into legislative and administrative action." Mr. Hoover was rather less articulate regarding his views on the subject, but according to Mr. Luce, an excellent authority, "he sent drafts of several important proposals to the Capitol to be introduced by leaders."[19] And thanks to his inaction at the time of framing the Hawley-Smoot Tariff, he had in retrospect the doubtful satisfaction of being responsible for that egregious exemplification of the gospel of hands-off.[20]

ROOSEVELT II AND CONGRESS—THE LAW OF EBB AND FLOW

While President Franklin D. Roosevelt's accomplishment as legislator first and last surpassed all previous records, yet the story of it, so far as it is of interest to us, offers little of novelty. Old techniques were sharpened and improved, sometimes with the aid of modern gadgets—radio, for instance—and there are certain lessons for the future which the record underlines. But for the most part, except for the dimensions which the familiar sometimes attains, the pleasure afforded by its study is that of recognition rather than of surprise.

First of all we perceive again the immense reinforcement which recognized "emergency" is capable of bringing to presidential leadership in this field of power as well as in others. For confronted with such a condition, Congress feels at once the need for action and its inability to plan the action needed; so it turns to the President. Contrariwise, once the pressure for action lessens, congressional docility speedily evaporates. Casting a backward glance in his first annual address to Congress upon the remarkable performance of the 73rd Congress in its first session, Mr. Roosevelt said:

"A final personal word. I know that each of you will appreciate that I am speaking no mere politeness when I assure you how much I value the fine relationship that we have shared during these months of hard and incessant work. Out of these friendly contacts we are, fortunately, building a strong and permanent tie between the legislative and executive branches of the Government. The letter of the Constitution wisely declared a separation, but the impulse of common purpose declares a union. In this spirit we join once more in serving the American people."[21]

In point of fact, the "strong and permanent tie" revealed even then to close observation several signs of fraying, and these rapidly became more generally evident.

Secondly, the late President's experience illustrates once more the aid which a President can derive from an active and widespread popular understanding of an announced program and from interest in his political good fortunes, a fact of which from the first he evinced constant awareness both in utterance and in practice. Within a few days of his first election Mr. Roosevelt took occasion to formulate his conception of the Presidency at some length. He said:

"The Presidency is not merely an administrative office. That is the least of it. It is pre-eminently a place of moral leadership.

"All of our great Presidents were leaders of thought at times when certain historic ideas in the life of the nation had to be clarified. Washington personified the idea of Federal Union. Jefferson practically originated the party system as we know it by opposing the democratic theory to the republicanism of Hamilton. This theory was reaffirmed by Jackson.

"Two great principles of our government were forever put beyond question by Lincoln. Cleveland, coming into office following an era of great political corruption, typified rugged honesty. Theodore Roosevelt and Wilson were both moral leaders, each in his own way and for his own time, who used the Presidency as a pulpit.

"That is what the office is—a superb opportunity for reapplying, applying to new conditions, the simple rules of human conduct to which we always go back. Without leadership alert and sensitive to change, we are bogged up or lose our way."[22]

Aside from the anachronistic attempt to foist upon Jefferson a preference for the word "democratic" over "republican" as descriptive of his creed,[23] there is little of originality here—indeed, except for the complimentary references to Jefferson and Wilson, one might easily parallel the passage from the writings of Roosevelt I. The late President's assiduity in reducing his philosophy to practical form has, however, never been surpassed. "T.R." traveled widely, but not nearly so widely as his relative, who by the time of his reëlection in November 1936 had journeyed nearly 83,000 miles by train, and undetermined thousands by automobile, and had visited all but three states of the Union.[24] "T.R.'s" relations with the press were excellent, but the press was not yet represented at Washington on its later scale, nor was the newspaper "columnist" the power in the land he has in recent years become. By his liberal employment of "off the record" remarks, "F.D.R." flattered the newspaperman's sense of honor, while by handing out "background information" he guaranteed the semi-weekly "story" that spelt for the latter butter and jam for his daily bread; and by both devices he assured publicity for an intelligent, if not always sympathetic, version of presidential policies.[25] Nor did Mr. Roosevelt's suavity, genial and impenetrable, often desert him in his conferences with the press's representatives until toward the end of his second term, when he suddenly developed considerable sensitiveness to being quizzed as to his intentions about running again; and whereas "T.R.'s" famous Ananias Club came finally to be the best "covered" organization in the country, "F.D.R." appears to have found it necessary to resort to the "short and ugly" only once.[26] And in the radio Mr. Roosevelt possessed an instrument that enabled him to bring his views to the immediate attention of millions of voters and to invite their response, which, as registered in the suddenly mounting White House mail, soon became prodigious.[27]

In the third place, however, before the dispersed energies of popular support can generate legislative current they must, of course, be adjusted to the organization and procedures of Congress. In the endeavor to accomplish this Mr. Roosevelt relied on the well-timed special message.[28] To the 73rd Congress nearly thirty such communications went; to the 74th about half that number; to the 75th something like seventy and during the war years the same tactic was continued. Some of these communications merely drew attention in general terms to the need for legislation on a particular subject; others contained specific recommendations as to the content of the needed legislation; a few were accompanied by draft bills to which Congress's attention was definitely directed; the "economy message" of March 9, 1933, the message of March 16 of the same year which led to the first AAA, the message of May 17 which led to the NRA, and—later—the Court Reform message of February 5, 1937, all belonged to this category, as did also the famous "H.R. 1776," which became in due course the Lend-Lease Act. But other important measures, especially during Mr. Roosevelt's first term, were also modeled in the first instance by administration draftsmen—the act establishing TVA, the hard-fought Holding Company Act, and the Social Security Act being outstanding illustrations. And more formal communications were frequently followed by letters to committee chairmen or even to private members.[29]

In the fourth place, Mr. Roosevelt's experience underscores a lesson to be drawn also from that of the first Roosevelt and of Woodrow Wilson, that presidential leadership is subject to a law of ebb and flow, or, as Professor Laski suggests, a "law of honeymoon." The remarkable achievement of the 73rd Congress bespoke almost continuous presidential stimulation and direction and equally continuous congressional response. The first session of the 74th Congress, on the other hand, convened amid cries of "dictatorship" and some of the most raucous voices were of Mr. Roosevelt's own party. The principal policy-making legislation of the session comprised the Wagner National Labor Relations Act and the Social Security Act. While the former, named for its author, represented legislative initiative and presidential sponsorship, the latter was largely the handiwork of the President's own Committee on Economic Security, consisting of the Secretaries of the Treasury, Agriculture, and Labor, the Attorney General, and the Federal Emergency Relief Administrator. Although there were times in the course of the session when it was predicted that the President's leadership had been broken, the final outcome refuted the Cassandras.[30]

On its face the election of 1936 was a tremendous endorsement of the New Deal and so of the methods of leadership by which it had been set up. ("Who wishes the end wishes the means.") The opening session of the 75th Congress witnessed nevertheless a definite crisis in the President's relations with that body, one largely of Mr. Roosevelt's own creation. For whatever else may be said of his startling and practically unheralded Court Reform message, it produced at a single stroke a serious cleavage in both his popular and his party support, and in so doing afforded his congressional critics a powerful handle for their accumulated discontents. Although special messages were never showered upon Congress more lavishly, the legislative product of the 75th Congress was chiefly by way of repairing the breaches which successive Supreme Court decisions had made in the New Deal; and final adjournment was followed by an attempt by the President, which proved unrewarding for the most part, to "purge" Congress of certain nonresponsive members of the Democratic party. The 76th Congress, with an increased representation of the Republican opposition, speedily disclosed a renewed independence on its part, which was evidenced in its first session by the enactment, despite many covert frowns from administration circles, of the first Hatch Act for the political sterilization of federal officeholders, by its drastic curtailment of the President's proposals for administrative reorganization, and by the refusal of the Senate Foreign Relations Committee to report out a presidentially sponsored measure to modify the Neutrality Act.

The first session of the 76th Congress marked, in fact, the low point up to that time of "F.D.R.'s" hold on Congress. But with Hitler's invasion of Poland the ebb in the President's influence with the legislative branch began to slacken; and following the fall of France, the bombing of London in the summer and autumn of 1940, and the November election, it was sharply reversed. The enactment of Lend-Lease in March 1941 advertised the new situation, which was nine months later brought to culmination by the Japanese attack on Pearl Harbor. But once again there came a recession in presidential influence, even in the midst of war. In April 1943 Congress, against the President's vehement protest, repealed his order setting a $25,000 limit to salaries; in June it enacted over his veto the War Labor Disputes Act; throughout the year it rebuffed repeated attempts by the administration to sequester further legislative powers through a Third War Powers Act. Nor did "F.D.R.'s" perfervid plea early in January 1944 meet any better reception. The climax came a month later when Mr. Roosevelt for the first time in the nation's history vetoed a revenue bill, and added insult to injury by the contumelious terms in which he couched his veto message.[31] Thereupon ensued one of the most remarkable scenes ever enacted in the Senate, when administration floor leader Barkley declared, with tears streaming from his eyes, that he "did not propose to take this unjustifiable assault lying down." When the day following Mr. Barkley resigned his post as floor leader to the Democratic caucus and was promptly reëlected by acclamation, it was made plain to all that a serious rift existed between the President and his party support in Congress, one not to be repaired by soothing words from the presidential desk to "Dear Alben."[32] Even the President's reëlection for a fourth term in November did not improve matters noticeably. Hardly had the 79th Congress convened for its first session than it became clear that "the law of honeymoon" was no longer in operation. The President's death on April 12 brought to a close a constantly renewed feud of more than two years' duration with Congresses in which his own party was in the majority.

Fifth and finally, passing reference must be made to a factor of presidential leadership nowadays which, although by no means totally novel when Mr. Roosevelt assumed office, became so in effect in view of the dimensions it attained under him. I mean "F.D.R.'s" consistent championship of the demands of certain groups, especially agriculture and labor. Congressional legislation meant to promote the general welfare via the welfare of particular groups is as old as Congress itself. The element of novelty presented by the New Deal legislation in this respect is furnished by the *size, permanency, and voting strength of the groups served by it*. One of the principal arguments for representative government has been that it assured the responsibility of the governors of society by imposing upon them the constant necessity of obtaining a fresh consensus. But when a powerful pressure group or groups furnish the core of a legislative majority, their easy maneuverability in respect of issues which do not touch their own central interest renders easy the descent into "government by bloc and by blackmail." Not to give the thought too fine a point, a President with a modicum of horse-trading sense will always be able to buy the support of expectant interest groups for policies as to which they have no policy; and what President ever failed to identify his own and his party's political prosperity with the general welfare? At least, such Presidents have been few and far between.

ANCILLARY WEAPONS OF PRESIDENTIAL LEADERSHIP — THE VETO POWER

We recur to the constitutional document, and first of all to Article I, section 7, paragraphs 2 and 3, dealing with the "veto power." They read as follows:

"Every bill which shall have passed the House of Representatives and the Senate shall, before it become a law, be presented to the President of the United States; if he approve he shall sign it, but if not he shall return it, with his objections, to that house in which it shall have originated, who shall enter the objections at large on their journal and proceed to reconsider it. If after such reconsideration, two-thirds of that house shall agree to pass the bill, it shall be sent, together with the objections, to the other house, by which it shall likewise be reconsidered, and if approved by two-thirds of that house it shall become a law. But in all such cases the votes of both houses shall be determined by yeas and nays, and the names of the persons voting for and against the bill shall be entered on the journal of each house respectively. If any bill shall not be returned by the President within ten days (Sundays excepted) after it shall have been presented to him, the same shall be a law, in like manner as if he had signed it, unless the Congress by their adjournment prevent its return, in which case it shall not be a law.

"Every order, resolution or vote to which the concurrence of the Senate and House of Representatives may be necessary (except on a question of adjournment) shall be presented to the President of the United States; and before the same shall take effect, shall be approved by him, or being disapproved by him, shall be repassed by two-thirds of the Senate and House of Representatives, according to the rules and limitations prescribed in the case of a bill."

This ingredient of presidential prerogative is to be accounted for in part by the mistaken belief, derived from Blackstone, that the King's veto was a still vital element of the British constitution, although in fact it had not in 1787 been employed for almost eighty years. Much more is the President's veto to be ascribed to the general conviction of the Framers that without some such defense against the legislature the executive would soon be "sunk into nonexistence." But what form was the veto to assume: was it to be absolute or qualified; if the latter, by what vote ought the houses of Congress be enabled to override it; and was the President to exercise it alone or in association with a Council of Revision, comprising also "a convenient number of the national Judiciary"? While the first question was speedily answered, the Convention vacillated almost to the hour of its adjournment between requiring a two-thirds and a three-quarters vote in both houses for overriding a veto; and only a little less pertinacious were the champions of the Council of Revision proposal. The final rejection of this idea, in leaving the President his own sole master in this field of power, was a decision of first importance.[33]

Naturally, the veto power did not escape the early talent of Americans for conjuring up constitutional limitations out of thin air. The veto was solely a self-defensive weapon of the President; it was the means furnished the President for carrying out his oath to "preserve, protect and defend the Constitution" and was not validly usable for any other purpose; it did not extend to revenue bills, never having been so employed by the King of England; it did not extend to "insignificant and trivial" matters like private pension bills; it was never intended to give effect merely to presidential desires, but its use must rest on considerations of great weight, and so on and so forth.[34] Although efforts of this nature to forge shackles for the power derived a certain specious plausibility from the rarity of the veto's use in English history, they met with failure from the first. Washington exercised the power twice, once on constitutional grounds, once on grounds of expediency. Neither Adams nor Jefferson exercised the power at all. Of Madison's six vetoes four urged constitutional objections to the measure involved, two objections of policy. Summing the matter up for the first century under the Constitution, the leading authority on the subject says: "From Jackson's administration to the Civil War vetoes on grounds of expediency became more frequent, but they were still in a decided minority. Since the [Civil] War constitutional arguments in a veto message have been almost unknown."[35] The latter statement applies moreover equally to the last sixty years, if exception be made for one or two vetoes by Presidents Taft and Coolidge, both of whom had a special penchant for constitutional niceties.[36] The notion that revenue bills are not subject to veto was punctured by Mr. Roosevelt's veto of February 22, 1944, mentioned a moment ago, although the veto in question was overridden. The precedent thus set was clinched by President Truman on June 16th last, and this time the veto stuck.[37]

Nor have attacks upon the veto via the amending process fared any better. In 1818 and once or twice later exasperated Congressmen have even proposed that the President be entirely stripped of the power, but their efforts were stalled at the first parliamentary hurdles. Proposals to supersede the requirement of a two-thirds vote in each house for overriding the veto with a simple majority vote have been more numerous but no more successful. On the other hand, several dozen amendments have been offered since 1873 to give the President what is sometimes termed the "selective veto," which would enable him to veto parts of an enactment and approve the rest.[38] A suggested device for obtaining much the same end by ordinary legislation will be mentioned in a moment.

Finally, the Court has within recent years shown itself generally diligent to repel all constitutional sophistries whereby the practical availability of the power might have been curtailed. Bills which have been passed within ten days of the end of a session may be kept from becoming laws by the "pocket veto," that is, by the President's failing to return them till an adjournment of Congress has intervened; nor does it make any difference that the adjournment was not a final one for the Congress which passed the bill, but a merely *ad interim* one between sessions.[39] Also, he may return a bill with his objections to the house of its origin via a duly authorized officer thereof while it is in temporary recess in accordance with Article I, section 5, paragraph 4—a holding, however, which is not without its dangers, since it leaves it open for either house to fail to provide such duly authorized officer.[40] It would have been better perhaps to hold, as Justice Stone suggested, that neither house acting separately can adjourn so as to prevent a return by the President of his objections to a measure without thereby decapitating the measure.[41] Again, the Court has held that the President may effectively sign a bill at any time within ten calendar days of its presentation to him, Sundays excepted, even though Congress has meantime adjourned, and whether finally or for the session.[42] But here again a criticism should be noted, for the Court's assertion in the course of its opinion that the ten-day limitation applies to the President's power to *approve* as well as to his power to *disapprove* is not borne out by the words of the constitutional clause. The Court seems to be going rather out of its way to supply an omission of the Constitution.[43]

And its further statement in this same opinion that "an incoming President, to whom a bill has not been presented by the Congress, cannot approve it" is more or less of this nature.[44] Thus let us suppose that a new Congress meets, in accordance with the Twentieth Amendment, on January 3 and that a new President takes office on January 20, and suppose also that Congress passes a bill on, say, January 13 and presents it to the outgoing President, who fails to sign it before leaving office. His successor, by the above dictum, would not be entitled to sign the measure. Yet suppose that he was his own successor, what would be the rule then? Or suppose that a President died while still considering a bill, could the succeeding Vice-President sign effectively? I see absolutely no reason why the legislative process should be interrupted in any of these situations. Formerly, it is true, the death of the British monarch involved the dissolution of Parliament, since Parliament meets on his personal summons; but this usage, which was abolished by statute in 1867, obviously furnishes no guidance for practice under the Constitution.

To turn again to the words of the Constitution—the fact that the President has ten days from their *presentation* rather than their passage in which to disapprove bills makes it possible for him to visit the remotest quarters of the globe without relaxing this control over Congress. Furthermore, by withholding their signatures from bills that have passed the houses, the presiding officers of those bodies can lengthen the period between the actual passage of a measure and its presentation to an absent President, so that on his return he will not be swamped with such measures.[45] Thus, by an extraordinary series of accidents, helped out by some contriving, President Roosevelt was enabled, on July 13, 1936, to sign a bill no less than twenty-three days after the adjournment of Congress.[46]

In fact, Mr. Roosevelt appears to have broken all records in this field of presidential endeavor as in several others. "The Roosevelt disapprovals," said a writer at the close of "F.D.R.'s" second term,

"represent over 30 per cent of the total measures disapproved since 1792, when the veto was first used (505 out of 1,635). The messaged vetoes have been nearly 30 per cent of the total returned measures inviting congressional action (262 out of 901). The pocketed measures, with or without comment, have been over 33 per cent of the total pocket vetoes (243 out of 734). The combined disapprovals of Grover Cleveland and Franklin D. Roosevelt represent two-thirds of the total disapproved measures of all veto presidents. The combined messaged vetoes total over 67 per cent of all messaged vetoes; the combined pocket vetoes total over 65 per cent of all pocketed measures. These two executives may justly be rated as our outstanding veto presidents.

"In contrast to Cleveland, who devoted his unfavorable attention to pension, military, and naval relief measures, the range of subjects drawing the adverse action of Roosevelt has been as wide as the activity of Congress. Nothing too large or too small has escaped the penetrating eye of the President and his advisers. The following indicate that range of vision: agricultural relief, general appropriations, adjusted service compensation for World War veterans, interstate commerce, alien deportation, judicial review of administrative tribunals, flood control, protection of fisheries, homestead administration, Indian relief, tax and tariff policy, national defense, Philippine independence, Memorial Day observance, cemetery approaches, short-hand reporting, homing pigeons, District of Columbia street designations, parking meters, credit for beer wholesalers, control of funerals, and the exemption of religious periodicals."[47]

As to the actual effectiveness of the President's veto as a check on Congress the testimony of statistics is conclusive. Between the first inauguration of George Washington and the second inauguration of Franklin D. Roosevelt 750 measures were vetoed, of which 483 were private bills. Of these 750 vetoes only 49 were overridden, six being vetoes of private bills. That is to say, 16 per cent of vetoes of public bills were overridden and 1 per cent plus of vetoes of private bills. Nor does this take account of the fact that 15 of the 43 overridden vetoes of public bills occurred during the vendetta between Andrew Johnson and Congress; nor yet of pocket vetoes, of which some 330 have been uncovered for the period from 1789 to 1936.[48] Later statistics conform substantially to this pattern. Altogether, it seems just to say that the President's veto is normally effective in nine cases out of ten.[49]

Moreover, the President's veto is not always a mere negative; it is at times a *positive* instrument of his legislative leadership. As Professor Finer has put it:

"It would be no wonder if the veto power were not only discriminatory among bills already passed, but if it became an ever-present, if unuttered, threat to promoters of bills (unless they were quite certain of a two-thirds majority in the ultimate resort), and tended to become an instrument of bargaining for other legislation—an instrument to be propitiated by timely and obvious surrenders. This, indeed, has happened."[50]

On the other hand, that a certain incompatibility exists at times between the President's possession of the veto power and his duty to "take care that the laws be faithfully executed" is plain. This was illustrated recently when President Truman felt it incumbent upon him to assure the country that he would "carry out his constitutional duty and administer" the Taft-Hartley Act, his ineffective veto of which he had accompanied with a bitter excoriation of the measure as "unworkable" and likely to "do serious harm to the country." As was pointed out in an earlier chapter, far from being a purely mechanical business, enforcement of the laws frequently involves the application of broad interpretative powers, which of course may be exercised sympathetically from the point of view of Congress's purpose in enacting a particular statute or quite otherwise.[51]

Likewise, certain recent happenings remind us that the obverse of the President's veto is his power to affix his signature to congressional measures of which he approves. Does such approval have to be unqualified or may it be qualified? The question is raised by President Truman's action in accompanying his approval on July 3, 1946, of the so-called Hobbs Anti-Racketeering Act of July 3, 1946,[52] with a message purporting to construe certain of its supposedly ambiguous or doubtful provisions—a performance which he repeated on May 14, 1947, in approving the Portal-to-Portal Act.[53]

Commenting in his column on this probably unprecedented course of the President, Mr. Krock said:

"Usually, when acts of Congress are disputed in the courts, judgment is based on what the judges interpret from the record as the meaning of Congress. But usually this record consists of hearings before the committees which drafted the laws, reports by these committees and the bi-cameral conferences, and the floor debates. If, however, a court test shall be made of the meaning of the Hobbs and portal-to-portal bills, and their effect on other statutes, the President's interpretation of what he believes he signed will become an essential part of that record."[54]

I strongly demur. There is a vast difference between the assumption that Congress's purpose in passing a bill can be gleaned from a study of reports, etc., which Congress had before it while the measure was under consideration and, on the other hand, the assumption that similar light can be obtained from the study of a presidential message which followed the measure's passage by the houses. Equally obvious is it that an act of Congress gets its intention from the houses, in which the Constitution specifically vests "all legislative powers herein granted." For a court to vary its interpretation of an act of Congress in deference to something said by the President at the time of signing it would be to attribute to the latter the power to foist upon the houses intentions which they never entertained, and thereby endow him with a legislative power not shared by Congress.

I return for a moment to the item veto. As was mentioned

above, proposals to amend the Constitution in this respect have been repeatedly offered in Congress, but have never got far along the legislative delivery belt. It was suggested in 1938 that the desired result could be achieved by the simple device of incorporating in appropriation bills a provision modeled on that which appears today in the Reorganization Act of 1939. Thus the President would be authorized to eliminate or reduce specific items of appropriation, and his orders to that end would become effective unless the houses disallowed them within a stipulated period by concurrent resolution. Although accepted by the House as an amendment to the Independent Offices Appropriation bill of 1938, the proposal failed in the Senate, and a like proposal met the same fate in 1942. The latest idea seems to be that the reform would require a constitutional amendment.[55]

Of the two remaining factors of the President's participation in legislation, so far as it has direct constitutional basis, his power in case of disagreement between the houses with respect to adjournment to "adjourn them to such time and place as he shall think proper" and his power to convene either or both houses on "extraordinary occasions" may be dealt with very briefly. The former meager remnant of the British monarch's power to prorogue Parliament has never been used, although Andrew Jackson once thought it worth while to pen a veto in its behalf;[56] and in the case of an atom bomb attack it might even today come in handy as to "place." The latter power, contrariwise, has been used so often that the word "extraordinary" in the constitutional clause has taken on a decidedly Pickwickian flavor. Today in common parlance "extraordinary" sessions are simply "extra" or "special" sessions.[57] On the other hand, there have been a few really extraordinary occasions when the President in power has disappointed expectations by not summoning Congress. Lincoln did this at the outset of his administration, to the vast aggrandizement of the presidential office for the time being at least, and Johnson followed his example four years later with the exactly opposite result. Under a majority of the state constitutions, when the governor calls the legislature together it may deal only with such matters as are specified in his call. Once, however, Congress has been convened by the President it is in full possession of its constitutional powers; and, of course, once in session, the houses are able by continuing so or by adjourning for only brief intervals to render this presidential prerogative altogether nugatory. Indeed, by legislation under Article I, section 4, paragraph 2, Congress could long since have rendered itself a practically perpetual body; and could still do the same under Amendment XX, section 2.

COLLATERAL FACTORS OF PRESIDENTIAL LEADERSHIP—
PATRONAGE, FILIBUSTERS, JUDICIAL REVIEW

While by Article I, section 6, paragraph 2, it is put out of the President's power to "corrupt" the houses directly, he may still attain the same noxious end indirectly by bestowing offices upon the political henchmen of members in return for the latter's votes, or by getting rid of members who are willing to exchange their seats for more desirable posts; nor can there be any doubt that Presidents have at times been able in this way to turn the scales in favor of desired legislation as, conspicuously, was President Cleveland in 1893 in his fight for the repeal of the discredited Sherman Silver Purchase Act.[58] Indeed, it may be asserted generally that so long as the President possesses patronage to dispense, he will often be compelled to use it in order to obtain, or hold, support which ought to be forthcoming on other grounds—will, in brief, have to submit to political blackmail. Yet the question remains whether his possession of "the loaves and fishes" really strengthens the President in the long run. The President's greatest weapon is always the power of a favoring public opinion. In the words of Lincoln, than whom no President ever dispensed offices more lavishly, "With public sentiment everything is possible; without public sentiment nothing is possible." Pertinent too is Mr. Taft's considered verdict that every time he made an appointment he created "nine enemies and one ingrate."[59] Furthermore, the elimination of federal patronage would tend to undermine the local party machines, and to that extent transform the parties into organs of opinion pure and simple, much to the aggrandizement of the President as party leader. It is more than possible, therefore, that the anxiety of certain authorities to discover some mode of "compensating" the President for the loss of patronage, which an extension of the merit system to the higher echelons would mean, is misconceived, that the President would gain by the reform in his legislative as well as in his executive capacity.[60]

Another collateral factor of presidential leadership is the power of the houses to shape their own rules of procedure, which may either help or hinder the enactment of measures desired by the President. The Senate's individualistic mode of doing business, which occasionally burgeons in the filibuster, must of course be set down as being of the "hinder" order, although it may pay for itself at times by the protection which it affords to "rights" of minorities, or for the maturing of a genuine public opinion on a presidential proposal. "It is a remarkable fact," says Professor Rogers in his excellent volume on the Senate, "that practically every proposal defeated by a filibuster has been unregretted by the country and rarely readvocated by its supporters"; but, he at once adds, "Such minority omniscience . . . must be more accidental than wise, and the danger is always present . . . that the interests of the country will be adversely affected."[61] Nor is the question simply whether the filibuster has killed good measures, but also whether it has led to the enactment of bad ones. The indefensible concessions which a small bloc of so-called "Silver Senators" have been able to wrest from Congress from time to time during the past seventy-five years are conclusive testimony on that point.

But whatever its advantages and disadvantages in the past, this institution—altogether unique among the parliamentary devices of popular governments—has been losing ground now for some time. Filibustering Senators can no longer defend their endless trivialities and irrelevancies by arguing that they are "ambassadors of sovereign states"—as if ambassadors ever spouted nonsense! And in March 1917 a filibuster against a presidential proposal led to the Senate's adopting a cloture rule for the first time in its history. Subsequently the Twentieth Amendment, by abolishing the "short session" which used to terminate the life of a Congress, has eliminated the situation in which the threat of a filibuster was most apt to prove effective in extorting special favors for its authors. I should add my belief that the watering-down process must be carried considerably further if Congress as a whole is to be capable of performing its part in dealing with modern emergency conditions, and so retain its intended place in the constitutional system.[62]

The manner in which the two houses can facilitate executive participation in legislation is illustrated on a small scale by the steps they have taken to adjust their procedures in financial legislation to the Budget and Accounting Act of 1921. A provision of the act reads:

"No estimate or request for an appropriation and no request for an increase in an item of any such estimate or request, and no recommendation as to how the revenue needs of the Government should be met, shall be submitted to Congress or any committee thereof by any officer or employee of any department or establishment, unless at the request of either House of Congress."[63]

To match this concentration of responsibility on the part of the executive branch the House has transferred the power of initiating appropriation bills, which had been shared theretofore by eight committees, to a single committee, and the Senate has taken similar action. This, however, is only a slight indication of what could be done to the same general end. Administration measures, which today have no status as such before either house, could be given preference over other bills to any extent deemed desirable. Imitating what was done during the Reconstruction Era, the houses could by concurrent resolution create a joint standing committee, or "legislative council," to maintain contact with the President for the purpose of discussing with him his legislative program and translating it into mutually satisfactory proposals. Indeed, a provision of the Administrative Reorganization Act of 1939 suggests that such arrangements may even be given the form of statute. Under this act, it will be recalled, the houses have the right by concurrent resolution to veto any presidential order issued under it, provided the disapproving resolution be passed within sixty days—otherwise the presidential order becomes effective. But suppose a Senate filibuster should develop in *support* of the order? In anticipation of this too obvious possibility the act itself provides that debate on a resolution of disapproval shall be limited in each house to ten hours, which shall be equally divided between opponents and advocates.[64] To be sure, any restriction of this nature on the constitutional power of each house to "determine the rules of its proceedings" has only the force of an agreement between the houses; for that very reason perhaps the more solemn form of statute may at times be preferable.[65] I shall return to the idea of a legislative council later.

Yet another collateral factor of presidential leadership is the Supreme Court's power of judicial review as it affects acts of Congress. It is a striking fact that of the Presidents who have made the Presidency what it is all except two sooner or later crossed swords with the Court. The exceptions were Washington, who appointed the first Bench and, indeed, first and last, appointed no fewer than 13 Justices; and Woodrow Wilson. And stemming from this fact are two others: first, the survival in face of the generally adverse opinion of the Bar of a potentially formidable challenge to the finality of Supreme Court interpretations of the Constitution affecting national legislative power; and, secondly, a series of measures whereby the Court has been subjected sometimes overtly, more often covertly, to political pressure.

Jefferson, invoking the principle of the separation of powers, denied that the President and Congress were bound by the views which the Supreme Court adopted of the Constitution any more than the Court was bound by their views. Jackson took the same position, urging also in its support the oath which every officer gives to uphold the Constitution. Lincoln argued that to identify the Court's version of the Constitution, formulated perhaps for the purpose of deciding a single private lawsuit, with the Constitution itself was incompatible with the idea of popular government.[66] Each of these Presidents, moreover, took a hand in legislation which altered the size of the Court. By the Judiciary Act of 1802, the Court, whose membership had been contingently decreased the year before from six Justices to five in order to prevent Jefferson from appointing a successor to the aged and ailing Cushing, was restored to six Justices for the diametrically opposed reason, and in 1807 a seventh Justice was added. One of Jackson's last acts was to sign a bill enlarging the Court to nine Justices, with the probably intended and certainly realized result of watering down the influence of the departed Marshall with his surviving brethren. During the Civil War the Court was temporarily en-

larged to ten Justices after it had sustained the blockade of the
Southern states by the narrow margin of one vote; and meantime
by the Act of March 1, 1863, slavery had been prohibited in the
territories, thus setting the Republican platform of 1861 above the
Dred Scott decision as the effective Constitution of the country.[67]

Nor is this the whole story by any means. Both in 1866 and
again in 1869 the size of the Court was changed by Congress of its
own initiative. In the former year it was prospectively shrunk to a
membership of seven Justices in order that Johnson should not be
able to make any appointments; in the latter year—Grant now
being President—it was restored to its ante-bellum membership
of nine Justices. As we know today, Grant utilized his opportunity to nominate, the same day that *Hepburn v. Griswold* was decided, two Justices who, he believed, could be relied upon to bring
about a reversal of that decision; and fifteen months later his confidence was rewarded by the event.[68]

"The traditional American way," it has been wittily remarked,
"of being radical with the Supreme Court" is to alter its personnel
rather than its structure and powers.[69] It should be added that the
procedure is expected to be accompanied by a certain amount of
indirectness and disavowal of political motivation; and President
Roosevelt's proposal of February 5, 1937, was shaped by its authors
to comply with the demands of the tradition.

The immediate instigation of the Roosevelt proposal came
from the general election of 1936. The huge popular endorsement
which this gave Mr. Roosevelt he not unreasonably interpreted as
a mandate to establish certain legislation which by theories then
dominant on the Court was clearly unconstitutional. The President was thus confronted with a difficult problem of political
leadership: was he to postpone his program indefinitely while

his political following dissolved, or was he to remove the principal obstacle to success within a comparatively brief time?[70]

In his address to Congress of January 6, 1937, Mr. Roosevelt said:

"With a better understanding of our purposes, and a more intelligent recognition of our needs as a nation, it is not to be assumed that there will be prolonged failure to bring legislative and judicial action into closer harmony. Means must be found to adapt our legal forms and our judicial interpretation to the actual present national needs of the largest progressive democracy in the modern world. . . .

"The judicial branch also is asked by the people to do its part in making democracy successful. We do not ask the courts to call nonexistent powers into being, but we have a right to expect that conceded powers or those legitimately implied shall be made effective instruments for the common good.

"The process of our democracy must not be imperiled by the denial of essential powers of free government."[71]

Unfortunately, the proposal of February 5 was not presented as a logical method of carrying out the message of January 6, but—in harmony with the evasive tradition mentioned above— was directed to the largely, although certainly not altogether, irrelevant problem of superannuation on the Bench.[72] It was consequently much more extreme than a measure addressed to the main purpose need have been, and furthermore supplied only a partial guarantee against the recurrence of the situation most demanding remedy, a haphazard system of recruitment which entirely ignores the place of the Court in the lawmaking process.

While the proposal was defeated, this did not occur until the emergency which had challenged the President's leadership had been to a large extent removed by the Court itself by its decisions sustaining the Wagner Labor Relations Act and the Social Security Act.[73] But that the proposal had some influence, in conjunction with the election of 1936 and the C.I.O. strikes early in 1937, in inducing the Court to restudy certain of its doctrines in the light of modern conditions, is not an extreme conjecture. At any rate, the time relationship between the proposal and the decisions just mentioned is something to take into account in estimating the present legislative role of the President. History does not regard very seriously the logician's criticism of the *post hoc ergo propter hoc*—to it the chronological *is* the logical.[74]

THE PRESIDENT AS "DICTATOR" VERSUS THE PRESIDENT AS LEADER — A NEW TYPE OF CABINET

The growth of presidential participation in legislation,[75] and indeed the vast expansion in recent decades of the President's role in all the departments of national power, invites our attention afresh to a question which has been repeatedly raised regarding the Presidency in the past, but never with more insistency than in recent years, nor for more cogent reasons. This is the question whether the Presidency is a potential matrix of dictatorship; and, if it is, whether there is a remedy.

"Dictatorship," I hardly need to point out, is a word with a highly ambiguous connotation, so much so in fact that I propose to dismiss it at the outset in favor of a less colorful word, "domination." "A nation," it has been well said, "does not have to have a genuine dictator in order to suffer some of the evils of too great executive domination." Imagine an historically minded member of the 81st Congress seeking to emulate Henry Dunning's exploit in 1781 in bringing George III's domination of Parliament to an end and with it, ultimately, British resistance to American independence. It would be the part of such a member to move a resolution declaring that "the power of the President has increased, is increasing, and ought to be diminished," and he would have little difficulty in making out an arresting case.

First off, he would point out that impeachment, the weapon which the Constitution provides against presidential "high crimes and misdemeanors," is, as Jefferson early discovered, a "scarecrow," and that to galvanize this scarecrow into life would be to run the risk of reducing the Presidency to a nullity, as almost happened in 1868. Then, noting the decision in *Mississippi v. Johnson*[76] shortly after the Civil War, he would assert, and quite correctly, that the President has no judicially enforcible responsibility either for nonperformance of his duties or for exceeding his powers. Congress's power of the purse, to be sure, still offers, he would concede, an obstacle to presidential usurpation which only an outright *coup d'état* could entirely overcome. Nevertheless, as Dr. Wilmerding points out in his volume on *The Spending Power*,[77] not only have Presidents been able repeatedly to break over statutory controls on expenditure, but such controls are usually much abated by Congress itself in times of emergency, exactly when expenditures are heaviest and presidential dominance is at its zenith. Indeed, generalizing from what happened during the Great Depression, the honorable member might urge that congressional largess in such situations, by the hold which it gives the executive branch upon millions of votes, enables the President to tighten his hold also upon Congress, and so creates a vicious circle whereby Congress pays for its own slow enslavement. And, continues our orator, when war activates the President's powers as Commander-in-Chief, the situation is still more disastrous from the point of view of opposing the power of the purse to presidential dominance. The sums which Congress is at such times under every compulsion to vote are colossal. The needs which they are designed to meet are forcefully represented, and are believed by the public, to be most urgent, while itemization is put out of the question by the demands of military secrecy; and unexpected turns in the military situation may aggravate all these difficulties. Moreover, the criticism which overworked congressional committees of varying competence can offer to the demands of the executive branch under such conditions will be haphazard in the extreme—an item of $50,000 may get more consideration, and certainly far better informed consideration, than a presidential demand for billions.

Turning then to the course which constitutional interpretation has taken more and more pronouncedly in consequence of our participation in two world wars and under the stimulation of economic crisis, our fictioned Dunning will sketch a system of constitutional law which attributes to Congress a legislative power of indefinite scope, and the further power to delegate this indefinite power to the President *ad libitum,* and which attributes to the President in his own right an indefinite power to proclaim "emergencies" and thereby appropriate an indefinite "aggregate of powers" in meeting them. At the same time, he will show that the President, not without judicial encouragement, has been able to cut loose from the two most important controls which the Constitution originally imposed upon his direction of foreign policy. With our four greatest wars directly ascribable to presidential policies, the exercise by Congress of its power "to declare war" has become, he will assert, an empty formality; while by means of the executive-agreement device the President has emancipated himself from his constitutional partner in pledging the national faith.

And at this point our hypothetical member will perhaps devote a word or two to the advantages which a President today enjoys in appealing to the multitude. Propaganda, he will point out, once the casual art of a gifted few, has been within recent times converted into a skilled technique, which is supplemented by the most ingenious gadgets of mechanical science. Today the President of the United States can at any time request that the nation's broadcasting channels be cleared so that he may "chat" with the people, and the request will be granted pronto, for are not all the available frequencies allocated to companies on federal licenses which terminate every six months? Besides, every member of his administration is a propagandist and has access to the radio at will, although a first-class radio voice may not be the heaven-sent gift of all.

Finally, our orator will note certain of the consequences of the demise of the anti-third-term tradition. A third-term—*a fortiori* a fourth-term—President is bound to dominate not only his party, and Congress through it, but the executive agencies, most of whose chief personnel he will have appointed, and even the courts, a large proportion of whose judges will be his appointees. And in proportion as a President displays reluctance to quit office will the strength of the vested interests supporting his continuance in it wax greater.

The picture is unquestionably overdrawn in some of its details. Thus, if it is true that impeachment is no longer to be reckoned with as an effective weapon in the arsenal of liberty, this is partly due to the fact that Presidents have in the past kept pretty clear of courses which might make people think seriously of so extreme a discipline. Again, although there is no court which is entitled to order a President to perform his duties or to enjoin him from exceeding his powers, yet the subordinates through whom he must ordinarily act do not share his immunity in this respect; and his orders are at all times subject to judicial inquiry into their validity when anybody bases on them any claim or justification whatsoever.[78] Also, his subordinates are, ordinarily, liable at any time to be summoned before a congressional investigating committee and put to the question regarding their official conduct.[79]

Nor is it by any means the case that Congress's control of the purse strings is ineffective as a restraint on the executive branch.

To the contrary, it is potentially a highly effective restraint, which with improved machinery within the power of Congress to provide could be made actual. Again, our orator did not find it to his purpose to mention that in the "concurrent resolution" a device today exists by which sweeping delegations of power to the President can be recalled by the houses without the necessity of obtaining presidential consent; nor that ordinarily executive agreements, unlike treaties, do not have the force of law unless they have been sanctioned by Congress. And other lesser exaggerations or omissions might be indicated were it worth while.

What is more, that is a seriously contracted point of view from which presidential domination appears as solely a *menace* to democratic institutions. Why, in the face of our democratic institutions, has presidential domination attained its present proportions? Indeed, must not this development be considered as a fulfillment in a measure of those institutions, and as an answer to some demand from public opinion, on which by hypothesis they are grounded? Without doubt, such is the case, and especially as regards presidential leadership in legislation; nor is it difficult to identify this demand—it is the demand that government assume an *active* role in matters of general concern, and especially in matters affecting the material welfare of the great masses of the people. This may eventually turn out to have been a demand impracticable of beneficial realization in the long run; but of its existence there can be no present question.

So we are not free to blame presidential leadership as such for those intrusions upon "liberty," as it has sometimes been understood, which present expanded theories of governmental function entail. This at least must be conceded. We are free, on the other hand, to ask whether presidential leadership, as we know it, is as good an instrument of the demand which brought it into existence as conceivably it might be. Presidential leadership sets itself the task of guiding legislation; and the critics are numerous who say that it does the job badly. To make the indictment more specific, it is asserted that presidential leadership is discontinuous, not to say spasmodic; that it is too dependent on the personality of the President rather than on the authority of the office; that it is often insufficiently informed, especially as regards the all-important matter of administrative feasibility; and, finally, that the contact between the President and Congress is most faulty, being, in fact, at the mercy of either's whim. These contentions also have too much obvious validity to make it worth while to attempt to refute them or even to qualify them nicely.

In short, we are confronted, not with a *single* problem, but with *two* problems: first, the problem of bringing presidential power in *all* its reaches under some kind of institutional control; secondly, the problem of relieving presidential leadership in the legislative field of its excessive dependence on the accident of personality and the unevenness of performance which this involves. Is it possible that these two problems admit of a common solution? At least, so far as they do, it is evident what form the solution must take—the *provision, namely, of some kind of improved relationship between President and Congress.*

It is not irrelevant in this connection to recur for a moment to the argument which the President's Committee on Administrative Management advanced a decade ago in support of its recommendation that the independent agencies be brought within the departments whose heads compose the President's Cabinet.[80] It was upon these agencies, the argument ran, that the most novel, most controversial, most interesting activities of the National Government had been lodged in recent decades, with the result that the President had been constrained to look increasingly outside the Cabinet for advice in shaping his legislative program. But let the Committee's recommendation be adopted, the argument continued, and the President would be forced, or at any rate would have incentive, to return to the bosom of his "official family" instead of consorting with this, that, and other anonymous adviser or dispenser of happy ideas. Thus, on the one hand the Cabinet would be revitalized, and on the other hand the President would become "the spokesman for the 'administration' in the real sense of the word, not merely the interpreter of his own fancies." He would be at all times what he had always been in times of his greatest power, the representative of the public.[81]

The argument overlooked certain facts, one of which is that "Kitchen Cabinets," far from being recent phenomena, on the contrary long antedate the first "independent agency." Nor is the reason far to seek. It is because the Cabinet seraglio has been recruited from an early date on principles which make it fairly certain that an active presidential imagination will frequently stray beyond its decorous precincts. One of these—the one which is of chief importance for the present discussion—is the idea that the heads of the great majority of the departments ought to be administrative experts, or at least capable of quickly becoming such. Unfortunately, an expert in a particular area of governmental activity is not likely to possess the breadth of outlook which is most desirable in a political adviser, or the time or inclination to interest himself in the problems of other departments or of the country at large. And obviously the Committee's proposal to increase his departmental duties was badly calculated to overcome these handicaps, if that was one of the ends in mind. The argument overlooks the fundamental distinction between Politics and Administration, between determining *what* government ought to do and *how* it should do it, and the exigent need of a President for responsible counsel in relation to the former. It overlooks too the considered opinion of competent critics that, even as an agency for the development of a unified *executive* policy among its own membership, the Cabinet has today "become an administrative anachronism."[82]

Two other plans for stabilizing presidential leadership, while also pivoting on the Cabinet, are directed primarily to the problem of creating a permanent link between the President and Congress. The less radical of these would give the Cabinet members the right to attend the houses in order to participate in debate on matters of official interest to them and impose upon them the obligation of doing so in order to impart information desired by the houses. The proposal, far from raising any constitutional difficulties, has the countenance of early practice under the Constitution. The first volume of the *Annals of Congress* records that "Secretary for Foreign Affairs Jefferson attended agreeably to order, and made the necessary explanations." Actually, it was Secretary for Foreign Affairs Jay, for this was on July 22, 1789, and Jefferson did not become Secretary of State till March 1790. Secretary of War Knox later visited the Senate Chamber with the President on at least one occasion, which was described in the preceding chapter, and by himself on two others. The Act of 1790, organizing the Treasury Department, provided that the head of the Department should digest plans for improving the revenue and public credit, and "make report and give information to either branch of the legislature, in person or in writing, as may be required," etc. That Hamilton, the first Secretary of the Treasury, was never asked to report in person was due, as we saw earlier, to the opposition of the rising Jeffersonian party as voiced by Madison.[83]

And so matters rested till near the end of the Civil War when George H. Pendleton of Ohio began an agitation, the principal result of which was a report many years later by a distinguished Senate committee supporting the idea both on grounds of policy and of constitutionality;[84] and since then at least four future or past Presidents are on record as having expressed themselves in its favor. Why then has the suggestion never produced tangible fruit? Chiefly because most of the legislative work of Congress is done by committees, and before such a body a head of department can always obtain a far more satisfactory hearing than would be conceivably possible before either of the houses in open session. Conversely, if it is Congress which is seeking information, it can do so through the investigatory process much more effectively and thoroughly than by the wasteful and pretentious methods of parliamentary interpellation.[85]

We come now to the more radical proposal referred to above. *It is simply that the President shall construct his Cabinet from a joint Legislative Council to be created by the two houses of Congress and to contain its leading members.*[86] Then to this central core of advisers may be added at times such heads of departments and chairmen of independent agencies as the business forward at the moment naturally indicates.

That the creation of a Cabinet with legislative members would not encounter constitutional difficulties was pointed out in an earlier chapter.[87] Nor would it amount to supplanting forthwith the "Presidential System" with the "Cabinet System." The President would not become a prime minister, bound to resign when outvoted in Congress, although circumstances might arise in which it might be expedient for him to do so, as Mr. Wilson contemplated doing in 1916 in the event of Mr. Hughes's election. Nor yet would he be a figurehead like the King of Great Britain or the President of Italy, for he would still retain all his constitutional powers and prerogatives although, again, he might choose to use them at times less for pushing a program of his own than for the purpose of mediating between the programs of others, as did Washington at the beginning.

The new Cabinet would, in other words, still be a body of *ad-*

visers. But there are advisers *and* advisers. The proposed Cabinet would comprise men whose daily political salt did not come from the presidential table, whose political fortunes were not identical with his, who could bring presidential whim under an independent scrutiny which today is lacking, and yet who, by putting the stamp of their approval upon his proposals, would be able to facilitate their enactment into law. It would be a body both capable of *controlling* the President and of *supporting* him; of guaranteeing that the things needing to be done would be done on time, but that, on the other hand, the judgment that they needed to be done represented a wide consensus, a vastly wider consensus than the President can by himself supply.[88]

But it may be objected that such an arrangement could not long be adhered to, or if it was it must at times cut athwart the two-party system, and so weaken the political responsibility of the President. The objection has reference to the evident possibility of the President's belonging to the party which is a minority in Congress. Actually, the supposed situation has obtained comparatively rarely—only four times since the turn of the century, covering eight years out of forty-eight. Furthermore, the objection overlooks the fact that the advantage which is supposed to accrue from President and Congress both being of the same party rarely outlasts the first two years of an administration, when indeed it lasts that long, while some of the bitterest feuding between the two branches has often occurred when both were of the same party. Such conspicuously was the case in the latter days of "F.D.R.," as I was at pains to point out earlier in this chapter. What kept the two branches coöperating at all was the common compulsion of a great emergency; and at such times, even under present arrangements, coöperation between President and Congress does not stop at the party line. *But why should it require a crisis to bring forth best methods, especially as with best methods operative crisis might often be avoided?* Suppose one takes the position that government is normally a species of *nation-keeping;* then it is clear that much of the fuss and fury of politics is really factitious and a sheer waste to the community; that the chief objective to be sought in political discussion, whether carried on in Cabinet council, on the floors of Congress, or elsewhere, is *consensus*—in what light does the above proposal then appear?[89]

Furthermore, it would seem that the principle of cycle holds in the matter of legislation, and especially of reform legislation, as it does in so many other things mundane. The mere enactment of laws is only the first step toward incorporating them in the social order; following it ensues a process of gradual absorption into the general institutional setup and outlook of the community; and this process is apt to be hindered rather than helped if reforms are pressed forward too fast and furiously. A wise legislative leadership will, therefore, reckon on a certain amount of reaction against its measures as inevitable and seek to forestall this. In such an endeavor the advice of potential political foes may easily be of more value than that of overenthusiastic supporters.

Kept within bounds, the power and prestige of the Presidency comprise the most valuable political asset of the American people; they are, moreover, in a very true sense the creation of the American people. But centering as they do in a single individual who is free to advise, or to refrain from advising, with whomsoever he chooses, this power and this prestige are apt to become unduly *personalized,* thus inviting two dangers: the slowing down of the legislative process to an extent that unfits it for a crisis-ridden world in which time is often of the essence, and—in consequence —autocracy. It is, therefore, an additional merit of the suggestion advanced above that it is calculated to meet, or at least abate, both these dangers. Effective presidential leadership is essential to the ready availability of the national lawmaking power; this ready availability reduces to a minimum the excuse for autocratic courses.[90]

To sum up: What is sometimes termed the question of "presidential responsibility" is not a single problem, but presents two quite different, even opposed, aspects: (1) that of concern for the *responsiveness* of government, and particularly the legislative branch of it, to public opinion; (2) that of concern for the *accountability* of the executive branch to the existing constitutional structure, which also presumably embodies public opinion. I am here suggesting that these two aspects admit of a common solution.

Practice under the Constitution clearly demonstrates that the legislative process requires presidential guidance. But it shows too that no President can long shape policy in any field without legislative support, *or*—as happened during the Civil War—an obvious breach of constitutional forms. The problem for which a constitutional solution is sought is, therefore, really the problem of equating easily, and without constant jar to society, the political forces which Congress at any time represents with those which the President represents at the same time, and of putting the relationship of the two *on a durable and understood basis*. For this purpose a reconstruction of the Cabinet, which in its present form has proved but an indifferent success for more than a century, is at least a promising expedient, and one to which the Constitution interposes no obstacles.

RÉSUMÉ

I T IS an axiom of American history that the Constitution came from the Framers "a bundle of compromises." Not so generally recognized is the confirmation which is lent this observation by those clauses of the Constitution most nearly affecting the office and powers of the President. The vagueness of the constitutional grants of power to the President has always furnished matter for comment, sometimes favorable, sometimes otherwise, depending on the commentator's bias.[1] "The executive power shall be vested in a President of the United States of America"; "the President shall be Commander-in-Chief of the Army and Navy"; with the advice and consent of the Senate he shall make treaties and appoint to office; he shall have power to "grant pardons for offenses against the United States," he shall "recommend . . . such measures to Congress, as he shall judge necessary and expedient"; and so on and so forth. Yet, in order to exercise any of these powers—in order, indeed, to subsist—he must have money, and can get it only when and if Congress appropriates it. Likewise, he is dependent on Congress for the very agencies through which he must ordinarily exercise his powers, and Congress is the judge as to the necessity and propriety of such agencies. Again, he is bound to "take care that the laws" which Congress enacts are "faithfully executed"—for this purpose all his powers are in servitude; and Congress has the power to investigate his every official act, and can, by a special procedure, if it finds him guilty of "high crimes and misdemeanors," impeach him and throw him out of office. Moreover, by the standard set by the prerogative of the British monarch in 1787, his "executive power" and his power to protect that power were both seriously curtailed.

The Notes to the Résumé begin on page five hundred twenty

The power to "declare war" was vested in Congress; the Senate was made a participant in his diplomatic powers; he was given a veto upon all legislative acts, but one which the houses may override by a two-thirds vote.

In short, the Constitution reflects the struggle between two conceptions of executive power: the conception that it ought always to be subordinate to the supreme legislative power, and the conception that it ought to be, within generous limits, autonomous and self-directing; or, in other terms, the idea that the people are *re-presented* in the Legislature *versus* the idea that they are *embodied* in the Executive. Nor has this struggle ever entirely ceased, although on the whole it is the latter theory which has prospered. To repeat what was said on an earlier page, "Taken by and large, the history of the Presidency has been a history of aggrandizement."

The office got off to a good start under a very great man. The principle of the separation of powers was not yet regarded as forbidding the executive to initiate legislation. In the act establishing the State Department Congress itself laid down a "practical construction" of the Constitution which, save for the interregnum of the Reconstruction Period, has left the President absolute master of his official family. A dangerous foreign situation in 1793 brought that family into existence, while it also enabled the President to translate his position as the organ of communication with other governments into a substantive, creative power. Finally, the Whiskey Rebellion provided the occasion for the first step in that course of legislation and of presidential action which has long since clothed the President in situations of widespread disorder, or threat thereof, with powers of dictatorship.

Under Jefferson and "the Virginia School of Presidents" a certain retrogression took place from the notion of presidential autonomy toward that of legislative supremacy. Under Jefferson himself the retreat was theoretical rather than actual. As the founder and leader of the first national party, Jefferson was able to dominate Congress by personal influence, and it was shown for the first time what accession of strength political skill can bring the Presidency. But Jefferson's successors, caught between the upper and nether millstones of their self-abasing conception of the Presidency and their lack of personal force, were reduced to official insignificance. The War of 1812 marked the near elimination for the time being of presidential prerogative in the field of foreign relations; the Monroe Doctrine announced to the world at large that opportunities for aggrandizing the Presidency from foreign adventuring were to be confined strictly to the Western Hemisphere.[2] Jefferson pronounced the dictum that no President could with safety to our democratic institutions be eligible for a third term, albeit he might nominate his successor; and the successors whom Jefferson himself nominated ratified the ban.

Jackson's Presidency was more than a revulsion to earlier ideas —it was a revolution. A new electorate was organized into a new party whose wide ramifications, focusing in the National Convention, rendered its continuance independent of accidents of personality. Guaranteed this powerful and persistent support among the people at large, Jackson extended the doctrine of the President's autonomy to embrace his obligation to the law; constitutional obligation was reduced—or exalted—to the level of *moral* obligation. At the same time the President's duty to "take care that the laws be faithfully executed" was asserted to comprise the right to read the law for any and every member of the Executive Department; and through a vigorous and expanded use of his veto and removal powers, Jackson for the time being made this claim good. Through the latter power, moreover, the Spoils System was for the first time engrafted on the National Government, thereby adding one more weapon to the presidential armory.

Except nevertheless for a few unfortunates like John C. Calhoun and Nicholas Biddle, the Jacksonian "dictatorship" was more bark than bite, more proclamation than performance. The Monroe Doctrine, the taboo on a third term, and, what was even more important, the States Rights conception of national legislative power, all set conspicuous landmarks which Jackson himself had not the slightest inclination to disturb. His most outstanding assertions of power, and especially in the field of legislation, were negative and exercised by veto. Moreover, despite the permanency of the party organization which was reared by his henchmen in every quarter of the Union, the prominence of the office during his incumbency was predominantly a reflection of his own energetic personality. When he left office he left behind him a political vacuum which a resuscitated Congress presently filled, and, thanks to the manipulations of the slavery interest, continued to fill—if exception be made for Slavery's tool, the sly, pious Polk—till the outbreak of the Civil War.

For all that, the Jacksonian conception of the Presidency was not forgotten. Indeed, its champions and its critics contributed about equally to render it more articulate than ever—a fact of the first magnitude when Lincoln became President and found himself confronted with a nation in dissolution. Lincoln's claim to "the war power" was derived from three sources: Jackson's doctrine that *all* the President's powers are autonomous; the Supreme Court's doctrine in *Luther v. Borden* (1849) that insurrection is "war"; and the measures which Pierce and Buchanan had taken in their efforts to put down civil war in Kansas, together with the budget of doctrine which the legal genius of Caleb Cushing had furnished them in justification of their policy.

At first, as was pointed out on an earlier page, Lincoln laid claim only to an *ad interim* war power, one which was operative only until Congress could ratify and reinforce its measures; but the Supreme Court's sweeping language in the Prize Cases (1863) encouraged him to take a more forthright stand, and this, combined with his indisposition to coöperate with Congress, led him to break over constitutional bounds and become a dictator even exceeding the Roman model.[3] Nor was the constitutional corrective applied until after the war was comfortably over, by the Court's decision in *ex parte* Milligan and by Congress's uprising against Johnson. The implication of Lincoln's course that the President has power to meet an emergency without awaiting action by Congress is accordant with the most ancient traditions of Anglo-American law; but when on this implication Lincoln sought to erect a plan of Reconstruction in which the role of the national legislative power was negligible, he brought the Presidency in the person of his too zealous apostle Johnson to the verge of disaster. Even so, it fell to Johnson, by escaping impeachment, to demonstrate the impracticability of this medieval method of controlling presidential power. Moreover, it was during his term that the Supreme Court virtually underwrote, in *Mississippi v. Johnson* (1867), Jackson's contention that the President's duty to the Constitution is solely the duty of conscience which his oath imposes.

But again the cyclical character of presidential power demonstrated itself. As from 1809 to 1829, so again from 1865 to 1885, the legislative power became the dominant element of the National Government. Indeed, except for the success of Presidents Hayes and Cleveland in using the Army to put down "domestic violence" within the states, the period of congressional preponderance reached to the death of McKinley. But meantime Congress had, by its own headiness, paved the way for the recrudescence of its constitutional rival, by forcing upon McKinley the war with Spain. By that act and the consequences which ensued from it, the restrictive effect of the Monroe Doctrine on presidential prerogative was seriously undermined. The United States was now a "World Power," and presently found itself involved in a World War.

The great accession to presidential power in recent decades has, however, taken place in the *internal* equally with the *external* field of government, and has been signalized by the breakdown of the two great structural principles of the American Constitutional System, the doctrine of dual federalism and the doctrine of the separation of powers; while along with this breakdown has gone a change of even more fundamental character in popular outlook regarding the purpose and scope of governmental power. I mean, of course, the replacement of the *laissez-faire* theory of government with the idea that government should make itself an *active, reforming* force in the field of economic enterprise, which means, necessarily, that the *National Government* should be active in this way, inasmuch as the field in question has long since come to transcend state lines.

The result for the Presidency has been twofold. On the one hand, Presidents have made themselves spokesmen of the altered outlook, have converted their parties to it—a conversion not infrequently accompanied by backsliding—and, with the popular support thus obtained, have asserted a powerful legislative initiative. On the other hand, Congress, in responding to the President's leadership in its own peculiar field, has found it convenient to aggrandize his executive role enormously, by delegating to him the power to supplement its measures by a type of sublegislation called "administrative regulations." Not all this delegated power, it is true, has gone to the President, but a vast proportion of it has; and it constitutes a realm of presidential power of which the

Framers had little prevision, although it began to appear in the field of foreign relations even as early as Washington's second administration.

The first exponent of the new Presidency was Theodore Roosevelt, but his achievement was to some extent negated by faults of method. Woodrow Wilson was enabled by the advantage of having critically observed his predecessor, by his knowledge of political methods abroad, by a taste for institution-building, which was later to divert him into an abortive effort at world organization, and finally by the opportunity afforded by our entrance into World War I, to illustrate on an unprecedented scale both the new roles of the President—that of legislative leader and that of recipient of delegated legislative power. World War I was prosecuted for the most part under laws which were drafted under the appraising eye of the President and which conferred upon him far greater powers than those which Lincoln had exercised as Commander-in-Chief.

But it is the second Roosevelt who beyond all twentieth-century Presidents put the stamp both of *personality* and *crisis* upon the Presidency as it exists at this moment. In the solution of the problems of an economic crisis—"a crisis greater than war"—he claimed for the National Government in general and for the President in particular powers which they had hitherto exercised only on the justification of war. Then when the greatest crisis in the history of our international relations arose, he imparted to the President's diplomatic powers new extension, now without consulting Congress, now with Congress's approval; and when at last we entered World War II he endowed the precedents of both the Civil War and of World War I with unprecedented scope.

The Presidency of this present year of grace, so far as it is explicable in terms of American constitutional law and theory, is the product of the following factors: (1) social acceptance of the idea that government should be active and reformist, rather than simply protective of the established order of things; (2) the breakdown of the principle of dual federalism in the field of Congress's legislative powers; (3) the breakdown of the principle of the separation of powers as defining the relation of President and Congress in lawmaking; (4) the breakdown of the corollary principle that the legislature may not delegate its powers; and (5) the impact on the President's power as Commander-in-Chief and the organ of foreign relationship of two world wars and the vastly enlarged role of the United States in the international field.[4]

Does the Presidency, then, in the light of these facts, constitute a standing menace to popular government and to those conceptions of personal liberty to which popular government is, in part, traceable? So far as concerns popular government in the sense of majority rule, the exact contrary is the case—all the above developments are the direct consequence of Democracy's emergence from the constitutional chrysalis. That, on the other hand, these developments leave private and personal rights in the same strong position as they once enjoyed would be quite impossible to maintain. Nor is it feasible in this connection to distinguish too acutely between the property and other rights. Not only in the past, but today as well, the property right is the right best capable of holding its own against political power. This is the principal lesson to be drawn from the history of Liberalism.

As matters stand today, presidential power is dangerously *personalized,* and this in two senses: first, that the leadership which it affords is dependent altogether on the accident of personality, against which our haphazard method of selecting Presidents offers no guarantee; and, secondly, that there is no governmental body which can be relied upon to give the President independent advice and which he is nevertheless bound to consult. As a rem-

edy calculated to meet both phases of the problem I have suggested a new type of Cabinet. At least, if a solution is to be sought
in *institutional* terms, it must consist in *stabilizing* in some way
or other the relationship between President and Congress. To
achieve such stabilization should be a foremost objective with
both the political branches.

[1] *Myers v. United States*, 272 U. S. 52, 118 (1926). Construing the term "all cases" in Art. III, §2, par. 1, counsel in *Osborn v. The Bank* remarked: "The pleonasm is here meant to perform its usual office, to be emphatic. It marks the intention, and affords a principle of construction." 9 Wheat. 738, 809 (1824). See also Hamilton's argument as "Pacificus," pp. 217–218 *infra*. *Cf.* note 50 *infra*.

[2] Constitution, Art. I, §8, cl. 18.

[3] *Ibid.*, Art. II, §3.

[4] 1 Cr. 137, 165–166.

[5] See Evarts B. Greene, *The Provincial Governor*, etc. (New York, 1898).

[6] Allan Nevins, *The American States During and After the Revolution* (New York, 1924), p. 166; also studies by W. C. Morey and W. C. Webster in *Annals of the American Academy of Political and Social Science* (1893).

[7] *Federalist* 48; Edward M. Earle (ed.) (Washington, 1938), p. 322. Cited hereafter as Earle.

[8] F. N. Thorpe (ed.), *American Charters, Constitutions,* etc. (Washington, 1909), VII, 3816–3817. A similar clause appeared also in the Maryland constitution of 1776. *Ibid.*, III, 1696.

[9] *Proceedings Leading to the Calling of the Conventions of 1776 and of 1790* (J. S. Wiestling, publ., Harrisburg, 1825), pp. 100–101; also at p. 75. This "supreme executive power," however, was "vested in a president and council." Thorpe, *op. cit.*, V, 3084.

[10] *Federalist* 69; Thorpe, *op. cit.*, V, 2632–2633.

[11] *Two Treatises of Government* (Morley, ed.), Bk. II, Ch. 14, §§ 159–166.

[12] *Ibid.*, Ch. 11, §134.

[13] *Politics* (Welldon, tr.), Bk. VI, Ch. 14. For Locke's contribution see *op. cit.*, Bk. II, Ch. 12.

[14] *Spirit of the Laws* (Nugent-Prichard, ed.) (London, 1905), Bk. XI, Ch. 3. For others who, besides Aristotle and Locke, are frequently set down as forerunners of Montesquieu, see John A. Fairlie, "The Separation of Powers," 21 *Michigan Law Review*, No. 3 (February 1923); and F. T. H. Fletcher, *Montesquieu and English Politics* (London, 1939), Ch. VIII. Most of the supposed forerunners, however, after Aristotle stopped short with pointing out the distinction between "legislative" and "executive" power. "Judicial power" does not reënter the picture to any great extent till after the British Act of Settlement of 1701, which guaranteed the judges security of tenure against the Crown. It is to be noted, too, that writers frequently confuse the notion of a balanced (or mixed) constitution, representing the three orders of society, with the principle of the separation of powers. Actually, Montesquieu is the first writer to bring the latter idea to the support of the former; and it is this fact which commended him so greatly to the founders of the American constitutional system, inasmuch as the social ingredients of a mixed constitution were absent in the United States.

[15] *Commentaries,* I, Intro., 49–51; Ch. 1, 154.

[16] *Ibid.*, Ch. 2, 161.

[17] *Ibid.*, Ch. 2, 154–155. Said George II to Walpole: "I will order my army as I see fit; for your scoundrels of the House of Commons, you may do as you please; you know I never interfere, or pretend to know anything about them." Quoted by Edgar Dawson in *The Sewanee Review*, July 1915, p. 264.

---

* *Chapter I (Conceptions of the Office) begins on page 1.*

[18] See generally Charles C. Thach's excellent volume, *The Creation of the Presidency, 1775–1789* (Johns Hopkins Press, 1922), especially Chs. 3–5.

[19] Max Farrand, *Records of the Federal Convention* (Yale University Press, 1911), I, 65. Cited hereafter as Farrand.

[20] *Ibid.*, 65, 68–69, 98. Two other important members of the "strong executive" party were Charles Pinckney, who probably deserves the credit for bringing the pertinent provisions of the New York constitution to the attention of the Committee of Detail, and also for proposing the title "President"; and Hamilton, who wished to see "the governor" chosen for life and vested with the power to appoint the governors of the states. Thach, *op. cit.*, pp. 92–94, 108–109, 116–117.

[21] Farrand, II, 181, 185–186.

[22] *Ibid.*, 541–542.

[23] *Ibid.*, 83, 132, 183, 185, 394, 498–499, 538–542, 547–550.

[24] *Ibid.*, 185.

[25] Wilson's original idea was that the President should be elected "by the people at large," i.e., *directly*, it would seem. *Ibid.*, I, 68 (June 1). The following day, however, he proposed a scheme of *indirect* election by Electors to be chosen in districts, who should come together into one body to elect "the Executive Magistracy." *Ibid.*, 80 (June 2). This would have been a real Electoral College, not the congeries of state electoral colleges which are so absurdly termed "the Electoral College." The proposal was voted down, 2 states to 8. Wilson later returned to his original proposal. *Ibid.*, II, 32. Altogether, no fewer than *eight* methods for choosing a President were first and last suggested in the Convention. *Ibid.*, IV, General Index, 148–149.

[26] *Ibid.*, II, 52–54.

[27] Summary of the July 17 debate, *ibid.*, 29–32.

[28] Herman Finer, *Theory and Practice of Modern Government* (New York, 1932), II, 1009–1010 (quoted with the consent of the publisher, The Dial Press); Farrand, I, 56–57, 72, 80; II, 29–31; *Federalist* 68. Mason thought that a majority of the Electors would rarely agree on a President and that therefore the election would often fall to the Senate (later changed to the House). Gouverneur Morris thought otherwise, partly because a successful President would be reëlected. Farrand, II, 512.

[29] Art. I, § 6, par. 2.

[30] Earle, pp. 436–437.

[31] *Ibid.*, pp. 454–455.

[32] *Ibid.*, p. 462.

[33] *Federalist*, Nos. 73–77. Necker, however, found it to his purpose to argue in 1792 that the President of the United States had more power than had the King of France in 1789. *An Essay on the True Principles of Executive Power in Great States* (London, 1792), II, Ch. 3. John Adams's initial evaluation of the Presidency was much the same: "Let us now consider what our constitution is, and see whether any other name can with propriety be given it, than of a monarchical republic, or if you will, a limited monarchy. The duration of our president is neither perpetual nor for life; it is only for four years; but his power during those four years is much greater than that of an avoyer, a consul, a podestà, a doge, a stadtholder; nay, than a king of Poland; nay, than a king of Sparta. I know of no first magistrate in any republican government, excepting England and Neuchatel, who possesses a constitutional dignity, authority, and power comparable to his. The power of sending and receiving ambassadors, of raising and commanding armies and navies, of nominating and appointing and commissioning all

officers, of managing the treasures, the internal and external affairs of the nation; nay, the whole executive power, coextensive with the legislative power, is vested in him, and he has the right, and his is the duty, to take care that the laws be faithfully executed. These rights and duties, these prerogatives and dignities, are so transcendent that they must naturally and necessarily excite in the nation all the jealousy, envy, fears, apprehensions, and opposition, that are so constantly observed in England against the crown." C. F. Adams, *Life and Works of John Adams* (New York, 1850–1856), VI, 430 (July 18, 1789).

34 "In the Constitution are provisions in separate articles for the three great departments of government—legislative, executive and judicial. But there is this significant difference in the grants of powers to these departments: The first article, treating of legislative powers, does not make a general grant of legislative power. . . . By reason of the fact that there is no general grant of legislative power it has become our accepted constitutional rule that this is a government of enumerated powers. . . .

"On the other hand in Article III, which treats of the judicial department—and this is important for our present consideration—we find that Section I reads 'the judicial power of the United States, shall be vested,' etc. By this is granted the entire judicial power of the Nation." *Kansas v. Colorado,* 206 U. S. 46, 81, 82 (1906).

"The difference between the grant of legislative power under Article I to Congress which is limited to powers therein enumerated, and the more general grant of executive powers to the President under Article II is significant." C. J. Taft, in *Myers v. United States,* 272 U. S. 52, 128 (1926).

35 See *Annals of Congress,* I, 462–463, 474, 481–482, 497, 515–519, *passim*; Edgar S. Maclay (ed.), *Journal of William Maclay* (New York, 1890), pp. 113–116; Adams, *Works,* III, 409.

36 See *Works of Alexander Hamilton* (J. C. Hamilton, ed.), VII, 76 ff.; and *Writings of James Madison* (Hunt, ed.) (New York, 1900–1910), VI, 138 ff.

37 It was Madison's contention precisely in 1793 that Hamilton was endeavoring to appropriate to the Presidency the royal prerogative of the King of England. *Ibid.,* 150. But in *Federalist* 69, Hamilton had disparaged all comparisons between the powers of the President and those of the British monarch; while in the Convention, Wilson, despite his belief in a strong executive, had remarked that "he did not consider the prerogatives of the British monarch as a proper guide in defining the Executive powers. Some of these prerogatives were of a Legislative nature." Farrand, I, 65. Most of the references by the Supreme Court to the British monarch's prerogative have been in elucidation of the President's pardoning power. *United States v. Wilson,* 7 Peters, 160; *ex parte* Wells, 18 How. 307, 311; *in re* Neagle, 135 U. S. 1; *ex parte* Grossman, 267 U. S. 109. Chief Justice Taft, however, endeavors to fortify his argument in the Myers Case by such a reference (272 U. S. 118); but seventy-five years earlier we find Chief Justice Taney writing: "In the distribution of political power between the great departments of government, there is such a wide difference between the power conferred on the President of the United States, and the authority and sovereignty which belong to the English crown, that it would be altogether unsafe to reason from any supposed resemblance between them, either as regards conquest in war, or any other subject where the rights and powers of the executive arm of the government are brought into question. Our own Constitution and form of government must be our only guide." *Fleming v. Page,* 9 How. 609, 618 (1851).

38 Act of September 2, 1789, c. 12; U. S. Code, tit. 5, § 242.

[39] *Works* (Ford, ed.), I, 160–165. See also *ibid.*, VII, 108.

[40] When President Washington reached New York City to take the oath of office, he found Congress already in session, and his so-called Inaugural Address of April 30, 1789, was addressed not to the citizenry of the country at large, as Inaugural Addresses are nowadays, but to his "Fellow-Citizens of the Senate and House of Representatives." The address was followed by answering addresses of a congratulatory nature from the two houses, whose members proceeded by carriage to present them in person; and in due course the President sent brief, formal replies. The procedure thus initiated was followed throughout Washington's two administrations and that of Adams, at the opening of each succeeding session of Congress, though not for the Inaugural Address. This, in fact, seemed at one time likely to disappear altogether, for Washington's second effort of the kind, addressed to his "Fellow-Citizens," contained fewer than 150 words, in which the President announced that he was about to take the oath of office and expressed the wish that if he should be discovered violating "willingly or knowingly the injunctions thereof," he might "besides incurring constitutional punishment, be subject to the up-braidings of all who are now witnesses of the present solemn ceremony." The inadequacies of this performance, however, were later more than compensated for by the famous Farewell Address of September 17, 1796, which, addressed to "Friends and Fellow-Citizens," was not delivered orally but reached the country through the press.

And meanwhile the outbreak of the Wars of the French Revolution, by creating a serious cleavage in American public sentiment, had put the ceremonies attendant upon the President's address to Congress in an altered light. Sympathizers with France denounced the whole business as "monarchical" in character. From the same cause it became increasingly difficult for the houses to frame responses to the President without precipitating long-drawn-out and sometimes angry debate. So when the government moved to the new capital on the Potomac, and it was found that Pennsylvania Avenue was no better than a quagmire which it was dangerous to life and limb to traverse by carriage, Jefferson, who was well aware that he wrote much better than he spoke, decided to replace "the speech from the Throne," as his partisans termed it, with a message sent by messenger. Though the change was bitterly criticized in the Federalist press, the precedent thus established continued in force until a follower of Jefferson upset it 113 years later. Charles Warren, "Jefferson and the Speech to Congress," *Proceedings of the Massachusetts Historical Society*, 1923, pp. 123–172; James D. Richardson, *Messages and Papers of the Presidents* (Washington, Government Printing Office, 1896–1899), I, 1–316, *passim*.

[41] Albert J. Beveridge, *Life of John Marshall* (New York, 1916–1919), II, 537. "His whole system of administration," wrote J. Q. Adams later, "seems founded on the principle of carrying through the legislature measures by personal or official influence." *Memoirs*, I, 403; quoted in W. E. Binkley, *The Powers of the President* (New York, 1937), p. 52—a first-class, though misnamed, volume. A revision of this work, which appeared in 1947 under the title *President and Congress*, is the volume referred to in the notes which immediately follow.

[42] Hamilton, who was moving heaven on earth to secure Burr's defeat, contradicted Marshall. Said he, in a letter dated January 6, 1801, to James A. Bayard: "But it is not true, as is alleged, that he is an enemy to the power of the Executive, or that he is for confounding all the powers in the House of Representatives. It is a fact which I have frequently mentioned, that, while we were in the administration together, he was

generally for a large construction of the executive authority and not backward to act upon it in cases which coincided with his views." *Works* (Fed. ed., 1904), X, 413. Apparently Hamilton was unaware of Jefferson's having instigated the "Letters of Helvidius." But as bearing Hamilton out, see Ch. III, n. 108, and Ch. VI, n. 5, *infra.*

43 Richardson, *Messages and Papers of the Presidents,* I, 331–332. Cited hereafter as Richardson.

44 See, e.g., his letter to Nicholson suggesting Chase's impeachment, Henry Adams, *History of the United States* (New York, 1889–1891), II, 150.

45 Binkley, *op. cit.,* p. 54; Ralph V. Harlow, *The History of Legislative Methods in the Period Before 1825* (Yale University Press, 1917), Ch. X; Norman J. Small, *Some Presidential Interpretations of the Presidency* (Johns Hopkins Press, 1932), pp. 164–167— another very competent and valuable study. It is interesting to note that Tocqueville, who visited the country at the beginning of the Jacksonian Era, but saw things governmental through the eyes of Webster and Story, records a very poor opinion of the Presidency and its potentialities, particularly in view of the nonparticipation of the United States in external affairs. "All his important acts are directly or indirectly submitted to the legislature; and where he is independent of it he can do but little." *Democracy in America* (New York, 1873), I, 126–132.

46 Small, *op. cit.,* p. 172 (quoted with the consent of the publisher, The Johns Hopkins Press).

47 See Binkley, *op. cit.,* Ch. III; Harlow and Small, *loc. cit.;* also H. J. Ford, *Rise and Growth of American Politics* (New York, 1898), pp. 165–167. Jefferson, writing in 1807, described his Cabinet as "my faithful and able fellow laborers in the Executive administration." *Writings* (Washington, ed.), VIII, 116. He also, the same year, set forth his theory of the Cabinet as follows: "All matters of importance or difficulty are submitted to all the heads of departments composing the Cabinet: sometimes by the President consulting them separately and successively, as they happen to call on him; but in the gravest cases, by calling them together, discussing the subject maturely, and finally taking the vote, in which the President counts himself but one. So that in all important cases the Executive is, in fact, a directory which certainly the President might control; but of this there was never an example, either in the first or the present administration" —that is, his own. *Works* (Ford, ed.), IX, 69. See also *ibid.,* 273.

48 The literature on the National Convention is enormous. For a few leading references see H. R. Bruce, *American Politics and Parties* (rev. ed.) (New York, 1932), p. 379. Writing in 1859 Thomas H. Benton excoriated the National Convention:

"An irresponsible body (chiefly constituted, and mainly dominated by professional office-seekers and office-holders) have usurped the election of the President (for the nomination is the election, so far as the party is concerned); and always making it with a view to their own profit in the monopoly of office and plunder." He considered this method of choosing a President to be one of the two great "trials" confronting the capacity of the American people for self-government, the other being slavery. *Thirty Years View* (1859), II, 787.

In 1872 Charles Sumner, in urging a constitutional amendment to provide for direct election of the President, voiced a like judgment: "Whereas, the caucus or convention, after being the engine for the nomination of President, allowing the people a little more than to record its will, becomes the personal instrument of the President when elected, giving him dictatorial power, which he may employ in reducing the people to conformity with his purposes and promoting his re-election, all of which is hostile to good government, and of evil example. . . ." Quoted by Chambrun in work cited in note 65 *infra*, at p. 43.

A current estimate of the National Convention is equally unfavorable:

"LOS ANGELES, Jan. 30—One of California's leading Democrats declined an invitation today to be a delegate at next summer's convention in Philadelphia, averring that the assemblages were a waste of time and should be supplanted by a more meaningful mechanism.

"John B. Elliott, an oil operator and an 'elder statesman' of the party here, in a letter to James Roosevelt, state chairman, wrote:

"'Frankly, I'm fed up on national party conventions. For nearly half a century I've been attending them either as a delegate or as a working newspaper reporter.

"'They have degenerated into nothing so much as super-colossal circuses with great noise, fanfare, disorder and loud oratory, climaxing usually in an outcome already previously and privately arranged.'

"He recommended 'some such common-sense procedure as a nation-wide direct primary' for Presidential and Vice Presidential nominations." *The New York Times,* January 31, 1948.

49 Richardson, II, 576, 582.

50 Beveridge, *op. cit.,* IV, 535n.; Binkley, *op. cit.,* pp. 80, 84. Webster, naturally, opposed the doctrine that the opening clause of Article II of the Constitution grants power. Speaking on the removal power in the Senate, February 16, 1835, he said:

"When they say it shall be vested in a President, they mean one magistrate, to be called a President, shall hold executive authority; but they mean, further, that he shall hold this authority according to the grants and limitations of the Constitution itself.

"They did not intend, certainly, a sweeping gift of prerogative. They did not intend to grant to the President whatever might be construed, or supposed, or imagined to be an executive power; and the proof that they meant no such thing is, that, immediately after using these general words, they proceed specifically to enumerate his several distinct and particular authorities; to fix and define them; to give the Senate an essential control over the exercise of some of them, and to leave others uncontrolled. By the executive power conferred on the President, the Constitution means no more than that portion which itself creates, and which it qualifies, limits and circumscribes." *Writings* (Constitutional ed., 1903), VII, 186–187; *Register of Debates in Congress,* XI, Pt. I, 462–463.

In the course of the same debate Calhoun confronted the idea of the equality of the three departments with that of legislative supremacy, in the following words:

"Permit each department to judge of the extent of its own powers, and to assume the right to exercise all powers which it may deem necessary and proper to execute the powers granted to it, and who does not see that, in fact, the Government would consist of three independent, separate, and conflicting departments, without any common point of union, instead of one united authority controlling the whole. . . . Under the opposite and true view of our system all these dangerous jars and conflicts would cease. It unites the whole into one, and the legislative becomes, as it ought to be, the center of the system; the stomach and the brain, into which all is taken, digested, and assimilated, and by which the action of the whole is regulated by a common intelligence. . . . Each [department] is left in possession of the powers expressly granted by the constitution, and which may be executed without the aid of the legislative department, and in the exercise of which there is no possibility of coming into conflict with the other departments; while all discretionary powers necessary to execute those granted, and in the exercise of which the sepa-

rate departments would necessarily come into conflict are . . . transferred to Congress.
. . ." *Ibid.,* 555–556.

This, in the main, was the position of the early Jeffersonians and of the later Whigs. For further expressions of the same point of view, both earlier and later, see statements by Sedgwick and Sherman in the First Congress, *Annals of Congress,* I, 511, 541; speech by Tucker of Virginia in House of Representatives, August 15, 1876, *Congressional Record,* 44th Congress, 1st sess., 5699; dissenting opinion of Holmes, J., in *Myers v. United States,* 272 U. S. 52, 177; dissenting opinion of McReynolds, J., *ibid.,* 183.

51 *A Brief Inquiry into the True Nature and Character of Our Federal Government* (1840), pp. 116–117.

52 Charles Warren, "Presidential Declarations of Independence," 10 *Boston University Law Review* (1930), 1–35, at 17 and *passim.* My authority for the statement about the Swiss constitution of 1848 is Professor Rappard. To the framers of the Weimar constitution the American Presidency appealed strongly—too strongly, it would seem. See Hajo Holborn in *The Constitution Reconsidered* (Conyers Read, ed.) (Columbia University Press, 1938), pp. 292–295.

53 A more positive assertion of power in the legislative field is, however, suggested by the Hon. Richard Fletcher's statement in a speech in Faneuil Hall in 1837 that "during Jackson's term of office the principal function" of the Ways and Means Committee, of which Fletcher had been a member, "was going through the form of approving the laws which Jackson prepared and handed down to them for acceptance." Speech of Representative Harlan of Ohio in the House, *Congressional Record,* February 27, 1935. Also Jackson gave as one of his reasons for vetoing Clay's Bank bill the failure of Congress to consult him prior to its passage. Richardson, II, 589. On the other hand, the first Harrison thought it worth while in his Inaugural to voice a very depreciatory construction of the President's power and duty to recommend measures to Congress. It was simply, he held, "a privilege which he holds in common with every other citizen." *Ibid.,* IV, 9. Similar views were later expressed by Polk, Taylor, and Fillmore. *Ibid.,* 517; V, 23 and 79.

54 The instrument by which the slaveholding interest was able to assure the nomination of manageable personalities was the "two-thirds rule," which was established by the first Democratic National Convention and was not abolished until 104 years later. Yet it is significant that even during this period the charge of "executive usurpation" was sometimes made. Warren, *loc. cit.,* pp. 17–20.

55 The following are characteristic laments of Mr. Welles on this point: "There is really very little of a government here at this time, so far as most of the Cabinet are concerned; certainly but little consultation in this important period." "All this has been done without Cabinet consultation, or advice with any one, except Seward and the President." "Cabinet-meetings, which should, at that exciting and interesting period, have been daily, were infrequent, irregular, and without system." "But little was before the Cabinet, which of late can hardly be called a council. Each Department conducts and manages its own affairs, informing the President to the extent it pleases." "Stanton does not attend one half of the Cabinet-meetings. When he comes, he communicates little of importance. Not unfrequently he had a private conference with the President in the corner of the room, or with Seward in the library." "The President did not join us today in Cabinet. He was with the Secretary of War and General Halleck, and sent word there would be no meeting. That is wrong, but I know no remedy." "This is a specimen of the management of affairs. A majority of the members of the Cabinet are not permitted to know what is doing." "Chase spent an hour with me on various subjects. Says the Ad-

ministration is merely departmental, which is true; that he considers himself responsible for no other branch of the Government than the Treasury, nor for any other than financial measures." "Chase . . . remarked that nothing could be expected where there were no Cabinet consultations and no concerted action." "Stanton has a cabinet and is a power in his own Department. He deceives the President and Seward, makes confidants of certain leading men, and is content to have matters move on without being compelled to show his exact position." *The Diary of Gideon Welles* (New York, 1911), I, 131, 134, 136, 274, 320, 351, 391, 401–402, 526; II, 17, 58, 59, 62, 84, 86, 91, 98, 166, 203.

In the conference of Lincoln with his Cabinet and certain Senators and Representatives, December 17, 1862, Senator Collamer stated the theory that "the early and uniform construction of the Constitution" required that the President "be aided by a Cabinet council" and that "important measures and appointments should be the result of their combined wisdom and deliberation," and he complained that Lincoln had disregarded this usage. Burton J. Hendricks, *Lincoln's War Cabinet* (Boston, 1946), p. 336. See also *ibid.*, 234, 313, and 328–329.

[56] Richardson, V, 626 ff.

[57] Message of July 4, 1861. *Ibid.*, VI, 20, 23–25, 31.

[58] These are Professor Randall's words, in his discerning *Constitutional Problems under Lincoln*, p. 514. Lincoln himself told Senator Chandler, in discussing his disapproval of the Wade-Davis Reconstruction bill (1864): "I conceive that I may in an emergency do things on military grounds which can not constitutionally be done by Congress." Nathaniel W. Stephenson, *Abraham Lincoln and the Union* (Yale University Press, 1921), p. 353.

[59] For new light on Lincoln's personal administrative habits in the White House see a letter of John Hay to Herndon in Emanuel Hertz, *The Hidden Lincoln* (New York, 1938), pp. 307–308. *Cf.* C. R. Fish, *The American Civil War* (New York, 1937), pp. 175–176, 356–362. Not only Lincoln's temperament, but his entire lack of previous administrative experience and the Western attitude that no elaborate bureaucratic machinery was needed must have contributed to this result.

[60] As a Whig member of Congress years before, Lincoln had written: "Were I President, I should desire the legislation of the country to rest with Congress, uninfluenced in its origin or progress, and undisturbed by the veto unless in very special and clear cases." *Complete Works* (John G. Nicolay and John Hay, eds.) (New York, 1890), I, 134. And on his journey to Washington as President-elect, referring in his speech at Pittsburgh to certain "indirect" means by which a President may influence legislation, he said: "My political education strongly inclines me against a very free use of any of these means by the executive to control the legislation of the country. As a rule, I think it better that Congress should originate as well as perfect its measures without external bias." *Ibid.*, 679. Even in his message to Congress of July 4, 1861, he wrote, after remarking that he had performed his duty, "you will now, according to your own judgment, perform yours." *Richardson*, VI, 31. In view of the *faits accomplis* with which he confronted Congress, the statement sounds a bit ironical, but Lincoln's acceptance of the principle of separation of powers saved it from insincerity. And in the main he undoubtedly adhered rather closely to his announced intention to avoid what he regarded as improper executive influence upon Congress. As Professor Randall points out, very little legislation was initiated or carried through by Lincoln, *op. cit.*, p. 387.

[61] Contemporary constitutional law was all with Congress in this dispute. Reciting Art. IV, §4, the Court had said in *Luther v. Borden:*

"Under this article of the Constitution it rests with Congress to decide what government is the established one in a State. For as the United States guarantee to each State a republican government, Congress must necessarily decide what government is established in the State before it can determine whether it is republican or not. And when the senators and representatives of a State are admitted into the councils of the Union, the authority of the government under which they are appointed, as well as its republican character, is recognized by the proper constitutional authority. And its decision is binding on every other department of the government, and could not be questioned in a judicial tribunal." 7 How. 1, 42 (1849).

And in *Texas v. White,* which was decided early in 1869, the Court reiterated this doctrine with direct reference to Reconstruction. Rehearsing the steps that Johnson had taken to restore civil government in Texas, Chief Justice Chase continued as follows:

"Whether the action then taken was, in all respects, warranted by the Constitution, it is not now necessary to determine. The power exercised by the President was supposed, doubtless, to be derived from his constitutional functions, as commander-in-chief; and, so long as the war continued, it cannot be denied that he might institute temporary government within insurgent districts, occupied by the National forces, or take measures, in any State, for the restoration of State government faithful to the Union, employing, however, in such efforts, only such means and agents as were authorized by constitutional laws.

"But, the power to carry into effect the clause of guaranty is primarily a legislative power, and resides in Congress. 'Under the fourth article of the Constitution, it rests with Congress to decide what government is the established one in a State. For, as the United States guarantee to each State a republican government, Congress must necessarily decide what government is established in the State, before it can determine whether it is republican or not.'

"This is the language of the late Chief Justice, speaking for the court, in a case from Rhode Island, arising from the organization of opposing governments in that State. And, we think that the principle sanctioned by it may be applied, with even more propriety, to the case of a State deprived of all rightful government, by revolutionary violence; though necessarily limited to cases where the rightful government is thus subverted, or in imminent danger of being overthrown by an opposing government, set up by force within the State.

"The action of the President must, therefore, be considered as provisional, and, in that light, it seems to have been regarded by Congress." 7 Wall. 700, 729–730 (1869).

[62] Edward McPherson, *History of the Rebellion* (2nd ed., 1865), p. 332. Cited hereafter as McPherson.

[63] *The New York Herald,* September 29, 1866; Binkley, *op. cit.,* p. 136. *Cf.* James A. Woodburn, *Life of Thaddeus Stevens* (Indianapolis, 1913), p. 447.

[64] 4 Wall. 475 (1867). The scope of the argument in the case is indicated by the following extracts from Attorney General Stanbery's address to the court:

"If, when the President is here by a service of the subpoena, the court proceed in the case, and find it a case in which they are ready to order an injunction to issue to the President to command him not to execute those laws, and notwithstanding, the President goes on to execute them, what follows? That the court must now sustain its own dignity, for the court has a dignity and a power to be observed as well as the President. The next step here, then, is to move for an attachment, or a rule on the President, to show cause why an attachment should not issue against him; for what? For a contempt of this court; that whereas the court ordered him to abstain from proceeding further in the execution of these laws, in defiance of that order the President has gone on to do some acts in execution of the laws. He is therefore brought here by what kind of process? by process *quasi* criminal; by process of attachment to answer for a contempt of the court. . . .

"What sort of a spectacle have we? One great department of this government has arraigned another, and the executive department of the government, represented by the President, brought before the judicial department—for what purpose? To be punished criminally. . . .

"What then? The President deposed; the President made incapable of performing the duties of his office! Certainly a jail, or a dungeon it may be, is not a fit place to perform the duties and functions of President. You have made the President incapable of performing his duties. What is the effect of that? You have removed the President, for that is one of the conditions in which the President's office becomes vacant, that he is incapable of performing his duties. You have done it more effectually than by impeachment, for an impeachment does not deprive him of liberty; an impeachment sets him at large, and simply takes from him his official character; but the order of this court under these circumstances takes him as President and puts him in jail, and keeps him there until he performs what this court orders him to perform. . . .

"You leave the government without a head; you leave the office vacant, and the people must go about to get another President to perform these functions and these duties. In the meantime, until that is done, everything is at large, and there is not a law of the United States that can be executed, not an officer that can be appointed or an officer that can be removed. There is no one left to proclaim insurrection, if that shall happen. There is no one left to perform all the duties which for the safety of this people as a nation are reposed in the President. To correct a particular evil, to guard a particular individual or a particular State against the acts of the President, there is no way, according to the gentlemen, but to depose that President by a proceeding like this, and, for the correction of this lesser evil, to produce that enormous evil which affects not merely the State of Mississippi, but every other State of the Union and every individual." 4 Wall. 486-488.

The Attorney General's main reliance was on Jefferson's defiance of the *subpoena duces tecum*, which Chief Justice Marshall issued during the trial of Aaron Burr for treason, ordering the President to produce certain documents in court. Marshall's position was that the President could claim no exemption from the law save possibly on the ground that his official duties "demand his whole time," while in fact "this demand is not unremitting." Beveridge, *Marshall*, III, 444–447. Jefferson communicated his refusal to the United States Attorney for the district, George Hay, in a letter dated September 7, 1807:

"As I do not believe that the district courts have a power of *commanding* the executive government to abandon superior duties and attend on them, at whatever distance, I am unwilling, by any notice of the subpoena, to set a precedent which might sanction a proceeding so preposterous." *Writings* (Mem. ed.), XI, 365.

He had earlier commented on the possibility that he would be summoned in characteristic vein, as follows:

"Laying down the position generally, that all persons owe obedience to subpoenas, he admits no exception unless it can be produced in his law books. But if the Constitution enjoins on a particular officer to be always engaged in a particular set of duties imposed on him, does not this supersede the general law, subjecting him to minor duties inconsistent with these? The Constitution enjoins his constant agency in the concerns of six millions of people. Is the law paramount to this, which calls on him on behalf of a single one? Let us apply the Judge's own doctrine to the case of himself and his brethren. The sheriff of Henrico summons him from the bench, to quell a riot somewhere in his county. The federal judge is, by the general law, a part of the *posse* of the State sheriff. Would the Judge abandon major duties to perform lesser ones? Again; the court of Orleans or Maine commands, by subpoenas, the attendance of all the judges of the Supreme Court. Would they abandon their posts to them, to serve the purposes of a single individual? The leading principle of our Constitution is the independence of the legislature, executive and judiciary of each other, and none are more jealous of this than the judiciary. But would the executive be independent of the judiciary, if he were subject to the *commands* of the latter, and to imprisonment for disobedience; if the several courts could bandy him from pillar to post, keep him constantly trudging from north to south and east and west, and withdraw him entirely from his constitutional duties?" *Ibid.*, 240–241.

Although the idea of presidential immunity arose early (see p. 138 *supra*), yet the notion that a President in office can be called to account judicially for his misdeeds still crops up now and then. When in 1922 President Harding dismissed the director and twenty-seven chiefs of divisions in the Bureau of Engraving and Printing "for the good of the Service," Senator Caraway (Arkansas) moved an investigation of what he termed "an indictment" of the discharged employees "both as to honesty and efficiency," and in the course of urging his resolution, said:

"The immunity against malicious slander does not clothe the Executive. Wisely or otherwise, the Constitution clothes us with the right to express opinions in debate in the Senate and in the House and not be required to answer elsewhere, but such immunity does not run with the President of these United States; and I feel certain, Mr. President, that what never happened before in the history of this country is going to happen now— that one of these discharged employees is going to sue the President of these United States for wilful, malicious defamation of character, and the President, like any other citizen, is going to the bar of justice in a court room in the city of Washington and answer that charge. That is their last resort. They hoped that the President would have regard for their rights, and restore their reputations he so ruthlessly destroyed; but he says now: 'I will not do it, and I am not sorry for what I did.' " *Congressional Record,* February 23, 1923.

No such action was brought, nor did the Senator get his investigation. Nor did an Atlanta lawyer make better headway when, early in 1937, he petitioned the Supreme Court to put President Roosevelt "in his place" by holding him to be in contempt of court on account of his message of January 6, 1937. Associated Press despatch of January 23, 1937.

[65] Lockwood, pp. 191–192.

"One of the most convincing evidences of the innate weakness of our form of Government is the fact that the people of this country are compelled, apparently, to turn to any one particular man in an emergency, for assistance and support. Woe to that country whose destinies are involved in the fortunes of any one man, however great and pure he may be!

"The true, logical, and efficient way to destroy imperialism in this country, is to abolish the system which makes it possible. With the destruction of presidential and the establishment of representative congressional government, we could, with impunity, place any man at the head of the executive branch, were he never so bad, ambitious, and inefficient, for it would then be known that at any moment he could be relieved from the cares of State." *Ibid.*, p. 195.

Note also the sweeping—too sweeping—language in which John Norton Pomeroy describes the President's affirmative powers" in relation to Congress's powers in his *Introduction to the Constitutional Law of the United States* (New York, 1877): "The acts done by virtue of these powers are completely political. The subjects themselves, over which the powers extend, do not fall within the province of congressional legislation; and that body cannot by any laws enlarge or diminish the President's capacity; it can do nothing more than pass such laws, if it thinks proper, as shall aid the Chief Magistrate in the execution of these powers, nor may the Courts interfere and assume to regulate the President's conduct." *Ibid.*, pp. 420–421. This work was first published in 1868, the year of Johnson's impeachment.

One other writing of this period should be mentioned briefly: *The Executive Power in the United States, A Study of Constitutional Law,* by Adolphe de Chambrun (Madeleine Vinton Dahlgren, tr.) (Lancaster, Pa., 1874). The writer, a grandson of Lafayette, was for many years Counselor of the French legation at Washington, and enjoyed the friendship of Caleb Cushing, Charles Sumner, and Carl Schurz, to all of whom he acknowledges indebtedness. The volume shows considerable discernment, and is notable for its discriminating choice of materials. It would, in fact, be unjust to term it out of date even today. Chambrun agrees, in effect, with Lockwood's evaluation of the Presidency. "If, then," he writes, "the exercise of popular sovereignty such as has been witnessed for more than eighty years, should cease, and the organization of the states lose its present strength, the powers of the central government, and especially the executive branch, would in a corresponding degree be enlarged. It is also quite true that a change of foreign policy and an undue territorial extension would, for different reasons, bring about an analogous transformation." *Op. cit.*, p. 286.

[66] Wilson, *Congressional Government,* pp. 6, 11, 23, 301.

[67] *Ibid.*, pp. 41–43 *passim.*

[68] *Ibid.*, pp. 44–45. It cannot be said that Wilson showed much discernment in this passage. For one thing, he entirely overlooks the way in which their labors in committee keep most Congressmen out of mischief much of the time.

[69] *The American Commonwealth* (New York, 1895), I, 61.

[70] *Ibid.*, 223–224. Lord Bryce's words reflect a conventional view, but the fact is that individual incumbents of an office can be just as tenacious of its supposed powers and of its traditions as an assembly is of its supposed powers and traditions.

[71] *Ibid.*, II, 712–713.

[72] *Rise and Growth,* pp. 279–293 *passim.*

"In the strictest meaning of the term the [United States] federal government is a limited or constitutional monarchy, and the events of recent years have left it the only real monarchy of first-class importance in the world." Herbert A. Smith, *Federalism in North America* (Boston, 1923). See also Seward's statement on the title page of this volume. It comes from Louis John Jennings, *Eighty Years of Republican Government in the United States* (1868), p. 36.

[73] *Congressional Government,* pp. xi–xii.

[74] *Constitutional Government,* pp. 67–73 *passim.*

[75] Washington, Jefferson, Jackson, Polk, Lincoln, Hayes, Cleveland, Wilson, the two Roosevelts are my nominees.

"Americans have seen and heard their late President described variously as the thirty-first and the thirty-second President of the United States, and Mr. Truman as the thirty-second and the thirty-third President. The difference in reckoning springs from the case of Grover Cleveland. He served two terms, but not consecutively. He served in 1885–1889, was succeeded by Benjamin Harrison in the latter year and in turn succeeded Harrison for the term 1893–1897. In a list of Presidents running down the page Grover Cleveland appears twice, whereas all other multiple-term Presidents appear only once; even Franklin D. Roosevelt, who was elected four times.

"Actually there have been only thirty-two persons who became President of the United States, of whom President Roosevelt was the thirty-first person and President Truman is the thirty-second person. This is the count adopted in the World Almanac. Its list makes Grover Cleveland twenty-second President, Benjamin Harrison twenty-third, and puts an asterisk instead of a number before Grover Cleveland on his second appearance. Mr. Roosevelt is the thirty-first President on the World Almanac list.

"It is not, however, the usual practice and what may be called the authoritative form. President Roosevelt called himself the thirty-second President in his personal sketch in Who's Who, where Mr. Hoover calls himself the thirty-first President, and so back to Theodore Roosevelt, who called himself the twenty-sixth President, though he is Number 25 on the World Almanac list. Similarly the Dictionary of American Biography follows the higher enumeration, making Grover Cleveland, constructively, two persons.

"To most of us this may seem not wholly logical. What people have in mind when they want to know how many Presidents we have had is the number of persons who have held that high office. If we start counting by terms or fractions of a term, we will have had not far from fifty Presidents, of whom Franklin D. Roosevelt will account for no less than four." "Topics of the Times," *The New York Times,* April 17, 1945.

76 "If both Houses represent the states and the people, so does the President. The President represents in the executive department the whole people of the United States, as each member of the legislative department represents portions of them." Polk's Fourth Annual Message, December 5, 1848. Richardson, IV, 665.

"He [Jackson] claims to be not only the representative, but the immediate representative of the American people. What effrontery! . . . . Why he never received a vote from the American people. He was elected by the electors—the colleges." John C. Calhoun, as quoted in Professor C. Perry Patterson's *Presidential Government in the United States—The Unwritten Constitution* (University of North Carolina Press, 1947), p. 52. I regret that this interestingly written and informative work came out too late to be of much use to me in the preparation of this volume.

NOTES TO CHAPTER II*

1 Floyd R. Mechem, *A Treatise on the Law of Public Offices and Officers* (Chicago, 1890), §§89–94. See also 14 *Opins. A. G.,* 406 (1874).

2 David Hutchison, *The Foundations of the Constitution* (New York, 1928), p. 176. *Cf.* Calvin's Case, 4 Co. Rep. 1 (1608). For a curious argument asserting that citizens of the United States born before independence remained subjects of the British monarch when in his dominions, despite the Treaty of 1783, see George Chalmers, *Opinions of Eminent Lawyers* (London, 1814), II, 422 ff. On the source of the "natural-born citizen"

* Chapter II (Election, Tenure, Impeachment, etc.) begins on page 39.

clause, see Thach, *The Creation of the Presidency*, p. 137; *cf.* Farrand, III, 161. John Tyler was the first President born after independence, and James K. Polk the first "natural-born citizen of the United States" to be *elected* President.

3 Act of March 26, 1790, 1 Stat. 415.

4 Act of February 10, 1855, 10 Stat. 604; R. S. §1993; Act of March 2, 1907, 34 Stat. 1229; Act of October 14, 1940, 54 Stat. 1136; U. S. Code, tit. 8, §601.

5 Art. I, §8, cl. 4.

6 See especially *Mackenzie v. Hare,* 239 U. S. at 311–312.

In *United States v. Wong Kim Ark,* 169 U. S. 649 (1898), Justice Gray, speaking for the Court, indicates quite clearly the opinion that the above legislation was passed under the "naturalization" clause, and that children born abroad of American parents are therefore *naturalized* citizens; that, in short, to be a natural-born citizen of the United States one has to be born "within the United States and subject to its jurisdiction." *Ibid.,* 674, 702–703. The point, however, was not involved in the case; nor does Justice Gray explain why Congress in the Act of 1855 declares children born abroad of American parents *"to be* citizens of the United States."

7 Mr. Hoover's eligibility was defended at length by Mr. Wickersham in an elaborate opinion late in 1927. One point much stressed was that, with all his absences abroad on business, Mr. Hoover had taken great pains to retain his legal domicile in the United States. *The New York Times,* December 20, 1927; see also editorial in the same issue, entitled "Residency and Presidency"; also C. K. Burdick, *ibid.,* February 2, 1920; and Farrand, II, 498, 536, 598.

When President Coolidge accepted membership of the Sioux tribe in August 1927, a correspondent of *The New York Times* expressed concern lest he might by so doing have lost his citizenship of the United States, and so his right to remain President. *The New York Times,* August 27, 1927.

It should be noted that political considerations or accident have confined the Presidency to residents of twelve states, of which five—Virginia (7), New York (6), Ohio (6), Tennessee (3), and Massachusetts (3)—have supplied 25 of the 32. Of New York's 6 Presidents, 4 had been Vice-Presidents.

8 U. S. Code, tit. 18, §§ 2, 4, 51, 192, 199, 203, 207, 235, 237, 238. Mr. Earl Browder's conviction in 1940 was under such a section. *The New York Times,* June 25, 1940.

9 Originally this was assumed to mean 12.01 a.m., March 4—a belief which underlies the yarn about President Adams's "midnight appointments." How it came finally to be practically settled that the presidential term ended at noon March 4 is told by Mr. Charles Warren in an interesting and learned article published in 1941. "For thirty years," says Mr. Warren, "it was tacitly assumed that, as a matter of constitutional law, the Presidential term ended at midnight on March 3 and that the Congress came to an end at the same hour and on the same date," but "at a very early date, Congress attempted to deceive itself as to the arrival of midnight by tampering with the clock; but it still recognized midnight as the crucial hour." And in 1821, when the fourth of March chanced to fall on Sunday (as it did later in 1849, in 1877, and in 1917), and the question was put to the Supreme Court as to when the incoming President should take the oath of office, the Court, through Chief Justice Marshall, rendered what amounted to an advisory opinion, which among other things stated: "The time of the actual President will expire and that of the President-elect commence, at twelve in the night of the third of March." Thirty years later, to wit, in 1851, it was authoritatively ruled by both houses that the Congress then in session did not expire until the noon of March

4. This was on the theory that the legislative day of the third of March did not expire until that hour; and all laws enacted after midnight March 3–4 were still enrolled as of "March 3." Not until 1909 did the *Statutes at Large* list certain acts of Congress enacted at the end of the term of Congress as having been enacted on March 4. Meantime, by 1881 it had become apparent that the construction of thirty years previous had "hardened into a legal construction of constitutional rights"—those of the President as well as of Congress, since no President ever "asserted his right to be sworn into office a minute after midnight and thereafter act as President." With the going into effect of the Twentieth Amendment, the question, of course, lost its practical importance. Charles Warren, "Political Practice and the Constitution," 89 *University of Pennsylvania Law Review* (June 1941), 1003–1025. Chief Justice Marshall's "advisory opinion" was in the form of a letter to Secretary of State John Quincy Adams. The document "has only recently come to light in the files of the State Department," says Mr. Warren.

10 Washington's announcement occurred at the outset of his Farewell Address. Richardson, I, 213. Jefferson's announcement was made December 10, 1807, in response to an address from the Vermont Legislature thirteen months earlier. It reads:

"I received in due season the address of the Legislature of Vermont, bearing date the 5th of November, 1806, in which, with their approbation of the general course of my Administration, they were so good as to express their desire that I would consent to be proposed again to the public voice on the expiration of my present term of office. Entertaining as I do for the Legislature of Vermont those sentiments of high respect which would have prompted an immediate answer, I was certain, nevertheless, they would approve a delay which had for its object to avoid a premature agitation of the public mind on a subject so interesting as the election of a Chief Magistrate.

"That I should lay down my charge at a proper period is as much a duty as to have borne it faithfully. If some termination to the services of the Chief Magistrate be not fixed by the Constitution, or supplied by practice, his office, nominally four years, will in fact become for life, and history shows how easily that degenerates into an inheritance. Believing that a representative Government responsible at short periods of election is that which produces the greatest sum of happiness to mankind, I feel it a duty to do no act which shall essentially impair that principle, and I should unwillingly be the person who, disregarding the sound precedent set by an illustrious predecessor [Washington], should furnish the first example of prolongation beyond the second term of office.

"Truth also requires me to add that I am sensible of that decline which advancing years bring on, and feeling their physical I ought not to doubt their mental effect. Happy if I am the first to perceive and to obey this admonition of nature, and to solicit a retreat from cares too great for the wearied faculties of age.

"For the approbation which the Legislature of Vermont has been pleased to express of the principles and measures pursued in the management of their affairs, I am sincerely thankful, and should I be so fortunate as to carry into retirement the equal approbation and good-will of my fellow-citizens, generally, it will be the comfort of my future days and will close a service of forty years with the only reward it ever wished." *Writings* (Mem. ed.), XVI, 293.

Similar addresses from seven other states at about the same time elicited like responses. Nearly two years earlier Jefferson had written his friend John Taylor of Caroline, under date of January 6, 1805, that he proposed to follow Washington's "example of voluntary retirement," hoping that "a few more precedents will oppose the obstacle of habit to anyone after a while who shall endeavor to extend his term" or even "beget a disposition to establish it by an amendment of the Constitution." Only "one circumstance," he continued, "could engage my acquiescence in another election; to wit, such a division about a successor, as might bring in a monarchist. But this circumstance is impossible." *Ibid.,* XI, 56–57. Indeed, even while the adoption of the Constitution was pending, he had expressed concern over the "perpetual reëligibility" of the President. Said he, in a letter to Washington, from Paris, which was dated May 2, 1788: "This, I fear, will make an office for life. I was much an enemy of monarchy before I came to Europe. I am ten thousand times more so since I have seen what they are. . . . I shall hope that before there is danger of this change taking place in the office of President the good sense and free spirit of our countrymen will make the change necessary to prevent it. Under this hope I look forward to the general adoption of the new Constitution with anxiety as necessary for us under our present circumstances." See *ibid.,* VI, 385, 447, 454.

Washington, however, deprecated these apprehensions. Writing Lafayette, April 28, 1788, from Mount Vernon, he said:

"There are other points in which opinions would be more likely to vary, as for instance, on the eligibility of the same person for President, after he should have served a certain course of years. Guarded so effectively as the proposed Constitution is, in respect to the prevention of bribery and undue influence in the choice of President, I confess I differ widely myself from Mr. Jefferson and you, as to the necessity or expediency of rotation in that department. The matter was freely discussed in the convention and to my full conviction.

"Though I cannot have time or room to sum up the argument in this letter, there cannot, in my judgment, be the least danger that the President will by any practicable intrigue ever be able to continue himself one moment in office, much less perpetuate himself in it, but in the last stage of corrupt morals and political depravity, and even then there is as much danger that any species of domination would prevail. Though when a people have become incapable of governing themselves, and fit for a master, it is of little consequence from what quarter it comes. Under an extended view of this part of the subject I can see no propriety in precluding ourselves from the services of any man who in some great emergency shall be deemed universally most capable of serving the public." *Writings* (W. C. Ford, ed.), XI, 254, 257.

And Hamilton in *The Federalist* came out strongly for indefinite reëligibility:

"Nothing appears more plausible at first sight, nor more ill-founded upon close inspection than a scheme which in relation to the present point has had some respectable advocates,—I mean that of continuing the chief magistrate in office for a certain time and then excluding him from it, either for a limited period or forever after. This exclusion, whether temporary or perpetual, would have nearly the same effects, and these effects would be for the most part rather pernicious than salutary.

"One ill effect of the exclusion would be a diminution of the inducements to good behavior. There are few men who would not feel much less zeal in the discharge of a duty, when they were conscious that the advantages of the station with which it was connected must be relinquished at a determinate period, than when they were permitted to entertain a hope of *obtaining,* by *meriting,* a continuance of them. . . .

"Another ill effect of the exclusion would be the temptation to sordid views, to peculation, and, in some instances, to usurpation. An avaricious man, who might happen to fill the office, looking forward to a time when he must at all events yield up the emoluments he enjoyed, would feel a propensity, not easy to be resisted by such a man, to make the best use of the opportunity he enjoyed while it lasted. . . .

"An ambitious man, too, . . . in such a situation, would be much more violently tempted to embrace a favorable conjuncture for attempting the prolongation of his power, at every personal hazard, than if he had the probability of answering the same end by doing his duty.

"Would it promote the peace of the community, or the stability of the government to have half a dozen men who had had credit enough to be raised to the seat of the supreme magistracy, wandering among the people like discontented ghosts, and sighing for a place which they were destined never more to possess?

"A third ill effect of the exclusion would be, the depriving the community of the advantage of the experience gained by the chief magistrate in the exercise of his office. . . .

"A fourth ill effect of the exclusion would be the banishing men from stations in which, in certain emergencies of the state, their presence might be of the greatest moment to the public interest and safety. . . .

"A fifth ill effect of the exclusion would be, that it would operate as a constitutional interdiction of stability in the administration. By *necessitating* a change of men, in the first office of the nation, it would necessitate a mutability of measures. It is not generally to be expected, that men will vary and measures remain uniform. The contrary is the usual course of things. . . .

"There is an excess of refinement in the idea of disabling the people to continue in office men who had entitled themselves, in their opinion, to approbation and confidence; the advantages of which are at best speculative and equivocal, and are overbalanced by disadvantages far more certain and decisive." Earle, pp. 470–472.

[11] For a compilation of "Statements of Various Presidents of the United States with reference to the Presidential Term," see Bulletin No. 3, April 22, 1940 (Library of Congress, Legislative Reference Service). Jackson was the most persistent champion of an amendment to the Constitution limiting Presidents to one term. Cleveland also favored a similar reform, both in his letter accepting the nomination for President and in his first Inaugural Address. Buchanan, on the other hand, speaking in the House of Representatives February 6, 1829, said: "This principle [that no President shall be more than once reëlected] has now become as sacred as if it were written in the Constitution. I would be inclined to leave to the people of the United States, without incorporating it in the Constitution, to decide whether a President should serve longer than one term. The day may come when danger shall lower over us, and when we may have a President at the helm of State who possesses the confidence of the country, and is better able to weather the storm than any other pilot; shall we, then, under such circumstances, deprive the people of the United States of the power of obtaining his services *for a second term?*" (My italics.)

[12] The evidence relating to President Wilson's desire for a third term comprises some notes which were made at the time by the Hon. Carter Glass, a friend and supporter of Wilson, and which are reprinted in Mr. Rixey Smith's recent *Carter Glass, a Biography* (New York, 1939) (I quote the passage with the consent of the publisher, Longmans, Green and Company, Inc.):

"June 10, 1920. Grayson [Wilson's physician] told me President seriously contemplates permitting himself to be named for third term and said it would kill him. Later in the day Burleson [Postmaster General] told me he believed President wanted third term, saying he had told President latter or McAdoo would be nominated, to which President made no answer.

"June 16, 1920. Grayson at Executive Office expressed to me greatest anxiety about

President's third term thoughts, saying he literally impossible to measure up to exactions of campaign. Would probably kill him. Said President's sole idea was to lead fight for covenant; he was totally indifferent to all other considerations. Would resign after covenant was adopted. I told Grayson I did not think convention could be induced to nominate man in President's disabled condition, and if President was in robust health, 'twas barely possible Democratic party and American people might submerge third-term antipathies in their desire for permanent guaranty against war; but not in present circumstances. Grayson begged me to do all possible to guard against such an untoward development in San Francisco. Tumulty also today expressed concern about this third-term manifestation." *Op. cit.*, pp. 205–206.

¹³ The Democratic Platform of 1912 had contained a single term pledge for the party's nominee, which Wilson repudiated in his letter to A. Mitchell Palmer, February 5, 1913:

"As things stand now, the people might more likely be cheated than served by further limitations on the President's eligibility. His fighting power in their behalf would be immensely weakened. No one will fear a President except those whom he can make fear the elections. . . . If we want our Presidents to fight our battles for us we should give them the means, the legitimate means, the means their opponents will always have. Strip them of everything else but the right to appeal to the people, but leave them that. Suffer them to be leaders."

Cleveland, in his first Inaugural Address, announced that eligibility to reëlection constituted a grave danger to democracy; in fact, he served two terms and, prior to 1940, was the one President in our history who three times received a popular plurality.

¹⁴ Irwin Hood Hoover, *Forty-Two Years in the White House* (New York, 1934), pp. 166–180, a circumstantial account which leaves little doubt in the reader's mind that Coolidge expected to be "drafted" and was chagrined to the point of positive illness when he was not. H. L. Stoddard's attempted refutation in *It Costs To Be President* (New York, 1938), pp. 91 and 124, and Chs. 13 and 14, is quite unconvincing. Coolidge issued his statement at Rapid City, South Dakota, August 2, 1927. Neither former Secretary of the Treasury Shaw nor ex-President Taft thought that the third-term tradition barred Coolidge from running in 1928. *The New York Times*, February 9, 1927; H. F. Pringle, *Taft* (New York, 1939), II, 1061–1063.

¹⁵ Three volumes have been published on the subject, one before, one during, and one since "the great betrayal": Willis Thornton, *The Third Term Issue* (New York, 1939); Fred Rodell, *Democracy and the Third Term* (New York, 1940); Charles W. Stein, *The Third-Term Tradition* (Columbia University Press, 1946). The late President Roosevelt's first discussion of the subject occurred in his address at the Democratic Victory Dinner, March 4, 1937:

"A few days ago a distinguished Member of the Congress came to see me to talk about national problems in general and about the problem of the judiciary in particular.

"I said to him:

"John, I want to tell you something that is very personal to me—something that you have a right to hear from my own lips. I have a great ambition in life.'

"My friend pricked up his ears.

"I went on: 'I am by no means satisfied with having twice been elected President of the United States by very large majorities. I have an even greater ambition.'

"By this time my friend was sitting on the edge of his chair.

"I continued: 'John, my ambition relates to January 20, 1941.' I could feel just what horrid thoughts my friend was thinking. So, in order to relieve his anxiety, I went on to say: 'My great ambition on January 20, 1941, is to turn over this desk and chair in the White House to my successor, whoever he may be, with the assurance that I am at the same time turning over to him as President a nation intact, a nation at peace, a nation prosperous, a nation clear in its knowledge of what powers it has to serve its own citizens, a nation that is in a position to use those powers to the full in order to move forward steadily to meet the modern needs of humanity—a nation which has thus proved that the democratic form and methods of national government can and will succeed.

" 'In these coming years I want to provide such assurance. I want to get the Nation as far along the road of progress as I can. I do not want to leave it to my successor in the condition in which Buchanan left it to Lincoln.' " *Congressional Record,* Appendix, 75th Congress, 1st sess., p. 422.

[16] H. J. Res. 27, 80th Congress, 1st sess. One objection to the proposal appears on the face of it, its apparent uncertainty whether to speak of "the office of *the* President" or simply "the office of President."

[17] Of 85 proposals, prior to 1929, 63 favored a single term of six years, and one of these was adopted by the Senate February 1, 1913, by a vote of 47 to 23, a bare constitutional majority. In the House it never got out of committee. M. A. Musmanno, *Proposed Amendments to the Constitution* (70th Congress, 2nd sess.; H. D. No. 551; Government Printing Office, 1929), pp. 51–60. Between 1789 and 1889 over twenty-five proposals to restrict presidential reëligibility were brought forward in Congress without result. *Ibid.,* pp. 51–52.

[18] There was, in fact, as early as September 1941, a good deal of talk in administration circles to the effect that national elections ought to be "suspended during the crisis," which as yet did not embrace war. See Mr. Krock's column in *The New York Times* of September 18, 1941.

[19] See Henry Steele Commager, "Only Two Terms for a President?," *The New York Times Magazine,* April 27, 1947.

[20] See Ch. VII, note 89 *infra.* An Associated Press despatch from Washington suggests one definite and rather important argument against extended presidential terms: "Chairman Alexander Wiley of the Senate Judiciary Committee said today that he had told Attorney General Tom Clark that 'I will do everything I can to reject any more New Deal appointments to the Federal judiciary.' The judiciary committee passes on nominations to the Federal courts. Mr. Wiley said in a statement that 'New Dealers already pack the courts in innumerable instances,' and made public statistics which Mr. Clark prepared at his request. Those showed only seventeen Republicans among the 231 Federal judges appointed since 1932." *The New York Times,* January 10, 1947. It is with this kind of situation in mind that the following proposed constitutional amendment was offered in the Senate by Messrs. Eastland and Bridges, June 18, 1946: "Constitutional Amendment—The number of Associate Justices of the Supreme Court of the United States shall not be fewer than 6, and not more than 10, as Congress shall by law provide. All justices shall hold office during good behavior. No more than three justices shall be appointed by one President. Vacancies in excess of three which occur during the tenure of any President shall be filled by the House of Representatives, on the basis of one vote for the delegation from each State, from among judges of inferior Federal courts or of State courts of last resort who do not reside in a judicial district in which any other person holding office as a Justice of the Supreme Court resided at the date of taking such office. A person thus chosen by the House of Representatives shall hold office as Justice of the Supreme Court only until another President takes office, at which time he shall

be restored to his former judicial office. If more than three persons holding office as Justices of the Supreme Court on the date of the ratification of this amendment shall have been appointed by the same President, all persons holding such office who were appointed by that President, except the first three appointed, shall be retired." S. J. Res. 167. Messrs. Eastland and Bridges; June 18, 1946 (Judiciary), 79th Congress, 2nd sess. The resolution was referred to the Committee on the Judiciary but has not been further heard from.

There is a good summary of the debate in Congress on the pending amendment by Professor Everett S. Brown, in 41 *American Political Science Review,* 447–452: "Despite frequent denials to the contrary, party politics entered definitely into the debates in Congress. The principal demand for setting the time-limit on the term of the President came from Republicans, and the strongest opposition to it was offered by Democrats, who professed to see in it a slur on the memory of President Franklin D. Roosevelt. All in all, however, the debate was maintained on a fairly high plane."

[21] Art II, §1, par. 2. The term "college of electors," according to Professor Mc-Laughlin, was used by Abraham Baldwin in 1800 and by John Randolph in 1809, and "officially" in 1845. *Constitutional History of the United States* (New York, 1935), p. 702, n. 14, citing *Miscellaneous Documents of the House of Representatives,* 44th Congress, 2nd sess., No. 13.

[22] 146 U. S. 1.

[23] *Ibid.,* 29.

[24] James Wilson made the suggestion. Farrand, II, 97.

[25] *McPherson v. Blacker* grew out of this legislation.

[26] Everett S. Brown, ed., *The Missouri Compromise and Presidential Politics* (Missouri, 1926), pp. 53–62; C. O. Paullin, 21 *American Historical Review,* 318–319, and *cf.* note 28 *infra.*

[27] George H. Haynes, *The Election of Senators* (New York, 1906), p. 132.

[28] Benjamin Harrison, *This Country of Ours* (New York, 1898), p. 77; quoted in H. W. Horwill, *Usages of the American Constitution* (Oxford University Press, 1925), p. 38. For other statements to the same general effect, see *ibid.,* pp. 40–41. Horwill's account of what happened in 1872 and 1912 when one of the candidates—fortunately of the minority party—died between the November election and the meeting of the Electors affords a further demonstration of the present status of the Electoral College:

"Is there any possibility of the Electors regaining their forfeited independence? A situation is conceivable which would put the matter to the test.

" 'Should accident so shape events,' writes Dr. Von Holst, 'that the Presidential candidate of the victorious party should die immediately before the meeting of the Electoral College, then the United States would again have a President who was, not only in form but in truth, elected by the Electors. The effects that such an accident might produce are incalculable.'

"Such a case has never yet occurred. The nearest approach to it was in 1872, but with the important difference that the man who died was the candidate not of the victorious but of the defeated party. Horace Greeley, who had been defeated as Democratic candidate at the popular election on November 5, died on November 29. The Electors met a week later, on the very day on which he was carried to his grave. Out of a total of 366 Electoral votes there were sixty-six that would have come to him if he had lived. These sixty-six votes belonged to Democratic Electors in six States. The three Democratic Electors in Georgia evaded the difficulty by voting for the dead man. They felt themselves under a sacred obligation to vote for Greeley, and vote for him they did, although at the time he was in his coffin. The other Democratic votes were divided among four candidates, T. A. Hendricks receiving forty-two, B. Gratz Brown (the official party candidate for the Vice-Presidency) eighteen, C. J. Jenkins, two, and D. Davis one. As there was not the remotest chance of the election of a Democrat, what the Democratic Electors did with their votes did not really matter in the least.

"Another interesting incident occurred in 1912. In that year also the popular election was held on November 5. The Electors were to meet on January 13, 1913. The Vice-President, James S. Sherman, who had been nominated for re-election on the Republican ticket, died on October 30. It so happened that in this instance provision had been made for meeting such a situation. In its closing hours the Republican convention in June had passed a resolution authorizing the national committee to fill any vacancy on the ticket that might be caused by the death or disability of Mr. Taft (who was the party's candidate for re-election to the Presidency) or Mr. Sherman. This was done in such a way that it attracted no attention at the time. It was due to the fact that the managers of the convention were aware that Mr. Sherman's death was expected in the near future. The Republican national committee met hurriedly after Mr. Sherman's death, and decided that, as it was a question not of the Presidency but of the Vice-Presidency, it would not be worth while to complete the ticket until after the popular election. So that year the Republicans throughout the country cast their votes for Electors without knowing who would be Vice-President if their party was successful. The polling on November 5 showed that here, again, the choice of a substitute would be a mere formality. The committee, however, solemnly conferred together on November 12 and decided on a distinguished University President as the person for whom the Republican Electors should vote. With equal solemnity four Republican Electors in Vermont and four in Utah met on the appointed day in their respective State capitals, and cast for this gentleman the eight votes which were all that had been saved, out of a total Electoral vote of 531, from the wreck of orthodox Republicanism." Horwill, *op. cit.,* pp. 51–52.

When, nevertheless, in 1924, it appeared not unlikely that the late Senator La Follette, who was running on a third-party ticket, would capture enough electoral votes to prevent either of the major party candidates from getting a majority in the College, the suggestion was advanced that Mr. La Follette might throw his strength in the College to the Democratic candidate, Mr. Davis, or to a compromise candidate to be selected by himself and the Democratic party management. *The New York Times,* October 12, 1924.

[29] Preceding the Democratic National Convention of 1944 opponents of a fourth term for Mr. Roosevelt in three or four of the Southern states started a movement to obtain "free" electoral states from those states; *i.e.,* "free" to cast their votes for somebody else than F.D.R., whose renomination was already assured. The movement came to nothing. See Mr. Krock's column in *The New York Times* for May 7 and 28, June 13, 14, and 21, 1944.

In the prosecution of his similar feud with President Truman, Governor Tuck of Virginia had introduced into the Virginia General Assembly on February 26, 1948, a bill which provided in part as follows: "The electors of any political party who are elected in the general election shall be obligated and pledged to support and vote in the electoral college for the candidates for President and Vice-President who have been nominated by the National Convention of said party unless otherwise authorized or instructed by the duly constituted authorities of said party in Virginia. In such a case they shall be obligated to conform to and comply with such authorization or instructions." In a substitute measure the word "obligated" was replaced by the word "expected." I am endebted for copies of the two bills to my friend Professor William A. Mitchell of the University of Virginia.

30 An informed writer has expressed the opinion that popular election of the President in 1860 would have postponed the Civil War and perhaps have prevented it. Arthur C. Cole, "Lincoln's Election," 36 *American Historical Review* (July 1931), 740 ff.

31 For an interesting account of the first three presidential elections, and the gradual emergence of party lines, see an Associated Press despatch from Washington to *The New York Times* of July 12, 1936. Speaking of the third election the despatch says, among other things:

"In spite of his [Hamilton's] manoeuvring, when the votes were counted in the Electoral College, Adams had been elected by three votes. And Jefferson was the runner-up, thus giving the Federalist President a Republican Vice President.

"Pinckney had 59 votes and Aaron Burr had 30. The remainder were strewn among nine other candidates. Washington got two votes, one North Carolinian and one Virginian refusing to take his farewell message seriously.

"Curiously enough four of the votes were of questionable legality. And they were the four that decided the Presidency. Vermont had not enacted a law specifying how the electors should be chosen. But the Legislature had named four electors and sent them down to vote.

"They voted for Adams, thus giving him three more votes than Jefferson. Adams, presiding over the electoral colleges as President of the Senate, stated the result and then sat down to await a protest against the Vermont vote. Hearing none, he then declared himself elected President of the United States.

"And thus ended a campaign which had been so heated in spots that one orator had proclaimed:

" 'Damn John Jay. Damn every one who won't damn John Jay. Damn every one who won't put lights in his windows and sit up all night damning John Jay.' "

For the remarkable Federalist intrigues that preceded and followed the election of 1800, see Beveridge's *Life of John Marshall* (Boston, 1916), II, 452–458 and 532–547.

32 See on this subject P. L. Haworth, *The Hayes-Tilden Disputed Election* (New York, 1906); W. A. Dunning, *Reconstruction Political and Economic* (New York, 1907), Chs. XIX–XXI; Henry L. Stoddard, *It Costs To Be President* (1938); Charles Bradley, *Miscellaneous Writings of the Late Honorable Joseph P. Bradley* (Newark, 1902), pp. 165–223.

33 The constitutional question had been raised several times before this, in 1812, 1837, 1857, 1865, 1869, and 1873, but in circumstances which permitted its evasion. Stoddard, *op. cit.,* p. 262.

34 The bill was passed January 26, 1877. In the total 186 Democrats and 52 Republicans voted for it, while 18 Democrats and 85 Republicans opposed it. Having the President *pro tem* of the Senate and being assured of the support of the army, the vast majority of the Republicans were opposed to compromise, or at least pretended to be. Stoddard, *op. cit.,* p. 264.

35 Bradley, *Miscellaneous Writings,* etc., pp. 193–194.

36 *Ibid.,* p. 195.

37 It should be noted that even after the Electoral Commission had completed its work, the Democrats of the House were in a position by filibustering to prevent the count of electoral votes by the houses from being completed. That they did not was due to the

assurance which the Southern leaders of the party received that Hayes, once seated, would withdraw the federal troops from the Southern states whose electoral votes had been in dispute. Thus, although the South lost that particular election, it became master of its own household for future elections. See Stoddard, *op. cit.*, p. 263.

38 The Act of February 3, 1887, has since been replaced in part by the more detailed provisions of the Acts of May 29, 1928, and of June 5, 1934. See U. S. Code, tit. 3, Ch. I.

39 *Ibid.*, §§ 5a and 17.

40 *Ex parte* Yarbrough, 110 U. S. 651 (1884).

41 289 U. S. 159 (1933).

42 The argument advanced by Justice Pitney in his partially concurring opinion in *Newberry v. United States*, in support of the power of Congress to control prenomination expenditures of candidates for Congress, is equally applicable to this question:

"It seems to me too clear for discussion that primary elections and nominating conventions are so closely related to the final election, and their proper regulation so essential to effective regulation of the latter, so vital to representative government, that power to regulate them is within the general authority of Congress. It is matter of common knowledge that the great mass of the American electorate is grouped into political parties, to one or the other of which voters adhere with tenacity, due to their divergent views on questions of public policy, their interests, their environment, and various other influences, sentimental and historical. So strong with the great majority of voters are party associations, so potent the party slogan, so effective the party organization, that the likelihood of a candidate succeeding in an election without a party nomination is practically negligible. As a result, every voter comes to the polls on the day of the general election confined in his choice to those few candidates who have received party nominations, and constrained to consider their eligibility, in point of personal fitness, as affected by their party associations and their obligation to pursue more or less definite lines of policy, with which the voter may or may not agree. As a practical matter, the ultimate choice of the mass of voters is predetermined when the nominations have been made. Hence, the authority of Congress to regulate the primary elections and nomination conventions arises, of necessity, not from any indefinite or implied grant of power, but from one clearly expressed in the Constitution itself (Art. I, §8, cl. 18)—'To make all Laws which shall be necessary and proper for carrying into Execution the foregoing Powers, and all other Powers vested by this Constitution in the Government of the United States, or in any Department or Officer thereof.' This is the power preservative of all others, and essential for adding vitality to the framework of the Government. Among the primary powers to be carried into effect is the power to legislate through a Congress consisting of a Senate and House of Representatives chosen by the people—in short, the power to maintain a law-making body representative in its character. . . .

"The passage of the act under consideration amounts to a determination by the lawmaking body that the regulation of primary elections and nominating conventions is necessary if the Senate and House of Representatives are to be, in a full and proper sense, representatives of the people. Not only is this true of those cases referred to in the report of the Senate Committee (*Senate Reports*, No. 78, 62nd Congress, 1st sess., p. 2) where the parties are so unequally divided that a nomination by the majority party is equivalent to election; but it is true in every case to the extent that the nominating processes virtually eliminate from consideration by the electors all eligible candidates except the few—two or three, perhaps—who succeed in receiving party nominations. Sinister influences exerted upon the primaries inevitably have their effect upon the ultimate election—are employed for no other reason. To safeguard the final elections while leaving the proceedings for proposing candidates unregulated, is to postpone regulation until it is comparatively futile. And Congress might well conclude that, if the nominating procedure were to be left open to fraud, bribery, and corruption, or subject to the more insidious but (in the opinion of Congress) nevertheless harmful influences resulting from an unlimited expenditure of money in paid propaganda and other purchased campaign activities, representative government would be endangered." 256 U. S. 285–286, 287–288.

The principal suggestions for legislation thus far have revolved about "the Presidential Primary," a sort of nine-day wonder, which has today lost most of its popular appeal. On the institution at its heyday, see Miss Louise Overacker's volume *The Presidential Primary* (New York, 1926). Woodrow Wilson, in his first annual message to Congress, urged "the prompt enactment of legislation which will provide for primary elections throughout the country at which the voters of the several parties may choose nominees for the Presidency without the intervention of nominating conventions." *Congressional Record*, 63rd Congress, 2nd sess., p. 44; Overacker, p. 188 n. Ten years later Professor P. Orman Ray suggested legislation providing for a presidential primary which should follow the national conventions, and at which the voters would choose the party candidates for President and Vice-President from five or six names submitted by the Convention for President. The person getting the highest popular vote of the party would be the party candidate for President and the second highest would be the party candidate for Vice-President. 106 *Annals of the Academy of Political and Social Science* (March 1923), 61–71. Neither proposal ever led to anything.

43 *United States v. Classic*, 315 U. S. 299 (1941); *Smith v. Allwright*, 321 U. S. 649 (1944).

44 U. S. Code, tit. 50, §§301–302, 331, 333, 341.

45 No. 68; Earle, p. 441.

46 Several proposals have been introduced in the 80th Congress, 1st sess., for direct election of the President: S. J. Res. 91; H. J. Res. 9, 21, 68, 69, 87, 106, 107, 108, 124. The substance of S. J. Res. 91 is as follows: "Provides for the election of the President and Vice President by direct vote of the qualified voters at a general election on the first Tuesday after the first Monday in November (unless determined otherwise by Congress). The President shall take necessary steps to prevent abridgment of citizen's right to vote on account of race, creed, or color. Within 30 days after such election, each State shall certify and transmit the results thereof to the President of the Senate who on January 6 shall, in the presence of the Senate and the House of Representatives, open the certificates and count the votes. The person having the greatest number of votes for President and Vice President shall be declared President and Vice President, respectively. In case of a tie, the House of Representatives shall immediately choose the President from those having the three highest votes for President, voting by State with each State having one vote, and the Senate shall choose the Vice President, with a majority in each case necessary for election." The substance of H. J. Res. 21 is as follows: "Abolishes the electoral college and provides that the President and the Vice President shall be elected at a general election. Each State shall have a number of electoral votes equal to the number of Senators and Representatives to which it is entitled in Congress. Each candidate shall be credited with such proportion of the electoral vote of each State as he received of the total popular vote therein, fractional numbers less than one-thousandth to be disregarded unless a more detailed calculation would change the result of the election. In case of a tie in the electoral vote, the person

for whom the greatest number of popular votes was cast shall be President. The Vice President shall be elected in the same manner as the President." *Digest of Public General Bills with Index,* 80th Congress, 1st sess. (Library of Congress, 1947).

47 On the discussion growing out of Garfield's fatal illness see especially the symposium of views in 133 *North American Review* (November 1881), 417–446, the participants in which were Senator Lyman Trumbull, General Benjamin F. Butler, Judge T. M. Cooley, and Professor Theodore Dwight of Yale; also Urban A. Lavery's article on "Presidential 'Inability,'" in 8 *American Bar Association Journal,* 13–17. For President Arthur's repeated and ineffectual efforts to get Congress to legislate on the whole subject of presidential succession, see Richardson, VIII, 65, 147, 187. Not until 1886 did Congress respond, and then it did not touch the question of "inability."

Mr. Wilson's illness produced several legislative proposals in Congress, none of which was debated in either house, although evoking some discussion in committee. Their purport is sufficiently indicated in the following excerpt from a despatch to the *New York Evening Post* of March 1, 1920:

"Out of this discussion has come a quartet of bills on which hearings are now being held, designed to settle a question for which a satisfactory answer has long been awaited, namely, What constitutes the inability of a President within the meaning of the Constitution, and who shall decide when this disability arises?

"Representatives Fess of Ohio, Rogers of Massachusetts, Madden of Illinois and McArthur of Oregon, all Republicans, have introduced bills or joint resolutions which they believe will furnish the answer, and which are now receiving consideration at the hands of the House Judiciary Committee.

"All of the measures except that of Mr. Fess are based on the assumption that the power to prescribe a method of determining a President's disability is already vested in Congress by the Constitution. Representative Fess, on the other hand, believes that an amendment to the Constitution is necessary.

"The Rogers bill provides that on the request of either House the Supreme Court shall determine whether the President is unable to discharge his duties, and that the court may on its own initiative or on the request of either House determine whether the inability has been removed. If so, the President shall resume his official duties. In discussing this measure Chairman Volstead of the Judiciary Committee raised the point that it confers original jurisdiction upon the Supreme Court, whereas under the Constitution it has only appellate jurisdiction, except in certain cases specifically enumerated. He gave it as his view that if the fact of disability is to be judicially determined, this must be done by some other body than the Supreme Court.

"The bills of Representatives Madden and McArthur place the determination of the question in the hands of the Cabinet. In their view this body, being in political harmony with the President, will not be suspected of ulterior motives if it decides that a President is incapacitated. Moreover, their close contact with the Chief Executive will enable the Cabinet officers readily to ascertain the facts and render a quick decision. The McArthur bill defines inability as illness for a period of thirty days or absence from the continental United States for a similar period.

"Representative Fess, assuming that a constitutional amendment is necessary, has introduced a joint resolution proposing an amendment that empowers the Supreme Court to determine the question of disability when requested by a concurrent resolution of Congress. If Congress should not be in session, the Vice President is authorized to call a special session for this purpose upon the recommendation of the Cabinet.

"In opposition to all these measures another view has developed, namely, that these questions are already settled by the Constitution itself, and that no further legislation or amendment is necessary. It is held that the very act of a Vice President in calling Congress into session would establish the fact that a Presidential disability exists. Further machinery for passing on this question would therefore be superfluous. The fact of disability being thus established, the Constitution already provides that the duties of the Presidential office shall devolve upon the Vice President, and nothing further is required.

"This opinion has been enunciated by Henry E. Davis, a Washington lawyer, who has given considerable study to the subject and has prepared a monograph which the Senate sometime ago had printed as a public document. A number of Congressmen accepted this view. Mr. Davis contends that the wording of the Constitution concerning the disability of the President was not the result of carelessness on the part of the framers, but that it was drafted with the same care as the other provisions and was regarded as 'self-explanatory, self-operative and self-sufficient.' He maintains that the Vice President alone is the person to decide when this disability has arisen. 'No Vice President would assume to insist to a President against his judgment that he was under a disability,' says Mr. Davis, 'and so long as a President would resist such an intimation there would be no inability.'

"It has been brought out at the committee hearings that the problem involves much more than merely a definition of a President's inability. Some of the questions raised were: Who shall say when the inability ceases—the President himself, the Vice President or some other officer or officers? During the period of inability is the Vice President merely acting President for the time being or does he succeed to the full status of President?" See also *The New York Times,* February 19, 20, and 27, 1920; and 59 *Congressional Record,* 3106, 3158, 3217 (February 18, 19, 20, 1920).

The question of "inability" is not discussed by either Story or Hare, and is dealt with by Willoughby in his famous work only briefly. He considers the primary responsibility to rest with the Vice-President, but adds:

"It is to be assumed, however, that he would not take this serious step without previous consultation with, and approval by, the members of the President's cabinet and members of Congress. Having taken this step, its constitutionality could be tested in the courts by bringing before them the validity of his official acts, or of the acts of lower executive officials committed in reliance upon his orders. Thus, in last resort, the Supreme Court of the United States might be called upon to determine whether, in fact, there had existed an inability of the President which would constitutionally justify the exercise of presidential powers by the Vice-President. Similarly, should it happen that the disability of the President should prove to be temporary, and he should again claim the right to exercise the powers of his office, and the acting President should refuse, upon any ground to yield to this claim, the question as to who is to be recognized as legally entitled to exercise the powers of the President could be determined by the courts in cases involving the validity of the acts of either or both of the two claimants to the office." *Willoughby on the Constitution* (2nd ed.) (New York, 1929), III, 1470–1471. See also *Tucker on the Constitution* (Chicago, 1899), II, 713; and J. W. Burgess, *Political Science and Comparative Constitutional Law* (Boston, 1890–1891), II, 241.

[48] "Mr. Wilson's serious illness befell September 26, 1919, while he was on tour in the West in behalf of the Treaty of Versailles, which was then pending in the Senate. Three days later he returned to Washington. On October 4th he had a stroke of paralysis and was unconscious for nearly a week and semiconscious for over a month. His partial re-

covery was very slow and for three months he saw no one but Mrs. Wilson, his doctors and his nurses. During that period all state papers were given to Mrs. Wilson first. If she was in doubt as to the possible effect they would have on the President she submitted them to Dr. Grayson. If he thought that Mr. Wilson was strong enough to pass judgment on them without excitement, they were shown to him. If not, they were passed upon by Secretary of the Treasury Houston and one or two others in whom Mrs. Wilson had confidence." Letter by "Pollio," editorial page of *The New York Times*, March 29, 1921.

This brief narrative is much amplified by George Sylvester Viereck's articles in *Liberty* for February 20 and 27, 1932, entitled "When a Woman was President of the United States." Though written in a somewhat sensational strain, the articles are borne out as to their most important assertions of fact by Messrs. Tumulty, Houston, and others, as well as by press despatches of the period. See especially Mr. Tumulty's communication to *The New York Times* of December 3, 1921, and his *Woodrow Wilson as I Know Him* (New York, 1921), pp. 435–456; also David J. Houston, *Eight Years with Wilson's Cabinet* (New York, 1926), II, 36–70. Mrs. Wilson's *My Memoir* (New York, 1939) adds certain personal details which are of no interest in the present connection. See *ibid.*, pp. 283–302.

As late as December 3, 1919, *The New York Times* recorded that Senator Hitchcock, who was conducting the fight for the Treaty in the Senate, was unable to see the President. Two days later, however, it was stated that the President had seen Hitchcock three times; also that he had received Attorney General Palmer, William G. McAdoo, Dr. Axson, the King of Belgium, and the Prince of Wales. The day previous (December 4), the Senate Foreign Relations Committee created a subcommittee consisting of Senators Hitchcock and Fall to interview Mr. Wilson ostensibly in regard to our Mexican relations, really to find out if possible the extent of the President's incapacity. The request was granted after Admiral Grayson, the President's physician, had consulted Mrs. Wilson, who was present throughout the ensuing forty-minute interview. The Senators came away, *The Times* of December 5 records, "convinced that his [Mr. Wilson's] mind is vigorous and active."

Nevertheless, it was not until April 13, 1920, that the President was able to convene his Cabinet, which had meantime been meeting at intervals at the call of Secretary of State Lansing. Word of this proceeding having reached the President, the latter, on February 7, wrote Lansing to learn if such was the case, for, if it was, he professed to believe, a most serious breach of "the Constitutional system" had occurred. Mr. Lansing's reply, dated February 9, 1920, follows:

> The Secretary of State,
> Washington, Feb. 9, 1920.

My Dear Mr. President:

It is true that frequently during your illness I requested the heads of the executive departments of the Government to meet for informal conference.

Shortly after you were taken ill in October, certain members of the Cabinet, of which I was one, felt that, in view of the fact that we were denied communication with you, it was wise for us to confer informally together on interdepartmental matters and on matters as to which action could not be postponed until your medical advisers permitted you to pass upon them. Accordingly, I, as the ranking member, requested the members of the Cabinet to assemble for such informal conference, and in view of the mutual benefit derived the practice was continued.

I can assure you that it never for a moment entered my mind that I was acting unconstitutionally or contrary to your wishes, and there certainly was no intention on my part to assume powers and exercise functions which under the Constitution are exclusively confided to the President.

During these troublous times, when many difficult and vexatious questions have arisen and when in the circumstances I have been deprived of your guidance and direction, it has been my constant endeavor to carry out your policies as I understood them and to act in all matters as I believed you would wish me to act. If, however, you think that I have failed in my loyalty to you and if you no longer have confidence in me and prefer to have another conduct our foreign affairs, I am of course ready, Mr. President, to relieve you of any embarrassment by placing my resignation in your hands.

I am, as always,   Faithfully yours,
                                              ROBERT LANSING.

Upon receipt of this letter, finding "nothing in your [Lansing's] letter which justifies your assumption of Presidential authority in such a matter," Mr. Wilson on February 11 asked for the Secretary's resignation, a request which Mr. Lansing met the following day.

As a matter of fact, Lansing had not merely called the Cabinet together at times, but he had at the outset of the President's illness endeavored to induce the President's secretary, Mr. Tumulty, to join with him in calling on Vice-President Marshall to take over the President's "powers and duties." The story is told by Mr. Tumulty with considerable indignation in his *Woodrow Wilson as I Know Him*, pp. 443–444.

That inability definitely existed early in Mr. Wilson's illness is clear. In addition to the evidence already presented, the following statistics compiled by Professor Lindsay Rogers at the time are pertinent:

"To mention only one evidence, twenty-eight bills became law during the special session of Congress owing to the failure of the Executive to act within ten days (exclusive of Sundays) after their receipt at the White House; and when full disclosures are made as to the nature and times of the President's complete inability to act, it will be interesting to check them up with the dates on which bills were signed. For example, the President was able to veto the Prohibition Enforcement act on October 27, but he did not approve two statutes which became law on October 22 and 25, and he failed to sign Public Laws Numbers 67 and 82 inclusive (October 28 to November 18), with the exception of Number 73, the first General Deficiency Law for 1920, which was signed on November 4. After November 18 practically all of the bills became law with the signature of the President." *The Review*, May 20, 1920.

Public opinion as reflected by the press was substantially universal in its condemnation of the principal ground which Mr. Wilson advanced for dismissing Secretary Lansing. The following extract from the editorial column of *The New York Times* is sufficiently typical to warrant quotation:

"Of all men in the United States, President Wilson should have been most wary of raising that question. It was known early in October that he could not attend Cabinet meetings. If Congress had then accepted the theory which Mr. Wilson now propounds, that the Cabinet could do nothing without his presence, and consequently that Government business was at a standstill, Congress might have felt it to be its duty to ascertain whether in respect to the President the condition described by Article II., Section 5, of the Constitution as 'inability to discharge the powers and duties of the said office' actually existed. Had constitutional inability been ascertained and declared, the powers and duties of the President's office would at once have been devolved on the Vice President. That eventuality, we are very sure, would have been much more distasteful to President Wilson than Secretary Lansing's temporary and, as it seems to us and to the people of the country, absolutely necessary assumption of the power to bring the Cabinet members together in informal conferences." *Ibid.*, February 15, 1920.

See also Secretary of Commerce Redfield's astonished comment on the President's action. *Ibid.*, February 17, 1920.

The question remains whether Mr. Lansing's action amounted to a usurpation of presidential function. The precedents are few and of uncertain bearing. Secretary Blaine called Cabinet meetings during Garfield's illness, and Secretary Knox during an absence of President Taft from Washington; also, the Cabinet met during the Boxer troubles at a time when President McKinley was absent from the Capital. But it does not appear that on any of these occasions presidential approval was lacking. Nor is it to the point, as some of Mr. Wilson's critics seemed to think it was, that members of the Cabinet are sometimes required by statute to consult with one another. Thus, the Grain Futures Act of 1922 is administered in part by a commission consisting of the Secretaries of Agriculture and Commerce and the Attorney General, and the Council of National Defense is made up of the Secretaries of War, Navy, Interior, Agriculture, Commerce, and Labor. In short, Lansing acted without the backing of substantial precedent in a situation that was also without precedent.

The question of Mr. Wilson's "inability" was once raised in court. This was when the government attorneys, in the suit to upset the Alien Property Custodian's sale of German dye and chemical patents to the Chemical Foundation, asked the United States district court at Wilmington to take notice of the fact that when President Wilson signed the order approving the sale, he was a sick man. *The New York Times,* October 30, 1923. The sale was upheld.

49 The story of Tyler's succession is graphically told in Henry W. Horwill's *Usages of the American Constitution,* pp. 69–74.

50 *Ibid.*, p. 75.

51 The Hon. Leslie M. Shaw, as quoted in *The New York Times,* February 9, 1927.

52 Horwill, pp. 58–66. He is supported, I admit, by J. Q. Adams. *Ibid.*, pp. 72–73.

53 Mr. Horwill also urges the fact that in the states of the Australian Commonwealth, when a governor leaves his state temporarily or becomes ill, the lieutenant-governor administers the government in the interval, but does not become governor. *Ibid.*, p. 67. He might have added that a like practice prevails in the states of the United States. By way of illustration see a decision of the Oklahoma Supreme Court on the point which is mentioned in *The New York Times,* February 20, 1927. It is possible too that Mr. Horwill might have bolstered his grammatical argument by stressing the verb "devolve" in the constitutional clause. At least, Mr. John Brook Leavitt argued that an "office" *passes,* but that "powers and duties" *devolve. Ibid.*, August 11, 1923. See also Fessenden's *Fessenden* (New York, 1907), II, 246–247.

54 Nevertheless, it was the opinion of Webster that there could be no temporary succession by the Vice-President, but that even though the President recovered from his "inability," the Vice-President, having once assumed the powers and duties of the presidential office, would continue to the end of the term for which both were elected. This, of course, was before the Twentieth Amendment, but it serves to strengthen the argument that the Vice-President was originally expected to succeed to the "office" and not merely its "powers and duties." See Thomas Ewing in *The New York Times,* December 10, 1921.

[55] Stressing those powers and duties of the President which can be best performed at the seat of government, former Attorney General Wickersham was strongly of the opinion that Mr. Wilson's absence abroad would amount to "inability" in the constitutional sense, and suggested that the Vice-President could be compelled by mandamus to exercise the powers and duties of the presidential office while the "inability" continued. In the latter connection he cited *Attorney General v. Taggart*, 66 N. H. 362, a state case. At the same time he admitted that this would be "rather an unsatisfactory remedy." Mr. Wickersham was answered by Mr. Samuel Untermeyer and Mr. Louis Marshall, who pointed out that the President had powers and duties which might well take him abroad, namely, as Commander-in-Chief and as treaty maker, and that therefore the Constitution must have contemplated his occasional absence from the seat of government. *The New York Times, supra*. Nor did Vice-President Marshall agree with Mr. Wickersham, as the following despatch in *The Sun* of December 10, 1918, indicates:

"The first Cabinet meeting directed to a certain extent by wireless from mid-ocean was held in the White House today, with Vice President Marshall officiating in the President's absence. It lasted one hour and a half and by all reports had many novel features, though the business of the nation was transacted in the usual way. So far as the records go no other Vice-President ever has presided at a Cabinet meeting.

"A wireless message from the *George Washington* asked Vice-President Marshall if he would preside and the latter assumed his temporary duty as acting President. At the outset of the meeting the Vice President said:

" 'Gentlemen: In assuming the chair and presiding over what is known as a meeting of the Cabinet, I deem it proper to make a brief statement so that my conduct may not be misunderstood or misinterpreted. I am here and am acting in obedience to a request preferred by the President upon the eve of his departure and also at your request. But I am here informally. I am not undertaking to exercise any official duty or function. I shall preside in an unofficial and informal way over your meetings out of deference to your desires and those of the President.'

"Mr. Marshall astonished his audience by saying he had been much interested and concerned over the various opinions offered by constitutional lawyers as to whether he was or was not rightfully entitled to Mr. Wilson's job. Not knowing just where he stood, he said, he had written to Newt Plum, a constable in Indiana, to ask his advice. In reply he had received a message saying: 'The President by leaving the country loses his office but retains his salary.'

" 'Under these conditions,' the Vice-President said, 'I don't want to have anything to do with the office.'

"A report of the day's proceedings will be sent to the President either by wireless or cable after he reaches France."

On Washington's refusal to enter Rhode Island before she entered the Union, see Jared Sparks, *Life of Washington* (Boston, 1839), pp. 421, 429; and see generally David Hunter Miller's article on "Some Legal Aspects of the Visit of President Wilson to Paris," 36 *Harvard Law Review* (November 1921), 51–78. While it seems not to have occurred to Washington, in connection with any of his numerous tours, to ask Adams to act for him during his absence, an unwritten rule later developed that when the President was on an extended jaunt, the Vice-President should hover in the neighborhood of the Capitol. But even this rule was violated in October 1935 when both President and Vice-President were out of the country. *The New York Times,* October 17, 1935.

[56] Richardson, VII, 364–366.

[57] The point was made several times in the course of the debate on the act. See Benton's *Abridgement,* I, 333–335.

[58] U. S. Code, tit. 3, §21. For an excellent discussion of the act against its historical and constitutional background, see Charles S. Hamlin, "The Presidential Succession Act of 1886," 18 *Harvard Law Review* (1905), 182–195.

[59] *Congressional Record,* June 19, 1945, pp. 6382–6383. See also Robert S. Rankin, "Presidential Succession in the United States," 8 *Journal of Politics* (February 1946), 44–56; and Lucius Wilmerding, "The Presidential Succession," *Atlantic Monthly* for May 1947.

[60] The following is the substance of several of the proposals offered: One proposed a special election to fill out the unexpired term when a vacancy occurred in the office of both President and Vice-President. Another provided for the resummoning of the Electoral College to elect a President and Vice-President to serve out the remainder of the unexpired term. A third provided for the election of a President by the House of Representatives from a list of three Senators presented by the Senate. H. J. Res. 362 provided that the ranking officer of the Army, of the Navy, and of the Army Air Forces should select a civilian as interim President who should act until "the State governors, at a meeting called by him, shall select from among their number by majority vote a President and Vice President" to serve out the unexpired term. H. J. Res. 230 provided "for a First, a Second, and a Third Vice President of the United States, who shall, in the order named, succeed to the office of the President or act as President" to fill out an unexpired term. *Digest of Public General Bills,* 79th Congress (Library of Congress, 1946). *Cf.* note 72 *infra.*

[61] Message of February 5, 1947, 80th Congress, 1st sess., H. D. No. 89.

[62] Public Law No. 199, 80th Congress, 1st sess. (July 18, 1947). For a good discussion of the measure, see Professor Joseph E. Kallenbach, "The New Presidential Succession Act," in 41 *American Political Science Review* (October 1947), 931–941.

[63] Although no President has ever resigned, Mr. Wilson contemplated doing so if Mr. Hughes was elected in 1916. Says Mr. Lansing, in a "most confidential" communication, "the President . . . suggested the following plan: In the event of his defeat he would ask me to resign as Secretary of State and then he would name Mr. Hughes as my successor; as soon as the latter had assumed office, Mr. Wilson himself would resign as President, and Mr. Marshall, the Vice-President, would also resign; thus Mr. Hughes would succeed to the Presidency by reason of his holding the office of Secretary of State." R. S. Baker, *Woodrow Wilson,* VI, 292–293.

Later, during the fight over the Treaty of Versailles, the suggestion was made in certain quarters that both Mr. Wilson and Mr. Marshall should resign, thus bringing Secretary of State Lansing into the succession, whereupon Mr. Lansing would summon Congress into session, in accordance with the provisions of the Act of 1886, and it would proceed to call a special election, which would amount to a popular referendum on the Treaty of Versailles. Indeed, after the election of 1920, which Mr. Wilson asserted would be just such a referendum, and "a great and solemn" one, Mr. Bryan called upon Mr. Wilson to resign, after first making Mr. Harding Secretary of State. *New York Tribune,* November 5, 1920.

The possibility of a President's resigning is dealt with in a provision of the Act of March 1, 1792, which in substance still remains on the statute books:

"Resignation or refusal of office. The only evidence of a refusal to accept, or of a resignation of the office of President or Vice President, shall be an instrument in writing, declaring the same and subscribed by the person refusing to accept, or resigning, as the case may be, and delivered into the office of the Secretary of State." U. S. Code, tit. 3, §23.

Following the recent November election, Senator Fulbright of Arkansas suggested that President Truman resign, but the President rejected "the soft impeachment." *The New York Times,* November 7, 1946 (Associated Press despatch), and November 8 (John D. Morris's despatch). Mr. Truman had been invited by a correspondent of *The New Republic* as early as March 4, 1946, to promise his resignation "if the opposition wins the congressional election."

On Calhoun's resignation from the Vice-Presidency December 28, 1832, see an interesting note by Professor Everett S. Brown in 22 *American Political Science Review* (August 1928), 732–733.

[64] In view of some of the things just said in the text it is pertinent to recall certain principles of the common law respecting public office. I quote another communication to the *Times:* "The United States is a corporation in a legal sense, as are all the individual States (*United States v. Maurice,* 2 Brock, 96, 109, by Chief Justice Marshall; *Respublica v. Sweers,* 1 Dall. 41; *Dugan v. U. S.,* 3 Wheat. 172; *State of Indiana v. Woram,* 6 Hill [N. Y.] 33, 38). It is, of course, the general rule as to all corporations that, in the absence of some positive law, charter or by-law to the contrary, the president continues in office until his successor is elected and qualifies (7 *Ruling Case Law* 427; 14a *Corpus Juris* 72). It is also the general rule that public officers, in the absence of any constitutional or statutory prohibition, hold over after the conclusion of their terms until their successors are elected and qualify (22 *Ruling Case Law* 554; *Jones v. Roberts County,* 27 So. Dak. 519). In particular, such is the rule with regard to the governor of a state (*Carr v. Wilson,* 32 W. Va. 419). The supreme court of appeals of West Virginia, in the case cited, decided, in 1889, that the provisions of the constitution of West Virginia expressly limiting the term of governor to four years and making him ineligible to re-election did not prevent him from continuing to discharge the duties of his office after his term and pending the decision of a contested election of a successor. It is particularly significant that the constitution in question expressly made the governor ineligible for a second term of four years, yet the court held that such clause did not operate to create a vacancy in the office of governor at the expiration of the term. The Constitution of the United States merely provides affirmatively that the President, 'shall hold office during the term of four years,' and nowhere therein can language be found expressly negativing a term of longer duration than four years or making the President ineligible for a second or third or greater term of office." John Edmund Hewitt, *The New York Times,* December 14, 1924. Relevant, too, in the same connection is the following communication to the same journal: "The New York Times's Washington dispatch stated that the first term of President Roosevelt and Vice President Garner ended at noon on January 20, and that it was twenty-eight minutes later before the country had a new head, because Vice President Garner was not sworn in until 12:28. While I do not claim to be an expert such as Charles Watkins, Senate parliamentarian, it seems to me that the Twentieth Amendment to the Constitution distinctly guards against a single moment when the nation shall be minus a head. Section 3 of Article XX says: 'If, at the time fixed for the beginning of the term of the President, the President-elect shall have died, the Vice President-elect shall become President; if a President shall not have been chosen before the time fixed for the beginning of his term, or if the President-elect shall have failed to qualify, then the Vice President-elect shall act as President until a President shall have qualified.' At

noon on January 20, when the terms of the President and Vice President ended, it is a fact that twenty-eight minutes elapsed before the Vice President took his oath of office, and that in the meantime the President had not qualified, but during that time, under the Constitution, the Vice President-elect was acting as President. The Constitution does not demand that the Vice President-elect shall qualify before he is able to act as President." Henry Litchfield West, *The New York Times*, January 23, 1937.

65 See Percy Ernst Schramm, *History of the English Coronation Oath* (Legg, tr.; Oxford, 1937), pp. 179–227. Coke's remark in Sutton's Hospital Case, 10 Rep. 23a (1615) is also good indirect evidence: "A thing which is not *in esse* but in apparent expectancy is regarded in law; as a Bishop who is elected before he is consecrated; an infant in his mother's womb before birth." Had he regarded an uncrowned king as falling in the same class, Coke could not have failed to mention the fact.

The Hon. David R. Atchison's claim, therefore, that as President *pro tem* of the Senate he was "President *de jure* of the United States" a single day, namely Sunday, March 4, 1849, in consequence of General Taylor's refusal to take the oath of office on the Sabbath, must be disallowed.

The taking of the presidential oath once at least occurred in highly picturesque circumstances. The following despatch to *The New York Times* of August 3, 1923, tells the story:

"Plymouth, Vt., Aug. 3.—Facing his father and with his wife at his side, Calvin Coolidge was sworn in as the thirtieth President of the United States at 2:43 this morning, standard time, in the parlor of the Coolidge homestead, directly across the road from the house in which he was born.

"The President's father, John Calvin Coolidge, 78 years old, like his son, of stalwart New England stock, administered the oath of office. It was the first time in the history of the Republic that a father installed his son as the Chief Executive of the nation.

"The ceremony took place in a typical New England parlor or sitting room, a comfortably furnished, livable room in the father's farm house at Plymouth Notch, in the southern part of the Green Mountains, nearly 2,000 feet above the level of the sea.

"The faint light of an old-fashioned kerosene lamp, with a fluted top chimney and etched sides, was sufficient to throw the faces of the President and his father into bold relief. The rest of the small group that witnessed the simple ceremony were in a half light, almost a shadow. Back of the President was a large framed portrait of himself, which occupies the position of honor in his father's home.

"The President's father, sturdy and active despite his years, stood at the south side of a small centre table that held the lamp, the family bible and a number of other books. . . .

"It was an impressive sight when Mr. Coolidge took his place opposite his father. The President's face was pale. His bearing was marked by the simple dignity and poise which has characterized him all through the difficult period of President Harding's illness.

"The elder Coolidge, who bears a marked resemblance to his son and has the same immobility of features, asked the President to raise his right hand. The President did so, and his father then read him the following oath, prescribed by the Constitution of the United States, the form of which had been received by telegraph and telephone only a few minutes before from Washington.

" 'I do solemnly swear that I will faithfully execute the office of President of the United States and I will to the best of my ability preserve, protect and defend the Constitution of the United States.'

"The President repeated the oath after his father. There was a tense moment as he paused, with hand still uplifted, and added in a voice deep with feeling: 'So help me God.' "

On his return to Washington, however, Mr. Coolidge took the precaution to be sworn in a second time, the oath on this occasion being administered by Justice Hoehling of the supreme court of the District of Columbia, in a room of the New Willard Hotel, and a Gideon Bible was used. Attorney General Daugherty pledged the justice to secrecy, and the transaction was not divulged till more than eight years later. *The New York Times,* December 3, 1932. No doubt Mr. Coolidge sensed the superior popular appeal of the original oath, whatever might be its constitutional deficiencies. See also H. B. Learned, "The Vice-President's Oath of Office," *The Nation,* March 1, 1917.

66 As a matter of fact the President enjoys many more "emoluments" from the United States than the "compensation" which he receives "at stated times"—at least, what most people would reckon to be emoluments.

"For compensation of the President of the United States, $75,000. For compensation of the Vice President of the United States, $15,000.

"OFFICE OF THE PRESIDENT: Salaries: For personal services in the office of the President, including the Secretary to the President, and two additional secretaries to the President at $10,000 each; $136,500: *Provided,* That employees of the executive departments and other establishments of the executive branch of the Government may be detailed from time to time to the office of the President of the United States for such temporary assistance as may be deemed necessary. Contingent expenses: For contingent expenses of the Executive Office, including stationery, record books, telegrams, telephones, books for library, furniture and carpets for offices, automobiles, expenses of garage, including labor, special services, and miscellaneous items to be expended in the discretion of the President, $50,000. For printing and binding, $2,700. Traveling expenses: For traveling and official entertainment expenses of the President of the United States, to be expended in his discretion and accounted for on his certificate solely, $25,000. Total, Executive Office proper, $304,200.

"EXECUTIVE MANSION AND GROUNDS: For the care, maintenance, repair and alteration, refurnishing, improvement, heating, and lighting, including electric power and fixtures of the Executive Mansion, the Executive Mansion greenhouses, including reconstruction, and the Executive Mansion grounds, and traveling expenses, to be expended as the President may determine, notwithstanding the provisions of any other Act, $146,750. Total, Executive Office, $450,950." Public Law No. 8, 76th Congress, 1st sess., approved March 16, 1939. See also B. Sparkes, "The President's Salary and Other Perquisites," *The Saturday Evening Post,* November 7, 1936.

The above provision is supplemented by Art. I, sec. 9, par. 8, which reads as follows: "No title of nobility shall be granted by the United States; and no person holding any office of profit or trust under them, shall, without the consent of the Congress, accept of any present, emolument, office or title of any kind whatever from any king, prince, or foreign state." But, of course, there are always other members of the family who do not hold "any office of profit or trust" under the United States.

Public taste has not invariably been quite as rigid as it is today as to what favors a President may properly accept from private givers. The following paragraphs from Mr. George Fort Milton's interesting volume, *The Age of Hate* (New York, 1930), are quoted with the consent of the publishers, Coward-McCann, Inc.:

"Early in the summer of 1865 a group of New York bankers and merchants opened a subscription to buy the President a span of horses, a handsome carriage and the requisite accoutrements. Johnson declined the gift in firm though courteous words which met with great approval through the whole country. 'Nothing has given more satisfaction to all patriots and thinking men than your refusal to accept the present,' Senator Dixon wrote from Hartford.

"It seems, however, that Johnson did accept a free insurance policy tendered by the Phoenix Mutual Life Insurance Company. At that time it was the custom of this company to vote policies free of cost to the President, the Vice-President, and Speaker of the National House of Representatives. On January 9, 1865, according to the minute book of the Board of Directors of the Phoenix, 'it was voted that the premiums on policies issued to President Lincoln, Vice President Hamlin, and Speaker Colfax, be tendered them as a gratuity.' On April 17, the minute book records that 'the policy of Andrew Johnson was made free for one year.' According to the legends of the company, Lincoln refused, while Johnson accepted the free policies." *Op. cit.*, p. 232.

[67] *Evans v. Gore,* 253 U. S. 245; *Miles v. Graham,* 268 U. S. 501.

[68] *O'Malley v. Woodrough,* 307 U. S. 277 (1939).

[69] See generally L. C. Hatch and E. L. Shoup, *History of the Vice-Presidency of the United States* (New York, 1934), especially Chs. III–V; also Oliver P. Field, "The Vice-Presidency of the United States," 56 *American Law Review* (1922), 365–400. There have been thirty-three Vice-Presidents, six of whom (Adams, Clinton, Tompkins, Calhoun, Marshall, and Garner) were chosen for a second term, and seven of whom (Tyler, Fillmore, Johnson, Arthur, T. Roosevelt, Coolidge, and Truman) succeeded to the Presidency through the death of the President. Of the latter group two (T. Roosevelt and Coolidge) succeeded themselves in the Presidency. Of the remaining Vice-Presidents only three were elected to the Presidency (Adams, Jefferson, and Van Buren), and this occurred in the first half century of the government.

[70] Adams was of a bilious and jealous disposition. Jefferson's attitude toward the office was very different. He professed to regard its "tranquil and unoffending" character as a recommendation, as assuring him "philosophical evenings in winter and rural days in summer."

[71] It is further characteristic of Adams that the first time he became Vice-President he delivered an Inaugural Address. The custom—perhaps fortunately—died "a-bornin'."

[72] Farrand, II, 536–537. Even as early as 1803 John Randolph had suggested that the office could be eliminated with advantage—a suggestion which was renewed recently in connection with the discussion of presidential succession. In this connection Mr. Wilmerding, pointing out that, while "we choose our President, our choice for Vice-President is forced," that "like Siamese twins, the two candidates come together or not at all," urged that the succession question be met by "the abolition of the Vice-Presidency, the holding of a mid-term election if the office of President becomes vacant, and the designation by Congress of the Secretary of State to act as a caretaker President until a new President is elected, or, in the case of a presidential disability, until the disability is removed." See note 59 *supra.* I would add: first, that a President should not be chosen under this plan if less than two years of the former incumbent's term remained; secondly, that a President so chosen should hold only until the end of the term of the former incumbent, in order to permit a new President, a new House, and a new one third of the Senate to be chosen at the same time; and, thirdly, that instead of the Secretary of State being designated as "caretaker President," the office of Assistant to the President be created, the holder of it to have such duties and powers

as the President cares to devolve upon him, plus the duty to take over if the Presidency becomes vacant. All this could be accomplished by mere act of Congress except the liquidation of the Vice-Presidency, which would call for a constitutional amendment. This feature of the plan, fortunately, while highly desirable, is not urgent. The country having already put up with the Vice-Presidency for 160 years will probably not succumb if the office continues for a while longer. Meantime, there is, theoretically, nothing to prevent the rise of a custom which would require that a Vice-President resign immediately upon his election. A pledge to this effect might, perhaps, be exacted of him by his running mate, as was in fact exacted by President Wilson of Vice-President Marshall against the contingency of Mr. Hughes's election in 1916. Inasmuch as Vice-Presidents are characteristically chosen only for the honor of the thing, such a pledge should be easy to obtain, provided it was accompanied by the understanding that persons practising this act of self-abnegation should be rewarded with a fat pension.

73 Maitland, *Constitutional History,* p. 99.

74 Richardson, II, 576. For an anticipation of Jackson's position, however, see a portentously pompous passage which Jefferson had originally intended to include in his first message to Congress, and where, citing his oath, he declared the Sedition Act "to be a palpable and unqualified contradiction to the Constitution," and announced his intention on that ground of pardoning convicted offenders under it. Inasmuch as the President is free to exercise the pardoning power for good reasons, bad reasons, or no reason at all, the argument was quite superfluous, and so Jefferson evidently decided finally. Beveridge, *Life of John Marshall,* III, 605–606.

75 Charles Warren, *The Supreme Court in United States History* (New York, 1926), II, 223–224.

76 The tale has no better source than Greeley's *American Conflict,* I, 106, where Greeley credits it to "the late Governor George N. Briggs, of Massachusetts, who was in Washington as a member of Congress when the decision was rendered." Mr. Warren thinks the tale a myth, but Mr. Marquis James holds otherwise, quoting the following from the *National Journal* of April 7, 1832: "The prerogative of nullifying laws and political decisions by denying their conformity to the court makes . . . [the President] supreme—the final arbiter—the very Celestial Majesty." *Andrew Jackson, Portrait of a President* (Indianapolis, 1937), pp. 304–305. The word "court" in the above quotation ought to be, I suspect, "constitution."

77 Richardson, VI, 25.

78 Evarts's words were:

"Much has been said about the duty of the people to obey and of officers to execute unconstitutional laws. I claim for the President no greater right in respect to a law that operates upon him in his public duty, and upon him exclusively, to raise a question under the Constitution to determine what his right and what his duty is, than I claim for every citizen in his private capacity when a law infringes upon his constitutional and civil and personal rights. . . . And are we such bad citizens when we advise that the Constitution of the United States may be upheld, and that anybody, without a breach of the peace and in an honest purpose, may make a case that the instance may be given whereby the judgment of the court may be had and the Constitution safe from violation?" *Trial of Andrew Johnson* (Washington, 1868), II, 293, 296.

79 *Ibid.,* 200.

80 *Ibid.,* 71. Boutwell was the speaker.

81 *Ibid.*, 256.

82 See Willoughby, III, 1502–1504, for substantially this view. In *United States v. Lee*, Justice Miller, speaking for a divided Court, said:

"No man in this country is so high that he is above the law. No officer of the law may set that law at defiance with impunity. All the officers of the government, from the highest to the lowest, are creatures of the law, and are bound to obey it.

"It is the only supreme power in our system of government, and every man who by accepting office participates in its functions is only the more strongly bound to submit to that supremacy, and to observe the limitations which it imposes upon the exercise of the authority which it gives." 106 U. S. 196, 220.

While these words state the general theory of the President's duty as Chief Executive to the law as it comes from the courts, yet in the light of the Court's earlier ruling in *Mississippi v. Johnson* that duty must be held to be *moral* rather than *legal* in character —one the final forum of which is the President's own conscience, not a court of law. 4 Wall. 475 (1867).

83 In the Chase impeachment the prosecution advanced the doctrine that impeachment is "an inquest of office," a political process for turning out of office any official whom a majority of the House and two thirds of the Senate wished to be rid of. The failure of the impeachment went to establish the opposed view that it is essentially a criminal proceeding. Beveridge, III, 198–216.

The same issue was nevertheless raised at Johnson's trial by Manager Bingham who at the outset defined an impeachable offense as follows:

"The result is, that an impeachable high crime or misdemeanor is one in its nature or consequences subversive of some fundamental or essential principle of government or highly prejudicial to the public interest, and this may consist of a violation of the Constitution, of law, of an official oath, or of duty, by an act committed or omitted, or, without violating a positive law, by the abuse of discretionary powers from improper motives or for an improper purpose." *Trial of Andrew Johnson* (1868), I, 147.

This position was rebutted with great acuteness by former Justice Benjamin R. Curtis, one of Johnson's counsel. Said Curtis, in part:

"In the front of this inquiry the question presents itself: What are impeachable offences under the Constitution of the United States? Upon this question learned dissertations have been written and printed. One of them is annexed to the argument of the honorable manager who opened the cause for the prosecution. Another one on the other side of the question, written by one of the honorable managers themselves, may be found annexed to the proceedings in the House of Representatives upon the occasion of the first attempt to impeach the President. And there have been others written and published by learned jurists touching this subject. I do not propose to vex the ear of the Senate with any of the precedents drawn from the middle ages. The framers of our Constitution were quite as familiar with them as the learned authors of these treatises, and the framers of our Constitution, as I conceive, have drawn from them the lesson which I desire the Senate to receive, that these precedents are not fit to govern their conduct on this trial.

"In my apprehension, the teachings, the requirements, the prohibitions of the Constitution of the United States prove all that is necessary to be attended to for the purposes of this trial. I propose, therefore, instead of a search through the precedents which were made in the times of the Plantagenets, the Tudors, and the Stuarts, and which have been repeated since, to come nearer home and see what provisions of the Constitution of the United States bear on this question, and whether they are not sufficient to settle it. If they are, it is quite immaterial what exists elsewhere.

"My first position is, that when the Constitution speaks of 'treason, bribery, and other high crimes and misdemeanors,' it refers to, and includes only, high criminal offences against the United States, made so by some law of the United States existing when the acts complained of were done, and I say that this is plainly to be inferred from each and every provision of the Constitution on the subject of impeachment.

"'Treason' and 'bribery.' Nobody will doubt that these are here designated high crimes and misdemeanors against the United States, made such by the laws of the United States, which the framers of the Constitution knew must be passed in the nature of the government they were about to create, because these are offences which strike at the existence of that government. 'Other high crimes and misdemeanors.' *Noscitur a sociis.* High crimes and misdemeanors; so high that they belong in this company with treason and bribery. That is plain on the face of the Constitution— in the very first step it takes on the subject of impeachment. 'High crimes and misdemeanors' against what law? There can be no crime, there can be no misdemeanor without a law, written or unwritten, express or implied. There must be some law, otherwise there is no crime. My interpretation of it is that the language 'high crimes and misdemeanors' means 'offences against the laws of the United States.' Let us see if the Constitution has not said so.

"The first clause of the second section of the second article of the Constitution reads thus:

" 'The President of the United States shall have the power to grant reprieves and pardons for offences against the United States, except in cases of impeachment.'

" 'Offences against the United States' would include 'cases of impeachment,' and they might be pardoned by the President if they were not excepted. Then cases of impeachment are, according to the express declaration of the Constitution itself, cases of offences against the United States.

"Still, the learned manager says that this is not a court, and that, whatever may be the character of this body, it is bound by no law. Very different was the understanding of the fathers of the Constitution on this subject." *Ibid.,* 408–409.

This view must be regarded as having prevailed, not only on account of the failure of the impeachment, but because of the emphasis given by the House Managers themselves to the contention that Johnson was guilty of a breach of law, the Tenure of Office Act.

Johnson and his Cabinet were much concerned over rumors that it was the intention of his enemies in the House, following impeachment and pending the trial, to put him under arrest and/or suspend him from office. Welles, *Diary,* III, 21, 27, 50, 57, 60, 62, 151, 200, 235, 237, 238, 291, 313. But, of course, no such step was attempted. Several state constitutions contain provisions authorizing suspension from office in such a case; but when, late in the Philadelphia Convention, a motion was offered to this effect, Madison objected, as follows:

"The President is made too dependent already on the Legislature, by the power of one branch to try him in consequence of an impeachment by the other. This intermediate suspension will put him in the power of one branch only. They can at any moment, in order to make way for the functions of another who will be more favorable to their views, vote a temporary removal of the existing magistrate." Farrand, II, 612. The motion failed by a vote of 3 states to 8.

Is impeachment the *only* way in which Congress, or either house thereof, is constitutionally entitled to call the President to account for his conduct in office? So far as the Senate is concerned this question was answered with a most emphatic "yes" by President Jackson in his famous "Protest" Message of April 15, 1834, which was evoked by a resolution of the Senate asserting "That the President, in the late Executive proceedings in relation to the public revenue, has assumed upon himself authority and power not conferred by the Constitution and laws, but in derogation of both." Richardson, III, 69.

Said Jackson, among many other things:

"The Constitution makes the House of Representatives the exclusive judges, in the first instance, of the question whether the President has committed an impeachable offense. A majority of the Senate, whose interference with this preliminary question has for the best of all reasons been studiously excluded, anticipate the action of the house of Representatives, assume not only the function which belongs exclusively to that body, but convert themselves into accusers, witnesses, counsel, and judges, and prejudge the whole case, thus presenting the appalling spectacle in a free State of judges going through a labored preparation for an impartial hearing and decision by a previous *ex parte* investigation and sentence against the supposed offender." *Ibid.*, 76.

And not only, the President continued, was the Senate's action a usurpation of power on its part but of a most pernicious tendency, for should the example thus set be followed, "all the independent departments of the Government, and the States which compose our confederated Union, instead of attending to their appropriate duties and leaving those who may offend to be reclaimed or punished in the manner pointed out in the Constitution, would fall to mutual crimination and recrimination and give to the people confusion and anarchy instead of order and law until at length some form of aristocratic power would be established on the ruins of the Constitution or the States be broken into separate communities." *Ibid.*, 91.

"The resolution of the Senate," Jackson concluded, "contains an imputation upon my private as well as upon my public character," one which "must stand forever on their journals." This gloomy view of the matter was not borne out by events, inasmuch as the Senate itself finally "expunged" the objectionable resolution from its Journal, thereby affording Jackson his most sensational triumph over his political foes.

A similar question, but this time involving the House of Representatives, came up in 1860, when the House authorized the so-called Covode Committee to investigate: "Whether the President of the United States or any other officer of the Government has, by money, patronage, or other improper means, sought to influence the action of Congress or any committee thereof for or against the passage of any law appertaining to the rights of any State or Territory; and, second, also to inquire into and investigate whether any officer or officers of the Government have, by combination or otherwise, prevented or defeated, or attempted to prevent or defeat, the execution of any law or laws now upon the statute book, and whether the President has failed or refused to compel the execution of any law thereof." Warren, 10 *Boston University Law Review*, 18; Richardson, V, 614.

Buchanan, who was the President in question, retorted that "the Constitution has invested the House of Representatives with no power, no jurisdiction, no supremacy whatever over the President" except in the sole matter of voting impeachments. "In all other respects," he continued, "he is quite as independent of them as they are of him. As a coordinate branch of the Government he is their equal. Indeed, he is the only direct representative on earth of the people of all and each of the sovereign States. To them, and to them alone, is he responsible whilst acting within the sphere of his constitutional duty, and not in any manner to the House of Representatives. The people have thought proper to invest him with the most honorable, responsible, and dignified office in the world, and the individual, however unworthy, now holding this exalted position, will take care, so far as in him lies, that their rights and prerogatives shall never be violated in his person, but shall pass to his successors unimpaired by the adoption of a dangerous precedent. He will defend them to the last extremity against any unconstitutional attempt, come from what quarter it may, to abridge the constitutional rights of the Executive and render him subservient to any human power except themselves." Richardson, V, 615.

Let Mr. Warren complete the story:

"This protest met with violent attack in the House. John Sherman of Ohio stated that the President could not claim exemption from investigation, and that the House had the 'right to examine into anything which may affect the conduct of any public officer under the Government from the Chief Executive down to the little page who runs your errands upon the floor. Everyone of the officers of this Government is subjected to the power of the House.' The Presidential doctrine, said he, was that of Charles I and Louis XIV— 'The King can do no wrong.'—'L'État c'est moi.'—'This doctrine set up by the President of the United States is, in my judgment, the very worst that has been enunciated since the foundation of the Republic.' John B. Haskins of New York said that the question was: 'Shall we or shall we not maintain the Legislative power and independence of the House of Representatives which have been insulted this day by a Napoleonic decree coming here as a Message from the President?' Buchanan's Message was finally sent to the Committee of the Judiciary, which reported a Resolution, adopted by the House (June 8, 1860, by a vote of 88 to 40), stating that the House dissented from the President's doctrine, and that to abandon its well-established power to investigate would 'leave the Executive Department without supervision or responsibility and would be likely to lead to a concentration of power in the hands of the President dangerous to the rights of a free people.' The Covode Committee proceeded to investigate in secret sessions, not only the subject set forth in the original Resolve, but also actions of the President relative to domestic and foreign questions entirely within the Executive sphere of action. In continued protest against this usurpation of authority, Buchanan sent to the House another Message, June 22, 1860, stating that 'the Star-Chamber, tyrannical and odious as it was, had never proceeded like this Committee. . . . For centuries, there has been nothing like it in any civilized country, except the Revolutionary Tribunal of France in the days of Robespierre.' If its proceedings should be allowed to become a precedent, 'the Presidential office will be dragged into the dust.' He denied that the Constitution authorized 'this terrible, secret, inquisitorial power.' While stating that he made this protest, for the protection of his successors, he pointed out, however, that the Committee, in concluding its work, had reported no resolution for impeachment or censure and had made no suggestions as to any improper acts in the Executive Departments." *Loc. cit.*, 19–20.

Both Jackson's position in 1834 and Buchanan's in 1860 are high-flown in the extreme. There is certainly nothing in the Constitution to prevent either house from investigating any subject on earth or passing resolutions thereon, whether they happen to be complimentary to the President for the time being or not. For a somewhat different point of view, however, see Mr. George Wharton Pepper's interesting little volume, *Family Quarrels, The President, The Senate, and the House* (New York, 1931), pp. 138 ff.

NOTES TO CHAPTER III*

[1] In the words of Hamilton in *Federalist* No. 69: "He [the King of Great Britain] not only appoints to all offices, but can create offices." Earle, 451. See further Alpheus Todd, *Parliamentary Government in England* (2nd ed.) (London, 1887), p. 609; *Encyclopaedia Britannica* (11th ed., 1913), XXII, 280; William R. Anson, *Law and Custom of the Constitution* (London, 1892), II, 405–406, 449–450.

[2] *United States v. Maurice*, 2 Brock. 96; 26 Fed. Cas. No. 15,747 (1823); 5 *Opins. A. G.* 88 (1849); 10 *ibid.*, 11 (1861); 18 *ibid.*, 171 (1890).

[3] *Ex parte* Robinson, 19 Wall. 505, 511 (1873); Chief Justice Taney's opinion in *Gordon v. United States*, 117 U. S. 697, 699 (Appendix). The date of the opinion is 1864.

[4] 7 *Opins. A. G.* 193–194 (1855).

[5] *Infra*, Ch. VI.

[6] "An office is a public station, or employment, conferred by the appointment of government. The term embraces the idea of tenure, duration, emolument and duties." *United States v. Hartwell*, 6 Wall. 385, 393 (1868). The term is often used, nevertheless, to comprehend any public employment even of the most transitory nature, as in the following dictum of a state court: "The essence of it is the duty of performing an agency, that is, of doing some act or acts, or series of acts for the State." See generally Mechem, *The Law of Public Offices and Officers*, pp. 1–3; also *People v. Tremaine*, 252 N. Y. 27 (1929) and cases there cited. It should be noted that the weight of congressional opinion seems to condemn acceptance by a Senator or Representative of any post which has been created by act of Congress, however lacking in other respects such post is in the tests of an office as set forth in the above quotation from the Hartwell Case. See Willoughby, I, 606; *Senate Reports*, No. 563, 67th Congress, 2nd sess., March 1922.

[7] *Theodore Roosevelt, An Autobiography* (New York, 1913), pp. 365–369. Cited hereafter as *Autobiography*. When President Tyler in 1841 appointed a nonstatutory commission to conduct an investigation of the New York Customs House, his action led to a demand by the House of Representatives that he inform it under what authority the commission "was raised." Tyler answered by citing his duty to "take care that the laws be faithfully executed." Richardson, V, 99–100. Still earlier precedents are listed by Carl Morey in his informative brochure *Presidential Commissions* (New York, 1945): "Caleb Cushing in his defense of Tyler's authority to create a commission to investigate the custom-houses cited a number of earlier presidential commissions. (See *Congressional Globe* [May 9, 1842], II, 481–482.) President Van Buren sent a commission to Europe to investigate the postoffice establishments and get information on which the President could act, and also sent an agent to get information on the armies of Europe. Jackson appointed two commissioners to investigate the Naval Department. Even the 'Father of our Country' sent a commission 'unauthorized by law' to deal with the rebellious elements of Western Pennsylvania; 'the report of the commissioners marks their firmness and abilities . . . and' shows 'that the means of conciliation have been exhausted.' " The commission was appointed August 7, 1794; the quoted words are from Washington's Sixth Annual Message. See Richardson, I, 158–164. On Jackson's appointments, see *House Reports*, No. 194, 24th Congress, 2d sess. The following item from

---

* *Chapter III (Administrative Chief) begins on page 82.*

Jefferson's first message to Congress (December 8, 1801) is also interesting in the same connection: "Several agencies created by Executive authority, on salaries fixed by that also, have been suppressed, and should suggest the expediency of regulating that power by law. . . ." Richardson, I, 328.

[8] 27 *Opins. A. G.* 309, 310 (1910).

[9] *Autobiography*, pp. 416–417.

[10] 34 *Current History* 1931, 491.

[11] U. S. Code, tit. 40, § 401; Resolution of June 21, 1938, c. 554; Act of August 10, 1917, §§ 1 and 2.

[12] Clarence A. Berdahl, *War Powers of the Executive in the United States* (University of Illinois Press, 1921), pp. 197–200, 211–212; the present writer's *Total War and the Constitution* (Princeton University Press, 1947), pp. 51–55.

[13] In *Marbury v. Madison* Marshall concedes that in the case of officers appointed by the President with the consent of the Senate, appointment and commissioning are practically indistinguishable and declines to say whether the latter completes the former or is merely evidence of it. 1 Cr. 137, 156–157. It is not surprising, therefore, that cases have occurred in which the President, by withholding the commission, refused to complete an appointment to which the Senate had consented. 12 *Opins. A. G.* 41 (1866); *ibid.*, 306 (1867). In the case, on the other hand, of officers whose appointment is vested by act of Congress in the heads of departments, appointment and commissioning are distinct, since the latter has, by the requirement of the Constitution, to be by the President. Yet even such officers are covered by the legislative provision that their commissions shall not have the seal of the department affixed to them "before the same shall have been signed by the President of the United States" (U. S. Code, tit. 5, § 11), which seems well designed to leave with the President the final say whether the appointment shall be consummated.

[14] On this and other constitutional questions raised by Justice Black's appointment, see Dudley O. McGovney, "Is Hugo L. Black a Supreme Court Justice De Jure?" 26 *California Law Review* (1937), 1–32. For a decision of the Supreme Court of Washington sustaining the thesis of eligibility in a case closely paralleling Justice Black's, see *State ex rel. Todd v. Reeves*, 196 Wash. 175 (1938).

[15] Willoughby, *op. cit.*, I, 607.

[16] See in this connection Madison's message of July 6, 1813, to the Senate, rejecting a suggestion that he confer with a committee of the Senate respecting a nomination. "The Executive and the Senate," said he, "in the cases of appointments and of treaties, are to be considered as independent of and coordinate with each other," and the appointment of a committee by the latter to confer with the former lost sight of the nature of this relationship. Richardson, I, 531. On the other hand, Mr. Roosevelt, in the controversy referred to in note 18, below, took occasion to state that all Presidents had recognized "that the constitutional procedure is for the President to receive advice, i.e., recommendations from Senators." *The New York Times*, February 8, 1939. I know of no other authority, however, for according the "recommendations" of individual Senators any higher status than those of Representatives, or indeed of private citizens. Besides, Senators generally make their recommendations prior to nomination, a stage in the procedure of appointment with which the Constitution does not associate them. *Vd.* note 32 *infra.*

[17] Richardson, I, 58. President John Adams wrote a kinsman in 1799 that before he would venture to nominate a kinsman of theirs for office he "must apply to the

senators and representatives of his own state for recommendations," and added, "The Samuel Adams appointed a customhouse officer, was named by the senators and representatives of New Hampshire. I know him not." *Works,* VIII, 636.

18 Earle, p. 494; Farrand, II, 523. "Senatorial courtesy"—in part an outgrowth of the secrecy of senatorial proceedings in executive session—was one of the early indications that the effort of the Constitution to make the Senate an executive council was not going to jell. See on the whole subject Professor George H. Haynes's admirable *The Senate of the United States* (New York, 1938), I, 54; II, 736–749; also Miss Dorothy Ganfield Fowler's informative article on "Congressional Dictation of Local Appointments," in 7 *Journal of Politics* (February 1945), 25–27.

On the classic struggles which Presidents Hayes and Garfield waged in succession with that redoubtable champion of "senatorial courtesy" in the late seventies and early eighties of the last century, Senator Roscoe Conkling of New York, see Binkley, pp. 155–161.

In the case of nominees to Cabinet posts the operation of "senatorial courtesy" is almost but not quite automatic. Taney was rejected for Secretary of the Treasury in 1834; three Tyler nominees were rejected in 1843 and 1844; and one Johnson nominee in 1868. The latest such victim of senatorial wrath was Charles B. Warren, whose nomination by President Coolidge to the Attorney Generalship was rejected in March 1925.

A word should be given the controversy in 1939 between the late President Roosevelt and Senators Glass and Byrd of Virginia, growing out of the Senate's rejection of the President's nominee, Judge Floyd H. Roberts, for a federal judgeship in that state. The President, in a letter to Judge Roberts, charged the Senators who invoked "senatorial courtesy" on this occasion with "usurping" the presidential power of nominating to office. Actually, it would seem that what happened—as in all such cases—was a temporary abdication by the *Senate* to one or two of its members of its participation in the appointing power. On the other hand, Senator Glass, in his answer to the President, was able to adduce facts which went some way to show that the President, in an effort to "purge" the Virginia Senators, had for the time being abdicated his nominating power to Governor Price and other political foes of Senators Glass and Byrd. *The New York Times,* February 8 and 9, 1939.

19 On this point, examine the vast mass of data brought together in Justice Brandeis's dissenting opinion in *Myers v. United States* and accompanying notes. 272 U.S., 52, 264–274. Hundreds of statutory provisions are cited. "Thus," the opinion summarizes, "Congress has, from time to time, restricted the president's selection by the requirement of citizenship [some thirty distinct acts of Congress]. It has limited the power of nomination by providing that the office may be held only by a resident of the United States [Act of Mar. 1, 1855, c. 133, dealing with ministers and their subordinates]; of a state [one act]; of a particular state [five acts]; of a particular district [two acts]; of a particular territory [three acts]; of the District of Columbia [Act of May 3, 1802, and four other acts]; of a particular foreign country [one act]. It has limited the power of nomination further by prescribing professional attainments [some fifty-six acts and joint resolutions], or occupational experience [eighteen acts and joint resolutions]. It has, in other cases, prescribed the test of examinations [seven acts, including the Civil Service Act of Jan. 16, 1883, c. 27, sec. 2, and the Foreign Service Act of May 24, 1924, c. 182, sec. 5]. It has imposed the requirement of age [three acts]; of sex [two acts]; of race [one act]; of property [Act of Mar. 26, 1804, c. 38, sec. 4, legislative council of Louisiana, to be selected from holders of realty]; and of habitual temperance in the use of intoxicating liquors [one act—re-

peated, perchance, by the Eighteenth Amendment]. Congress has imposed like restrictions on the power of nomination by requiring political representation [eighteen acts, including those organizing the interstate commerce and federal trade commissions]; or that the selection be made on a nonpartisan basis [twenty-three acts]. It has required, in some cases, that the representation be industrial [six acts]; in others that it be geographic [seventeen acts and joint resolutions]. It has at times required that the President's nominees be taken from, or include representatives from, particular branches or departments of the government [twenty-six acts and joint resolutions]. By still other statutes, congress has confined the president's selection to a small number of persons to be named by others [five acts, including act of February 23, 1920, c. 91, sec. 304, requiring that the railroad labor board consist of three to be appointed from six nominees by employees, and three to be appointed from six nominees by carriers]."

Cf. an opinion by Attorney General Sargent advising against a similar feature of the McNary-Haugen bill, *The New York Times,* February 26, 1927; also a protest by President Harding against a proposal to require that one member of the Federal Reserve Board be "a farmer." *Ibid.,* February 6, 1922.

²⁰ The following item from *The New York Times* of May 20, 1916, affords an illustration:

"Another joker in the Army Reorganization bill is very interesting to those who know of the circumstances connected with it. This joker, slipped into the bill behind the closed doors of the Conference Committee, as jokers frequently are, is contained in a paragraph providing for the appointment of Judge Advocates in the reorganized regular army. Probably there never was more peculiar language employed to frame a joker than that which reads this way: 'Provided further, That of the vacancies created in the Judge Advocate's Department by this act, one such vacancy, not below the rank of Major, shall be filled by the appointment of a person from civil life, not less than forty-five nor more than fifty years of age, who shall have been for ten years a Judge of the Supreme Court of the Philippine Islands, shall have served for two years as a Captain in the regular or volunteer army, and shall be proficient in the Spanish language and laws.'

"The one man in the world that this description seems to fit is Judge Adam C. Carson of the Supreme Court of the Philippine Islands. Judge Carson is now in the United States on leave of absence. His home is at Riverton, Va., in the Congressional district of Representative James Hay, Chairman of the House Committee on Military Affairs, and Chairman of the House conferees on the Army Organization bill. Judge Carson went to Cuba after the Spanish war as an officer of one of the immune regiments. Afterwards he was an officer in the Philippine army which supplemented the work of the regular troops in suppressing the Aguinaldo insurrection. President Taft, while Governor General of the Philippines, appointed him a judge of the Court of First Instance and later he was appointed a judge of the Philippine Supreme Court." Judge Carson got the job.

With this episode should be compared President Arthur's veto, July 2, 1884, of "an act for the relief of Fitz John Porter," the enacting clause of which read as follows:

"That the President be, and he is hereby, authorized to nominate and, by and with the advice and consent of the Senate, to appoint Fitz John Porter, late a major-general of the United States Volunteers and a brevet brigadier-general and colonel of the Army, to the position of colonel in the Army of the United States, of the same grade and rank held by him at the time of his dismissal from the Army by sentence of court-martial promulgated January 27, 1863. . . ." Richardson, VIII, 221.

To this the President objected:

"It is apparent that should this bill become a law it will create a new office which can be filled by the appointment of the particular individual whom it specifies, and cannot be filled otherwise; or it may be said with perhaps greater precision of statement that it will create a new office upon condition that the particular person designated shall be chosen to fill it. Such an act, as it seems to me, is either unnecessary and ineffective or it involves an encroachment by the legislative branch of the Government upon the authority of the Executive. As the Congress has no power under the Constitution to nominate or appoint an officer and cannot lawfully impose upon the President the duty of nominating or appointing to office any particular individual of its own selection, this bill, if it can fairly be construed as requiring the President to make the nomination and, by and with the advice and consent of the Senate, the appointment which it authorizes, is in manifest violation of the Constitution. If such be not its just interpretation, it must be regarded as a mere enactment of advice and counsel, which lacks in the very nature of things the force of a positive law and can serve no useful purpose upon the statute books." *Ibid.*

The veto prevailed. Congress has, nevertheless, repeatedly designated individuals, sometimes by name, more frequently by reference to a particular office, for the performance of specified acts or for posts of a nongovernmental character; e.g., to paint a picture (Jonathan Trumbull), to lay out a town, to act as Regents of Smithsonian Institution (note 41 *infra*), to be managers of Howard Institute, to select a site for a post office or a prison, to restore the manuscript of the Declaration of Independence, to erect a monument at Yorktown, to erect a statue of Hamilton, and so on and so forth. 42 *Harvard Law Review*, 426, 430–431.

²¹ The above note; also 13 *Opins. A. G.* 516 (1871). In his message of April 13, 1822, President Monroe stated the thesis that, as "a general principle," "Congress have no right under the Constitution to impose any restraint by law on the power granted to the President so as to prevent his making a free selection of proper persons for these [newly created] offices from the whole body of his fellow citizens." Richardson, II, 129, 132. The statement is ambiguous, but its apparent intention is to claim for the President unrestricted power in determining who are "proper persons" to fill newly created offices.

²² U. S. Code, tit. 5, § 633 (2).

²³ *Ibid.*, tit. 22, §§ 4, 5.

²⁴ U. S. Code, tit. 39, §§ 31a and b.

²⁵ *Shoemaker v. United States,* 147 U. S. 283, 301 (1893).

²⁶ *Ibid.; United States v. Ferreira,* 13 How. 40 (1851); *ex parte* Siebold, 100 U. S. 371 (1879).

²⁷ *United States v. Germaine,* 99 U. S. 508 (1878) is the leading case. For further citations see *Auffmordt v. Hedden,* 137 U. S. 310 at 327 (1890). The Court will, nevertheless, be astute to ascribe to a head of department an appointment made by an inferior of such head. *Ekiu v. United States,* 142 U. S. 651, 663 (1892). For the view that there is an intrinsic difference between a "public office" and a "public employment," see Mechem, *op. cit.,* pp. 3–5.

²⁸ On this subject see an extensive correspondence in *The New York Times* for February 12, 19, 21, and 26, and March 12, 1939, which was precipitated by Mr. Carr Van Anda's contention that "inferior officers" comprise all civil officers of the National Government except "ambassadors, other public ministers and consuls," and "judges of the Supreme Court," and that Congress could therefore at any time deprive the President of his appointing power except as to these. Mr. Van Anda relied chiefly on the following statement from the Court's opinion in the Germaine Case, cited in the previous note:

"The Constitution for purposes of appointment very clearly divides all its officers into two classes. The primary class requires a nomination by the President and confirmation by the Senate. But foreseeing that when offices became numerous, and sudden removals necessary, this mode might be inconvenient, it was provided that, in regard to officers inferior to those specially mentioned, Congress might by law vest their appointment in the President alone, in the courts of law, or in the heads of departments." 99 U. S. at 509.

The statement is purely *obiter* and is furthermore ambiguous; "the President alone," "the courts of law," and "the heads of departments," are also "specially mentioned." The view adopted in the text is stated by the Court of Claims in the case of *Collins v. United States,* in the following words:

"The word inferior is not here used in that vague, indefinite, and quite inaccurate sense which has been suggested—the sense of petty or unimportant; but it means subordinate or inferior to those officers in whom respectively the power of appointment may be vested—the President, the courts of law, and the heads of departments." 14 Ct. Cls. 568 (1878).

Mr. Van Anda's suggestion that Congress divest the President of a large part of his appointing power is, of course, quite academic so far as officers appointed by him with the Senate's concurrence are concerned, inasmuch as it would at the same time divest the Senate of its part in such appointments. Besides, where could it lodge the appointment of "heads of departments" except with "the President alone"?

However, a question remains—why does the Constitution make specific mention of "ambassadors," etc., and of "judges of the Supreme Court"? Possibly as reflecting the theory mentioned on p. 84; more probably because the original intention of the Framers was to leave the appointment of ambassadors and judges of the Supreme Court to the Senate alone and they were accordingly listed specially for this purpose in the report of the Committee of Detail. Farrand, II, 183.

"From March 4, 1933, to the end of 1942, 100,328 nominations were submitted to the Senate. Of these, 58,912 were commissioned officers of the armed forces. Postmasters totaled 33,966." The remainder included commissioned personnel in the Public Health Service and the Coast and Geodetic Survey and career positions in the foreign service. Arthur W. MacMahon, "Senatorial Confirmation," 3 *Public Administration Review* (autumn 1943), 281–296. The article sketches senatorial efforts from 1937 to increase its patronage in the "inferior offices" category.

29 286 U. S. 6 (1932); *cf. United States v. Le Baron,* 19 How. 73 (1856).

30 *The New York Times,* January 11, 1931.

31 *Ibid.,* July 14, 1939.

32 *Writings of James Madison,* IX, 112–113; Earle, pp. 493–494; Adams, *Life and Works of John Adams,* III, 575–576. "The Senate cannot originate an appointment. Its constitutional action is confined to the simple affirmation or rejection of the President's nominations, and such nominations fail when it rejects them. The Senate may suggest conditions and limitations to the President, but it cannot vary those submitted by him, for no appointment can be made except on his nomination, agreed to without qualification or alteration." 3 *Opins. A. G.* 188 (1837). The opinion cites two unsuccessful attempts by the Senate, one in J. Q. Adams's administration, one in Jackson's, to reshape a nomination to a military grade to the advantage of the nominee.

33 U. S. Code, tit. 4, § 6; *Marbury v. Madison,* 1 Cr. 137 (1803).

34 1 *Opins. A. G.* 631 (1823); 2 *ibid.,* 222 (1830); 3 *ibid.,* 673 (1841); 4 *ibid.,* 523 (1846); 10 *ibid.,* 356 (1862); 11 *ibid.,* 179 (1865); 12 *ibid.,* 32 (1866); 12 *ibid.,* 455

(1868); 14 *ibid.*, 563 (1875); 15 *ibid.*, 207 (1877); 16 *ibid.*, 523 (1880); 18 *ibid.*, 28 (1884); 19 *ibid.*, 261 (1889); 26 *ibid.*, 234 (1907); 30 *ibid.*, 314 (1914); 33 *ibid.*, 20 (1921).

In 4 *Opins. A. G.* 361, 363 (1845), the general doctrine was held not to apply to a yet unfilled office which was created during the previous session of Congress, but this distinction is rejected in 12 *ibid.*, 455 (1868); 18 *ibid.*, 28; and 19 *ibid.*, 261.

There have been no fewer than twelve recess appointments to the Supreme Court, and only one of the appointees, John Rutledge, whom Washington appointed as Chief Justice in 1795, was later rejected by the Senate. *The New York Times,* July 29, 1937.

35 23 *Opins. A. G.* 599 (1901); 22 *ibid.*, 20 (1898). A "recess" may, however, be merely "constructive," as when a regular session succeeds immediately upon a special session. It was this kind of situation that gave rise to the once famous Crum incident. See Willoughby, III, 1508–1509.

36 U. S. Code, tit. 5, § 56.

37 The following extracts from a Washington press despatch of December 18, 1914, tell how President Wilson once violated the understanding:

"The Bloom case is unprecedented so far as Senators can recall. John H. Bloom was nominated for postmaster. Five hundred citizens of Devils Lake protested. The charges against Bloom were serious and involved his personal character. The Senate Committee rejected it in August.

"The President then sent to the Senate the nomination of Mrs. Marjorie Bloom, wife of the man whose nomination had been rejected. This nomination was in turn rejected. The President then conferred a recess nomination on Mrs. Bloom as soon as Congress adjourned and she took the office under a commission. Today her name was again sent to the Senate.

"It is probable that when the Senate comes to deal with the case at Devils Lake it may go even further than a formal rejection and refer the nomination of Mrs. Bloom back to the President with a direction to the Secretary of the Senate to call his attention to the fact that the nomination was rejected by the Senate in October and citing the Constitution of the United States, which provides that such nominations shall be made 'by and with the advice and consent of the Senate.' "

The Senate has occasionally confirmed nominees whom it originally rejected, upon the nomination being renewed. Willoughby, III, 1508.

38 6 *Opins. A. G.* 358 (1854); 12 *ibid.*, 41 (1866); 25 *ibid.*, 259 (1904); 28 *ibid.*, 95 (1909). Probably the most extreme case on record of the assignment of a person—and one apparently without official status at the time—to the duties of an absent official occurred in Jefferson's second term. Henry Adams tells the story in his *History* as follows:

"When Congress met, Dec. 2, 1805, Breckenridge was attorney-general under a temporary commission, and Robert Smith who had ceased to be Secretary of the Navy on the confirmation of his successor, March 3, was acting as secretary under no apparent authority. Dec. 20, 1805, the President sent a message to the Senate making nominations for vacancies which had occurred during the recess, for which commissions had been granted 'to the persons herein respectively named.' One of these persons was John Breckenridge of Kentucky to be Attorney-General of the United States, and the nomination was duly confirmed. Breckenridge's permanent commission bore date Jan. 17, 1806.

"These dates and facts are curious for the reason that Robert Smith, who had ceased to be Secretary of the Navy, March 3, 1805, ceased necessarily to be attorney-general on the confirmation of Breckenridge, and continued to act as Secretary of the Navy without authority of law. The President did not send his name to the Senate, or issue to him a new commission either permanent or temporary. On the official records of the Department of State, not Robert Smith, but Jacob Crowninshield, was Secretary of the Navy from March 3, 1805, till March 7, 1809, when his successor was appointed, although Jacob Crowninshield died April 15, 1808, and Robert Smith never ceased to act as Secretary of the Navy from his appointment in 1801 to his appointment as Secretary of State in 1809. During the whole period of Jefferson's second administration, his Secretary of the Navy acted by no known authority except the verbal request or permission of the President." *History of the United States* (New York, 1893), III, 11–12. Adams might have added that from March 4, 1803, till his death in 1808, Crowninshield was a member of Congress. I must say, the story seems to me rather fishy. For legislation governing this matter today, see U. S. Code, tit. 5, §§ 4–8.

39 The most dramatic cases of the President exercising his prerogatives directly prior to World War II were Washington's accompanying his forces part of the way at the time of the "Whiskey Rebellion" and Wilson's attendance at the Versailles Peace Conference.

40 7 *Opins. A. G.* 453, 464–465 (1855).

41 *Williams v. United States*, 1 How. 290, 297 (1843). By the Act of August 19, 1846 (9 Stat. 102), as amended, the President, Vice-President, the Chief Justice, and the heads of the executive departments are constituted the Smithsonian Institution, over whose meetings "the President, and in his absence the Vice-President, shall preside." U. S. Code, tit. 20, §§ 41 and 45. This is doubtless a personal duty, but not a very arduous one. Earlier, expenditures from the secret-service fund had to be vouched for by the President personally (2 Stat. 78), but this provision has long since dropped out of the statute book.

The New York Times of March 12, 1923, contained the following item:

"A little less than two years ago Judson C. Welliver, executive clerk at the White House, stepped across the corridor which separates his office from that of President Harding to place some papers on the President's desk. To his surprise, for it was but a few minutes after 8 o'clock in the morning, he found the President already seated and busily signing papers from a two-foot stack.

" 'Good morning, Mr. President,' Mr. Welliver said. 'I didn't know you had come to the office.'

" 'Yes, I came in just now,' the President replied. 'I had a lot of papers to sign, and thought I might as well get them out of the way.'

" 'Anything important?'

" 'Yes and no,' said the President. 'I am beginning to find out something about being President and the amount of time it demands. You can hardly imagine what I am doing now. This stack of papers is just so much routine. They are the wills of Indians. The President has to countersign the will of every Indian with whom the Government has dealings. If the will is not so countersigned it is null and void. And so I expect to put in the next hour or so countersigning these wills.'

" 'But can't someone else sign them for you?' Mr. Welliver inquired.

" 'No; not under the law. There are only two—possibly three—persons in the United States authorized to sign the President's name. They are employees of the General Land Office and they sign the President's name, under certain safeguards and precautions, to the patents granted by that office. But there is no one else who may do so.'

" 'I am beginning to find out,' Mr. Harding went on, 'that this job of being President is one that makes almost inordinate demands upon a man's time.' "

I can find no justification in the U. S. Code for the statement that the President is required to sign the wills of Indians; that seems to be the duty of the Secretary of the Interior. *Ibid.*, tit. 25, §373. The statement, however, that the President's name is affixed to land patents by authorized clerks of the General Land Office is correct. *Ibid.*, tit. 43, §§ 8, 9. Originally it had to be affixed by the President himself. 1 Stat. 109 (April 10, 1790).

More recent efforts to ease the President's lot by relieving him of minor statutory duties are mentioned in the following Associated Press despatch:

"WASHINGTON, Aug. 30 [1942]—Many steps were being taken, official sources related today, to clear President Roosevelt's desk of petty routine so he can concentrate on the war.

"Until recently, for instance, the President was forced to examine hundreds of orders putting a few acres of land in the public domain or taking this property off. The Budget Bureau and the Justice and Interior Departments worked out a procedure by which, for the first time in history, the President was relieved of these matters.

"More hundreds of orders were being signed by Mr. Roosevelt authorizing experienced government workers to stay in service after reaching the retirement age of 70. A study of Civil Service laws showed that the same goal could be gained without bothering the President by technically retiring the employes and rehiring them instantaneously.

"Officials are sponsoring legislation to permit department heads to settle the hundreds of 'personal injury' claims—up to $1,000—of citizens against the government. At present special acts of Congress to pay the claims must be signed by the President.

"No one but the President can sign an act of Congress, but this situation has been improved, too. The President usually asks his various departments to study these new acts before he signs or vetoes them. Formerly the one official copy of the act was passed around for this purpose until, in some cases, the copy was lost or became so soiled and dog-eared it was illegible.

"Now, however, the same printing type from which the official copy is made is used to make duplicates which subordinates can handle safely, while the President has the clean, official copy before him during the full ten days within which he must act."

42 *Runkle v. United States*, 122 U. S. (1887). By the theory of the case the President was in this instance exercising a judicial, and hence nondelegable, function; from which it followed that his approval of the decree "must be authenticated in a way to show" that it was "the result of his own judgment." *Cf. in re Chapman*, 166 U.S. 661 (1897), and other cases there cited as establishing that "the presumptions in favor of official action . . . preclude collateral attack on the sentences of courts-martial." Confirmation by the President of sentences of courts-martial is still required in several instances. U.S. Code, tit. 10, § 1519. How this may be shown, however, still remains a question, in view of the Chapman Case.

43 *Wilcox v. Jackson*, 13 Pet. 498 (1839); *United States v. Eliason*, 16 Pet. 291 (1842); *Williams v. United States*, 1 How. 290 (1843); The Confiscation Cases, 20 Wall. 92 (1874); *Wolsey v. Chapman*, 101 U.S. 755 (1879); 7 Opins. A. G. 479 (1855).

44 *Opins. A. G.* 470.

45 *Writings of James Madison*, V, 392; also 398, 401, 402, etc., where he insists upon the *unity* of the Executive Department; although in other passages (*ibid.*, 362, 364, 399–400), he seems to regard the power of removal as primarily a power to get rid of malfeasant subordinates. Hamilton's position in *The Federalist* is not entirely clear of doubt either. In No. 70 (Earle, p. 455), he insists upon the value of *unity* in the Executive, and in No. 72 he writes as follows:

"The administration of government, in its largest sense, comprehends all the operations of the body politic, whether legislative, executive, or judiciary; but in its most usual and perhaps in its most precise signification, it is limited to executive details, and falls peculiarly within the province of the executive department. The actual conduct of foreign negotiations, the preparatory plans of finance, the application and disbursement of the public moneys in conformity to the general appropriations of the legislature, the arrangement of the army and navy, the direction of the operations of war,—these, and other matters of a like nature, constitute what seems to be most properly understood by the administration of government. The persons, therefore, to whose immediate management these different matters are committed, ought to be considered as the assistants or deputies of the chief magistrate, and on this account, they ought to derive their offices from his appointment, at least from his nomination, and ought to be subject to his superintendence." Earle, pp. 468–469.

The removal power, on the other hand, he divided between the President and the Senate. *Ibid.*, 497. Later, as Secretary of the Treasury, Hamilton regarded himself as standing in a very immediate relation to Congress. Says H. C. Lodge: "He could not rid himself of the idea that he was really the prime minister, a notion encouraged by the way in which Congress had thrown all sorts of questions into his hands for decision." *Alexander Hamilton* (Boston, 1898), p. 156.

[46] Act of September 2, 1789, c. 12, § 2; U. S. Code, tit. 5, § 242.

[47] *Cf.* U. S. Code, tit. 5, §§ 156, 190, 361, 412, 481, 485.

[48] 1 Cr. 137, 165–166 (1803).

[49] 1 *Opins. A. G.* 624 (1828). Wirt continued: "To interpret this [the "take care"] clause so as to throw upon the President the duty of personal interference in every specific case of an alleged or defective execution of the laws, and to call upon him to perform such duties himself, would not only be to require him to perform an impossibility himself, but to take upon himself the responsibility of all the subordinate executive officers of the government—a construction too absurd to be seriously contended for." See also 4 *ibid.*, 515 (1846); 5 *ibid.*, 287 (1851) and 630 (1852); 11 *ibid.*, 109 (1864); 15 *ibid.*, 94 (1876); etc. "The President has, under the Constitution and laws, certain duties to perform, among these being to take care that the laws be faithfully executed; that is, that the other executive and administrative officers of the government faithfully perform their duties; but the statutes regulate and prescribe these duties, and he has no more power to add to, or subtract from, the duties imposed upon subordinate executive and administrative officers by the law, than those officers have to add to or subtract from his duties." 19 *Ibid.*, 686 (1890). The decision of a United States consular officer refusing a visa to an alien may not be overruled by a Cabinet officer. *United States ex rel. Ulrich v. Kellogg*, 30 F. (2nd) 984 (1929). "President Roosevelt decided today [May 11] that he was powerless to override the judgment of any one of six Cabinet officers and direct the sale of helium to Germany. Accordingly, an act of Congress modifying the existing authorizing statute appeared necessary if the transaction was to be carried out." *The New York Times*, May 12, 1938. See further note 60 *infra;* also note 94.

[50] See generally Mary L. Hinsdale, *A History of the President's Cabinet* (Ann Arbor, 1911); and Henry B. Learned, *The President's Cabinet* (New Haven, 1912).

For firsthand Cabinet interiors see the *Memoirs of John Quincy Adams* (Philadelphia, 1874–1877); *Diary of James K. Polk During His Presidency* (Chicago, 1910); *The Diary of Gideon Welles* (Chicago, 1911); and other similar works listed by Wilfred E. Binkley in his *President and Congress*, pp. 301–312.

[51] Art 1, § 2, par. 1. This clause is the modest residuum of numerous efforts in the Convention of 1787 to load the President with a "Council of State." H. B. Learned, *op. cit.*, Ch. III. An "exclusive" construction of Art. 1, § 2, par. 1, such as was applied in *Marbury v. Madison* to the opening clause of Art. III, § 2, par. 1, defining the Supreme Court's original jurisdiction, would render the Cabinet "unconstitutional."

[52] *Vd.* pp. 253–255 *supra.*

[53] Learned, *op. cit.*, p. 127. Earlier steps in the "evolution" of the Cabinet are summarized in Andrew C. McLaughlin's *Constitutional History of the United States* (New York, 1935), pp. 245–246. See also Charles Marion Thomas's excellent volume, *American Neutrality in 1793, A Study in Cabinet Government* (Columbia University Press, 1931), for much incidental light. Even after the definite emergence of the Cabinet written opinions of the heads of departments—and especially those of Hamilton and Jefferson—were of great importance in illuminating the presidential mind. See John Marshall, *Life of Washington* (1807), V, 403 ff. The idea that the President was bound to consult the Cabinet on important matters (see Ch. I, notes 47 and 55, pp. 378, 380–381 *supra*) arose very early. See Hamilton, *Works* (J. C. Hamilton, ed.), VII, 708.

[54] For a reliable although rather caustic narrative of the episode, see W. G. Sumner, *Andrew Jackson* (Boston, 1899).

[55] Wyman, Willoughby, Fairlie, Finley, and Sanderson all seem to take this general position. Wyman's language is as follows: "This account of this event is worth a hundred cases from the law reports. The President, it appears, has the power in all matters whatsoever to force any officer whatsoever to do any act which the officer has the power to do. He can dictate in all matters because of his power of instant dismissal, without giving reasons therefor, and thereupon the right to immediate appointment without limitation therein. . . . Might makes Right. *Whatever the superior commands will be done by the inferior.* Because of this sanction, an administration which is centralized in its organization will always prove to be centralized in action." Bruce Wyman, *Principles of the Administrative Law* (St. Paul, 1903), p. 233.

[56] Richardson, III, 79–80. The issue involved in Duane's removal had been anticipated in connection with the enforcement of Jefferson's Embargo, and had been decided judicially in the opposite way. Mr. Warren tells the story in his *The Supreme Court in United States History:*

"It was a matter of considerable astonishment and resentment to Jefferson that the first judicial act of interference with his Embargo Laws should come from his own Republican appointee to the Court, the young Judge, William Johnson, and from the strongly Republican State of South Carolina. The episode forms one of the most striking illustrations of judicial independence in American history, and deserves more detailed notice than has hitherto been given to it. The case in which Judge Johnson felt called upon to act arose in the United States Circuit Court for the District of South Carolina— *Ex parte Gilchrist.* Under the Embargo Act of April 25, 1808, collections of customs were required to detain any vessel ostensibly bound with cargo to United States ports, whenever *in their opinion* the intention was to evade the Embargo. In the enforcement of this law, Jefferson had assumed to direct the Secretary of the Treasury to instruct collectors to detain *all* vessels loaded with provisions and such a letter of instruction was sent out, in spite of the fact that the statute expressly vested the collectors with the right of determination as to detention. This action had aroused intense excitement, especially at the North. . . . A test of its legality was at once made in the Circuit Court, when on May 24, a vessel owner in Charleston petitioned for a mandamus to require the collector to grant a clearance of a vessel bound for Baltimore and loaded with rice, clearance of which had been refused by the collector, acting under the Presidential instructions, though he personally was of the opinion that the vessel was not intending to evade the Embargo. Four days later, Judge Johnson announced his decision, granting the mandamus and holding Jefferson's instructions to the collector to have been illegal and void, as unwarranted by the statute. 'We are of opinion,' he said, 'that the Act of Congress does not authorize the detention of this vessel,' under the facts presented; that without the sanction of law, 'the collector is not justified by the instructions of the Executive in increasing restraints upon commerce . . . . At the utmost, the collector could only plead the influence of advice, and not the authority of the Treasury Department, in his justification.' " Warren, I, 324–326, citing 5 Hughes 1; *Hall's American Law Journal* (1808); and Federal Cases No. 5420.

57 12 Pet. 524 (1838).

58 *Ibid.*, 539–540.

59 The following extract from the argument for Kendall is worth quoting:

"The argument of the postmaster general, and of the attorney general, assumes that the post office department is an essential part of the executive department of the government; and from this position infers the want of the jurisdiction claimed. The assumption has been shown to be inaccurate; but even if true, it is not easy to perceive the connection between the premises and the conclusion.

"We are referred to the debates in the convention, to show the anxiety of that body to preserve separate and distinct the three great departments. I will, in return, refer to the 47th and to the succeeding numbers of the Federalist, for a correct exposition of this maxim of political philosophy, and its practical adoption in our constitution.

"Starting from this basis, the constitution is appealed to; and by the aid of some interpolation and some extravagant interpretation, we are told substantially, if not in terms:

"1. That the clause in the constitution which provides that the executive power shall be vested in the President, actually confers upon him all that power which, in any age of the world and under any form of government, has been vested in the chief executive functionary; whether king or czar, emperor or dictator.

"2. That the clause which imposes upon the executive the duty of seeing that the laws are faithfully executed, contains another large grant of power.

"3. That, as a means to the performance of this duty, he is invested with the power of appointment to and removal from office.

"4. That the power of appointment and removal carried with it the power to direct, instruct, and control every officer over whom it may be exercised, as to the manner in which he shall perform the duties of his office.

"My observations upon these points shall be few and brief:

"The first proposition was, perhaps, for the first time distinctly advanced by General Hamilton, in his Letters of Pacificus, No. 1, p. 535. A great and revered authority, but subject to occasional error. It was fully answered by Mr. Madison in the Letters of Helvidius, p. 594, etc., and has since remained dormant. The second is now for the first time broadly asserted. Its dangerous tendencies—its hostility to every principle of our institutions, cannot be exaggerated. The true signification of this part of the constitution, I take to be simply this, that the President is authorized to employ those powers which are expressly entrusted to him to execute those laws which he is empowered to administer; or, in the language of the late Chief Justice, he is at liberty to employ any means which the constitution and laws place under his control. 2 Brockenb. 101.

"The third proposition is a palpable and unwarrantable interpolation of the constitution. The fourth, if the power claimed is derived from the power of appointment, would make the judges dependent upon executive dictation; if from that power and that of removal, conjointly, would make it the true theory of the English constitution, that the king might instruct, direct, and control the lord chancellor in the performance of his judicial duties. It would make him the keeper of the chancellor's conscience.

"The right to command, direct and control, involves the correlative duty of obedience. No officer can be criminally or civilly punished for obedience to the lawful command of a superior, which he is bound to obey. This doctrine, then, asserts the entire irresponsibility of all officers, except to this one superior.

"One of the practical inferences from these premises is, that the judiciary department cannot execute its own judgments; a proposition distinctly avowed by the postmaster general in his return, p. 127–8–9, and asserted, in terms equally distinct, by the attorney general, in p. 152." *Ibid.*, 571–572.

[60] *Ibid.*, 610. Further along the Court adds: "It is urged at the bar, that the postmaster general was alone subject to the direction and control of the President, with respect to the execution of the duty imposed upon him by this law; and this right of the President is claimed, as growing out of the obligation imposed upon him by the constitution, to take care that the laws be faithfully executed. This is a doctrine that cannot receive the sanction of this court. It would be vesting in the President a dispensing power, which has no countenance for its support in any part of the constitution; and is asserting a principle, which, if carried out in its results, to all cases falling within it, would be clothing the President with a power entirely to control the legislation of Congress, and paralyze the administration of justice.

"To contend that the obligation imposed on the President to see the laws faithfully executed, implied a power to forbid their execution, is a novel construction of the constitution, and entirely inadmissible." *Ibid.*, 612–613.

Although Stokes got his mandamus, it seems to have netted him little, and his later attempt to recover damages from Kendall was thrown out of Court on the ground that he had already exhausted his right to a remedy. *Kendall v. Stokes et al.*, 3 How. 87 (1845). President van Buren sharply criticized the decision, "such a power having never before been asserted or claimed by that [the District] court." He asked Congress to abolish this branch of jurisdiction, but Congress failed to respond. Richardson, III, 504–505.

[61] Art. I, § 4.

[62] 272 U.S. 52. Much of my discussion here of the Myers Case is taken from my *Removal Power of the President* (New York, 1927).

[63] In *Wallace v. United States*, 257 U.S. 541 (1922) it was held that the limitations imposed on the President's power to remove an army officer (119 Art. of War, 39 Stat. 699) do not apply when the removal is approved by the Senate through its consent to a new appointment to the post. Chief Justice Taft's opinion contains a suggestion that when the removal power is thus exercised it is illimitable—which is bad logic, but at any rate indicates the Court's perception of the special risks likely to attend judicial intervention in such a case.

[64] 19 Stat. 80, 91. To this day the Postmaster General and the Assistant Postmaster Generals are appointed and removable "by and with the advice and consent of the Senate." U. S. Code, tit. 5, §§ 361, 363.

[65] *Annals of Congress*, I, 368 ff., or 383 ff., according to the printing used.

[66] *Federalist* 77; Earle, p. 497. Earlier, however, in No. 72 Hamilton had indicated the

opinion that the heads of departments ought always to be the choice of the incumbent President; Earle, p. 469. "In the Federalist, he, Hamilton, had so explained the removal from office as to deny the power to the President. In an edition of the work at New York, there is a marginal note to the passage that 'Mr. Hamilton had changed his view of the Constitution on that point.'" Madison to Rives, January 10, 1829. *Letters and Other Writings* (Philadelphia, 1865), IV, 5.

67 My *Removal Power of the President* (note 62 *supra*), pp. 26–31. Webster's position, as set forth in his answer to Jackson's Protest Message, was as follows:

"The regulation of the tenure of office is a common exercise of legislative authority, and the power of congress in this particular is not at all restrained or limited by anything in the constitution, except in regard to judicial officers. All the rest is left to the ordinary discretion of the legislature. Congress may give to offices which it creates (except those of judges) what duration it pleases. When the office is created and is to be filled, the President is to nominate the candidate to fill it; but when he comes into office, he comes into it upon the conditions and restrictions which the law may have attached to it."

"If Congress," he continued, "were to declare by law that the Attorney General, or the Secretary of State should hold office during good behavior," its action might be unwise, but it would not be unconstitutional. *Writings and Speeches of Daniel Webster* (National ed.) (Boston, 1903), VII, 196–199.

68 13 Pet. 225, 230 (two cases). The argument of counsel on both sides affords an exposition of the common law theory of office. Jones, who appeared against Hennen's application for a mandamus, set forth the theory adopted by the Court, as follows:

"The right to remove is an incident to the power of appointment. It is essential to the exercise of the power to appoint; and the power which is given by the law cannot exist without this incident.

"If the common law has any bearing on this question, it is very remote. The Constitution of the United States, and the laws made in conformity with the provisions of the Constitution, are essentially different from the common law, as to appointments to offices, and as to the tenure by which they are held. 2 Black. Commentaries, 36, 37. The law of the tenure of office in England is regulated not by any principles of ethics, or express provision, but by immemorial usage. Office is there an incorporeal hereditament, as a right of way. There is, under the common law, an estate in an office.

"But in the United States this is not so. There is in this country no estate in any office. No property in an office. Offices are held for the benefit of the community in which their functions are exercised. As to the tenure and nature of office in England: cited Coke Litt. 378a. 4 Institute, 117. Coke Litt. 233b. 2 Institute, 388.

"The position in England is, that unless the statute which creates the office limits its tenure, at the time of the creation; it is an office for life, as at the common law. But here no such principles prevail. The common law does not apply to offices, which are all created by the Constitution, or by express statute." *Ibid.*, 253–254.

69 P. 100 *supra*.

70 *Removal Power*, pp. 36–41.

71 Pp. 83–84 *supra*.

72 272 U. S. at 134.

73 All these provisions can be easily traced through the index to the U. S. Code.

74 *Ibid.*, tit. 31, § 43.

75 *Ibid.*, tit. 29, § 153.

76 295 U. S. 602 (also styled *Rathbun, Executor v. United States*).

[77] These facts are given at the outset of Justice Sutherland's opinion for the Court. See also *The New York Times*, October 8, 1933. The Federal Trade Commission at once recognized "the validity of said Executive order removing Mr. Humphrey"; and declined "to further recognize" him as a member of the commission. *Ibid.*, October 10, 1933. Also, in due course, Comptroller General McCarl ruled that Humphrey was no longer entitled to the salary of the post from which he had been ousted. *Ibid.*, November 12, 1933. Both actions were doubtless based upon the decision in the Myers Case.

But suppose a like situation should arise today, what attitude would the Trade Commission, or other similar body, and the Comptroller General be apt to take? Or suppose the Senate to have joined in a removal contrary to statute, would the Court itself interpose? Theoretically it ought to; but it would unquestionably be very astute to obviate such a situation. *Cf. Blake v. United States*, 103 U. S. 227 (1880), and *Wallace v. United States*, 257 U. S. 541 (1922).

[78] 295 U. S. 627–629.

[79] *Ibid.*, 631.

[80] But this interpretation of the decision still leaves doubtful the constitutionality of the Act of August 24, 1912, c. 389, 36, 37 Stat. 555, which provides that "no person in the classified civil service of the United States shall be removed therefrom except for such cause as will promote the efficiency of said service and for reason given in writing, and the person whose removal is sought shall have notice of the same and of any charges preferred against him, and be furnished with a copy of the same, and also be allowed a reasonable time for personally answering the same in writing; and affidavits in support thereof; but no examination of witnesses nor any trial or hearing shall be required except in the discretion of the officer making the removal. . . ." U. S. Code, tit. 5, § 652.

Even if this be considered as restrictive of the President's removal power, it seems to me to be entirely constitutional so far as it protects officers with merely ministerial duties vested in them by statute. The distinction in the Humphrey Case between such an officer and those protected by that decision is not logical. For there is no reason why Congress should not have power to protect against *arbitrary* removal even the humblest agents of its delegated powers, a conclusion to which *Shurtleff v. United States*, 189 U. S. 311, lends aid and comfort. On the other hand, once Congress designates any officer or agency of the government as an instrument of the President's constitutional or statutory powers, it thereby automatically renders such officer or agency, whatever may be its other powers or duties, removable by the President at will. *Cf.* opening paragraph of note 59 *supra*.

[81] 277 U. S. 189, 202 (1928).

[82] The Comptroller's office is, of course, a direct descendant of the British Comptroller and Auditor, "who holds his office during good behavior, with a salary paid by statute out of the Consolidated Fund and who considers himself in no sense a servant of the Treasury but an officer responsible to the House of Commons." A. Lawrence Lowell, *The Government of England* (1908), I, 289.

[83] That Justice Sutherland probably did not appreciate the logical bearing of his dictum is indicated by the following anecdote by Professor Cushman:

"In 1937 Mr. Justice Sutherland was on the bench during the oral argument in the *Shipping Board* cases. One who was present in Court at this time reported the following interesting colloquy which took place. Mr. James W. Ryan, counsel for the shipping company, was urging upon the Court the argument, earlier summarized, that the United States Shipping Board could not constitutionally be put by executive order or by act of Congress '*in*' the executive branch. The Shipping Board, he argued, was not an 'executive agency' and could not be an 'executive agency' because it was not *in* the executive branch of the government.

"Justice Sutherland, who had been sitting back in his chair and asking occasional questions during the course of the argument, leaned forward quickly when he heard this.

" 'Did you say that the Shipping Board was not *in* the executive branch of the government?' he said—as though he did not believe he had heard correctly. Several other Justices smiled condescendingly at counsel as though he were making a farfetched proposition.'

" 'Yes, your Honor,' Mr. Ryan replied.

" 'What makes you think that? Where do you find any legal basis for such a conclusion?' the Justice wished to know.

" 'Why in your Honor's opinion in the Humphrey case, this Court held that the Federal Trade Commission and similar regulatory agencies were not in the executive branch of the government. The Shipping Board fell within the same general category as the Federal Trade Commission and the Interstate Commerce Commission.' Mr. Ryan then proceeded to read certain portions of that opinion.

" 'What branch of the Government do you think the Shipping Board was in, if it was not in the executive branch?' the Justice wanted to know.

" 'In the legislative branch, your Honor.'

"Justice Sutherland shook his head, as though he disagreed, and seemed to be thinking the question over as the discussion went on to other points." Robert E. Cushman, *The Independent Regulatory Commissions* (Oxford University Press, 1941), pp. 447–448. Professor Cushman further comments: "An arm of Congress is not a distinctive designation. Every officer and agency created by Congress to carry laws into effect is an arm of Congress . . . . The term may be a synonym; it is not an argument." *Ibid.*, p. 451.

[84] U. S. Code, tit. 16, §§ 831c and e.

[85] The President stated his own case very satisfactorily, *The New York Times,* March 19, 22, and 24, 1938; see also note 49 *supra*; and *Morgan v. T.V.A.*, 28 Fed. Supp. 732 (August 1939). For the view that the President had no power to remove Morgan, see Arthur Larson, "Has the President an Inherent Power of Removal of His Non-Executive Appointees?" reprinted from the *Tennessee Law Review* for March 1940. Professor Larson's major premise is indicated in his title; it is that TVA lies outside the Executive Department. He accordingly gives the provisions of the TVA Act which makes members of the Authority removable by concurrent resolution of the houses an exclusive interpretation. Granting this premise, the conclusion follows logically enough, but I reject the premise. As appears from what I say in the text, I regard all nonjudicial agencies for carrying out the law as being "executive" in the sense of the Constitution, and think that the vast body of practice and doctrine under the Constitution sustains this view.

[86] See note 80 *supra*.

[87] President Coolidge attempted at least once, although unsuccessfully, to evade statutory restraints upon his removal power by demanding a blank resignation beforehand from the person whom he contemplated appointing. The story is told in the following memorandum of a conversation between the President and Hon. William F. Culbertson, Vice-Chairman of the Tariff Commission at the time, and a letter from Culbertson to the late Senator Costigan of Colorado:

"Contemporary memorandum of the interview with the President, Sept. 8, 1924:

"Shortly after I reached my office this morning, about 9:30, I received a request over the telephone to come to the White House to see the President. I went over immediately. The President was reasonably cordial. He began by saying that the subject of the interview was Mr. David J. Lewis's reappointment. Mr. Lewis's term as a member of the Tariff Commission expired yesterday. The President stated that he intended to reappoint Mr. Lewis, but that he desired that Mr. Lewis prepare and give to him a letter of resignation as a member of the Tariff Commission. At first I did not fully comprehend the nature of this request.

"I spoke of Mr. Lewis's term having already expired. Then the President explained that he wanted Mr. Lewis to submit his resignation under the new commission, to be effective in case he (the President) desired at any time in the future to accept it.

"The President at this point called in Mr. Forster, one of his secretaries, and instructed him to make out Mr. Lewis's commission of reappointment as a member of the Tariff Commission, effective today.

"The President then handed me a sheet of White House paper so that I could take down the tenor of the letter which he wished Mr. Lewis to write. I wrote down the following words: 'I hereby resign as a member of the Tariff Commission, to take effect upon your acceptance.'

"I raised the objection at this point that an unqualified resignation of this kind would imply on the record that Mr. Lewis did not desire to continue as a member of the Tariff Commission.

"The President replied that this was a matter for Mr. Lewis to decide. In explanation of his request, the President said he desired to be free after the election concerning the position filled by Mr. Lewis. He said that if he were not elected, the Democrats might undertake to hold up other appointments which he made during the next session of the Senate, and he implied that he desired to use the appointment of Mr. Lewis for trading purposes in case of necessity.

"I thereupon asked the President whether I could have his assurance that if he were re-elected Mr. Lewis could be continued as a member of the Tariff Commission. He said that he could not at this time make any commitments.

"We then talked of other matters, and at the end the President asked me to have Mr. Lewis see him during the afternoon, when he said he would give him his commission."

Mr. Lewis declined to sign the letter, but Mr. Coolidge, though greatly annoyed to see his little scheme thwarted, gave him his commission just the same. *The New York Times,* January 17, 1926. See also *Congressional Record,* January 13 and 16, 1926. Of course, a really successful enterprise of this sort, in evasion of the laws, would not be apt to leak out.

88 The Senate still retains a large control over the removal power through its power to ratify the appointment of a successor. In Coolidge's administration the terms of certain members of the ICC ran out whom Coolidge did not wish to reappoint, but was compelled to when information was conveyed to him by underground channels that the Senate would not ratify other appointees.

89 The Committee was set up March 20, 1936, in accordance with Public Law No. 739, 74th Congress, 2nd sess. Its membership was distinguished, comprising Messrs. Louis Brownlow, Chairman, Charles E. Merriam, and Luther Gulick. It was aided by a highly competent research staff, including among others Professors Joseph P. Harris, Director, Robert E. Cushman, William Y. Elliott, James Hart, Arthur N. Holcombe, Arthur W. MacMahon, Harvey C. Mansfield, Schuyler C. Wallace, and Edwin E. Witte. It transmitted its report to the President January 8, 1937, and he in turn forwarded it to Congress on January 12, with a covering message.

90 The quotations in the text can be readily found in the *Report of the Committee*

with Studies of Administrative Management in the Federal Government (United States Government Printing Office, 1937), pp. iii–v, 1–53.

91 Dean James M. Landis criticized this feature of the Committee's report as especially ill-founded, saying:

"Only a year ago a distinguished group of scholars, reporting to the President of the United States—in language hardly indicative of academic restraint—described the independent administrative agencies of the federal government as constituting 'a headless "fourth branch" of the Government, a haphazard deposit of irresponsible agencies and uncoordinated powers,' whose institution did 'violence to the basic theory of the American Constitution that there should be three major branches of the Government and only three.'

"Such apotheosizing obscures rather than clarifies thought. Despite this chorus of abuse and tirade, the growth of the administrative process shows little sign of being halted. Instead, it still exhibits the vigor that attends lusty youth, and, if we have defined our subject rightly, it is a youth with which we are concerned. For here is an institution that has existed for less than a century and which, with a few exceptions, has been of public moment for only a little more than half that time. Yet, its extraordinary growth in recent years, the increasing frequency with which government has come to resort to it, the extent to which it is creating new relationships between the individual, the body economic, and the state, already have given it great stature." *The Administrative Process* (Yale University Press, 1938), pp. 4–5 (quoted by permission of the publisher).

The late Commissioner Eastman had expressed similar views as far back as 1927: "The commissions are not irresponsible. Their members are appointed by the President, their decisions are subject to judicial review, and Congress, which establishes them, determines their policy and can change it at will. Quasi-legislative work through quasi-judicial procedure—that is the secret of the independent regulatory commissions.

". . . The place of the independent commissions in the Federal Government in my judgment is the place which they now occupy. I would not increase their dependence on any branch of the Government. . . . They are the evolutionary product of experience in meeting very genuine public needs and I know of no other way in which such needs can be met. . . ."

In his testimony before the Senate Select Committee on Government Reorganization, August 9, 1937, he further developed these views. His testimony was largely repeated by representatives of the other commissions before the same committee in oral testimony, reënforced by letters and written transcripts.

92 In this connection the following passages from Robert MacGregor Dawson's volume on *The Principle of Official Independence* (London and Toronto, 1922) seem extremely well worth quotation:

"Independence is not a mystical formula that will solve all the problems which confront a modern government; but it does give scope for the development of the positive side of the official's character. Instead of the physical threat of loss of office, independence supplies the moral inducement to do well; in place of distrust, it gives confidence; it calls forth a host of qualities that otherwise might have remained dormant—the official's vanity, his conscience, his desire for applause, his zeal for the public good, his feeling of special fitness for his post, his craftsman's delight in his skill—any one or all of these are given freer play."

Elsewhere, referring to certain remarks of Carlyle, Mr. Dawson adds:

"Carlyle thought that he was pointing out the absurdity of democracy; instead of that he was merely showing, what modern experience has confirmed, that the use of skilled officials is an essential condition of a democracy's existence. It is clear that to ascertain the will of the people is not sufficient; there must also be the means to ensure that what they desire will be carried out in the best possible manner. The real democracy demands a subtle combination of election and appointment, of non-expert minds and expert minds, of control and trust, of responsibility and independence. The size of the modern state and the complexity of our civilization may make it extremely difficult to attain this combination; but the survival of democratic government nevertheless depends on its attainment."

Again quoting Mr. Dawson:

"Removal may vary from a mere formality and simple dismissal in some cases to a long and weary procedure in others, as necessitated by statute, constitutional custom or both. Its effect on independence is obvious and may be expressed almost algebraically: the more involved and numerous are the formalities of removal, the greater are the opportunities for independence, and in proportion as the process becomes more simple the independence tends to diminish."

93 Don K. Price, "Staffing the Presidency," 40 *American Political Science Review* (December 1946), 1154–1168. The most thoroughgoing criticism of the Committee's proposals from a "pluralistic" point of view was that by Messrs. Lewis Meriam and Laurence F. Schmeckebier, in their *Reorganization of the National Government—What Does It involve?* (The Brookings Institution, 1939). See also note 91 *supra*.

94 It should be noted, however, that Presidents have more than once virtually ordered independent agencies to exercise their powers. President Wilson was reported in Washington despatches of June 23, 1920, to have "urgently requested" the Railroad Labor Board "to expedite" a then pending wage decision; and twenty years later President Roosevelt instructed the Federal Power Commission, through its chairman, to coöperate with the National Power Policy Committee and the Advisory Commission to the Council of National Defense for certain purposes in connection with the national defense. *The New York Times,* June 16, 1940. I know of no direct statutory warrant for either of these interventions, which must therefore be justified by reference to some kind of executive prerogative. President Roosevelt ordered the RFC in 1933 to loosen up its loan policy and grant loans to small concerns and to enterprises that would put people to work. Frances Perkins, *The Roosevelt I Knew* (New York, 1947), p. 174. Recently President Truman was reported to have stated that he considered the members of the NLRB "responsible" to him alone. *United States News,* August 29, 1947.

95 See George A. Graham, "Reorganization—A Question of Executive Institutions," 32 *American Political Science Review,* 708–718. The organization of the Executive Branch is again under inquiry by a bipartisan commission of twelve, created under the Act of July 7, 1947. It is headed by ex-President Hoover and will report to the 81st Congress.

96 Executive Order 9835; 12 *Fed. Reg.* 1935.

97 Stanton, on the day of his confirmation as Secretary of War, January 15, 1862, "consulted with the 'committee on loyalty of Federal Employes,' in order to learn who in his Department . . . could be trusted and who must be arrested or dismissed." Frank Abial Flower, *Edwin McMasters Stanton* (Boston, 1905), p. 119.

98 Report of the President's Temporary Commission on Employee Loyalty (created November 25, 1946, by Executive Order 9806), p. 3. The report was handed to the press along with Order 9835. *Cf.* U. S. Code, tit. 5, § 663.

[99] *Abrams v. United States,* 250 U. S. 616; Zechariah Chafee, Jr., *Free Speech in the United States* (Harvard University Press, 1941), pp. 108–140.

[100] Confidential.

EXECUTIVE ORDER.

In the exercise of the power vested in the President by the Constitution and the resolution of Congress of April 5, 1917, the following order is issued:

The head of a department or independent office may forthwith remove any employee when he has ground for believing that the retention of such employee would be inimical to the public welfare by reason of his conduct, sympathies or utterances, or because of other reasons growing out of the war. Such removal may be made without other formality than that the reasons shall be made a matter of confidential record, subject, however, to inspection by the Civil Service Commission.

This order is issued solely because of the present international situation, and will be withdrawn when the emergency is passed.

Woodrow Wilson

The White House,
7 April, 1917.

United States Civil Service Commission,
Washington, D.C.

Confidential. April 10, 1917.

The Honorable
The Attorney General.

My dear Sir:

There is transmitted herewith a copy of an Executive order issued by the President April 7, 1917, addressed to heads of Departments and independent offices, authorizing each such head to remove forthwith any employee when he has ground for believing that the retention of such employee would be inimical to the public welfare by reason of his conduct, sympathies or utterances, or because of other reasons growing out of the war, the only formality required in such removal being that of making the reasons a matter of confidential record subject to inspection by the Civil Service Commission. You will note from its last clause that this order is issued solely because of the present international situation and will be withdrawn when the emergency has passed.

This order has not been promulgated, as is usual with Executive orders, because the Commission deems it confidential and also because it is assumed that you will prefer to act under this authority in accordance with its terms but without reference to the authority appearing in your action.

The Commission requests that in each case of removal under this order you advise it under confidential cover of the name of the person removed and of the fact that the removal is made under this order.

By direction of the Commission:

Very respectfully,
John A. McIlhenny
President.

April 12, 1917.

The Civil Service Commission,
Washington, D.C.

Sirs:

Permit me to acknowledge receipt of your confidential letter of the 10th instant, transmitting a copy of an Executive order issued by the President April 7, 1917, authorizing the heads of Departments and independent offices to remove forthwith any employee when he has ground for believing that the retention of such employee would be inimical to the public welfare by reason of his conduct, etc.

Respectfully,

For the Attorney General,

Assistant Attorney General.

I am indebted to Miss Sarah L. Davis, a graduate student in Columbia University, who did a paper on the "Loyalty Order" under my direction, for these documents. She tracked them down and procured me photostats of them.

[101] U. S. Code, tit. 18, § 61i.

[102] Report cited in note 98 at pp. 4–5; Department of Justice "Release," September 2, 1947, at twelve noon, pp. 2–3; *Digest of Public Bills,* 79th Congress, 2nd sess., H.R. 5201, 5400, 5605, 5671, 5890, 5990, 6056, 6335, 6429, 6496, 6601, 6739, 6777, 6837, 6885; H. J. 390.

[103] Above "Release," at pp. 13–20. See also Professor Cushman's excellent article on "The President's Loyalty Purge," in the *Survey Graphic* for May 1947.

[104] Report cited in note 98, pp. 5–7.

[105] The provision was repeated with unimportant change the following June; Public Law No. 490, 79th Congress, Ch. 541; Public Law No. 166, 80th Congress, Ch. 211.

[106] H.R. 3813, 80th Congress, 1st sess.

[107] *The Report of the Royal Commission. . . to Investigate the Facts Relating to and the Circumstances Surrounding the Communication, by Public Officials and Other Persons in Positions of Trust, of Secret and Confidential Information to Agents of a Foreign Power* (Ottawa, June 27, 1946). See especially pp. 11 ff., 57 ff., and 89. The existence of the conspiracy was revealed in the first instance by Igor Gouzenko, one of the Soviet agents, early in October 1945. *Ibid.,* pp. 637–648.

[108] See especially Chs. IV and VI of this volume.

"It is further to be considered that the Constitution gives the executive a general power to carry the laws into execution. If the present law had enacted that the service of thirty thousand volunteers should be accepted, without saying anything of the means, those means would, by the Constitution, have resulted to the discretion of the executive. So if means specified by an act are impracticable, the constitutional power remains, and supplies them. Often the means provided specially are affirmative merely, and, with the constitutional powers, stand well together; so that either may be used, or the one supplementary to the other. This aptitude of means to the end of a law is essentially necessary for those who are executive; otherwise the objection that our government is an impracticable one, would really be verified." Jefferson to Governor Cabell, August 7, 1807, explaining certain points of law regarding the act of Congress for accepting thirty thousand volunteers, at the time of the *Chesapeake* affair. See James Hart, "Some Notes on Public Administration and Administrative Law by Thomas Jefferson," 9 *Journal of Politics* (February 1947).

[109] 272 U. S. 1 at 161.

[110] *McAuliffe v. New Bedford*, 155 Mass. 216 at 220 (1891).

[111] *Ibid.*, 218.

[112] *United Public Workers, CIO v. Mitchell*, 67 Sup. Ct. 556 (1947).

[113] *Friedman v. Schwellenbach*, 159 Fed. (2nd) 22 (app. D.C. 1946); *certiorari* denied, 67 Sup. Ct. 979 (1946); rehearing denied, 67 Sup. Ct. 1302 (1947).

[114] Communication to *The New York Times*, April 13, 1947, by Professors Chafee, Griswold, Katz, and Scott.

[115] See, e.g., article cited in note 103 *supra;* also statements of American Civil Liberties Union, April 7, 1947, and November 10, 1947; also *To Secure These Rights, The Report of the President's Committee on Civil Rights* (1947), pp. 49–51. This last publication should be compared with the document cited in note 121 below.

[116] It would seem that the Court would do well to decline jurisdiction under the Declaratory Judgment Act except in cases in which the principle of *res judicata* is capable of affording a valuable substitute for execution. Obviously, *res judicata* can have no application in such cases as *Public Workers v. Mitchell.*

[117] *Myers v. United States*, 272 U. S. 1 (1926); *Humphrey v. United States*, 295 U. S. 602 (1935); *United States v. Lovett*, 328 U. S. 303 (1946).

[118] I do not stop to consider what may be done in consequence of *quo warranto* proceedings, which are ordinarily brought on the initiative of the Attorney General and affect only the higher grades of functionaries. U. S. Code, tit. 28, § 377 a, b, c. See also the able note by an anonymous writer, "Restrictions on the Civil Rights of Federal Employees," in 47 *Columbia Law Review*, 1161–1187, at 1162–1163. The doctrine of estate in office, though recognized in *Marbury v. Madison*, 1 Cr. 137 (1803), has long since ceased to be acknowledged by the Supreme Court. See *Butler v. Pa.*, 10 How. 402 (1851); *Taylor v. Beckham*, 178 U. S. 547, 577 (1900); *Alvarez v. United States*, 216 U. S. 167 (1910); *Higginbotham v. Baton Rouge*, 306 U. S. 535 (1939).

[119] See *Knox v. Lee*, 12 Wall. 457 (1871); *Omnia Com'l Co. v. United States*, 261 U. S. 502 (1923); *Norman v. Balt & O. R. R. Co.*, 294 U. S. 330 (1935).

[120] U. S. Code, tit. 5, § 652.

[121] The statement is accompanied by several "directives." It appears without these in *The New York Times* of December 29, 1947. The following citations are to the original release.

[122] The President's statement in *The New York Times*, November 15, 1947.

[123] *The New York Times*, December 11.

[124] "All Communist practices in use anywhere on the globe are being applied and perfected inside the United States. This country is so large, so highly industrialized and complex, that Communist organizational machineries in America are more widely expanded and carefully perfected than anywhere else." Quoted by Arthur M. Schlesinger, Jr., in *The New York Times Book Review* of February 1, 1948, from Martin Ebon's *World Communism Today.*

[125] Richardson, II, 278 (January 10, 1825).

[126] 6 *Opins. A. G.* 220 (November 14, 1853).

[127] *The New York Times*, July 13 and September 15, 1943; *United States v. Lovett*, 328 U. S. 303 (June 3, 1946).

[128] 1 Cranch 137 at 144–145 (1803).

[129] *Maclay Journal*, p. 167. See also note 64 on pp. 382–384 *supra.*

[130] Albert J. Beveridge, *John Marshall*, III, 436, n. 1. Henry Adams, *History*, pp. 208 and 450.

[131] *The New York Times*, February 8, 1947. And see generally Ch. V, n. 41.

[132] Opinion of the Attorney General of April 30, 1941.

[133] On this paragraph see *The New York Times*, February 29 and March 5, 1944; July 10, 1943; January 27 and June 11, 1944; May 2, 1947. See also note 41 on pp. 467–469 *infra.*

[134] *The New York Times*, March 5, 14, 16, 21, April 8 and 23, 1948.

"WASHINGTON, May 13—In the face of renewed expressions of opposition by President Truman, the House passed today a bill designed to force executive departments and agencies to produce information demanded by Congress. The vote was 219 to 142.

"The measure, providing jail sentences and fines for recalcitrants from Cabinet rank on down, now goes to the Senate, where little interest has been manifested in it.

"A few hours before the action, President Truman told a news conference that Congress had no power to compel members of his Cabinet to divulge confidential information. The courts have passed on the question time and again, he asserted.

"Mr. Truman observed, moreover, that the bill could not become law until he had signed it. He said he did not think it would be enacted over a veto.

"At the same time the President stated that he was not going to make public a report by the Federal Bureau of Investigation on the loyalty of Dr. Edward U. Condon, director of the Bureau of Standards.

"He said it was a matter of principle. Congress has no right to the confidential records of his office, he asserted.

"Efforts to obtain the Condon report have been unsuccessful despite a committee subpoena and a House resolution calling for it." *The New York Times*, May 14, 1948 (John D. Morris).

Would the House itself have had the right to send Mr. Harriman to jail for disobeying the resolution just mentioned? It seems so; and also the right to keep him there till he complied, or till the end of the session; and the President's power to pardon could not have released him. See note 132 on p. 457 *infra.*

And that the principle of immunity may easily be carried to dangerous lengths has been well pointed out by Mr. Krock, always and commendably alert to bureaucracy's latest crochets:

"WASHINGTON, Oct. 23—With remarkable regularity, officials of the government draw up plans to keep the public from getting legitimate information, and with the same regularity the scheme never gets beyond the planning stage. This probably will be the history of the newest effort—a code drawn up by the Security Advisory Board of the State and Defense Departments and now in circulation before being submitted in final form for the President's approval. . . .

"In the code as projected by the SAB confidential government information is described as information 'the unauthorized disclosure of which, although not endangering the national security, would be prejudicial to the interests of the nation, any governmental activity or an individual; and (or) would cause serious administrative embarrassment or difficulty.' The President's good sense would surely prevent him from signing a rescript like that. And his memory would remind him that the wartime Senate

Committee which bore his name and made him a national figure turned many official faces red. . . .

"This code lists classified information as top secret, secret, confidential and restricted. The test given above of what is 'confidential,' so convenient to official blunderers and politicians, offers a rough idea of the range of information which the codifiers would consider 'secret' and 'top secret.' And they define 'restricted' as news which cannot be published or disclosed save for an 'official purpose.' Under this precious formula nothing could be published out of Washington except what government officials released, and in that form without supplement, interpretation or background.

"This latest attempt at suppression was done in response to a Presidential direction that rules be drafted 'applicable to the handling and transmission of confidential documents and other documents and information which should not be publicly disclosed.' The purpose, as is not always the case, was constructive. The bureaucratic response, as always, was destructive—in this instance of the free flow of legitimate public information.

"The last time this was tried was in February, 1942, by Francis Biddle, then Attorney General. The excuse was a state of war, which cannot be given now. But even under that pressure Congress declined to have anything to do with the proposed 'War Secrets Act.' On that occasion, however, Congress and the public had to be aroused to the threat by representatives of the press, for the bill went to the Capitol with administration approval. In wartime, support from that quarter was even more politically powerful than in time of peace. Also whenever that administration saw an opportunity to restrict public information or discredit the press, official spokesmen got on the job with exceptional enthusiasm." *The New York Times,* October 24, 1947.

NOTES TO CHAPTER IV*

[1] The basis was laid for this doctrine by the protests of the judges leading up to Hayburn's Case, 2 Dall. 409 (1792). See also Chief Justice Taney's opinion, with note, in *United States v. Ferreira,* 13 How. 40 (1851); and the same Justice's posthumous opinion in *Gordon v. United States,* 117 U. S. 697 (1864). Interesting cases illustrating judicial review of executive interpretation of the law are *Morrill v. Jones,* 106 U. S. 466; *United States v. Symonds,* 120 U. S. 46; *United States v. George,* 228 U. S. 14; *Waite et al. v. Macy et al.,* 246 U. S. 606; *International Railway Co. v. Davidson,* 257 U. S. 506; the decisions sustaining in 1927, the cancellation of the notorious Fall leases of oil reserves of the United States to the Doheny and Sinclair interests, *Pan American Petroleum . . . Co. v. United States,* 273 U. S. 456; and *Mammoth Oil Co. v. United States,* 275 U. S. 13. The decision of the United States court of appeals for the District of Columbia in *Lukens Steel Corp. et al. v. Frances Perkins et al.* (October 3, 1939), setting aside the Secretary of Labor's very extreme interpretation of the word "locality" as used in the Public Contracts Act of June 30, 1936 (U. S. Code, tit. 41, §35b), was itself overruled by the Supreme Court in *Perkins v. Lukens Steel Co.,* 310 U. S. 113. The Court, speaking by Justice Black, held in effect that prospective bidders for government contracts cannot challenge judicially an executive interpretation of statutes applicable to such contracts—in that field the executive, so long as it has a statute to work behind, is endowed with the absolute power of the National Government to determine whom it will deal with and on what terms!

* *Chapter IV (Chief Executive) begins on page 146.*

² The principle was early stated as follows: "In the construction of a doubtful and ambiguous law, the contemporaneous construction of those who are called upon to operate under the law and were appointed to carry it into effect is entitled to very great respect"; *Edwards' Lessee v. Darby*, 12 Wh. 206, 210 (1827). See also *Stuart v. Laird*, 1 Cr. 299, 309 (1803). The doctrine holds especially in regard to public land and pension legislation, in which the government appears in the role of distributor of gratuities. See *United States v. Midwest Oil Co.*, 236 U. S. 459; and *Decatur v. Paulding*, 14 Pet. 497 (1840). In the latter case executive construction of statutes is put on a peculiarly exalted plane, showing the contemporary influence of the Jacksonian doctrine of the equality of the three departments. In recent cases the doctrine has been put with varying degrees of positiveness. *Cf.* 321 U. S. 542, 552, and 323 U. S. 134, 140.

³ *Autobiography*, Ch. XI.

⁴ U. S. Code, tit. 43, §141.

⁵ See note 2 *supra*.

⁶ *Grisar v. McDowell*, 6 Wall. 364, 381 (1867).

⁷ 2 *Opins. A. G.* 482. The episode occurred in 1831, and so anticipated by two years the removal of the deposits, which Taney justified by substantially the same argument.

⁸ U. S. Code, tit. 5, §317; *ibid.*, tit. 28, §765.

⁹ During World War I the government sought from the Supreme Court postponement of argument in certain pending prosecutions under the Sherman Act on grounds solely of public policy.

" 'In order that the Government in this time of stress may not meet with competition from private enterprises in its financial operations,' said the Government's brief filed in connection with the motion, 'and the flotation of its loans, the Treasury Department has been constrained to urge that all private financing on a large scale shall be avoided as far as is at all possible.

" 'It is quite clear that the dissolutions which are sought in the pending cases will require financial operations on a large scale if they are to be genuine and effective. Important as the remedy sought in these cases is believed to be, it must give place for the moment to the paramount needs of the hour.' "

Against the strong protest of some of the defendant companies the Court granted the motion. *The New York Times*, January 3, 1918.

The extent to which executive interpretation may often make or break a statute is well illustrated by the proceedings in Johnson's Cabinet over the Reconstruction Acts of 1867, when Attorney General Stanbery's hostile interpretation of these measures was confronted with Secretary Stanton's sympathetic interpretation. *The Diary of Gideon Welles*, III, 59, 60, 63, 64, 93, 96–99, 105, 109–117. See also judicial comment critical of President Cleveland's interpretation of the Federal Election Laws. 32 Fed. 576; 34 Fed. 25; 35 Fed. 269; 39 Fed. 62. The rule of sympathetic interpretation is stated by Justice McKenna for the Court, in the following words: "If it fulfills the purpose of the law it cannot be said to be an addition to the law. . . . The purpose of the law is the ever insistent consideration in its interpretation." *United States v. Antikamnia Chemical Co.*, 231 U. S. 654, 667. See also the same Justice's opinion for the Court in *United States v. Janowitz et al.*, 257 U. S. 42.

Instructive, too, of the problems of interpretation which the President has frequently to face without any possibility of assistance from or review by the courts was Mr. Roosevelt's action in 1939 discouraging the transfer of certain American vessels to Panama registry, on the vague ground that it would not be right "for the United States to put any other American nation in a position which he does not think proper for the United States." *The New York Times,* November 22, 1939.

Sometimes it appears to be assumed that the President has power to *dispense* with the law. Thus we find the National Lawyers Guild petitioning President Roosevelt to cancel certain deportation proceedings against Harry Bridges on the ground that they would do Bridges grave injustice and also "will, we fear, jeopardize the acceptance of a view with respect to the unified functioning of democratic world forces which is crucial to the realization of the United Nations program for a durable peace." The memorandum adds:

"If Harry Bridges, a well-loved leader of a strong American trade union," the memorandum asserts, "were permitted to suffer the punishment of exile from a land in which he has lived almost twenty-five years for an alleged course of conduct, which is today the key to both the success of our arms and of a durable peace, would not fair-minded men everywhere tend to suspect the good faith of our commitments and the sincerity of our program for a lasting peace?" *The New York Times,* March 19, 1945. Mr. Bridges is still in the country.

Presidential enforcement of the law has sometimes been directly stimulated by Congress. By the Joint Resolution of February 8, 1924, which he signed and promptly acted upon, President Coolidge was directed "immediately to cause suit to be instituted and prosecuted for the annulment and cancellation" of the notorious Fall oil leases; also, to "appoint special counsel who shall have charge and control of such litigation"—a provision which took the matter out of the hands of a suspect Attorney General. See the narrative by Justice Van Devanter in *McGrain v. Daugherty,* 273 U. S. 135, 151 (1926).

Congress has sometimes incorporated in an act provision for its own participation in its enforcement, as in the following instance:

"President Roosevelt signed today the bill to permit increased oil production from the Navy's Elk Hill reserve in California, but stated his objections to provisions in the measure which, he contended, would vest the Congress with 'what amounts to executive powers over the administration of the naval petroleum reserves. . . . This legislative assumption of executive functions takes form in two requirements—first, that the Secretary of the Navy, even with the approval of the President, may produce petroleum from these reserves only in the quantities from time to time specified by the Congress, and, secondly, that the Secretary may not condemn lands or enter into joint or unit contracts, or other contracts or leases, without prior consultation with the Naval Affairs Committees of the Congress.' " *The New York Times,* June 18, 1944. Likewise the enactment of the Taft-Hartley Labor-Management Relations Act was followed by the creation of a joint congressional committee to aid General Counsel of NLRB in the act's interpretation; that is, to guarantee its sympathetic interpretation from an unsympathetic administration. *Ibid.,* July 24, 1947 (Joseph A. Loftus).

[10] Presidential *proclamations* may be simply announcements by the President over the seal of the United States, his own signature, and the countersignature of the Secretary of State, of the construction put by the executive department upon specified acts of Congress, or they may represent, like proclamations of amnesty, the exercise by the President of one of his constitutional prerogatives. See the interesting collection of proclamations issued by President Wilson during World War I. *Statutes of the U. S. A.,* 65th Congress, 2nd sess., Pt. II (Government Printing Office, 1918). The diplomatic characteristics of a presidential proclamation are apparently a matter of precedent merely, although by an act of Congress passed in 1794 the seal of the United States may not be affixed to "any other

instrument" than official commissions "without the special warrant of the President therefor"; U. S. Code, tit. 4, §4.

In the famous *Case of the Proclamations*, 12 Co. Rep. 74 (1611), Chief Justice Coke and three of his brother judges answered certain queries regarding the legality of royal proclamations with the following propositions: "1. The King by his proclamation cannot create any offence which was not one before. . . . 2. But the King, for the prevention of offences, may by proclamation admonish his subjects that they keep the law. . . . the neglect of such proclamations aggravates the offence. 3. . . . " In the main these principles undoubtedly govern the legality of presidential proclamations. The President cannot add to his constitutional or legal powers by proclamation, but it is possible that the issuance of a proclamation may sometimes impart to an authorized act of the President, particularly a pardon, a public character that it would not otherwise have had. See pp. 194–195 *supra* for comment on *Burdick v. United States*, 236 U. S. 79. See further Hans Aufricht, "Presidential Proclamations and the British Tradition," 5 *Journal of Politics* (May 1943), 142–162.

Some presidential proclamations can hardly be said to be official at all; they are the social acts of the highest official of government, the best known example being the Thanksgiving Proclamation. The first such proclamation under the Constitution was "authorized" by Congress, though not without certain constitutional scruples finding expression. *The New York Times,* November 24, 1932. The resolution was passed nevertheless, and a proclamation thereupon issued by President Washington. Richardson, I, 64. The first Adams and Madison issued several proclamations, on special occasions and at the instigation of Congress, calling for days of prayer, fasting, or thanksgiving, as the case might be. See Richardson, Index, under "Thanksgiving Proclamations." The first, however, of the since uninterrupted series of annual Thanksgiving Proclamations was issued by Lincoln in 1863, and without suggestion from Congress. It was dated October 3, the same date as Washington's proclamation in 1789, and set the last Thursday of the ensuing November as the festive day, November 26, 1789, the date of the Thanksgiving proclaimed by Washington having fallen on that day. Two Presidents at least refused to act upon suggestions that they should proclaim days of feast or fast, on account of constitutional scruples, Jackson and Taylor. *The New York Times,* November 26, 1931. For the only partially successful effort of the late President to promote Christmas buying by moving Thanksgiving up a week, see *The New York Times* for August 15 and 16, 1939.

For a presidential proclamation *"quo ad terrorem populi,"* see Jackson's famous Proclamation of December 10, 1832, of remonstrance and warning to South Carolina. Richardson, II, 640–656.

Executive *"laws"* fall into two categories: first, those which concern primarily the internal organization of the administration, and so are of interest chiefly to the members, or would-be members, thereof; secondly, those which supplement the general law. As to the former, each head of department is authorized by act of Congress "to prescribe regulations, not inconsistent with law, for the government of his department, the conduct of its officers and clerks, the distribution and performance of its business," etc. U. S. Code, tit. 5, §22. "Codes" of this character, determining the internal organization of administration, are those which govern the postal service, the Patent, Pension, and Land Offices, the Indian service, the customs, internal revenue, and consular services, the rules governing civil service examinations, and so on. Most such regulations stand in the name of some departmental head; but some, like those governing the consular service and civil service examinations, appear in the name of the President. Many rest on the explicit statutory basis just mentioned; but others arise simply from the discretion impliedly allowed by the statutes, and this is ordinarily so with those less formal orders, rules, and instructions which are issued to members of the administration as necessity arises.

Such regulations may not, of course, transgress the constitutional acts of Congress; and from this it follows that they are subject to judicial review in a case properly before the Court, and this even though the rights alleged to be infringed are those of a member of the administration as such. In *United States v. Symonds,* 120 U. S. 46, the question at issue was whether appellee, a lieutenant in the Navy, had performed certain services "at sea" within the meaning of §1556 R. S. Under an order of the Secretary of the Navy the services in question, which were performed aboard a training ship, were designated "shore services." But the Court held that it was not for the Secretary of the Navy to "fix by order and conclusively what was and what was not sea service"; that the facts of the case made appellee's service "sea service." See also *United States v. Hill,* 120 U. S. 169.

On the other hand, when such a regulation is within the law, it is endowed as against state authority with the supremacy of national law in general. Thus, in *Boske v. Comingore* a United States collector of revenue had been adjudged by a Kentucky court to be in contempt because he had refused, while giving a deposition in a case pending before the court, to file copies of certain reports made by distillers, basing his refusal upon a regulation of the Treasury Department which forbade the use of such reports for any other purpose than the collection of the revenues of the United States. The Supreme Court sustained the regulation in question as "a wise and proper one," and on this basis confirmed the order of the district court of the United States for Kentucky discharging the collector from the custody of the Kentucky court. 177 U. S. 459. For an executive order, on the other hand, which was designed to aid the enforcement of state criminal law, see *Ponzi v. Fessenden,* 258 U. S. 254 (1922). Many illustrations of the second category of executive "laws" are given in the text.

Presidential proclamations and orders are today published in the *Federal Register,* the first number of which appeared March 14, 1936, as a result, it may be assumed, of the following episode in connection with the argument before the Supreme Court of the "Hot Oil" Cases, December 10, 1934:

In the course of the argument Mr. Fischer, one of counsel opposing the government, complained that his client "Smith was arrested, indicted and held in jail for several days and then had to put up bond for violating a law that did not exist, but nobody knew it." Thereupon ensued an interesting fifteen minutes in Court, albeit "a bad quarter of an hour" for Mr. Stephens, the government counsel.

In reply to a question, Mr. Fischer said he had not been able to obtain a true copy of the petroleum code or regulations. He said the only copy he had ever seen was in "the hip pocket of an agent sent down to Texas from Washington."

"Are the facts recited in connection with this code applicable in general to the other codes?" asked Justice Louis D. Brandeis.

"You'll have to ask the Attorney General," replied the Texan.

Mr. Stephens, who had completed his argument, arose and Justice Brandeis asked him the question.

"I think that is so," Mr. Stephens replied.

"Who promulgates these orders and codes that have the force of laws?" asked the Justice.

"They are promulgated by the President and I assume they are on record at the State Department," he replied.

"Is there any official or general publication of these executive orders?" Justice Brandeis continued.

"Not that I know of," replied Mr. Stephens.

"Well, is there any way by which one can find out what is in these executive orders when they are issued?"

"I think it would be rather difficult, but it is possible to get certified copies of the executive orders and codes from the NRA," Mr. Stephens explained.

"And that advantage is open to the staff of the Justice Department?" asked Justice Willis Van Devanter.

"Yes, sir," Mr. Stephens replied as a titter swept the room.

"How many of these orders and codes have been issued in the last fifteen months—several thousand?" asked Justice James Clark McReynolds, who earlier had quizzed Mr. Stephens about the omitted provision of the code.

"I am not certain, Your Honor, but I should say several hundred," the attorney replied. *Washington Post,* December 11, 1934.

11 The maxim that the legislature cannot delegate its power is commonly traced to the more general maxim which is discussed in the learned article by Patrick Duff and H. E. Whiteside, entitled "Delegata Potestas non Potest Delegari: A Maxim of American Constitutional Law," 14 *Cornell Law Quarterly*, 168. This form of the maxim, we here learn, is from Branch's *Maxims,* a work which was published in 1753. Coke, 2 *Inst.,* 597 (which Branch cites) gives a variant; while the phrase *"delegatus non potest delegare"* occurs as a gloss on certain texts of the *Digest,* "restricting subdelegation of delegated jurisdiction." In the *Digest* itself the same restriction is expressed as follows: *"Mandatam sibi jurisdictionem mandare alteri non posse manifestum est,"* D. 1.21.5. (See also D. 2.1.5, and Code 3.1.5.) Bracton's *De Legibus,* f. 55b, also contains the maxim, though his precise wording of it is a matter of dispute. All earlier printings give it thus: ". . . *sicut jurisdictio delegata non delegari poterit, quin ordinaria remaneat cum ipso rege,"* which Sir Travers Twiss translates, ". . . as delegated power cannot be delegated, but ordinary jurisdiction remains with the king." The most recent editor of Bracton, however, gives the passage as follows: ". . . *sicut jurisdictio delegata, nec delegari poterit, quin ordinaria remaneat cum ipso rege"* (Woodbine, ed., II, p. 167), which Messrs. Duff and Whiteside translate "[unless it be given from above] like delegated jurisdiction; nor can it be so delegated that the primary [or regulating] power does not remain with the king himself." The older reading seems to me the authentic one, both on account of its close similarity in sense to the text from the *Digest,* and also because of its obvious bearing upon the problem, pressing in Bracton's day, of subinfeudation.

Locke's application of the maxim to forbid a transference "of the power of making laws to any other hands" occurs in his *Second Treatise on Civil Government* (Ch. XI). It has played a twofold role in American constitutional law: (1) as restrictive or prohibitive of legislative efforts to condition the going into effect of statutes upon approval by popular vote—referendum measures, in other words; and (2) as restrictive or prohibitive of legislative delegation of conditional or discretionary powers to the executive. The latter role, in relation to the National Government, is, of course, the one in which we are interested. For the former role, which it is not pertinent to treat here, see the above mentioned article, and more extensively Ellis P. Oberholtzer, *The Referendum in America* (2nd ed.) (New York, 1911).

Two competent but today out-of-date works, dealing with presidential legislative power, are James Hart, *The Ordinance Making Powers of the President* (Johns Hopkins

Press, 1925); and John Preston Comer, *Legislative Functions of National Administrative Authorities* (Columbia University Press, 1927).

[12] See also Ch. I, at pp. 2–3 *supra*.

[13] Thomas M. Cooley, *Constitutional Limitations* (2nd ed.) (Boston, 1927), p. 191* and cases there cited.

[14] Indeed, the first and second categories are merged in the justification which has been sometimes offered for laws to go into effect upon the favorable vote of the locality affected. *Ibid.*

[15] 7 Cr. 382 (1812). A few years later the case of *Wayman v. Southard,* 10 Wheat. 1 (1825), arose, involving a provision of the Judiciary Act of 1789, which authorized the courts of the United States "to make and establish all necessary rules" for the conduct of business in the said courts. Sustaining this measure, Chief Justice Marshall hinted a distinction between those powers which are "strictly and exclusively legislative" and those which are not so, although Congress is constitutionally empowered to exercise them. Although anticipated on the floor of the Philadelphia Convention (see Farrand, I, 67), this doctrine has produced little fruitage. Another and frequently recurrent formula in the cases is that which distinguishes between the making of "general rules" and the filling in of "details," or between discretion as to what the "law"—that is, as it comes from the legislature—"shall be" and discretion as to its "execution"—"an observation which derives its importance from the applications thereof." See, e.g., *Interstate Com. Commission v. Goodrich Transit Co.,* 224 U. S. at 214.

One of the most sweeping delegations of power ever made by Congress was to the Supreme Court itself, by the Act of June 19, 1934, to regulate civil proceedings in the district courts of the United States. U. S. Code, tit. 28, §723 b and c.

[16] 143 U. S. 649.

[17] *Ibid.*, at 692–693.

[18] 276 U. S. 394.

[19] "All in all, if the President exercised every power delegated to him in section 315 of the Tariff Act of 1922, he could rewrite the entire tariff bill as soon as the Congress had finished it." John Day Larkin, *The President's Control of the Tariff* (Harvard University Press, 1936), p. 2.

[20] The leading case is *State ex rel. R. R. and Warehouse Commission v. C. M. and St. P. R. Co.,* 38 Minn. 281, at 298–302 (1889); 37 N. W. 782 (1889).

[21] 192 U. S. 471; 220 U. S. 506; 242 U. S. 311.

[22] 192 U. S. at 494.

[23] 216 U. S. 614.

[24] 220 U. S. at 516. Note also Justice McKenna's words as quoted in note 9 *supra*.

[25] 242 U. S. at 326. For a general account of such congressional delegations to the states, and of resulting cases, see my *Court Over Constitution* (Princeton University Press, 1938), pp. 148–157.

[26] In this connection should be noted Story's remark that the principle of the separation of powers means "that the whole power of one of these departments should not be exercised by the same hands which possess the whole power of either of the other departments." *Commentaries,* §525. To the same effect are Madison's words in *Federalist* 47.

[27] *Panama Refining Co. v. Ryan,* 293 U. S. 388 (1934); *Schechter Bros. v. United States,* 295 U. S. 495 (1935).

[28] U. S. Code, tit. 7, §§ 601, 608c, 674. The act is now merged into the amended Agricultural Adjustment Act of August 24, 1935.

29 307 U. S. 533, especially at 574–580. It is impossible not to sympathize with Justice Roberts's dissenting opinion on this point:

"I am of opinion that the Act unconstitutionally delegates legislative power to the Secretary of Agriculture. Valid delegation is limited to the execution of a law. If power is delegated to make a law, or to refrain from making it, or to determine what the law shall command or prohibit, the delegation ignores and transgresses the Constitutional division of power between the legislative and the executive branches of the government.

"In my view the Act vests in the Secretary authority to determine, first, what of a number of enumerated commodities shall be regulated; second, in what areas the commodity shall be regulated; third, the period of regulation, and fourth, the character of regulation to be imposed and, for these reasons, cannot be sustained.

"The statute is an attempted delegation to an executive officer of authority to impose regulations within supposed limits and according to supposed standards so vague as in effect to invest him with uncontrolled power of legislation. Congress has not directed that the marketing of milk shall be regulated. Congress has not directed that regulation shall be imposed throughout the United States or in any specified portion thereof. It has left the choice of both locations and areas to the Secretary. Congress has not provided that regulation anywhere shall become effective at any specified date, or remain effective for any specified period. Congress has permitted such a variety of forms of regulation as to invest the Secretary with a choice of discrete systems each having the characteristics of an independent and complete statute." *Ibid.*, 603–604.

30 Art. I, § 9, par. 7. See my article "Constitutional Aspects of Federal Housing," 84 *University of Pennsylvania Law Review* (December 1935), 131–156.

31 1 Stat. 95, 104–106, 190.

32 5 Stat. 17–31.

33 7 *Opins. A.G.* 186, 201 (1855), citing 2 Stat. 188 (1802), 214 (1803), 269 (1804), 321 (1805), 388 (1806), 436 (1807), 466 (1808), 524 (1809).

34 U. S. Code, tit. 31, §1; 42 Stat. 20.

35 *Encyclopedia of the Social Sciences,* III, 38, 42 (1930). But "his plan of operations" can be easily upset, in consequence of the theory that appropriations are mandatory. A threat by President Harding early in 1923 that he would order the War Department to keep expenditures on rivers and harbors within the amount fixed by the Budget Bureau and ignore an additional appropriation by Congress (*The New York Times,* February 11, 1923) led to the following protest by the late Senator Caraway of Arkansas:

"I hope that this report is not true. The President is the Chief Executive and it is his duty to see that the law is enforced. If it shall transpire that the President, instead of enforcing the laws, shall himself issue an executive order, forbidding the officers of this Government to obey the law, it will certainly be a very unfortunate circumstance. . . .

"The situation which will develop if the President makes good that threat will be one he will certainly regret. The time has not yet come when the people will tamely submit to executive domination, no matter who the President happens to be." *Ibid.*, February 13, 1923.

36 Because of its own almost unlimited power in the premises, Congress is not governed by the maxim when legislating for unincorporated territory of the United States. From the time of the purchase of Louisiana to the acquisition of the Panama Canal Zone, the first step taken by Congress in the case of recently acquired territory has invariably been to delegate unlimited power to the President to establish a government in such territory. Of course, the government so established has usually been quite temporary, but during

its existence it has rested on power delegated to the President by Congress—that is to say, has represented a *twofold* delegation of legislative power. See also *Cincinnati Soap Co. v. United States*, 301 U. S. 308, 323 (1937).

37 See U. S. Code, tit. 22, §412c; tit. 50—War Ap.—§§621, 901b, 966, and 1510.

38 *Hollingsworth v. Va.*, 3 Dall. 378 (1798).

39 See notes 27 and 29 *supra*.

40 The point was much debated in the press at the time of the pendency of the Lend-Lease bill: "Suppose," it was urged, "Congress could write such a provision into any law, as it could if this attempt were successful. No law including treaties would have any enduring quality. The President could be omitted by statute from his constitutional part in legislation, and the whole purpose and strength of his veto power would be demolished. Congress could thereafter engage in new legislation by concurrent resolution, and only two of the three constitutional factors in lawmaking would legislate from that time." As reported by Mr. Krock in *The New York Times*, February 11, 1941. The answer, however, is simple. The only question is whether certain kinds of laws can be made to terminate this way.

" It is a strong point and one never decided by the courts, but it certainly would be a strange result if Congress can, in part, suspend the Constitution by a majority vote but can't restore it by less than a two-thirds majority, when the Constitution itself provides that an amendment may not even be proposed except by a two-thirds majority ratified by three-fourths of the states. The contrary view is that whenever Congress grants an extraordinary power it can condition what it grants. It can put a time limit on it and thus work its repeal without any legislation whatever. It can make it depend on any contingency it likes, such as some administrative finding of fact or future conditions of time, tide and weather. If those conditions do not occur it does not speak. It speaks while they continue. It becomes silent when they cease regardless of Presidential veto power and with no new vote. If that is so in principle then in practice Congress could condition its grant on the President's favorite assumption—whether the cow jumps over the moon—or whether Congress passes a concurrent resolution." General Hugh S. Johnson in his syndicated column for February 12, 1941.

"The Supreme Court could contend that in signing a bill which provides for this possible method of terminating his delegated powers the President is in fact agreeing in the prescribed constitutional way to this method. Indeed, if the final lend-lease bill makes its grant of powers to the President on the condition specified in this proviso, it becomes a real question whether the Supreme Court could nullify this proviso without at the same time nullifying the rest of the act. . . . Extraordinary grants of power in times of emergency may properly be and ought to be accompanied by unusual safeguards. Certainly the framers of the Constitution could not deliberately have intended to prevent Congress from reserving the right to take back by a majority vote extraordinary powers granted by a majority vote. Fears have been expressed that if Congress were conceded to have this power it would upset our constitutional balance by permitting the legislative to usurp some of the powers of the executive branch. These fears seem misplaced. Congress would be doing little more in the present instance than if it chose instead to accomplish precisely the same purpose by the much clumsier device (the constitutionality of which, however, is beyond doubt) of putting very short time limitations on these extraordinary powers and forcing the Executive to ask for constant renewals. As Congress has never abused this power, there seems no reason to fear that it would abuse the special method provided in the lend-lease bill for accomplishing much the same object."

Mr. Stuart Piebes in "Letters to the Times," *The New York Times,* February 20, 1941.

Is the President entitled to take power under an act of Congress which he intends to repudiate in part, or *vice versa?* See 272 U. S. 1, 179. Would the Court be warranted by the doctrine of separability in upholding and enforcing a delegation of power to the President while overturning a provision for the termination of the delegation by a concurrent resolution?

[41] 1 Stat. 264.

[42] *Ibid.,* 424.

[43] 12 Wheat. 19, 31–32 (1827).

[44] 2 Stat. 443.

[45] "Federal Aid in Domestic Disturbances," *Senate Documents,* 209, 59th Congress, 2nd sess., p. 51.

[46] Richardson, V, 104–105.

[47] 6 *Opins. A. G.* 466 (May 27, 1854).

[48] Richardson, V, 358.

[49] 12 Stat. 282; U. S. Code, tit. 50, §202.

[50] 32 Stat. 776; U. S. Code, tit. 32, §81a.

[51] 7 How. 1 (1849).

[52] *Op. cit.,* in note 45, at pp. 188–205. See also *Senate Documents,* 263, 67th Congress, 2nd sess.; and Bennett Milton Rich, *The Presidents and Civil Disorder* (Brookings Institution, 1941).

[53] On the whole episode, see Cleveland, *Presidential Problems* (New York, 1904).

[54] 158 U. S. 564, 582.

[55] 17 Stat. 14; U. S. Code, tit. 50, §203.

[56] This and the documents mentioned in the next paragraph are from the files of the War Department.

[57] Richardson, VII, 530–531.

[58] This seems a fair interpretation. See *Autobiography,* pp. 552–553. Other instances of the same sort are listed in Lucius Wilmerding's *The Spending Power: A History of the Efforts of Congress to Control Expenditures* (Yale University Press, 1943), as follows: (1) In 1807 when relations with Great Britain were still strained over the attack on the *Chesapeake,* Jefferson made "certain purchases of a military character although no appropriation had been made for that purpose." At the *next* session of Congress he reported the expenditure, explained the emergency, and asked Congress to give its sanction ex post facto. Congress "in due course" complied. (p. 9.) (2) At the beginning of his first term Lincoln "authorized and directed the Secretary of the Treasury to advance, without requiring security, $2,000,000 of public money to John A. Dix, George Opdyke, and Richard M. Blatchford, of New York, to be used by them in meeting such requisitions as should be directly consequent upon the military and naval measures necessary for the defense and support of the government." (p. 14.) (3) In 1873 when relations with Spain were strained over the *Virginius* affair, Secretary of the Navy Robeson was directed to place the Navy on a war footing which included the enlistment of 1,500 additional men, "[President] *Grant and* [Secretary of State] *Fish assuring him that Congress would legalize any overdraft on his appropriations."* (p. 16.) Congress, in fact, eventually did just that. (4) At the time of the San Francisco earthquake and fire in 1906 Secretary of War Taft directed all available stores of the Army to be used for relief purposes. Altogether, almost one and one-half million dollars worth of stores were so used, but in the next appropriation Congress provided for their replacement. (p. 17.) (5) In 1926 President Coolidge authorized Secretary of Agriculture Jardine

to use about $253,000 out of the appropriation for the eradication of the foot-and-mouth and other contagious diseases of animals for the purpose of making advances to destitute farmers in the storm-stricken areas of Florida for the purchase of seed, fertilizer, and other items. Although this, says Wilmerding, was a "clear diversion of appropriated moneys from one purpose to another," and hence unlawful, Congress, at the President's request, validated the action, despite some opposition in the House. (pp. 17–18.) (Quotations made with the consent of the Yale University Press.)

Wilmerding also quotes John Randolph as saying: "You have fixed limits, but expenditures exceed the appropriation. . . . As to appropriations I have no faith in them. We have seen that so long as there is money in the Treasury there is no defence against its expenditure." And this was said in 1806. See 15 *Annals of Congress*, 1063; Wilmerding, p. 67.

59 Act of March 3, 1809, 2 Stat. 535; U. S. Code, tit. 31, §628. See also *ibid.*, §§665, 712–713, 715.

60 20 Stat. 152; U. S. Code, tit. 10, §15.

61 Richardson, VII, 526.

62 Note 57 *supra.*

63 Some other discussions of "the power of the purse" may be mentioned briefly. In 1796 the House formally declared itself free in principle to refuse the legislation needed —including an appropriation—to carry the Jay Treaty into effect, but then voted the required legislation. The year following Nicholas of Virginia expressed himself in the House on the general issue to the following effect:

"The power of this house to control appropriations has been settled. It was indeed an absurdity to call a body a legislature, and at the same time deny them a control over the public purse; if it were not so, where would be the use of going through the forms of that house with a money bill? The executive might as well draw upon the treasury at once for whatever sums he might stand in need of. A doctrine like this would be scouted even in despotic countries." Elliot, *Debates* (1836), IV, 451.

Gallatin avowed a like opinion. Yet a year later Bayard of Delaware contended that Congress was constitutionally obliged to vote a sum asked for by the President for the conduct of foreign relations:

"It had been supposed by gentlemen, that he might appoint an indefinite number of ministers, and were the house, in that case, he asked, blindly to appropriate for them? This question was predicated upon an abuse of power, whilst the constitution supposed it would be executed with fidelity. Suppose he were to state the question in an opposite light. Let it be imagined that this country has a misunderstanding with a foreign power, and that the executive should appoint a minister, but the house, in the plenitude of its power, should refuse an appropriation. What might be the consequence? Would not the house have contravened the constitution by taking from the president the power which, by it, is placed in him? It certainly would. So that this supposition of the abuse of power, would go to the destruction of all authority. The legislature was bound to appropriate for the salary of the Chief Justice of the United States, and though the president might appoint a *chimney sweeper* to the office, they would still be bound. The constitution had trusted the president, as well as it had trusted that house. Indeed it was not conceivable that the house could act upon the subject of foreign ministers. Our interests with foreign countries came wholly under the jurisdiction of the executive. The duties of that house related to the internal affairs of the country, but what related to foreign countries and foreign agents, was vested in the executive. The president was responsible for the manner in which this business was conducted. He was bound to communicate from time to time, our situation with foreign powers, and if plans were carried on abroad for dividing or subjugating us, if he were not to make due communication of the design, he would be answerable for the neglect." *Ibid.*, 452–453.

And in 1826, when the opponents of the Panama Congress sought to attach certain conditions to the appropriation for the mission, Webster took a similar position, saying:

"He would recapitulate only his objections to this amendment. It was unprecedented, nothing of the kind having been attempted before. It was, in his opinion, unconstitutional; as it was taking the proper responsibility from the Executive and exercising, ourselves, a power which, from its nature, belongs to the Executive, and not to us. It was prescribing, by the House, the instructions for a Minister abroad. It was nugatory, as it attached conditions which might be complied with, or might not. And lastly, if gentlemen thought it important to express the sense of the House on these subjects, or any of them, the regular and customary way was by resolution. At present, it seemed to him that we must make the appropriation without conditions, or refuse it. The President had laid the case before us. If our opinion of the character of the meeting, or its objects, led us to withhold the appropriation, we had the power to do so. If we had not so much confidence in the Executive, as to render us willing to trust to the constitutional exercise of the Executive power, we have power to refuse the money. It is a direct question of aye or no. If the Ministers to be sent to Panama may not be trusted to act, like other Ministers, under the instructions of the Executive, they ought not to go at all." Benton, *Abridgment,* IX, 91.

Congress, in 1860, in appropriating money for the completion of the Washington Aqueduct, provided that it should be expended under the superintendence of one Captain Meigs of the Army. This provision evoked from President Buchanan the following protest:

"The first aspect in which this clause presented itself to my mind was that it interfered with the right of the President to be 'Commander in Chief of the Army and Navy of the United States.' If this had really been the case, there would have been an end to the question. Upon further examination I deemed it impossible that Congress could have intended to interfere with the clear right of the President to command the Army and to order its officers to any duty he might deem most expedient for the public interest. If they could withdraw an officer from the command of the President and select him for the performance of an executive duty, they might upon the same principle annex to an appropriation to carry on a war a condition requiring it not to be used for the defense of the country unless a particular person of its own selection should command the Army. It was impossible that Congress could have had such an intention, and therefore, according to my construction of the clause in question, it merely designated Captain Meigs as its preference for the work, without intending to deprive the President of the power to order him to any other army duty for the performance of which he might consider him better adapted." Richardson, V, 598.

In 1912 Senator Bacon of Georgia proposed an amendment to the Army Appropriation bill of that year, that "except as herein provided, or specifically otherwise provided by statute," none of the monies appropriated by the bill should be used for "the pay or supplies of any part of the army of the United States employed or stationed in any country or territory beyond the jurisdiction of the laws of the United States, or in going to or returning from points within the same." Senator Root objected that the amendment would encroach upon the President's powers as Commander-in-Chief, and it was defeated without a record vote. *Congressional Record,* 62nd Congress, 2nd sess., pp. 10,921–10,930.

Ten years later the same situation occurred during President Harding's administration. Said Representative Mann of Illinois, regarding a proviso similar to that which Senator Bacon had championed: "Our power to limit appropriations is so conclusive that we can say that no money shall be given in this bill except to red-headed men. . . . I question the advisability of exercising this power, but the right is there." Representative Rogers of Massachusetts, on the other hand, denounced the proviso as both "unconstitutional and unwise" and, like its predecessor, it was rejected. *The New York Times,* March 23, 1922. A third effort of the sort occurred in 1928, and resulted similarly. An extract from the debate in the Senate states the issue in conventional terms:

"MR. BLAINE: Mr. President, just one other question of the distinguished Senator from Idaho. I know that ordinarily he does not hedge. . . .

"I repeat; assuming that Congress has created an army and has created a navy, after that is all done, then may Congress not limit the uses to which money may be put by the President as Commander-in-Chief in the operation and in the command of the Army and Navy?

"The Senator has said that, of course, if we do not create an army and navy, then there is nothing over which the President has command. But we have an Army and Navy. Cannot Congress limit, by legislation, under its appropriation acts, the purposes for which money may be used by the President as Commander-in-Chief of the Army and Navy?

"MR. BORAH: I do not know what the Senator means by 'purposes for which it may be used.' Undoubtedly the Congress may refuse to appropriate and undoubtedly the Congress may say that an appropriation is for a specific purpose. In that respect the President would undoubtedly be bound by it. But the Congress could not, through the power of appropriation, in my judgment, infringe upon the right of the President to command whatever army he might find. Congress might, by refusing to make an appropriation or by limiting it to a specific purpose, make it physically impossible for the President to discharge his duty in a particular instance. . . . But if the Army is in existence, if the Navy is in existence, if it is subject to command, he may send it where he will in the discharge of his duty to protect the life and property of American citizens. Undoubtedly he could send it, although the money were not in the Treasury." *Congressional Record,* April 20, 1928. See also *ibid.,* December 27, 1922; and 37 Stat. 913.

[64] It is on this ground that Attorney General Daugherty advised President Harding, September 13, 1923, that he was not authorized, in the absence of specific legislation giving him the power, to employ the Navy in enforcing National Prohibition, there being "no unlawful obstructions, combinations or assemblages of persons, or rebellion against the authority of the United States" rendering ordinary methods of enforcement impracticable. Daugherty found "but one instance in the history of the country in times of profound peace when Congress did authorize the use of naval vessels to enforce the civil or criminal statutes of the United States directed against individuals," and this was the Act of March 2, 1807, forbidding the slave trade from January 1, 1808. One provision of this measure made it "lawful" for the President to employ the Navy in its enforcement. 2 Stat. 426, 428. However, five years before this Congress had authorized the use of troops to expel intruders from the public lands (March 3, 1802, 2 Stat. 445), while by a provision that still remains on the statute books he is authorized to employ the land or naval forces of the United States, and the militia, to aid the execution of judicial process, in enforcement of the anti-peonage statutes, and to prevent the rescue of prisoners in the custody of the United States. U. S. Code, tit. 8, § 55. See also § 49.

That the President has no power to use the armed forces to enforce the law except what comes from statute appears to be the doctrine of the early case of *Gelston v. Hoyt,* 3 Wheat. 246, 332 (1818).

65 Collateral to the subject discussed in the above section is the power of the President to repel invasions. By the Acts of 1795 and 1807 he is authorized to call upon the militia and to employ the armed forces of the United States not only in cases of actual invasion, but also whenever there is "imminent danger of invasion," a question to be determined exclusively by himself. *Martin v. Mott,* 12 Wheat. 19 (1827). President Wilson, in 1916, interpreted the power thus conferred as authorizing him to send punitive forces into Mexico in pursuit of the bandit Villa. Some of these forces proceeded as far as 400 miles from the American border, and remained on Mexican soil more than nine months. The Judge Advocate General ruled that the situation was technically "war," so that the soldiers involved were amenable only to military courts. *The New York Times,* October 22, 1916.

The question was raised as early as the War of 1812 whether the militia may be constitutionally sent out of the country and has continued to trouble commentators ever since. See Clarence A. Berdahl, *War Powers of the Executive in the United States,* pp. 131–134. Cited hereafter as Berdahl.

Sometimes it has been difficult to get the troops out of a state on account of the attitude of the local authorities themselves. Such a case occurred in 1907 when President Theodore Roosevelt responded to a call for aid from the Governor of Nevada. "The Governor," Mr. Roosevelt narrates, "became so well satisfied that he thought he would like to have them permanently." Ultimately the President notified him that "If within five days . . . you shall have issued the necessary notice to convene the Legislature of Nevada, I shall continue the troops during a period of three weeks. If when the term of five days has elapsed the notice has not been issued, the troops will immediately return to their former stations." *Autobiography,* p. 416. This proved effective.

66 An illustration of the use of soldiers as police was furnished by the "slacker raids" in New York City and elsewhere in September 1918. *The New York Times,* September 6, 1918. The employment of soldiers for this purpose was, however, without authorization of the President, and was condemned by Attorney General Gregory as "unlawful" and "ill-judged." The raids themselves the Attorney General defended as legal and necessary. *Ibid.,* September 12.

67 *Martial law* theoretically exists for the purpose of restoring civil government as soon as possible; *military government* offers no such apology for its existence, and is a relatively permanent order. The best example of the latter is furnished by the government of conquered territory. The distinction, however, often vanishes in practice. See the case cited in note 77 *infra.*

68 Charles Fairman, *The Law of Martial Rule* (Chicago, 1930), pp. 20–22. This work and Professor Robert S. Rankin's volume, *When Civil Law Fails* (Duke University Press, 1939), are both excellent in their different ways and supplement each other at important points.

69 *Law of the Constitution* (7th ed.), pp. 283–287.

70 See James F. Stephen, *A History of the Criminal Law of England* (1883), I, 203–204, 213–215.

71 7 How. at 62, 70–75.

72 2 Bl. 635 (1863). Years before this John Quincy Adams had asserted in the House that insurrection in a state was "war," and that if the United States entered a state for the

purpose of putting down such an insurrection it would be vested with the war power, which was limited only by the laws of war. Citing, then, what had happened in South America, he warned the slave states that in such a situation their slaves would be liable to confiscation. "I lay this down," he continued, "as the law of nations. I say that the military authority takes for the time the place of all municipal institutions, and of slavery among the rest; and that under this state of things . . . not only the President of the United States, but the commander of the army has power to order the universal emancipation of the slaves." *Congressional Globe*, XI, 429 (April 15, 1842).

It must be said that "Old Man Eloquent" was here indulging his penchant for baiting the minions of slavery, at the expense of strict accuracy. Said Marshall, C. J., in 1833: "It is very unusual, even in cases of conquest, for the conqueror to do more than displace the sovereign and assume dominion of the country. The modern usage of nations, which has become law, would be violated . . . if private property should be generally confiscated, and private rights annulled." *United States v. Perchman*, 7 Pet. 51 (1833). He acknowledged, however, that enemy property could be confiscated by legislative decree, though only thus. *Brown v. United States*, 8 Cr. 110 (1814).

73 4 Wall. 127. See also *United States v. Diekelman*, 92 U. S. 520, 526.

74 *Moyer v. Peabody*, 212 U. S. 78 (1909).

75 *Ibid.*, 84-85.

76 287 U. S. 378 (1932).

77 327 U. S. 304 (1946).

78 Art. I, §9, par. 2.

79 Taney's *Reports*, 246 (1861); McPherson, *History of the Rebellion* (1865), pp. 154-158.

80 §§ 1338-1342; also to the same effect is 8 *Opins. A. G.* 365 (1857).

81 McPherson, *op. cit.*, pp. 158-161.

82 *Ibid.*, pp. 161-162. I have also had the use of a volume of contemporary pamphlets on the subject in the Pierson Civil War Collection of Princeton University Library.

83 *Constitutional Problems under Lincoln* (New York, 1926), pp. 136-137.

84 14 Stat. 46 (1866). That Congress cannot indemnify for acts which it could not have authorized in the first place is the doctrine of *Mitchell v. Clark*, 110 U. S. 633 (1884). If, therefore, suspension of the writ does not authorize arbitrary arrests in the sense above indicated, then a statute of indemnity would not protect officers making them. I know of no case, however, precisely on the point.

85 *Vd.* especially Hughes, C. J.'s, language in *Coleman v. Miller*, 307 U. S. 433, 454-455 (1939).

86 See Ch. I, pp. 6-8 *supra*.

87 135 U. S. 1.

88 *Ibid.*, 64.

89 *Ibid.*, 69; U. S. Code, tit. 28, §504 (R.S., §788).

90 *Dugan's Executors v. United States*, 3 Wheat. 172.

91 *United States v. Tingy*, 5 Pet. 115 (1831).

92 *Ibid.*, 122.

93 See also *United States v. Bradley*, 10 Pet. 343; *United States v. Linn*, 15 Pet. 290. As early as *Chisholm v. Georgia*, 2 Dall. 419 (1792), it was held that the process of the United States courts would run in the name of the President until Congress otherwise provided—which it has never done.

94 6 *Opins. A. G.* 28; also to same effect is 4 *ibid.*, 248 (1843).

452   PRESIDENT: OFFICE AND POWERS

95 6 *Ibid.*, 220.

96 *Ibid.*, 466.

97 See p. 163 *supra;* also Richardson, VI, 13; *United States v. Hughes,* 11 How. 552; *Wells v. Nickles,* 104 U. S. 444; *United States v. San Jacinto Tin Co.,* 125 U. S. 273—all of which are mentioned by Justice Miller in his opinion. *Cf.* 28 *Opins. A. G.* 143 and 511; and 33 *ibid.*, 436, 438.

98 158 U. S. 564 (1895).

99 *Ibid.*, 586. See also 128 U. S. 315, 367; and 224 U. S. 413, 438–442. Out of the Debs Case, in the main, has grown "government by injunction," a danger which was early recognized. See *Senate Reports.* No. 827, 54th Congress, 1st sess., p. 166.

100 2 Dall. 409 (1792); Homer Cummings and Carl McFarland, *Federal Justice* (New York, 1937), pp. 27–28.

101 U. S. Code, tit. 29, §§101–105; Act of March 23, 1932, ch. 90.

102 330 U. S. 258 (1947).

103 The recent order of the United States district court for the District of Columbia (Justice T. Alan Goldsborough), making permanent an injunction against a nation-wide strike by three railroad brotherhoods, and the opinion accompanying it, correct the deficiencies of the Chief Justice's opinion and revive the doctrine of the Debs Case for a widespread transportation strike. The Norris-La Guardia Act, says the opinion, was not intended to permit "the disintegration of society." *The New York Times,* July 2, 1948.

"It is true that the general rule in England is that the king is not bound by a statute if he be not named in it. But this rule has many exceptions. All statutes made to suppress wrong, to take away fraud, to prevent the decay of religion, to prevent tortious usurpations, or to secure to electors the right to make free election, are excepted out of this rule in England, and bind the king although he be not named: 5 *Coke's Rep.* 14b; Dwarris on Statutes, 27, 28." *Commonwealth v. Garrigues,* 28 Pa. St. 9 (70 Am. Dec. 103). *Cf.* in this connection two opinions by Attorney General Biddle, dated respectively June 18, 1941, and May 8, 1942.

104 Public Law 101, 80th Congress, 1st sess. §§206–210.

105 *Autobiography,* pp. 388–389. In June 1908, and so some months before leaving the Presidency, Roosevelt wrote Sir George Otto Trevelyan as follows:

"While President I have *been* President, emphatically; I have used every ounce of power there was in the office and I have not cared a rap for the criticisms of those who spoke of my 'usurpation of power'; for I know that the talk has been all nonsense and that there had been no usurpation. I believe that the efficiency of this Government depends upon its possessing a strong central executive, and wherever I could establish a precedent for strength in the executive, as I did for instance as regards external affairs in the case of sending the fleet around the world, taking Panama, settling affairs of Santo Domingo, and Cuba; or as I did in internal affairs in settling the anthracite coal strike, in keeping order in Nevada . . . or as I have done in bringing the big corporations to book . . . in all these cases I have felt not merely that my action was right in itself, but that in showing the strength of, or in giving strength to, the executive, I was establishing a precedent of value. I believe in a strong executive; I believe in power; but I believe that responsibility should go with power, and that it is not well that the strong executive should be a perpetual executive." Joseph B. Bishop, *Roosevelt and His Time,* II, 94.

106 Taft, *Our Chief Magistrate,* pp. 139–140. The same issue had been thrashed out earlier in the famous Ballinger-Pinchot quarrel in 1910, in the course of which Mr. James R. Garfield, who had been Mr. Roosevelt's Secretary of the Interior, advanced the theory

of a residual executive power and Ballinger's defenders took the other end of the argument. See, e.g., Senate debate in *Congressional Record* for May 11, 1910; also Rose M. Stahl, *The Ballinger-Pinchot Controversy* (Smith College, 1926). A statement of the residual power theory which attracted considerable attention at the time was that made by Senator Works of California in the Senate, January 5, 1917; see *Congressional Record* for that date.

107 *Autobiography*, pp. 474–476; see also Henry F. Pringle, *Theodore Roosevelt* (New York, 1931), pp. 268–274. Apparently President Wilson contemplated a similar step at the time of the Colorado coal strike in 1916. *The New York Times,* October 29 and 30, 1916. For information regarding the Knox opinion I am indebted to Mr. Hugh B. Cox, formerly Assistant Attorney General of the United States.

Roosevelt's plans for the protection of the treaty rights of Japanese in the United States in 1906, at the time of the San Francisco School controversy, also contemplated the possible use of troops, and on very doubtful legal warrant. See Thomas A. Bailey, *Theodore Roosevelt and the Japanese-American Crises* (Stanford University Press, 1934), pp. 28–29, 45, 80–84, 100–101.

108 For the following list of major labor disputes in which Presidents have intervened in other than a purely police capacity, I am endebted to my friend and former student, Professor Robert Dishman of the Department of Political Science of Dartmouth College:

1. The anthracite coal strike of 1902. See Roosevelt, *Autobiography*, p. 474.

2. Strike threatened on the Southeastern Railroads, 1908. See *ibid.*, pp. 496–498.

3. Strike threatened by conductors and trainmen on Eastern Railroads, 1913. See W. Jett Lauck, *Railroad Labor Arbitrations,* 64th Congress, 1st sess., S. D. 493, pp. 259, 263 (1916).

4. Strike threatened by engineers and firemen on Western Railroads, 1914. See *Report of the Commissioner of Mediation and Conciliation, 1913–1919,* pp. 21–22 (1920).

5. Colorado coal strike, 1913–1914. See Edward Berman, *Labor Disputes and the President of the United States* (New York, 1924), pp. 76–99.

6. Threatened railroad strikes of 1916 and 1917. See *Report of the Eight-Hour Commission, passim* (1918). Also 64th Congress, 1st sess., S. D. 549, *Hearings before the Senate Committee on Interstate Commerce on the Threatened Strike of Railway Employees,* p. 97 (1916).

7. Railway shopmen's strike of 1919. See 58 *Congressional Record,* pt. 5, pp. 4344–4345 (August 26, 1919).

8. Steel strike of 1919. See 66th Congress, 1st sess., S. R. 289, *Report of the Senate Committee on Education and Labor Investigating the Steel Strike, passim.*

9. Bituminous coal strike of 1919. See *Eighth Annual Report of the Secretary of Labor, 1920,* pp. 100–106.

10. Anthracite coal strike of 1920. See *Eighth Annual Report of the Secretary of Labor, 1920,* pp. 109–113.

11. General coal strike of 1922. See 62 *Congressional Record,* pt. 11, pp. 11,537 ff. *Tenth Annual Report of the Secretary of Labor, 1922,* pp. 14–18.

12. Railway shopmen's strike of 1922. See *Monthly Labor Review* (December 1922), pp. 1175 ff. *Decisions of the Railroad Labor Board.*

13. Running dispute over railway wages, 1933–1935. See Samuel I. Rosenman, compiler, *The Public Papers and Addresses of Franklin D. Roosevelt* (1934), Vol. III, pp. 98–99, 155–156, 187–189; (1938), p. 201.

14. Threatened automobile strike, 1934. See *The Public Papers and Addresses of Franklin D. Roosevelt* (1934), pp. 166–169; (1935), pp. 74–76.

15. Pacific Coast longshoremen's strike, 1934. See *The Public Papers and Addresses of Franklin D. Roosevelt* (1934), p. 157.

16. Threatened bituminous coal strike, 1935. See Edwin F. McGrady to Rodier, Roosevelt Papers, Franklin D. Roosevelt Memorial Library, Hyde Park, New York. Also *The Public Papers and Addresses of Franklin D. Roosevelt* (1935), pp. 306–307.

17. Little steel strike, 1937. See *The New York Times*, June 30, 1937, p. 1. *The Public Papers and Addresses of Franklin D. Roosevelt* (1937), pp. 270–272.

18. General railroad strikes threatened in 1938. See *Report to the President by the Emergency Board Appointed September 27, 1938.*

19. Bituminous coal strike, 1939. See *The Public Papers and Addresses of Franklin D. Roosevelt* (1939), pp. 304–305.

20. Captive coal mine strikes, 1941. See *Report on the Work of the National Defense Mediation Board, March 19, 1941–January 12, 1942,* pp. 118–134, 268–276.

21. Threatened railroad strike, 1941. See *Report to the President by the Emergency Board Appointed September 10, 1941.* Also *Supplementary Report* to the above.

22. Threatened railroad strike, 1943. See *Report to the President by the Emergency Board Appointed February 20, 1943. Supplementary Report* to above. *Report to the President by the Emergency Board Appointed May 31, 1943. Report to the President by the Emergency Board Appointed September 25, 1943.*

23. Coal strikes of 1943. See *Monthly Labor Review* (August 1943), pp. 290–295. *Ibid.* (May 1944), pp. 945–947.

24. Steel strike of 1946. See *The New York Times*, January 1–February 16, 1946, inclusive.

25. Engineers' and trainmen's strike, 1946. See Alexander F. Whitney, *Railroad Rules —Wage Movement in the United States, 1944–45–46* (1946), *passim.*

26. Bituminous coal strikes of 1946. See *The New York Times*, December 8, 1946, pp. 1, 3. Also *United States v. United Mine Workers of America* and associated cases, 330 U. S. 258 (1947).

It will be observed that only Taft, Coolidge, and Hoover failed to intervene personally in at least one major labor dispute for the purpose of hastening or influencing its settlement, and this no doubt was due as much to the absence of serious industrial strife during their incumbencies as it was to their conservative and legalistic eschewal of strong presidential leadership.

[109] See "Executive Powers under National Emergency," 76th Congress, 2nd sess., *Senate Documents*, No. 133; also Acts of Congress Applicable in Time of Emergency, *Public Affairs Bulletin*, No. 35 (Library of Congress Legislative Reference Bureau, 1945); also Louis William Koenig, *The Presidency and the Crisis, Powers of the Office from the Invasion of Poland to Pearl Harbor* (King's Crown Press, 1944), which is valuable especially for its digests of "emergency" legislation. *Cf.* President Truman's statement of December 31, 1946, listing laws that were to end immediately or six months hence, or later (*The New York Times*, January 1, 1947); also his message to Congress of February 19, 1947. *Ibid.*, February 20, 1947.

[110] 4 *Commentaries*, 397–398.

[111] Art. II, §2, par. 1 "It is declared in parliament, by statute 27 Hen. VIII. c. 24, that no other person hath power to pardon or remit any treason or felonies whatsoever; but that the king hath the whole and sole power thereof, united and knit to the imperial crown of this realm." Preceding note.

[112] Farrand, II, 426, 526–527. Sherman characteristically wanted pardons conditioned

on the consent of the Senate, a suggestion which received the support of only his own state. *Ibid.*, 419.

113 Earle, p. 484.

114 7 Pet. 150 (1833).

115 The argument for the United States was made by Taney as Attorney General and was based exclusively upon British authorities. Marshall invoked British practice as furnishing the proper rule of constitutional interpretation for the "reprieves and pardons" clause thus:

"As this power had been exercised from time immemorial by the executive of that nation whose language is our language, and to whose judicial institutions ours bear a close resemblance; we adopt their principles respecting the operation and effect of a pardon, and look into their books for the rules prescribing the manner in which it is to be used by the person who would avail himself of it." *Ibid.*, 160.

The rule was reiterated in *ex parte* Wells, 18 How. 307, 310–311 (1855), but met with strenuous protest in a dissenting opinion by Justice McLean: "The executive office in England and that in this country is [sic] so widely different that doubts may be entertained whether it would be safe for a republican chief magistrate, who is the creature of the laws, to be influenced by the exercise of any leading power of the British sovereign." *Ibid.*, 318. This was certainly good Jeffersonian doctrine. To the contrary effect, however, see 4 *Opins. A. G.* 456 (1843) and 5 *ibid.*, 536 (1852); also the Grossman Case, which is discussed below. But the McLean dissent may be said to have come into its own in the Perovich Case. Today, as is indicated in the text, the Court follows the Marshall rule at discretion—it has, in short, a choice.

116 *Armstrong v. United States,* 13 Wall. 154, 156. For presidential proclamations of amnesty, see Richardson, I, 181 (Washington), 303 (Adams), 512, 514, 543 (Madison); VI, 213–216 (Lincoln), 310, 547, 655, 708 (Johnson); X, 496 (Roosevelt). This power was the pivot of "Presidential Reconstruction," just as the power of the houses of Congress to determine the qualifications of their respective members was the pivot of "Congressional Reconstruction." By a clause of the Confiscation Act of July 17, 1862 (12 Stat. 592), Congress purported to authorize the President to extend to participants "in the existing rebellion" "pardon and amnesty," with such exceptions and on such conditions as he deemed expedient. Lincoln, in his Proclamation of December 8, 1863, refers to this provision merely as "according with well-established judicial exposition of the pardoning power." He based his action on the Constitution. In consequence of the quarrel between Johnson and Congress over Reconstruction, Congress repealed the above provision of the Confiscation Act January 21, 1867; and in its Report of December 25, 1868, the Senate Committee on the Judiciary directly challenged the title of the President to the power of amnesty, which it claimed for Congress alone. *Senate Reports* 239, 40th Congress, 3rd sess. Royal amnesties, the committee argued, were always by virtue of parliamentary authorization. The contentions of the committee were, however, pretty well met and refuted by one "L.C.K.," writing in 7 *University of Pennsylvania Law Review and American Law Register* (New Series), 523–532 (September 1869). In point of fact, Hamilton seems clearly to assume in the passage in *The Federalist* already referred to that the power to pardon includes amnesty. In *United States v. Padelford,* 9 Wall. 542 (1870), which involved Lincoln's amnesty, the Court said: "This proclamation, if it needed legislative sanction, was fully warranted by the Act of July 17, 1862." Three years later, in *United States v. Klein,* it is stated flatly "Pardon includes amnesty," a proposition which the dissenting minority does not challenge. 13 Wall. 128, 147; also to the same effect are

Armstrong v. United States, supra, and *Jenkins v. Collard,* 145 U. S. 560. See also W. H. Humbert, *The Pardoning Power of the President* (American Council on Public Affairs, Washington, 1941), pp. 36–42.

[117] 236 U. S. 79 (1915).

[118] *Ibid.,* 90–91.

[119] Equally surprising is the Court's failure to take account of its own words in *Brown v. Walker,* 161 U. S. 591 (1896): "It is almost a necessary corollary of the above propositions that, if the witness has already received a pardon, he cannot longer set up his privilege, since he stands with respect to such offense as if it had never been committed." *Ibid.,* 599, citing British cases. To the same effect was a suggestion by the late Justice Cardozo, when he was Chief Judge of the New York Court of Appeals, that "the quickest and easiest way" to get the testimony of one Doyle, who was pleading his constitutional privilege, would be for the governor to pardon him. *The New York Times,* July 28, 1931.

[120] For a most absurd tempest in the teapot, which first and last involved, besides President Coolidge and Craig, the United States Supreme Court, Attorney General Daugherty, Judge Mayer, Senator Copeland, Representative La Guardia, several labor organizations, and still others, see *The New York Times,* November 20 to December 11, 1923.

[121] *Chapman v. Scott,* 10 F (2nd.) 156, 161 (December 14, 1925).

[122] *Biddle v. Perovich,* 274 U. S. 480.

[123] *Ibid.,* 486. Mr. Humbert thinks my inference that *Biddle v. Perovich* dismisses "the doctrine of acceptance" a little too confident. *Op. cit.,* p. 73. I have to admit that the Court has not yet passed on the precise question.

[124] 267 U. S. 87.

[125] *The New York Times,* May 16, 1924. See also Story, 2 *Commentaries,* § 1503.

[126] Especially difficult to meet was the proposition that an "offense against the United States" must be violative of a statute of the United States (*United States v. Hudson,* 7 Cr. 32); nor can it be said that the Chief Justice's opinion entirely disposes of the question. 267 U. S. 114–115.

[127] *Ibid.,* 110.

[128] *Ibid.,* 118–119, citing 3 *Opins. A. G.* 622; 4 *ibid.,* 317 and 458, and 19 *ibid.,* 476.

[129] *Ibid.,* 121.

[130] *Ibid.,* 122. It may be remarked in passing that in classifying "criminal" contempts as "offenses against the United States," the Grossman Case would seem to throw down every barrier in the way of requiring that "contempts fully completed" be tried by jury, thus rendering obsolete the halfway doctrine of the slightly earlier Michaelson Case (266 U. S. 18). For being offenses against the United States, it is the public interest which is primarily involved in the punishment of "criminal" contempts, and only secondarily the dignity of the offended court. Indeed, as Chief Justice Taft takes pains to note in his opinion, such acts were triable in England at the time of the framing of the Constitution in both ways, that is, by the Court alone or by a court and jury, following indictment of the offender (267 U. S. at 110). See also J. Holmes on the same point in the Gompers Case, 233 U. S. 604; and compare the Court's ignorant denial of this in the Eilenbecker Case, 134 U. S. 3.

Instructive cases which are illustrative of the judicial power to punish "criminal contempts" are *ex parte* Robinson, 19 Wall. 505; *ex parte* Wall, 107 U. S. 265; *ex parte* Terry, 128 U. S. 289; *Gompers v. United States, supra; Toledo Newspaper Co. v. United*

States, 247 U. S. 402, which was overturned in *Nye v. United States,* 313 U. S. 33 (1941). *Cf. Bridges v. California,* 314 U. S. 252 (1941).

131 The passage in Blackstone alluded to is to the effect that coercive measures of a court in support of the rights of a suitor, "being properly the civil remedy of individuals for a private injury, are not released or affected by a general pardon." 4 *Commentaries,* 285. But as general pardons, according to Blackstone, are by act of Parliament, what he here has in mind is apparently a rule of statutory construction rather than of constitutional limitation binding on the King. It may be granted, nevertheless, that the rule of restriction stated in the Grossman Case is a fairly logical application of the ancient maxim that the "King may not use his grace to the injury or detriment of others [*non poterit rex gratiam facere cum injuria et damno aliorum*]." Brac., lib. iii, f. 132; 3 *Inst.,* 236; 4 *Commentaries,* 398. See, however, *Young v. Chamberlain,* Tothill, 41, for a late use of the power to pardon what we should today term a civil contempt; *cf. ex parte* Whitechurch, 1 Atk. 37 (1749).

132 The case referred to is *Besette v. McConkey Co.,* 194 U. S. 324, in which the Court, speaking by Justice Brewer, takes the distinction from Judge Sanborn's opinion in *in re* Nevitt, 54 C. C. A. 622, 632; 117 Fed. Rep. 448, 458 (1902). Justice Miller, speaking for the Court in *in re* Chiles, 22 Wall. 157 (1874), recognizes the twofold use of contempt proceedings, the punitive and the coercive, but does not distinguish "criminal" from "civil" contempts. Nor does the Act of 1831 (§725 R.S.) recognize such a distinction; nor yet does Story in his *Commentaries* (see §1503). In his article, however, in 21 *Harvard Law Review,* 161–174, on "Contempt of Court, Civil and Criminal," Professor Beale is able to supply a very different ancestry for each of the two types. *Criminal* contempts he traces to insults to the royal authority, and terms them "active contempts," while *civil* contempts he traces to disobedience of the Lord Chancellor's orders. "Punishment" in such cases, he explains, is not punitive in intention, but coercive and therefore is indefinite—that is, it continues until the order is performed by the recalcitrant party, or until he has restored the *status quo ante.* The comparatively recent formulation of the distinction is probably due to the tendency of the two concepts to merge.

The question is naturally suggested by the Grossman Case whether the President could pardon contempts of the houses of Congress. The general argument against the suggestion on the ground of the principle of separation of powers is logically invalidated by the holding; but the silence of precedent is a strong counter-consideration, and precedent is the basis of the decision. Moreover, the Chief Justice mentions specifically an opinion by Rawle about 1830 that the pardoning power did not extend to "contempts of a House of Congress." 267 U. S. 118. And suppose that one of the houses should order the incarceration of a Cabinet officer *until* he complied with its subpoena to testify or to produce certain papers. By analogy at least this would seem to be a case of "civil contempt," to which consequently the President's power to pardon would not extend. It is probable, however, that with the adjournment of Congress the imprisonment would end, the legislative power which brought it about being now in abeyance.

133 Another interesting aspect of the case is its manipulation of the separation of powers principle, wherein it presents a striking contrast to the same Justice's opinion in the Myers Case. *Ibid.,* 119–121.

134 4 Wall. 333.

135 *Ibid.,* 380.

136 *Ibid.,* 396–397.

137 See especially Professor Williston's article, "Does a Pardon Blot Out Guilt?" in 28 *Harvard Law Review*, 647–663; and Mr. Henry Weihofen's article "The Effect of Pardon" in 88 *University of Pennsylvania Law Review*, 177–193.

138 142 U. S. 450 (1892).

139 See Professor Everett S. Brown's valuable article, "The Restoration of Civil and Political Rights by Presidential Pardon," 34 *American Political Science Review*, 295–300. On the question whether a presidential pardon is capable of relieving a federal convict of legal or political disabilities imposed by state laws, doctrine has varied somewhat. Attorney General Cushing's opinion in 7 *Opins. A. G.* 760–761 (1856), which is cited by Professor Brown as negativing the proposition, applied only to "a supplemental or special pardon," but apparently recognized that "a general pardon" would have been efficacious for the purpose. And four years later Attorney General Black ruled in unqualified terms that a person disfranchised as a citizen by conviction for crime under the laws of the United States could be restored to his rights by a pardon issued either before or after he had suffered the other penalties incident to his conviction. 9 *Ibid.*, 478 (1860). See also 21 *ibid.*, 242–243 (1893).

140 233 U. S. 51.

141 The provisions of the Act of February 5, 1917, for the deportation of aliens convicted of certain offenses involving "moral turpitude" do not apply "to one who has been pardoned" (U. S. Code, tit. 8, §155); and on this ground the Attorney General has occasionally advised the President to pardon alien offenders against United States statutes upon completion of sentence.

Nor is the efficacy of this provision confined to presidential pardons for federal offenses, in which connection the following item from the *Boston Transcript* of December 24, 1938, is of interest:

"Pasquale Vallarelli, 30 year-old Boston alien, walked out of the East Boston Immigration Station today a free man after Washington authorities ruled that the pardon granted him by Governor Hurley and the Executive Council automatically canceled a deportation warrant for his detention.

"Vallarelli was pardoned by the Council Thursday night after serving more than nine years of a 21 to 24-year sentence for robbery. He was released from State Prison yesterday afternoon and was immediately taken into custody by immigration authorities.

"James H. Brennan, attorney for Vallarelli, contacted officials of the Labor Department in Washington last night and today word was received here by Immigration Commissioner Mary A. Ward that the pardon dismissed the deportation warrant."

142 *Ex parte* Wells, 18 How. 307 (1855), the leading case, relies principally on British authority. Some early Attorneys General were reluctant to admit the propriety of conditional pardons or of pardons prior to the trial of the applicant. 1 *Opins. A. G.* 342 (1820); 2 *ibid.*, 275 (1829); 5 *ibid.*, 687 (1795). The broader view is based in 4 *ibid.*, 433 on the maxim *"quod omne majus continet minus"* (1845). See also *Senate Documents*, No. 123, 26th Congress, 2nd sess. For an interesting case growing out of a conditional pardon, see 21 *Harvard Law Review*, 541. On the royal dispensing power prior to the Revolution of 1688, see Frederic W. Maitland, *The Constitutional History of England* (Cambridge University Press, 1908), pp. 302–306.

143 Art. I, §9, par. 7; *Knote v. United States*, 95 U. S. 149 (1877); *The Laura*, 114 U. S. 411 (1885); 5 *Opins. A. G.* 580 (1852); 6 *ibid.*, 393 (1853); 16 *ibid.*, 1 (1878).

144 *The Laura, supra; Brown v. Walker*, 161 U. S. 591 (1896); *ex parte* United States, 242 U. S. 27 (1913).

145 *Ex parte* United States, preceding note.
146 Farrand, II, 185; *cf.* 4 *Bl. Commentaries,* 399–400.
147 Art. I, §3, par. 7.

NOTES TO CHAPTER V*

1 At no point did the Framers depart more conspicuously from their materials than in dispersing among the President, Congress, and the Senate the powers most immediately touching the conduct of foreign relations—the war power, the treaty-making power, and the power to appoint ambassadors, etc. Blackstone, Locke, and Montesquieu were all in agreement in treating the direction of foreign relations as a branch of "executive," or royal, power. Said Blackstone:

"With regard to foreign concerns, the king is the delegate or representative of his people. It is impossible that the individuals of a state, in their collective capacity, can transact the affairs of that state with another community equally numerous as themselves. Unanimity must be wanting to their measures, and strength to the execution of their counsels. In the king therefore, as in a center, all the rays of his people are united, and form by that union a consistency, splendor, and power, that make him feared and respected by foreign potentates; who would scruple to enter into any engagement, that must afterwards be revised and ratified by a popular assembly. What is done by the royal authority, with regard to foreign powers, is the act of the whole nation; what is done without the king's concurrence is the act only of private men. And so far is this point carried by our law, that it hath been held, that should all the subjects of England make war without the royal assent, such war is no breach of the league. . . . The king therefore, considered as the representative of his people, has the sole power of sending embassadors to foreign states, and receiving ambassadors at home." 1 *Commentaries,* 252.

Locke expressed himself on the topic as follows:

"There is another power in every commonwealth which one may call natural, because it is that which answers to the power every man naturally had before he entered into society. For though in a commonwealth the members of it are distinct persons still, in reference to one another, and, as such, are governed by the laws of the society, yet, in reference to the rest of mankind, they make one body, which is, as every member of it before was, still in the state of Nature with the rest of mankind, so that the controversies that happen between any man of the society with those that are out of it are managed by the public, and an injury done to a member of their body engages the whole in the reparation of it. . . . This, therefore, contains the power of war and peace, leagues and alliances, and all the transactions with all persons and communities without the commonwealth, and may be called federative if any one pleases. So the thing be understood, I am indifferent as to the name. . . .

"Though, as I said, the executive and federative power of every community be really distinct in themselves, yet they are hardly to be separated and placed at the same time in the hands of distinct persons. For both of them requiring the *force* of the society for their exercise, it is almost impracticable to place the force of the commonwealth in distinct and not subordinate hands, or that the executive and federative power should be placed in persons that might act separately, whereby the force of the public would be

---

* *Chapter V (Organ of Foreign Relations) begins on page 207.*

under different commands, which would be apt some time or other to cause disorder and ruin." *Two Treatises on Civil Government* (Morley, ed.), Bk. II, §§145–146, 148.

Montesquieu's words are as follows:

"In every government there are three sorts of power: the legislative; the executive in respect to things dependent on the law of nations; and the executive in regard to matters that depend on the civil law.

"By virtue of the first, the prince or magistrate enacts temporary or perpetual laws, and amends or abrogates those that have been already enacted. By the second, he makes peace or war, sends or receives embassies, establishes the public security, and provides against invasions. By the third, he punishes criminals, or determines the disputes that arise between individuals. The latter we shall call the judiciary power, and the other simply the executive power of the state." *Spirit of the Laws* (Nugent tr.), Bk. XI, Ch. 6.

While these views were, of course, known to the Framers, their acceptance of them— so far as it went—was qualified from the outset by the allocation of the war-declaring power with Congress, where it had been lodged by the Articles of Confederation. *Cf.* Farrand, *Records,* I, 65–66, 70, 244, 292; II, 104; *Federalist* 75 (Hamilton); Elliot's *Debates* (1836), IV, 124.

2 "The War of Jenkins' Ear" commenced in 1739, seven years after the sanguinary cause of it occurred.

3 For some particulars, see John Bassett Moore, *Digest of International Law* (Washington, 1906), VI, 651 ff.; Quincy Wright, *The Control of American Foreign Relations* (New York, 1922), pp. 18, 24, 25, 30, 60, 67, 206, 225, 229, 265; *United States v. Jeffers,* 4 Cranch, C. C. 704 (Fed. Cas. No. 15,471). While in attendance at the Paris Peace Conference President Wilson was forced to intervene through Secretary of State Lansing against certain legislative proposals in the California legislature having an anti-Japanese slant. *The New York Times,* April 11, 1919.

Indeed, presidential messages and less formal communications have at times disturbed good relations with foreign governments. As an example of the former, see the reference in Jackson's message of December 1, 1834, to the failure of the French government to execute certain claims conventions. France protested, and was answered by Secretary of State Forsythe in the following words:

"The first reflection produced by Mr. Serurier's note is that it brings into discussion the propriety of a message of the President to Congress, for the contents of which, until the recommendations it contains are adopted by Congress, the United States are not responsible to foreign governments. . . . The President corresponds with foreign governments, through their diplomatic agents, as the organ of the nation. As such he speaks for the nation. In his messages to Congress he speaks only for the Executive to the legislature. He recommends, and his recommendations are powerless, unless followed by legislative action. No discussion of them can be permitted. All allusions to them, made with a design to mark an anticipated or actual difference of opinion between the Executive and legislature, are indelicate in themselves, and if made to prejudice public opinion will immediately recoil upon those who are so indiscreet as to indulge them. If they contain anything injurious to foreign nations, the means of self-justification are in their own power without interposing between the different branches of this government, an interposition which can never be made, even by those who do not comprehend the true character of the Government and the people of the United States, without forfeiting the respect of both." Richardson, III, 97, 100–105.

Eighty-six years later Ambassador Jusserand, acting under instructions from his gov-

ernment, expressed hurt surprise at references by President Wilson, in a letter to Senator
Hitchcock, to "French militarism." *The New York Times,* March 12, 1920. Debates in
Congress may once have excited foreign governments, but apparently do so no more.
The houses were able in 1919 to pass resolutions favoring Irish independence without
evoking an answering roar from the British Lion. Wright, *op. cit.,* pp. 33–34. And a year
later 88 members of the House of Representatives cabled Prime Minister Lloyd George
and the British Parliament a protest against the imprisonment without arraignment or
trial of certain political offenders in Ireland, without producing any unfortunate repercussions on our diplomatic relations. See *The New York Times,* May 5, 1920.

The Dominion of Canada in 1925 requested our government to interpret a ruling of
the Supreme Court bearing on the diversion of water from the Great Lakes by Chicago.
Associated Press despatch, Ottawa, May 19, 1925. The fact that a foreign government
may take cognizance at times of acts of American state legislatures does not prove that
the latter have status as an organ of foreign relationship (*cf.* Wright, *op. cit.,* p. 30) any
more than—for example—an American mob, of whose acts, too, a foreign government
may take notice if they injure its citizens or subjects. See however note 12 below.

The very downright language being used currently at Lake Success may actually
contribute to the cause of international peace by making ridiculous the extravagances of
wounded *amour-propre* which old-time diplomats habitually affected. The hardy school
of Marshall, Bevin, and Molotov would never dream of parading such outmoded sensi-
bilities.

4 No. 64; Earle, pp. 418–419.

5 In No. 43 he wrote:
"The circumstances that endanger the safety of nations are infinite, and for this
reason no constitutional shackles can wisely be imposed on the power to which the care
of it is committed. This power ought to be co-extensive with all the possible combinations
of such circumstances; and ought to be under the direction of the same councils which
are appointed to preside over the common defence." Earle, p. 142.

6 *Ware v. Hylton,* 3 Dall. 199, 281 (1796).

7 On the general subject of the international obligation of the United States to enact
legislation adequate to protect the treaty rights of aliens, see an informed note by Wright,
op. cit., p. 18, with citations. Illustrative of the general power of Congress to enact legislation in furtherance of the rights of foreign governments and of international comity, see
United States v. Arjona, 120 U. S. 479 (1887). See also note 29 *infra.*

8 3 Dall. 54 (1795), especially at 80–81 (Paterson), and 91–95 (Iredell).

9 299 U. S. 304, 316–317 (1936). In the Philadelphia Convention, King of Massachusetts denied that the states had any international capacity whatsoever:
"The states were not 'sovereigns' in the sense contended for by some. They did not
possess the peculiar features of sovereignty,—they could not make war, nor peace, nor
alliances, nor treaties. Considering them as political beings, they were dumb, for they
could not speak to any foreign sovereign whatever. They were deaf, for they could not
hear any propositions from such sovereign. They had not even the organs or faculties of
defence or offence, for they could not of themselves raise troops, or equip vessels, for
war." Farrand, I, 323.
It is significant that nobody challenged this position.

10 Attorney General Cushing argued to this effect in 8 *Opins. A. G.* 411 (1857).

11 14 Pet. 540.

12 *Ibid.,* 570–576. Taney accordingly concludes that the Framers "anxiously desired to

cut off all connection or communication between a state and a foreign power"—a conclusion which is hardly borne out by the precise terms of Art. I, § 10.

Two years prior to the Jennison Case, Daniel Webster had stated a very different doctrine in a letter to the Barings of London, as follows:

"Your first inquiry is, 'whether the Legislature of one of the States has legal and Constitutional power to contract loans at home and abroad?' To this I answer, that the Legislature of a State has such power; and how any doubt could have arisen on this point, it is difficult for me to conceive. EVERY STATE IS AN INDEPENDENT, SOVEREIGN POLITICAL COMMUNITY, except in so far as certain powers, WHICH IT MIGHT OTHERWISE HAVE EXERCISED, have been conferred on a General Government, established under a written Constitution, and exerting its authority over the people of all the States. This General Government is a limited Government. Its powers are specified and enumerated. All powers not conferred upon it still remain with the States and with the people. The State Legislatures, on the other hand, possess all usual and extraordinary powers of Government, subject to any limitations which may be imposed by their own Constitutions, and with the exception, as I have said, of the operation on those powers of the Constitution of the United States." W. O. Bateman, *Political and Constitutional Law of the United States* (1876), p. 211.

In point of fact, state governmental agencies do (even today) sometimes assume international significance temporarily. An instance is furnished by the action of the governors of Texas, New Mexico, and Arizona early in 1924 in according President Obregon of Mexico, in response to a request to that effect by Secretary of State Hughes, the right to transport troops from Naco, Arizona, to a point on the border between Texas and Mexico. Like permission was granted Carranza in 1915. News despatches of January 18 and 19, 1924. Nor should the following Associated Press despatch of August 20, 1924, from Geneva be overlooked:

"Philip S. Henry, bearing a signed and sealed document from Gov. Cameron Morrison of North Carolina, appointing Mr. Henry a special commissioner from North Carolina, arrived in Geneva today. League of Nations officials are somewhat puzzled over how to receive him.

"Mr. Henry has not yet presented his credentials, but it was said today the league officials were going to welcome him as a representative American, anxious to learn about the league, and particularly as the Governor's impressive document concludes with the words, 'I do hereby confer on him all rights, privileges and powers useful and necessary to the just and proper discharge of the duties of his appointment.'"

Governor Morrison later explained that he had given Mr. Henry his commission "more as an introduction than anything else."

[13] 299 U. S. at 318. See also The Chinese Exclusion Case, 130 U. S. 581, 604 (1889); *Fong Yue Ting v. United States,* 149 U. S. 698, 711 (1893); *Mackenzie v. Hare,* 239 U. S. 299, 311 (1915).

[14] Note 6 *supra.*

[15] I trace the history of judicial opinion on this subject in some detail in my *National Supremacy* (New York, 1913).

[16] 252 U. S. 416 (1920).

[17] *Ibid.,* 432–434; *cf.* argument of counsel, *ibid.,* 422.

[18] *University of Illinois v. United States,* 289 U. S. 48, 59 (1933). See also p. 261 *supra.* The "dual principle" has, nonetheless, even within recent years, furnished the

State Department at Washington a pretext for declining to undertake international engagements the discharge of which would, to its way of thinking, obtrude upon "the police functions of the several states of the Union and which the Federal Government would not in consequence be capable of fulfilling." It was on this totally fallacious and deliberately specious reasoning that the United States based its declination to sign both the Geneva Convention of 1910 and that of 1921, concerning the traffic in women and children. Letter of the Undersecretary of State to the present writer, May 27, 1922.

Indeed as late as 1929 an American representative had the effrontery to base the refusal of the United States to assent to a convention for "equal treatment for foreigners and foreign enterprises" on the ground that it "proposed to give aliens the right to own real estate, which in the United States is a matter under the jurisdiction of the States." *The New York Times,* November 7, 1929. The truth is that the very first foreign treaty which the United States entered into under the Constitution, the Jay Treaty, dealt with this very subject.

The most recent rebuff administered by the Court to the "dual principle" is that in *United States v. California,* 332 U. S. 19 (1947). Here the National Government was held to be the owner of the three-mile marginal belt along the coast of California and hence to be vested with "paramount rights in and power over that belt, an incident to which is full dominion over the resources of the soil under that water, including oil." The holding is based on the general principle of national sovereignty in the international field, and involves the overruling or elbowing aside of many judicial dicta and some decisions. See Justice Gray's opinion in *Shively v. Bowlby,* 152 U. S. 1 (1894); *Louisiana v. Mississippi,* 202 U. S. 1 (1906); *The Abby Dodge,* 223 U. S. 166 (1912).

[19] The classic statement of this principle was that made in Jackson's Veto Message of July 10, 1832 (*ante,* p. 24). But the principle arose, it will be perceived, in the field of foreign relations.

[20] "Letters of Camillus," *Works* (Hamilton, ed.), VII, 556 ff.; Marshall, *Washington,* V, 650–665; S. B. Crandall, *Treaties, Their Making and Enforcement* (Washington, D. C., 1916), pp. 170–171.

[21] The main purport of Madison's argument appears in the following passages from his speech in the House, March 7, 1796:

"It was an important, and appeared to him to be a decisive, view of the subject, that if the Treaty power alone could perform any one act for which the authority of Congress is required by the constitution, it may perform every act for which the authority of that part of the Government is required. Congress have power to regulate trade, to declare war, to raise armies, to levy, to borrow, and to appropriate money, etc. If, by Treaty, therefore, as paramount to the Legislative power, the President and Senate can regulate trade, they can also declare war, they can raise armies to carry on war, and they can procure money to support armies. . . .

"The force of this reasoning is not obviated by saying, that the President and Senate would only pledge the public faith, and that the agency of Congress would be necessary to carry it into operation. For, what difference does this make, if the obligation imposed be, as is alleged, a constitutional one; if Congress have no will but to obey, and if to disobey be treason and rebellion against the constituted authorities? Under a constitutional obligation with such sanctions to it, Congress, in case the President and Senate should enter into an alliance for war, would be nothing more than the mere heralds for proclaiming it. In fact, it had been said that they must obey the injunctions of a Treaty, as implicitly as a subordinate officer in the Executive line was bound to obey the Chief Magistrate, or as the Judges are bound to decide according to the laws. . . .

"He came next to the fifth construction, which left with the President and Senate the power of making Treaties, but required at the same time the Legislative sanction and cooperation in those cases where the constitution had given express and specific powers to the Legislature. It was to be presumed, that in all such cases the Legislature would exercise its authority with discretion, allowing due weight to the reasons which led to the Treaty, and to the circumstances of the existence of the Treaty. Still, however, this House, in its Legislative capacity, must exercise its reason: it must deliberate; for deliberation is implied in legislation. If it must carry all Treaties into effect, it would no longer exercise a Legislative power; it would be the mere instrument of the will of another department, and would have no will of its own. Where the constitution contains a specific and peremptory injunction on Congress to do a particular act, Congress must, of course, do the act, because the Constitution, which is paramount over all the departments, has expressly taken away the Legislative discretion of Congress. The case is essentially different where the act of one department of Government interferes with a power expressly vested in another, and nowhere expressly taken away: here the latter power must be exercised according to its nature; and if it be a Legislative power, it must be exercised with that deliberation and discretion which is essential to the nature of Legislative power." Benton, *Abridgment*, I, 650–651.

In the interest of strict accuracy it should be noted that Madison rejects the term "concurrent powers" as descriptive of his own position, as well as the view to which in the text I have applied this term. The latter he phrases as follows: "The Treaty Power and the Congressional power might be regarded . . . as each of them supreme over the other, as it may be last exercised." This position he repels as involving "the absurdity of an *imperium in imperio* of two powers, both of them supreme, yet each of them liable to be superseded by the other." *Ibid.*, 649. This, nonetheless, is the view which has come to prevail, it being today established doctrine that, when a treaty and a statute conflict, the maxim *"leges posteriores priores contrarias abrogant"* applies in the same way that it would in the case of conflict between two treaties or two acts of Congress. *The Cherokee Tobacco*, 11 Wall. 616, 621 (1870); *United States v. McBratney*, 104 U.S. 621, 623 (1881); Head Money Cases, 112 U.S. 580, 599 (1884); *Whitney v. Robertson*, 124 U.S. 190, 194 (1888); *Botiller v. Dominguez*, 130 U.S. 238, 247 (1889); The Chinese Exclusion Case, *ibid.*, 581, 600 (1889); *Fong Yue Ting v. United States*, 698, 720–721 (1893); *DeLima v. Bidwell*, 182 U.S. 1, 195 (1901); *Johnson v. Browne*, 205 U.S. 309, 321 (1907); *Charlton v. Kelly*, 229 U.S. 447, 463 (1913); *Rainey v. United States*, 232 U.S. 310, 316 (1914); 6 *Opins. A. G.* 291 (1854); 13 *ibid.*, 354 (1870); 21 *ibid.*, 80 and 347.

It should be noted, however, that all the above references have to do with situations in which an act of Congress was held to have superseded a treaty provision of earlier date. So far as I know there is only one case in which the Supreme Court has held that the converse had occurred, and this case is, for several reasons, not entitled to be taken seriously as a binding construction of the Constitution. The reference is to *Cook v. United States*, 288 U.S. 102 (1933). Speaking by Justice Brandeis, the Court held that Section 581 of the Tariff Act of 1922 had been repealed by the Treaty of May 22, 1924, with Great Britain, but that the reënactment of the same section in 1930 did not repeal the treaty provision involved! The only precedent cited for the proposition that treaties may repeal inconsistent statutes of earlier date is *Whitney v. Robertson*, 124 U. S. 190 (1888), where the question was the obverse one; namely, whether an act of Congress had repealed a treaty, and this question was answered in the affirmative. The assertion, too, in the Cook Case that the treaty involved was "self-executing" is a simple ipse dixit. The holding is a prize example of judicial strong-arm methods, for which, I suspect, the Department of State was primarily responsible.

"The House would not in any case consider itself under a constitutional obligation to appropriate money in support of a treaty the provisions of which it will not approve." James G. Blaine, *Twenty Years of Congress* (New York, 1884–1886), as quoted by Noel Sargent in *The New York Times,* November 18, 1928.

22 The preceding note; *ex parte* Grossman, 267 U. S. 87, 119–120 (1925).

23 For a considerable list of treaty provisions affecting especially the war power and collateral powers of Congress, see a communication from Professor J. P. Chamberlain in *The New York Times* of December 11, 1927. Among others are mentioned the Treaty of Alliance of 1778 with France, which continued in formal effect till 1798 and contained a guarantee by the United States of French possessions in the West Indies; the Treaty of December 12, 1846, with Colombia by which the neutrality of the Isthmus of Panama was guaranteed; the Treaty of Paris of 1856 abolishing the right of privateering, to which President Lincoln offered to accede in 1861, notwithstanding Congress's power to issue "letters of marque and reprisal"; the Hague Convention of 1907 limiting the rights of belligerency, although the Constitution gives Congress the power to "make rules concerning captures on land and water"; etc. See further 155 Fed. 842 (1907).

24 2 Pet. 253 (1829).

25 *Ibid.,* 309.

26 *Oetjen v. Cent. Leather Co.,* 246 U. S. 297 (1918), and cases there cited.

27 Benton, *op. cit.,* II, 466–467.

28 Jefferson to Genêt, November 22, 1793, *Writings of Thomas Jefferson* (Mem. ed.), IX, 256; *Writings* (Ford, ed.), VI, 451. Note also his statement that "the transaction of the business with foreign nations is executive altogether." *Ibid.,* V, 162.

29 Charles M. Thomas, *American Neutrality in 1793* (Columbia University Press, 1931), disposes of the persistent idea that the author was Chief Justice Jay. *Ibid.,* 43–49. The proclamation proceeded on the theory that violations of it would be subject to prosecution in United States courts for violation of "the Law of Nations," which was assumed to be embodied in "a common law of the United States"; and in the case of Gideon Henfield this theory was sustained by the federal circuit court at Philadelphia, though other federal courts rejected it. Charles Warren, *The Supreme Court,* I, 112–118. Washington, in his message of December 3, 1793, suggested to Congress that it "correct, improve, or enforce" the "procedures" for carrying the policy of the proclamation into effect, including an extension of the jurisdiction of the United States courts. Richardson, I, 139. The Neutrality Act of June 5, 1794, was the outcome of this suggestion.

30 *Works* (Hamilton, ed.), VII, 76 ff.; my *President's Control,* pp. 8–15.

31 The passage in question (*ibid.,* 10–12) reads:

"The second article of the Constitution of the United States, section first, establishes this general proposition, that 'the EXECUTIVE POWER shall be vested in a President of the United States of America.'

"The same article, in a succeeding section, proceeds to delineate particular cases of executive power. It declares, among other things, that the president shall be commander in chief of the army and navy of the United States, and of the militia of the several states, when called into the actual service of the United States; that he shall have power, by and with the advice and consent of the senate, to make treaties; that it shall be his duty to receive ambassadors and other public ministers, *and to take care that the laws be faithfully executed.*

"It would not consist with the rules of sound construction, to consider this enumeration of particular authorities as derogating from the more comprehensive grant in the general clause, further than as it may be coupled with express restrictions or limitations; as in regard to the cooperation of the senate in the appointment of officers, and the making of treaties; which are plainly qualifications of the general executive powers of appointing officers and making treaties. The difficulty of a complete enumeration of all the cases of executive authority, would naturally dictate the use of general terms, and would render it improbable that a specification of certain particulars was designed as a substitute for those terms, when antecedently used. The different mode of expression employed in the constitution, in regard to the two powers, the legislative and the executive, serves to confirm this inference. In the article which gives the legislative powers of the government, the expressions are, 'All legislative powers herein granted shall be vested in a congress of the United States.' In that which grants the executive power, the expressions are, '*The executive power* shall be vested in a President of the United States.'

"The enumeration ought therefore to be considered, as intended merely to specify the principal articles implied in the definition of executive power; leaving the rest to flow from the general grant of that power, interpreted in conformity with other parts of the Constitution, and with the principles of free government.

"The general doctrine of our Constitution then is, that the *executive power* of the nation is vested in the President; subject only to the *exceptions* and *qualifications*, which are expressed in the instrument."

32 *Ibid.*, 14.

33 *Writings* (Ford, ed.), VI, 338. Madison accepted Jefferson's commission with great reluctance, as is shown in his letter of July 23, 1793, to the latter: "As I intimated in my last I have forced myself into the task of a reply. I can truly say I find it the most grating one I ever experienced." *Writings* (Hunt, ed.), pp. 138–139.

34 *Writings* (Hunt, ed.), VI, 138 ff.; *President's Control*, pp. 16–27. "He [Madison] therefore entered the lists against Mr. Hamilton in the public journals and in five papers under the signature of Helvidius, scrutinized the doctrines of Pacificus with an acuteness of intellect never perhaps surpassed and with a severity scarcely congenial to his natural disposition and never on any other occasion indulged." J. Q. Adams, *Eulogy on James Madison* (Boston, 1836), p. 46. Adams notes that Madison's "most forcible arguments are pointed with quotations from the papers of *The Federalist* written by Mr. Hamilton." *Ibid.*, p. 48.

35 *President's Control*, pp. 20–21.

36 The authoritative work for the subject, as it stood prior to World War I, is Charles G. Fenwick, *The Neutrality Laws of the United States* (Washington, D. C., 1913). Madison's cause was greatly aided of course by the breakdown of the theory that there was a common law of the United States for violation of which offenders could be prosecuted by the National Government even in the absence of statute. Note 29 *supra.*

37 7 *Opins. A. G.* 190, 209. Similarly, the President's power to nominate and, with the advice and consent of the Senate, to appoint "ambassadors, other public ministers and consuls" comprehends "all officers having diplomatic functions, whatever their title or designation." *Ibid.*, 192–193. For the expression of a different view, apropos of President J. Q. Adams's nomination, December 26, 1825, of three persons to be "envoys extra-

ordinary and ministers plenipotentiary to the Assembly of American Nations at Panama,"
see Benton, VIII, 463–464; my *President's Control*, pp. 56–57.

³⁸ *Ibid.*, pp. 24–25. In *The Federalist*, interestingly enough, Hamilton manifests no
prevision of the potentialities of the power of reception. In No. 69 he writes:
"The President is also to be authorized to receive ambassadors and other public
ministers. This, though it has been a rich theme of declamation, is more a matter of
dignity than of authority. It is a circumstance which will be without consequence in the
administration of the government; and it was far more convenient that it should be
arranged in this manner, than that there should be a necessity of convening the legislature, or one of its branches, upon every arrival of a foreign minister, though it were
merely to take the place of a departed predecessor." Earle, p. 451.

³⁹ Moore, *Digest*, IV, 484–549. See especially *ibid.*, 507, for the case of Dupuy de
Lome, whose recall was demanded shortly preceding the war with Spain. For Bernstorff's
dismissal February 3, 1917, see press despatches of this and following day; also *War
Cyclopedia*, 37. J. Q. Adams introduced a bill in the Senate to authorize the President to
dismiss foreign diplomatic representatives, arguing that, as such action was tantamount
to a declaration of war, it was beyond his normal constitutional powers. The proposal
was defeated by a vote of 74 to 24. Charles Warren, 10 *Boston University Law Review* 4
(1930), citing 9th Congress, 1st sess., March 3, 7, 1806.

⁴⁰ *Writings* (Hunt, ed.), VI, 266.

⁴¹ *President's Control*, p. 197. For a catalogue of congressional calls for documents, see
Senate Miscellaneous Documents, No. 7, 52nd Congress, 2nd sess., pp. 232–272. For
several instances of refusal of documents by the President, see Warren, article cited in
note 39, at pp. 4, 8, 11, 12, 15, 16, 17, 29. Apropos of a resolution by Senator Penrose
early in December 1906, "That the President be requested to communicate to the Senate,
if not incompatible with the public interests, full information bearing upon the recent
order dismissing from the military service of the United States three companies of the
Twenty-fifth Regiment of Infantry, United States troops (colored)," Senator Spooner of
Wisconsin said:

"Mr. President, I am opposed to the resolution offered by the Senator from Pennsylvania. My opposition to it is based entirely upon the form of it. This resolution does not,
so far as the subject-matter goes, fall within the class of inquiries which the Senate has
ever been accustomed to address to the President. It implies on its face, Mr. President, a
doubt here which I think does not exist; as to whether the Senate is of right entitled to
all the facts relating to the discharge of the three named companies or not. Always the
Senate, in passing resolutions of inquiry addressed to Cabinet officers, except the Secretary
of State, make them in form of *direction*, not *request*. It rarely has happened that a
request has been addressed to any Cabinet officer where foreign relations were involved.
Where such a resolution has been adopted it has been addressed to the President, with the
qualification that he is requested to furnish the information only so far as, in his judgment, the transmission of it is compatible with the public interest.

"There are reasons for that, Mr. President. The State Department stands upon an
entirely different basis as to the Congress from the other Departments. The conduct of
our foreign relations is vested by the Constitution in the President. It would not be admis-
sible at all that either House should have the power to force from the Secretary of State
information connected with the negotiation of treaties, communications from foreign
governments, and a variety of matters which, if made public, would result in very great
harm in our foreign relations—matters so far within the control of the President that it

has always been the practice, and it always will be the practice, to recognize the fact that there is of necessity information which it may not be compatible with the public interest should be transmitted to Congress—to the Senate or to the House.

"There are other cases, not especially confined, Mr. President, to the State Department, or to foreign relations, where the President would be at liberty obviously to decline to transmit information to Congress or to either House of Congress. Of course, in time of war, the President being Commander in Chief of the Army and Navy, could not, and the War Department or the Navy Department could not, be required by either House to transmit plans of campaign or orders issued as to the destination of ships or anything relating to the strategy of war. . . ."

In the ensuing discussion it was agreed that information had been sought from the President from time to time on all sorts of subjects; that "we request the President and we direct the Cabinet officers"; that there had "been cases within comparatively recent years where Cabinet officers having been directed by resolution of the Senate to send certain information to it, had withheld entirely, or withheld in part, such information by order of the President"; and that there had been no remedy when this happened. *Congressional Record,* December 6, 1906.

President Hoover's refusal to furnish the Senate letters, cablegrams, minutes, memoranda, etc., with reference to the London Naval Treaty (*The New York Times,* July 12, 1930), evoked from Senator McKellar of Tennessee a claim of absolute right on the part of the Senate to such documents. The learned Senator said:

"Does anybody doubt that proposition of law, first, that the Senate and the President are co-equal partners in the business of treaty-making, and secondly, that the possession of one or all of the papers and documents in reference to a partnership matter makes them the joint property of all, and that they are all entitled to them? . . . He has the documents and we would have to take them away from him in order to get them. The law says they are the joint property of the two partners—namely, the Senate and the President —but the President withholds them." *The New York Times,* July 17, 1930.

The documents were not forthcoming. See also 72nd Congress, 1st sess., *Senate Hearings on S. R. 19* (December 1931 and January 1932).

Although the controversy arose outside the area of foreign relations President Cleveland's special message to the Senate of March 1, 1886, vindicating the Attorney General in refusing to comply with a demand for certain documents which bore on the suspension of one George M. Duskin from office (Richardson, VIII, 375 ff.) is instructive; as is also President Theodore Roosevelt's special message of January 6, 1909, setting out his reasons for directing the Attorney General not to reply to a resolution of the Senate asking whether or not certain proceedings had been instituted against the Tennessee Coal and Iron Company for an alleged violation of the Sherman Act, and if not, why not. The latter message reads in part:

"I have instructed the Attorney General not to respond to that portion of the resolution which calls for a statement of his reasons for non-action. I have done so because I do not conceive it to be within the authority of the Senate to give directions of this character to the head of an executive department, or demand from him reasons for his action. Heads of executive departments are subject to the Constitution, and to the laws passed by the Congress in pursuance of the Constitution, and to the direction of the President of the United States, but to no other direction whatever."

The Senate then tried to get certain documents bearing on the same matter from the head of the Bureau of Corporations, whereupon Roosevelt ordered that official to hand the papers in question to him, and defied the Senate to do its worst. Archibald Butt, *Letters,* pp. 305–306.

42 *Senate Documents,* No. 56, 54th Congress, 2nd sess., p. 9 note; Moore, *Digest,* IV, 462; *cf.* notes 46 and 56 *infra.* No doubt, the discarded practice was a leftover from Revolutionary days, when all such communications were sent to the Continental Congress.

43 For debate on the act see *Annals of Congress,* December 27, 1798, to January 25, 1799, *passim.* The measure, amended by the Act of March 4, 1909, 35 Stat. 1088, is now U. S. Code, tit. 18, § 5. See further "Memorandum on the History and Scope of the Laws Prohibiting Correspondence with a Foreign Government," *Senate Document,* No. 696, 64th Congress, 2nd sess. (1917). The author was Mr. Charles Warren, then Assistant Attorney General.

44 *The New York Times,* October 19, 1920; *The Woman Patriot* (Washington, D. C.), May 1, 1922; *The New York Times,* June 22 and 23, 1930, and January 11, 1933. Mr. Ford's "Peace Ship" project early in 1915 did not of course fall within the purview of the Logan Act, not being intended "to influence the measures or conduct of any foreign government or of any officer or agent thereof, in relation to any disputes or controversies with the United States, or to defeat the measures of the government of the United States." A like enterprise would later on have appeared in a far different light. The latest American citizen to have the Logan Act shaken at him is Mr. Henry Wallace. This occurred when in April 1947 he went abroad to stir up sentiment against "the Truman Doctrine." See Mr. Krock's column in *The New York Times* of April 15, 1947.

45 For Mr. Wilson's reaction to Grey's indiscretion see Washington despatches of February 5, 1920. For the exchange between Wilson and Harding see *The New York Times* of October 19, 1920. Mr. Hoover's invitation to Roosevelt was sent from Yuma, Arizona, November 13, 1932; and the latter's invitation to Sir Ronald Lindsay was sent January 28, 1933. An Associated Press despatch of December 23, 1920, mentioned two other breaches of official etiquette by foreign representatives. One was the action of the Guatemalan minister in discussing with Senator Moses a resolution introduced into the Senate by the latter with regard to the detention by Guatemalan authorities of former President Cabrera; the other was the action of the first secretary of the British embassy in sending direct to a Senate committee a denial of testimony before it to the effect that the British government censored cable messages from Great Britain to the United States.

46 Presidential assertions of the principle have not always escaped a flavor of pedantry. In 1876 the governments of Pretoria and Argentina both sent congratulations to *Congress* on the occasion of the Centennial, and the following January Congress adopted joint resolutions of "high appreciation," which, however, were vetoed by President Grant on the constitutional ground:

"The usage of governments generally confines their correspondence and interchange of opinion and of sentiments of congratulation, as well as of discussion, to one certain established agency. To allow correspondence or interchange between states to be conducted by or with more than one such agency would necessarily lead to confusion, and possibly to contradictory presentation of views and to international complications.

"The Constitution of the United States, following the established usage of nations, has indicated the President as the agent to represent the national sovereignty in its intercourse with foreign powers and to receive all official communications from them. It gives him the power, by and with the advice and consent of the Senate, to make treaties and to appoint ambassadors and other public ministers; it intrusts to him solely 'to receive ambassadors and other public ministers,' thus vesting in him the origination of negotiations and the reception and conduct of all correspondence with foreign states, making him, in the language of one of the most eminent writers on constitutional law, 'the constitutional organ of communication with foreign states.'

"No copy of the addresses which it is proposed to acknowledge is furnished. I have no knowledge of their tone, language, or purport. From the tenor of the two joint resolutions it is to be inferred that these communications are probably purely congratulatory. Friendly and kindly intentioned as they may be, the presentation by a foreign state of any communication to a branch of the Government not contemplated by the Constitution for the reception of communications from foreign states might, if allowed to pass without notice, become a precedent for the address by foreigners or by foreign states of communications of a different nature and with wicked designs." Richardson, VII, 431.

Earlier, on August 14, 1876, Grant had sent a special message to the House protesting against a clause of the diplomatic appropriations act for the ensuing year which directed the President to notify certain diplomatic and consular officers "to close their offices." "In the literal sense of this direction," he asserted, "it would be an invasion of the constitutional prerogatives and duty of the President." *Ibid.,* 377. Late in 1928 Congressman Britten of Illinois, Chairman of the House Naval Committee, sent Prime Minister Baldwin of Great Britain a proposal that the latter call a naval limitation conference. When the British Premier sought to reply through the State Department, the latter declined to transmit the reply. Subsequently Mr. Britten and Commander Kenworthy, a member of Parliament, exchanged correspondence looking to an "unofficial conference" on the same subject between American M. C.'s and British M. P.'s. United Press despatch, Washington, D. C., December 29, 1928. Nothing came of the idea.

"The very delicate, plenary and exclusive power of the President as the sole organ of the Federal Government in the field of international relations" is invoked by the Court in *United States v. Curtiss-Wright Corp.,* 299 U. S. at 320. *Cf.* note 130 *infra.*

47 On the general subject of recognition, see *Senate Documents,* No. 56, cited in note 42 *ante;* Moore, *Digest,* I, 67–255 *passim.*

48 *Senate Documents,* No. 56, p. 30.

49 *Ibid.,* p. 31.

50 *Memoirs,* IV, 205–206.

51 Benton, *Abridgment,* VI, 168.

52 *Senate Documents,* No. 56, p. 36.

53 *Ibid.,* pp. 41–43; Richardson, III, 266–267; Thomas Hart Benton, *Thirty Years View* (Boston, 1854–1856), I, 665–670.

54 *President's Control,* pp. 79–83; Warren, article cited in note 39 *supra,* 31–32.

55 *Senate Documents,* No. 56, pp. 21–22.

56 It should be noted, however, that Lincoln, in his message of December 3, 1861, asked for congressional approbation before recognizing "the independence and sovereignty of Haiti and Liberia." This deference may have encouraged Henry Winter Davis, April 6, 1864, to present the following resolution in the House apropos of Napoleon III's enterprise in Mexico:

"Resolved, That the Congress of the United States are unwilling, by silence, to leave the nations of the world under the impression that they are indifferent spectators of the deplorable events now transpiring in the Republic of Mexico; and they therefore think fit to declare that it does not accord with the policy of the United States to acknowledge a monarchical government, erected on the ruins of any republican government in America, under the auspices of any European power." McPherson, p. 349.

The resolution, which was voted unanimously, was transmitted to Dayton, our minister at Paris, by Secretary Seward, who at the same time took pains to indicate that it did not state the policy of the American government, that being "a purely Executive question" and one the decision of which constitutionally belonged "not to the House of Representatives but to the President of the United States." *Ibid.*, pp. 349–350.

Secretary Seward's despatch having been communicated by the President to the House at its request, Davis on June 27 made an elaborate report from the Committee on Foreign Affairs which concluded with the following resolution:

"Resolved, That Congress has a constitutional right to an authoritative voice in declaring and prescribing the foreign policy of the United States, as well in the recognition of new powers as in other matters; and it is the constitutional duty of the President to respect that policy, not less in diplomatic negotiations than in the use of the national forces when authorized by law; and the propriety of any declaration of foreign policy by Congress is sufficiently proved by the vote which pronounces it; and such proposition while pending and undetermined is not a fit topic of diplomatic explanation with any foreign power." *Ibid.*, p. 354.

The resolution passed the House in a somewhat diluted form, but failed to come to a vote in the Senate.

The residence of the power of recognition was found by Story, writing in 1833, to be still "open to discussion," but his own opinion evidently was that it belonged to the President alone:

"The constitution has expressly invested the executive with power to receive ambassadors, and other ministers. It has not expressly invested congress with the power, either to repudiate, or acknowledge them." 2 *Commentaries*, §1566. Story noted, however, the contrary opinion of Rawle, *On the Constitution.*

57 On this controversy see Washington despatches of September 4, 24, 25, and October 4, 1920; also Jesse S. Reeves, "The Jones Act and the Denunciation of Treaties," 15 *American Journal of International Law* (January 1921), 33–38. Congress has often passed resolutions denouncing treaties or treaty provisions, sometimes by the invitation of the President, and Presidents have "usually carried out such resolutions," though not always. Wright, *op. cit.*, p. 258. Late in 1922 Senator McKellar proposed two amendments to the Jones Act, one of which abrogated outright the twenty-one treaties affected by it, and the other of which purported to notify the governments concerned. Washington despatches of December 26, 1922. Nothing came of these proposals. See also note 21 *supra.*

58 Richardson, XVII, 7934. For a similar appeal by Wilson from Paris early in 1919 in support of the three-year naval building program which was then pending in the House, see Washington despatches of February 4, 1919.

59 U. S. Code, tit. 22, §262.

60 *Ibid.*, tit. 8, §213c. For the story of the passage of the provision, see George H. Haynes, *The Senate of the United States* (Boston, 1938), II, 648–651; *cf. ibid.*, 676, n. 3. On the relation of the measure to the "Gentleman's Agreement" of 1907, see Max J. Kohler, *The New York Times*, January 9, 1924. The constitutional question had been settled by the cases cited in notes 13 and 21 *supra.*

61 The Johnson Act is U. S. Code, tit. 31, §804a. Even in the absence of the principle of Congress's sovereignty in the external field, the act would be justifiable as a measure to implement Congress's power over property of the United States (Art. IV, §3, par. 2); the property in question being debts due the United States from certain foreign governments. By the Act of July 31, 1945, the Export-Import Bank of Washington is exempt

from the Johnson Act. U. S. Code, tit. 12, §635h. The Neutrality Act of 1939 was repealed at presidential insistence, November 13, 1941.

[62] *Total War and the Constitution*, pp. 23–25; James F. Green, "The President's Control of Foreign Policy," *Foreign Policy Reports*, April 1, 1939, pp. 17–18.

[63] *House Reports*, No. 1569, 68th Congress, 2nd sess., p. 10.

[64] *House Reports*, No. 1569, etc.

The attitude of Presidents toward such congressional expressions of opinion has naturally varied with circumstances—and also with the temperaments of Presidents. Monroe's cordiality toward congressional collaboration in the matter of recognizing the South American republics was noted above. The same President also expressed his acquiescence in a resolution passed by the House February 28, 1823, requesting the President to enter upon negotiations with the maritime powers of Europe and America for the abolition of the slave trade. Richardson, II, 244. The Joint Resolution of April 27, 1846, requesting the President to give notice to Great Britain of the termination of the Convention of 1827, was approved by Polk—was, in fact, procured by him as a part of his efforts to disentangle himself from the embarrassment of his "Fifty-four Forty or a Fight" pledge.

Grant's and Wilson's response to congressional "interferences" was quite different, as we have seen. A further illustration of the latter's generally jealous attitude is furnished by his letter of December 8, 1919, to Senator Fall anent a resolution which had just been introduced by the latter advising the President to sever diplomatic relations with Mexico. The letter reads:

"Thank you very much for your kind promptness in complying with my request that you send me a copy of the memorandum report of the sub-committee on Mexican affairs of the Committee on Foreign Affairs [*sic*]. I shall examine it with the greatest interest and care. What you told me of the investigation, on Friday last, prepares me to find it matter of the greatest importance.

"You ask an indication of my desire with regard to the pending resolution to which you and Senator Hitchcock called my attention on Friday, and I am glad to reply with the utmost frankness that I should be gravely concerned to see any such resolution pass the Congress. It would constitute a reversal of our Constitutional practice which might lead to very grave confusion in regard to the guidance of our foreign affairs. I am confident that I am supported by every competent Constitutional authority in the statement that the initiative in directing the relations of our Government with foreign governments is assigned by the Constitution to the Executive and to the Executive only. Only one of the two houses of Congress is associated with the President by the Constitution in an advisory capacity, and the advice of the Senate is provided for only when sought by the Executive in regard to explicit agreements with foreign governments and the appointment of the diplomatic representatives who are to speak for this Government at foreign capitals. The only safe course, I am confident, is to adhere to the prescribed method of the Constitution. We might go very far afield if we departed from it.

"I am very much obliged to you for having given me the opportunity to express this opinion."

Woodrow Wilson

The New York Times, December 9, 1919.

Resolutions which were passed by the Senate and House separately in the 2nd session of the Fifty-third Congress, warning President Cleveland against the employment of force to restore the monarchy of Hawaii, probably saved his administration from a serious misstep. *Congressional Record,* 53rd Congress, 2nd sess., pp. 1814, 1825, 1838, 1879, 1942, 2000, 5127, 5499. Likewise, the once hotly debated "McLemore Resolution," requesting President Wilson "to warn all citizens of the United States to refrain from travelling on armed merchant vessels," while resented by him, did unquestionably afford him a valuable hint as to the state of the public mind, and one which he was quick to take. *House Reports,* No. 147, 64th Congress, 1st sess. Similarly, the *failure* of the Senate in August 1937 to adopt a resolution authorizing the loan of six superannuated destroyers to the government of Brazil saved Secretary Hull, the author of the proposal, from embarrassing our government's relations with Argentina.

65 James M. Landis, "Constitutional Limitations on the Congressional Power of Investigation," 40 *Harvard Law Review* (December 1926), 153–266. See also *infra,* pp. 513–514, note 79.

66 I am indebted in this matter to an unpublished thesis by Dr. James A. Perkins of Princeton University, entitled *Congress Investigates Our Foreign Relations* (Princeton University Library).

67 135 U. S. 1, 64.

68 1 *Opins. A. G.* 566, 570–571.

69 My *President's Control,* p. 15.

70 The most elaborate statement of this point of view, that by Mr. J. Randolph Tucker of Virginia as Chairman of the House Judiciary Committee (1887), relates to the incidence of treaty provisions on the revenue laws. 57th Congress, 1st sess., *House Reports* No. 4177; Henry St. George Tucker, *Limitations on the Treaty-Making Power* (Boston, 1915), Ch. XI. See the excellent discussion of this whole subject in *Willoughby on the Constitution* (2nd ed.) (New York, 1929), I, 548–560; also S. B. Crandall, *Treaties, Their Making and Enforcement* (2nd ed.) (Washington, D.C., 1916), Chs. XI–XIII.

71 "Where a treaty is law of the land, and as such affects the rights of parties litigating in court, that treaty as much binds those rights and is as much to be regarded by the court as an act of Congress." Chief Justice Marshall, for the Court, in *United States v. Schooner Peggy,* 1 Cr. 103, 110 (1801). See also to the same effect *Foster v. Neilson,* 2 Pet. 253, 314 (1829). The principle was, in fact, assumed in the first case to come before the Court involving a treaty. *Ware v. Hylton,* 3 Dall. 199 (1796).

72 Note 21 *supra.*

73 Crandall, pp. 458–465; Wright, pp. 258–260. While treaties sometimes provide for their own termination upon notice to the other party, or upon the lapse of a certain period following notice, the presence or absence of such a provision seems not to have influenced the procedure of termination for the United States. Our earliest treaties, those of 1778 with the King of France, were "abrogated" by act of Congress, July 7, 1798, on the justification that they had been violated by France. Whether the act of Congress was formally brought to the attention of the French government does not appear. In *Bas v. Tingy,* 4 Dall. 37 (1800), it was treated by some of the Justices as amounting to a partial declaration of war. In *Ware v. Hylton,* two years earlier, J. Iredell had expressed the opinion that a treaty of the United States could be cast off only in this way, namely, by a solemn declaration by Congress that the other party had violated it. 3 Dall. 260. In his message of March 1, 1879, vetoing a bill restrictive of Chinese immigration to the United States, President Hayes distinguished between outright termination of a treaty "by expressing the will of the nation no longer to adhere to it" and the power to modify an existing treaty. The former, he conceded, belonged to Congress; the latter, however, was lodged by the Constitution in the President and Senate. Richardson, VII, 514–518. Needless to

say, the record of practice under the Constitution does not support this distinction. The broad power which Hamilton attributed to the President in connection with the interpretation and suspension of treaties (*ante,* p. 237) leads logically to conceding him the power to terminate them; and Jefferson's view as Secretary of State closely approximated Hamilton's on this point. Moore, IV, 681. See also 229 U. S. 447, 473, where the question whether a treaty is still binding on the United States is held to be one for "the political branch of the government," by which is meant in this instance "the Executive." President Taft in 1911 headed off a resolution of Congress "directing" the abrogation of the Treaty of 1832 with Russia by giving notice "couched in a friendly and courteous tone" and inviting negotiations for a new treaty. *Our Chief Magistrate,* pp. 115–117; Washington despatches of December 18, 1911. Our extradition treaty with Greece, having proved of no aid in enabling us to get hold of Samuel Insull, was peremptorily denounced by the Roosevelt administration without stimulation or assistance from either Congress or the Senate. Washington despatches, November 4, 1933. On the other hand, when the question arose of reviving the Patents Convention of 1909 with Germany, President Harding consulted the Senate, February 17, 1922, and that body gave its approval by a two-thirds vote. Haynes, *op. cit.,* II, 590.

The most recent instance of denunciation of a treaty was that of Treaty of Commerce and Navigation of February 21, 1911, with Japan, which was effected by the State Department's giving on July 26, 1939, the Japanese government six months' notice, in accordance with the terms of the treaty. A proposal to the same end, offered by Senator Vandenberg, was at the time before the Senate Foreign Relations Committee. *The New York Times,* July 27 and 31, 1939.

74 229 U. S. 447, 472–474, and authorities there cited.

75 I am indebted to Professor Zurcher for drawing my attention to this matter.

76 For the above data, see Moore, *Digest,* II, 452–466. By the Act of May 27, 1921 (42 Stat. 8), "no person may land or operate in the United States any submarine cable directly or indirectly connecting the United States with any foreign country" without a written license from the President, who "may withhold or revoke such license when he shall be satisfied after due notice and hearing that such action will assist . . . in maintaining the rights or interests of the United States or of its citizens in foreign countries or will promote the security of the United States." U. S. Code, tit. 47, §§34–35.

77 30 *Opins. A. G.* 217.

78 37 Stat. 302, which has been superseded by the Act of June 19, 1934, 48 Stat. 1064 ff. Under the latter no station license can be granted any alien or representative, any foreign government or representative, or "any corporation organized under the laws of any foreign government." U. S. Code, tit. 47, §310.

79 30 *Opins. A. G.* 291; Richardson (1926 ed.), XVII, 7962, 8006. Washington's Proclamation of Neutrality was, of course, a further illustration of presidential action in execution of a national duty under international law; and there have been numerous instances of the return by executive authorization of property of foreign governments or their citizens found, for some reason or other, within the confines of the United States. *Senate Executive Documents,* No. 123, 26th Congress, 2nd sess., pp. 379, 384, 853, 1288. The doctrine seems early to have been established, however, that the President may not deliver up fugitives from justice taking refuge in the United States except under an act of Congress or a treaty. This was on the ground that there is no such duty owing by the law of nations. 1 *Opins. A. G.* 509, 521 (1821); 3 *ibid.,* 661 (1841); Moore, *Digest,* IV, 245–246. And although President Lincoln delivered up one Arguelles, a Spanish subject, in

1864 upon the demand of the Spanish government, with which we had no extradition treaty at the time (*ibid.*, 249–250), the case of *Valentine v. United States*, 299 U. S. 5 (1936), approves the more generally accepted doctrine. *Ibid.*, 8.

For a recent illustration of the President's "residuary" powers in protecting the national interest, as this is defined by international law, see President Truman's Proclamation of September 28, 1945, respecting coastal oil lands. Executive Proclamation No. 2667, 10 *Fed. Reg.* 12303.

80 For expert authority urging such action by the President, see *The New York Times*, March 5, 1917. Said Chief Justice Marshall, with reference to a seizure under the Act of February 9, 1799, suspending intercourse with France:

"It is by no means clear that the president of the United States whose high duty it is to 'take care that the laws be faithfully executed,' and who is commander in chief of the armies and navies of the United States, might not, without any special authority for that purpose, in the then existing state of things, have empowered the officers commanding the armed vessels of the United States, to seize and send into port for adjudication, American vessels which were forfeited by being engaged in this illicit commerce." *Little v. Barreme*, 2 Cr. 170, 177 (1804).

81 For a list of "incidents" reaching from 1798 to 1941, see James Grafton Rogers, *World Policing and the Constitution* (Boston, World Peace Foundation, 1945), pp. 92–123. Also pertinent for the period 1811 to 1934 is J. Reuben Clark's Memorandum as Solicitor of the Department of State entitled *Right to Protect Citizens in Foreign Countries by Landing Forces* (Government Printing Office, 1912, 1934). The great majority of the landings were for "the simple protection of American citizens in disturbed areas," and only about a third involved belligerent action.

82 Moore, *Digest*, II, 24, 409; VI, 261; VII, 919.

83 *Ibid.*, V, 478, 479, 482, 500, 502, 507, 508, 510.

84 Richardson, V, 284.

85 *Durand v. Hollins*, 4 Blatch 451, 454 (1860).

86 *Works* (Hamilton, ed.), VII, 745–748.

87 Richardson, IV, 442–443.

88 Benton, *Abridgment*, XV, 491, 500.

89 *Ibid.*, 503.

90 2 Black at 659–660.

91 Richardson, IV, 317–318. Benton assailed Tyler's "bedlamite conduct" with heavy sarcasm. *Globe*, XIII, 498–499. For the correspondence between the United States and Texas at this time, see *ibid.*, Appendix, 572 ff.

92 *Globe*, 42nd Congress, 1st sess., Pt. I, p. 294; *ibid.*, Appendix, pp. 52 and 65.

Grant's Santo Domingo adventure was vastly improved upon by the first Roosevelt, both as to audacity and outcome, when late in 1903 he "took Panama." The debate on the matter, which was precipitated in the Senate early in January 1904, when the Hay-Herran Treaty was laid before that body for ratification, centered upon a resolution which declared the President's course to have been violative of the law of nations, our treaty with Colombia, and the Neutrality Act. Said Senator Morgan:

"The President has paused in his usurpation of the war power, but not until he had gone to so great a length that he believed Congress would be compelled to follow the flag to save appearances and adopt a war that he was actually waging against Colombia under guise of treaty obligations to protect the transit across the Isthmus of Panama. . . . To obtain ratification of his excessive adventure he comes to the Senate and appeals to its special treaty-making power to join him in giving sanction to the war he had begun and is conducting with a display of war power at sea that is far greater than was mustered in the war with Spain, all under the pretext of protecting the isthmian transit. He asks the Senate to usurp the power of Congress to declare war, instead of making his appeal to Congress." *Congressional Record,* January 4, 1904, pp. 426–437.

On our Latin-American diplomacy from 1900 on see Thomas A. Bailey, *A Diplomatic History of the American People* (2nd ed.) (New York, 1946), Chs. XXXII, XXXIII, XXXV, XXXVI, XLII, and XLVII, *passim.*

93 Most of the presidential utterances referred to are conveniently assembled in Albert H. Putney's article on "Executive Assumption of the War Making Power," *National University Law Review* (May 1927), 1–41. See also Moore, *op. cit.,* VII, 162–168. That the power of Congress comprises the power to "declare a general war" and also the power to "wage a limited war" was asserted by the Supreme Court in *Bas v. Tingy,* 4 Dall. 37 (1800) and *Talbot v. Seeman,* 1 Cr. 28 (1801). The language of the Justices in these early cases implies that any act of war, to be entitled to judicial recognition as such, must be ascribed to congressional authorization. President Cleveland is said by one of his biographers to have asserted in 1897 that, if Congress declared war on Spain on account of Cuba, he would refuse to order the Army and Navy to fight. Robert M. McElroy, *Grover Cleveland* (New York, 1923), II, 249–250.

94 The following extract from the 3rd revised edition of Clark's Memorandum (cited in note 81 above) is interesting in this same connection: "On February 3, 1914, President Wilson by proclamation revoked the previous proclamation of March 14, 1912, making it unlawful to export arms or munitions of war to Mexico. Shortly thereafter, on April 9, 1914, the famous U.S.S. *Dolphin* incident occurred. The facts are briefly these: A squad of men of the Mexican military forces arrested and marched through the streets of Tampico a commissioned officer of the U.S.S. *Dolphin,* together with seven men composing the crew of the whaleboat of the *Dolphin.* Active negotiations took place with Mexico looking to an adequate form of redress, which finally terminated in Huerta's refusal to meet this Government's demand to unconditionally salute the United States flag. Huerta was willing to make the salute on condition that the American Chargé sign a protocol providing for simultaneous salutes from both Mexico and the United States. On April 20, 1914, President Wilson delivered an address at a joint session of the two houses of Congress on 'The Situation in our Dealings with General Victoriano Huerta at Mexico City.' As a part of his remarks, the President said (*Foreign Relations,* 1914, p. 476):

" ' . . . I, therefore, come to ask your approval that I should use the armed forces of the United States in such ways and to such an extent as may be necessary to obtain from General Huerta and his adherents the fullest recognition of the rights and dignity of the United States, even amidst the distressing conditions now unhappily obtaining in Mexico.

" 'There can in what we do be no thought of aggression or of selfish aggrandizement. We seek to maintain the dignity and authority of the United States only because we wish always to keep our great influence unimpaired for the uses of liberty, both in the United States and wherever else it may be employed for the benefit of mankind.'

"The following Joint Resolution was approved on April 22, 1914 (38 Stat. L., 770):

" 'In view of the facts presented by the President of the United States in his address delivered to the Congress in joint session on the twentieth day of April, nineteen hundred and fourteen, with regard to certain affronts and indignities committed against the United States in Mexico: Be it

" '*Resolved by the Senate and House of Representatives of the United States of Amer-*

ica in Congress assembled, That the President is justified in the employment of the armed forces of the United States to enforce his demand for unequivocal amends for certain affronts and indignities committed against the United States.

" *'Be it further resolved*, That the United States disclaims any hostility to the Mexican people or any purpose to make war upon Mexico.

" 'APPROVED, April 22, 1914.'

"On the morning of April 21, 1914, armed naval forces of the United States occupied the port of Vera Cruz, Mexico. On April 28, 1914, the strength of this force was approximately 316 officers and 6,362 men. On April 30, 1914, the United States naval forces formally turned over the port of Vera Cruz to the army, and on May 2, 1914, General Funston established a military government. Plans for evacuation of the United States forces were completed November 23, 1914, at which time the American troops left Mexican territory." *Op. cit.* (1934 ed.), pp. 118–119.

95 *Total War and the Constitution*, pp. 29–31. For the vigorous criticism stirred up in Congress by the late President's intervention in behalf of the French air mission which came to this country in the autumn of 1939 to purchase planes, when the facts were developed in "secret" testimony before the Senate Military Committee, see *The New York Times*, February 17, 1940.

96 *Total War*, pp. 32–33.

97 See pp. 50–52 *supra*.

98 *President's Control*, pp. 49–56.

99 Pp. 93–94 *supra*.

100 P. 157 *supra*. The maximum salaries of the different diplomatic grades were, however, often stipulated in early appropriation acts. Jefferson to Gallatin, February 19, 1804. *Works* (Mem. ed.), XI, 4–13.

101 10 Stat. 619.

102 7 *Opins. A. G.* 186 and 242.

103 U. S. Code, tit. 22, §§1–231; §§31–40. The restriction as to ambassadors comes from the Act of March 2, 1909, 35 Stat. 672. In the face of this provision, when President Wilson sent Mr. Elihu Root to Russia on a special mission in May 1917, he conferred upon him "the rank of ambassador" and upon certain of his associates "the rank of envoy extraordinary." The mission was not authorized by Congress, nor were the names of its members referred to the Senate. President Harding imitated his predecessor to the extent of conferring the "rank of ambassador" upon the American delegates at the Washington Conference, but submitted their names to the Senate, despite the fact that some of them were Senators, and hence incapable of holding "any civil office under the authority of the United States" (Art. I, §6, par. 2). Later, too, Mr. Harding conferred "the rank of ambassador extraordinary where matters of diplomatic precedence are involved" upon his "High Commissioner" in Haiti, Brigadier General John H. Russell of the Marine Corps. Washington despatches of April 25, 1922.

The New York Times of February 14, 1940, carried the information that Mr. Myron Taylor, whose choice by President Roosevelt as a "personal representative" to the Holy See had been announced a few days earlier, would be accorded the status of "ambassador" by the Papal authorities.

It is interesting to note that as late as 1876 James A. Garfield contended that diplomatic offices were "constitutional offices," a view which was repelled by J. Randolph Tucker of Virginia. *Congressional Record*, August 15, 1876, 44th Congress, 1st sess., pp. 5685, 5688.

Whichever view be accepted, Congress's control over salaries would often enable it, if it chose, to force a practical severance of diplomatic relations, such as was threatened when the House came within three votes of cutting out of the State Department Supply bill the provision for the annual salary of the ambassador to Russia. *The New York Times,* February 8, 1940. For an earlier similar incident see note 46 *supra.*

[104] *President's Control,* pp. 49–70; Wright, *op. cit.,* pp. 328–334; Henry M. Wriston, *Executive Agents in American Foreign Relations* (Johns Hopkins Press, 1929). The great majority of such designations have been agents to conduct negotiations. Crandall, *op. cit.,* pp. 76–77, n. 52; *Senate Document,* No. 231, 56th Congress, 2nd sess.

[105] Benton, *Abridgment,* XI, 221–222.

[106] Richardson, I, 96–98.

[107] *Congressional Record,* 53rd Congress, 2nd sess., pp. 127, 132, 196–197, 199, 205, 431–432; *Senate Reports,* No. 277, same Congress and session.

[108] Henry L. Stoddard, in *It Costs To Be President,* gives the curious code which was sometimes used by Mr. Wilson and Colonel House in their correspondence with each other. *Ibid.,* p. 59. It was doubtless the product of the mystery-loving Colonel's mind. The President could hardly have had time for such nonsense.

[109] Note 37 *supra.*

[110] Note 103 *supra.* Washington despatches of October 10, 1928, told of an agreement among twenty-two "career men" at the head of diplomatic posts of the United States not to follow precedent by resigning the following March 4th, at the beginning of Mr. Hoover's administration. President Coolidge demurred to the agreement on the ground that such heads of diplomatic posts were "primarily personal representatives of the President."

[111] Nos. 64 and 75.

[112] Farrand, III, 424–425. Yet two years before this the first standing Committee on Foreign Relations asserted in a report to the Senate:

"The President is the constitutional representative of the United States with regard to foreign nations. He manages our concerns with foreign nations and must necessarily be most competent to determine when, how, and upon what subjects negotiation may be urged with the greatest prospect of success. For his conduct he is responsible to the Constitution. The committee considers this responsibility the surest pledge for the faithful discharge of his duty. They think the interference of the Senate in the direction of foreign negotiations calculated to diminish that responsibility and thereby to impair the best security for the national safety. The nature of transactions with foreign nations, moreover, requires caution and unity of design, and their success frequently depends on secrecy and dispatch." 299 U. S. at 319, citing *United States Senate Reports, Committee on Foreign Relations,* VIII, 24.

[113] *Constitutional Government in the United States* (Columbia University Press, 1908), pp. 138–141. Ten years later, December 2, 1918, with the Versailles Peace Conference pending, Senator Cummins of Iowa introduced a resolution in the Senate which, reciting the Senate's participation in treaty making, proposed that a Senate committee of four Democrats and four Republicans be sent to Paris to keep the Senate informed of proceedings there in connection with the making of peace. The proposal did not come to a vote.

[114] Haynes, *op. cit.,* I, 62–67; *Journal of William Maclay* (Edgar S. Maclay, ed.), pp. 128–133; J. Q. Adams, *Memoirs,* VI, 427, where the story is told, on the authority of Crawford, that, as Washington strode out of the Senate chamber, he declared "that he

would be damned if he ever went there again." The account given in Maclay seems to prove Crawford's anecdote to be apocryphal.

[115] Norman J. Small, *Some Presidential Interpretations,* etc., p. 69; Ralston Hayden, *The Senate and Treaties* (New York, 1920), Chs. II and III.

[116] Pp. 98–99 *supra.*

[117] Hayden, *op. cit.,* Ch. VIII.

[118] See especially "Treaty-making Powers of the Senate," *Foreign Policy Information Service,* IV, No. 16 (October 12, 1928); also, entry "Treaties" in Index to W. Stull Holt, *Treaties Defeated by the Senate* (Johns Hopkins Press, 1933). For the pro's and con's of senatorial participation in treaty making see Frank D. Fleming's *Treaty Veto of the American Senate* (New York, 1930), especially Ch. XII, and R. J. Dangerfield, *In Defense of the Senate* (University of Oklahoma Press, 1933). A well-balanced account of the classical struggle over the Treaty of Versailles is to be found in Professor Holt's work, cited above, where the defeat of the treaty is laid to "politics," and blame is equally awarded to Wilson and Lodge. *Cf.* note 137 *infra.*

[119] For this and other instances of prior consultation of the Senate, usually by message, see Crandall, *op. cit.,* pp. 67–72.

[120] "He [the President] alone negotiates." Justice Sutherland, for the Court, in 299 U. S. at 319. The late Senator Lodge had stated this conclusion in an article in *Scribner's* in 1902. Hayden, *op. cit.,* p. 17.

[121] Wallace McClure, *International Executive Agreements* (Columbia University Press, 1941); Myres S. McDougal and Asher Lans, "Treaties and Congressional Executive or Presidential Agreements: Interchangeable Instruments of National Policy," reprinted from 54 *Yale Law Journal* (1945), Nos. 2 and 3; the excellent article by David M. Levitan in 35 *Illinois Law Review* (December 1940), 365 ff.; *Senate Documents,* No. 244, 78th Congress, 2nd sess. Between 1789 and 1929, over 1,200 agreements were consummated with foreign governments without the participation of the Senate, and between 1929, when the State Department inaugurated the separate Executive Agreement series, and 1939 more than another hundred.

[122] The story is told by Mr. Roosevelt as follows:

"The Constitution did not explicitly give me power to bring about the necessary agreement with Santo Domingo. But the Constitution did not forbid my doing what I did. I put the agreement into effect, and I continued its execution for two years before the Senate acted; and I would have continued it until the end of my term, if necessary, without any action by Congress. But it was far preferable that there should be action by Congress, so that we might be proceeding under a treaty which was the law of the land and not merely by a direction of the Chief Executive which would lapse when that particular Executive left office. I therefore did my best to get the Senate to ratify what I had done. There was a good deal of difficulty about it. . . . Enough Republicans were absent to prevent the securing of a two-thirds vote for the treaty, and the Senate adjourned without any action at all, and with the feeling of entire self-satisfaction at having left the country in the position of assuming a responsibility and then failing to fulfil it. Apparently the Senators in question felt that in some way they had upheld their dignity. All that they had really done was to shirk their duty. Somebody had to do that duty, and accordingly I did it. I went ahead and administered the proposed treaty anyhow, considering it as a simple agreement on the part of the Executive which would be converted into a treaty whenever the Senate acted. After a couple of years the Senate did act, having previously made some utterly unimportant changes which I ratified and persuaded Santo Domingo to ratify. In all its history Santo Domingo has had nothing happen to it as fortunate as this treaty, and the passing of it saved the United States from having to face serious difficulties with one or more foreign powers." *Autobiography,* pp. 551–552; see also Bishop, *Roosevelt,* I, 433–434.

[123] Richardson, X, 198.

[124] The agreements which bear the redolent names of Cairo, Teheran, Yalta, and Potsdam were primarily military agreements. For the texts of these now notorious instruments, see *The New York Times,* March 25, 1947. Prior to these the most remarkable secret "executive agreement," at least the most remarkable one to come to light, is the "agreed memorandum," dated July 29, 1905, of an exchange of opinion between Count Katsura of Japan and Secretary of War Taft, acting as personal representative of President Theodore Roosevelt. The document was discovered among Mr. Roosevelt's unpublished papers by Mr. Tyler Dennett, who described his find in an address before the Williamstown Institute of Politics, August 7, 1924, as follows:

"In the course of the conversation the American representative of President Roosevelt remarked to the Japanese, 'I suppose that you do not desire to take the Philippine Islands away from us.' The Japanese replied that he was glad to assure the American Government that Japan had no such desire or intention, and that Japan would be best satisfied to see the United States remain in the Philippines and establish and maintain a stable government.

"The Japanese representative then said in substance: 'You realize how difficult it is to preserve the peace of the Far East. There is danger that following the conclusion of the Russo-Japanese War, Korea will lapse again into a condition of anarchy. We are aware of the provision of the American Constitution which make alliances so difficult, but it seems to us as though it would be possible for the United States to enter into a secret agreement with Japan and England for the preservation of the peace of the Far East.'

"The American replied that under our Constitution such a secret agreement would be impossible. However, he thought he could assure the Japanese Government that the American people would be glad to act with the Japanese and British people for the preservation of the peace of the Far East.

"The Japanese representative then inquired of the American representative what, in his opinion, Japan should do with reference to Korea. The American replied that in his judgment Japan would be fully justified in establishing a military protectorate over Korea and in taking charge of her foreign relations.

"This document was approved by President Roosevelt only twelve days before the formal publication of the terms of the second Anglo-Japanese alliance and two weeks before the opening of the Portsmouth Peace Conference." *The New York Times,* August 8, 1924; also, Tyler Dennett, *Roosevelt and the Russo-Japanese War* (New York, 1925), pp. 112–114.

Nor, as Mr. Dennett further pointed out, did this action "stand alone." At the outbreak of the Russo-Japanese War, eighteen months earlier, Roosevelt had, according to a letter which also Mr. Dennett was the first to bring to light, "notified"—the words are Roosevelt's—"Germany and France in the most polite and discreet fashion that in the event of a combination against Japan to try to do what Russia, Germany, and France did to her in 1894, I should promptly side with Japan . . . to whatever length was necessary on her behalf." Dennett, *op. cit.,* p. 2. The exhumation of the records of such adventurings as these greatly aided the agitation for the War Referendum proposal a few years ago.

[125] 301 U. S. 324; followed in *United States v. Pink,* 315 U. S. 203 (1942).

[126] 143 U. S. 649 (1892); followed and expanded in *Hampton v. United States,* 276 U. S. 394 (1928). As early as 1792 Congress authorized the Postmaster General to enter into postal conventions. Crandall, *op. cit.,* p. 131; 19 *Opins. A. G.* 520.

[127] The above cases; also *Altman and Co. v. United States,* 224 U. S. 583 (1912).

[128] Bertram D. Hulen in *The New York Times,* February 17, 1935.

[129] *The New York Times,* July 9, August 18 and 19, 1943, and January 13, 1944.

[130] Lucile Cardin Cram, in *The New York Times* of May 25, 1944. Senator Vandenberg's resolution of June 11 last, by which the Senate, by a vote of 64 to 4, undertook to pledge the United States to give aid by "constitutional process" to regional blocs for mutual self-help, where the security of the United States would be promoted, was a highly unusual but not entirely unique effort on the part of the Senate to speak for the country in the diplomatic field. *The New York Times,* June 12, 1948 (W. S. White). *Cf.* the Senate Resolution of August 2, 1912, *in re* the Magdalena Bay episode, 48 *Congressional Record,* 10,045–10,046; also note 139 *infra.*

[131] U. S. Code, tit. 22, §271. A vigorous attack was later made on the resolution's constitutionality by Representative Tinkham. *Congressional Record,* February 5, 1935. Mr. David J. Lewis of Maryland introduced in the House on March 19, 1934, a similar measure to end, as he declared, "the impasse which has for years enabled thirty-three Senators to delay final action upon American membership in the World Court." *The New York Times,* March 19, 1934.

[132] See pp. 210–211 and 213 *supra.*

[133] Arthur Krock in *The New York Times,* October 11 and December 13, 1944. The change of the administration's policy on this point was announced by Senator Connally in his speech of April 11, 1945, before the Washington Rotary Club. James B. Reston, *The New York Times,* April 12, 1945.

[134] *Ibid.,* October 23, 1944.

[135] See a communication in *The New York Times* of November 5, 1944, signed by Messrs. John W. Davis, W. W. Grant, Philip C. Jessup, George Rublee, James T. Shotwell, and Quincy Wright; also the excellent article by Harry Wilmer Jones entitled "The President, Congress, and Foreign Relations," 29 *California Law Review* (July 1941), 565–585.

[136] Public Law No. 264, 79th Congress, 1st sess.

[137] It is interesting to note the extent to which the Participation Act was anticipated by the provision made in the "Lodge Reservations" for congressional consent to American action under the League of Nations Covenant. The following are the pertinent Reservations (the italics are mine):

"1. The United States so understands and construes Article 1 that in case of notice of withdrawal from the League of Nations, as provided in said article, the United States shall be the sole judge as to whether all its international obligations and all its obligations under the said Covenant have been fulfilled, and *notice of withdrawal by the United States may be given by a concurrent resolution of the Congress of the United States.*

"2. *The United States assumes no obligation to preserve the territorial integrity or political independence of any other country by the employment of its military or naval forces, its resources, or any form of economic discrimination,* or to interfere in any way in controversies between nations, including all controversies relating to territorial integrity or political independence, whether members of the League or not, under the provisions of Article 10, or to employ the military or naval forces of the United States, under any article of the treaty for any purpose, *unless in any particular case the Congress, which, under the Constitution, has the sole power to declare war or authorize the employment of the military or naval forces of the United States, shall, in the exercise of full liberty of action, by act or joint resolution so provide.*

"3. *No mandate* shall be accepted by the United States under Article 22, Part I, or any other provision of the Treaty of Peace with Germany, *except by action of the Congress of the United States.* . . .

"7. *No person is or shall be authorized to represent the United States,* nor shall any citizen of the United States be eligible, as *a member of any body or agency established* or *authorized by said Treaty of Peace with Germany, except pursuant to an act of the Congress of the United States* providing for his appointment and defining his powers and duties.

"8. *The United States understands that the reparation commission will regulate or interfere with exports from the United States to Germany,* or from Germany to the United States, *only when the United States by act or joint resolution of Congress approves such regulation or interference.*

"9. *The United States shall not be obligated to contribute to any expenses of the League of Nations,* or of the secretariat, or of any commission, or committee, or conference, or other agency, organized under the League of Nations or under the treaty or for the purpose of carrying out the treaty provisions, *unless and until an appropriation of funds available for such expenses shall have been made by the Congress of the United States: Provided,* That the foregoing limitation shall not apply to the United States' proportionate share of the expense of the office force and salary of the secretary-general.

"10. *No plan for the limitation of armaments proposed by the Council of the League of Nations under the provisions of Article 8 shall be held as binding the United States until the same shall have been accepted by Congress,* and the United States reserves the right to increase its armament without the consent of the Council whenever the United States is threatened with invasion or engaged in war. . . .

"13. *The United States withholds its assent to Part XIII* (Articles 387 to 427, inclusive) *unless Congress by act or joint resolution shall hereafter make provision for representation in the organization established by said Part XIII,* and in such event the participation of the United States will be governed and conditioned by the provisions of such act or joint resolution.

"14. *Until Part I, being the Covenant of the League of Nations, shall be so amended as to provide that the United States shall be entitled to cast a number of votes equal to that which any member* of the League and its self-governing dominions, colonies, or parts of empire, in the aggregate shall be entitled to cast, the United States assumes no obligation to be bound *except in cases where Congress has previously given its consent,* by any election, decision, report, or finding of the Council or Assembly in which any member of the League and its self-governing dominions, colonies, or parts of empire, in the aggregate have cast more than one vote. . . ."

[138] See Mr. Hanson W. Baldwin's column in *The New York Times* for January 7, 1948, where is pointed out the secrecy attending the sending of 1,000 marines to the Mediterranean, the evident intention being to mislead public opinion on the importance of the step. Congress owed its knowledge of the move, says Mr. Baldwin, "neither to

the Navy nor to the State Department but to the enterprise and initiative of the American press." See also note 141 *infra*.

139 I like the tone of the following editorial from *The New York Times* of September 8, 1947:

"CONGRESS AND EUROPE: While we strongly favor the calling of a special session of Congress to deal with the European situation, we agree with Senator Vandenberg that the initiative in this matter must come from the President rather than from the majority leaders of the Senate and the House, even though these leaders are empowered, under the new rules of Congress, to take such action if they choose to do so. There are two sound reasons for this judgment. In the first place, the formulation of foreign policy— and we are about to deal here with a most important foreign policy indeed—is properly and inescapably an executive rather than a legislative function. In the second place, it is the executive and not the legislative branch of the Government that is in possession of the relevant information regarding Europe's problems. To be sure, a Congressional committee under able leadership is now making its own on-the-spot investigation. But the whole conduct of the official inquiries and negotiations in Paris and in London, as well as the surveys made on our own side of the Atlantic into the ultimate capacity and necessary limitations of American assistance, has been in the hands of the Administration. Mr. Truman and the State Department have the facts. Congress, thus far, is in a position to see only that the European situation is deteriorating and that the insatiable Mr. Stalin waits hopefully for a collapse.

"The case for calling a special session rather than marking time until next January is that it is neither proper nor practicable to attempt to rush Congress into insufficiently considered action in a matter of such grave importance, and that the customary procedures in Congress in such matters eat up time. Committee hearings must be held, the case examined on both sides, legislation drafted, opportunity afforded for a debate that will satisfy the country on the score of its thoroughness, time allowed for the almost inevitable adjustment in conference of points of difference between House and Senate bills. Even under the pressure of great events and crying need the wheels turn slowly. Two closely analogous cases may be cited. It was on Jan. 30, 1946, that President Truman recommended the present British loan to Congress, and not until July 13—165 days later—that Congress gave him a completed bill. And it was on March 12 of this year that the President proposed to Congress the adoption of the 'Truman Doctrine' of urgently needed aid to Greece and Turkey; whereas, on July 19—129 days later—the State Department was still pleading with Congress for the appropriation of funds with which to implement this program. In the present state of affairs in Europe, the prospect of an interval of anywhere from 100 to 200 days between recommendation and action is a sufficient and conclusive argument for making a beginning before autumn is well advanced rather than temporizing until midwinter."

140 For further illustration of presidential-congressional coöperation in the conduct of our foreign relations, see President Truman's message of May 26, 1947, urging military collaboration among the Western Hemisphere nations and submitting a bill for the purpose. *The New York Times*, May 27, 1947.

141 The tendency in this direction is well illustrated by President Truman's claim on April 22 last that he would have the power, without the consent of Congress, to dispatch troops for service in Palestine as part of an international force which was provided by the United Nations. This claim was supported by Mr. Warren R. Austin and by Senator Vandenberg. *The New York Times*, April 23, 1948.

NOTES TO CHAPTER VI*

[1] Earle, p. 448.

[2] *Commentaries*, §1492.

[3] 9 How. 603.

[4] See proclamations of April 15 and May 3, 1861, Richardson, VI, 13–16; message of July 4, 1861, *ibid.*, 20–31; special message of May 26, 1862, in which the facts regarding the "advance" the year previous of $2,000,000 to Messrs. Dix, Opdyke, and Blatchford for confidential services were divulged for the first time, *ibid.*, 77–79; special message of February 14, 1862, giving other details, *ibid.*, 102–104. The militia call was under the Act of 1795. See also James G. Randall, *Constitutional Problems Under Lincoln* (New York, 1926), and Carl B. Swisher, *American Constitutional Development* (Boston, 1943), Ch. XIV.

[5] Richardson, VI, 120. It is interesting to contrast President John Adams's doubts regarding his powers, as reflected in a memorandum which was addressed January 29, 1799, by the Secretary of the Navy to other Cabinet members:

"Sir, The President requested me to consult the Heads of Departments, whether the President, in whom is vested the Executive Power of the Nation, possesses the Constitutional power of regulating the exchange of Prisoners, & all matters belonging to that subject." *Naval Documents—Quasi-War with France* (Washington, 1938). It should be noticed that no mention is made of the President's role as Commander-in-Chief. Jefferson, on the other hand, reveals in his seventh annual message (October 27, 1807) an attitude quite akin to that of Lincoln: "The moment our peace was threatened I deemed it indispensable to secure a greater provision of those articles of military stores with which our magazines were not sufficiently furnished. To have awaited a previous and special sanction by law would have lost occasions which might not be retrieved. I did not hestitate, therefore, to authorize engagements for such supplements to our existing stock as would render it adequate to the emergencies threatening us, and I trust that the Legislature, feeling the same anxiety for the safety of our country, so materially advanced by this precaution, will approve, when done, what they would have seen so important to be done if then assembled. Expenses, also unprovided for, arose out of the necessity of calling all our gunboats into actual service for the defense of our harbors; of all which accounts will be laid before you." Richardson, I, 428. Writing Caesar Rodney February 10, 1810, Jefferson said: "In time of peace the people look most to their representatives; but in war to the Executive solely." *Writings* (Mem. ed.), XII, 359.

[6] Richardson, VI, 98–99.

[7] *Ibid.*, 96–98. For the final draft, see *ibid.*, 157–159. It is notable that in this draft no mention is made of the Confiscation Act of July 17, 1862, although it might easily have been treated as furnishing complete legal justification of the Proclamation. *Cf.* Edward McPherson, *History of the Rebellion* (2nd ed.) (Washington, 1865), pp. 196–197, 227–229. It was also in 1862 that Lincoln issued General Order No. 100, which was a code of Laws of War, prepared by Francis Lieber, to regulate the conduct of the armies in the field, although under the Constitution this power is specifically vested in Congress. See note 97 *infra*.

The extent to which Lincoln's thinking was influenced by William Whiting's *War Powers under the Constitution* is impossible to say; but it is not improbable that Whiting's

---

* Chapter VI (*Commander-in-Chief in Wartime*) *begins on page 275.*

views were frequently brought to his attention through Stanton. The first edition of this work appeared in 1862, the forty-third—the one cited here—in 1870. It was Whiting's task as Solicitor of the War Department to provide legal and constitutional justifications for the policies and acts of that department, and especially for its policy in the matter of military arrests. Whiting's central proposition is the maxim that "amidst arms the laws are silent" (p. 52), which applied especially, he held, to the Bill of Rights of the Constitution. This was made for peacetime, not for wartime (p. 176). "The sovereign and almost dictatorial military powers" he wrote, "existing only in actual war, ending when war ends, to be used in self-defense, to be laid down when no longer necessary, are, while they last, as lawful, as constitutional, as sacred, as the administration of justice by judicial courts in time of peace" (p. 52). And again: "It [the Constitution] does not prescribe any territorial limits, within the United States to which his [the President's] military operations shall be restricted. . . . It does not exempt any person making war upon the country, or aiding and comforting the enemy, from being *captured*, or arrested wherever he may be found. . . . It requires the President, as Chief Executive Magistrate in time of peace to see that the laws existing in time of peace are faithfully executed—and as commander-in-chief, in time of war, to see that the laws of war are executed." *Op. cit.*, pp. 89, 165–166.

In short, Whiting contends that in time of war, the President's powers range over the entire country, and are subject to no constitutional limitations whatsoever. And, furthermore, Congress's auxiliary powers under the "necessary and proper" clause have equal scope, *provided* they be employed to *aid* and not to *hinder* "the war-making power."

One or two items may be added which bear upon the evolution of Lincoln's final position. In a confidential letter dated exactly a year before his Emancipation Proclamation, Lincoln wrote, with reference to Frémont's proclamation of martial law in Missouri, that he saw no difference between slaves and other forms of property:

"If the general needs them, he can seize and use them; but when the need is past, it is not for him to fix their permanent future condition. That must be settled according to laws made by law-makers, and not by military proclamations. The proclamation on the point in question is simply 'dictatorship.' . . . Can it be pretended that it is any longer the Government of the United States—any government of constitution and laws—wherein a general or a president may make permanent rules of property by proclamation? I do not say Congress might not pass a law on the point. . . . What I object to is, that I, as President, shall expressly or impliedly seize and exercise the permanent legislative functions of the government." Nicolay and Hay, *Complete Works,* II, 80–82.

Yet when he publicly revoked a similar proclamation of General Hunter in May 1862, he said:

"Whether it be competent for me, as commander in chief of the army and navy, to declare the slaves of any State or States free, and whether, at any time, in any case, it shall have become a necessity indispensable to the maintenance of the government to exercise such supposed power, are questions which, under my responsibility, I reserve to myself. . . ." Richardson, VI, 91.

The final Emancipation Proclamation simply spoke of the action "as a fit and necessary war measure for suppressing said rebellion . . . sincerely believed to be an act of justice, warranted by the Constitution upon military necessity. . . ." *Ibid.,* pp. 157–159.

It is also interesting to recall that as a Whig member of Congress years before, Lincoln had been one of Polk's severest critics and had voted for the Ashmun resolution of censure which declared that the President had "unconstitutionally" begun war with Mexico. Justifying his conduct in a letter to Herndon at the time, Lincoln said:

"Let me first state what I understand to be your position. It is that if it shall become necessary to repel invasion, the President may, without violation of the Constitution, cross the line and invade the territory of another country, and that whether such necessity exists in any given case the President is the sole judge. . . . Allow the President to invade a neighboring nation whenever he shall deem it necessary to repel an invasion and you allow him to do so whenever he may choose to say he deems it necessary for such purpose, and you allow him to make war at pleasure. Study to see if you can fix any limit to his power in this respect, after having given him so much as you propose. . . . The provision of the Constitution giving the *war-making* power to Congress was dictated, as I understand it, by the following reasons: Kings had always been involving and impoverishing their people in wars, pretending generally, if not always, that the good of the people was the object. This our convention understood to be the most oppressive of all kingly oppressions, and they resolved to so frame the Constitution that no one man should hold the power of bringing this oppression upon us. But your view destroys the whole matter, and places our President where kings have always stood." Nicolay and Hay, I, 111–112.

⁸ On the interesting question as to when, under international law, the Emancipation Proclamation took effect, see McLaughlin, *Constitutional History,* p. 633, note 28.

⁹ 2 Bl. 635 (March 10, 1863).

¹⁰ 4 Wall. 2 (1866).

¹¹ 2 Bl. at 648.

¹² Writing with Lincoln's suspension of habeas corpus particularly in mind, Fisher said:

"What, then, is the whole law of England in reference to the two vital points of personal liberty and the public safety? Is it not that both are placed under the care of the whole Government, each branch acting in its appropriate sphere and manner; that the Executive is subordinate to the Legislature, and cannot act without its consent, expressly given before or after action; that the Executive represents the whole Government in the absence of the Legislature, and may, to protect the public safety, arrest and detain individuals at its discretion, subject to the subsequent approval of Parliament?" *Op. cit.,* p. 216.

And English law on this point had, Fisher contended, been incorporated in the Constitution: "By that law Executive power, even in its primary and essential attributes, is subjected to legislative power. By our Constitution the subordination of Executive authority to the Legislature, is made even more complete than in the English model which was before the minds of the Convention. It is, therefore, reasonable to suppose, that in a matter so vital as personal liberty, and about which the American people were so sensitive, the founders of our Government would not intentionally depart from the English system, which, in other respects they copied so closely, or that if they meant to depart from it, they would have expressly said so. It cannot be implied that they intended to confer upon the Executive Magistrate a power so dangerous, so liable to abuse, as that of arbitrary and secret imprisonment, to be exercised without the knowledge or consent, or even against the will and protest of the Legislature, a power which it had cost the English people five centuries of effort to take from their kings. To this extent is authority now claimed for the President, not by himself, but by eminent jurists, whose names have just influence on public opinion. But not in the language of the Constitution, in reference to the writ of Habeas Corpus, nor in the provisions that confer and limit Executive power, nor in the analogy between the British Constitution and our own, is such a claim to be found. Neither is it supported by judicial or other authority, subsequent or contemporaneous." *Ibid.,* pp. 220–221.

Presidential war power was, in short, an *ad interim* power, operative when Congress was not in session, but subject to congressional review and supervision when Congress came together.

13 Sumner continued:

"It is true, the President is commander-in-chief; but it is for Congress to make all laws necessary and proper for carrying into execution his powers, so that, according to the very words of the Constitution, his powers depend upon Congress, which may limit or enlarge them at its own pleasure. Thus, whether you regard Congress or regard the President, you will find that Congress is the arbiter and regulator of the War Powers.

"Of the pretension that all these enormous powers belong to the President, and not to Congress, I try to speak calmly and within bounds. I mean always to be parliamentary. But a pretension so irrational and unconstitutional, so absurd and tyrannical, is not entitled to respect. The Senator from Ohio [Mr. Wade], in indignant words worthy of the Senate, has branded it as slavish, and handed it over to judgment. Born in ignorance, and pernicious in consequences, it ought to be received most sternly, and, just in proportion as it obtains acceptance, with execration. Such a pretension would change the National Government from a government of law to that of a military dictator. It would degrade our proud Constitutional Republic, where each department has its appointed place, to one of those short-lived, vulgar despotisms appearing occasionally as a warning to mankind. That this pretension should be put forward in the name of the Constitution is only another illustration of the effrontery with which the Constitution is made responsible for the ignorance, the conceit, and the passions of men. Sir, in the name of the Constitution, which I have sworn to support, and which, according to my ability, I mean to maintain, I protest against this new-fangled effort to foist into it a pretension abhorrent to liberty, reason, and common sense." *Works of Charles Sumner* (Boston, 1872), VII, 138–140; *Congressional Globe,* 37th Congress, 2nd sess., 2188–2196 (June 27, 1862).

Browning, in answer, denied "that Congress may decide upon the measures demanded by military necessities and order them to be enforced. . . . However great the apparent necessity for such measures now, the events of an hour may so change the face of affairs that the necessity will be found in leniency, forbearance, and protection. . . . These necessities may be determined by the military commander, and to him the Constitution has entrusted the prerogative of judging of them. When the Constitution made the President 'Commander in Chief of the Army and Navy of the United States' it clothed him with all the incidental powers necessary to a full, faithful and efficient performance of the duties of that high office; and to decide what are military necessities, and to devise and execute the requisite measures to meet them, is one of these incidents. It is not a legislative, but an executive function, and Congress has nothing to do with it. . . . And whenever Congress assumes the control of the Army in the field, it usurps the powers of a coordinate department of the Government, destroys the checks and balances provided for the safety of the people, and subverts the Constitution." *Ibid.,* 2919.

However, the President was not irresponsible. Indeed, he was more responsible than Congress:

"If these extreme war powers be prostituted to the purposes of tyranny and oppression by the President, to whom the Constitution has intrusted them, when peace returns he is answerable to the civil power for that abuse. If Congress usurps and prostitutes them, the liberty of the citizen is overthrown, and he is hopelessly without remedy for his grievances . . . there is absolutely no remedy to be found anywhere." *Ibid.,* 1136.

This was said, of course, some years before *Mississippi v. Johnson,* where it was held that the President could not be prevented by injunction from doing an illegal act. 4 Wall. 475 (1866).

[14] 12 Stat. 334–335. Amended by 12 Stat. 625.

[15] Earle, p. 143. This view was, even then, an illusion, arising from the fact that the Revolution had been fought under the direction of the Continental Congress, which had no real governing power. Actually, when we turn to the state records of the period, we encounter a considerable mass of legislation which, though it had no direct reference to either recruiting or supply, was often stimulated by Congress and had the character of emergency measures meant to aid the prosecution of the war.

Thus on November 22, 1777, Congress recommended to certain of the state legislatures that they appoint commissioners "to regulate and ascertain the price of labour, manufactures, internal produce," and so forth. J. Reuben Clark, *Emergency Legislation,* pp. 211–212. A month later the same body further recommended "to the respective legislatures of the United States, forthwith to enact laws, appointing suitable persons to seize and take, for the use of the Continental Army of the said States, all woollen cloths, blankets, linens, shoes," and so on. *Ibid.,* pp. 214–217. Also, under date of October 2, 1778, Congress recommended laws for "the seizure of all grain and flour purchased up or engrossed" under such limitations as might be thought expedient. *Ibid.,* pp. 220–222.

Nor did Congress address only the state legislatures. In August and September 1777, it resolved that "whereas the States of Pennsylvania and Delaware are threatened with immediate invasion from a powerful army . . . and whereas, principles of policy and self-preservation require all persons who may be reasonably suspected of aiding or abetting the cause of the enemy may be prevented from pursuing measures injurious to the public weal," "that the Executive authority" of the states in question apprehend, disarm, and secure all disaffected persons within their limits, and confine them "in such manner as shall be consistent with their respective character." It should be added that "these arrests were made with the knowledge and approbation of Washington. A writ of habeas corpus was issued at the instance of the prisoners, but it was disregarded by the officer in charge of them, and soon afterwards, on September 16, 1777, the Legislature [of Pennsylvania] passed a bill indemnifying the Executive Council and suspending the writ of habeas corpus." Sidney G. Fisher, *Trial of the Constitution* (Philadelphia, 1862), pp. 223–225.

Likewise, when we turn to the statute books of the individual states during this period we find measure after measure enacted which entrenched upon the normal life of the community drastically: laws penalizing engrossing and forestalling, and trading with the enemy; laws forbidding the exportation of necessaries for limited periods; laws forbidding the distillation of whiskey and other spirits, in order to conserve grain supplies (Clark, pp. 250, 332, 380, 438, 497, etc.); laws fixing prices of labor and commodities, sometimes in the greatest detail (*ibid.,* pp. 420, 466, 535, 595, etc.); laws levying requisitions upon the inhabitants for supplies needed by the Army (*ibid.,* pp. 482, 963, 969, etc.); in one instance a law impressing Negro slaves for labor on fortifications (*ibid.,* p. 280, Georgia); laws prohibiting auctions on account of their tendency to depress the currency of the United States (*ibid.,* p. 480 and *passim*); in one instance a law punishing dealers for withholding necessaries and refusing to take bills of credit of the state or the United States (*ibid.,* p. 466, Massachusetts); laws encouraging the manufacture of salt and of iron products; in one instance, a law for the erection of an arms manufactory for the United States (*ibid.,* p. 916, Virginia); and so on and so forth. Nor is this to mention the numerous acts of attainder, bills of pains and penalties, and confiscation measures which were passed by the states on their own initiative in the prosecution of their more or less private war upon the Loyalists. *Works of Charles Sumner,* VII, 59–64.

Thus, the actual prosecution of the War of Independence summoned into activity an immense range of legislative power. The fact, however, that this legislation came from the state legislatures whereas the war power was attributed to the United States in the Continental Congress served to obscure the fact that the former was really an outgrowth of the latter. Today, with World War II in mind, this lesson is clear.

¹⁶ *Ibid.*, Chs. V–VII; Berdahl, Chs. VI, XI, XII. The extraordinary breadth of these legislative delegations of power is illustrated by the clause of the Lever Act which empowered the President to create "agencies" for carrying the act into effect (*ante*, Ch. III, note 11). Proceeding under this general authorization, President Wilson ordered Food Administrator Hoover to obtain charters under the laws of Delaware for two corporations, the "United States Grain Corporation" (1917) and the "Sugar Equalization Board, Inc." (1918). These organizations, the operating capital of which was furnished from funds which Congress had appropriated for the enforcement of the act, were treated as being endowed with the powers of ordinary business corporations in the matter of buying, selling, borrowing money, and so forth, although Congress had initially withheld such powers from the Food Administration. The borrowings of the Grain Corporation, whereby it was enabled through market operations to maintain grain prices, amounted at one time to $385,000,000. See generally, Harold Archer Van Dorn, *Government Owned Corporations* (New York, 1926); also note 44 *infra*.

¹⁷ On presidential delegation of delegated power, see *Runkle v. United States,* 122 U. S. 543 (1887); *United States ex. rel. French v. Weeks,* 259 U. S. 326 (1922). Delegation was, of course, frequently—perhaps usually—succeeded by redelegation. "In one case, four successive redelegations were involved." Arthur T. Vanderbilt, "Administrative Law," *1942 Annual Survey of American Law* (New York University School of Law, 1945), p. 103, citing *United States v. Barreno,* 50 Fed. Supp. 520, 526–528 (U. S. D. Ct., Md.). See also the Opinion of Attorney General Biddle of August 29, 1942.

¹⁸ *Hamilton, Collector v. Distils. and Warehouse Co.,* 251 U. S. 146 (1919); *Jacob Ruppert v. Caffey, ibid.,* 264 (1920). See also *Northern Pac. Ry. Co. v. No. Dak.,* 250 U. S. 135 (1919).

¹⁹ See especially *Schenck v. United States,* 249 U. S. 47 (1919); *Abrams et al. v. United States,* 250 U. S. 616 (1919).

²⁰ 245 U. S. 366 (1918).

²¹ The Court entirely ignored Mr. Hannis Taylor's striking brief as *amicus curiae* on this essential point. *Cf.* Maitland, *Constitutional History,* pp. 455–456.

²² *Block v. Hirsh,* 256 U. S. 135; *Marcus Brown Co. v. Feldman, ibid.,* 170 (1921).

²³ The opinion of Chief Justice White in *United States v. Cohen Grocery Co.,* in which section 4 of the Food Control Act of August 10, 1917, as amended October 22, 1919, was set aside, perhaps militates against this view to some extent. But it should be noted that the decision came more than two years after the cessation of hostilities, and received on the constitutional point the approval of only six Justices. Chief Justice White's statement, therefore, in support of which *ex parte* Milligan is cited, that "the mere existence of a state of war could not suspend or change the operation upon the power of Congress of the guaranties and limitations of the Fifth and Sixth Amendments as to such questions as we are here passing upon," should be read with careful attention to the qualifications it contains. 255 U. S. 81 (1921).

On the whole subject of the impact of war on constitutional rights, see my *Total War and the Constitution* (New York, 1947), Ch. III, and material cited there.

²⁴ The Committee on Public Information was created by a presidential order, April

12, 1917. It consisted of the Secretary of State, the Secretary of War, the Secretary of the Navy, and a civilian who was charged "with the executive direction of the Committee." The civilian was Mr. George Creel, who to all intents and purposes *was* the Committee. The Committee's principal function at the outset was the exercise of a so-called "voluntary censorship," in connection with which it from time to time issued "requests" to the press to suppress information of military value. Later it published an *Official Bulletin* containing executive proclamations and orders, rules and regulations promulgated by the departments, statutes, and judicial decisions, bearing on the conduct of the war, and directed the propagandist efforts of the government, both at home and abroad. All of which it did "on the sole authority of the President," even operating for a considerable time on the executive budget, though it later secured some appropriations from Congress. Berdahl, pp. 197–199. Even more noteworthy from the present point of view was the War Industries Board. This body was originally created, on July 28, 1917, by the Council of National Defense, with the approval of the President, to serve "as a clearing-house for the war industry needs of the government"; but in March 1918 its functions were by a mere letter of the President continued, expanded, and vested almost exclusively in the chairman, Mr. Bernard M. Baruch, while by an executive order, dated May 18 of the same year, "the President formally made the War Industries Board an independent administrative agency acting directly under his authority," thus creating what was "in effect an industries administration analogous in all essential respects to the Food and Fuel Administrations," which had been created by direct authorization of Congress. "The Board derived its legal powers directly from the President. It therefore had the power to exercise, within its field, all the powers of the President over industry entrusted to him by statute or possessed by him in virtue of his position of head of the armed forces of the Nation." Berdahl, p. 211. For details concerning the widespread activities of the War Industries Board, see Bernard M. Baruch, *American Industry in War* (New York, 1941); "Universal Mobilization for War Purposes," *Hearings before the Committee on Military Affairs*, 68th Congress, 1st sess. (March 11, 13, 20, 1924), pp. 1–144 *passim;* "specials" to *The New York Times* of March 6, April 8, August 6, October 4, and October 18, 1918, in which orders by the Board curtailing production in various lines, fixing the price of clothing, etc., are given. Creation of a Labor Board was taken up by the Secretary of Labor January 4 1918, when the matter was referred to President Wilson, who thereupon chose an advisory council, which recommended a conference of twelve persons representing employers' organizations, employees' organizations, and the public for the purpose of establishing principles and policies to make possible the prosecution of production without stoppage of work. This became the War Labor Conference Board, which was established by the Secretary of Labor January 28, 1918, and which on March 29 reported unanimously a plan for a National War Labor Board. On April 8 President Wilson announced the creation of a NWLB consisting of the membership of the Conference Board, and with Messrs. W. H. Taft and Frank P. Walsh as joint chairmen. The Board thus established by the President without legislative sanction was not only successful for the immediate purpose of preventing work stoppage, but it created the precedent of government-enforced noninterference by employers in worker's organization and collective bargaining through representatives chosen by a majority; its decisions paved the way for the Wagner Act of 1935 and the Fair Labor Standards Act of 1938. The Board relied on the political and administrative pressure of the President and various departments and agencies ("indirect sanctions") and public opinion. Only three times in its sixteen months' history was its authority challenged.

It should be added that Mr. Hoover was appointed Food Administrator April 17, 1917, four months before the Food Control Act was passed, Berdahl, p. 205. Nor should all mention be omitted of the "heatless," "meatless," "sweetless" days, which represented the public's response to executive appeals to patriotism.

25 *Ibid.*, p. 200; *War Cyclopedia*, pp. 112, 208. The status of German insurance companies and patent rights was eventually determined by the Trading with the Enemy Act.

26 James Hart, *op. cit.*, pp. 92–96.

27 For a fuller narrative of the evolution of the Lend-Lease Act, see my *Total War and the Constitution*, pp. 23–29.

28 Arthur Krock in *The New York Times*, January 22, 1943.

29 Thomas A. Bailey, *A Diplomatic History of the American People, Supplementary Chapters* (New York, 1942), p. 769.

30 *Ibid.*, pp. 769–772, and citations; my communication to *The New York Times*, October 13, 1940; U. S. Code, tit. 34, §§492, 493a, 546c; tit. 18, §33.

31 For the final steps leading to the enactment for Lend-Lease see my *Total War and the Constitution*, pp. 27–29.

32 U. S. Code (1940), Supp. IV, tit. 22, §§411–413.

33 U. S. Code, tit. 50, §80.

34 *Ibid.*, §82.

35 *Ibid.*, tit. 50—War, Appendix—§309 (Supp. IV to 1940 ed.).

36 *Ibid.*, §1152.

37 *Ibid.*, §633 (also §1152).

38 John Lord O'Brian and Manly Fleischmann, *The War Production Board, Administrative Policies and Procedures* (pamphlet, reprinted from the *George Washington Review* for December 1944), p. 11.

39 See note 37. In §§633 and 1152 of tit. 50—War, Appendix (Supp. IV), the statutory provisions distinguished in the text are all jumbled together.

40 *Ibid.*, §§901–946.

41 321 U. S. 414 (1944).

42 *Ibid.*, p. 460.

43 P. 287 *supra*.

44 For an alphabetical list of "Federal Government Agencies, showing origins . . . ," see U. S. Code (1940), Supp. V (1941–1946), pp. 1382–1391. In the case of each of the presidentially created agencies, the number of the executive order is given and its location in the *Federal Register*.

For a "Chronological List of Wartime Agencies" (including government corporations) and some account of their creation down to the close of 1942, see the excellent chapter on "War Powers and Their Administration" by Dean Arthur T. Vanderbilt in *1942 Annual Survey of American Law* (New York University School of Law, 1945), pp. 106–231. At the close of the war there were 29 agencies grouped under OEM, of which OCD, WMC, and OC were the first to fold up. At the same date there were 101 separate government corporations, engaged variously in production, transportation, power generation, banking and lending, housing, insurance, merchandising, and other lines of business and enjoying the independence of autonomous republics, being subject to neither congressional nor presidential scrutiny, nor to audit by the General Accounting Office.

45 When Congress desired to authorize the President to *create* offices, it was able to do so in unmistakable terms. See note 16 *supra;* also Ch. III, at pp. 85–86 *supra*.

46 No. 8680 (June 2, 1944). The decision occurred at a very opportune moment for

the Government in its feud with Ward's. Associated Press despatch in *The New York Times,* June 3, 1944. A year earlier the Board had written Senator Van Nuys, expressing its preference that its orders remain "without specific legal sanctions," *Congressional Record,* June 12, 1943, p. 5883 (unofficial paging), and this plea prevailed with Congress, which was then considering the bill that became the War Labor Disputes Act of June 25, 1943. Its purely advisory character, however, did not prevent WLB, it should be noted, from claiming the right to override state laws. Associated Press despatch in *The New York Times,* August 29, 1943; *New York Herald Tribune,* October 27, 1944.

[47] June 25, 1943, ch. 144, §1; 57 Stat. 163.

[48] Executive Order 9017 (January 12, 1942), creating the National War Labor Board, read in part as follows:

"Whereas, by reason of the state of war declared to exist by certain resolutions of Congress . . . the national interest demands that there shall be no interruption of any work which contributes to the effective prosecution of the War; and Whereas, as a result of a conference of labor and industry which has met at the call of the President on December 17th, 1941, it has been agreed that for the duration of the war there shall be no strikes or lock-outs, and that all labor disputes shall be settled by peaceful means, and that a National War Labor Board be established for a peaceful adjustment of such disputes. Now, therefore, by virtue of the authority vested in me by the Constitution and the statutes of the United States, it is hereby ordered: 1. There is hereby created in the Office for Emergency Management a National War Labor Board." The order further provided that the Board was to be composed of twelve special commissioners to be appointed by the President, of whom four should be representatives of the public, four of employees, and four of employers; and that it was to have "jurisdiction to settle all labor disputes likely to interrupt work which contributed to the effective prosecution of the war." Its jurisdiction was not to fall, however, until direct negotiations and the procedures of conciliation provided by the Department of Labor had proved fruitless and the dispute had been certified to it by the Secretary of Labor. 7 *Fed. Reg.* 237.

[49] See, e.g., "special" to *The New York Times,* June 17, 1943, and an Associated Press despatch, *ibid.,* two days later, dealing with the subject of appropriations to the war agencies. The War Labor Disputes Act of June 25, 1943, constituted a further legislative recognition of WLB, giving it power to issue subpoenas (§7, 4B).

[50] McKellar's proposal, backed by Senator O'Mahoney, was that all persons receiving a salary of $4,500 or better, including "all persons whose duties include the preparation or issuance of rules, regulations, or orders made or issued under authority of any act of Congress or any executive order," should be appointed by the President with the advice and consent of the Senate, that is to say, from 25,000 to 30,000 persons altogether. *The New York Times,* March 4, 1943. Presidential opposition finally killed the measure.

[51] *The New York Times,* June 10, 1941.

[52] *Report on the Work of the National Defense Mediation Board, March 19, 1941–January 12, 1942,* Bureau of Labor Statistics Bulletin, No. 714 (1942), pp. 185–192, 194–199, 265–268.

[53] *The New York Times,* March 22 and April 21, 1942; and Howard S. Kaltenborn, *Governmental Adjustment of Labor Disputes* (Chicago, 1943), pp. 129–130. See further note 61a *infra.*

[54] See *Total War and the Constitution,* pp. 49–50.

[55] See Hearings cited in note 24 *supra,* at p. 21.

[56] *Ibid.,* at pp. 67, 101, 110.

57 In Executive Order 9370 of August 16, 1943, the President personally authorized certain "indirect sanctions." The order read:

"By virtue of the authority vested in me by the Constitution and the statutes of the United States, it is hereby ordered:

"In order to effectuate compliance with directive orders of the National War Labor Board in cases in which the board reports to the Director of Economic Stabilization that its orders have not been complied with, the director is authorized and directed, in furtherance of the effective prosecution of the war, to issue such directives as he may deem necessary:

"(a) To other departments or agencies of the Government directing the taking of appropriate action relating to withholding or withdrawing from a noncomplying employer any priorities, benefits or privileges extended, or contracts entered into by executive action of the Government, until the National War Labor Board has reported that compliance has been effectuated;

"(b) To any Government agency operating a plant, mine or facility, possession of which has been taken by the President under Section 3 of the War Labor Disputes Act, directing such agency to apply to the National War Labor Board, under Section 5 of said act, for an order withholding or withdrawing from a noncomplying union any benefits, privileges or rights accruing to it under the terms of conditions of employment in effect (whether by agreement between the parties or by order of the National War Labor Board, or both) when possession was taken, until such time as the noncomplying labor union has demonstrated to the satisfaction of the National War Labor Board its willingness and capacity to comply; but, when the check-off is denied, dues received from the check-off shall be held in escrow for the benefit of the union, to be delivered to it upon compliance by it.

"(c) To the War Manpower Commission, in the case of noncomplying individuals, directing the entry of appropriate orders relating to the modification or cancellation of draft deferments or employment privileges, or both.

FRANKLIN D. ROOSEVELT.

The White House.
Aug. 16, 1943."
8 Fed. Reg. 11463.
The order was called forth by John L. Lewis's defiance of some of WLB's directives, and proved completely futile.

58 7 Fed. Reg. 10177. Prior to this by Executive Order 9247, September 17, 1942, the USES, certain defense functions of OE (Office of Education) and the employment functions of SSB (Social Security Board) and of the NYA (National Youth Administration) were transferred to WMC. 7 Fed. Reg. 7379. On December 5, by Executive Order 9279 a similar operation was attempted on the Selective Service System, but was soon given up on account of military opposition. See Executive Order 9410 (December 23, 1942), 8 Fed. Reg. 17319.

59 8 Fed. Reg. 1996–1997.

60 The New York Times, February 10, 1943.

61 Labor Relations Reporter, August 21, 1944.

61a "During the course of the year [1945] the President directed the seizure of many of the nation's industries in the course of labor disputes. The total number of facilities taken over is significant: two railroad systems, one public utility, nine industrial companies, the transportation systems of two cities, the motor carriers in one city, a towing company and a butadiene plant. In addition thereto the President on April 10 seized 218 bituminous coal mines belonging to 162 companies and on May 7, 33 more bituminous mines of 24 additional companies. The anthracite coal industry fared no better; on May 3 and May 7 all the mines of 365 companies and operators were taken away from the owners, and on October 6 the President ordered the seizure of 54 plants and pipe lines of 29 petroleum producing companies in addition to four taken over prior thereto.

"During the year disputes between railroad companies and the Brotherhoods resulted in the establishment of twelve *Railroad Emergency Boards* to investigate disputes and to report to the President. The President also established on October 9 a *Railway Express Emergency Board* to investigate the dispute between the Railway Express and a union.

"To implement the directives of the National War Labor Board, the Office of Economic Stabilization directed the cancellation of all priority applications, allocation applications and outstanding priorities and allocations in the cases of three clothing companies and one transportation system which refused to comply with orders of the National War Labor Board." Arthur T. Vanderbilt, "War Powers and their Administration," *1945 Annual Survey of American Law* (New York University School of Law), pp. 271–273.

[62] While the proposal was not adopted, the federal district courts were given exclusive jurisdiction to enjoin suspension orders. 78th Congress, 2nd sess. Public Law No. 509 (December 20, 1944); U. S. Code, tit. 50—War Appendix—§633, sec. 2(a), (9). The enactment came too late in the war to have much effect.

[63] Thomas J. Graves, *The Enforcement of Priorities, Conservation and Limitation Orders of the War Production Board* (Princeton University Ph.D. thesis, 1946). Mr. Graves was a member of the Compliance Division of WPB. "More than three million PD-1A priority certificates were issued from January, 1941, through May 31, 1944; 5,353 orders, regulations and amendments were issued by the Office of Production Management and the War Production Board. There is no record available as to the individual directions and allocations issued. When it is recalled that all this gigantic spate of legal and executive activity finds its basis in three sentences of a statute, some notion can be gained of the scope and complexity of the undertaking from the standpoint of legal supervision and direction." O'Brian and Fleischmann, *op. cit.*, p. 28.

[64] *United States v. Eaton*, 144 U. S. 677, is the leading case.

[65] 322 U. S. 598 (1944).

[66] *Ibid.*, p. 405.

[67] "Montgomery Ward's statement to the special Investigating Committee of the House of Representatives," June 6, 1944; *The New York Times*, "special," May 14, 1945; Associated Press despatch, Washington, June 30, 1943; same July 14, 1945; same, February 9, 1943; same, January 7, 1945.

[68] *The New York Times*, September 8, 1942.

[69] See pp. 189–190 *supra*.

[70] See pp. 7–8 *supra*. The classic expression of Stuart theory is Justice Vernon's statement in the Ship Money Case: "The King *pro bono publico* may charge his subjects for the safety and defense of the kingdom, notwithstanding any act of Parliament, and a statute derogatory from the prerogative doth not bind the king, and the king may dispense with any law in cases of necessity." *Rex v. Hampden,* 3 S.T. 825 (1637).

[71] While Congress complied with Mr. Roosevelt's demand with respect to the Emergency Price Control Act, it was able to express its resentment a few weeks later when it

refused to pass a "Third War Powers Act," which was planned, among other things, to give the President power to suspend any laws hampering "the free movement of persons, property and information into and out of the United States." The President made his request November 2, 1942. The anti-administration trend of the congressional elections a few days later, plus the President's ill-advised order of October 27, 1942, to set a $25,000 limit to all salaries, which he purported to base upon the Act of October 2, sealed the fate of this fresh demand. See Mr. Krock's column in *The New York Times,* issues of November 27 and December 13; also Mr. Dorris's and Mr. Barkley's "specials" in the issues of November 28 and December 4, 1942. The $25,000 limit order was repealed by Congress in the Act of April 12, 1943, raising the public debt limit from 125 billions to 210 billions. Mr. Roosevelt strongly assailed the practice of "attaching extraneous riders to any bill," but was forced to sign the measure.

[72] See, e.g., 4 Wall. at 17 and 87–88.

[73] *Duncan v. Kahanamoku,* Sheriff, 327 U. S. 304 (1946); *White v. Steer, ibid.*

[74] *Ibid.,* p. 350.

[75] *Ibid.,* p. 357. As late as April 12, 1944, both General Richardson, in command in Hawaii, and Admiral Nimitz testified in the federal court in Honolulu that the Islands were "constantly subject to Japanese air raids or a commando operation from submarines despite precautions." *The New York Times,* April 13, 1944.

[76] Executive Order 9066, 7 *Fed. Reg.* 1407.

[77] 56 Stat. 173; U. S. Code (1940), Supp. IV, tit. 18, §97a.

[78] *Hirabayashi v. United States,* 320 U. S. 81; *Korematsu v. United States,* 323 U. S. 214.

[79] On this entire, most regrettable episode see my *Total War and the Constitution.* pp. 91–100, and citations.

[80] *Ex parte* Quirin, 317 U. S. 1 (July Special Term, 1942). The opinion in the case was not published till October. The Court found it unnecessary to construe the phrase "cases arising in the land or naval forces" of Amendment V, holding that cases involving enemy personnel had never been deemed to fall within the guaranties of Amendments V and VI. In this connection the Chief Justice cited Section 2 of the Act of Congress of April 10, 1806, which, following the Resolution of the Continental Congress of August 21, 1776, imposed the death penalty on alien spies "according to the law and usage of nations, by sentence of general court martial." He also pointed to the close similarity of the case before the Court and that of Major André in the Revolution.

[81] U. S. Code, tit. 10, ch. 36; and see note 8 *supra.*

[82] *Ibid.,* tit. 50, §21.

[83] *Re* Yamashita, 327 U. S. 1 (1946).

[84] *Total War and the Constitution,* pp. 122–124, note 46, and Preface.

[85] See the excellent and authoritative article on "The Criminality of Aggressive War" by Leo Gross, in 41 *American Political Science Review* (April 1947), 205–225.

[86] During the War of 1812 the curious contention was advanced that the President could not delegate his power of command as to militia in the service of the United States. Berdahl, pp. 136–137.

[87] Rhodes, III, 581. See also *ibid.,* pp. 616–617.

[88] Burton J. Hendrick, *Lincoln's War Cabinet* (New York, 1947), p. 297. On the remarkable—and unquestionably unconstitutional—"rider" to the Army Appropriation Act of March 3, 1867, by which President Johnson's power as Commander-in-Chief was partially transferred to General Grant, see McLaughlin, *op. cit.,* p. 662.

[89] The feature of American military policy in World War I for which President Wilson was most criticized was the despatch of troops to Siberia and their retention there after the Armistice. Several resolutions of a censorious nature were introduced in Congress, but none was adopted in either house, showing, as Professor Berdahl puts it, "that even under the stress of bitter partisanship and despite all its mutterings and criticisms of executive policy, Congress will be slow to deny the power of the President as Commander-in-Chief to send and maintain troops of the army and navy abroad at his discretion, or to assert any definite claim of control for itself." Berdahl, pp. 124–125.

[90] See Art. I, §8, cls. 10 and 11. *Miller v. United States*, 11 Wall. 268 (1870); *United States v. Arjona*, 120 U. S. 479 (1887); *Mitchell v. Harmony*, 13 How. 115 (1852); *United States v. Russell*, 13 Wall. 623 (1872).

[91] *Foreign Relations, 1898*, p. 829.

[92] See *supra*, Ch. V, note 124.

[92a] The President at the same time furnished a list of the statutory provisions involved, which was accompanied by the following statement:

"I have today issued a proclamation terminating the period of hostilities of World War II as of 12:00 noon today, Dec. 31, 1946.

"Under the law, a number of war and emergency statutes cease to be effective upon the issuance of this proclamation. It is my belief that the time has come when such a declaration can properly be made and that it is in the public interest to make it.

"Most of the powers affected by the proclamation need no longer be exercised by the Executive branch of the Government. This is entirely in keeping with the policies which I have consistently followed, in an effort to bring our economy and our Government back to a peacetime basis as quickly as possible.

"The proclamation terminates Government powers under some twenty statutes immediately upon its issuance.

"It terminates Government powers under some thirty-three others at a later date, generally at the end of six months from the date of the proclamation.

"This follows as a result of provisions made by the Congress when the legislation was originally passed.

"In a few instances the statutes affected by the proclamation give the Government certain powers which in my opinion are desirable in peacetime, or for the remainder of the period of reconversion. In these instances recommendations will be made to the Congress for additional legislation.

"It should be noted that the proclamation does not terminate the states of emergency declared by President Roosevelt on Sept. 8, 1939, and May 27, 1941. Nor does today's action have the effect of terminating the state of war itself. It terminates merely the period of hostilities. With respect to the termination of the national emergency and the state of war, I shall make recommendations to the Congress in the near future." *The New York Times*, January 1, 1947.

[93] *Fleming v. Page*, 9 How. 603 (1850). *Leitensdorfer v. Webb*, 20 How. 176 (1857), however, shows a decided slant toward the conquest theory.

[94] *Fleming v. Page, supra;* The Insular Cases, 182 U. S. 1 (1901).

[95] *Cross v. Harrison*, 16 How. 164 (1853); *Santiago v. Nogueras*, 214 U. S. 260 (1909). The President's powers in conquered territory are measured only by the laws of war as interpreted by himself. 182 U. S. 222, 231–232.

[96] See 15 *Opins. A. G.* 297 and note; 30 *ibid.*, 303. The early view was to the contrary. 1 *ibid.*, 233, 234 (Wirt).

[97] General Orders, No. 100, *Official Records, War of Rebellion*, ser. III, vol. III, 148.

[98] By the Act of May 18, 1917 (40 Stat. 83), Congress forbade the keeping or setting up of houses of ill fame in the vicinity of military stations. The provision was sustained in *McKinley v. United States*, 249 U. S. 397 (1919). Meantime it was supplemented by presidential orders or "requests" regulative of saloons in similar proximities. See New York papers of July 11 and August 18, 1917. Later, zones were created about certain naval stations from which saloons were banned entirely. *The New York Times,* March 8, 1918. See also *ibid.*, April 21, 25, and 29, for items showing federal intervention, or at least remonstrance, with the police authorities of Philadelphia and New York, in the interest of the health and morals of the troops in those vicinities.

[99] See *Congressional Record* for December 3, 19, and 20, 1906, and January 19, 1907. Mr. Henry F. Pringle points out that in his *Autobiography* Roosevelt omits all mention of the Brownsville affair. *Theodore Roosevelt,* p. 464.

[100] Congress did, however, during World War I confer power on President Wilson, acting with the consent of the Senate, to appoint for the period of the war *to such grades as he might determine,* in the case of general officers. Berdahl, p. 126. Polk was bitter because Congress would not create during the Mexican War the grade of Lieutenant General, in order that he might appoint somebody over the heads of Scott and Taylor. "My situation," he lamented, "is most embarrassing. I am held responsible for the War, and I am required to entrust the chief command of the army to a general in whom I have no confidence." *Diary*, II, 393–394. It is to be suspected that Polk's concern was largely of political motivation, Scott and Taylor both being Whigs. See the debate in the Senate, May 5, 8, 10, 12, 1848; *Globe*, 30th Congress, 1st sess.

[101] See p. 417 *supra*. On the other hand, the President and the Senate have sometimes collaborated successfully to side-step the rules of eligibility laid down by statute. William Howard Taft, *Our Chief Magistrate*, pp. 127–128.

[102] U. S. Code, tit. 10, §1590.

[103] *Mullan v. United States*, 140 U. S. 240 (1891); *Wallace v. United States*, 257 U. S. 541 (1922).

NOTES TO CHAPTER VII*

[1] F. D. G. Ribble, *State and National Power Over Commerce* (Columbia University Press, 1937), pp. 117–119. (The passage is quoted with the consent of the publishers.)

[2] The clause was probably suggested by a similar one of the New York constitution of 1777. Article 19 of this instrument declared it to be the "duty of the governor to inform the legislature, at every session, of the condition of the State, so far as may respect his department; to recommend such matters to their consideration as shall appear to him to concern its good government, welfare, and prosperity." Thorpe, V, 2633.

[3] Except for the case of McKinley, regarding whose success as President Professor Binkley waxes enthusiastic: "The inauguration of William McKinley marked the beginning of a new era in the operation of the national government. Not since the presidency of Thomas Jefferson, had there been achieved such an integration of the political branches of the federal government and such consequent coherence and sense of direction in its functioning." *President and Congress* (New York, 1947), p. 187. (Quoted with the consent of Alfred A. Knopf, Inc.) The trouble with McKinley is that he worked for the

---

* *Chapter VII (Legislative Leader) begins on page 319.*

wrong people, so that in the era of reform inaugurated by his successor his real achievement was blacked out; and much the same thing must be said of "T. R.'s" successor.

4 *Autobiography*, p. 282.

5 Mark Sullivan, *Our Times* (New York, 1926), I, 74.

6 In his *Autobiography* Roosevelt calls the Washington correspondents "the most useful of all agents in the fight for efficient and decent government." *Ibid.*, p. 354. On "T. R.'s" popularity with the correspondents, see Oscar K. Davis, *Released for Publication* (New York, 1925), pp. 123–124.

7 When in 1908 Congress had got entirely out of hand, Roosevelt is reported to have told a congressman that "he wished he had sixteen lions to turn loose in Congress with which august assembly he was just then having some difficulty." The congressman asked the President whether he thought they might not make a mistake. "Not if they stayed long enough," answered "T. R." Archibald Butt, *Letters* (New York, 1924), p. 104. I can testify of my own recollection to the wide-eyed amazement with which some students of mine returned from an interview at the White House during the fight over the Hepburn bill. Mr. Roosevelt's characterizations of some of the Senators who resented his desertion of the Chandler bloc were uncomplimentary to a degree. On reaching Princeton the young men were met by telegrams asking them to consider what the President had said as confidential, but the caution came too late in some cases.

Late in his second administration the impression gained currency that Mr. Roosevelt was using the Secret Service to trail members of Congress, and a provision was inserted in the Sundry Civil Appropriation bill of 1908 limiting the activities of the Secret Service. This action the President condemned in his annual message the following December, thereby precipitating a mutually irritating wrangle with the House of Representatives. Richardson, XI, 1398 ff. (In this "revised" edition of Richardson, dated 1909, Vol. XI is paged continuously with Vol. X.)

That the Secret Service watched Senator Foraker at the time of the Brownsville affair and also tampered with his mail is asserted positively by Mrs. Foraker in her *I Would Do It Again* (New York, 1932), pp. 286–288.

8 *Autobiography*, pp. 382–383.

9 *Some Presidential Interpretations*, p. 182.

10 Mr. Wilson's appeal of October 24, 1918, read in part as follows:

"My Fellow-Countrymen: The Congressional elections are at hand. They occur in the most critical period our country has ever faced or is likely to face in our time. If you have approved of my leadership and wish me to continue to be your unembarrassed spokesman in affairs at home and abroad, I earnestly beg that you will express yourselves unmistakably to that effect by returning a Democratic majority to both the Senate and the House of Representatives.

"I am your servant and will accept your judgment without cavil. But my power to administer the great trust assigned to me by the Constitution would be seriously impaired should your judgment be adverse, and I must frankly tell you so because so many critical issues depend upon your verdict. No scruple of taste must in grim times like these be allowed to stand in the way of speaking the plain truth.

"I have no thought of suggesting that any political party is paramount in matters of patriotism. I feel too deeply the sacrifices which have been made in this war by all our citizens, irrespective of party affiliations, to harbor such an idea. I mean only that the difficulties and delicacies of our present task are of a sort that makes it imperatively necessary that the nation should give its undivided support to the Government under a unified leadership, and that a Republican Congress would divide the leadership.

"The leaders of the minority in the present Congress have unquestionably been pro-war, but they have been anti-administration. At almost every turn since we entered the war they have sought to take the choice of policy and the conduct of the war out of my hands and put it under the control of instrumentalities of their own choosing."

It will be noted that Mr. Wilson was not appealing to the people against Congress in behalf of a specific measure or program, but was asking the country for a vote of confidence for himself and party. His action is, therefore, in line with his own peculiar conception of the President as Prime Minister rather than with the Andrew Jackson–"T. R." procedure of endeavoring to bludgeon the President's own party. "F. D. R.'s" "purge" in 1938 was, of course, modeled on the latter procedure. See, e.g., his "Fireside Chat" of June 25, 1938, and his anti-Tydings speech at Denton, Md., September 5, 1938. *The New York Times,* June 26 and September 6, 1938.

On the other hand, Mr. Wilson repeatedly asked Congress during the War for what was in effect a "vote of confidence." Two items from *The New York Times* illustrate the point:

"Washington, July 23.—A virtual threat to veto the Administration Food Bill if the conferees retain the Senate amendment creating a joint committee to supervise war expenditures is contained in a letter sent tonight by President Wilson to Chairman Lever of the House Committee on Agriculture. The latter says the President would interpret 'the final adoption of Section 23 as arising from a lack of confidence in myself.'" *Ibid.,* July 24, 1917.

"Washington, May 15.—Three moves of prime importance were made today in connection with the aircraft controversy:

"President Wilson in a letter to Senator Martin, the Democratic floor leader, vehemently opposed the Chamberlain resolution for an investigation of the conduct of the war by the Committee on Military Affairs of the Senate. He said passage of the resolution would be 'a direct vote of want of confidence in the Administration,' and would constitute 'nothing less than an attempt to take over the conduct of the war.' The President called upon supporters of the Administration in the Senate to rally in his support." *Ibid.,* May 16, 1918.

Mr. Wilson also contemplated resignation had he been defeated on the Panama toll's issue and in his opposition to the McLemore Resolution of March 1906, warning American citizens to refrain from traveling in armed belligerent vessels. Binkley, pp. 207–208. He got his way in all four cases.

[11] *Theory and Practice of Modern Government,* II, 1034.

[12] *Congressional Record,* April 5 and June 19, 1906. On the latter occasion Senator Isidor Rayner became heavily sarcastic regarding Mr. Roosevelt's proceedings:

"Here we were day after day struggling with questions of constitutional law, as if we really had anything to do with their settlement, laboring under the vain delusion that we had the right to legislate; that we were an independent branch of the Government; that we were one department, and the Executive another, each with its separate and well-defined distinctions, imagining these things, and following a vision and a mirage, while the President was at work dominating the legislative will, interposing his offices into the law-making power, assuming legislative rights to a greater extent than he could possibly do if he were sitting here as a member of this body; dismembering the Constitution, and exercising precisely and identically the same power and control as if the Constitution had declared that Congress shall pass no law without the consent of the President; adopting a system that practically blends and unites legislative and executive functions, a system that prevailed in many of the ancient governments that have forever gone to ruin, and which today still obtains in other governments, the rebellious protests of whose subjects are echoing over the earth, and whose tottering fabrics I hope are on the rapid road to dissolution." *Ibid.* See also a speech of similar import by Representative Charles A. Towne, *ibid.*, June 11, 1906; and another by Senator Tillman, *ibid.*, March 16, 1908.

[13] See *ante*, note 10.

[14] *Public Papers of Woodrow Wilson* (New York, 1925–1927), I, 32. It is sometimes stated that Mr. Wilson delivered his messages as governor in person and orally, but the researches of Professor John E. Bebout seem to refute this belief. *Documents and Readings in New Jersey Government* (Copyright, Photo-Lithographers, 1931), p. 191.

[15] Tumulty, *Woodrow Wilson as I Know Him*, p. 176.

[16] Dr. Franklin Burdette tells the story in his excellent volume, *Filibustering in the Senate* (Princeton University Press, 1940), pp. 117–128.

[17] See J. S. Bassett, *Our War With Germany* (New York, 1919), pp. 117, 139–141, 150, 163, 173–177; J. B. McMaster, *The United States in the World War* (New York, 1920), pp. 36–37; Black, *op. cit.*, p. 58; Baker is singularly disappointing on such matters.

[18] "The Future of the Presidency," *The New Republic*, September 29, 1917; quoted in Black, *op. cit.*, pp. 38–39.

[19] Robert Luce, *Legislative Problems* (New York, 1935), p. 260.

[20] See also Binkley, pp. 227–233.

That Mr. Coolidge's constitutional views did not stand in the way of his drafting legislation to be laid before Congress is shown by the fact that in 1927 he drew legislation to apply the unexpended balance of the Deficiency Appropriation bill of July 3, 1926, to the prosecution of litigation to cancel the Fall-Sinclair-Doheny oil leases. *House Journal*, 69th Congress, 2nd sess., p. 194.

[21] *Public Papers and Addresses of Franklin D. Roosevelt* (New York, 1938), III, 14 (cited later as *F. D. R.*).

[22] *The New York Times*, November 13, 1932. On his western trip in 1937, Mr. Roosevelt remarked at Cheyenne that "it was part of the duty of the Presidency to keep in touch, personal touch, with the nation." *Ibid.*, September 25, 1937. See also his letter to Senator Barkley of July 15 of the same year: "On the Congress of the United States falls the primary responsibility for the adoption of methods, but on the President falls the responsibility of recommending objectives. This is in accordance with the Constitution."

[23] J. P. Foley's *Jeffersonian Cyclopedia* contains 110 entries under the headings "Republic," "Republicanism," and the like and precisely seven entries under the headings "Democracy," "Democratic," and "Democrats." It appears that Jefferson was equally well affectioned toward both "Republicans" and "Democrats," and of course his party came to be known as "Republican-Democratic."

[24] *The New York Times*, November 15, 1936.

[25] The authoritative work on this subject is James E. Pollard's *The Presidents and the Press* (New York, 1947), which covers the relations of Presidents with the press and the press's opinions of the successive Presidents from the first. The author has shown surpassing skill in reducing the voluminous materials gathered by his researches to an interesting narrative which is characterized by balance and good sense. I must confess that I do not

gather from Mr. Pollard's careful pages the impression that lightsome gaiety invariably featured Mr. Roosevelt's press conferences. His continually renewed complaint that the bulk of the newspaper press of the country was anti-administration could hardly have inspirited a good many of the correspondents. In general, however, I should say that as "F.D.R.'s" relations with Congress deteriorated, so did his relations with the press; and *pari passu* his health was deteriorating—which is the basic explanation no doubt of the other phenomena. See also Mr. Merriman Smith's engaging, if less critical, little volume, *Thank You, Mr. President* (New York, 1947), which deals with the press conference under "F.D.R." and Mr. Truman.

"On one thing, White House correspondents were agreed: under Harry Truman's administration, the presidential press conferences had become a mess. The fumbles, the off-the-cuff, foot-in-mouth answers had made news all right—but of a kind that needlessly and repeatedly embarrassed the U.S., if not its President." *Time*, October 21, 1946. Three days later Mr. Krock reported that the President was showing "improved footwork." "He made no errors, but he made no hits or runs either, and his audience got the same row of goose eggs. Changing the metaphor, Mr. Truman went underground, very often a saf eand sensible place for him to be." *The New York Times*, October 25, 1946.

26 This was when he was quoted as having said that "our frontier is on the Rhine," or words to that effect.

27 "Letters to the President that were 400 a week in the time of T.R. increased in number to more than 5,000 a day in the time of F.D.R.

"Just recently Ira Smith, who for fifty years, since McKinley, has been in charge of the mail room at the White House, celebrated his 50th anniversary and gave out an interesting interview. He said that he and he alone took care of all mail that came to the President from McKinley's time until the end of the Hoover administration. During that time there had been two peaks. One was in the administration of Theodore Roosevelt, when during the anthracite coal strike the letters got up to a thousand a day for a short time. They didn't write very much to Mr. Taft, and the volume dropped to about 200 a week. Then Wilson came in and the letters went up to an average of a thousand a day during periods of crises, dropping after he became ill. They dropped again under Mr. Hoover, and Mr. Smith, having no aid at all, took care of all the letters.

"Then F.D.R. came in. One sentence at the conclusion of his inaugural address so electrified the nation, recreating its hope: 'We have nothing to fear but fear itself,' that it alone brought into the White House 460,000 letters.

"Mr. Smith had to get two additional rooms in the State Department building and had to accumulate a staff of 50 persons to help him. Throughout the entire twelve years of Franklin D. Roosevelt's administration, the average was more than 5,000 letters a day. It rose at times on the March of Dimes birthday celebration as high as 150,000 to 175,000 a day. In times of great crises, it would frequently run for a week as much as 25,000 a day. The average of 5,000 over the twelve years includes a great falling off in the war years, when sometimes there would be a week or two with only 2,000 or 3,000 letters a day.

"The mail under the Truman administration is continuing at about the rate that it was toward the end of the Roosevelt administration, something around 4,000 letters a day. I think it is interesting to see how much closer the people seem to feel toward the President than they used to. Perhaps the radio is largely responsible. Of course, these

letters are not all of praise, by any means. Many of them are denunciation and admoni-
tion, and some are appeals, but that is a measure of the direct representation." *The
President and the Presidency,* III. "What We Expect the President To Do," lecture by
Louis Brownlow, April 14, 1947, Social Science Building, The University of Chicago,
Chicago, Illinois. Furnished the author through Mr. Brownlow's courtesy.

[28] This, of course, is not to say that Mr. Roosevelt invented the special message. Mr.
Cleveland devoted his third annual message to the tariff. Richardson, VIII, 580. The
first Roosevelt submitted special messages on Cuban reciprocity, naval armament, and
other topics. Wilson comparatively early in his first administration had addressed Congress on tariff revision, currency reform, trusts and monopolies, and repeal of the Panama
Tolls Exemption Act.

[29] One of these less formal communications was "F.D.R.'s" unfortunately worded
letter to Chairman Snyder in which he expressed the hope, with reference to the pending
Guffey-Snyder coal bill, that "your committee will not permit doubt as to its constitutionality, however reasonable, to block the suggested legislation." He could just as easily
have invoked the highly reasonable doubt as to the bill's *unconstitutionality* as an argument *for* its passage. *F.D.R.,* IV, 297–298. A memorandum by Attorney General Mitchell
advised President Hoover that it would be proper for him to sign the Norris-La Guardia
Act of 1932, restricting the equity powers of federal courts, despite doubts as to the
measure's constitutionality. The memorandum was attached to President Hoover's communication to Congress approving the act. *The New York Times,* March 24, 1932.

[30] For the doings of "F.D.R.'s" Congresses and his relations with them see articles by
Messrs. Herring, Altman, and Riddick in Volumes XXVII to XL of the *American Political Science Review;* also Professor Herring's *Presidential Leadership; the Political Relationships of Congress and the Chief Executive* (New York, 1940).

[31] "It is not a tax bill but a tax-relief bill providing relief not for the needy but for the
greedy. . . . The nation will readily understand that it is not the fault of the Treasury
Department that the income taxpayers are flooded with forms to fill out which are so
complex that even certified public accountants cannot interpret them. No, it is squarely
the fault of the Congress of the United States in using language in drafting the law which
not even a dictionary or a thesaurus can make clear."

[32] *The New York Times,* February 23 and 24, 1944. Answering the President's complaint as to the complexity of tax forms, Mr. Barkley asserted that the congressional
draftsmen had in every instance taken their language from the Treasury's experts.

[33] On the foregoing paragraph, see Farrand, I, 21, 98, 103–104, 138–140; II, 71, 78–
80, 104, 181, 298, 301, 568–569, 587. For the sources of the veto clause see the opinion
of Judge Nott in *United States v. Weil,* 29 Ct. Cl. 538 (1894); also Thomas H. Calvert,
The Constitution and the Courts (New York, 1924), I, 379–381.

[34] See generally Edward C. Mason, *The Veto Power* (1891); and Clarence A. Berdahl,
"The President's Veto of Private Bills," 52 *Political Science Quarterly,* 505–531.

[35] Mason, *op. cit.,* p. 120.

[36] In his veto of the Webb-Kenyon Act of 1913, which was promptly repassed over
his objections and later upheld by the Supreme Court (242 U.S. 311), President Taft
took the ground that his oath of office did not permit him to assent to an act of doubtful
constitutionality.

[37] See Mr. Krock's column, *The New York Times,* June 18, 1947.

[38] Musmanno, *Proposed Amendments,* pp. 67–70; R. L. Baldridge, *Record of Bills*

Vetoed and Action Taken Thereon by the Senate and House of Representatives, Fifty-first Congress to Seventy-Eighth Congress, Inclusive (Washington, 1941).

[39] *Okanogan Indians v. United States,* 279 U. S. 655 (1920). In his opinion of July 16, 1943, Attorney General Biddle held the doctrine of this case to "apply to adjournments of Congress within as well as at the end of a Session."

[40] *Wright v. United States,* 302 U. S. 583 (1938).

[41] See Justice Stone's separate opinion, 302 U. S. 598–609.

[42] *Edwards v. United States,* 286 U. S. 482 (1932). The opinions of the Court in this and the Okanogan Case contain valuable historical data on the points decided.

[43] The source of the Court's doctrine is *La Abra Mining Co. v. United States,* 175 U. S. 423, 453–454. Compare *The Cherokee Tobacco,* 11 Wall. 616 (1871), for a similar example of judicial embroidery to fill up an admitted constitutional gap.

[44] 286 U. S. at 493.

[45] "Arranging for the uninterrupted performance of his official functions during his proposed visit to Europe, President Wilson is represented as having reached an agreement with Vice-President Marshall, in his capacity as President of the Senate, and Representative Champ Clark, the Speaker of the House, under which these public servants would withhold their signatures from bills passed by the Congress until the President returns to this country, thereby delaying the presentation to him of such measures, and thus permitting him to exercise his power of veto when he is again established at the national capital." *The New York Tribune,* November 21, 1918.

[46] The story is told by Dr. L. F. Schmeckebier in 33 *American Political Science Review,* 52–54. The important parts of the narrative are as follows:

"The House Calendar for June 20 under H. R. 8875 contains the following notation: 'Passed Senate, amended, June 18, 1936.' The same notation appears in the House Calendar for June 22, and in the final edition of the Calendar published about July 1. In the list of 'Bills and Resolutions which have become Laws' in the final edition of the House Calendar, no mention of the bill is made.

"Congress adjourned on June 20, with the bill on the Speaker's table. The record showed that the bill had been amended by the Senate, and that the House had not concurred in the amendments; therefore, on the face of the record, the bill was dead.

"After adjournment, the error was discovered and steps were taken to remedy it. According to a reliable source, this was accomplished through alteration of the House *Journal,* although it has been impossible to prove this, inasmuch as access to the manuscript *Journal* was refused. However, such an examination might not be conclusive, since if a few pages of the manuscript *Journal* were copied the alteration would not be apparent. However, the contemporary records cited above all point conclusively to alteration of the *Journal.*

"The entries relating to the bill in the *Congressional Record* were also altered. The entry regarding H. R. 8875 in the list of amended bills on page 10215 of the daily *Record* was deleted from the bound *Record;* a new entry for H. R. 8875 was added to the message from the Senate stating that certain House bills have been passed without amendment (bound *Record,* p. 10175).

"As the *Journal* now showed passage, the bill was enrolled. It is reported that it was sent by airplane messenger to the presiding officers, and was signed by the Speaker at Jasper, Alabama, on July 9, and by the Vice-President at Uvalde, Texas, on July 10. This was probably the first time that a bill had been signed by the presiding officers when not in Washington and so long after adjournment. On the face of the altered *Journal*, this procedure was regular enough, as House Concurrent Resolution 54 gave the presiding officers power to sign after adjournment. The place of signing was immaterial."

47 Note by George C. Robinson in 36 *American Political Science Review* (February 1942), 76.

48 Berdahl, *loc. cit.*, pp. 508–511, including footnotes.

49 References in note 38 *supra*. The Civil Rights Act of 1866 was the first important measure to be enacted over a presidential veto according to Mr. Binkley. *Op. cit.*, p. 135. By providing for "the meeting of the fortieth and all succeeding Congresses immediately after the adjournment of the next preceding one," Congress paralyzed the "pocket veto" for the time being. *Ibid.*, p. 138.

50 Finer, *op. cit.*, II, 1033.

51 See 80th Congress, 1st sess., Public Law No. 101 (June 23, 1947); *The New York Times*, June 24, 1947; *ibid.*, January 8, 1948 (the President's annual message), where the pledge of faithful enforcement is repeated.

52 79th Congress, 2nd sess., Public Law No. 486.

53 80th Congress, 1st sess., Public Law No. 49.

54 *The New York Times*, May 16, 1947.

55 See the House proceedings in the *Congressional Record* for January 14, 1938, and appendix of the same issue; also *The New York Times* for January 6 and March 6, 1938. The President's request for this power read as follows:

"Appropriation item veto: An important feature of the fiscal procedure in the majority of our States is the authority given to the Executive to withhold approval of individual items in an appropriation bill, and, while approving the remainder of the bill to return such rejected items for the further consideration of the legislature. This grant of power has been considered a consistent corollary of the power of the legislature to withhold approval of items in the Budget of the Executive; and the system meets with general approval in the many States which have adopted it. A respectable difference of opinion exists as to whether a similar item-veto power could be given to the President by legislation or whether a constitutional amendment would be necessary. I strongly recommend that the present Congress adopt whichever course it may deem to be the correct one."

The constitutional issue was apparently conceded to turn solely on the matter of delegation.

In his earlier correspondence with Senator Vandenberg, who thought a constitutional amendment necessary, Mr. Roosevelt among other things remarked:

"I want you to know that I completely agree with your criticism of legislative 'riders' on tax and appropriation bills. Regardless of the merits or demerits of any such 'riders'— and I do not enter that phase of the discussion at the moment—the manifest fact remains that this practice robs the Executive of legitimate and essential freedom of action in dealing with legislation." *The New York Times*, January 6, 1938.

And again:

"About two months ago you wrote me in regard to the problem of the 'item veto.' Since then I have talked with Alben Barkley and he agrees with us that riders are foreign to the objectives of appropriation bills or other specific subject legislation; that they constitute a bad practice and that the President ought to have, as many Governors have, the right to veto such a rider without having to veto the whole bill." *Ibid.*

It should be noted that the House proposal did not cover "riders." It would have given the President only the right to *reduce* appropriations, not the right to eliminate restrictions on their expenditure. Nor, to my way of thinking, would it be desirable to do the latter. "Riders" are frequently objectionable, but they may also be an indispensable means of checking the executive. Doubtless the most remarkable "rider" in our legislative history is the one by which the Reconstruction Congress in effect transferred the command of the Army from President Johnson to General Grant. Binkley, *op. cit.*, p. 137.

56 The vetoed measure fixed the first Monday in November as the meeting day of Congress and the second Monday of May as its time of adjournment; and the latter provision, the President argued, invaded both the prerogative of the houses to agree on a date of adjournment and the President's contingent prerogative, in the event of their not agreeing. Richardson, III, 231–232. The date of the message is June 9, 1836. There was considerable talk that President Wilson might have to employ this unused prerogative to get Congress officially adjourned in October 1914. *The New York Times,* October 24, same year.

57 The threat of an extra session has sometimes been employed by Presidents to speed compliance with their demands. Small, *op. cit.*, p. 181. Professor Everett S. Brown draws my attention to the question which arose when at noon of November 17, 1947, the 80th Congress, which on the previous July 27 had adjourned until January 2, 1948, reconvened in response to the President's proclamation of October 23. What was the legal effect of the convening of Congress during this recess by the President's summons? Did it begin a special session which terminated the first regular session; or did it begin a special session within a regular session without terminating the latter; or was the special session only a resumption of the regular session? On the advice of experts and for reasons of convenience, the third view was adopted. See Memorandum from the Library of Congress to the Senate Committee on the Judiciary. *Congressional Record,* November 17, 1947 (No. 148), pp. 10,696–10,697 (unofficial paging).

58 Paul L. Haworth, *The United States in Our Own Times* (New York, 1920), p. 209.

59 "I am tired of an office where I can do no more good than many others, who would be glad to be employed in it. To myself, personally, it brings nothing but unceasing drudgery and daily loss of friends. Every office becoming vacant, every appointment made, *me donne un ingrat, et cent ennemis.* My only consolation is in the belief that my fellow citizens at large will give me credit for good intentions." Jefferson to John Dickinson, January 1807, *Writings* (Ford, ed.), IX, 10.

60 Speaking of President Roosevelt's relations with his first Congress, Professor E. Pendleton Herring, an excellent political observer, wrote in February 1934 as follows:

"His influence perhaps in greatest measure rested upon public confidence, together with his personal as well as official prestige. But for weathering the many political vicissitudes of putting through a complicated legislative program he was not forced to rely entirely upon these intangible factors. A second line of defense of undoubted significance was his control of patronage. In the distribution of jobs, the test of pre-convention support of Roosevelt was applied, but to this was added the query: 'How did you vote on the economy bill?' The President postponed all appointments except those that could not possibly be delayed, and owing to this (as one observer remarked) 'his relations with Congress were to the very end of the session tinged with a shade of expectancy which is the best part of young love.' His control of patronage was the only means that he had of touching individual members of Congress directly. The President could defy pressure groups and appeal to the country over the radio. But when he wished to marshal Congress behind his program and to persuade congressmen to risk the displeasure of important interests in their districts, he needed some means of strengthening their position at home. The dangers, the faults, and the limitations of this method are obvious. Yet the session indicated that the consummation of a national program of legislation is greatly aided by transmuting through patronage the localism of our politics into support of the Chief Executive." 28 *American Political Science Review,* 82–83.

Professor W. Y. Elliott expresses the view in his *The Need for Constitutional Reform* (New York, 1935) that "no President can surrender patronage unless he is given some other hold on Congress," and proposes in this connection that the President be empowered to dissolve both houses once during his term. *Ibid.,* pp. 234–235. It is possible I am a bit overconfident in my position; but all that seems certain is the fact that, as long as the President *has* offices to hand out, he will be subject to being held up by those whose support he courts for his projects.

[61] Lindsay Rogers, *The American Senate* (New York, 1926), pp. 168–169.

[62] See generally Dr. Franklin L. Burdette's volume cited in note 16 *supra.* In a memorandum which he kindly prepared at my request, Dr. Burdette lists the following Senate filibusters as having been directed against the President of the day or presidential policies:

1837 Brief obstruction against the resolution to expunge the Senate censure of President Jackson. Filibuster unsuccessful.

1846 Filibuster against a resolution to serve a year's notice of termination of "joint occupancy" of Oregon with obstruction eventually unsuccessful.

1846 (August 10) Filibuster of John Davis of Massachusetts, in effect against the Polk measure for an appropriation to be used for acquiring territory and in making peace with Mexico. Successful for the time. (See *The Diary of James K. Polk* [Chicago, 1910], II, 77, for the President's bitter complaint.)

1847 The same issue (an appropriation for peace with Mexico) was debated in the Senate from February 4 till March 1. Obstruction finally unsuccessful.

1863 (March 2–3) Democratic filibuster against a measure to "indemnify" the President for suspending the writ of habeas corpus. Obstruction unsuccessful because of arbitrary action of the chair.

1865 Filibuster of Charles Sumner and others against recognition of a reconstructed Louisiana. Successful.

1881 Final nominations of President Hayes were held in the Senate through factional Republican obstruction.

1893 Prolonged obstruction of President Cleveland's program for silver repeal. Eventually unsuccessful. For a detailed account of this filibuster see Jeannette Paddock Nichols, "The Politics and Personalities of Silver Repeal," 41 *American Historical Review* (October 1935), 33.

1903 John T. Morgan filibustered in executive sessions against President Roosevelt's treaty with Colombia for the Panama Canal. A special session of the Senate was necessary to secure ratification.

1907 Democratic filibuster led by Edward W. Carmack against Republican ship subsidy legislation supported by President Roosevelt. Obstruction successful.

1908 The record for continuous occupancy of the Senate floor was established this year by the late Robert M. La Follette of Wisconsin when, for more than eighteen hours, he filbustered against the Aldrich-Vreeland Currency Bill. But the Wisconsin Senator was relieved during the course of his remarks by twenty-nine quorum calls and three roll-call votes on questions of order.

1911 Robert L. Owen filibustered in an effort to force admission of Arizona to the Union against the wishes of President Taft, who disliked Arizona constitutional provisions. The filibuster failed in its ultimate purpose, but it contributed toward the failure to admit New Mexico at that session.

NOTES TO CHAPTER VII

1913 Taft's final appointments blocked by Democratic obstruction.

1913 Minor Republican obstruction delayed confirmation of Wilson's appointee to the position of Director of the Census. Republican threats of filibuster also served to postpone currency adjustments.

1914 Long debates on the Panama Canal Tolls, the Federal Trade Commission bill, and the Clayton Anti-Trust bill. It is doubtful whether these debates were genuine filibusters; and the President's program was eventually successful in each instance.

1914 President Wilson's Ship Registry bill was briefly delayed, but the President had his way.

1915 Republicans were successful in their filibuster against the Ship Purchase bill, supported by President Wilson.

1917 Republicans filibustered to delay business in order to force a special session and embarrass the administration. Obstruction continued from February 23 to February 28, but was abandoned when the Armed Ship bill was ready for consideration.

1917 Successful obstruction of the President's Armed Ship bill by "willful men."

1919 Republicans delayed business in order to force a special session "to keep representatives of the people closely in touch with peace negotiations in Paris."

1922 The Fordney-McCumber tariff supported by President Harding was long delayed.

1922–1923 Democrats successfully filibustered against a ship subsidy measure proposed by the Harding administration.

1926 A filibuster against adherence to the administration-supported World Court Protocol was broken by cloture.

1935 (May 21) Huey Long petulantly sought to prevent a joint session of Congress to hear President Roosevelt read his veto of the soldiers' bonus. The obstruction was unsuccessful.

1935 (June 12–13) Huey Long sought to force adoption of the Gore amendment providing for Senate confirmation of personnel under the proposed "skeletonized" NRA. This most celebrated of the Long filibusters was unsuccessful.

1937–1938 This winter during consideration of an antilynching measure, Southern loquaciousness occupied the time of the Senate almost exclusively for six weeks.

1939 Republicans and anti-administration Democrats won a technical though probably hollow victory by delaying a vote on renewal of the President's monetary powers until after their expiration at the end of the fiscal year.

On the other hand, the President has a few times been the intended beneficiary of a filibuster, as in the following instances:

1879 Republicans filibustered to defeat a Democratic rider to an appropriation bill intended to prevent use of federal troops "as a police force to keep the peace at the polls." President Hayes had previously vetoed similar but more drastically worded legislation. Republican obstruction was finally abandoned when leaders became convinced that the ambiguous rider was really a Democratic retreat and therefore essentially a compromise. The rider was allowed to pass, and Hayes approved it.

1901 Thomas H. Carter, Republican, of Montana, defeated by filibuster a river and harbor bill. It was understood widely that the Montana Senator acted in accordance with the wishes of President McKinley in order to save the executive the possible embarrassment of a veto.

1936 Bennett Champ Clark and others obstructed Treasury and Post Office appropriations until the House finally agreed to a ship subsidy law supported by President Roosevelt.

Senate filibusters sometimes receive an adventitious justification from the fact that while the filibusterers are a minority in the Senate they represent a majority of the voters. Rogers, *op. cit.*, p. 175, n. 13. The theme that the Senate filibuster is indispensable as a check on the President was harped on continuously during the debate on the Ship Purchase bill of 1915, which succumbed to the filibuster against it. See 52 *Congressional Record*, pp. 904–4020 *passim* (January 4–February 18, 1915).

63 U. S. Code, tit. 31, §15.

64 Public Law No. 19, 76th Congress, 1st sess.

65The constitutional problem raised by such a statute was the theme of the following colloquy in the Senate a year or two since. The passage is worth rescuing from oblivion not only for its immediate relevancy, but also for the light which it throws on the limitations of judicial review in certain situations.

"Mr. BARKLEY. If we could abrogate or nullify by statute the constitutional right of each House to adopt its own rules in a particular case, such as the joint resolution referred to in the amendment now pending, we could by statute enact a law which would bind both Houses with respect to all their rules of procedure on any sort of legislation. Could we not pass a law making the rules of the House and the Senate identical with respect to all matters?

"Mr. NORRIS. Probably we could. Let us take the other side of the question. If we are to regulate the country by rule, could we not adopt a rule providing that when any bill comes to the Senate from the House it shall lie on the table for 30 days, then be referred to a committee, that the committee shall be powerless to report it for 30 days more, and that when the bill comes on the floor of the Senate it shall not be voted on for another 30 days, or 60 days, even though a statute fixed the procedure by which such matters should be considered?

"Mr. BARKLEY. I suppose that when the Constitution provided that each House should fix its own rules of procedure it took the chance that the Senate or the House might be foolish in the determination of its rules.

"Mr. NORRIS. No; I think it took the chance that it would not be foolish.

"Mr. BARKLEY. That is just what I was about to say.

"Mr. NORRIS. Yes.

"Mr. BARKLEY. Of course it would be possible for the Senate to provide by rule that a bill coming over from the House shall not be referred to a committee for 30 days, but shall lie on the table; that it shall then be held in committee for 30 days; and then it shall not be passed for 30 days more. That, however, would be a ridiculous exercise of the constitutional authority to establish rules.

"Mr. NORRIS. The same thing is true of any activity of Government. The Constitution makes the President the Commander in Chief of the Army and Navy. Everybody knows that with that power in his hands, in 30 days we could make war against all the world, or any part of the world. He could go so far that he could not get out of what he had done. Everybody knows that the Constitution says that we shall be the judge of the qualifications of our own Members. If a man came here who was a Democrat, we could say, 'We will not take him in because he is a Democrat.' We could keep him out because of his color or because of his nativity.

"We could keep him out by reason of his age. We could do any ridiculous or foolish thing we chose to do; but it is impossible to put together a government on paper without having all those possibilities. If power is to be given to anybody to do anything under a government, it is possible for him to misuse and abuse the power and make it disreputable and destructive.

"Mr. Connally. Mr. President, will the Senator yield?

"Mr. Norris. I yield to the Senator from Texas.

"Mr. Connally. I am very much interested in the Senator's discussion of the constitutional provision giving the Senate the power to make its own rules. That power is not in anywise limited or restricted. If the Senate should foolishly adopt a rule such as the one suggested by the Senator from Kentucky, providing that a bill shall lie on the table for 30 days, and then go to a committee for 30 days, no power on earth could prevent it.

"Mr. Norris. I agree with the Senator.

"Mr. Connally. Any power which the Constitution gives to Congress, when properly exercised, is just as strong as the Constitution itself, is it not?

"Mr. Norris. Yes.

"Mr. Connally. So if we should enact a statute providing the manner in which a bill should be considered, so long as the Senate observed the statute and did not adopt a rule contrary to it, of course, the statute would be a rule of this body. But if the Senate should decide, under its constitutional authority, to adopt such a rule, the Rules Committee could bring in a resolution providing the manner in which a bill should be considered, thus overturning the statute. Will not the Senator agree to that?

"Mr. Norris. Yes.

"Mr. Connally. That is true, is it not?

"Mr. Norris. That is true. There would be a conflict.

"Mr. Connally. And the constitutional provision would override the statute.

"Mr. Norris. We cannot change the Constitution, so far as I know.

"Mr. Connally. Certainly not.

"Mr. Norris. There is no provision in the Constitution giving any Federal official anything to do which we could not disregard if we wanted to do so. Suppose a Governor appointed somebody who was only 15 years old to fill a vacancy in the Senate. The Senate is the judge of the qualifications of its own Members. It is supreme. There is no appeal. When the Senate decides such a matter, it is ended. The Constitution plainly states what the age must be. But suppose the Senate, in passing on the question, should say, 'We will accept this 15-year-old boy and make him a Senator.' What power could change it? Is there anybody in our Government who could change it? The Senate would have decided it. Everybody might say, 'The Senate itself has violated the Constitution.' What of it? The Constitution gives the Senate authority to pass upon the qualifications of its own Members. When the Senate decides such a question, that is the end of it.

"The Supreme Court is given certain authority under the Constitution. Suppose the Supreme Court should hold unconstitutional every act passed by the Congress. What could we do about it? It would be foolish, it would be silly; but the Supreme Court has the power to do it. So, in order to have power to perform the functions of their offices in a decent, methodical way, the Supreme Court must have power, which, if abused, might make them and the country ridiculous." *Congressional Record,* March 16, 1938.

[66] See my *Court Over Constitution,* pp. 68–74.

[67] For this paragraph see Warren, *op. cit.,* I, 185–214; II, 123–129, 313–316; III, 81–83, 102, 145, 171, 188–192, 214–216, 223; Carl B. Swisher, *Roger B. Taney* (New York, 1935), pp. 565–566.

[68] On this episode see Sidney Ratner's well-known article, "Was the Supreme Court Packed by President Grant?" 50 *Political Science Quarterly,* 342–356.

[69] Mr. Alexander Sachs, in a letter to the present writer.

[70] In his Victory Dinner address of March 4, 1937, the late President interpreted the election as meaning that the people expected the government to meet their needs "immediately." *The New York Times,* March 5, 1937.

[71] *F. D. R.,* V, 641–642; *The New York Times,* January 7, 1937.

[72] See Charles E. Fairman, "The Retirement of Federal Judges," 51 *Harvard Law Review,* 397–443. Nor is it surprising that "the man in the street" usually fastened on the age question as the main issue involved, as is shown in the following extracts from Richard Neuberger's amusing article in *Current History,* entitled "America Talks Court":

"Youthful service station operator: Sure the President ought to get rid of those old fossils. I've an uncle who is sixty-eight and I certainly wouldn't want him running the government. We have to help him around all the time, and he's never out of the doctor's office. He lives almost all the time on broth or milk toast. And by golly, he's younger than most of these Supreme Court justices.

"Young nurse: I didn't know whether to be for or against the President's plan until I saw a picture in a magazine showing the Supreme Court's dining room. All the judges had different knives and forks, and special salt and pepper shakers. That settled me. I've had enough experience with crotchety old patients to know that people who insist on all sorts of special favors sometimes aren't up to standard. If those judges can't use regular silverware and dishes, then they're too finicky and peculiar to run the government.

"Wife of a successful businessman: I know the President has never seen those dignified old men in their majestic black robes. If he had he would never propose such a terrible thing. When I was in Washington my husband took me to see the Court in session. It was the most wonderful sight I ever saw. It inspired me. If someone could only persuade the President to see the Supreme Court in that marvelous new hall, I know he would change his mind about the situation.

"A Townsendite: The President has no respect for the aged citizens of this country. He has made a political prisoner of their champion, Dr. Townsend, and now he claims that old people are not fit to serve on the Supreme Court. Providence will punish the President for this treatment of those who are old and gray. 'The hoary head is a crown of glory' says Proverbs, XVI, 31. Evil days will come on Americans if this Court plan is passed.

"Elderly lady: The founders of our country knew what they were doing when they provided for nine judges. If nine were good enough for President Washington, they should be good enough for President Roosevelt. I don't see why he needs fifteen.

"Young union man: I'll be for the bill if the President promises he won't appoint any more lawyers to the Court. The lawyers are the ones who have wrecked everything for the common people. If I had my way, no lawyers would be judges, Senators, or Congressmen." 46 *Current History,* 33–38.

[73] 301 U. S. 1, 548, 619. A common criticism of the Court for its decisions sustaining the New Deal and the correct answer thereto are given in the following communication to the *New York Herald Tribune* by Mr. Roger Hinds of the New York Bar:

"In Mr. Archibald E. Stevenson's letter in your paper he said:

" 'I cannot help wishing that the Supreme Court, when it uncovers a long-standing mistake in constitutional interpretation, would forgo the satisfaction of correcting it itself. A better and more democratic plan, it seems to me, would be to let the people do it themselves in the manner prescribed by the amending clause.'

"The suggestion, however, overlooks the fact that the judges have taken oath to uphold the Constitution, not to follow judicial precedents which are contrary to the Constitution. If any judge who conscientiously concluded that a precedent, no matter how long standing, was erroneous, should follow that precedent rather than uphold the Constitution, he would be unworthy to hold office and would deserve impeachment. In fact, the most effective opposition to the recent so-called court plan, was from those opponents who, conceding that the court had erred on important constitutional questions, held that the court could be trusted eventually to remedy its own mistakes, making 'packing' unnecessary. They refused to brand the court as incorrigible.

"There is no provision in our Constitution for judicial amendment. Under Mr. Stevenson's plan an erroneous judicial interpretation, after a sufficient lapse of time, would become part of the Constitution, in effect an amendment thereof, requiring a still further amendment to restore the Constitution to its original state, as intended by its founders. The Constitution does not prescribe amendment as the remedy for judicial error. Where the Constitution is all right as it stands, and the only fault is in its judicial interpretation, there is no occasion for amendment. The remedy should be applied to the interpretation, which is at fault, rather than to the Constitution which is not at fault.

"Not only is there no occasion for judicial amendment, accomplished through incorrigible adherence to erroneous precedents, but if we are first to make the unreasonable assumption that the judges are incorrigible, amendment by means of the amendment clause would be ineffectual to correct judicial error. The same judges who would flout the Constitution by consciously adhering to erroneous interpretations would be no more likely to obey the correcting amendments than to obey the original Constitution.

"If, for example, the court should now conclude that the Sixteenth Amendment means what it says, it is to be hoped that the court will candidly reverse its previous decisions to the contrary. Certainly it would unnecessarily and inartistically encumber our Constitution to adopt a new amendment stating that a previous amendment means what it says and not what the judges have erroneously said that it means.

"I think that we may properly assume that the judges are not only wise but are conscientious, and may be relied upon eventually to correct their own mistakes of interpretation, leaving the amending clause as a rarely used method for changing the Constitution itself.

Roger Hinds"

New York Herald Tribune, April 25, 1939.

Pertinent too—doubly pertinent, in fact—is the following passage from a speech by Senator William Jackson in the course of debate on the bill for abolishing the system of circuit courts which had been set up the year before. Answering the Federalist argument that the thing ought to be done by constitutional amendment, Jackson said:

"There is required first, then, two-thirds of both houses of Congress. Can this two-thirds be found now, or is there any probability of its being found for twenty years to come, who will concur in making the necessary alterations in the judiciary system that are now, or may hereafter, be required. . .? How, then, can we expect three-fourths of the legislatures of the several states to agree when we cannot agree among ourselves? There is, in fact, no amendment which could reach the case, and exhibit to view all requisite and necessary regulations for such an extent of the country. Such an attempt must form a volume, a Constitution by itself and after all fall short of the subject.

"I am clearly, therefore, of opinion that if the power to alter the judiciary system vests not here, it vests nowhere." Sen. William Jackson (Georgia). Judiciary Debate, January 1802, Annals, 7th Congress, 1st sess., col. 49.

74 In a formal statement issued to the press, August 9, 1939, Mr. Roosevelt, with much justification, pronounced the objectives of his Court Reform bill "fully attained." He listed the objectives as follows:

"1. Extending to Supreme Court justices of retirement privileges available to other Federal judges.

"2. Ending the Court's 'narrow interpretations' which he blamed for impeding social and economic reforms, and the Court's 'assumption . . . of legislative powers.'

"3. Eliminating the Federal courts' congested dockets and delay in disposing of cases, and obtaining 'new blood' in the judiciary and additional judges.

"4. Obtaining greater flexibility in assignment of judges.

"5. Giving the Government the right to intervene in private cases involving constitutional issues.

"6. Providing direct and immediate appeal to the Supreme Court in cases involving constitutionality of Federal statutes.

"7. Reforming the administrative machinery of the courts."

75 The most careful attempt that has been made to evaluate presidential leadership in terms of legislative product is that of Professor Lawrence H. Chamberlain in his *The President, Congress and Legislation* (Columbia University Press, 1946). Tracing the history of the conception, gestation, and birth of ninety major acts of Congress, the earliest of which became law in 1882, the latest in 1940, Professor Chamberlain finds that "presidential influence" was "preponderant" in the enactment of nineteen of these measures, that "congressional influence" was "preponderant" in the enactment of thirty-five, that "joint presidential-congressional influence" brought about the enactment of twenty-nine, and that "pressure group influence" was "preponderant" in the case of seven measures. The tests by which presidential preponderance is determined are liberal (*ibid.*, pp. 26–27), but in reaching so far back the investigation unmistakably favors congressional claims. Of the nineteen measures in the enactment of which presidential influence is reckoned to have been preponderant, ten became law between 1932 and 1938, while only two of the thirty-five credited to Congress were enacted during these years. Nor is this more than partially compensated for by the fact that twelve of the twenty-nine measures credited to the President and Congress jointly belong to the same period. *Ibid.*, pp. 450–452.

In his own evaluation of his results Professor Chamberlain points out the important difference between regarding the President as the *creator of legislation* and as *catalyst* bringing to fruition earlier ineffective efforts in and out of Congress. As is apparent, the latter is the vastly more important role. Except in wartime or extreme crisis, like that of 1933, few measures of the scope and importance of those treated of by Professor Chamberlain but have undergone a long term of incubation in congressional committee files prior to their final enactment.

Professor Chamberlain's volume supplies a needed corrective to swollen ideas of accomplishment of Presidents as legislators, but has not avoided altogether the opposed error. One can readily agree that the President frequently appears to be "the initiating agent of a particular law when as a matter of fact he is little more than the conveyance— sometimes the reluctant one—upon which it moves to fruition," that "presidential leadership has been and probably will continue to be uneven"—a matter that is considered in the text—and that "the atomized nature of the congressional approach to our legislative needs has supplied something without which the executive leadership would be less effective," "an inexhaustible flood of observations, suggestions, and proposals." *Ibid.,* pp. 463–464. Three things, however, Professor Chamberlain seems to me to overlook. One is that in our crisis-driven world "time is often of the essence." The second is that the President occupies a superior position from which to descry the approach of crisis, especially crisis in the international field. The third is the concentrated political weight which the presidential office alone can bring to bear in support of an urgently needed measure. For all these reasons presidential leadership is a factor of ever increasing indispensability to the adequate functioning of the legislative process, and so of its survival.

With Mr. Chamberlain's volume it is interesting to compare on the subject of executive leadership in legislation Emile Giraud's *La Crise de la démocratie et le renforcement du pouvoir exécutif* (Paris, 1938). While the argument is mainly directed against the deficiencies of the French constitution—now defunct—it is rich in observations of interest to American readers, as that the executive must direct the legislature, being the organ with "unity of thought," "capacity to acquire a view of the whole" (p. 110), and possessing, by virtue of its participation in administrative and diplomatic activities, adequate information (p. 115). M. Giraud systematically attacks the *laissez-faire* conception of democracy as "the organization of resistance to power" (p. 72, n. 2). To the contrary, he asserts, it is "a power of action and realization" (p. 99). "A feeble executive," he continues, "means a feeble state, one which fulfills badly its function of protecting the individual against political, economic, and social forces which, without the state, tend to swallow him up, to exploit and oppress him" (pp. 101–102). All of which is true within limits, but furnishes no reason for compressing the Constitution into the opening clause of Article II.

[76] *Mississippi v. Johnson,* 4 Wall. 475 (1867).

[77] Lucius Wilmerding, *The Spending Power; A History of the Efforts of Congress to Control Expenditures* (Yale University Press, 1943).

[78] Ever since the time of the great leading case of *Marbury v. Madison,* 1 Cr. 137 (1803), heads of departments have occasionally been subjected to proceedings, brought usually in the first instance in a District of Columbia court, in which a writ of mandamus or a writ of injunction was sought, and such writs have now and then been awarded against them. See, e.g., *Kendall v. Stokes,* 12 Pet. 524; *Decatur v. Paulding,* 14 Pet. 497; *Garfield v. United States,* 211 U. S. 249; *Smith et al. v. Hitchcock,* 226 U. S. 53; *Morgan v. United States,* 304 U. S. 1. Two cases 130 years apart in which presidential orders were held by the court to be without legal warrant are *Little v. Barreme,* 2 Cr. 170 (1904) and *Panama Refining Co. v. Ryan,* 293 U. S. 388 (1934). See also *Ex parte Orozco,* 201 F. 106 (1912).

[79] See generally Marshall E. Dimock, *Congressional Investigations* (Johns Hopkins Press, 1926); M. Nelson McGeary, *The Development of Congressional Investigative Power* (Columbia University Press, 1940); and George B. Galloway, "The Investigative Function of Congress," 21 *American Political Science Review,* 46–70.

"A careful survey of the history of committee activity from 1789 to the expiration of the Sixty-eighth Congress in 1925 discloses that there have been, all told, about 285 investigations by the select and standing committees of the House and Senate. Only three Congresses have been barren of legislative inquests, while no administration has been immune. The high-water mark was reached during Grant's eight turbulent years, when incompetence and corruption ran riot through public life; between 1869 and 1877 Congress undertook thirty-seven different inquiries aimed at remedying bad conditions in the administration.

"Much American history can be gleaned from the reports of these nearly three hundred investigating committees. For the houses of Congress have employed the inquisitorial function over a wide range of governmental activity. Beginning with the inquiry into the defeat of General St. Clair by the Indians in 1792, and continuing down to the current investigation of the Tariff Commission, this device has been put to many uses. The record shows that the War Department has come most frequently under the inquiring eye. Congressional committees have scrutinized the conduct of all the wars in which the United States has engaged except the Spanish-American war, when President McKinley forestalled legislative inquiry by appointing the Dodge commission. They were responsible for the impeachment of President Johnson and Secretary of War Belknap. They have examined the conduct of the Treasury Department fifty-four times and of the Interior Department forty-one times, with attention centered most frequently on the Indian Bureau and the Patent Offices. The Government Printing Office has also been submitted to frequent inspection; likewise the Navy and Postoffice Departments. The President has been the subject of investigation twenty-three times, commencing with John Adams and ending with Woodrow Wilson. In fact, no department or activity of the government has escaped inquiry unless it be the Departments of Commerce and Labor since their separation in 1913." Galloway, *ibid.,* 47–48.

As stated in Chapter III, I know of no instance in which a head of department has testified before a congressional committee in response to a subpoena, nor been held for contempt for refusal to testify. All appearances by these high officials seem to have been voluntary.

[80] See, e.g., George A. Graham, "Reorganization—A Question of Executive Institutions," 32 *American Political Science Review* (August 1938), 708–718.

[81] *Ibid.*

[82] Don K. Price, "Staffing the Presidency," 40 *American Political Science Review* (December 1946), 1168.

[83] Luce, *Legislative Problems,* pp. 325–326.

[84] *Senate Report,* No. 837, 46th Congress, 3rd sess. (1881).

[85] Luce, *op. cit.,* pp. 327–330. Secretary of State Hull's unexpected appearance before Congress November 18, 1943, to report on the Moscow Conference, just then concluded, appears to have resuscitated the idea recently. Its great champion in Congress is Representative Kefauver of Tennessee. See his brief history of the notion and plea for its adoption in 38 *American Political Science Review* (April 1944), 317–325.

Justice Story seems to have been the first to suggest the idea. Commenting on the exclusion of officeholders from membership in Congress, he said:

"If it would not have been safe to trust the heads of departments, as representatives, to the choice of the people, as their constituents, it would have been at least some gain to have allowed them a seat, like territorial delegates, in the house of representatives, where they might freely debate without a title to vote. In such an event, their influence, whatever it would be, would be seen, and felt, and understood, and on that account would have involved little danger, and more searching jealousy and opposition; whereas, it is now secret and silent, and from that very cause may become overwhelming.

"One other reason in favor of such a right is, that it would compel the executive to make appointments for the high departments of government, not from personal or party favorites, but from statesmen of high public character, talents, experience, and elevated services; from statesmen, who had earned public favor, and could command public confidence. At present, gross incapacity may be concealed under official forms, and ignorance silently escape by shifting the labors upon more intelligent subordinates in office. The nation would be, on the other plan, better served; and the executive sustained by more masculine eloquence, as well as more liberal learning." *Comms.*, §§ 869, 870.

Story wrote with Andrew Jackson's second Cabinet, recruited from his "Kitchen Cabinet," before him.

"I have long believed that the official relations between the Executive and Congress should be more open and direct. They are now conducted by correspondence with the presiding officers of the two Houses, by consultation with committees, or by private interviews with individual members. This frequently leads to misunderstandings, and may lead to corrupt combinations. It would be far better for both departments if the members of the Cabinet were permitted to sit in Congress and participate in the debates on measures relating to their several departments,—but, of course, without a vote. This would tend to secure the ablest men for the chief executive offices; it would bring the policy of the administration into the fullest publicity by giving both parties ample opportunity for criticism and defense." James A. Garfield, *Works*, II, 483.

W. F. Willoughby, writing with modern conditions in mind, gives his verdict in these words: "It is believed that examination will show that the proposal is not a desirable one to incorporate into our political system." See Ch. XIII of his excellent *Principles of Legislative Organization and Administration* (The Brookings Institution, 1934).

[86] In 1879, his senior year at Princeton, Woodrow Wilson published an article in the *International Review* entitled "Cabinet Government in the United States." In his introductory note to a reissue of this piece last year, under the auspices of the Woodrow Wilson Foundation, Mr. Thomas K. Finletter says, "The key suggestion . . . was to set up a Cabinet from among members of the House and Senate." This is apparently a misinterpretation of Wilson's words. Thus, putting the question, "What is the change proposed?" Wilson answers: "Simply to give to the heads of the Executive departments —the members of the Cabinet—seats in Congress, with the privilege of the initiative in legislation and some part of the unbounded privileges now commanded by the Standing Committees"; and he quotes "Chief-Justice Story" as favoring a similar proposal. See pp. 8–9. That Wilson did not contemplate putting members of Congress at the head of the Executive departments or, on the other hand, making the latter *members* of Congress seems also to be indicated by his total failure to allude to the constitutional obstacle to either of these steps. It is true that he hoped his design would lead eventually to the practice on the part of the President of maintaining a Cabinet "who represent the majority in Congress," when this was of a different party than the President. But apparently what he meant by "represent" is "belong to" the same party as the majority in Congress. A different construction would show Wilson to have been unaware or indifferent to the constitutional ban on officeholders being members of Congress.

In his *Can Representative Government Do the Job?* (New York, 1945), Mr. Finletter himself urges a joint executive-legislative Cabinet. Commenting on the suggestion, Mr. George B. Galloway remarks: "The joint cabinet idea, it will be recalled, was first suggested by Senator La Follette in July, 1943, and was first adopted at the state level in 1931 by Wisconsin. Since 1931, nine states have created legislative councils, whose experience should be useful in evaluating the merits of this proposal, which certainly deserves a fair trial." I feel justified in pointing out that my suggestion of the idea came three years earlier than Senator La Follette's. See the first edition (1940) of this work at page 304.

Writing in October 1934, Professor Herring described "F.D.R." as evolving "informally a 'master-ministry' of congressional leaders, cabinet officers and executive officials working through the White House," and adds: "Recognizing and implementing this rather inchoate group of leaders might serve to introduce the coordination now left to personal and informal contacts."

At the outset of our entrance into World War II a joint bipartisan committee to advise the President on the conduct of the war was suggested in the Senate, and the suggestion was not opposed by Mr. Roosevelt. United Press despatch in *The New York Times,* under date line, Washington, November 10, 1942. Though the suggestion was renewed early in January 1943 (United Press despatch in *The Times,* of January 4), nothing came of it, possibly on account of the bad odor still attaching to the memory of the famous, or notorious, Joint Committee on the Conduct of the War which was created at the opening of the Civil War and which dogged Lincoln's footsteps throughout that struggle. See the informative article in *The New York Times* of January 10, 1943, by Professor T. Harry Williams of Louisiana State University. The Truman Committee and the parallel committee in the House were purely investigating committees and stuck strictly to the job of investigating past happenings, especially as they affected national expenditure. They did not venture to intrude their opinions concerning policy upon the President.

The serious breakdown in the relations between the President and Congress in 1943 led to considerable writing on the related problems of a better organization of Congress and a closer coördination between the two branches. Besides Judge Finletter's notable volume, see Merle J. Pusey, *Big Government—Can We Control It?* (New York, 1945); Roland Young, *This Is Congress* (New York, 1943); and George B. Galloway, *Congress at the Crossroads* (New York, 1946), not to mention dozens of articles in periodicals, newspaper editorials, etc. Congressional reorganization was the subject of investigation by a special committee of the American Political Science Association, headed by Mr. Galloway, who was also Director of the La Follette-Monroney Joint Committee which framed the Act of August 2, 1946. The act unfortunately ignored the suggestion, strongly supported by Mr. Galloway, "that a Legislative Council be established, to be composed of the Vice President, the Speaker of the House, the majority leaders in both chambers, and the chairmen of the reorganized standing committees (sitting separately in each house); and that it be the duty of this Legislative Council to plan and coordinate the legislative program of Congress and to promote more effective liaison and cooperation with the Executive." One of the most notable periodical studies appeared in *Fortune,* November 1943. It was called "The Rehabilitation of Congress," and was one of a group of studies entitled "Our Form of Government," in a series on "The United States in a New World." See also the "leader" in *The New York Times,* March 15, 1943; and Henry Hazlitt's plea for an approach to the Cabinet System, *ibid.,* February 8, 1942. *Cf.* with the last Don K. Price article, "The Parliamentary and Presidential Systems," in 3 *Public Administration Review* (October 1944), 317–334.

[87] Pp. 14–15 *supra.*

[88] A critical volume on the Cabinet is something badly needed. Its success as an advisory body has been highly discontinuous, to say the least.

Writing of Jackson's relations with his Cabinet, Sumner says:

"Jackson introduced two innovations. He put the Secretaries back more nearly into the place in which they belong by the original theory of the law. He made them executive clerks or staff officers. The fashion has grown up of calling the Secretaries the President's 'constitutional advisers.' It is plain that they are not anything of the kind. He is not bound to consult them, and, if he does, it does not detract from his responsibility. Jackson, by the necessity of his character and preparation, and by the nature of the position to which he had been elected, must lean on somebody. He had a number of intimate friends and companions on whom he relied. They did not hold important public positions. They came to be called the 'Kitchen Cabinet.' The men were William B. Lewis, Amos Kendall, Duff Green, and Isaac Hill. If the Secretaries had been the 'constitutional advisers' of the President, their first right and duty would have been to break off his intimacy with these irresponsible persons, and to prevent their influence. Jackson's second innovation was that he did not hold cabinet councils. Hence his administration lacked unity and discipline. It did not have the strength of hearty and conscious cooperation. Each Secretary went his way, and gossip and newsmongering had a special field of activity open to them." *Andrew Jackson*, pp. 181–182.

Lincoln's relations with his Cabinet were equally haphazard, or even more so (*ante*, pp. 27 and 380–381). And like Lincoln, the first Roosevelt failed often to keep his Cabinet informed of important decisions, consulting instead individual heads of departments and outsiders. Only Attorney General Knox knew that the Northern Securities suit was to be brought; and the taking of Panama was a similar surprise move. Mr. Oscar Straus describes Roosevelt's "Kitchen Cabinet" as consisting of "unofficial advisers who met round the luncheon and dinner table and afterwards in the White House study, where the President spoke without reserve on his executive problems, and read for our criticism and counsel his rough drafts of congressional messages, speeches, and notes to foreign governments." "This group," Mr. Straus adds, "served Roosevelt as energetically and loyally as if the grave responsibilities of state were upon their own shoulders." *Under Four Administrations* (New York, 1922), pp. 206–207. Likewise, Mr. Wilson regarded his Cabinet as a body of administrators rather than of political advisers. At no time were there more than two or three members whose opinions he valued on problems arising outside their departments. "When the Lusitania was torpedoed, it was dwelt on by the Washington correspondents that Mr. Wilson did not call together his Cabinet nor consult with any member of it, but, just as Lincoln had done, awfully communed with himself." Luce, *op. cit.*, p. 313. Nor did Wilson read his War Message to the Cabinet; and when Colonel House asked him why he had not done so he replied that if he had every man in it would have had some suggestion to make, and it would have been too picked to pieces if he had heeded their criticism. He said he preferred to keep it to himself and take the responsibility entirely upon his own shoulders. Charles Seymour, *The Intimate Papers of Colonel House* (1926–1928), II, 468.

The following entries are culled from the late Franklin K. Lane's diary at the time he was in Mr. Wilson's Cabinet: "To-day's meeting has resulted in nothing, though in Mexico, Cuba, Costa Rica, and Europe we have trouble. . . .For some weeks we have spent our time at Cabinet meetings largely in telling stories. Even at the meeting of a week ago, the day on which the President sent his reply to Germany . . . we were given no view of the Note which was already in Lansing's hands and was emitted at four o'clock; and had no talk upon it, other than some outline given offhand by the President to one of the Cabinet who referred to it before the meeting; and for three-quarters of an hour told stories on the war, and took up small departmental affairs." *The Letters of Franklin K. Lane* (New York, 1922), pp. 237, 293.

Early in President F. D. Roosevelt's first administration the so-called "Brain Trust" rather put the Cabinet in the shade, and later some of the men brought into notice by the new Federal agencies, NRA, TVA, RFC, etc., did the same. And even when Mr. Roosevelt had free recourse to his official family for counsel, he turned to individual members of it quite as frequently as to the Cabinet as a body, and this on large questions of policy.

The following extracts from his *On Our Way* (New York, 1934) are illustrative:

"I discussed the banking situation with the Secretary of the Treasury and the Attorney General, asking them to be prepared the next day to outline a constitutional method of closing all banks."

"During these first five days, the Vice-President, the Cabinet, the Director of the Budget and I had been considering another vitally important factor necessary to the restoration of confidence [governmental economy]."

"Under the leadership of Secretary of Agriculture Wallace, we held many conferences with the leaders of farm organizations. . . ."

"Every day that went by . . . brought before me and the Cabinet and the Congress some new emergency which cried out for action."

"It took much courage on the part of Secretary of the Interior Ickes when he told me, about the middle of March, that he was ready to tackle a task which had baffled many others who had sought to limit production of oil to the needs of the consuming public. . . ."

"It was at this point that Secretary Woodin and I decided that the time had come to prevent the export of any more gold." *Ibid.*, pp. 1, 18, 38, 46, 49, 59.

Recently published extracts from Mr. Morgenthau's diary confirm this picture. The following is a sample:

"Beginning on Oct. 25, each morning the President conferred with Mr. Morgenthau and Jesse Jones to set the price of the gold for the day. While the President breakfasted, usually on scrambled eggs, the trio discussed the gold reports from abroad. On the first day, gold was $31.02 in London and $31.09 in Paris. Mr. Morgenthau suggested $31.36 for the first day price, $1.56 over the previous American price. 'All right,' said the President, 'we will make it $31.36.'

"The actual price on any given day made little difference and was determined arbitrarily, the diary says. One day, for example, the bedside conference decided on a rise of 21 cents.

" 'It's a lucky number,' the President remarked, 'because it's three times seven.'

"In his diary, Mr. Morgenthau commented: 'If anybody ever knew how we really set the gold price through a combination of lucky numbers, etc., I think they would really be frightened.' " *The New York Times,* December 31, 1946.

"In the early days, there had been many cabinet meetings with just that flavor—full cabinet decision and expression on matters of policy. But as the years went on, Roosevelt's cabinet administration came to be like most previous ones—a direct relationship between a particular cabinet officer and the President in regard to his special field, with little or no participation or even information from other cabinet members. Certainly almost no 'cabinet agreements' were reached. Something about our governmental forms and tensions between the legislative and executive functions seem to make fully responsible action unlikely." Frances Perkins, *The Roosevelt I Knew* (New York, 1946), p. 377. (Quoted with the consent of the Viking Press.)

Dr. Price, in the article cited in note 82 *supra,* speaks of "Cabinet anarchy" (*ibid.,* p. 1155); see also Binkley, p. 235. Before President Truman decided to cross swords with the redoubtable John L. Lewis in January 1947, he did not content himself with getting the support of his Cabinet, but polled the governors, all of whom except Governor Arnall backed him. Felix Blair, Jr., in *The New York Times,* January 31, 1947. Mr. Truman claimed he was following Jefferson in this, but we have Jefferson's own word that "General Washington sometimes wrote them, and probably Mr. Adams did, as you mention his having written to you. On the whole, I think a free correspondence best, and shall never hesitate to write myself to the Governors even in a federal case, where the occasion presents itself to me particularly." Jefferson to Monroe, May 1801, *Writings* (Ford, ed.), VIII, 59.

89 Washington's warning in his Farewell Address against "the spirit of party" still merits attention for its eminent good sense:

"It serves always to distract the public councils and enfeeble the public administration. It agitates the community with ill-founded jealousies and false alarms; kindles the animosity of one part against another; foments occasionally riot and insurrection. It opens the door to foreign influence and corruption, which find a facilitated access to the government itself through the channels of party passion. Thus the policy and the will of one country are subjected to the policy and will of another.

"There is an opinion that parties in free countries are useful checks upon the administration of the government, and serve to keep alive the spirit of liberty. This within certain limits is probably true; and in governments of a monarchical cast patriotism may look with indulgence, if not with favor, upon the spirit of party. But in those of the popular character, in governments purely elective, it is a spirit not to be encouraged. From their natural tendency it is certain there will always be enough of that spirit for every salutary purpose; and there being constant danger of excess, the effort ought to be by force of public opinion to mitigate and assuage it. A fire not to be quenched, it demands a uniform vigilance to prevent its bursting into a flame, lest, instead of warming, it should consume." Richardson, I, 219.

It is a serious question to my mind whether the Presidency, considering its vast accumulation of powers today, could not be advantageously neutralized politically to the extent that this could be effected by a constitutional amendment forbidding a President to succeed himself. The two roles of the President, recognized by Woodrow Wilson, as "leader of the nation" and "leader of his party," are frequently incompatible, owing to the fact that in the latter capacity the President must make his own and his party's political future a primary concern.

90 Of some significance in this connection is the fact that the crisis of 1932–1933 evoked several suggestions of dictatorship in the United States. Mr. Ralph Adams Cram wanted President Hoover to suspend the Constitution, abolish the income tax and prohibition, dissolve Congress, and so on. *Boston Globe,* July 16, 1932. The Hon. Alfred E. Smith was for laying the Constitution "on the shelf." This was in February 1933; and at the same time *Pacific Banker,* a San Francisco publication, was urging a "National Manager," who was to be "of commanding ability" and was to be selected by "the business leaders of the country"—this although the country had just elected a President! *The New York Times,* February 5, 1933. Abroad there were predictions that the President would be presently vested with dictatorial powers. *Ibid.,* January 25, 1933.

It is, of course, in the field of foreign relations that the personalization of the Presidency has appeared most strikingly in the past and that Presidents have most frequently disported themselves uncontrolled by responsible counselors. Mr. Hull's *Memoirs* gives one or two illustrations; e.g., the late President's famed "quarantine against aggressors" speech of October 5, 1937, Mr. Hull considers to have had most unfortunate results for our peace-seeking diplomacy; and Arthur Bliss Lane, in his recent *I Saw Poland Betrayed,* gives another example. "I was disturbed," he writes, "by President Roosevelt's exaggerated confidence in the power of his charm to persuade diplomatic and political adversaries to his point of view. He seemed to feel that this charm was particularly effective on Stalin. Close advisers of Mr. Roosevelt confided to me that this overconfidence had been noticeable at Teheran. Yet Roosevelt had been unable to gain the principal decisions over Stalin." Quoted by Drew Middleton in *The New York Times Book Reviews,* February 15, 1948. Of course, the United Nations Participation Act assumes that this kind of presidential adventuring is now at an end, but President Truman's erratic Palestinian policy hardly supports the assumption.

NOTES TO *RÉSUMÉ**

¹ "Indeed, the organization of the Executive Power in a republican form of government always presents the greatest difficulties. If its powers are defined with exact precision, events may at some critical juncture occur which will baffle all calculations. Then the republic will be placed between the danger of violating its fundamental law and the imperious necessities of public safety. Nor is it much to be feared that, in moments of imminent peril, the majority would decide in favor of usurpations of power, and suffer the Constitution to be sacrificed. The only means of avoiding these dangers is to mould the fundamental law so that the President, always prominent in times of crisis, may be able to stretch his privileges, in case circumstances shall absolutely require it. . . . Happily for the United States, the framers of the Constitution . . . vested certain powers in the President, but did not declare that these powers should form a limit to his authority. Besides, the prerogatives thus conferred upon him admit on certain occasions of an almost indefinite extension." Chambrun, *op. cit.,* pp. 153–154.

Cf. Upshur, p. 25 *supra.*

² "An active and energetic foreign policy necessarily implies that the executive who directs it is permanent and clothed with powers in proportion to his vigor of action. At the same time, combinations with other governments can be of value only so far as they are upheld by an exhibition of adequate strength, or in other words, they cannot be formed without strongly organized land and sea forces.

"If, then, a passion for conquest and territorial acquisitions should take root and spread in the United States, it would soon and inevitably lead to an increase of the powers of the President." Chambrun, *op. cit.,* p. 284.

³ Speaking of the Roman dictatorship, which was a "temporary concentration of powers for emergency purposes," and with which the Framers of the Constitution had a literary acquaintance, Professor Friedrich makes the following interesting observations:

"The Roman example is significant, because for several centuries dictatorship there remained a bulwark for the Republican government, and did not lead to any usurpation of powers. The conditions of this state of affairs seem to have been essentially four. In the first place the appointment of the dictator took place according to precise constitutional forms. Secondly, the dictator himself could not at his discretion declare the state of emergency. The dictatorship occurred, thirdly, always in defense of the existing constitutional order, never with a view to changing it (as under Caesar). And a fourth condition of great importance was a strict time limit imposed upon the dictator for the

---

* *The Résumé begins on page 365.*

fulfillment of his task, never to exceed six months. Obviously, all these conditions are themselves dependent upon the constitutional order, and can therefore be properly called constitutional limitations." *Constitutional Government and Politics* (New York, 1937), p. 211. (The above passage is quoted from Professor Friedrich's work by permission of the publishers, Harper and Brothers.)

4 The effect of the breakdown of States Rights in aggrandizing the Presidency became a theme for gloomy prophecy very early. Gouverneur Morris, in the great debate on the Judiciary Act of 1802, said in the Senate:

"While I was far distant from my country, I felt pain at some things which looked like a wish to wind up the general government beyond its natural tone; for I knew, that if America should be brought under one consolidated government, it could not continue to be a republic. I am attached to republican government, because it appears to me favorable to dignity of sentiment and character. . . . But if a consolidated government be established, it cannot long be republican. We have not the materials to construct even a mild monarchy. If therefore the States be destroyed, we must become the subjects of despotism." *Annals,* 7th Congress, 1st sess., pp. 15–16, 23.

Chambrun repeated the warning more than seventy years later in these words: "We may readily see that, should the autonomy of the States disappear, the Executive Power would at once essentially change and assume inordinate proportions. It is to a great extent confined by State governments to that sphere of action prescribed for it by the Constitution. In fact, incessant conflicts would take place between the executive, which is independent within the scope of its constitutional authority, and the Legislature, with the increased powers that would almost necessarily attach to it on the destruction of the governments of the separate States. From that time one might foresee that the President, although a person of limited ability, would succeed in gaining the sympathy and influence of a majority of the people. Doubtless the latter might at times declare in favor of a deliberative assembly, but it would not be safe to depend on their permanent support. Called upon to choose between an abstract sovereignty and the concrete idea of power centered in one man, they would in the end almost always prefer the living personality, and recognize him as the elect of the nation, without scarcely remembering that they had also chosen their representatives." *Op. cit.,* pp. 233–234.

TABLE OF CASES

INDEX

Page numbers from 1 to 373 refer to the text; page numbers from 374 to 521 refer to the notes.

PAGE

PAGE

PAGE

PAGE

PAGE

OTHER PUBLICATIONS
ON THE STOKES FOUNDATION

(James Stokes Lectureship on Politics
Anson G. Phelps Lectureship on Early American History)

NEW YORK UNIVERSITY

Representative Government in the United States
By William Howard Taft, 1921

Sovereign States and Suits before Arbitral Tribunals
By James Brown Scott, 1925

American Foreign Policies: An Examination and Evaluation of Certain Traditional and Recent International Policies of the United States
By James Wilford Garner, 1928

The Pilgrim Fathers from a Dutch Point of View
By D. Plooij, 1932

The Foundations of American Constitutionalism
By Andrew McLaughlin, 1932

Our Earliest Colonial Settlements: Their Diversities of Origin and Later Characteristics
By Charles M. Andrews, 1933

The Puritan Pronaos: Studies in the Intellectual Life of New England in the Seventeenth Century
By Samuel Eliot Morison, 1936

The Role of Politics in Social Change
By Charles E. Merriam, 1936

Yankees and Yorkers
By Dixon Ryan Fox, 1940

American Neutrality: Trial and Failure
By Charles G. Fenwick, 1940

Religion and the State: The Making and Testing of an American Tradition
By Evarts B. Greene, 1941

The Golden Age of Colonial Culture
By Thomas J. Wertenbaker, 1942

The Forces That Shape Our Future
By Clyde Eagleton, 1945

Conservatism in Early American History
By Leonard W. Labaree, 1948

New York University Press . Washington Square . New York

This is the pictorial history of the American wars as seen by artists in uniform, a unique compilation of the work in sketch book and on canvas of the men who recorded history as they made it. Through the trained eye of the military artist, sharper even than the undiscriminating lens of the camera, the most stirring moments of the past two hundred years of American history come to life in this lavish picture book.

Soldiers sketched as they appeared in the field, fortifications, battle arrays are here; here also are portraits and battle scenes, drawn by eyewitnesses, some after the event, but all dramatic with the first-hand knowledge of the artist. Here is the array of America's military greats, beginning with the young George Washington; here are the people, places, and events you have read about, brought to life in pictures you will never forget.

Many of the pictures here have never before been published, but the work of famous men is here too, some like Frederic Remington noted as artists, some like Peyton C. March more famous for their distinguished military careers. But one thing is common to all: a sharp eye for artistic detail and the talent for setting down accurately on paper and canvas what the eye sees. This is living, breathing experience, retold in a form that can be understood — and thrilled to — by all.

In his captions, and in the brief introductory text to each section of the book, Roy Meredith, noted for his brilliant historical exposition and research, knits the pictures together to tell a connected story of action on all fronts — from the French and Indian War, through the Revolution and the Civil War, the Indian fighting in the West, both World Wars, right up through the Korean conflict. This is history as it should be told — and seen — in a blending of word and picture that makes even more memorable the immortal deeds of America's heroes.

ROY MEREDITH

The American Wars

A Pictorial History from Quebec to Korea

1755–1953

THE WORLD PUBLISHING COMPANY

CLEVELAND AND NEW YORK

Library of Congress Catalog Card Number: 54–5341

First Edition

AH955

To Bobby

Contents

The American Wars

Even so, when the framework of the world is dissolved and the final hour, closing so many ages, reverts to primeval chaos, then all the constellations will clash in confusion, the fiery stars will drop into the sea, and the earth, refusing to spread her shores out flat, will shake off the ocean: The moon will move in opposition to her brother, and claim to rule the day, disdaining to drive her chariot along her slanting orbit: and the whole distracted fabric of the shattered firmament will overthrow its laws.

Great things will come crashing down upon themselves—such is the limit of growth ordained by heaven for success.

LUCAN (MARCUS ANNAEUS LUCANUS)
44 B.C. in *The Civil Wars (Pharsalia)*

Introduction

For a nation not given to military aggression or wilful warfare, the United States has been involved in many serious wars. The purpose of this book is to chronicle and bring to their proper place in history the combat artists and military engineers who have provided such a magnificent pictorial record of the American wars. The saga of the American wars, depicted with pencil and brush by these artists, is an indelible, awe-inspiring, and sometimes ghastly story of crashing battle, sudden death, disease, and unspeakable horror.

In our earliest wars, military and naval artists recorded on canvas and paper critical battles and naval engagements that more or less decided the future of the nation. Their inestimable services to the armed forces and their contribution to the military and naval history of the United States certainly deserve to be recorded. During the Civil War, many artists, though not in uniform, were attached to the army as "war artists" for *Harper's Weekly* and *Leslie's*. With few exceptions, these men sketched from sight, under the most difficult conditions imaginable, reams of drawings that today can be seen in the old bound copies of these wonderful magazines. Until the outbreak of the Civil War, military pictorial reporting was held as not too important. But many soldiers and sailors, awed by the history-making action in which they were taking part, recorded it of their own volition in untutored but graphic sketches.

Of no small importance is the military art of Cap-

tain John Montresor and Captain Hervey Smyth, officers and military engineers of the British Army during the French and Indian War. Our own army had its beginnings in that war. Colonel George Washington was himself, in 1755, a British Colonial officer. Moreover, the military procedure and the tactics used by the British Army at that time were afterward heavily drawn upon and embellished with many novel improvements by the Americans, notably the deadly technique of Indian tactics. Little known is the fact that Ulysses S. Grant, George Gordon Meade, William Tecumseh Sherman, Henry N. Walke, David Porter, Seth Eastman, and many other graduates of West Point and Annapolis were artists of no mean ability, particularly Seth Eastman, who contributed a brilliant portfolio of life on the American frontier and in the Western territories.

The United States Army Corps of Engineers in World War I employed a large staff of combat artists, commissioned as captains. Among them were George Harding, Harvey Dunn, Kerr Eby, and Wallace Morgan, who, in civilian life, were among the finest illustrators of that era. The United States Marine Corps can claim great distinction in its combat artists both in World War I and II in the persons of the late Colonel John W. Thomason, Colonel Donald Dickson, who took part in the campaigns in the South Pacific in our recent war with Japan, as well as many other Marine combat artists. World War II, by volume of work alone, had the greatest coverage. Never in the history of warfare was every phase so well pictured by the combat artists. The United States Army Air Forces can claim particular distinction in the brilliant work of Francis Beaugureau, Captain Ogden Pleissner, and Major Milton Marx. The skillful men of the Army, Navy, Marine Corps, Air Force, Coast Guard, and the many special units with their own staff of artists, articulate with pencil and brush, depicted the thrilling actions in the South Pacific, Asia, and Europe. They were adventurous soldiers and sailors, given to sketching at sight with engaging frankness what they saw of war.

The inspiring inheritance of pictorial military material which they produced presented no easy problem in the matter of selection. Many anxious hours of intensive search and study went into the final selection of pictures for the chapter on World War II. It was not the dearth of material but the bulk from which to select that was at times frightening to contemplate. Therefore, the non-inclusion of any picture of an action or scene in the over-all picture of World War II is due not to oversight nor as a reflection on the work of these men, but is entirely incidental to limited space. For, after all, it was a big war, and the combat art produced would fill many volumes.

Long after the Civil War, Edward Lamson Henry, the military artist who served on an Army transport as clerk during the war, was invited to the White House for a visit with President Grant. During the course of their pleasant conversation, Mr. Henry mentioned the trouble he had had making his pictures because of stringent Army regulations barring unattached artists from the combat zones. President Grant informed the artist that he should have come to him for a blanket permit. "We are the men who make history, Mr. Henry," said the President, "but you are the men who perpetuate it."

The military drawings and paintings of our combat artists at war prove, beyond the shadow of a doubt, that if it came about that the mold of mankind's baser nature, forged through the centuries in the fiery furnace of war, should be shattered on the anvil of the better elements of his inherent instincts for peaceful pursuits, man would not seek a solution to his vexing, perplexing problems on the battlefield.

I

Powder, Pigtails, and Warpaint

The French and Indian War

1755–1763

The French and Indian War began in 1755, an outgrowth of French schemes of conquest in North America. An undeclared war, it was the result of fifty years of violent border raids and Indian massacres, war of the knife, the tomahawk, firebrand, and musket. The first action took place near Great Meadows in July of that year, and fighting came to an end eight years later in a classic battle on the Plains of Abraham.

The French had "lost their geographical senses" and claimed all of North America as their own. The flag with the fleur-de-lis flew from the Alleghenies to the Rockies, from Mexico and Florida to the North Pole. Except for some "ill-defined" British land holdings bordering Hudson's Bay, the vast region was given the imposing name of Northern New France. Most important of all, France controlled the Mississippi and St. Lawrence rivers, which gave her access to the rich, fertile inland regions. England, her thirteen colonies situated along the Atlantic coast line from Maine to Georgia, had no such inland highroads. To consolidate her position on the northern American frontier, England in 1749 had founded and fortified the city of Halifax.

The numerical insignificance of her American colonial population notwithstanding, France undertook a bold move toward further territorial expansion by constructing a chain of forts along the British colonial frontier. To forestall this French aggression, Governor Robert Dinwiddie of Virginia dispatched Lieutenant Colonel George Washington to Fort Le Boeuf to demand the immediate withdrawal of the French garrison from Virginia territory.

Colonel Washington, with a company of regulars and some militia, in May, 1754, marched to the country of the Monongahela River and met the French at Great Meadows, "a level tract of grass and bushes," which the twenty-two-year-old Washington called "a charming place for an encounter." The first volley fired from the muskets of his backwoodsmen touched off a war that for numbers engaged was probably the bloodiest, most savagely fought contest ever to take place on the American continent. A short time later, Washington and his little army were besieged and defeated at an improvised fort which he had named "Necessity." The French, superior in numbers, forced a surrender. Washington was gallantly accorded all the honors of war and allowed to march out of the fort with his paroled men.

Aware that the French had begun their new conquests, King George II made a speech to Parliament on November 14, 1754, proclaiming that he would further trade with his colonial subjects "and protect those possessions which constitute one great source of their wealth." The implication was plain, and a campaign was implemented at once. Two regiments, the Forty-fourth and the Forty-eighth Foot, numbering a thousand men, embarked on transports at Cork,

13

Ireland. Major General Edward Braddock was placed in command of these forces and, on the day before Christmas, 1754, sailed for Virginia. The great and far-reaching question, "Shall France remain here, or shall she not?" was at last to be tested on the battle-ground of the North American forest.

The pictorial records of the French and Indian War include portraits of the leading personalities involved in the conflict painted by Benjamin West, George Romney, Joseph Highmore, John Singleton Copley, and Sir Joshua Reynolds. Whatever other talent existed, aside from primitive art, was found chiefly among the military engineers of the contending armies. Those artists included Captain Hervey Smyth, aide-de-camp to Major General James Wolfe; Captain (?) Ince of the Thirty-fifth Regiment; Major Patrick MacKellar, a sub-engineer; Captain Robert Orme, who made maps to illustrate his copious *Journal*; Richard Short, a British cartographer; and Lieutenant John Montresor, aide-de-camp and engineer to Major General James Abercrombie and engineer to Major General Edward Braddock.

On March 14, 1755, General Braddock, his aide Captain Robert Orme, and Ensign John Montresor, his engineer, landed from the warship *Centurion* at Hampton, Virginia. One month later, on April 14, Governor Dinwiddie called for a council of war with the provincial governors at Alexandria to act on a plan, originally conceived by the Duke of Cumberland, that called for simultaneous attacks on the four strongest French outposts: Forts Duquesne, Niagara, Crown Point, and Beauséjour in Acadia. The council agreed to the plan and selected General Braddock to lead his own forces against Fort Duquesne.

On June 10, Braddock's army started its ill-fated march from Fort Cumberland, led by 300 pioneers, axmen, and scouts to cut and clear the road. Foot by foot, the little army advanced into the waste of lonely mountains. The road, but twelve feet wide, forced the army's line of march to extend often for miles, over a forest trail that led past waterfalls, chasms, and stony ridges, the wild forest enveloping the army with its green towering mountains. The French made no attempt to interrupt the march, though they knew of the advance, except to send an occasional raiding party to harass the column, now and then scalping a straggler. Their passage was so slow that Washington feared for their safety and suggested to Braddock that he detach a large, fast-moving body of chosen troops and push on ahead rapidly. Braddock accepted the plan, but Washington's "hopes were brought very low indeed" when he found that ". . . instead of pushing on with vigor . . . they were halting to level every mole-hill, and to erect bridges over every brook . . ."

One month after leaving Fort Cumberland, Brad-

dock's column reached Turtle Creek, a stream entering the Monongahela River eight miles from Fort Duquesne. It was a beautiful day and not a cloud overhead. To avoid a perilous trek through the woods, Braddock decided to cross the Monongahela twice. The troops, inspirited by the prospect of easy victory, caused Washington to speak with admiration of the spectacle: "The music, the banners, the mounted officers, the troops of light cavalry, the naval detachment, the red-coated regulars, the blue-coated Virginians, the wagons and tumbrils, cannon, howitzers, and coehorns, the trains of packhorses, the droves of cattle, passed in a long procession through the rippling shallows, and slowly entered the bordering forest. Here, when all was over, a short halt was ordered for rest and refreshment."

Contracoeur, commandant of Fort Duquesne, accepted the suggestion of his second in command, Captain Daniele Hyacinthe de Beaujeu, that he attack the British on the march and ambush them before they reached the fort, but the Indians refused to fight when Beaujeu first offered them the war hatchet. Determined to carry out his plan, Beaujeu shamed the Indians into putting on their war paint. Beaujeu, himself dressed and painted like an Indian, left the fort followed by 600 Indians, 36 French officers and cadets, some regulars, and about 146 Canadians.

Warned of the approach of the slow-moving British column, the French and Indians quietly lay in ambush. General Gage's advance column, unaware of the trap, moved slowly along the narrow path, the green wilderness hanging over them. Suddenly a man, dressed like an Indian, was seen to wave his hat. A bloodcurdling war whoop broke the silence of the forest, filling the air with the howls and shrieks of the Indians. The French and Indians, fanning out among the trees, opened fire.

Wheeling into line with good discipline despite the surprise, Gage's column began firing by volley at the shadowy enemy, but the trees caught most of the bullets. The scarlet coats of the British soldiers made bright red targets for the alert Indians. Surrounded by an unseen and deadly enemy, the British soldiers huddled in close groups, loading and firing blindly into the deep woods. Many, overwhelmed with terror, broke and ran, the Indians after them. One officer said: "They would fight, if they could see someone to fight with." Many officers and men, under fire all afternoon, could not remember once having seen an Indian. Soon the ground was strewn with the red-coated bodies of the dead and wounded. The terrifying, screeching war cries, mingled with the sounds of rifle shots and the cries of wounded men and horses, "formed a chaos of anguish and terror scarcely paralleled even in Indian warfare."

Though mortally wounded in the action, Braddock, showing "great strength of character and reso-lution," tried to rally his men. While endeavoring to cover the retreat, he was struck in the arm by a bul-let, which penetrated his lung. The dying Braddock was placed on a litter and carried off the field by his aide, Captain Robert Orme, who bribed the terri-fied litter-bearers with "promises of rum and a guinea a piece." Captain Orme, though severely wounded himself, stayed with his wounded general till his death. Sometime afterward, Captain Orme told Ben-jamin Franklin that Braddock was silent all next day except for the utterance, "Who could have thought it?"

Destroying the remaining stores, powder, and am-munition that could not be carried away, the terri-fied fugitives of Braddock's army, with the yells and shrieks of the Indians still in their ears, fled to Fort Cumberland, some even "going as far as Philadel-phia." The French returned to Fort Duquesne with their wounded. The battlefield abandoned, the In-dians swarmed over the ground scalping the dead, and killing the helpless, wounded British soldiers.

Ensign Montresor did not come off unscathed. He, too, was seriously wounded in the engagement. Oddly enough, he received his wound five days before his promotion to lieutenant in the now blooded Forty-eighth Regiment of Foot. General Braddock, who had befriended him and was probably responsible for his promotion, was dead. Lieutenant Montresor's first experience in Indian warfare was ended.

The first stroke against French expansion ended in disaster. Meanwhile, the campaign against Crown Point, the French colonial fortress on lower Lake Champlain, got under way. An unusual campaign, because of its incredible outcome, it reached its cli-max near Lake George on September 8, 1755. "The Crown Point expedition," wrote Francis Parkman, "was a failure disguised under an incidental suc-cess." Located on a small peninsula at the south end of Lake Champlain, Crown Point had for years been a threat to the northern colonies.

The French had learned early of the British plan to attack this key stronghold and "prepared to de-fend it." Command of the British expedition was given to William Johnson, a jovial Irishman, who "had never seen service and knew nothing of war." His great influence with the Indians of the Five Na-tions was the prime factor in gaining him the com-mand. Johnson's "crude" army of untrained, undis-ciplined New England farmers who had "volun-teered for the summer campaign" assembled on the "Flats" and hills above Albany. Among his officers were General Israel Putnam, General Phineas Ly-man, and Colonel Ephraim Williams, whose legacy founded the school that later became Williams Col-

lege and who died during the battle at Lake George. After many unaccountable delays, Johnson finally got the expedition moving.

Almost at the same time, Baron Dieskau, "a man of great penetration and quickness of apprehension," also started for Crown Point from Canada with 3,500 picked troops and Indians, transporting them by way of the River Richelieu. News of Dieskau's advance reached General Johnson, but his Indian scouts ex-aggerated the size of the French force, and Johnson immediately called for reinforcements, meanwhile moving his army up-river to the Great Carrying Place, where General Lyman had constructed a for-tified storehouse, later called Fort Lyman. Leaving 500 men behind to finish the fort, Johnson marched his main body of troops to the head of Lake George. Arriving that same afternoon, he made camp at the water's edge, his men "pitching their tents among the stumps of the newly felled trees."

Dieskau had no intention of waiting for Johnson to attack him at Crown Point. Instead, he "prepared to surprise him" and issued marching orders speci-fying that his officers were "to take nothing with them but one spare shirt, one spare pair of shoes, a blanket, a bearskin, and provisions for twelve days," adding succinctly that the "Indians are not to amuse themselves by taking scalps until the enemy are en-tirely defeated, since they can kill ten men in the time required to scalp one!"

Dieskau marched his army to Fort Carillon (Ti-conderoga), which commanded the routes Johnson would have to take to reach Crown Point. At Caril-lon, a captured provincial soldier "invented a pa-triotic falsehood," informing Dieskau that Johnson and his army had fallen back to Albany, leaving Fort Lyman lightly garrisoned. Dieskau, believing the false information, prepared to leave at once for Fort Lyman. With a thousand men of his total force, he embarked in canoes and sailed for South Bay, where he entered the woods at the Drowned Lands and struck out for Fort Lyman. On the march, he surprised and captured some of Johnson's teamsters. In the skirmish, two were killed, two were captured; the others, escaping, made their way back to John-son's camp. The prisoners, under threat of Indian torture, divulged Johnson's whereabouts and num-bers. Dieskau, "daring to rashness," decided to at-tack Johnson's main body and turned his army in that direction.

Upon reaching camp, the escaped teamsters told Johnson of the French advance, and he sent out two small columns to head them off, one to Fort Lyman, the other to South Bay. Dieskau made plans to am-bush the latter column. The big clash came when this column, under Lieutenant Colonel Whiting, carelessly fell prey to the ambush. Suddenly out of the thickets roared deadly rifle fire amid a burst of war whoops. According to Dieskau, "the head of Johnson's column doubled up like a pack of cards." From behind every tree and bush poured heavy rifle fire, the British column recoiling when the enemy rushed them with shouts and screeches. Johnson's men fought back desperately, killing great numbers of Frenchmen, who were "seen to drop as pigeons."

Falling back on the main body, Johnson's men barricaded themselves in the camp with everything they could find to use as cover, Massachusetts men on the right, Connecticut men on the left. They had hardly taken their posts when the white-coated French soldiers were seen moving toward them with fixed bayonets. According to Colonel Pomeroy, "the Canadiens and Indians, helter-skelter, the woods full of them, came rushing with undaunted courage right down the hill upon us, expecting us to flee." Johnson's officers threatened instant death to any man who left his post. When the French ranks got within range, Johnson's three-gun battery opened up with grapeshot and broke their ranks. General Lyman it was who rallied the men, and to him should have gone the credit for the victory. But Johnson did not see fit to even mention his name in the report of the engagement. Dieskau was killed during the fighting.

Thus ended the battle of Lake George and the ill-fated expedition against Crown Point.

Major General William Shirley's expedition to capture Fort Niagara assembled at Albany that summer of 1755. He started up the Mohawk River with three regiments. After a grueling trek through swamp and forest, they reached Lake Oneida. Twenty days later, they arrived at Lake Ontario "where on a bare hill at their left stood the miserable little fort of Oswego." Shirley's whole force soon arrived, but without provisions. Fort Frontenac lay to the north, 60 miles across the lake; Niagara, his objective, was "a distance of four or five days by boat or canoe along the south shore." Both of these forts were well garrisoned with greater numbers than Shirley's little army.

His strategic position was precarious, for if he set out for Niagara the French garrison at Frontenac could cut his supply and communication lines and easily take Oswego. His field officers advised that it was "too rash an attempt" and Shirley accepted their council and abandoned the enterprise. Finally, at the end of October, leaving a small garrison at Oswego, Shirley returned to Albany.

So far, the three major points in the strategic plan had been failures. The one bright spot of the campaign was Colonel Robert Monckton's expedition against Acadia, which was entirely successful, both

Forts Beauséjour and St. John being captured. But this victory also had its sour undertones. The Acadians, in greater numbers than the invading army, refusing to take the oath of allegiance to the British Crown, were banished because of a possible insurrection.

That winter, military operations ended, saw the beginning of one of the worst outbreaks of furious Indian raids against the settlements of the northern colonies. "Every day," wrote Major George Washington, "we have accounts of cruelty and barbarity as are shocking to human nature. It is not possible to conceive the situation and danger of this miserable country. Such numbers of French and Indians are all around that no road is safe." These war parties prowled the snow-covered forests, leaving in their wake the smoldering logs of cabins, the scalped and mangled bodies of women and children. Life was short for the isolated farmer and his family, for these human marauders would spring out of the woods with tomahawk and firebrand, execute their grisly work, and vanish almost without trace. Occasionally there was some resistance, but for the most part the raiders were free to roam at will, and it was a common sight, Adam Hoops wrote, "for the husband to see the wife of his bosom, her head cut off and the children's blood drunk like water by these bloody and cruel savages."

On May 18, 1756, England formally declared war on France and turned her fleet against French commerce. General Louis Joseph, Marquis de Montcalm was placed in command of the French forces in America. After a shuffling in the British high command, Earl Loudon was made commander in chief of the British forces. In August, Montcalm crossed Lake Ontario and, in a quick dash, attacked and captured the garrison at Oswego, completely destroying the old fort. Shortly thereafter, he marched his army to Fort Carillon, where he left a small garrison, and returned to Montreal. Earl Loudon withdrew his army and went into winter quarters.

The main attack on Fort William Henry at the south end of Lake George came in August, 1757. Lieutenant General Montcalm, taking full advantage of the new British commander in chief Earl Loudon's absence with his army at Louisbourg, attacked with 8,000 regulars, Canadians, and Indians, laid siege to the fort, and forced its surrender. English paroles were accepted and all honors of war granted in the terms of capitulation. What followed when the fort surrendered is told in a report by General Webb to his commander in chief Earl Loudon. "On leaving the Camp Yesterday Morning they [the English soldiers] were stript by the Indians of everything they had both Officers and Men the Women and Children drag'd from among them and most inhumanly butchered before their faces . . . a great many men and we are afraid several Officers were massacred." The morning after the massacre, the Indians set out in a body for Montreal. The French soldiers demolished the fort, setting fire to the mass of logs and the dead bodies that filled the casements. The armies had gone and "no living thing was left but the wolves that gathered from the mountains to feast upon the dead."

The following year, 1758, William Pitt, who was acting premier of England, recalled Earl Loudon from America and placed two of Britain's generals, Jeffrey Amherst and James Wolfe, in command. By the end of May, 1758, the British fleet and army were again at Louisbourg. Admiral Edward Boscawen was in command of the fleet, General Amherst and General Wolfe commanded the land forces. On June 3, Amherst's army effected a landing, while Boscawen's fleet guarded the harbor entrance, bottling up the French fleet of twelve men-of-war. Amherst then laid siege to the fortress and, after a month of considerable fighting, the Louisbourg garrison surrendered on July 27, 1758.

While Amherst and Wolfe were attending to the reduction of Louisbourg, General James Abercrombie, with an army of 15,000 men, camped on the site of the ruins of Fort William Henry at Lake George. Montcalm was at Ticonderoga with only 3,600 troops to defend it. The morning of July 5 saw Abercrombie's army embarked in whaleboats headed for the north end of the lake where, after landing, they marched through the forest to the fort. Abercrombie made five frontal assaults against the strong French fortress and "was repulsed with great slaughter." Suddenly losing his nerve, Abercrombie withdrew in panic and took to his boats. After that the American soldiers serving with the British Army nicknamed him "Mrs. Nabby Crombie."

Louisbourg had fallen. And with the loss of Lake Ontario and Frontenac, New France was now cut in two. In another effort to capture Ticonderoga, Amherst joined Abercrombie with five regiments at Lake George, but with winter coming on the enterprise was abandoned. Fort Duquesne was abandoned by the French garrison and fell into the hands of the willing British. So ended the campaign of 1758.

That same winter William Pitt planned the expedition against Quebec, a final campaign that would bring all the French possessions on the American continent under the British crown. Major General James Wolfe, who had distinguished himself at Louisbourg, was wisely given command of the British army and, on June 26, 1759, the fleet of transports bearing his troops anchored just below Quebec, where his army went into camp on the Island of Orleans.

The campaign for Quebec opened on July 31, 1759, when General Wolfe attacked the strongly fortified shores of the St. Lawrence River near the heights and cataract of the Montmorenci. The man-of-war *Centurion* and two other warships opened the engagement with a heavy fire on the French batteries and forts on the mud flats along the shore. Wolfe's troops, landing in boats, made a rush for the redoubt. They were met with "a hailstorm of musket-balls and buckshot, and dead and wounded in numbers rolled down the slope." Strangely enough, there was a cloudburst, the rain coming down in torrents. Their ammunition wet, and climbing the slippery heights impossible, the British soldiers fell back, "in good order," set fire to the stranded vessels, and rowed across the river for Point du Orleans, some rowing to Point Levi.

Thus ended the first attempt at taking Quebec. Wolfe, despondent over the defeat and suffering from an incurable disease, nevertheless did not abandon the idea of taking Quebec. When he recovered sufficiently, he directed that detachments of soldiers lay waste the farmhouses and villages surrounding the fortified city, in retaliation for outrages committed on his troops by the French citizens. Many atrocities were committed during these attacks.

During the weeks that followed in camp on the Montmorenci, Captain Hervey Smyth and Captain John Montresor, at headquarters, seem to have amused themselves by sketching when their duties permitted. According to the existing records, Captain Smyth made the only existing portrait sketch of himself at that time. Captain Montresor, also on General Wolfe's staff as engineer, also engaged himself in portraiture, "and it is to his talent that we are indebted for an excellent profile of General Wolfe taken in his camp at Montmorenci near Quebec, September, 1759."

A note attached to the frame of the Montresor portrait says that Montresor had received his promotion to Captain when he joined General Wolfe's staff. Captain Smyth also made a sketch of General Wolfe at about the same time, as is indicated by the comment of the relative of General Wolfe.

Finally, on September 12, after many weeks of reconnoitering the ground for a landing place for an attack, he found one, "a path that ran with a long slope up the face of a woody precipice at the Anse du Foulon, now called Wolfe's Cove." Above those heights was the plateau called the Plains of Abraham. With 3,600 men and officers aboard the British fleet of Admiral Holmes, Wolfe was ready for the attack on Quebec. For him there was no turning back. If his move were discovered by the French, it could mean defeat and capture.

At two o'clock on the morning of September 13, Wolfe's warships, thirty large bateaux lashed to their sides, quietly dropped downstream on the ebb tide.

Wolfe was aboard the *Sutherland*. Captain Hervey Smyth was aboard with him. Two hours later they rounded the headland above the Anse du Foulon. The men disembarked on a narrow strand at the foot of the heights. Twenty-four volunteers silently climbed the steep hill, reaching the heights where they overpowered the guard. Wolfe's main body of troops waited in their boats for a signal.

The signal to Wolfe was the loud shouts and musket shots coming from the heights. The morning revealed a long file of red-coated soldiers climbing the hill and forming in battle order on the plateau. Wolfe's army, six battalions drawn up in ranks three deep, stood at arms. Montcalm discovered the long ranks at six o'clock in the morning and rushed his troops into position. The French soldiers formed hastily into line and came rushing toward the English line firing and shouting. The British advanced but a short distance and waited. When the French were within forty paces, the word of command rang out along the line, followed by the tearing crash of rifle fire, "delivered with remarkable precision." When the smoke cleared, the ground was covered with dead and wounded. The British charged with fixed bayonets, Wolfe in the lead at the head of the Louisbourg grenadiers. Suddenly a shot struck his wrist. Wrapping a handkerchief about the wound, he went on. Two more shots struck him, and he still rushed forward. A third shot struck him in the breast, and he staggered and fell to the ground. A Lieutenant Brown, a grenadier, and two other soldiers carried Wolfe to the rear. Asked if he would have a surgeon, Wolfe answered, "There's no need, it's all over with me." At that moment, one of the soldiers, looking across the field, shouted, "They run; see how they run!" "Who run?" asked the dying general. "The enemy, sir!" Wolfe murmured, with his last breath, "Now, God be praised, I will die in peace." Montcalm also lost his life in the action. Thus ended a battle that, despite the small numbers engaged, was to be regarded as one of the world's greatest.

Captain Hervey Smyth executed most of his drawings on board the H. M. S. *Vanguard* while that warship covered the landing of the troops. Captain Smyth was wounded in the battle. Shortly thereafter he received permission "to attend to his private affairs" and to accompany the remains of his friend General Wolfe back to England. After Wolfe's death, Captain Smyth learned that he had been mentioned in the General's will. "All my Books and Papers," it read, "both here and in England, I leave to Colonel Carleton. I leave Major Barre, Captain Delaine, Captain Smyth, Captain Bell, Captain Calwall each a hundred Guineas, to buy swords and rings in remembrance of their friend."

The year 1759 saw the fall of Quebec and Major Robert Rogers' punitive expedition to St. Francis to attack the stronghold of the Abnaki Indians. The following years, 1760 and 1761, Captain Montresor engaged in two scouts across Maine, carrying dispatches for Brigadier General James Murray, and in other services and surveys on the St. Lawrence. Captain Montresor writes in his *Journal* of a "scout from Quebec to New England on Snowshoes in 1760, to fix the Plan for the Junction of the Armies at Montreal . . ." Montresor, in company with some Abnaki Indians, set out from Quebec on January 26, 1760, for Topsham, Maine, the nearest New England settlement. For nearly four weeks he and his party trudged through heavy forest and deep snows, suffering terribly from hunger and fatigue. Lost in the snow-haze, Montresor and his little band of Abnakis wandered and trudged through the inhospitable Maine forest in the dead of winter, the snow and icy blasts in their faces. How they struggled through that painful march in a hell of trees, snow, bitter cold, and biting winds which could reduce the bravest man to a stumbling maniac in a day or two is recorded in Montresor's *Journal*. Writing with blunted pencil and benumbed fingers, later rewriting in ink when he reached Topsham, Montresor noted on February 9, "the first day my party fell short of provisions." On Thursday the 14, "The party almost wasted, so faint from want of food. Several got sick eating Alderberries, continuing eating their moccasins, and bullet pouches, snowshoes, netting and strings." The 15th, "the party reduced to eating their leather breeches and raw woodpeckers." The 16th, "Everybody ready to drop for food—began eating their bullet pouches and belts."

Recovered from the hardships of the scout, Montresor set out on another expedition the following year. His list of "Extra Services" to his government states that ". . . discovery in 1761 of the unexplored Lands between Canada and Fort Halifax on Kennebec River, with a party of savages" inspired the exploration. Montresor suggested the expedition to the English ministry in 1760, and the plan was accepted by Sir Henry Erskine and Major Dalrymple. The necessity of military secrecy is evident in a little couplet Montresor penned in red ink in his *Journal*:

Hail, happy Country! that can disclose
Thy inmost secrets to thy deadliest foes.

Captain Montresor mapped the entire region of the Chaudière and Kennebec rivers throughout northern Maine. His original maps are beautifully executed and are now in the British Museum in London. At the outbreak of the American Revolution, the able Colonel Benedict Arnold used them in his expedition through the Maine forest to Quebec.

General George Washington, Commander in Chief, Continental Army, 1776–1799

Painted by James Peale, brother of Charles Willson Peale, who also served in the Continental Army. James Peale is famous for his miniature paintings of Colonial figures of the Revolution.

Colonel John Montresor

Chief military engineer for North America,
British Army, 1775–1779.

From an original painting by John Singleton Copley. Courtesy Detroit Institute of Arts

Captain Daniele Hyacinthe
Marie Lienard de Beaujeu

French Army officer in command of the detachment that
attempted to halt the expedition of Major General Braddock
against Fort Duquesne on the Monongahela River. Dressed
like an Indian, Captain de Beaujeu led the attack that
smashed Braddock's army. Like Braddock, he lost his life in
the battle, being killed by the first volley fired by the British
soldiers.

Courtesy Public Archives of Canada

Sketches from the Field Book of Lieutenant John Montresor

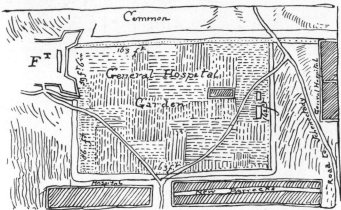

From the Journal of Lieutenant John Montresor. Courtesy New York Public Library

Plan of fort and hospital gardens

Erected at Schenectady by assistant engineer
Lieutenant John Montresor in 1757

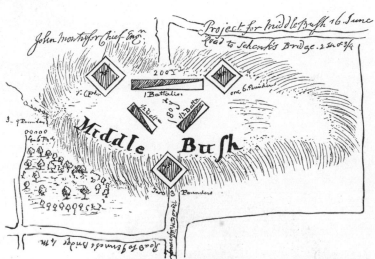

From the Journal of Lieutenant John Montresor. Courtesy New York Public Library

Project for Middle Bush, 16 June

Plan showing a strategic position for guarding
roads and bridges. The symbols used by Montresor to indicate battalions and artillery lunettes
would, in American Civil War maps, indicate
cavalry.

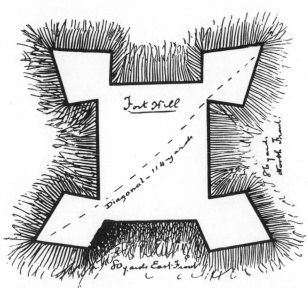

Plan of a redoubt for 150 men

"Open to the north and East Fronts but trespassed on the
other two, close upon their Exterior Lines."

Sketch from the Journal of Lieutenant John Montresor. Courtesy New York Public Library

*Military Sketches of the Battle of the Monongahela
Drawn by Major Patrick Mackellar, Sub-engineer,
British Forces Attacking Fort Duquesne*

From a contemporary print

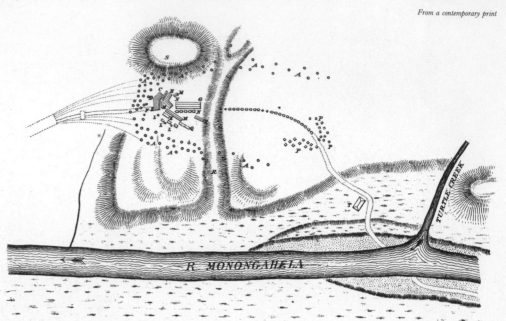

"A sketch of the field of battle of the 9th of July, upon the Monongahela, seven miles from Fort Du Quesne, shewing the disposition of the troops when the action began"

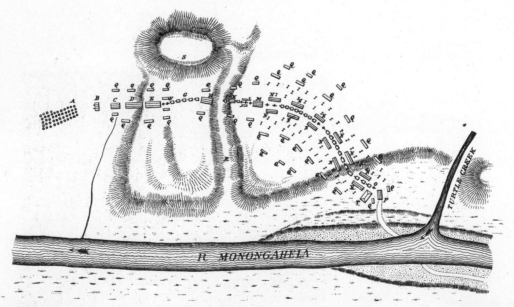

"A sketch of the field of battle, shewing the disposition of the troops about 2 o'clock, when the whole of the main body had joined the advanced and working parties, then beat back from the ground they occupied as in Plan I"

From an original painting by Edwin Willard Deming. Courtesy The State Historical Society of Wisconsin

Death of Major General Edward Braddock at the Battle of the Monongahela

"I cannot describe the horrors of that scene," wrote one of General Braddock's officers three weeks after. "No pen could do it. The yell of the Indians is fresh on my ear, and the terrific sound will haunt me till the hour of my dissolution." In the painting General Braddock is seen falling from his horse, struck in the chest by a bullet which had penetrated his arm. The young officer reaching for the bridle of Braddock's horse is Colonel George Washington.

Death of General Edward Braddock

From an engraving by Edmund Scott, probably executed from an original drawing made on the spot.

From a contemporary print

23

Major General Sir William Johnson

Officer in the British service, he was beloved by the Indian Nations, whom he had befriended and with whom he had great influence. Sir William went so far as to adopt their ways and was a master of Indian rhetoric. Upon the death of his German wife, he married a young Mohawk squaw, sister of the infamous Thayendanegea, "Joseph Brant."

Major Israel Putnam

Major Putnam took part in General William Shirley's expedition against Crown Point. He was also with General Howe at Ticonderoga. The Indians captured him, dragged him to the rear, lashed him to a tree so that he could not move a limb, and a savage amused himself by throwing a tomahawk at Putnam's head, coming as close as possible to the mark without hitting him. Another time they almost burned him alive at the stake. Putnam later made his escape.

Fort Frederic
or Crown Point—North View

French key fortress and advance post on Lake Champlain. Built along medieval lines, of masonry, it was a formidable work and withstood many attacks. After it was captured by the British, it was used as a base by General Amherst.

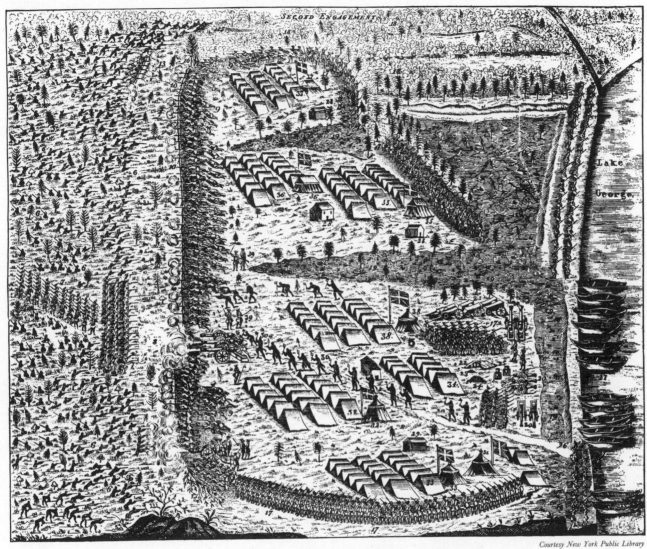

Courtesy New York Public Library

REFERENCES: 5. Site of proposed Monument—Memorial of Battle. 6. Canadians and Indians. 7. French regulars attacking the centre. 8. The road. 9. Provincials in action posted in front. 10. The trees felled for the breastworks. 11. Cannon. 12. A cannon posted "advantageously" on the eminence. 13. Place where Dieskau fell. 14-15. Canadians' attack. 16. The man that shot Dieskau. 17. Reserves. 18. Woods and swamps. 19. Morass. 20. Cannon defending the flank. 21. Baggage wagons. 22-23-24. Stores and ammunition. 25. Mortars. 26. Road to the Lake. 27-28-29. Storehouses. 30. Mohawks. 31. Gen'l Johnson's tent. 32. Lyman's Regiment. 33. Col. Harris's Company. 34. Col. Cockroft. 35. Col. Williams. 36. Col. Ruggles. 37. Col. Titcomb. 38. Col. Guttridge. 39. Officers.

The map, besides being unique, possesses great historical value. Blodgett appears to have been a sutler for the rangers.

Samuel Blodgett's "Perspective Plan of the Battle near Lake George"

This view was published in Boston by E. B. O'Callahan soon after the battle in 1755. The artist accompanied it "with an explanation thereof containing a full, though short history of that important affair, by Samuel Blodgett, occasionally at the camp when the battle was fought."

25

From an original water color by Captain Henry Rudyerd, Royal Engineers. Courtesy William Coverdale Collection, Manoir Richelieu, Murray Bay, Quebec

A view of Ticonderoga taken from the sand-redoubt

"shewing the Piers for a Bridge constructed by the Americans in the year 1776 intended to form a communication with Ticonderoga and Mount-Independence." The celebrated fortress was built by the French in 1755 and was originally named Carillon from the music of the Upper and Lower Falls. It was the headquarters of Montcalm in 1757, was suc- cessfully besieged by Abercrombie in July, 1758, and was taken July 26, 1759. The Americans captured it May 10, 1775, but retired in July, 1777. After the war it fell into ruins. The fort has since been restored. Noted by Captain Goden- rath, November, 1946.

A view of Fort Niagara

Captured by Sir William Johnson, on July 25, 1759.

Drawn on the spot in 1758. Artist unknown. Courtesy Public Archives of Canada

From a contemporary print (mezzotint). Courtesy Public Archives of Canada

Earl Loudon

In one of the strangest shufflings of military command in history, Earl Loudon superseded Major General William Shirley as commander in chief of the British Forces in North America after the first expedition against Fort Niagara was abandoned at Oswego.

Map of Fort William Henry

Situated at the south end of Lake George, Fort William Henry was often a scene of battle in the French and Indian War. In 1757 the fort capitulated to a French force under Montcalm and became the scene of one of the worst Indian massacres in military history.

Profile section of the Fort

Showing the underground corridors, firing step, and glacis.

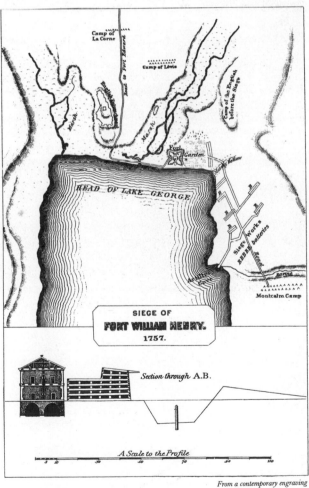

From a contemporary engraving

27

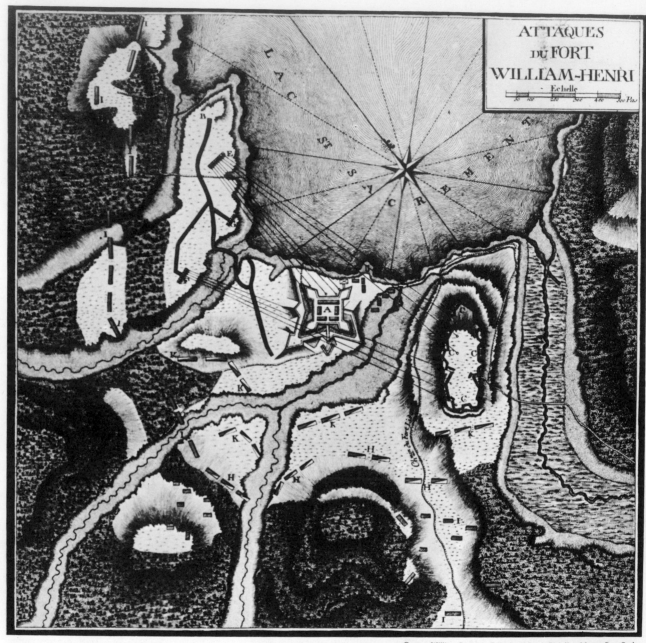

(A) Fort William Henry. (B) Outer works on the night of 4th–5th August. (C) Camp and entrenchments occupied by the English when the French arrived. (D) Battery of French artillery. (E) Battery of eight cannon and one mortar. (F) Battery of ten cannon and one mortar. (G) Battery of six cannon which saw no use. (H) Position of Monsieur de Levi during the attack on the fort. (I) Position of the troops during the siege. (K) Position of the troops after the fort was taken and while the English were demolishing their entrenchments. ▬▬▬ Symbol indicating Indian troops.

Attacks on Fort William Henry in America with troops under the command of the Marquis Louis de Montcalm, August 1757

General Jeffrey Amherst

General Jeffrey Amherst was appointed commander of the Louisbourg expedition, having been recalled from the German war by the young William Pitt, who did not have much confidence in the supine General James Abercrombie. An energetic officer, sometimes overly cautious, he fought with the tenacity of a bulldog. He is reputed to be the first soldier to introduce germ warfare. His method was dosing Indian blankets with smallpox germs and giving the infected blankets to the Indians.

From an engraving by James Watson taken from an original painting by Joshua Reynolds.
Courtesy Public Archives of Canada

Courtesy Public Archives of Canada

Admiral Edward Boscawen, Commander of the British Fleet

This British naval officer was sent to intercept the French expedition to Canada but failed. He was then sent to Louisbourg where, against the advice of other British naval officers, he attempted a landing. The French opened a fierce cannonade on his ship. A signal to withdraw was mistaken and caused another officer to land his troops. General James Wolfe saw the movement, hastened to support it. The rest of the troops followed and effected a beachhead. Louisbourg was surrendered after many battles and a long siege.

29

Lieutenant Colonel Robert Monckton

Lieutenant Colonel Robert Monckton, assigned to command the Acadian expedition, was an officer of merit. He led the successful attack against Fort Beauséjour. Later he commanded a brigade in Wolfe's attack on Quebec. He was responsible for the removal of the Acadians, all adult males in the neighborhood of Beauséjour, for refusal to take the oath of allegiance to King George II. The order originated with Major Charles Lawrence, Governor of Halifax, but Colonel Monckton executed the order, which was "to clear the whole country of such bad subjects."

After a painting by Benjamin West. Courtesy Public Archives of Canada

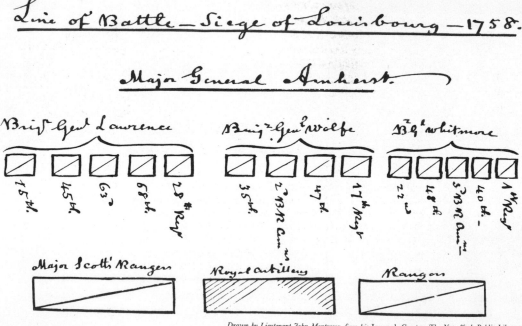

Drawn by Lieutenant John Montresor, from his Journal. Courtesy The New York Public Library

Line of Battle, Siege of Louisbourg

Plan of the line of battle in the attack on Louisbourg, showing troop formations. The brigades on the right and left have five regiments, the brigade in the center four, under the command of Brigadier General James Wolfe. The entire command was under Major General Jeffrey Amherst.

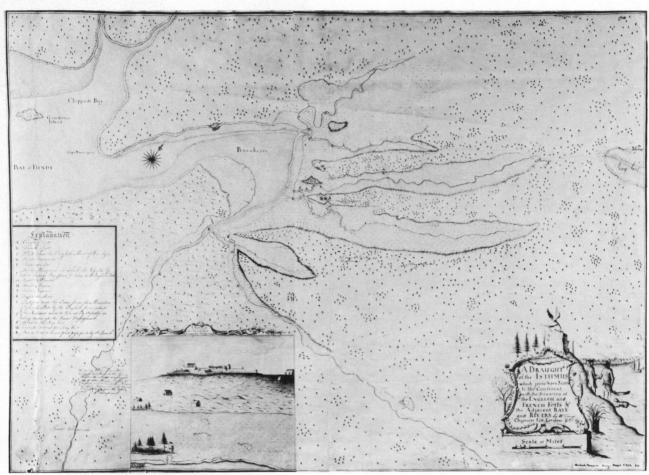

KEY AND EXPLANATION OF THE CHIGNECTO FORTS: "A. English fort. B. French fort. C. Place where the English man-of-war lyes. D. River Tintamar. E. River du Sac. F. River Mesiguash in which the vessels ly that bring provisions and stores to the English fort. G. River La Planche. H. River Macan. I. River Napan. J. River de Mine. K. Dykes to keep the tides from the marshes. O. Dykes levelled by the English from which the Indians used to fire at the vessels as they came up the River Messiguash. P. Road to the Bay Vert. Q. French fort at the Bay Vert. R. Pom a Piquot, a small post possessed by the French."

"A Draught of the Isthmus which joyns Nova Scotia to the Continent, with the Situation of the English and French Forts & the Adjacent Bays and Rivers."

31

Joseph Brant or Thayendanegea, a Mohawk Chief

whose sister was the wife of Sir William Johnson, commanded the British Indians under St. Leger in the bloody attacks on the Mohawk Valley and at Cherry Valley. Brant was defeated at the Battle of Oriskany in 1777.

A View of the Fortifications of Louisbourg

In the lower left-hand corner can be seen army engineer officers surveying and directing the placement of cannon. In the middle foreground a group of soldiers is hauling a cannon. The group of laborers in the lower foreground is carrying bound sticks for the making of gabions.

Courtesy William Coverdale Collection, Manoir Richelieu, Murray Bay, Quebec

PLAN: (A) Fort Carillon. (B) Entrenchments which the French began to construct on the morning of July 7. (C) Camp of the French Army, occupied by them on the 6th, where they remained under arms during the night of the 7th and 8th. At daybreak on the 8th the Army took position (D) in battle order behind the entrenchments. (E) Grenadiers and troops in reserve behind each battalion. (F) Columns of English troops which attacked at 12:30 P.M. (G) Platoons of light provincial troops firing from between these columns. (H) The Canadians leave their entrenchments and attack a column of English on the flank. (I) English sloops which appeared during the attack and were repulsed by the fort's artillery. (K) Retreat of the English columns to their first camp near the sawmills about 7 P.M.; their light troops covered this retreat until evening with prolonged firing. (L) Position of the French after the retreat of the English. (M) French batteries, redoubts, and entrenchments established after the battle.

Attack on the Entrenchments before Fort Carillon (Ticonderoga) in America

By the English, under the command of General Abercrombie, against the French under the command of the Marquis de Montcalm, on July 8, 1758.

33

Pierre François Rigaud, Marquis de Vaudreuil

The Marquis de Vaudreuil, Governor of French America, succeeded the Marquis Duquesne in that post. He organized a war party and expedition against Fort William Henry. The expedition met with disaster, many men dying in the retreat back to Canada. Others, becoming snow-blind, were led homeward by their comrades. Vaudreuil was responsible for many of the Indian massacres in northern New England.

From a painting in possession of Countess Clerniort-Tonnerre, Chateau Brugny, Marne, France.
Courtesy Public Archives of Canada

Lithograph from a contemporary sketch. Courtesy New York Public Library

Penaubsket Alnambay Udenek, Old-Town Indian Village

The Abnakis had five villages, two among the French colonies, located between the Kennebec and Lake Champlain in New Brunswick, Nova Scotia, and Maine. St. Joseph, or Sillery, and St. Francis were in French colonial territory.

34

From a painting by Joseph Highmore. Courtesy Public Archives of Canada

Major General James Wolfe

Commander in Chief of the British forces in the attack on Quebec.

From an original painting by Joseph Highmore. Courtesy Public Archives of Canada

Lieutenant General Louis Joseph Gozon de Saint-Véran, Marquis de Montcalm

Commander of the French military forces in North America. He was defeated in the classic battle on the Plains of Abraham, losing his life in the action, September 13, 1759.

Captain Hervey Smyth (Circa 1759) Aide-de-camp to Major General James Wolfe

Military engineer and artist, author of the portfolio, "Six Elegant Views of the . . . Gulph of St. Laurence."

A self-portrait. Courtesy Public Archives of Canada

35

Major General James Wolfe

"After a sketch from life by Captain John Montresor in Camp at Montmorenci, near Quebec, 1st September 1759." A relative of Wolfe says: "Thus the Hervey Smith, and Montresor sketches are so Valuable, showing as they do What he was really like at the time—On placing them side by side it is at once evident they are Sketches of the same man—done at the same period—They were both serving with him and were done—not more than 3 Months prior to his death."

A General View of Quebec From Point Levi

36

A South View of the Isle-Aux-Noix on Lake-Champlain

representing the Works erected by the French in the year 1759, also the Block-houses built in the year 1776." "Isle-Aux-Noix, Province of Quebec, lies in the Richelieu River twelve miles from St. John. In 1759, Bourlamaque fortified it and held up the British advance from the south for months. In 1775, American invaders seized and rebuilt it; from it Montgomery set out to attack Quebec. In 1812, the British built a new fort, named Fort Lennox. Finished in 1818 and occupied by troops until 1869. The site is now a National Historical Park."—Dr. C. Webster.

Infcribed to the Right Honourable WILLIAM PITT, Efq; one of his Majefty's moft Honourable Privy Council, and Principal Secretary of State.

SIX
ELEGANT VIEWS
OF THE
Moſt Remarkable Places
IN THE
RIVER and GULPH
OF
ST. LAURENCE,

From the ORIGINALS, drawn on the Spot,

By Captain *HERVEY SMYTH,*

Aid de Camp to the late General *WOLFE.*

Engraved by Meſſ. *CANOT, SANDBY, ELLIOT,* and others.

1. The City of QUEBEC, the Capital of *Canada.*
2. The FALLS of MONTMORENCY, and the Attack made by Gen. *Wolfe,* July 31, 1759.
3. Cape ROUGE, called by the *French* CAROUGE, Bay and River.
4. The Bay of GASPE, a *French* Settlement in the Gulph of *St. Laurence.*
5. MIRAMICHI, a *French* Settlement in the Gulph of *St. Laurence.*
6. The PERCED ISLAND, a remarkable Rock in the Gulph of *St. Laurence.*

LONDON:

Publiſhed, according to Act of Parliament, by *THOMAS JEFFERYS,* at *Charing-Croſs.*

Price ONE GUINEA.

Engraving on the Cover of the Portfolio of Captain Hervey Smyth's Collection of Drawings of Major General Wolfe's Attack on Quebec, September 13, 1759

37

A View of the City of Quebec, the Capital of Canada, Taken Partly from Pointe des Peres, and Partly on Board the Vanguard Man of War, by Captain Hervey Smyth

A View of Cape Rouge or Carouge, Nine Miles above the City of Quebec on the North Shore of the River St. Laurence. From this Place 1500 Chosen Troops at the Break of Day Fell Down the River on the Ebb of Tide to the Place of Landing 13 Sept. 1759

38

A View of the Fall of Montmorenci and the Attack Made by General Wolfe, on the French Intrenchments near Beauport, with the Grenadiers of the Army, July 31, 1759

A View of Gaspe Bay, in the Gulf of St. Laurence

This French Settlement used to supply Quebec with fish till it was destroyed by General Wolfe after the surrender of Louis-bourg in 1758. During the stay of the English fleet in 1759, General Wolfe resided at the house on the beach.

A View of the Pierced Island, a Remarkable Rock in the Gulf of St. Laurence.
Two Leagues to the Southward of Gaspée Bay

A View of the Taking of Quebec

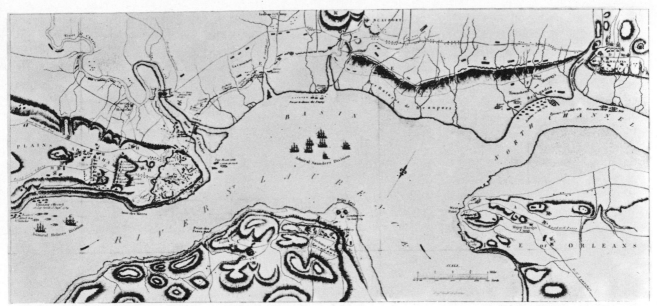

Plan of Quebec and Adjacent Country Showing the Principal Encampments and Works of the British and French Armies during the Siege by General Wolfe in 1759

This excellently detailed military map was drawn by Captain J. B. Clegg of the British Army at the time of attack.

A View of the Taking of Quebec, September 13, 1759

"Shewing the manner of debarking the English Forces & of the resolute scrambling of the light Infantry up a Woody Precipice to dislodge the Captains post, which defended a small entrenched path, through which the Troops were to pass. Also a view of the signal Victory obtained over the French regulars, Canadians and Indians, which produced the surrender of Quebec." This drawing, made by an unknown combat artist with General Wolfe's forces, is here published for the first time since November, 1797.

41

Battle on the Plains of Abraham, September 13, 1759

"On the 13th of September, 1759, the English reached the Plains [of Abraham] coming from the side of the Anse des Mères. The French, surprised, engaged in a battle that lasted almost all day and ended with their defeat and the death of the two generals Wolfe and Montcalm. On the 17th Quebec surrendered."

From a rare original print, published for the first time, in possession of the late Sir Arthur Doughty, Dominion Archivist.
Courtesy Public Archives of Canada

From the original painting by Benjamin West. Courtesy Public Archives of Canada

Death of General James Wolfe, Quebec, September 1759

Sir Joshua Reynolds had suggested to West that he paint the subjects of his masterpiece dressed in "classical clothes" instead of their uniforms. West replied "that the event intended to be commemorated took place on 13th of September, 1759, in a region of the world unknown to the Greeks and Romans, and at a period of time when no such nations nor heroes in their costumes existed."

A View of the Church of Notre Dame de la Victoire

Showing the destruction caused by the shelling from the artillery of General Wolfe.

A View of the Bishop's House and the Ruins as They Appear in Going Up the Hill
from the Lower to the Upper Town

43

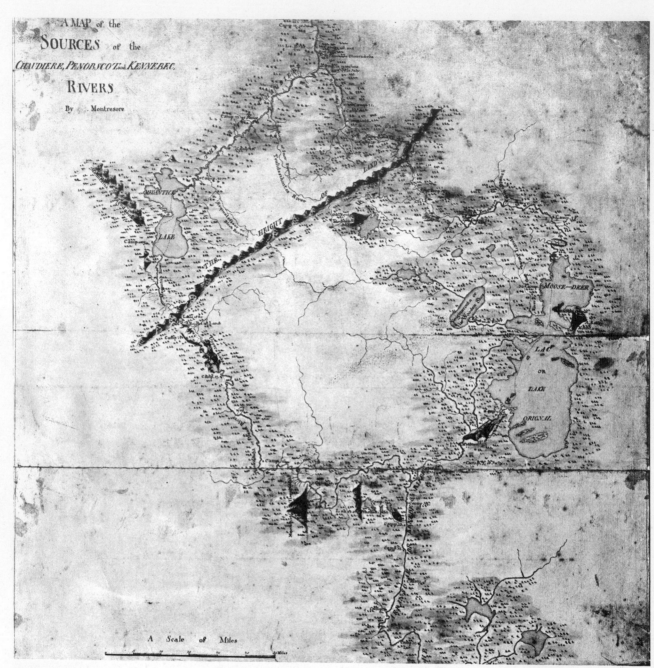

Captain John Montresor's Map of the Sources of the Chaudière, Penobscot, and Kennebec Rivers, 1761

The original of this map is in color, 22½″ x 18½″, and shows the terrain along the rivers, the route of exploration and survey, and the campsites, numbered consecutively.

The second map, of which the original is in the British Museum, covers the same area as the one described above, but is in a much larger scale and appears as an inset on another map. The scale of the first map is about 1:390,000. The second is on a scale of about 1:129,000.

Colonel Benedict Arnold followed these maps on his great march to Quebec. He was misled by omission of the swamps, but his foresight and warning, "By no means keep to the brook which will carry into the swamp, out of which it will be impossible for you to get," went unheeded, and a detachment of his command almost paid with their lives for their disregard of his orders.

2

"Disperse, Ye Rebels!"

War of the American Revolution

1775–1783

On a quiet Sunday, November 28, 1773, when the wharves and docks of Boston were deserted, there sailed into the harbor the English merchantman *Dartmouth,* with a consignment of tea belonging to the British East India Company. Behind this deceptive mask of tranquillity a large body of American colonists broke their traditional observance of the Sabbath to meet in a warehouse a short distance away to find means of legally preventing Captain Rotch of the *Dartmouth* from landing his cargo.

To Samuel Adams and 5,000 enraged Bostonians it was a meeting of necessity. Overtones of violence alarmed the committee when cries of "throw it overboard!" were heard, but the demonstration was held in check long enough for the committee to arrive at the decision that the tea would not be landed. Day and night designated individuals watched the *Dartmouth* to prevent any attempt to land the tea. Thirteen days later an order was issued by the committee, now swelled to 7,000, that the tea would be sent back to London. There remained, however, the task of obtaining from Governor Thomas Hutchinson an order to allow the *Dartmouth* to clear port and pass the King's ships on guard at the harbor entrance. On December 16, Captain Rotch was ordered by the committee to apply to Governor Hutchinson for the pass to clear his ship, and while Captain Rotch sought his clearance papers some of the committee members went to church to await the Governor's reply. But the Governor refused to issue the sailing order.

In defiance of the Governor, 50 men, disguised and painted as Mohawk Indians, raised the war whoop at the church and under cover of darkness descended on the wharf where the *Dartmouth* was moored, climbed aboard, and in three hours emptied 340 chests of tea into the dark waters of Boston Harbor. Bostonians slept peacefully that night, deluded in the thought that the affair was nothing more than an amusing prank. By morning, many Bostonians felt, the tea dumping would be forgotten.

But British reaction to the demonstration was immediate and decisive. When news of the confiscation reached the British Government, the Lords of the Council were called into session to decide what punitive measures would be taken to prevent similar incidents. During the heated session Dr. Benjamin Franklin, agent for the Colony of Massachusetts, had the temerity to present to the Council the Massachusetts Petition calling for the removal of the imperious Governor Hutchinson and Lieutenant Governor Oliver as unfit for their high offices. The Council, smarting under the humiliation of the Boston Tea Party, subjected Franklin to a torrent of abuse and invective, and some members laughed at his discomfiture. Franklin bore the insults with customary dignity and equanimity.

When the tongue-lashers had spent themselves, the Council coldly announced that the petition of Massachusetts was "groundless, vexatious, and scandalous." Two days later, Franklin was dismissed as colonial mediator and deputy postmaster general. Far from dismayed at the treatment of the Council, the sagacious Franklin later reflected that the cause in which he bore these insults was one of "the best actions of his life."

The rebellion's most outspoken advocate was fiery Samuel Adams. In a letter to Lord Dartmouth, British Colonial Secretary, Governor Hutchinson wrote that Samuel Adams "was the first person that openly, and in any public assembly, declared for total independence." To Governor Hutchinson Samuel Adams had full control of the people of Boston, the House of Representatives, and the Council and, consequently, "does as he pleases."

On April 19, 1775, the first gun was fired at Lexington and the War for American Independence began. The British General Thomas Gage, in an attempt to capture rebel military stores and supplies at Concord and seize the arch conspirators, John Hancock and Samuel Adams, sent a regiment of 800 troops to Concord in a night march from Boston. Paul Revere, a Boston silversmith, learning of Gage's sudden move, saddled his horse and rode to lasting fame that night.

Patriotic farmers and shopkeepers, shouldering their muskets and fowling pieces, gathered in a body, shot Gage's men up, marched to Boston, and besieged the British garrison. One month later, on May 10, 1775, the daring and capable Benedict Arnold and Ethan Allen, with a small company, attacked and captured Ticonderoga and Crown Point, two strong British fortresses on Lake Champlain. Later that same month three British generals, William Howe, John Burgoyne, and Henry Clinton arrived at Boston with reinforcements amounting to 10,000 men. The war was now more than a series of incidents.

The British regulars occupied Boston almost at once and the city was cut off from all outside communication. The British fleet of warships of 100 guns, swinging at anchor in the Charles River and Boston Harbor, watched, as did British generals Gage and Howe, the movements of the rebel army as it encircled the city, trapping the British army in the peninsula. John Trumbull, attached to General Joseph Spencer's First Connecticut Regiment as adjutant, marched with the regiment for Boston on the first of May. The following is an excerpt from his memoirs:

" . . . The regiment reached the vicinity of Boston early in May, and was stationed in Roxbury: the parade and alarm post was a field on the hill between the meeting-house and the then road, in full view of the enemy's lines at the entrance of Boston . . . On the 17th of June, I was out at daybreak, visiting the piquet-guard of the regiment, which was posted in full view of Boston and the bay behind it, when I was startled by a gun, fired from a small sloop of war, lying at anchor between the town and Letchmere's

point, about where Cambridgeport bridge now is. It was the hour for the morning gun, but what, I thought, has this little thing to do with the morning gun, which is always fired by the admiral, on the other side of town. It was very soon followed by another, apparently from the *Somerset,* sixty four, which lay between the north end of Boston and Charlestown.

"It soon became apparent to us in Roxbury, that some movement was making in that quarter, but we knew not what. Although the distance between Roxbury and Charlestown, measured on the bay, on a direct line, might not exceed four miles, yet by road, over the bridge, and through the town of Cambridge, it was not far from twelve. As the day advanced the firing continued to increase, and our anxiety to know the cause was extreme; when at length, near noon, we learned that a detachment from Cambridge, had, during the preceding night, taken post on the hill behind Charlestown, and were engaged in throwing up a work. They had been discovered from the ships at daybreak, and fired upon. Charlestown and the hills behind it were in full view from the upper windows of headquarters, but the distance was too great for the naked eye to ascertain what was doing.

"It was about three o'clock when the firing suddenly increased, and became very heavy and continuous; and soon after, with the help of glasses, the smoke from fire-arms became visible along the ridge of the hill, and fire was seen to break out among the buildings of the town, which soon extended rapidly, and enveloped the whole in flames. We could ascertain by the receding of the smoke on the ridge of the hill, that our troops were losing ground, but we had no correct information of the result of the battle of Bunker's Hill, until late at night.

"In the meantime, when the firing became frequent and heavy, the troops in Roxbury were ordered under arms, and to their posts. General Spencer's regiment was drawn up on parade, in full view of the enemy's lines, and it was not long before we attracted their attention and their fire. Several of their heavy shot passed over us, and we were soon ordered to fall back to the hill above the meeting-house. It was my duty as adjutant to bring up the rear and pick up stragglers.

"The regiment fell back to the summit of the hill, and we there passed the night on our arms. Charlestown, at the time, contained six hundred buildings of various sizes, almost all of wood, and lay full in our view, in one extended line of fire. The British, victorious indeed so far as possession of the field went, but fearfully cut up, were apparently not without apprehensions that their obstinate enemy might rally and renew the action, and therefore kept up during the night a frequent fire of shot and shells in the direction of Cambridge. The roar of artillery—the bursting of shells, (whose track, like that of a comet, was marked on the dark sky, by a long train of light from the burning fuze)—and the blazing ruins of the town, formed altogether a sublime scene of military magnificence and ruin. That night was a fearful breaking in for young soldiers, who there, for the first time, were seeking repose on the summit of a bare rock, surrounded by such a scene. . . .

"Soon after that memorable day, General Washington arrived and assumed command of the army. A few days after his arrival, I was told by my eldest brother, the commissary general, that the commander in chief was very desirous of obtaining a correct plan of the enemy's works, in front of our position on Boston neck; and he advised me (*as I could draw*) to attempt to execute a view and plan, as a means of introducing myself (probably) to the favorable notice of the general. I took his advice and began the attempt by creeping (under the concealment of grass) so high that I could ascertain that the work consisted of a curtain crossing the entrance of the town, flanked by two bastions, one on the western and the other on the eastern side, and I had ascertained the number of guns mounted on the eastern, (their calibre was already known), when my further progress was rendered unnecessary by the desertion of one of the British artillerymen, who brought with him a rude plan of the entire work. My drawing was also known to the general, and their correspondence proved that as far as I had gone I was correct. This probably led to my future promotion; for, soon after, I was presented to the general, and appointed his second aide-du-camp. . . . "

Colonel Benedict Arnold's daring expedition to attack Quebec took place that year, its large aims the dual purpose of preventing an advance of the British southward through the valley of the Hudson River and of inciting rebellion among the British and French Canadians. Basing his decision on intelligence reports that the British strongholds in Canada were weakly garrisoned and that the population of the region was sympathetic to the American cause, General Washington, who conceived it, decided to put the plan in operation at once.

The route through the Maine wilderness to Quebec had been surveyed and mapped by Captain John Montresor, the talented British military engineer, in 1760. Colonel Arnold was in possession of this map. Arnold's plan was to move troops northward up the Kennebec River to the Carrying Place near the Dead River, turn westward on that river to the headwaters near Lake Megantic, thence down the Chaudière River northward to the St. Lawrence. Directly opposite the mouth of the Chaudière was the heavily fortified British military base, Quebec. Then began one of the most heartbreaking, most grueling military expeditions in history.

The energetic and capable Colonel Arnold, and his little army of 1,100 picked troops and riflemen, started on the difficult enterprise from Cambridge on September 16, 1775. From the start the rigors of the campaign contradicted all high hopes for its success. Through the inhospitable Maine woods, with winter coming on, trudged the soldiers of Arnold. Over rocky crevasses and carrying places, through swampy bogs struggled the weary men, often standing waist-deep in the rushing, icy waters of the Kennebec and the Chaudière. Before a week passed much of their food was either spoiled or lost at the bottoms of the racing, treacherous rivers.

Exerting supreme effort, without adequate food, their clothing in rags, and suffering from disease and exposure to the northern cold, Arnold's troops reached Quebec numbering only 800 of the original 1,100 who started from Cambridge. In the meantime, General Richard Montgomery, with another detachment acting in concert with Arnold's, engaged the forces of General Guy Carleton, defeated them, and captured Montreal. When Montgomery joined Arnold under the walls of Quebec, their total force numbered no more than 1,000 men. The Americans laid siege to the town and, on December 31, 1775, attacked the fortress and were repulsed with much loss. Montgomery was killed and Arnold received a painful wound in the leg. During the bitter winter the remnants of Arnold's army continued the siege, while the men of Carleton, well clothed and fed, watched the Americans freeze and starve below the walls. That spring, Washington dispatched reinforcements but it was too late; British reinforcements had arrived first. Arnold, his little army disintegrating before his eyes by smallpox, complication of wounds, and lack of food, retreated, the British army close on his heels in pursuit. At Deschambault, 40 miles up the St. Lawrence from Quebec, near Three Rivers, the rout was halted by General Thomas at the head of a detachment sent to assist Arnold in the retreat.

After the British withdrawal to Halifax, following the siege of Boston, Washington transferred his army to New York where it was expected the British would strike next. On June 28, 1776, General Howe landed his excellent army on Staten Island. Realizing that he could not hold New York, Washington wanted to withdraw his forces from the city in order to have more room for maneuver in the open. But the Continental Congress ordered the city held at all costs. Acting on these impossible orders, Washington divided his army, leaving a token force in New York; the greater part of his total strength he placed on Brooklyn Heights under the command of General Israel Putnam. In August the situation became critical. General Howe, with 15,000 men and 40 cannon, executing a skillful turning movement against Putnam, landed on Long Island, defeated and routed him. The British fleet was supposed to have sailed up the East River, but the wind, coming from the northeast, prevented the movement. Meanwhile, Washington, in an effort to extricate Putnam from his plight, arrived from New York with reinforcements. The vacillating Howe, his lack of effort almost amounting to treason, failed to consolidate his victory, and Washington, under cover of darkness and in a driving rain, succeeded in saving his army, getting them back to New York. Howe did not pursue but stayed in Long Island for two weeks while his officers wondered and chafed at his supineness.

Washington withdrew his little army to Harlem Heights, then outside New York. Howe finally crossed over to New York, took possession of the defenseless city, and, on September 16, 1776, attacked Washington at Harlem Heights and was repulsed with some loss. Leaving a small force to guard the fortifications of New York, Howe with a large force headed for Throgg's Neck to cut the American supply line based in Connecticut. Another force set sail up the Hudson River to prevent Washington from crossing into New Jersey.

But again Howe delayed. Washington, needing precious time to withdraw his army to White Plains, got the needed time when Howe took six days to cross a small creek which could have been waded. Washington fortified his position at White Plains and awaited Howe's attack, which came on October 28. The attack was repulsed, and Washington took up a stronger defensive position at North Castle, a short distance away. Howe meanwhile retired to Dobbs Ferry to await the arrival of Carleton with a force coming down from Canada.

Washington then took the initiative. Leaving General Charles Lee in command of 7,000 men to guard North Castle, Washington crossed to the west side of the Hudson River with 5,000 men, sending a small force to West Point to build forts and guard the northern approaches.

Returning from special duty at Crown Point and Ticonderoga where he assisted in the examination and strengthening of those fortifications, Trumbull started for Fort George. His narrative continues:

"Late in the night we reached Fort George, at the head of the Lake, and thence proceeded to Albany by land. There the general met an order from General Washington to hasten on with all disposable troops, and join him behind the Delaware River. The best troops were selected, (the remainder being discharged into winter quarters,) and with these we proceeded by water as far as Esopus [Kingston], thence by land through the then uncultivated country of the Minisink, nearly on the route of the present Delaware and Hudson Canal—inclining to the left to Sussex courthouse, in the hope of falling in with and joining the division of General Lee, which we learned was crossing Jersey. At Sussex, having learned of Lee's unfortunate capture, we inclined to the right, crossed the Delaware at Easton, and marched through Bethlehem to Newton, where we joined the commander in chief, a few days before his glorious success at Trenton."

In December, while the army set about refurbishing its equipment and replenishing its stores, Washington planned a surprise movement against Trenton and Bordentown. Colonel Johaan Gottlieb Rall with about 1,500 Hessian mercenaries held Trenton, while Colonel Carl von Donop, with a small force, occupied Bordentown. The entire maneuver was set for Christmas night, December 25, 1776.

The Delaware River, clogged with grinding, jagged blocks of ice, and with biting winter winds howling across it from the glazed snow-covered roads and fields, presented formidable obstacles to the operation. Undaunted by these difficulties, the Marblehead Regiment of Massachusetts fishermen under General John Grover began moving the troops in the memorable crossing. The river was high and flowing rapidly, great blocks of ice striking the long, narrow hulls of the "Durham" boats. It was not until three o'clock on the morning of December 26 that men and guns were landed on the Jersey shore. It was then near dawn, and there were still nine miles of icy roads to travel. The sole disquiet was whether or not the movement had been discovered by some alert sentry. But Washington's fears were groundless, for the Hessians were deep in a drunken carouse in celebration of Christmas. Thus far everything had gone without hitch. The night was terribly cold and the howling north wind swirled around the shivering troops as they stumbled down the glassy roads that rain and sleet had turned into jagged ribs of ice.

Just before daybreak the first vagrant streaks of dawn's light silhouetted the struggling, ghostlike troops of Nathanael Greene, still two miles from their objective. Greene's advance became slower as the wind-swept road became more treacherous with every drop of freezing rain. About eight o'clock the American advance column was challenged, the Hessians rushing into line firing a volley that went wild over the heads of the Continentals. The Hessians then fell back through the fields. Soon the sound of musket firing was heard to the south in the direction of John Sullivan's advance. Rushing cannon to the head of King Street and into battery, Henry Knox's men opened fire. Above the sound of the storm, solid shot screamed down King and Queen streets, ripping up and disorganizing the defense. The Continentals, entering into the spirit of the engagement, poured into town, and before long they were breaking into houses, routing out the Hessians who had taken refuge in them. One regiment of Hessians tried to form for a charge at the end of the street, bringing up their artillery as Washington had done, but this was soon broken up by Knox's men serving Washington's artillery. Things were going well and there was not a man in the Continental Army who did not realize what had come to pass. The surprise was complete.

Washington, apprised of the victory when the last Hessian regiment had surrendered, turned to Major James Wilkinson and said elatedly, "This is a glorious day for our country." A few days later, on January 3, 1777, Washington met the British at Princeton and defeated them. The balance of the winter was spent raiding British foraging parties. Beyond that nothing was done except for the everlasting effort of trying to fill the ranks with new troops.

A revealing incident occurred during the march on Trenton. Coming upon a ragged group of Continentals on the road, Captain Charles Willson Peale found his brother James, the miniature painter, as ragged as the rest and suffering with the intense cold. "He had lost all his clothes," wrote Peale, "he was in an old, dirty blanket jacket, his beard long, and his face so full of sores he could not clean it, which disfigured him in such a manner that he was not known to me at first sight."

Early in May, 1777, General John "Gentleman Johnny" Burgoyne, with an army of 10,000 men, started on an ill-fated march from Canada toward Albany in the high hope of making a junction with Lord Howe and Lieutenant Colonel Barry St. Leger coming up the Hudson and Mohawk valleys, its purpose to sever New England from the other warring colonies. Burgoyne crossed the Hudson River on September 13 and approached Bemis Heights, south of Saratoga, where the Continental Army had taken up a strong position. Burgoyne, fully prepared to sacrifice the last belt-buckle, opened an attack on the American left flank. The attack was met at Freeman's Farm by Arnold with a force of 3,000 determined Continentals. For two hours the discouraging battle swayed back and forth, neither side gaining the advantage. While the battle thus hung in the balance, Arnold begged Gates to send reinforcements. But the scheming Gates preferred to stay behind his fortifications with 10,000 men and do nothing. Had Gates co-operated with Arnold the victory would have been overwhelming. Despairing of any support from Howe, Burgoyne broke off the battle and camped on the field. On October 7, Burgoyne renewed the battle by attacking the American left

wing again. "The struggle here was obstinate and sanguinary," wrote E. S. Creasy, " . . . but the Americans made good the ground which they had won, and captured baggage, tents, artillery, and a store of ammunition, which they were greatly in need of." After a retreat to Saratoga, Burgoyne, realizing the hopelessness of his position, opened negotiations for surrender. Gates received all the credit for the victory, but the victory was indeed Arnold's.

After the battles of the Brandywine and Germantown, Washington renewed his efforts to hold the forts of the Delaware and to reconcentrate his army, and, one week before Christmas, arrived at the new winter camp site—Valley Forge—located on the south side of the Schuylkill River, 18 miles to the west of Philadelphia. There, during those first days in winter encampment, the soldiers spent a pitiful Thanksgiving. For them it was starvation. There was no meat. There were no shoes. Many of the soldiers were naked altogether, with no more than a dirty blanket to cover them. Their plight moved Washington to draft a letter to Congress warning that " . . . unless some great and capital change suddenly takes place . . . this army must inevitably be reduced to one or other of these three things. Starve, dissolve or disperse in order to obtain subsistence in the best manner they can . . . three or four days bad weather will prove our destruction." All the Continental Army owned was the ground it camped on. Exposure of the men to the biting cold, rain, and snow increased sickness in the ranks, and there was so little medicine many men died from lack of it. Yet, while the fate of the Continental Army hung in the balance, the work of fortifying the position went on.

Strategically, at least, the location defied assault. Even General Howe admitted that fact. "The entrenched position was a strong point," he wrote, " . . . having good information in the spring that the enemy had strengthened his camp by additional works, I dropped all thoughts of attack."

After Valley Forge little of military importance immediately occurred except for the resignation of Lord Howe. Sir Henry Clinton, placed in command of the British army in America, had every intention of conducting a far more vigorous campaign than did Howe. Accordingly, Clinton evacuated Philadelphia on June 18, 1778, marching his army across New Jersey. At Monmouth Clinton's and Washington's forces met and locked in battle. But for the treachery of General Charles Lee, Washington would have won a resounding victory. With victory within his grasp, Lee ordered a withdrawal at the critical moment and thus lost Washington the opportunity to destroy Clinton and end the war. Following the battle Clinton marched his army to New York. Washington marched his army to White Plains, and both armies were right back to where they had started two years before.

Then the emphasis of the war shifted to the south. On August 14, 1781, Lafayette sent Washington urgent word that "Cornwallis had established himself at Yorktown, where he had deep water on three sides of him and a narrow neck in front." Upon receiving the message Washington determined to move his army 400 miles to Virginia. Maneuvering his army in such a manner as to give Clinton in New York the impression that he was going to attack him, Washington crossed the Hudson at King's Ferry and began his march to Virginia.

The final action of the Revolution is set forth in General Richard Butler's account: "The batteries were opened and fired with great success, which silenced the chief of the enemy's batteries; many of their men were killed, and the whole of the garrison thrown into confusion. . . . the British spiked the guns of Captain Savage with the points of bayonets, but our smiths and artillerymen soon cleared all the guns,

and in six hours chastised the enemy for their temerity with the same pieces. Our loss was very trifling, though the British really executed the sortie with secrecy and spirit."

In desperation Cornwallis tried to break out of the trap by transporting his army across the York River to Gloucester Point, with the idea of then marching overland to New York, but the attempt was doomed to failure. "As the boats were all on the York side of the river, in order to bring over the troops," wrote Colonel Tarleton, "it required some time to row them to Gloucester Point, to carry back the infantry of the first embarkation; but soon after daybreak they returned under fire of the enemy's batteries to Earl Cornwallis at Yorktown. Thus expired the last hope of the British Army."

The Marquis de Lafayette exulted in the victory. In a letter to M. de Maurepas and M. de Vergennes, on October 20, 1781, he wrote: "The play is over, Monsieur le Comte, the fifth act has just come to an end."

From an original painting by Colonel Trumbull. Courtesy Museum of Fine Arts, Boston

Colonel John Trumbull

Self-portrait painted by the young colonel after he resigned his commission in the Continental Army. Trumbull was then twenty-one years of age and living at Lebanon, Connecticut. The carefully planned palette, and the leather-bound volume of Hogarth's *Analysis of Beauty,* form part of the composition of the picture.

51

Colonel John Trumbull's Pencil Studies
of Soldiers and Officers of the Continental Army

Pencil studies of Major General Horatio Gates, General Arthur St. Clair, and soldiers of the Continental Army reveal the expert draftsmanship of Colonel Trumbull. The sketches were made by him in New York in 1790.

From the original sketch by Trumbull made in New York, December 6, 1790.
Courtesy Metropolitan Museum of Art

Major General Horatio Gates, Continental Army

From an original sketch by Trumbull. Courtesy Yale University Art Gallery

Study of a Continental soldier, identity unknown

From the original sketch made by Trumbull in New York in 1790.
Courtesy Metropolitan Museum of Art

Major General Arthur St. Clair, Continental Army

Drawn by Colonel John Trumbull. Courtesy Yale University Art Gallery

Pencil study of a Continental soldier, unidentified

52

Two Major Generals and
a Captain of Dragoons of the Continental Army

These miniatures were executed by Colonel John Trumbull in 1790 and were probably used for studies for later paintings. They were done in oils on mahogany in the artist's most delightful manner.

Captain Thomas Young Seymour, 2nd Continental Dragoons

Courtesy Yale University Art Gallery

Major General Horatio Gates

Courtesy Yale University Art Gallery

Major General Philip Schuyler

Courtesy Yale University Art Gallery

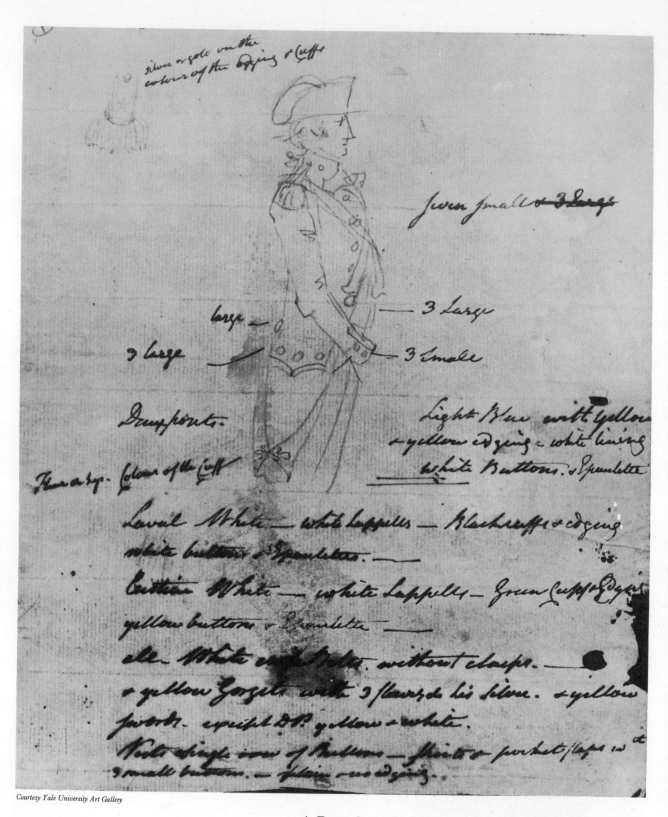

A Page from Colonel John Trumbull's Sketchbook

Showing a Continental infantryman, with notes on the coloring and trappings of the regulation uniform.

54

Two Military Maps Drawn by Colonel John Trumbull for General George Washington, 1775–1776

These maps by Trumbull are excellent examples of his ability as a military cartographer. Trumbull's eye for ground and meticulous attention to detail brought him to the notice of General Washington. The general promptly recognized his talent and appointed Trumbull his aide.

Boston and the Surrounding Country, and Posts of the American Troops, Sept. 1775, J.T.

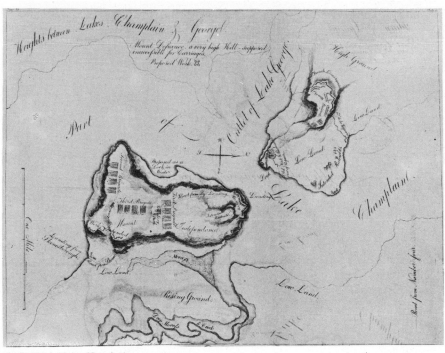

Ticonderoga and Its Dependencies, August 1776, J.T.

Colonel Andrew Porter,
4th Pennsylvania Artillery,
Continental Army, 1776–1790

John Dickinson,
Continental Army, 1776

Colonel Henry Lee,
Continental Army, 1776

Captain James Biddle,
Continental Army, 1776

General George Washington at the Battle of Trenton.
"First in War, First in Peace, and First in the Hearts of His Countrymen"

It was noted in Washington's diary that he sat for Colonel Trumbull five times in February, three in March, and four in July, 1790.

Death of General Warren at the Battle of Bunker's Hill

Bunker's Hill (actually Breed's Hill), near Boston, was defended by some 1,500 farmers and American Minutemen. It was attacked on June 17, 1775, by 2,500 British redcoats, after they had set fire to the suburb of Charleston to clear it of American snipers. Twice repulsed, the British finally won after a bayonet charge when the Americans ran out of powder. Almost half the British force was killed or wounded.

Death of General Richard Montgomery at Quebec

Colonel Benedict Arnold and General Richard Montgomery received orders to attack the British stronghold at Quebec, in Canada. Colonel Arnold made the famous but ill-fated march through the wilds of Maine and Canada and reached his objective before Montgomery, but many of his men perished. With his small remaining force Arnold laid siege to Quebec but was unable to take it until supported by Montgomery. He finally captured the city, but was unable to hold it.

58

From an original painting by Colonel John Trumbull. Courtesy Yale University Art Gallery

Capture of the Hessians by Washington's Continentals
at Trenton, New Jersey, Christmas Night, 1776

From an original painting by Colonel John Trumbull. Courtesy Yale University Art Gallery

Death of the American General Hugh Mercer
at the Battle of Princeton

Most of the fighting at Princeton took place south of the town. Here on the open fields the British fought in the well-disciplined, close-order-formation type of fighting at which they were superb. General Mercer was killed in the engagement.

59

From an original painting by Colonel John Trumbull. Courtesy Yale University Art Gallery

Surrender of General John "Gentleman Johnnie" Burgoyne at Saratoga

The Battle of Saratoga, one of the decisive victories of the Revolutionary War, was made possible by the impromptu rally and charge by General Benedict Arnold. Burgoyne began his advance down the Lake Champlain waterway, while Colonel Barry St. Leger advanced up the St. Lawrence, intending a junction at Albany. Neither army got there. Burgoyne slogged his way through the forest to Saratoga, his army in poor shape to fight after the grueling march. In the final engagement the Americans, under General Horatio Gates, but led by Arnold in a classic charge, defeated the British. The great victory caused the French to ally themselves with the Americans. But the victory belonged to Arnold.

Curiously enough, the flag appearing atop the tent in the background is unlike previously noted likenesses of the American flag. The Continental Congress, on June 14, 1777, authorized that the "Flag of the United States be thirteen stripes alternate red and white, that the Union be thirteen stars white on a blue field, representing a constellation."

Colonel Trumbull has placed these stars, representing the thirteen original colonies, along the edges of the rectangle with one star in the center. This representation has apparently not been noted before, the stars always appearing in a circle. Colonel Trumbull was a meticulous worker, he having spent a number of years doing research for his military paintings. It is highly unlikely that he would have been mistaken about his arrangement of them.

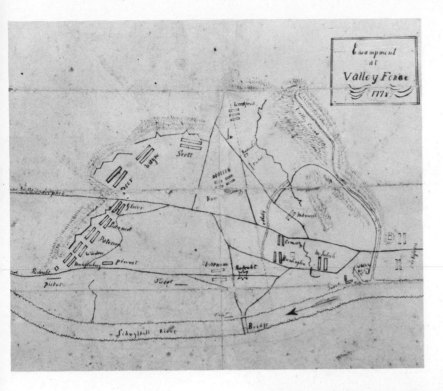

Manuscript Military Map of the Encampment at Valley Forge on the Schuylkill River, near Philadelphia

This map by an unidentified military cartographer, made for General Washington, shows the command of Major General Lord Stirling, including the positions of the Carolina Brigade, Virginians, La Fayette Brigade, and Valley Forge road. It is probably an early, and scantily detailed, map of the Valley Forge encampment.

Courtesy Historical Society of Pennsylvania

Manuscript Military Map of the Lower New York and Jersey Combat Zone

Made for General Washington's personal use, the map is the only one of its kind in existence. The cartographer is unknown.

Courtesy Historical Society of Pennsylvania

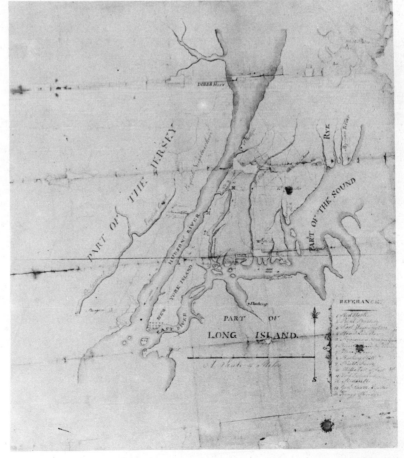

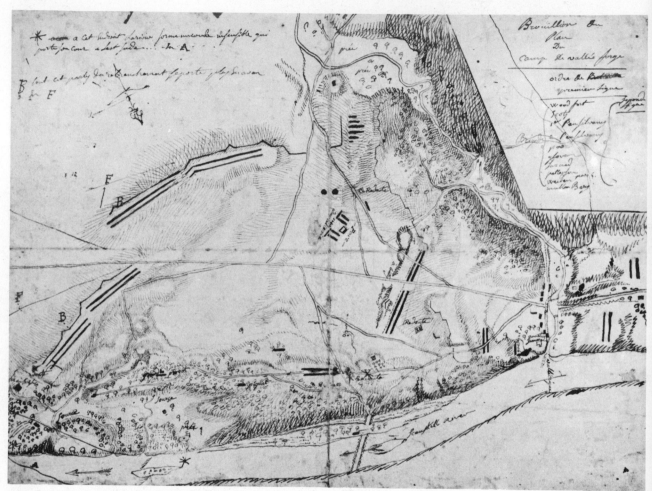

Brigadier General Louis du Portail's Map of the Defenses of Valley Forge

This military map by the Chief Engineer of the Continental Army, Brigadier General Louis Le Beque du Portail, is an excellent example of this officer's ability and talent. He was the best military engineer in the army and was beloved by Washington.

The map of Valley Forge, though probably incomplete, shows definitely where the defenses should be—and were later—located. His notes on the map are written upside down, but are precise in detail. The only contemporary map of real accuracy, it can be compared with the map on page 61.

From an original painting by Colonel John Trumbull. Courtesy Yale University Art Gallery

Surrender of Lord Charles Cornwallis to General George Washington at Yorktown, Virginia

By James Peale of the Continental Army. Courtesy The Maryland Historical Society

Meeting of the Generals of the American and French Armies at Yorktown after the Surrender

63

3

The Girls They Left
Behind Them

The War of 1812

The War of 1812 was mainly a naval war, immediately resulting from the indiscriminate impressment of American merchant seamen by British men-of-war on the high seas. The United States Navy was small then, almost insignificant when compared with the British fleet. But this lack of capital ships, strangely enough, did not alter the face of the war at sea. Rather, it embellished it. A new type of fighting seaman was introduced—the privateersman. Fast brigs, built in New England and outfitted with naval guns, were commissioned, along with their captains, by the United States government to augment the regular fleet.

The new privateersmen learned their lessons of war well and quickly. Before long they made themselves felt by their slashing attacks and hit-and-run tactics against British shipping. The British called it piracy, but they were powerless against it.

It was left to the frigates *Constitution* and *Constellation* to cope with the British men-of-war. Soon these great ships, with their superior seamanship and gunnery, reduced to burning hulks some of the finest warships of the British Navy. After the failure of the British fleet in 1814 to subdue Fort McHenry at Baltimore, Great Britain made no further attempt to subjugate the young nation.

The four artists most prominent for their work in delineating the War of 1812 in paintings and drawings were Captain David Porter, William Bain-

bridge Hoff, Thomas Birch, and Nicolas Pocock. Since the war was fought mainly on the sea, most of these artists' paintings depicted the many naval actions which took place over the vast ocean territory. The United States Navy, at the declaration of war, comprised only four ships of the line: the *Constitution,* "the ship that was a navy," the *United States,* the *Constellation,* and the *Essex.*

Captain David Porter, of the United States frigate *Essex,* was a man who knew where he stood in life to an altogether unusual degree. He had a profound knowledge of navigation and seamanship. As commander of a ship of war, his daring, his strategic judgment, and his shrewd and careful handling of his men followed in the finest tradition of American naval history.

A remarkably versatile man, he wrote a *Journal* of the celebrated cruise of the *Essex* which was later published by the firm of Bradford and Inskeep of Philadelphia in the spring of 1815. The *Journal* was wonderfully illustrated with engravings of drawings by Porter's own hand. The stirring events pictured in these drawings were those of an active participant with a retentive memory, who could describe in charcoal and white chalk American naval battles in the South Pacific.

Although Captain Porter's *Journal* is a serious professional Navy man's work, the events in the story read like fiction. Never in any narrative has a man's personality been more pronounced than in the pages of this remarkable book. His character and personality are apparent on every page. Porter's reflections on life among the natives of the Marquesas Islands, and of the habits of these unclad children of nature, are made unforgettable by his loving description of them. He wrote as he sketched, forcibly and with broad sweeping strokes and plain unvarnished language. David Porter, a naval officer, was telling exactly what he had seen of war at sea and of life in the lush islands of the South Pacific.

Porter was compelled, in the second edition of his *Journal,* to make some revisions. The vivid description of the natural habits, morals, and general behavior of the Marquesans was all too shocking for the sensitive minds of patrician gentry of his day. Yet the book aroused a great deal of interest at home and abroad and was later translated into Italian and published in a three-volume edition in Milan in 1820. Porter's *Journal* is an extremely rare book, for it was suppressed soon after publication by the American government because of a mutiny that took place on board his ship, a mutiny which the resolute Porter put down single-handed.

THE *ESSEX* IN THE SOUTH PACIFIC

1812–1814

In October, 1812, Captain David Porter was given secret orders to rendezvous with the *Constitution,* under the command of Commodore William Bainbridge, at the island of Fernando de Noronha off the Brazilian coast. That same day the *Essex* left the mouth of the Delaware River bound for South America.

The ship, in view of the long voyage, wrote Captain Porter, "had on board stock, vegetables, and other stores, in as large quantities as could be stowed." The realization that he might run into acute difficulties when he reached the Brazilian coast, and the somber prospect of sailing alone in the mid-Atlantic without support or escort of any kind, compelled Porter to overload his ship. "The ship being very deep," he wrote, "we found her unusually laborsome and uncomfortable; her straining occasioned by her deep rolling opened her waterways, and kept the berthdeck full of water, where many provisions were stored."

Once clear of the American coast the *Essex* was alone on the great Atlantic. Neutral ports were closed to her officially. Only by the personal favor of local officials of small ports along Porter's route could he depend on bases where he could put in for repairs and supplies. Porter's wise precautions and foresight were manifest when, "previous to leaving the river [Delaware] the crew had been put on allowance of half a gallon of water." The bread ration reduced to half, an extra portion of potatoes and apples was issued in its place. Wrote Captain Porter, "Every other article of provisions were reduced one-third, excepting rum."

On March 3, while cruising in search of the *Constitution,* the *Essex* ran into a heavy gale. Much of the food and provisions on board were spoiled. "An enormous sea broke over the ship," wrote Porter, "and for an instant destroyed every hope. Our gundeck ports were burst in; both boats on the quarterdeck stove; our spare spars washed from the chains; our headrails washed away, hammock stanchions burst in, and ship perfectly deluged and waterlogged, immediately after the tremendous shock."

The desperate need of fresh food for his crew compelled Captain Porter to head for the Portuguese Cape Verde Islands, the port of Porto Praya. While en route, the *Essex* overhauled and captured a Peruvian privateer, the *Neyreda.* Porter learned from the Peruvian crew that "an embargo had been laid on American vessels in the Brazils on the news of the war." The place was approached with extreme caution, the *Essex* standing offshore before the anchor was dropped. Porter sent Lieutenant Downes ashore to report to the Governor that the ship was "an American Frigate wanting supplies." But to Porter's complete surprise, the Governor of Porto Praya was very co-operative. The islanders were badly in need of bread because of the cessation of American commerce brought on by the war, and Porter, the diplomat, taking advantage of the chance their plight afforded, sent the Governor "a barrel of flour and one of pork." The gift won over the Governor, and the *Essex* was permitted to take on board large quantities of water and fresh fruit. The *Essex* again set sail for the Brazilian mainland. On the way to Brazil, Porter's main concern was for the physical welfare of his men. "My chief care was now the health of my people," he wrote, "and all means that suggested themselves to my mind to effect this great object were adopted." The utmost cleanliness was required. The crew was mustered on the deck every morning and "strictly examined by their officers."

Porter now sailed to keep his rendezvous with the *Constitution.* But the great warship failed to arrive at the appointed time. While cruising in the vicinity of the place of rendezvous, Porter overhauled a small British ship. "She proved to be His Majesty's Ship *Nocton,*" wrote Porter, "bound to Falmouth, of ten guns and thirty-one men." A careful search of the cargo disclosed that the *Nocton* "had on board $55,000 in specie."

Porter, after putting a prize crew of fifteen aboard the *Nocton,* continued his search for the *Constitution* and again failed to locate her. Finally, on December

13, the *Essex* arrived at Fernando de Noronha, the first rendezvous fixed by Bainbridge.

Taking no unnecessary chances, Porter disguised his ship as a merchantman, and Lieutenant Downes was again sent ashore, this time in civilian clothes. Downes obtained secret instructions left by Bainbridge to rendezvous with the *Constitution* at Cape Frio, farther south. Porter, meanwhile, went on a concerted hunt for British whalers reported to be in those waters. Soon thereafter, he again became in need of food and water and put in at the island of St. Catherine's.

While there, he heard rumors of a superior British naval force prowling the vicinity. Upon receiving this disquieting intelligence and fearing a blockade, Porter "left port after dark on January 25th, leaving two stragglers ashore." Having no base in that part of the world, Porter had now to decide between returning home or continuing the cruise to disrupt British shipping. The alternative of returning to the United States was eliminated at once; to return home "at a season of the year when our coast would be swarming with the enemy's cruisers," he wrote, "would be running too much risk." Moreover, such action was directly contrary to his orders. Porter then toyed with the idea of "going off to St. Helena's to intercept returning British Indiamen." But the state of his food supplies precluded this bright prospect.

Porter "therefore determined to pursue that course which would be best calculated to injure the enemy and would enable me to prolong my cruise. This could be done by going into a friendly port, where I could increase my supplies without the danger of blockade, and the first place that presented itself to my mind was the Port of Conception, on the coast of Chile. The season, to be sure, was far advanced for doubling Cape Horn; our stock of provisions was short, and the ship in other respects not well supplied with stores for so long a cruise; but there appeared no other choice for me, except capture, starvation, or blockade."

Having made his decision to round the Horn, Porter took immediate measures to conserve his existing supplies. He devised a special arrangement for catching rain water; one half-gallon of water was a week's allowance for each man. Bread rations were reduced to one half. All other rations were reduced one third with the exception of extra potatoes and "a full rum ration."

Desperately in need of a base from which to operate, Porter had no choice other than to round Cape Horn, despite the bad season for such an attempt. It took a dangerous cruise of three weeks for the *Essex* to round the Horn. Stopping at Mocha, an island off the Chilean coast, Porter took care of immediate supply needs. He then "found it necessary

to again reduce the allowance of rum, in the same proportion as the salt provisions. Every man in the ship refused to receive any of that precious liquor unless he could get full allowance; stating that when there should be no more on board, they would willingly go without; but so long as it lasted they wished their full allowance. However, as there was but a small quantity in the ship, and believing that a sudden privation of it altogether would cause dejection and sickness among them, I determined that the grog-tub should be upset fifteen minutes after they were called to grog; the consequence was that every man hastened to the tub for fear of losing his allowance. After this no further complaint was made."

Porter and his crew found Mocha uninhabited except for droves of wild horses and hogs, replenishing his food supply from the latter. He then set sail for Valparaiso. According to Porter the ship looked like "a latter day Noah's Ark," for the deck was loaded with squealing hogs and chattering wild fowl. After an uneasy trip up the west coast of South America, the battered *Essex* arrived with her ragged and hungry crew at Valparaiso, Chile, in March, 1813, having by-passed Concepción in a dense fog.

Porter sent Lieutenant Downes ashore with a message to the Governor that they "were an American frigate greatly in need of supplies of every kind . . ." Instead of finding reluctant assistance, he found an ally. Chile, having thrown off the yoke of Spain, "looked up to the United States of America for example and protection."

The Chilean government had been constantly harassed by Peruvian privateers sent out by the Spanish viceroy, and several American ships had also suffered capture by these marauders. The friendly Chileans liberally restocked the *Essex*. After a week of repairs, the ship was able to sail for the Galápagos Islands. British whalers habitually cruised among those islands, and Porter accordingly proceeded to this vicinity, arriving there on April 17, 1813, and put into the harbor of Charles Island (now known as Santa María).

When they landed on the island, they found sea lions and green turtles in countless numbers. The turtles were easy to catch as they came up on the beaches at night to lay their eggs. Moreover, a short exploratory trip around the island disclosed an acre of giant iguanas. These lizards were found to be quite edible, having a taste like chicken when cooked. Giant tortoises, almost six feet long and four feet across the back, also proved edible, and many were captured and stored in the hold for food. The Galápagos Islands were green though arid, and the water surrounding them had bewildering currents and calms and was alive with whales and tortoises. They were everywhere. In his *Journal* Porter wrote, ". . . land tortoises are to be found in great numbers, which are esteemed for their excellence, and remarkable for their size, weighing from 300 to 400 weight each."

Fresh drinking water was still a serious problem, and Porter solved it by the capture of the British whaler *Atlantic,* which "had on board about one hundred tons of water, an article of more value to us than anything else. . . ."

The *Essex* had, to date, captured in all twelve British whalers, which included the *Montezuma, Georgianna, Policy, Atlantic,* and *Greenwich,* nearly half the total in the Pacific. These ships were larger than the average merchant ship and were exceedingly "well found." The *Atlantic,* a fast sailer and a "smart ship," which had been pierced for only six guns, was rebuilt above decks to carry a battery of twenty, and became the *Essex Junior,* under the command of Lieutenant Downes.

From the rest of his prizes Porter obtained "an abundant supply of cordage, canvas, paint, tar, and every other article necessary for the ship, all of which she stood in great need, as our slender stock brought from America had now become worn out and useless." After six months of cruising in the Galápagos Islands Porter found the *Essex* urgently in need of extensive overhauling. To make matters worse she was overrun with giant rats which could be killed only by smoking out the ship. The rats destroyed food, clothing, sails, and water casks, according to Porter, "even getting into the magazine and destroying our cartridges."

Porter's nearest base was 11,000 miles away and to solve his problems of refitting and repair he chose the Marquesas Islands as a base. "The repairs and smoking of my ship were paramount to every other consideration," he wrote, "and I knew of no place where I could be more likely to do it undisturbed." On the way to Callao, Peru, Porter ran down a Peruvian privateer which had captured two U. S. whalers. Overtaking her, he had his men strip the ship of her guns, throwing them overboard, and sent the Peruvian home with a warning to the viceroy. At the entrance to Callao the *Essex* again recaptured an American whaler from a Peruvian prize crew, after which she proceeded to the Marquesas Islands. In October, 1813, the *Essex* dropped anchor in the harbor of Nuku Hiva (Nukahiva) with her prizes, the first ship instrumental in establishing an American South Pacific naval base.

The natives were friendly, and they paddled out in dugout canoes and outriggers to greet the ship. But this friendliness did not last long. Porter immediately established an armed fort on shore, everything from the flagship being removed in order that extensive re-

pairs could be at once undertaken. Porter then placed the natives under requisition, compensating them for all the fresh provisions they could bring to camp. The tribe whose village was near the new naval base was frequently attacked by the Happas natives who inhabited a near-by valley on the island.

Despite Porter's warnings, the depredations continued. Taking a small detachment of his men, which included a number of Marines, together with a six-pounder, Porter went in search of the troublesome Happas. Seeing this determined show of force, the Happas quickly established good relations with the American seamen. Meanwhile, Porter took formal possession of the island for the United States on November 19, 1813, renaming it Madison's Island. He named the stockade Fort Madison, the native village Madisonville, and the harbor Massachusetts Bay. With all due ceremony Porter read the formal declaration, and the Stars and Stripes was hoisted over the fort and saluted with seventeen guns.

"Nukahiva," admits Porter, "had many charms for the sailor." The easy, lush, island living attracted the sailors of his crew to the charms of native life, and it was not surprising that the men felt disposed to settle there for the rest of their lives.

The free and easy habits of the native girls were a constant source of temptation to Porter's men difficult to overcome. These women were straight and lusciously golden; high-breasted, proud, handsome, and well formed. Flirtatious daughters of chiefs and petty chiefs, from the ages of twelve to eighteen, roamed at will and gave their full attention to the pursuits of pleasure, offering their favors to whom they pleased. The girls spent their time swimming and bathing naked. They ornamented themselves so as to be more attractive to the man of the moment who held their fancy, and they overran Porter's ships, consorting with the crew. For the price of a whale's tooth a sailor could have any wench he desired. All in all the native girls were playful, willing, and by habit wore no more clothes than Aphrodite. Some of the crew formed permanent attachments with these native girls.

Porter found the men of Nuku Hiva to be generally handsome and well made, and of a curious copper color except where their bodies were covered with intricate tattooing. Shades of skin varied so that many were no darker than many of Porter's crew members who had spent time in the sun.

Before long trouble again began brewing among the Typees, a warlike tribe living on the coast, but separated from Madisonville by high mountains. Their disaffection spread rapidly to the friendly tribes near-by. The situation became so serious, wrote Porter, "that it was absolutely necessary to bring the Typees to terms or endanger our good understanding with the other tribes, and consequently our own safety."

In an effort to quell the rebellious natives, Porter took a small detachment of his men with him, expecting the friendly natives to join the expedition, but he made the mistake of employing too small a force and his detachment of thirty-five sailors and Marines had to do all the fighting despite the "support" of five thousand friendly natives. Porter's naval detachment, upon reaching the jungle, was greeted with a shower of stones hurled by several thousand entrenched Typees. In this attack the loyal Lieutenant Downes, commanding the advance, had his leg bone shattered and had to be carried to the rear.

After the fight in the tropical thickets had lasted several hours, the detachment was safely withdrawn. The withdrawal convinced Porter that, unless American prestige was quickly restored, the friendly natives would immediately go over to the enemy. In full expectation of this, Porter quickly organized a force of 200 picked men and again marched into the jungle against the Typees. The detachment met with determined resistance, and it was only after two days and three nights of hard fighting, and the necessity of burning most of the Typees' villages, that peace with the unruly natives was established.

By early December the repairs to the *Essex* were completed, and Porter made preparations for another foray against the British. This time the *Essex Junior* was to accompany the flagship. One of the captured prizes, the *New Zealander,* was dispatched to the United States. The others, the *Greenwich,* the *Seringapatam,* and the *Hammond,* wrote Porter, "were safely moored under the fort, and placed under the charge of Lt. Gamble of the Marines, who, with Midshipman Feltus and twenty-one men, volunteered to remain until my return, or until they should receive further orders from me.

"On the ninth of December," Porter continued, "I had all my provisions, wood, and water on board, my decks filled with hogs and a most abundant supply of cocoanuts and bananas with which we had been furnished by the liberality of our Nooaheevah friends, who had reserved for us a stock of dried cocoanuts, suitable for taking to sea, and calculated for keeping for three or four months.

"I now found it necessary to restrain liberty I had heretofore given to my people, and directed that every person should remain on board, and work late and early to hasten the departure of the ship. But three of my crew swam on shore at night, and were caught on the beach and brought to me. I immediately caused them to be confined in irons, and determined to check any further disobedience of my orders by the most exemplary punishment. Next morning I had them punished at the gangway, and

set them to work in chains with my prisoners. This severity excited some discontent and murmurings among the crew, but it effectually prevented a recurrence.

"Nooaheevah had many charms for a sailor; and had part of my crew felt disposed to remain there, I knew they would not absent themselves until the moment before my departure. This severity had the desired effect; whatever might have been their disposition, none thought proper to absent themselves except a lazy negro, whom I took on board through charity at Tumbez. This affair had, however, liked to have ended seriously; my crew did not see the same motives for restraint as myself; they had long been indulged, and they thought it now hard to be deprived of their usual liberty."

Restless, discontented, and unhappy, Porter's crew began to show signs of disaffection and rebellion. Their situation, they said, was worse than slavery, and one Robert White declared, on board the *Essex Junior,* that the crew of the *Essex* had come to a resolution not to weigh her anchor, or if they should be compelled to get the ship under way, in three days time after leaving the port to hoist their own flag. When this situation was reported to Porter he recognized that it had become vitally necessary to take heed, and with none but quick energetic measures. "I was willing to let them ease their minds by a little grumbling," wrote Porter. "It was no more than what I expected, but a threat of this kind was carrying matters rather too far."

David Farragut, at that time a midshipman of twelve years and five months, wrote his account of the mutiny from memory many years afterward: "I suppose from having received some intimation that the ships were about to sail, dissatisfaction was expressed, as the sailors were loath to give up the demoralizing pleasures of the island.

"On Monday morning I saw that all was not right. The Captain took his cutlass in his hand, which he laid on the capstan. He then, though shaking with anger, addressed the crew, who had been mustered on the larboard side of the deck with forced composure. 'All of you who are in favor of weighing the anchor when I give the order, pass over to the starboard side; you who are of a different determination, stay on the larboard side.' All of them, to a man walked over to the starboard. He called up a man named Robert White, an Englishman, and said to him in a severe tone: 'How is this? Did you not tell them on board the *Essex Junior* that the crew of this ship would refuse to weigh anchor?' The man tremblingly replied: 'No, sir.' 'You lie, you scoundrel,' said the Captain. 'Where is the list of the men who visited the *Essex Junior* on Sunday?' He then made several of them step forward and put the question to

THE WAR OF 1812

them one after the other: 'Did you not hear of this thing on board the *Essex Junior?*' 'Yes, sir,' was the response. Then, turning to White, he exclaimed: 'Run, you scoundrel, for your life!' and the fellow went over the starboard gangway. I believe Captain Porter would have killed the man at the moment, if he had caught him, but it was equally evident he did not make any great exertion to do so. White got into a passing canoe, and we never saw him again. Captain Porter then addressed the crew in a hearty manner, praising their good conduct, and holding up to reprobation such miserable villainies. At the same time, he gave them to understand that he always intended to act summarily when such disgraceful affairs came to his notice, and intimated to them that he 'would blow them all to hell before they should succeed in a conspiracy.' Having delivered his address, he wheeled around and ordered them to man the capstan and the music to play 'The Girl I Left Behind Me.' The fiddle struck up, the anchor fairly flew to the bows, and we made sail and stood out to sea. Taken altogether, it was the most exciting scene I had ever witnessed, and made such impression on my young mind that the circumstance is as fresh as if it occurred yesterday."

With the island secured, Porter, on December 9, 1813, sailed for Mocha, which had been his first anchorage after rounding Cape Horn almost a year before. Thence he cruised toward Valparaiso on the lookout for prizes. Upon his arrival in February, the Chileans again showed their engaging hospitality. Porter, holding a scrupulous regard for Chilean neutrality, was put to great provocation with the arrival of the British frigate *Phoebe,* and her consort, the *Cherub.*

Captain Hillyar of the *Phoebe,* bent on trouble even though in a neutral port, inexcusably almost fouled the *Essex* as he came into the harbor. Porter realized at once that he was in imminent danger of having to face a powerful British naval concentration in the South Pacific. The American commander "had gained certain intelligence that the *Tagus,* rated 38 guns, and two other frigates" were heading in from the Atlantic. Also known to Porter was intelligence that the *Raccoon* was sailing from the northwest United States. Sifting this information and realizing its portent, Porter wisely decided to escape at the first opportunity. On March 28, "the wind came on to blow fresh from the south, when I parted my larboard cable and dragged my starboard anchor directly out to sea." This initial attempt to escape the British failed when "a heavy squall struck the ship and carried away her main topmast, precipitating the men who were aloft into the sea who were drowned." This accident delivered the *Essex* into British hands.

With her main topmast gone, her speed broken, the gallant *Essex* gave the best that was in her in a furious battle with the two British vessels, both carrying heavier and longer range guns. The gallant *Essex* gave a great account of herself, and struck her colors only when there was nothing left to surrender but a burning hulk. Thus in the printed word and masterful drawings of two great naval officers is left to American heritage the history of a gallant ship, a gallant crew, and a brilliant American naval officer— Captain David Porter.

There were many major naval engagements between the heavier ships of the line, notably between the U. S. S. *Constitution* and H.M.S. *Guerrière* and *Java,* and the frigates *United States* and *Macedonian.* These famous naval battles were delineated in oil on canvas by Thomas Birch in a series of beautiful paintings, faithful in every degree to fact.

The thrilling and decisive battle between the *Constitution* and the *Guerrière* was fought off the coast of Nova Scotia on August 4, 1812. The *Constitution,* commanded by Captain Isaac Hull, sailed from Boston Harbor on August 2, on a patrol of the coast "in hopes of falling in with some British cruisers." After cruising along the coast of Nova Scotia to Newfoundland, the *Constitution* took up a station off Cape Race. Before long Captain Hull made out a large sail "bearing E.S.E. and to leeward." The day was cloudy with a strong wind blowing from the northwest. Soon the *Guerrière,* commanded by Captain J. R. Dacres, came within range and hoisted her ensigns. The *Constitution* accepted the challenge by running up her colors "one at each mast-head and one at mizzen-peak." The *Guerrière* opened the battle, coming in on the starboard tack, "wore round," and fired her port broadside.

To quote Admiral Jurien de la Gravière: "In an engagement which terminated in less than half an hour, the English frigate *Guerrière,* completely dismasted, had fifteen men killed, sixty-three wounded, and more than thirty shot below the water line. She sank twelve hours after the combat." The other naval events depicted by Thomas Birch ended in much the same manner, in favor of the ships of the young United States Navy.

"The *United States* took an hour and a half to capture the *Macedonian,*" wrote Admiral de la Gravière, "and the same difference made itself felt in the damage suffered by the two ships. The *Macedonian* had her mast shattered, two of her main-deck and all her spar-deck guns disabled; more than a hundred shot had penetrated the hull, and over a third of the crew had suffered by hostile fire. The American frigate, on the contrary, had to regret but five men killed and seven wounded; her guns had been fired each sixty-six times to the *Macedonian's* thirty-six." Admiral de la Gravière goes on to say: "The combat of the *Constitution* and the *Java* lasted two hours, and was the most bloody of these three engagements. The *Java* only struck when she had been razed like a sheer hulk; she had twenty-two men killed and one hundred and two wounded."

The military engagements of the War of 1812 brought forth once again the familiar names of Oswego, Fort Erie, and Niagara as battlegrounds. Most of these sporadic engagements could not lightly be termed "battles," but General Winfield Scott's forces fought a "struggle of the most desperate character" at Niagara, or Lundy's Lane, in which Scott was defeated. Moreover, the seacoast of the United States was harried by small British raiding parties, but for the most part the war was fought on the sea and on the Great Lakes where Oliver Hazard Perry earned everlasting fame in the battle of Lake Erie.

A small British army raided and burned Washington, and the British Navy attacked, but failed to take, Fort McHenry near Baltimore. And "The Star-Spangled Banner" was born.

One of the smaller battles, smaller by virtue of the number of casualties sustained by both sides, took place on October 5, 1813, at the Moravian Settlement near the town of Oxford, on the Thames River, Ontario, Canada. An American army composed of 3,000 Kentucky volunteers, led by General William Henry Harrison, engaged a British force, under General Proctor, numbering about 650 whites and some 2,000 Indians led by Tecumseh. The British had been retreating before the American force for several days, pursued by Harrison and his riflemen, before they decided to make a stand.

The battle opened with an American cavalry charge that all but ended the engagement as it began. The British broke and fled under the weight of the charge, General Proctor leading the rout. Tecumseh and his Indians put up the only serious resistance, a show of valor which cost the Indian chieftain his life. Tecumseh's death settled the matter and gave the victory, such as it was, to Harrison. The victory had little bearing on the outcome of the war, but it did have a profound nullifying effect on the powerful Northwestern Indian confederacy against the United States.

One major land battle of the War of 1812 was fought at Lundy's Lane on the Canadian side of the border near Niagara Falls. The battle was fought on July 25, 1814, between General Winfield Scott's forces and a large British contingent commanded by General Riall. That afternoon the American army, comprising about 1,300 men, stationed at Chippewa, made its cast into Canadian territory by advancing on Queenstown.

It was late in the afternoon when the American forces, after marching two miles, suddenly flushed the superior British army in line of battle in the little road known as "Lundy's Lane." Scott opened the attack at once, turned the British left flank, and captured some prisoners, including General Riall. Although the American forces put up a stiff battle, no gain was made by either side. Scott's army held the initiative for about an hour and at nightfall broke off the engagement and retired to its original position at Chippewa. No further advance was made into Canadian territory.

The battle of New Orleans, the most decisive battle of the land war, was fought at Chalmette, near New Orleans, on January 8, 1815. The first signs of the impending engagement arrived at Borgne Bay on December 10, 1814, when a British fleet of 50 warships and transports, carrying 7,000 troops, arrived at the entrance to Lake Borgne. Two weeks later, a division of British troops, guided by a Spanish fisherman, trudged its way through Bayou Bienvenu on the right bank of the Mississippi River, eight miles below New Orleans.

The American forces under Major General Andrew Jackson, aware of the British invasion, inflicted considerable loss on the British troops in a night attack, later falling back and establishing lines behind an old mill race that stretched along a strip of dry land, the only solid ground at the edge of a cypress swamp. There Jackson threw up earthen field works, not breastworks of cotton bales as was once believed. The only cotton bales on hand were those used as artillery embrasures.

On January 8, 1815, Major General Edward Pakenham opened the engagement with a heavy bombardment of the American lines which failed of its purpose. Pakenham then began an attack on one of Jackson's batteries on the right flank, at the same time ordering two British columns to attack the left. The British attack was delivered with precision, but the veterans of Spain were no match for Jackson's Tennessee and Kentucky riflemen. In less than thirty minutes 2,000 British soldiers and three British generals, including Pakenham, were dead in the Louisiana swamps. Jackson's losses were eight killed and thirteen wounded.

The battle was unnecessary, for the peace treaty had been signed at Ghent on December 24, though the news did not reach America until the middle of February. Ten days after the battle, the British troops had embarked on their ships never to return. "The English had thrown for high stakes," wrote Theodore Roosevelt, "and had lost everything, and they knew it."

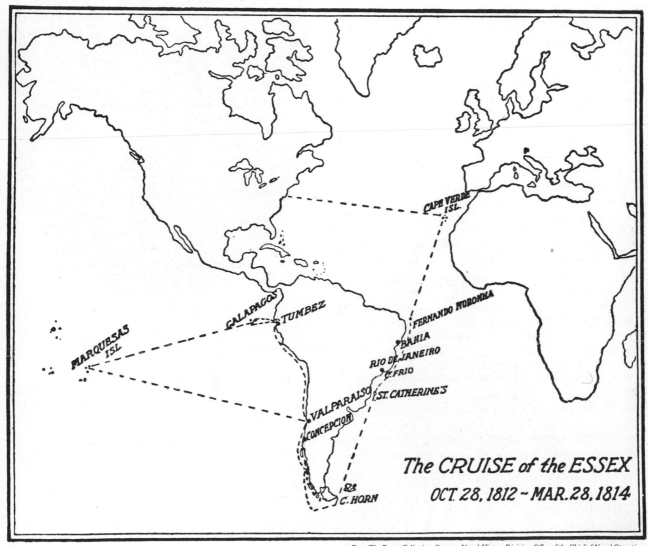

The CRUISE of the ESSEX
OCT. 28, 1812 ~ MAR. 28, 1814

Cruise of the United States frigate *Essex*
to the South Pacific, October 28, 1812–March 28, 1814

This map, from Captain Porter's *Journal,* shows the route sailed by the *Essex* in
her raids on British shipping in the War of 1812.

Commodore David Porter,
U. S. Navy, Commander of the frigate *Essex*

From a hand painting on ivory, artist unknown. The original of this painting is owned by Mr. William Porter, April, 1930.

Courtesy Naval History Division, Office of the Chief of Naval Operations

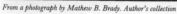

From a photograph by Mathew B. Brady. Author's collection

Admiral David Farragut, U. S. N.

Commander of the United States Fleet in the Civil War, he was a midshipman on the *Essex* during the cruise to the South Pacific in 1812.

From an original drawing by Captain William Bainbridge Hoff in The Porter Collection. Courtesy Naval History Division, Office of the Chief of Naval Operations

United States frigate *Essex* capturing the *Alert* off the coast of
South America, 1812

From an original drawing by Captain William Bainbridge Hoff in The Porter Collection. Courtesy Naval History Division, Office of the Chief of Naval Operations

United States frigate *Essex* capturing the *Nocton,* South Pacific, 1812

From an original drawing by Captain William Bainbridge Hoff in The Porter Collection. Courtesy Naval History Division, Office of the Chief of Naval Operations

United States frigate *Essex* and her prizes making Washington Island, South Pacific, 1812

From an original drawing by Captain William Bainbridge Hoff in The Porter Collection. Courtesy Naval History Division, Office of the Chief of Naval Operations

United States frigate *Essex* and her prizes leaving Tumbez Bay, South Pacific, 1812

United States frigate *Essex* and her prizes at Markahewah (Nukahiva), South Pacific, 1812

United States frigate *Essex* at anchor in Massachusetts Bay,
Nukahiva Island, the Marquesas group, South Pacific, 1812

From an original drawing by Captain William Bainbridge Hoff in The Porter Collection. Courtesy Naval History Division, Office of the Chief of Naval Operations

United States frigate *Essex* offering battle to the British frigates,
Phoebe and *Cherub*, South Pacific, 1812

From an original drawing by Captain William Bainbridge Hoff in The Porter Collection. Courtesy Naval History Division, Office of the Chief of Naval Operations

Battle between the United States frigate *Essex* and British frigates
Phoebe and *Cherub* in Valparaiso Harbor, 1812

From an engraving of an original drawing of the event by Captain Porter, commander of the Essex.
Copied from his Journal, Vol. II, 1812–1814. From The Porter Collection.
Courtesy Naval History Division, Office of the Chief of Naval Operations

The Victory: battle between the United States frigate *Essex* and the
British frigates *Phoebe* and *Cherub*, Valparaiso Harbor, Chile, 1812

Opening of the battle between the U.S.S. *Constitution* and H.M.S. *Guerrière*, 1812

The frigate *Constitution* and British man-of-war *Guerrière* circle for raking position as they prepare to engage in battle.

Battle between the U.S.S. *Constitution* and H.M.S. *Guerrière*, 1812

The *Constitution* and *Guerrière* exchange broadsides as both ships sail into position.
The *Guerrière* is losing her mizzenmast in the first encounter.

78

"Falling Astern": battle between the U.S.S. *Constitution* and H.M.S. *Guerrière*

Her mizzenmast falling into the sea, the *Guerrière* drops astern of the *Constitution* after taking a raking broadside from the *Constitution*'s "Long Toms." The fighting, becoming personal, has developed into exchanges of rifle fire between the Marines aboard the two vessels. The battle is over in less than twenty minutes.

The wreck of the H.M.S. *Guerrière*

End of the battle between the *Constitution* and *Guerrière*. The *Guerrière*, her rigging torn away, is a smoking wreck.

Battle between the U.S.S. *Constitution* and H.M.S. *Java*, 1812

The engagement opens as the *Constitution* cuts across the bow of the *Java* and fires a broadside with her starboard battery which rakes the British man-of-war, toppling her foremast.

From an old print, artist unknown. Courtesy Naval History Division, Office of the Chief of Naval Operations

Battle between the U.S.S. *Constitution* and H.M.S. *Java*, 1812

The *Constitution* coming up on the *Java's* starboard quarter, fires a salvo from her port battery.
The *Java*, her foremast gone, has difficulty in maneuvering.

From an engraving drawn and etched by Nicolas Pocock after an original sketch by Lieutenant Buchanan. Courtesy Naval History Division, Office of the Chief of Naval Operations

Battle between the U.S.S. *Constitution* and H.M.S. *Java*, 1812

The *Java*, totally dismasted, endeavors to steer by the assistance of a jury staysail hoisted to the stump of the foremast and bowsprit. The *Constitution* crosses the *Java's* bow in a raking position and compels her surrender at "50 minutes past 5."

81

From an engraving drawn and etched by Nicolas Pocock after an original sketch by Lieutenant Buchanan. Courtesy of Naval History Division, Office of the Chief of Naval Operations

Battle between the U.S.S. *Constitution* and H.M.S. *Java*, 1812

The *Java*, in a sinking state, blows up as the fire reaches her magazine. The *Constitution*, standing by some distance ahead, "laying to," unbends her sails, repairing her rigging: evening of December 29, 1812.

From an original painting by Nicolas Pocock. Courtesy Naval History Division, Office of the Chief of Naval Operations

End of the battle between the U.S.S. *Constitution* and H.M.S. *Java*, 1812

The *Java*, her stern awash and bow rising out of the water, awaits her final plunge to the bottom. Fires have just reached her powder magazine. In the distance the *Constitution* "lays to" ready to pick up the survivors, while her crew repairs damage done to the rigging.

"Drawn on the battlefield and painted in 1815." By H. de Laclotte. From a copy of a lithograph

The Battle of New Orleans, January 8, 1814

4

Forts on the Prairie

The Western Frontier

Fort Crawford, a few miles above the mouth of the Wisconsin River, typified the frontier military posts of the middle of the first half of the nineteenth century. It stood near the left bank of the Mississippi, on low ground close to the ancient Indian village called by the French Prairies du Chien, or Dog Plains. "Prairie du Chien," wrote George Catlin, "was the concentrating place of the Winnebagoes and Menomonees who inhabit the waters of the Ouisconsin and Fox Rivers, and the chief part of the country lying east of the Mississippi and west of Green Bay."

John Carver, an English Army officer, "traveling through the interior parts of North America," came upon the large Indian town. Carver wrote the village contained a total of something like "three hundred families;—the houses are well built after the Indian manner. . . ." He adds, "The town is a great mart." Shortly after Carver's visit, a group of French colonists from Canada established their own village for the purpose of trading with the Indians and maintained a garrison in the vicinity for several years.

Fort Crawford, begun in 1816, was designed and built by Major Stephen H. Long, who "spent the day in measuring the planning of Fort Crawford and its buildings." The work was a "square of 340 feet upon each side; and constructed entirely of wood, as were all its buildings, except the magazine, which was of stone; it accommodated five companies of soldiers." The thriving French village near-by soon became a center for Indian trading and an important gathering place for tribes that received annuities. From far and near came Menominees, Winnebagos, and Foxes, then occupying the lands east of the Mississippi, as well as the Sioux tribes from farther up the river. H. R. Schoolcraft, the historian, gathering data for his history of the American Indian, visited the fort soon after its construction.

"While at Prairie du Chien," wrote Schoolcraft, "the murder of twenty-six Menomonee Men, Women and children, by a War Party of Sacs and Foxes, which had transpired a few days previous, was the subject of exciting interest. It was narrated in all its atrocious circumstances. A flag waved over the common grave of the slain, and several of the wounded Menomonees, who had escaped massacre, were examined and conversed with. This affray unparalleled for its boldness and turpitude, having occurred in the village of Prairie du Chien, within the hearing of its inhabitants, and in sight of the fort, was made the subject of demand by the Government for surrender of the murderers, and produced the concentration of troops on that frontier which eventuated the Indian Act of 1832."

Lieutenant Seth Eastman, stationed at the fort with the First Infantry beginning in late summer, 1829, had many opportunities to make sketches and drawings of the Indian tribes that visited the fort. Eastman's earliest sketch, later the subject of one of his greatest paintings, was made as he watched a game of ball played between the Menominee squaws and the squaws of another tribe. The game, somewhat resembling today's modern game of lacrosse, was also observed by Major Zebulon Pike when he visited the Indian village in 1806, attending a council of the Winnebago chiefs. "They had a great game of Cross on the Prairie," he wrote, "between the Sioux on one side, and the Puants [Winnebagos] and Reynards [Foxes] on the other. The ball is made of some hard substance and covered with leather, the cross sticks are round and net work with handles of three feet long. In the game which I witnessed, the Sioux were victorious, more I believe, from the superiority of their skill in throwing the ball than by their swiftness, for I thought the Puants and Reynards the swiftest runners."

George Catlin had visited the fort in 1835, after Eastman was stationed there. "Wa-be-sha's band of Sioux came there," Catlin wrote, "and remained several weeks to get their annuities. A day came when the men wanted a little more amusement, and felt disposed to indulge the weaker sex in a little recreation also; it was announced amongst them, and through the village, that the women were going to have a ball-play! For this purpose the men, in the very liberal trades they were making and filling their canoes with goods delivered to them on a year's credit, laid out a great quantity of ribbons, calicos and other presents well adapted to the wants and desires of the women; which were hung on a pole on crotches, and guarded by an old man, who was to judge and umpire the play which was to take place among the women, who were divided into two equal parties, and were to play a desperate game of ball, for the valuable stakes that were hanging before them."

Lieutenant Eastman remained at Fort Crawford for about a year, and during that time made a number of spirited sketches and drawings of military and Indian life on the prairie. In the late fall of 1829 Lieutenant Eastman packed his drawing material and his baggage and, with his regiment, moved to Fort Snelling, an outpost located at the junction of the Mississippi and Minnesota rivers. He traveled with his regiment by water from Fort Crawford, up the Mississippi River to the mouth of the Minnesota. The edges of the river banks were luxuriant with vegetation typical of the country, and his sketchbook is filled with material believed to have been noted while he was traveling to his new base. Lieutenant Eastman had easy traveling, the canoes and boats gliding over the smooth waters along the same route Father Marquette had traveled many years before.

Fort Snelling, in appearance, differed little from Fort Crawford, except for its location on the summit of a high cliff at the junction of the Mississippi and Minnesota rivers. The fort had been constructed in 1817 by Major Long, who had built Fort Crawford, and who had, long before, recommended the establishment of a military post at the confluence of these streams. Lieutenant Leavenworth, with a detachment of the Fifth Infantry, arrived at the mouth of the Minnesota River September 17, 1819, "and on the 10th of September, 1820, the cornerstone of Fort St. Anthony was laid." Shortly thereafter Colonel Josiah Snelling arrived at the new post and relieved Leavenworth, and the name of the fort was later changed in honor of its new colonel.

Lieutenant Eastman remained at Fort Snelling for about a year and occupied what time he had free from military duties making sketches and drawings of the fort and its surroundings. Eastman was soon ordered "on topographical duty," however, a special assignment which kept him busy until 1833, when he was recalled to the Military Academy to fill the post of assistant teacher of drawing.

Early in 1836 he began the preparation of some paintings for exhibition. In Eastman's day every city of consequence had an art association. New York, being the largest, had, as might be expected, the largest and most important National Academy of Design. A satellite of the New York Academy of Fine Arts, it was born during a revolt instigated by Samuel F. B. Morse. Sometimes these institutions were helpful to young artists, providing a reference library and lectures. All had picture galleries, and exhibitions were made up entirely of the works of members. Asher B. Durand, Thomas Cole, and followers of the "Hudson River School" were the leading artists of the era, and large paintings were the rage— the larger the better. Seth Eastman's paintings of the American West were something of an innovation at the Academy. For natural subject matter they were the finest and most authentic Western scenes to have been painted up to that time. The exhibition was a success, and Eastman's paintings were exhibited every year from 1836 to 1840. The exhibition of 1838 included Eastman's paintings of Fort Snelling and Fort Crawford, done from original sketches made in 1830 or 1831 when Eastman was stationed there. That they were successful is evidenced by the fact that he was elected an honorary member of the National Academy while he was still an instructor at West Point.

At the outbreak of the War with the Seminoles in Florida, Lieutenant Eastman was assigned to active duty. ". . . In the Florida War, 1840–1841, whereabouts unknown" says the entry in the record.

Major General Alexander Macomb, Commander in Chief of the Army, left Washington, D. C., on March 22, 1839, "for Garey's Ferry, on Black Creek in Florida." General Macomb arrived on April 5. His main purpose in coming to the peninsula was to make peace with the Seminoles. Indian runners were sent to all the Seminole tribes throughout the Everglades to notify the scattered, hostile Indians of the General's arrival and to request the tribal chiefs to meet in a council of peace at Fort King. But the chiefs did not respond to the call as readily as expected, which was not strange, since only a year and a half before the Seminoles' military leader Osceola had been captured at just such a meeting and died in prison three months later. Not until the middle of May did "Lt. Colonel Harney, accompanied by Chitto Tustenuggee, the great war chief of the tribes associated with Arpeika, attended by Ochi-Hajo, a brother of Blue Snake, arrive from Cape Florida the day before council." The council was held on May

18. Later that same day, after the Indians had met the Army officers in council, General Macomb issued the following General Orders:

"Headquarters Army of the U.S.
Fort King, Florida
May 18, 1839

"The Major General, Commander in Chief, has the satisfaction of announcing to the army in Florida, to the authority of the Territory, and to the citizens generally, that he has this day terminated the war with the Seminole Indians by an agreement entered into with Chitto Tustenuggee, principal chief of the Seminoles and successor to Arpeika, commonly called Sam Jones, brought to this post by Lieutenant Colonel Harney, 2nd Dragoons, from the southern parts of the peninsula . . ."

General Macomb's sensational report of peace was premature; because of hostile action on the part of the Indians, quiet was not restored for months afterward. This document, however, served to "identify Sam Jones as the Great Chief of the Seminoles, Chitto-Tustenuggee."

Captain Eastman visited the southern part of Florida during the Army's occupation and made several sketches in pencil and water colors of picturesque subjects that interested him. One is a view of "Sam Jones's Village," showing a group of shelters, typical of those seen in the Everglades, with roofs of palmetto thatch supported by upright posts set in the ground. These primitive native structures are surrounded by semitropical vegetation, with the open water in the distance. A large wooden mortar and pestle are shown in the extreme lower right hand corner of the drawing, with a large venomous-looking snake on the left. The exact location is unknown, but it is probably far south on the Florida peninsula.

Regrettable it is that Captain Eastman did not keep a journal of his adventures in the Indian Country and in Florida. His writings would have been an invaluable adjunct to his wonderful paintings and drawings. Captain Eastman's meticulous descriptions of his paintings in the vivid captions attached to them show his attention to accuracy and detail, thanks to his training at the Military Academy.

When war with Mexico was declared in 1846, Captain Eastman was assigned to recruiting service for the Army. Just exactly what his duties were in this regard is not set forth in the record. But, we again find him on active duty as commandant at Fort Snelling. From the standpoint of drawing output, this period was probably the most productive and interesting part of his life. Many of the sketches

Eastman made while on this tour of duty served him as reference drawings for paintings in the years that followed.

Unscrupulous individuals, and some of the post traders, had introduced whisky into the tribes. The problem had apparently fallen into the lap of Captain Eastman. A letter written from Fort Snelling, Indian Territory, to Major Thomas H. Harney, Superintendent of Indian Affairs, on August 6, 1848, and signed "S. Eastman, Captain 1st Infantry, Commanding Fort Snelling," mentioned "means as will effectually stop the Indians from smuggling ardent spirits into the country." Just what those "means" were and whether or not they were effective was never reported.

Eastman remained at Snelling until October, 1848, when he left for New Orleans. Four weeks later he arrived in San Antonio, Texas, where he remained a very short time preparatory to traveling to Camp Houston. Following his short stay in San Antonio, Captain Eastman left that historic city and traveled to Camp Sam Houston, 65 miles away. He remained at this army post near Fredericksburg until March 10, 1849, taking part in the march from San Antonio to Fredericksburg and the Nueces River— a march which seemed more a transferring of troops than an operation. When Captain Eastman returned to Washington in the winter of 1849, he was assigned to undertake the preparation of a series of illustrations for Schoolcraft's *History, Conditions, and Prospects of the Indian Tribes of the United States.* To illustrate this monumental work, he executed a great number of water-color illustrations done from the original pencil sketches made during service in the Western Territories. Not until 1855 did he return to active duty, "with his regiment at Forts Duncan and Chadburn, Texas."

Eastman attained the rank of lieutenant colonel in 1861 and served in various capacities during the Civil War, but there is no evidence of his having seen action in any of the great battles. In 1867, he retired to his home in Washington, D.C. On March 6 Congress jointly resolved ". . . if the President shall deem it proper to assign Brevet Brigadier General Seth Eastman, of the United States Army, now on the retired list, to duty, so as to entitle him to full pay, emoluments, and allowances of his lineal rank . . . " The main purpose of returning General Eastman to active duty was to have him execute a series of oil paintings for the rooms "of the Committee on Indian and on Military Affairs of the Senate and House of Representatives" under the supervision of the architect of the Capitol. General Eastman completed this assignment, but while he was engaged on another project, that of painting a series of forts, he was stricken and died in Washington.

Mississippi River, Fort Armstrong, Rock Island, 357 miles above St. Louis

Mississippi River, Fort Crawford, Prairie du Chien, 557 miles above St. Louis

87

Drawing by Lieutenant Seth Eastman: Courtesy Peabody Museum, Harvard University

Mississippi River, 574 miles above St. Louis, 17 miles above Prairie du Chien

Water-color sketch by Lieutenant Seth Eastman. Courtesy Peabody Museum, Harvard University

Sioux Indian Medicine Bag

mountain that soaks in the Water – miss. River – 690 above St. Louis

Drawing by Lieutenant Seth Eastman. Courtesy Peabody Museum, Harvard University

The Mountain that Soaks in the Water, Mississippi River, 690 miles above St. Louis

Indian Grave in Pilot Knob, opposite Fort Snelling

View of an Indian Graveyard, above Fort Snelling, Minnesota

90

Squaws Playing Ball on the Prairie

Medicine Dance: Dakotah or Sioux Indians

"A large party of Indians beside their wigwams engaged in mystic ceremonies of the Medicine Dance."

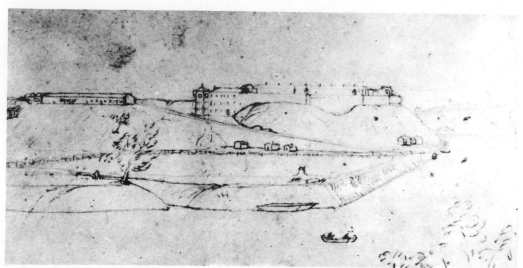

Drawing by Lieutenant Seth Eastman. Courtesy Peabody Museum, Harvard University

Fort Snelling, Minnesota

Sketched by Lieutenant Seth Eastman. Signed lower left: "Lt. Eastman 1830."

Water color by Lieutenant Seth Eastman. Courtesy Peabody Museum, Harvard University

View of Fort Snelling, Minnesota

Oil by Lieutenant Seth Eastman. Courtesy Peabody Museum, Harvard University

Fort Snelling, 1841

93

Water color by Lieutenant Seth Eastman. Courtesy Peabody Museum, Harvard University

Women Dancing at a Sioux Village near Fort Snelling, 1848

Oil by Lieutenant Seth Eastman in the Karolik Collection. Courtesy Museum of Fine Arts, Boston

Sioux Indians Breaking Up Camp

Buffalo Hunt of the Sioux Indians

"A herd of buffaloes are attacked by the Indians, one of whom is dismounted by a furious bull, which his comrade dispatches with a lance."

The Indian Council

General Seth Eastman painted this picture sometime in 1865 for Peter Force, his friend and neighbor in Washington.

Sam Jones's Village in Florida, 1841

Chitto Tustenuggee or "Sam Jones" was Great Chief of the Seminoles
and one of their leaders in the war against the United States.

Character Studies of Indians of the Great Plains
Painted by George Catlin

These are types of the Indians of the Great Plains of the American West among whom Lieutenant Seth Eastman lived while on duty at Forts Crawford and Snelling.

Toh-to-wah-kon-da-pee, The Blue Medicine, a noted medicine man, is seen here in his ceremonial paint, with mystery drum and rattle in his hands; his looking glass on his chest is made of hammered silver, the rattle of antelopes' hoofs, and the drum of deer skin. Stu-mick-o-sucks, Buffalo's Back Fat, Chief of the Blackfeet, is splendidly dressed in a costume richly garnished with porcupine quills, fringed with scalp locks. Ten-squat-a-way, the Open Door, called the Shawnee Prophet, was the brother of Tecumseh who led an army of warriors operating with the British army against the American forces in the War of 1812.

Buffalo's Back Fat,
Chief of the Blackfeet

The Shawnee Prophet, Brother of Tecumseh

The Blue Medicine,
Medicine Man of the
Eastern Dakotas

97

5

Great Virtues, Great Deeds

West Point

The United States Military Academy at West Point was established July 4, 1802, for the training of young officers who would one day form the nuclear officer personnel of the U. S. Army. From the beginning the subject of drawing has been an important part of the Academy's curriculum. Traditional with the Academy is its appreciation of the fine arts. Early in its history the Academy provided drawing instruction for the cadets by engaging French miniaturists and engravers as instructors. The basis of instruction, however, was the training of each student in mechanical draughtsmanship and topography. The cadet was also trained in the method of plotting land elevations and in the sketching of landscapes for purposes of reconnaissance. The cadet also studied star-shaped fortifications in the manner of Vauban, the French military engineer, such as Fort Jefferson on Garden Key in the Dry Tortugas, the Gibraltar of the Gulf of Mexico, and Fortress Monroe in Virginia, which figured so prominently in the Civil War.

The first American artist to become Colonel-Professor of Graphics and Drawing was Charles R. Leslie. The assistant instructor in those subjects was Lieutenant Seth Eastman, the frontier artist. Eastman, a graduate of the class of 1829, was assigned to the Academy in January, 1833, after a long tour of duty in the Western Territories. Charles Leslie resigned the following year, and Colonel Robert Weir, father of the distinguished impressionist J. Alden Weir, was appointed by Lieutenant Colonel Lewis Cass, Secretary of War. The appointment was approved by the Senate, and Colonel Weir assumed his duties as Professor of Drawing at the military school. Eastman remained as assistant instructor until 1840,

when he was transferred to active service. Many cadets who were to become distinguished soldiers studied under these instructors. Among those cadets were Ulysses S. Grant, William Tecumseh Sherman, Robert E. Lee, George Gordon Meade, and Jefferson Davis. Colonel Weir was James A. McNeill Whistler's first teacher in painting and drawing. Whistler, of the class of 1855, was an excellent draughtsman, as was his father, Major G. W. Whistler, before him. Whistler did not graduate, having failed in chemistry. But he was always devoted to the Academy.

The majesty of Hudson's River, and the beauty and charm of the surrounding mountainous countryside which had cast its magic spell over Washington Irving, stirred something more than martial spirit in Robert Weir. "At West Point," he wrote, "the beautiful scenery of the Hudson gave me full opportunity to indulge my love of landscape." Seth Eastman had also discovered a bounty of subjects for his brush. He made many sketches and paintings in the vicinity of the Academy and of many historic spots along the Hudson. A cadet with a gift for description put into words his impressions of nature's handiwork that provided the backdrop setting of the Academy. "It would seem as if nature had specially prepared the place, directing the very forces and adjustment of rock and stone for the purpose of creating a military post. Time never dulls the feeling of overwhelming beauty. I have sometimes thought it conspired to bring the intellectual vision the spiritual significance of great virtues and great deeds . . . I have a feeling that a noble feeling never rises in the heart, that an heroic deed is never performed, but the hills with their laurel, the ridges with their strong limbed oaks, feel a responsive thrill, and impart to the winds and streams their secret joy."

The twilight hours and the night struck a responsive chord in the mind and thoughts of Walter Weir, Robert's son, who wrote of his impressions:

"It is night; the great candle uplifted on the top of the Eastern hills and the thousand wax-tapers of the stars, with their flickering, twinkling lights tell that nature's vesper time is come. As the blaze in the great fire goes out in the west, the evening gun on the plain announces that the sun is set, and the day is done.

"Its thunders roll among the hills; Old Cro' Nest passes them on to Butter-hill, Butter-hill to Bull-hill, and Bull-hill to Breakneck.

"How the Highlands toss the thunder-ball among themselves, till, tired of the sport, like children at play, they send it with spent speed hovering across Newburg bay to the town that lies asleep on the hill-side."

The beauty of the West Point countryside left a lasting impression on young Walter Weir that was not easily erased by time, for he remembered the happy scenes of his youth for the rest of his life. But to the cadets as well as the professors all was not gazing at the beautiful scenery, awesome though it was. The sterner and more serious aspects of military and academic matters occupied their daytime hours. Even in those days before the Civil War the importance of drawing as a requisite study is set forth in a report: "The first five graduates in each year, those most distinguished for their acquirements and good conduct, are the men selected to enter the engineer department. For the Staff, Engineers, Ordnance, and Artillery, high scientific attainments are required. But also the cadet has been drilled in military exercises; he has served as a soldier for years in the ranks, or as a sergeant or corporal; and he has had experience as a commissioned officer performing on the field all appropriate duties, as Engineer, Infantry, Light Infantry, Cavalry, and Artillery both mounted and on foot. From his training he delineates maps and plans, and explains maneuvers of Battalions, Brigades, Divisions and Army Corps. His moral character has been developed by virtuous habits and the influence of wise, experienced and honorable men. For this the government bears the expense of the cadet's education and fits him not only for the military education alone, but also for high position in civil life."

Robert Weir was an observant instructor when it came to evaluating the drawing talents of his pupils. Among the pupils who attended his classes in drawing at the Academy at West Point were Grant, Sherman, G. H. Thomas, "Stonewall" Jackson, P. T. G. Beauregard, Philip Sheridan, Winfield Hancock, Fitz-John Porter, Maxcy Gregg, Truman Seymour, George Gordon Meade, and J. A. McNeill Whistler. Colonel Weir did not include the works of Ulysses Grant and Jefferson Davis in the exhibition gallery in Academic Hall, "for the reason that they stood at the wrong end of their class." "The rough sketches by Whistler," wrote Colonel Weir, "even at this early date, exhibit decided talent and singular independence of thought; indeed this latter characteristic so got the better of him that he was finally obliged to leave the Academy, expelled for his eccentricities—but he later expressed his great admiration for his training and discipline there. He was the 'gentleman of the nocturnes in blue and silver.' He drew beautifully and rapidly with a pen, and had a fine eye for color. He had all these natural artistic tendencies as a lad . . . " Colonel Weir could not say the same for Ulysses Grant, however, for he wrote, "I can't say that General Grant had a very artistic tendency; he was rather a poor hand at it . . . "

Looking at Grant's drawing "Trading with the Indians," which he made when a cadet at the Academy, one could take exception to Colonel Weir's verdict. A fine, sensitive piece of work, Grant's drawing reveals another and little-known side of the "brutal Suvarov" of the Union Army, as Mrs. Chesnut referred to him in her vehemence and resentment toward things Federal. Mrs. Chesnut was prone to overlook much in Grant's character.

One of the most controversial figures in American art was James Abbott McNeill Whistler. After the disappointed Whistler left the Academy, Colonel Weir wrote, "The Army lost but an indifferent soldier, but the world of art was recruited by one of the brilliant lights of his time." Whistler was, indeed, an "indifferent soldier," but he always recalled with affection his student days at the Academy. When Whistler was pursuing his impoverished art career in London, a friend inquired about his short military career. His reply was, "If silicon had been a gas, I would have been a Major General."

In an extract from *A Discussion in Congress* appeared the following: "In reference to the drawing department over which Mr. Weir presides, the Committee may not be aware that it is one of the most important branches of military education. . . . Those skilled in that science, the officers of the engineering department, have performed most important services during the progress of the war with Mexico. We know of a young man in Louisiana who drew for General Scott the whole plan of the fortifications around the city of Mexico; for which services he received only the approval of the General, while in its performance he encountered as much peril as an officer in battle." Although the young man is not mentioned by name it was probably James Walker.

The curriculum at the Academy placed heavy emphasis on mathematics—calculus, analytical and descriptive geometry, and conic sections. These mathematical studies were co-ordinated with the course in drawing, which included perspective, shading and shadow, and the study of the human figure in free-hand drawing. A course in drawing was given by Thomas Gimbrede, a Frenchman and amiable teacher, and an accomplished miniaturist and engraver with a broad sense of humor.

"There are only two lines in drawing," he said to his class, "the straight line and the curved line. Everyone can draw a straight line and everyone can draw a curved line—therefore, everyone can draw." Robert E. Lee had shown exceptional talent in map making and topography which manifested itself when, as Captain of Engineers on General Winfield Scott's staff in Mexico, he made a map of the field of Cerro Gordo under fire, almost getting himself captured in the process. Later, at a council of war called by General Scott, Captain Lee was the subject of close observation by Lieutenant Raphael Semmes of the Navy. Greatly impressed, Semmes wrote: "The services of Captain Lee were invaluable to his chief. Endowed with a mind which has no superior in the corps, and possessing great energy of character, he examined, counselled, and advised with a judgment, tact, and discretion worthy of all praise. His talent for topography was peculiar, and he seemed to receive impressions intuitively, which it cost other men much labor to acquire . . . "

A View of the Hudson from West Point

Painting by Colonel Robert W. Weir,
Professor of Drawing at the Military
Academy. Circa 1864.

Photograph by Mathew Brady. Author's collection

Colonel Robert Walter Weir, 1840

Professor of Drawing, United States Military Academy, West Point, New York.

Lieutenant General
Thomas Jonathan Jackson

Commander of the Army of the Valley, C.S.A.

Photograph by George Cook. Author's collection

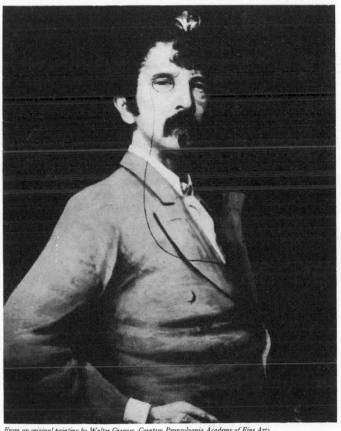

From an original painting by Walter Greaves. Courtesy Pennsylvania Academy of Fine Arts

James Abbott McNeill Whistler

Whistler's father was a major of engineers. Like Edgar Allan Poe, Whistler was sent to West Point to become a soldier, but he soon discovered that he was not cut out for the military and resigned from the Academy.

103

Names	Cadets Signature.	Date of Report	Age 1st July September		Cadets place of residence	
			Yrs.	Mos.	Town	County
F. M. W. Burton	Frank Mark William Burton	June 3rd	17	8	Murfreesboro	Rutherford
Francis M. Lea x	Francis Lytle Ells Lea (Register)	Aug. 26	18	7	Cleveland	Bradley
R. Hazlett	Robert Hazlett ✓ +	June 10	18	5	Warren	Trumbull
U. S. Grant	Ulysses Hiram Grant ✓ x	May 25	17	2	Georgetown	Brown
W. F. Reynolds	William Franklin Reynolds	June 10	19	3	Canton	Stark
Chas. S. Gillespie						

Courtesy U. S. Military Academy

Signature of Ulysses Grant on Reporting at West Point

I, Cadet U. S. Grant, of the State of Ohio, aged Seventeen years and Two months, do hereby engage, with the consent of my guardian, to serve in the Army of the United States for eight years, unless sooner discharged by the proper authority. And I, Cadet U. S. Grant, do hereby pledge my word of honor as a gentleman, that I will faithfully observe the Rules and Articles of War, the Regulations for the Military Academy; and that I will in like manner, observe and obey the orders of the President of the United States, and the orders of the officers appointed over me, according to the rules and discipline of War.

Subscribed to at West Point, N.Y., this 14th day of September eighteen hundred and thirty nine, in presence of

U S Grant

Courtesy U. S. Military Academy

First Signature of Cadet Ulysses S. Grant as U. S. Grant, on the Articles of War and Academy Regulations

Lieutenant General
Ulysses Simpson Grant

Commander in Chief of the Armies of the
United States, 1864–1865

From a painting by Paul Louvrier given to the Military Academy by Mrs. Julia Dent Grant.
Courtesy U. S. Military Academy

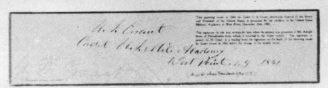

Water-color drawing by U. S. Grant, Cadet, Class of 1843, U. S. Military Academy

Trading with the Indians

"This painting made in 1841 by Cadet U. S. Grant, afterwards General of the Army and President of the United States, is presented by his children to the United States Military Academy at West Point December 25, 1902.

"The signature in ink was written by him when the picture was presented to Mr. Adolph Borie of Philadelphia from whom it reverted to the Grant family. The signature in pencil—U. H. Grant—is a tracing from the signature on the back of the drawing made by Cadet Grant in 1841 before the change of his middle initial."

Original Grant signature on the reverse side of the painting which was presented to the Academy by his children on December 25, 1902

105

Photograph by Mathew Brady. Author's collection

Major General William Tecumseh Sherman, Commander of the Military Division of the Mississippi

The great invader who, with 60,000 men, marched from Atlanta to the sea, in one of the greatest military marches in history.

Courtesy U. S. Military Academy

Copy from the Antique

Drawn by Cadet William T. Sherman, Class of 1840.

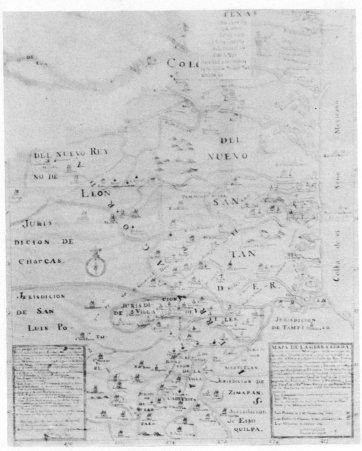

From the original map. Courtesy Confederate Memorial Museum

Map of La Sierra Gorda, Mexico

Drawn by Cadet Robert E. Lee, Class of 1829.

General Robert Edward Lee, Commander in Chief, Army of Northern Virginia, C.S.A.

Former Superintendent of the Military Academy at West Point, Robert E. Lee resigned his commission and became commander of the Confederate forces.

From a photograph by Mathew Brady made after the surrender at Appomattox, on the back porch of the Lee residence in Richmond. Author's collection

Major General George Gordon Meade

Commander of the Army of the Potomac
at Gettysburg, Pennsylvania, July 1, 1863.

Photograph by Mathew Brady. Author's collection

Courtesy U. S. Military Academy

View of a Town

Drawn by Cadet George Gordon Meade, Class of 1835.

Courtesy U. S. Military Academy

Copy from the Antique

Drawing by Cadet Jefferson Davis, Class of 1828.

Jefferson Davis

Former Secretary of War of the United States;
Colonel, United States Army; and President of
the Confederate States of America.

Photograph by Mathew Brady. Author's collection

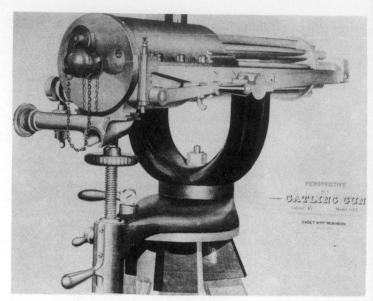

Perspective of a Gatling gun
Caliber .45—Model 1877

By Cadet Wirt Robinson, Class of 1887.
Drawn under the direction of Professor Charles W. Larned.

Perspective view of a field howitzer

Drawn under the direction of Professor Charles W. Larned, U.S.M.A.,
by Cadet I. W. Littel, Class of 1883.

Perspective view of a Gruson turret
In process of construction, showing exterior, Fort Longlutjen.

Drawn and colored by Cadet Peyton C. March, Class of 1888, under the direction of
Professor Charles W. Larned, U.S.M.A., June, 1888.

Elevation of a 10 horse
Baxter engine, scale 1:3

Drawn under the direction of Professor Charles W.
Larned, U.S.M.A., by Cadet Lawton M. Fuller,
Class of 1891.

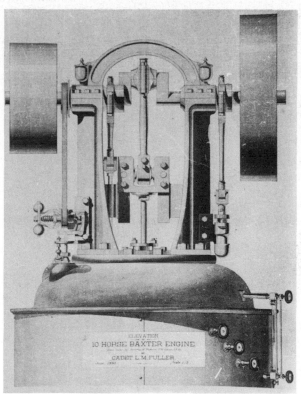

III

6

On the Banks
of the Rio Grande

The Mexican War

1846–1848

James Walker, and Lieutenant Henry N. Walke of the bomb-brig *Vesuvius,* dominate the artists' record of the battlegrounds and scenes of the war with Mexico. One an artist-interpreter, the other a naval officer-illustrator, though they did not know each other, had one thing in common—illustrating the war in paintings, lithographs, and water colors.

The Mexican War began in 1846, its causes many and varied. Since the days of De Soto and Cortez, Mexico had languished under fearfully despotic Spanish rule. Laws for Mexico, enacted in Spain, were executed with cruelty and treachery. After years of bloody resistance, Mexico finally won her independence.

Mexico's ordeal, however, did not end with freedom from her Spanish tormentors. Texas and New Mexico, within her boundaries, and empires in territory, became the objects of the next land grab of her growing neighbor to the north. Texan colonists, former American citizens who received grants to settle the territory, flouted Mexican laws and openly engaged in slavery even though the Mexican republic did not sanction the institution. Savage border warfare flared up between Texas and Mexico. To fight the war, Texans organized a military force, routed the Mexican Army at San Jacinto, and captured Mexican President Santa Anna. Elated by her victory, but realizing she could not hold the territory for long, Texas declared her independence and then

offered herself to the United States. On July 4, 1845, the United States announced the annexation of Texas. Mexico denounced the partition of her territory, and after months of bitter dispute over boundary lines ordered her army to the Rio Grande.

President James Knox Polk ordered General Zachary Taylor at Fort Jessup, Louisiana, to prepare an army of occupation for a march into Texas; the army's goal was the Rio Grande at Matamoros. Taylor's small force, consisting of four regiments of artillery, five regiments of infantry, and a regiment of dragoons, less than 4,000 men of all arms, established itself at Corpus Christi Bay, near the mouth of the Nueces River.

Many of Taylor's soldiers and officers had little sympathy with this action of their government. Lieutenant Ulysses S. Grant of the Fourth Regiment of Infantry, realizing the military aspects of the situation, was keenly aware of the political intent as well. "We were sent to provoke a fight," he wrote, "but it was essential that Mexico commence it. It was very doubtful whether Congress would declare war; but if Mexico should attack our troops, the Executive could announce, 'Whereas, war exists by acts of, etc.,' and prosecute the contest with vigor. Once initiated there were but few public men who would have the courage to oppose it. . . . " Lieutenant Grant further observed after a long period of boredom and inactivity at Corpus Christi that "Mexico showing no willingness to come to the Nueces to drive the 'invaders' from her soil, it became necessary . . . to approach within convenient distance to be struck. Accordingly, preparations were begun for moving the army to the Rio Grande, to a point near Matamoras."

The march of the American army to the Rio Grande was weary and painful—the ground underfoot hot sand broken by volcanic rock and covered with mesquite, jimson weed, and cactus. There was no enthusiasm among the men. The sun got hotter and the men's thirsts got sharper. "We had fourteen miles to march to get water," wrote Captain Henry, "and were forced to halt repeatedly;—and the men sat down with parched mouths upon the hot sand, with the tropical sun beating down on them. The prairie had a few sickly blades of grass upon it;—the sand was like hot ashes, and when you stepped upon it you sank up to the ankles. The last two miles I could not help but pity the men; many gave out and lay down by the roadside, perfectly exhausted and looking as if they did not care for life."

Sometimes the soldiers would see mirages of ships reflected in the sky from the Gulf 60 miles away. When the army had marched 125 miles the men ahead saw the chaparral, bluffs 30 feet high or more covered with dense thickets and dwarf evergreen oak stretching for miles, snarled, twisted, and forbidding, infested with poisonous snakes and other reptiles. Near-by was the Little Colorado River. At the base of the chaparral the advance columns were halted. Some men of the Fourth Regiment broke ranks and made a rush for the stream. Plunging their heads into the water to drink, the soldiers found it salt. The army halted long enough for the engineers to cut a roadway through the bluffs to the water's edge. The road completed, the army crossed the river, unopposed; but as the "Yanquis" scrambled up the opposite bank, the Mexican soldiers kept up a continual blowing of bugles and shouting to give the impression of a large army. Once on the opposite side, the Americans made camp and waited two days for the ox-drawn supply wagons to catch up.

Then began the final march of 30 miles to the Rio Grande. The going was now much better and the men's spirits rose. Marching four abreast, the soldiers presented a spectacle not soon forgotten by those who participated. The desert gave way to green grass, thick underfoot. Beautiful cactus blossoms of red and gold showed in bursts of color. As the long columns moved southward, the sun, setting in the west, backlighted the silhouettes of blue uniforms against the flowering acacia, casting soft shadows on the bright grass. Captain Henry wrote of the following morning: "I do not think I have ever felt a sweeter or fresher morning. The morning-star and moon were about setting; the former, even as day broke, looked like a diamond set in a clear blue sky . . . the country was beautiful . . . the air from the sea was delightful, and everything in nature appeared so happy, that it was perfectly exhilarating." But the harsh note of war broke in on this reverie. A rumor ran through the ranks that a force of 10,000 Mexicans were awaiting the "Yanquis." At last the army was drawn up on the bank of the Rio Grande. Across the river was Matamoros.

The scene was one to gladden the heart of the painter of military epics. American sentries, posted at the river bank in full sight of the Mexican sentries across the river, saw the gleaming white, flower-covered walls of beautiful buildings. On tiled roof tops, Mexican soldiers, in colorful red and green uniforms and wearing large sombreros, stared across the stream at the soldiers in blue. Companies of Mexican soldiers marched through the streets behind blaring brass bands. The gardens, riots of color, further tempered the martial background.

But the idyllic pause ended abruptly with the arrival of General Mariano Arista at Matamoros. The American camp experienced a somber moment when the body of Major Trueman Cross, "the first victim of the Mexican War," was discovered by searching parties a short distance from the river. The body "had been stripped, and flesh afterwards torn off by vultures, recognizable only by portions of clothing, scalp and teeth." The remains of Major Cross were later brought into camp and buried with military honors on the right bank of the river "in sight of both armies." The event cast a cloak of gloom over both armies. Matters remained fairly quiet until Mexico declared "defensive war" against the United States. Then, on April 24, General Arista ordered General Torrejón, with a heavy detachment, to cross the Rio Grande at La Palangana, six miles above Matamoros. The following day Captain Thornton and a small scouting party of dragoons flushed a Mexican detachment. One of Thornton's officers and sixteen men were killed, the rest captured. General Torrejón, anxious to take the initiative, marched to Palo Alto. About noon of May 8, Taylor came upon the Mexican army in battle formation. The weak Mexican left flank became Taylor's point of attack. Torrejón attempted an attack on the right and rear of the American army but was repulsed with loss by the Fifth Infantry.

Taylor soon discovered that his force was outnumbered and getting the worst of it, until the prairie grass was set afire by the exploding shells. Screened by the smoke, the Mexican army broke off the battle and fell back to Matamoros. Taylor, close on their heels, attacked them again the next day. There began the battle of Resaca de la Palma. Lieutenant Grant wrote of his first experience under fire.

"On the ninth of May about noon we left the field of battle [Palo Alto] and started on our way to Matamoras. When we advanced about six miles we found that the enemy had taken up a new position in the midst of a dense wood, and as we have since learned they had received a reinforcement equal to our whole numbers.

"Grape shot and musket balls were let fly from both sides making dreadful havoc. Our men continued to advance and did advance in spite of the shots, to the very mouths of the cannon and killed and took prisoner the Mexicans with them, and drove off with their own teams, taking cannon, ammunition and all to our side. In this way nine of their big guns were taken and their own ammunition turned against them. The Mexicans fought hard for an hour and a half but seeing their means of war fall from their hands in spite of all their efforts they finally commenced to retreat helter skelter. A great many retreated to the banks of the Rio Grande and without looking for means of crossing plunged into the water and no doubt many of them were drowned.

"After the battle the woods were strewed with the dead. . . . How many wagon loads [of bodies] have already come in and how many are left would be too hard to guess. . . ."

The battles which James Walker illustrated, fought in the Valley of Mexico, would today be considered minor affairs of arms. The main engagements took place at Buena Vista, Vera Cruz, Contreras, Churubusco (a costly blunder), and Chapultepec, the most unusual battle of the war. In these battles Zachary Taylor and Winfield Scott demonstrated the power of an ably handled, small, aggressive force. The American army fought its way across hostile desert country between the forbidding ranges of the Sierra Madre. The country was dry desert of bare flinty rocks, mesquite infested with snakes and lizards.

After the battle of Monterey, General Taylor, at Victoria, received a dispatch from General Scott ordering most of his troops "to assist that Officer in his contemplated attack on Vera Cruz." With a small force, Taylor remained at Monterey until January, 1847. General Santa Anna, after a brush with a detachment of Taylor's main force near Saltillo, marched for Buena Vista.

Buena Vista, a small farm or rancho, was situated five miles west of Saltillo, on the road to San Luis Potosí. American supply trains and baggage were stationed here. In a narrow valley of broad tableland, surrounded on three sides by high mountains, Buena Vista was almost inaccessible to attack. The American army, drawn up in battle array on this broad plateau, with artillery in the center and on each flank, received a desperate charge by Mexican cavalry and a column of nearly 2,000 infantry. The

American artillery did fearful execution. The wily General Santa Anna then called a truce which enabled him to change the position of his army, moving it northward over the hills in perfect order of battle near the American left flank.

Then took place one of the grandest spectacles seen by the American troops in the entire war. The Mexican soldiers, "their new uniforms and burnished arms, glittering in the morning sun, and quivering with thousands of reflections, seemed like a sea of steel:—while the rows of cavalry presented a pomp and grandeur of appearance far beyond anything in the American army. All morning long they continued to arrive, until the whole southern horizon blazed on every side with this intolerable splendor of their arms." But no attack came that day. All that night the Americans bivouacked on the bleak ground and rocks, without fires and on their arms. The night was excessively cold. Now and then a scream was heard through the stillness of the night when a vulture "moved heavily through the gloom of the battlefield attacking the wounded of the day before."

The battle opened noisily the next morning. Thousands of Mexican soldiers, pouring out of the defiles and mountain passes, attacked the American lines in an effort at annihilation. American cannon, firing grape and canister, swept men and horses to destruction. Three thousand Mexican infantrymen poured showers of bullets into the American lines. No matter how many gaps were ripped open in the Mexican lines by the American batteries, the ranks were filled up almost at once by fresh soldiers. At one time the Mexican cavalry, in dress uniforms, their arms glittering in the bright sun, dashed into the lines of Colonel Jefferson Davis' riflemen. Volleys from hundreds of rifles brought mangled heaps of Mexican cavalrymen and horses tumbling to the ground, screaming horses crushing the wounded and dying beneath their hooves. The fearful slaughter caused by the American artillery halted the Mexican attack for the moment. Then the Mexican army again opened the battle with thrilling intensity. Finally, after ten hours of furious fighting, the Mexicans withdrew to the hills.

The night was one of horror. The chill night air was filled with the piercing shrieks of the wounded. Every defile and gully, filled with the dead and the helpless wounded, attracted wolves and coyotes to the battlefield. The next morning the Mexican army was gone.

Vera Cruz and its fortress of San Juan de Ulloa were 123 miles away, on the coast. The next campaign was the reduction of this Mexican stronghold, a formidable position with "three hundred cannon" covering the channel of approach from the sea. The fortress of San Juan de Ulloa "had walls five yards in thickness," with 52 cannon, "impervious to shot as the sides of Mount Orizaba." On March 9, the American flotilla, with 2,800 men, arrived at Vera Cruz.

Aboard the U.S. bomb-brig *Vesuvius* was a young naval officer and talented artist, Lieutenant Henry N. Walke, the only naval officer to make a complete pictorial record of the naval operations of the Mexican War. In command of the *Vesuvius,* Lieutenant Walke took part in the actions on the winding, treacherous Tabasco River which finally ended in the battle for Vera Cruz. The men were transferred from the ships to the surfboats for the landing on the beaches.

One of the most startling things about Lieutenant Walke's water colors is the similarity of the amphibious landings to those made on the Pacific atolls in World War II. The only apparent difference is the type of ship, the paddle-wheel steamer towing landing barges being replaced by the Landing Ship, Tanks. The U.S. naval vessels *Spitfire* and *Vixen* and five gunboats ran close to shore to cover the landing. On March 22, General Scott opened bombardment of the city. All that night the bombardment continued, the bombs "flying into Vera Cruz like hail," every naval gun concentrated on the city with terrible effect. The next morning saw Vera Cruz in ruins. The governor, persuaded to capitulate by the civilian population, surrendered the city to General Scott; and the Mexicans evacuated the city, marched to an open plain, stacked their arms, and proceeded toward the interior.

The great event of the war, the one that captured the country's imagination, was the taking of Chapultepec, outside Mexico City, in September. Chapultepec was a formidable position. It stood on "a high swell of ground near the center of an irregular basin, and is girdled with a ditch in its greatest extent—a navigable canal of great breadth and depth —very difficult to bridge in the presence of an enemy." On top of this great mound, the "Hill of Grasshoppers," stood the Military Academy of Mexico. General Scott ordered General Quitman's division to join that of General Pillow, *"by daylight,"* before the southern gates to attract Mexican fire from the garrison and to deceive the enemy as to the real point of attack. The whole army was then divided into two sections, "each performing duties distinct from the other."

Scott opened a heavy bombardment on the southern side of the fortress, preventing the arrival of Mexican reinforcements from without or escape from within. The bombardment continued until nightfall. In the meantime the Mexican garrison held themselves in readiness on the hill and awaited the assault. At eight o'clock on the morning of September 13, the American forces assaulted the fortress by storm. The Mexican batteries opened fire and swept the front of the attacking troops, but the enemy was steadily driven from shelter to shelter. Armed with scaling ladders, the American regulars fought their way to their objectives. The Mexican batteries, behind the walls, poured shells and shot over the heads of the American soldiers. When the Americans reached the top, the fighting became hand to hand. Swords, bayonets, and clubbed rifles came into play. For a while, friend and foe mingled in one great struggling mass. The desperate Mexican resistance came to nothing. Before long the heights of Chapultepec were carried, and the enemy surrendered.

Chapultepec was the last great battle of the war. There followed the attack on Mexico City, the siege of Puebla, the action at La Paz, and Atalixco which ended the war.

From an original painting by James Walker. Courtesy Office of Military History, Department of the Army

March from Puebla in the order they were on the road

After the battle and occupation of Puebla, Winfield Scott decided to push on into Mexico. Ahead, he knew he faced at least 20,000 Mexican troops. General Worth's division marched out on August 9, followed by Pillow's division, one day behind the division of Quitman. On the march a heavy fog, "an immense inland sea," settled over them. When the fog lifted the soldiers were greeted with an awesome spectacle. One of Quitman's men described it as "a great garden dotted with bright lakes, fields of emerald, and white domes and glittering spires of the villages that environ the Mexican Capitol City . . . far to the south, gleaming like snow—tiny Mexican Lancers moved slowly among olive groves and straggling villages."

From an original painting by James Walker. Courtesy Office of Military History, Department of the Army

Detour around Lake Chalco

The advanced brigades of Garland and Quitman made camp on the shores of Lake Chalco for three days. Meanwhile General Scott, at his headquarters near another lakeside, dispatched dragoons and engineers to look for the best approach to Mexico City. Scott decided that the approach should be made by way of the southern route, thinking it would be less costly in the lives of his soldiers, though the way was laid through swamps and rocks.

From an original painting by James Walker. Courtesy Office of Military History, Department of the Army

Camp of Valencia Contreras

Here at Contreras, General Worth received orders to demonstrate up the Acapulco Road, while the rest of the army passed around to the south. Santa Anna, divining Scott's plan, blocked the army at the village of Contreras. For two days the army bombarded the mountain breastworks. By noon of the third day, the Mexicans fled. Captain Robert E. Lee, who had "a peculiar talent for topography," won distinction here by his efforts to chart the roads under the most dangerous conditions, performing the "greatest feats of physical and moral courage . . ."

117

From an original painting by James Walker. Courtesy Office of Military History, Department of the Army

Convent of Churubusco, Mexico

The Convent of San Pablo at Churubusco made a powerful fortress. "We rushed our heads against Churubusco," Richard Stoddart Ewell wrote home, "and a bloody field it was." Here the men were shot down by rows of hidden Mexican gunners along the high banks on the riverside. To the red-haired Nathaniel Lyon, "Our advance through the corn was necessarily confused, so that, when within range of the enemy's guns, we were compelled to stand exposed to fire from men concealed in the maguey plants, behind breastworks, and in the Convent." It was 6,000 Americans against 15,000 Mexicans. "We must succeed or the army is lost," said Lieutenant Colonel Ethan Allan Hitchcock. As if by a miracle the Mexican fire slackened from lack of ammunition. The American attack was pressed and the Mexicans broke and fled.

118

From an original painting by James Walker. Courtesy Office of Military History, Department of the Army

Molino del Rey, Mexico

The main objective of the U. S. Army, before reaching Mexico City, was the formidable chief Mexican fortress of Chapultepec. The building was the Mexican Military College situated on the "Hill of the Grasshoppers," an elevation of about 200 feet. One of the defenses at the foot of this fortress was a group of stone buildings called El Molino del Rey—the King's Mill. Here Santa Anna was making cannon from bronze church bells. A spy informed Scott that a surprise attack could put a stop to this work. After a brief preliminary shelling with two cannon, and believing the building to be lightly garrisoned, General Worth ordered a charge. General George Wright, with the 4th Infantry, attacked. Suddenly, his whole front blazed with cannon and musket fire. In five minutes of action Wright lost thirteen officers and nearly half of his men. It was the blackest moment of the war. Finally, a regiment under Captain E. Kirby Smith, in a desperate sortie, routed the enemy.

General Gideon Pillow's attack—advancing through the woods of Chapultepec

On the night of September 11, U. S. Army Engineers hauled cannon close to Chapultepec. On the following day General Scott opened a heavy bombardment on the fortress. Next morning, at five o'clock, the volunteer divisions of Pillow and Quitman, shouting and cheering, running through a grove of cypress trees under heavy fire from the Mexican fort, charged up the "Hill of the Grasshoppers." General Pillow received a minor wound in the foot. His men, however, had suffered a lapse of memory, for they had forgotten to bring the scaling ladders and had to cower at the base of the fortress, pinned down by Mexican gunfire. Finally the scaling ladders were brought to them. From that point the charge up the hill was successful, and the Mexican defenders were overwhelmed.

South side of the castle of Chapultepec

From an original painting by James Walker. Courtesy Office of Military History, Department of the Army

North side of the castle of Chapultepec

Scene of the action of Robert Garland's brigade, which circled around to the north side of Chapultepec to block the San Cosme route to Mexican reinforcements. Lieutenant Tom Jackson, the "Stonewall" Jackson of Civil War fame, was seen by Garland standing in the middle of a pile of dead and dying horses working a cannon his men had deserted, they being unable to stand the Mexican fire. Garita de Belen was the strongest of the *garitas*, as the Mexicans called their gates

From an original painting by James Walker. Courtesy Office of Military History, Department of the Army

South side of the Garita de Belen

From an original painting by James Walker. Courtesy Office of Military History, Department of the Army

North side of the Garita de Belen

From an original painting by James Walker. Courtesy Office of Military History, Department of the Army

Aqueduct

Fighting was heavy around the Aqueduct in the attack on Chapultepec. Built of heavy white masonry, it was a causeway which ran down the center of a carriage road and supplied Mexico City with water. The one appearing in the painting is near El Molino del Rey. Scott's troops can be seen here seeking protection under the archways. On the road are the dead and wounded of Scott's command, lying where they fell.

122

James Walker

Combat artist and interpreter with
the American Army in Mexico,
1846–1848.

General Zachary Taylor

Commander of the United States
Army in its march to Mexico,
1846–1848.

General Winfield Scott

Commander in chief, United States Army,
in the war with Mexico.

Battle of Buena Vista, Mexico

Buena Vista was a victory for General Zachary Taylor, "Old Rough and Ready." General Scott, on March 15, received word that "Old Zach," with only 6,000 men, had whipped Santa Anna, whose force numbered more than 15,000. "Old Zach's" losses amounted to no more than 600 as against 4,000 for Santa Anna. One of the most colorful battles of the Mexican War, it was Zachary Taylor's fourth victory since entering Mexico with his army.

The United States naval battery during the bombardment of Vera Cruz on the 24th and 25th of March, 1847

The battery was composed of heavy guns from the U. S. squadron under Commodore M. C. Perry.

124

The United States steam frigate *Mississippi*, Commodore M. C. Perry

Going out to the relief of the American steamer *Hunter*, a French bark (her prize), and an American
pilot boat wrecked on Green Island Reef near Vera Cruz, March 21, 1847.

From an original painting by Lieutenant Henry N. Walke. Courtesy U. S. Naval Academy Museum

The United States naval expedition under Commodore M. C. Perry

Ascending the Tuspan River, destroying the forts, and taking possession of the Port of Tuspan, with the following vessels and their commanders: Steamer *Spitfire,* Commodore J. Tattnall; Steamer *Vixen,* Commodore J. R. Sands; Steamer *Scourge,* Lieutenant commanding J. S. Lockwood; Schooner *Reefer,* Lieutenant commanding T. Turner; Schooner *Bonita,* Lieutenant commanding T. G. Benham; Schooner *Tampico,* Lieutenant commanding Wm. P. Griffin; Schooner *Petrel,* Lieutenant commanding T. D. Shaw; with a detachment of officers and men in 35 barges from the U. S. Steamer *Mississippi,* Commodore A. S. Mackenzie and Lieutenant A. De Camp; *Ohio,* Commander L. M. Goldsborough; *Potomac,* Lieutenant E. R. Tompson; *Raritan,* Captain C. F. Forrest; *Albany,* Captain S. L. Breese; *Germantown,* Commander F. Buchanan; *John Adams,* Commander Wm. J. M. Clancy; *Decatur,* Commodore R. S. Pinckney; Bomb-Brig *Vesuvius,* Commander G. M. Magruder; Bomb-Brig *Etna,* Commander G. J. Van Brunt; Bomb-Brig *Hecla,* Lieutenant Commander A. B. Fairfax. Mexico, April 19th, 1847.

From an original lithograph by Lieutenant Henry N. Walke. Courtesy U. S. Naval Academy Museum

The United States steamers *Scorpion, Spitfire, Vixen,* and *Scourge:*

with 40 barges in tow, crossing the bar at the mouth of the Tobasco [Tabasco] River (Mexico)

Commodore M. C. Perry in command, supported by the commands of Captains J. Mayo, S. L. Breese, F. Forrest; Commanders Wm. J. McCluney, A. Bigelow, F. Buchanan, H. A. Adams, A. S. Mackenzie, G. A. Magruder, C. J. Van Brunt; Lieutenants commanding S. S. Lee, S. Lockwood, and J. M. Berrien, June 14th, 1847.

From a lithograph by Lieutenant Henry N. Walke. Courtesy U. S. Naval Academy Museum

Commodore M. C. Perry's naval expedition ascending the winding Tabasco River, June, 1847

The steam frigate *Mississippi,* followed by the *Scorpion* and *Scourge,* leading the procession of schooners and bomb-brigs up the winding Tabasco River. Each steam-driven vessel is towing its own complement of troop-laden barges.

From a lithograph by Lieutenant Henry N. Walke. Courtesy U. S. Naval Academy Museum

The attack of the Mexicans from the chaparral
on the First Division of the naval expedition to Tabasco, June, 1847

The U. S. S. *Scorpion,* Commodore Perry, Captain Breese, and Commander Bigelow, and Bomb-Brig *Vesuvius,* Commander Magruder, with Brig *Washington,* repel an attack by the Mexicans from the chaparral. Following the *Scorpion* are three barges with detachments of seamen and Marines from the Steam Frigate *Mississippi,* under Commanders Mackenzie and H. A. Adams. The detachment of Marines was commanded by Captain Edson.

From a drawing by Lieutenant Henry N. Walke. Courtesy U. S. Naval Academy Museum

The naval expedition under Commodore Perry ascending the
Tabasco River at the Devil's Bend, June 15, 1847

Drawing made the following day, showing the position of the Second Division of the
fleet in the advance up the Tabasco River, Mexico, 1847.

United States warships at anchor in the Tabasco River,
Tabasco in the background, Mexico, June, 1847

This tranquil scene shows the United States warships at anchor after the capture of the City of Tabasco, Mexico. In the right foreground is the captured Mexican fort guarding the entrance, now flying the American flag.

7

"The Brave Men, Living and Dead"

The Civil War

1861–1865

"A dog fight now might cause the gutters of the Capital to run with blood," said aging General Winfield Scott to an aide before the Electoral College was to announce whether or not Abraham Lincoln of Illinois would be certified as president of the United States. Such was the tension in the nation's capital on February 13, 1861, on the eve of the Civil War. The smoldering resentment of the southern states toward the northern states' interference with the institution of slavery had reached the point where, at St. Andrew's Hall, in Charleston, South Carolina, in secret session the Ordinance of Secession was passed without debate in 45 minutes.

On March 4, 1861, Chief Justice Roger Taney administered the oath of office to President-elect Abraham Lincoln, and the guns that fired the salute to the sixteenth president of the United States also ushered in one of the bloodiest wars in which the nation has ever taken part. "In *your* hands, my dissatisfied countrymen, and not in *mine,*" said President Lincoln in his First Inaugural Address, "is the momentous issue of civil war. . . ."

On April 12, 1861, Edmund Ruffin of Virginia pulled the lanyard of a cannon aimed at Fort Sumter and the war began.

Standing on a forlorn patch of ground called Gapland, near South Mountain, Maryland, is a somber monument commemorating the correspondents and artists of the Civil War. Designed and built by George Alfred Townsend, a war correspondent, the monument towers fifty feet in the air on the summit of a mountain. Terra cotta horse's heads, and niches containing small statues representing Mercury, Poetry, and Electricity, embellish its façade. Its motif, essentially not like any other, is Moorish, and the monument is capped by Roman arches and a turret. On both sides of the great arch are marble tablets containing the names of 157 war correspondents and artists who left a remarkable record of drawings, sketches, and stories of that war.

Among the artists commemorated are Winslow Homer, Alfred R. Waud, Edwin Forbes, Theodore R. Davis, James E. Taylor, and Frank Schell. Soldier-artists whose names do not appear on the roster but who took part in the fortunes and misfortunes of the Army of the Potomac were Colonel Julian Scott, U. S. V.; Captain James Hope, Company B, 2nd Vermont Volunteers; Corporal J. Nep Roesler, Color Guard, Company G, 47th Regiment, Ohio Volunteers; Lieutenant James Dickinson; Captain Alexander Lawrie, 121st Pennsylvania Infantry, and Lieutenant Frederic F. Cavada, 14th Pennsylvania Volunteers.

Combat artists without military rank or rating who, nevertheless, were "attached" to the Army were David Gilmour Blythe and Eastman Johnson.

Outstanding military artists in the Confederate service were Lieutenant Allen Carter Redwood, 55th Regiment, Virginia, and Sergeant Conrad Wise Chapman, 59th Regiment, Wise's Brigade.

Alfred R. Waud and Theodore R. Davis were

among the first war artists to sketch the opening military actions. Theodore Davis was at Charleston for *Harper's Weekly* and witnessed the drama taking place at Fort Sumter, and Alfred Waud's participation in the first battle of Bull Run is testified to by Mathew B. Brady, the Washington society photographer who embarked on the venture of making a pictorial history of the tragic conflict. "I went to the first battle of Bull Run," he told George Alfred Townsend, the correspondent, "with two wagons from Washington. My companions were Dick McCormick, a newspaper writer, Ned House, and Al. Waud, the sketch artist. . . ."

At the outset the battle of Bull Run or Manassas seemed like an act in a comic opera. The Union army approached the field of battle hilariously. Napoleon's colorful hordes could not challenge the originality and striking appearance of this nondescript American army. The 79th New York Highlanders marched in plaid fatigues, their colonels in kilts. The 11th New York, as French Colonial Zouaves, marched in bright red pantaloons, white gaiters, and blue kepis. The Garibaldi Guards marched in the uniforms of the Italian Carabinieri; the Fighting 69th marched "stripped to the pants"; Michigan regiments came as lumberjacks, sheath knives and horse pistols stuffed in their belts. One New York regiment sported light summer suits and straw hats. The only professional soldiers were two regiments of U. S. regulars.

This untrained, undisciplined army, commanded by General Irvin McDowell, himself a novice at war, looted houses, violated every regulation, and talked back to their officers. To Colonel William T. Sherman, commanding the Third Brigade, "there was no greater curse than an invasion by a volunteer army." The day was unbearably hot, the sky like brass, and "ambling along the dusty turnpike in the wake of the army, came the white-topped wagon train, and in its midst rolled Brady's two photographic wagons. . . ." On the wagon box rode Brady, Waud, and Dick McCormick. Crowds of spectators, congressmen, their wives in crinoline carrying lunch hampers, rode to the battlefield in horse and buggy; but the picnic was short-lived.

The battle began explosively, civilian gaiety swallowed up in the crises of dangerous military effort. Men shot and mangled, screaming with pain, were no less terrifying to Colonel Sherman than "horses running about with blood streaming from their nostrils or lying on the ground hitched to guns, gnawing their sides in death." The battle raged all that day in the hot sun, swirling in a tornado about the Henry House and Henry Hill.

Crossing Stone Bridge, Brady and Waud saw the battlefield strewn with dead men and horses, all about them the sickening confusion seen in battle.

Victory, within the grasp of the Union army, was lost when Colonel T. J. Jackson and his brigade of Virginians, hiding quietly behind a stone wall, on command suddenly fired a disciplined blast of rifle fire into a charging column of Union troops. What began as a retirement became a stampede. Yankee soldiers, streaming across Stone Bridge, overturned wagons and carriages in their haste to escape.

Attempts by the officers to avert panic were useless. Fleeing soldiers, catching the panic of the civilians, dazed with fright and mortification, swarmed down the roads to Washington, crossed Long Bridge over the Potomac, and dropped exhausted on the streets and sidewalks of the capital city. In the wake of the stragglers came Waud and Brady. Some days later their pictures and drawings appeared in *Harper's Weekly,* signed "A. R. W." and "From a photograph by Brady." For the next few years their signatures would underline many war pictures.

THE KANAWHA CAMPAIGN

September 1861

J. "Nep" Roesler, Company G, 47th Regiment, Ohio Volunteers, "sketched from nature" the pictorial record of a little known campaign fought in a wild region of the Kanawha Valley, West Virginia. The battle took place near Carnifex Ferry, on the Gauley River, between the forces of General William Starke Rosecrans and General John B. Floyd.

Rosecrans fought his battle near Carnifex Ferry in deep, tangled woods, heavy enemy artillery fire accounting for the deaths of 17 and the wounding of 141 of his men. Floyd retreated during the night, having to ease his artillery down a steep cliffside in darkness. After crossing the Gauley River on flatboats, he sank them when his army was safely on the other side. Floyd then retired to Big Sewell. Rosecrans, close on his heels, crossed the river, scaled the mountain, fought for and secured a position just below the summit. Rosecrans' determined assault again forced Floyd to retire and there ended the Kanawha campaign. Corporal Roesler completed his portfolio of sketches of the operation from which he made his lithographic stones. His drawings were entered in the Clerk's Office of the Southern District of Ohio, and printed in a limited number of copies by Ehrgott, Forbriger & Company, Cincinnati.

THE PENINSULA CAMPAIGN

When the Civil War broke out, Winslow Homer accepted a position as artist-correspondent for *Harper's Weekly*. The Provost Marshal in Washington issued the customary pass, and Homer joined McClellan's Army of the Potomac and sailed on an army transport for Fortress Monroe. McClellan fought a minor action at Big Bethel, then laid siege to York-town; and Homer, attached to the staff of young Colonel Francis Barlow, witnessed the action from the fortifications.

Homer remained with the army until the evacuation of Yorktown on May 3, when McClellan, finding no enemy on his front, moved up the peninsula toward Richmond. Winslow Homer then returned to New York, where in his studio, working from drawings made in the field, he made his paintings. Homer did not return to the army until Grant's battle in the Wilderness, in 1864. There are no drawings published in *Harper's Weekly* during the following two years to indicate that Homer was with the army during this period.

THE SEVEN DAYS' BATTLES

The battles of the Seven Days, which began at Beaver Dam Creek on June 25, 1862, were a series of sanguinary engagements fought in Virginia from Gaines' Mill just outside Richmond to Harrison's Landing on the James River. Lieutenant Allen Carter Redwood, one of the finest draughtsmen to emerge during the war, served with the Confederate Army in the 55th Regiment, Virginia, as courier and aide to Major General Lensford L. Lomax. An entertaining writer, Allen Redwood later wrote of his first experience under fire:

"The first engagement in which the writer took a modest part had been entirely forseen. . . . it was the beginning of a series which resulted in frustrating McClellan's campaign on the peninsula and raising the siege of Richmond in 1862. We had been holding the left of the Confederate line on the Meadow Bridge Road, picketing the bridges spanning the fork of the Chicahominy at this point—, a Union picket post being at the crossing of another branch, about a hundred yards distant, and in plain view from our outpost . . . it was the turn of our regiment for this duty . . . holding the advance post at the bridges. Thus when the advance began, we were the first to cross the river

"Thus far we had seen no Federals except the picket, which had promptly retired before our advance . . . the column, marching in fours, was halted in a shallow cut in the road . . . someone called an order to 'clear the road for artillery!' A wild scramble up the banks ensued, under the apprehension that we were about to be raked by McClellan's guns. Meanwhile, we had formed a line on the right of the road and approached the wooded camp-site in which, as we supposed, the foe was concealed and awaiting us. When almost up to it, some excited soldier discharged his musket; at once, and without orders, the entire right wing of the regiment blazed away at the numerous collection of tent-poles,

cracker-boxes, reminders of its late occupation. At that time there probably was not a Federal soldier nearer than the further side of Beaver Dam Creek, nearly a mile distant. . . .

"We were halted again just beyond a dip of the ground through which coursed a small rivulet, and some of us took the opportunity to fill canteens . . . while waiting there we received the first hostile shots from the guns beyond the creek. They soon got our range and it began to look like real war at last. At this point, for the first time, I saw a man killed in battle. We were standing to arms awaiting orders to advance; another regiment of the brigade was supporting us a short distance to the rear—the Sixtieth Virginia, under Colonel Starke, who was killed later at Sharpsburg. A shell plowed the crest of the elevation in front, and our line made a profound obeisance as it passed over . . . as I ducked I glanced back and witnessed its effect. . . .

"The body of a stalwart young fellow suddenly disappeared, and on the ground where he had stood was a confused mass of quivering limbs which presently lay still—the same shell as I learned afterward, carried away the top of a man's head in our own regiment.

"Another took effect soon after, as we were moving out by the left flank, knocking over several men and killing one of them. By this time the fire had grown quite brisk, and we lost more men as we lay in the open field before entering some woods still more to the left, where the regiment commenced firing, against an imaginary foe, I have cause to believe. Yet, these same skittish troops, under fire for the first time just four days later charged and captured a regular battery of twelve-pounder guns and were complimented on the field by General Longstreet. . . ."

The battle developed into a raging inferno of hissing steel and crashing explosives. McClellan's army, along the entire front, fell back slowly and began a retrograde movement that ended in disaster at Harrison's Landing, down-river from Richmond. McClellan, on the morning of June 27, was attacked by the entire Confederate army. Stuart's cavalry fell on his right and turned it at Old Church. McClellan then formed a new line of battle from Gaines House along Mill Road to New Cold Harbor. By three o'clock that afternoon his whole army had been driven back two miles.

"Their fire never slackened nor abated," wrote George Alfred Townsend. "They loaded and moved forward, column on column, like so many immortals that could not be vanquished. The scene from the balloon, as Lowe informed me, was awful beyond comparison—of puffing shells and shrieking shrapnel, with volleys that shattered the hills and filled the air with deadly whispers. Infantry, artillery, and horse turned the Federal right from time to time, and to preserve their order of battle the whole line fell back toward Grapevine Bridge.

"It was with difficulty that I could make my way along the narrow corduroy, for hundreds of wounded were limping from the field to the safe side, and ammunition wagons were passing the other way, driven by reckless drivers who should have been blown up momentarily. Before I had reached the north side of the creek, immense throngs of panic-stricken people came surging down the slippery bridge. A few carried muskets, but I saw several wantonly throw their pieces into the flood, and as the mass were unarmed, I inferred that they had made similar dispositions. ... Along the sides of the bridge many of the wounded were washing their wounds in the water; and the cries of the teamsters echoed weirdly through the trees that grew in the river At nine o'clock, we got under way—horsemen, batteries, ambulances, ammunition teams, infantry, and finally some great siege thirty-twos that had been hauled from Gaines's House. One of these pieces broke down the timbers again, and my impression is that it was cast into the current. When we emerged from the swamp timber, the hills before us were found brilliantly illuminated with burning camps."

Some time later, Colonel Julian Scott made a painting of the Union rear-guard action at White Oak Swamp which allowed McClellan time to wreck all the bridges after his hard-pressed troops were across. After Malvern Hill, McClellan made no further attempt to check the Confederate juggernaut. Thus ended the grand enterprise of 1862.

Major General John Pope succeeded McClellan in command of the Army of the Potomac, met Lee on August 30 at Manassas for the second time, lost the sanguinary battle, and paved the way for Lee's invasion of Maryland.

SHARPSBURG OR ANTIETAM

September 13, 1862

Antietam battlefield lies in a little peninsula bounded by Antietam Creek and the Potomac River, a short distance up-river from Harper's Ferry. The Hagerstown Pike runs atop a ridge northward out of town. Within that area are several little valleys that drop eastward from the ridge toward Antietam Creek.

Suddenly, this lovely countryside about Sharpsburg became of vital importance to Lee. For the present the combined forces of Lee, Longstreet, and Daniel Harvey Hill amounted to nearly 18,000 men. McClellan's host numbered 87,000!

Mid-afternoon of September 16, McClellan feinted at Lee's left and ran head on into Hood's veteran "Texicans." By dawn the next morning, Lee's army had increased to 25,000 men. Before sunrise Hooker attacked Jackson on the Confederate left, destroying the brigades of Lawton, Hayes, and Trimble, and opening a large gap in Lee's line. Then a boiling swell of men in blue—Hooker's men—climbing over the post-and-rail fence, rolled down the Hagerstown Pike toward the Dunker Church. Hood's men desperately fought them off, exhausting their ammunition until Mansfield attacked and drove them from the field.

At the critical moment, Lee ordered up the brigades of Anderson and Walker, then four miles away. But the Hagerstown Pike, swept by murderous enfilading fire, proved a terrible obstacle. Sumner's corps attacked again, only to be thrown back by McLaws' reinforcements. In mid-morning McClellan opened his second battle against the Confederate center. Then began the terrible struggle in the "Bloody Lane" where again enfilading fire left windrows of Confederate dead in the fence corners. At 1 P.M. Burnside's men attacked across a stone bridge over the Antietam. Once across they could have turned Lee's right flank. But a miracle happened. Three thousand men, belonging to Ambrose Powell Hill, after a forced march from Harper's Ferry, rushed onto the field and swept Burnside's men down the slopes and back across the bridge. Hill had saved the day. The battle was over by sunset. McClellan, though he had 20,000 troops in reserve, had no further interest in continuing the contest. A month later Lincoln fired him for good.

FREDERICKSBURG

December 13, 1862

The battle of Fredericksburg, on the Rappahannock, was by all odds the greatest Federal military blunder of the war. Charge after charge was ordered by Burnside against Lee's solidly entrenched army on Marye's Heights. Even his own officers, sickened by the wanton, senseless slaughter, balked at carrying out his orders, but not until almost 20,000 men were wounded or dead. The battle raged all afternoon, and the field was littered with the wrecks of men and horses, the dead "rolled out for shelter for the living, dead artillery horses breast-works for little groups of blue-coated men."

With darkness came the end of the battle, but Stonewall Jackson opened a cannonade, the muzzle flashes of his guns scorching the cold night sky. Later that night, as if to illuminate the carnage, the awesome spectacle of the northern lights flickered over the wounded and the dead.

On January 20, 1863, following the disaster at Fredericksburg, there began what was referred to as "Burnside's Mud March," an utterly useless expedition conceived by the hapless General Burnside to turn Lee's flank. A heavy rain began falling at the outset, continuing day and night until the roads were so muddy it was virtually impossible to travel. Many of the soldiers "left their shoes stuck in the mud . . . after they themselves had to be extricated by their comrades." The storm continued unabated until even the artillery and pontoon trains had to be pulled out by the infantry. "The army was, in fact, stuck in the mud and could not budge one way or another." Finally, five days later, the army managed to get back to camp at White Oak Church "more dead than alive, the worst looking set of Yanks possible to imagine."

CHANCELLORSVILLE

May 1, 1863

The classic battle at Chancellorsville, Virginia, where Stonewall Jackson "crossed the T" of the 11th Corps, spelled disaster for the Federal army and its commander, Fightin' Joe Hooker. The way was now open for Lee to strike into the north up the Shenandoah Valley. Hooker lost his command and Meade replaced him as chief of the Army of the Potomac. But the South's victory was not without its price. Jackson gained immortality and died, shot accidentally by his own men.

That summer of 1863, Lee made his last cast toward ending the war in northern territory.

GETTYSBURG

July 1863

Gettysburg should never be lightly termed a victory. At best it was a draw. At Gettysburg the Confederate soldiers again met their old antagonist, the Army of the Potomac. Lee's army, coming from Virginia, moving from one victory to another, marched hundreds of miles across hostile country, only to pile up on the crest of a little ridge now called the "High Water Mark." At Round Top, Little Round Top, Big Round Top, the Peach Orchard, the Wheatfield, Devil's Den, Bloody Angle, Lee's veterans fought and learned what it meant to waver under fire. At the Clump of Trees the war became personal, Yankee and Rebel soldiers slugging it out hand to hand. Then on that third day, July 3, the Union army pushed the gallant Confederates down the fatal slope never to return. But there was no shame connected with the setback. They had done their human best at Gettysburg in one of the most brutal battles in all of history.

"We accidentally stumbled into this fight," a Confederate officer of high rank was heard to say. It seemed that way, at least to Lieutenant Redwood, then serving in Henry Heth's division of the 3rd Corps, which opened the engagement the morning of July 1, 1863. "Usually we knew there must be trouble ahead," he wrote, "but not always how imminent it might be. The column would be marching for some days . . . the heat, fatigue, dust, and the general discomfort being far more insistent on the thoughts of the men than any consideration of the military objective.

". . . but hello! look yonder! the battery men who have been lounging about, are standing to their pieces now, and immediately executing mysterious movements in the methodical fashion distinctive of their arm. Those about the nearest gun suddenly break away to right and left. A dense white stream of smoke leaps from the muzzle, and a crashing report strikes our ears a few seconds later as the gunners step forward again, lay hold of the hand-spike and spokes, and run the gun back in position. Another shot and another, and yet another, and the smoke thickens and we discern only vaguely the movements at the cannon—but the war music has begun and we know the battle has opened."

Some time after the battle had developed, Lieutenant Redwood made an excellent drawing of Doubleday's Pennsylvania Bucktails near the Chambersburg Pike. Alfred Waud, also busy that first day, sketched Lieutenant Bayard Wilkeson's Battery G, 4th United States Artillery, in a spirited rendition of artillerists in action.

Edwin Forbes got there on the morning of July 3, some time before 10 A.M. His drawings, three in number, are all dated and captioned "July 3rd, 10 A.M. Battle of Gettysburg—3rd Day." The day before, Waud, working from a signal station on Little Round Top, was with General Warren when he discovered Sickles' exposed position. Waud, also with the Union skirmishers when they struggled in the Devil's Den, sketched the action from the Union position. That same evening he witnessed Early's charge upon East Cemetery Hill.

Meanwhile, Lee had been preparing for the final assault. By noon of July 3, 138 guns lined up in battery from the Peach Orchard to the Seminary buildings, less than 800 yards from the Union center. Also massed to the west of the Emmettsburg Road, screened by low ground, were the brigades of General G. E. Pickett, commanded by Kemper, Armistead, and Garnett, nearly 15,000 men, awaiting orders to attack, guiding on a clump of trees on the ridge in plain sight.

Except for some sporadic sniping by sharpshooters, an ominous silence fell over the field. On the ridges the Federal soldiers, lounging behind hastily thrown up breastworks of logs and stones, talked and drank coffee and munched hardtack, now and then looking anxiously toward the Rebel lines. At 1 P.M. Lee's artillery began a rolling barrage to open the way for Pickett's attack. The Union guns answered immediately with heavy return fire. Thus began an artillery duel that seemed to last interminably.

Then came a lull in the Union firing to allow the guns to cool. The silence was startling. Colonel Frank A. Haskell of Wisconsin, carrying a message to Webb, looked at his watch. It was exactly 3 P.M. Breaking from cover behind Seminary Ridge, an awe-inspiring array of 15,000 Confederate soldiers in a double line nearly a mile long, a third brigade guarding their right flank, formed for the attack. Across 1,400 yards of fields and fences in parade order marched the Confederates, their ranks closing up as fast as Federal shells tore holes in them, advancing steadily toward the Union lines.

Meade's men, crouching behind stone walls, held their fire. The Confederates, reaching the last rise of ground, broke into a run. Then Federal infantry and artillery opened up. Fighting quickly became hand to hand at the Bloody Angle at the stone wall. About a hundred men, led by General Armistead, drove a wedge into Webb's Philadelphia brigade and reached the "High Water Mark." Webb's men, rallying, hit Armistead on both flanks, driving his men back in confusion; Armistead was killed. The dazed survivors—only one in four of those who had begun the charge—of Pickett's brigades moved slowly and sullenly back down the slope, stepping over the bodies of their fallen comrades. There ended the battle. On July 4, Meade failing to counterattack, Lee marched the remnants of his army back to Virginia.

THE MISSISSIPPI CAMPAIGN

The battle for control of the Mississippi River began at St. Louis. The Confederate fortifications, constructed at strategic points along the Mississippi for a distance of 80 miles, were powerful and well situated. Early in 1861 preparations for a special type of war vessel, capable of carrying heavy armament and guns and light enough of draft to negotiate the shallow water, got under way. These were the "Turtles," devised by Alfred Eads and Charles Ellet, 45 gunboats and rams that comprised the Fleet.

One of the first of these vessels, the *Carondelet,* commanded by Henry N. Walke, saw service in the attacks on Fort Donelson and Fort Henry, where the *Carondelet* operated in close concert with Grant's land operations. With a flotilla of ships comprising the *Carondelet, Pittsburg, Tyler,* and *Lexington* under his command, Walke set out for Fort Donelson.

"When within four hundred yards of the fort," wrote Walke, "and while the Confederates were running from their lower battery, our pilot house was struck again and another pilot wounded, our wheel was broken, and shells from the rear boats were bursting over us. All four of our boats were shot away and dragging in the water. On looking out to bring our broadside guns to bear, we saw that the other gunboats were rapidly falling back out of line. The *Pittsburg* in her haste to turn, struck the stern of the *Carondelet,* and broke our starboard rudder, so that we were obliged to go ahead to clear the *Pittsburg* and the point of rocks below . . . there was no alternative for the *Carondelet* in that narrow stream but to keep her head to the enemy and fire into the fort with her two bow guns, to prevent it, if possible, from returning fire effectively. The enemy saw that she was in a manner left to his mercy, and concentrated the fire of all his batteries upon her. In return, the *Carondelet*'s guns were well served to the last shot."

By January, 1862, both sides were fairly well prepared for intensive operations. At the end of the next month Brigadier General Ulysses S. Grant attacked and captured Forts Henry and Donelson. The Confederate first line of defense was destroyed. Fort Pillow, Corinth, Chattanooga, Island No. 10, and New Madrid would now fall to the Union forces.

SHILOH, OR PITTSBURG LANDING

April 6–7, 1862

At six o'clock on the morning of April 6, 1862, near a little church called Shiloh, near the Tennessee River, the Confederate army, under General Albert Sidney Johnston, advancing in line of battle, surprised, attacked, and dispersed the advance units of the Union army of General U. S. Grant, overrunning their camps and forcing Prentiss's division back on the Federal second line. In no time at all, the Confederates enveloped the whole division. After several hours of bloody fighting, the Union army was pushed back to within 600 yards of the Landing on an overhanging bluff near the river's edge. After desperate work on the part of Grant and his officers, the Union line was finally restored. Because of the confusion in the Confederate ranks and the poor communications between units of the Confederate forces, the initial advantage of their surprise attack was lost.

By nightfall, the battle settled down to the sporadic firing of pickets. During the night Buell's forces arrived, 25,000 men who crossed the river on pontoon bridges by torchlight. Grant opened his counterattack by 5 o'clock the next morning, supported by his gunboats in the river. But the heavy-caliber naval rifles of the gunboats failed to make any impression in the Confederate line, their fire being inaccurate. Finally, after sustained attacks lasting five hours, the battle ended. The Confederate army withdrew and Grant's forces reoccupied their old camps. Both armies, weakened by losses and fatigue, did not renew the contest.

After completing his line of communications with the Yazoo River, Grant attacked Vicksburg vigorously in May and June, 1863, and tried to carry the works by force, but the attempt failing, Grant settled down to a siege. Cut off on all sides, supplies running out and with all hope of aid gone, General Pemberton prepared for a long siege and hoped for a miracle. The people of Vicksburg fared as badly, if not worse, than the army. They dug caves in the clay hillsides and lived on mule meat, rats, and dogs. Daily bombardment from the Union land batteries and gunboats killed many civilians foolish enough to venture forth during the regular shelling. Outside Vicksburg, Grant tightened his hold on the doomed city, planning the final attack to be staged on July 6. But Lieutenant General John C. Pemberton, his army starved out, asked for surrender terms on July 3 and Vicksburg fell on July 4. After holding out for 47 days, the "City of a Hundred Hills," called by Jefferson Davis "the Gibraltar of the West," fell to a determined and skillful soldier.

Thus ended the Vicksburg campaign. The Confederacy now was split in two; Port Hudson, above Baton Rouge, fell to General Nathaniel Prentiss Banks on July 8 and the whole length of the Mississippi was open.

After the battle of Murfreesboro (Stone River) at the beginning of January, 1863, General William Starke Rosecrans, commander of the Army of the Cumberland, marched his army through wild country and maneuvered Braxton Bragg out of Chattanooga, thereby placing his army in a commanding strategic position. On September 19, 1863, at Chickamauga Creek, near Crawfish Springs, in Georgia, the two armies met. After two days of desperate fighting along a line six miles long through thick woods, the Union army fell back upon the adjoining crests of Missionary Ridge. Then, in November, followed the battles of Missionary Ridge and Chattanooga, and the Confederates fell back into Georgia. Grant and Sherman had cleared Tennessee and driven a deep wedge into the heart of the Confederacy.

The year 1864 saw some of the bloodiest military actions ever witnessed. Grant had taken full command of the Union armies, taking personal command of the Army of the Potomac with the conviction that he would fight Lee on the line of the James River "if it took all summer."

"The battle of the Wilderness," wrote General Grant, "was renewed by us at 5 o'clock on the morning of [May] the 6th, and continued with unabated fury until darkness set in, each army holding substantially the same position that they had on the evening of the 5th. After dark the enemy made a feeble attempt to turn our right flank, capturing several hundred prisoners and creating considerable confusion but the promptness of General Sedgwick . . . soon reformed it and restored order . . ."

The second operation of Grant's campaign came on May 7 when Grant, seeing that Lee was determined to wait for him behind entrenchments, made a rapid "shift to the left" movement to Spotsylvania Court House with the 5th Corps, the object to get between Lee and Richmond. Grant's movement was divined by Lee, and Richard Anderson's division reached Spotsylvania first, precipitating a battle lasting three days.

The Army of the Potomac then advanced to Cold Harbor and, on May 29 and 30, engaged the Army of Northern Virginia in a battle that even Grant said "was the only general attack made from the Rapidan to the James which did not inflict upon the enemy losses to compensate for our own losses."

Executing a skillful maneuver, Grant brought his forces to the south bank of the James River in an effort to capture Petersburg and the Petersburg and Richmond Railroad, and thereby to cut off Lee's Richmond supply artery. On July 30, 1864, Petersburg was invested by the Army of the Potomac. A vast network of trenches and redoubts, forts and redans was hastily thrown up on both sides, and the war in Virginia settled down to a siege of almost a year.

During the long siege of Petersburg, Lieutenant Colonel Henry Pleasants, a mining engineer from Pennsylvania, devised a mine that could be run under the enemy's entrenchments. Burnside approved the plan and for a month "the spade took the place of the musket." When the gallery was ready, eight magazines of powder were placed in the two lateral galleries directly beneath the Confederate trenches and exploded before dawn on July 30. "It was a magnificent spectacle," wrote Major William Powell, "and as the earth went up into the air, carrying with it men, guns, carriages, and timbers, and spread out like an immense cloud as it reached its altitude, so close were the Union lines that the mass appeared as if it would descend immediately upon the troops waiting the charge."

Alfred Waud was an eyewitness to the "magnificent spectacle," and his drawing clearly shows what General Grant characteristically described as "a stupendous failure." The Union forces had lost 4,000 men in the abortive operation.

At 9 A.M. on March 29, 1865, Grant opened his last campaign. Since before 3 A.M. the Federal columns had been in motion. The weather had been favorable for operations and the roads in fair condition. Lee evacuated Petersburg and Richmond and headed in the general direction of Five Forks, where he and his devoted army made a last stand. On Sunday, April 2, Lee's decimated army was in full retreat toward Danville. With his supply lines cut, his army without food and shoes, his only escape route cut off by General George Armstrong Custer, Lee under a flag of truce asked terms for surrender. Shortly after 1 P.M. on April 9, 1865, Lee met Grant in the McLean House at Appomattox Court House and arranged terms of surrender for all the Confederates who remained under arms in Virginia.

Theodore R. Davis marched with Sherman's army to Savannah and "thence through the Carolinas," making drawings of the last and perhaps most colorful campaign of the war. In the years after the war the artists went their separate ways. Davis and Waud followed Western trails with the surveys and expeditions to chart the West. There is no record of Edwin Forbes. Winslow Homer went on to become one of America's greatest painters. Colonel Julian Scott and Captain James Hope became famous painters in their own right. Theodore R. Davis, after returning from the Western surveys, retired to New Jersey, where he opened a studio. He died in Asbury Park. Alfred R. Waud died in Marietta, Georgia, a sick man from his exertions and privations. All that is left is the monument at South Mountain—and their work.

From a drawing by Theodore R. Davis. Courtesy the Century Company

Sergeant John Carmody firing the barbette guns—Fort Sumter, 1861

A Soldier's Sketches
of General William Starke Rosecrans'
West Virginia Campaign—1861–1862

The drawings depicting General William Starke Rosecrans' campaign in West Virginia during the first year of the war were executed by Corporal Nep Roesler, Color Guard, Company G, 47th Regiment, Ohio Volunteers. Corporal Roesler made his spirited drawings during the campaign in late 1861 in which he participated.

The footnotes accompanying these drawings are taken from notes written in pen and ink on the borders of the original drawings by the Assistant Provost Marshal of General Rosecrans' staff, the former owner of the originals now in the possession of the author.

"These sketches were drawn by a soldier (Corporal Roesler) of the 47th Regiment, Ohio Volunteers, and represent scenes of our first year of army life from Kanawa Falls to Big Sewell [Mountain], West Virginia."

March to the landing, West Virginia

Crossing to Fayetteville

Advance in the woods, West Virginia

Tompkins' farm, Camp Gauley Mount, West Virginia

"Camp, near Gauley Bridge"

Pickets in the woods

"After the engagement near the drill ground, Camp Anderson."

Skirmishing near New River

Battle at Carnifex Ferry

"My first experience under fire. I was assistant provost marshal on
Gen. Rosecrans' staff and had charge of the captured property."

View from Hawk's Nest, towards the east

Thunder storm, Big Sewell Mountain

From an original sketch in charcoal and white crayon on gray paper by Winslow Homer.
Courtesy Cooper Union Museum for the Arts of Decoration

Sketch of a Federal soldier loading his rifle

The rifle used by the soldier in the Civil War was a muzzle-loading Enfield musket. The soldier seen in the sketch is in the act of tamping the powder and ball down the barrel with a ramrod. Homer probably made this sketch during the campaign of 1864 when he visited the front for the last time.

Study of a Union cavalryman

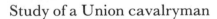

From a crayon drawing by Winslow Homer. Courtesy Cincinnati Art Museum

145

Studies of Civil War soldiers
by Winslow Homer

These studies of "Billy Yank" were probably sketched during the campaign of 1862 in Virginia, when Homer was with McClellan's Army of the Potomac advancing up the Peninsula to Richmond.

From original sketches in charcoal on brown paper by Winslow Homer.
Courtesy Cooper Union Museum for the Arts of Decoration

From original sketches by Winslow Homer.
Courtesy Cooper Museum for the Arts of Decoration

Two studies of Union Army
cavalrymen by Winslow Homer

The Union cavalryman was the "glamour boy" of the Federal Army in the Civil War. These beautiful sketches, done in black crayon on brown paper, typify the Union horse trooper in different attitudes.

On the left, the trooper is shown astride his horse, riding at a gallop. In the sketch on the right he is seen wielding his saber.

146

From sketches by Winslow Homer. Courtesy Cooper Union Museum for the Arts of Decoration

Four studies of infantrymen of the Army of the Potomac

Four sketches executed in charcoal on white paper. In the first sketch, upper left, the soldier is reaching for a cartridge. In the upper right, he is seen charging. The two lower figures depict different attitudes of soldiers who have just been shot.

The Military Drawings
of Lieutenant Allen Carter Redwood

Trooper of the Virginia Cavalry, 1861

Drawing by Lieutenant Allen C. Redwood. Courtesy The Century Company

From a drawing by Lieutenant Allen C. Redwood. Courtesy The Century Company

Confederate sharpshooter

Allen Carter Redwood, one of the finest illustrators the Confederacy produced, took part in all the major battles in the eastern theater of the war. He was a member of the 55th Regiment, Virginia, and served as courier on the staff of General Lensford L. Lomax. His drawings have a style all their own, equaling Homer at their best. Although many of Redwood's drawings were made after the war, they nevertheless were done from personal experience and are accurate in every detail.

Confederate types, 1862

A Confederate soldier of 1862

A Louisiana Pelican

Member of a Confederate Zouave Regiment, whose uniform was patterned after one worn in the French Army.

A rainy day in camp

A camp scene similar to many of Brady's photographs. Homer's painting shows a group of cavalrymen trying to keep warm and dry over the campfire. On the left are the Sibley tents. At the right is a row of cavalry horses.

From a drawing by Alfred R. Waud. Courtesy Library of Congress

Colonel Ambrose Everett Burnside's brigade, 1st and 2nd Rhode Island and the 17th New York Regiment, with their artillery, attacking the Confederate batteries at Bull Run, July 21, 1861

From a drawing by Thure de Thulstrup. Courtesy The Century Company

Battle of Bull Run, July, 1861

Rallying the troops of Bee, Bartow, and Evans, behind the Robinson House.

151

"Feeling the enemy"

Skirmishers advancing in front of the main body of troops.

"Beating the long roll"

Drummer boys of the Union Army.

From a wartime sketch by Winslow Homer. Courtesy The Century Company

The 61st New York Regiment in camp at Ship Point, below Yorktown

From a wartime sketch by Winslow Homer. Courtesy The Century Company

"Union camp scene—a quiet game"

153

From a drawing by Alfred R. Waud. Courtesy Library of Congress

Scene of the battle of Fair Oaks, Virginia, 1862

Drawn a day or two before the Confederate advance.

From a drawing by Alfred R. Waud. Courtesy The Century Association

Sumner's corps crossing the overflowed "grapevine" bridge
to reinforce Couch at Fair Oaks

From an engraving of a painting by Colonel Julian Scott. Courtesy The Century Company

The rear guard at White Oak Swamp

General W. H. Smith's division fighting a rear-guard action at White Oak Swamp in the battles of the Seven Days, Virginia, 1862.

From a sketch made at the time by Alfred R. Waud. Courtesy The Century Company

Burying the dead, and burning houses, at Twin Houses near Casey's redoubt

155

From a painting by Colonel Julian Scott. Courtesy The Smithsonian Institution

Battle scene

The battle of Cedar Creek, Virginia, 1862.

156

From a painting by Winslow Homer. Courtesy Harold T. Pulsifer and W. H. Tobey, Waterville, Maine

Army teamsters or "contraband"

Winslow Homer was always interested in the lowly members of the army. The Negro "contraband," freed from slavery and given jobs as army teamsters and officers' servants, formed subjects for his paintings of army camp life. The comic figure poking his head through the Sibley tent flap reflects the northern stereotype of the happy Negro indifferent toward his lot.

From a painting by Winslow Homer. Courtesy the Fogg Museum of Art, Harvard University

Pitching quoits

Zouave regiments were common in the early part of the war, but the uniform was later largely discarded for regulation blue. Several regiments, to retain their identity, continued to wear them.

157

From a drawing by Edwin Forbes. Courtesy The Century Company

The battle of Shiloh, Tennessee, April 6 and 7, 1862

Checking the Confederate advance on the evening of the first day of the battle. General Grant wrote, "Above this ravine, near the landing [Pittsburg Landing], the Federal reserve artillery was posted, and it was on this line the Confederate advance was checked, about sunset, Sunday evening. The Confederates then . . . bivouacked in the Federal camps."

From a drawing by Alfred R. Waud. Courtesy Library of Congress

Defeat of the army of General Pope at Manassas on the old Bull Run battleground, Saturday, August 30, 1862

From a painting by James Hamilton. Courtesy Historical Society of Pennsylvania

Battle between the *Monitor* and the *Merrimac*
at Hampton Roads, Virginia, March 8, 1862

Inscription: "Action between *Merrimac* and *Monitor*—Craney Island in middle ground—fog clearing off—."

Battle of Sharpsburg or Antietam, September 17, 1862

McClellan's troops, advancing toward the Confederate center, cross the "Bloody Lane" filled with the dead of Walker's and Anderson's brigades, the result of the enfilading fire of the Union forces.

Battle of Sharpsburg or Antietam, September 17, 1862

Stephen D. Lee's battery in action near the Dunker Church. The long lines of Union troops are men of Hooker's division. Three times Hooker broke the Confederate line, three times Hood's men threw them back. Then Mansfield and Sumner attacked and both were repulsed by McLaws.

Battle of Sharpsburg or Antietam, September 17, 1862

The "Bloody Lane," name given to a sunken road on Farmer Piper's farm, was well earned. In it the corpses of the men of Hill and Anderson, victims of a terrible concentration of enfilading fire, stare sightless at the sky. Meagher's Irish Brigade, the New Hampshire and New York regiments, gained the road and broke the Confederate line back to the village.

Gathering the dead for burial in slit trenches on the battlefield of Sharpsburg

Frank Schell has here caught with his pencil the horror of the scene following the battle of Antietam. The burial details have dug slit trenches. Curious civilians, some with children, are witnessing the grisly undertaking.

From a drawing by Lieutenant Allen C. Redwood. Courtesy The Century Company

The Washington Artillery of New Orleans on Marye's Hill
firing on the Union columns forming for the assault

Fredericksburg, December 13, 1862.

From a drawing by Alfred R. Waud. Courtesy Library of Congress

The charge of Humphrey's division, battle of Fredericksburg, December 13, 1862

Courtesy Historical Society of Pennsylvania

Battle of Fredericksburg, Virginia, December 13, 1862

From a painting by Lieutenant Frederick F. Cavada, 14th Pennsylvania Volunteers, a unit participating in the battle.

From a drawing by Lieutenant Allen C. Redwood. Courtesy The Century Company

Cobb's and Kershaw's troops behind the stone wall,
Marye's Heights, Fredericksburg, May, 1863

From a painting by J. Linton Chapman. Courtesy Victor D. Spark

View of Fort Sumter, South Carolina

"Fort Sumter, painted by J. Linton Chapman after the original painted by his brother, Conrad Wise Chapman, of the 59th Regular Virginia Volunteers—Wise's Brigade, while stationed at Charleston in 1862–63."

From a painting by Sergeant Conrad Wise Chapman. Courtesy The Confederate Museum, Richmond

Battery Rutledge

Between Battery Bee, on the west side, and Fort Moultrie was Battery Marion and a work called Battery Rutledge. This latter was the eastern flanking work of Fort Moultrie.

165

From a painting by Sergeant Conrad Wise Chapman. Courtesy The Confederate Museum, Richmond

Battery located on Laurens Street, Charleston, February 7, 1864

Battery Laurens, at the foot of Laurens Street, Charleston, was one of many such batteries within the city itself. Depicted is the fort's interior, a Columbiad on a sea-coast carriage, magazines, and a row of spherical shells. In the channel, a Confederate ironclad gunboat, similar to the *Merrimac*, moves up the channel. A lone sentry stands on the parapet.

From a painting by Sergeant Conrad Wise Chapman. Courtesy The Confederate Museum, Richmond

Battery Wampler, March 4, 1864

Directly west of Fort Duncan was Battery Wampler on James Island, flanking Fort Ripley. Typical of small Confederate coastal fortifications, it boasted two Columbiads mounted on siege carriages.

From a painting by Sergeant Conrad Wise Chapman. Courtesy The Confederate Museum, Richmond

Battery Bee on Sullivan's Island

Named after the Confederate General Barnard E. Bee, who lost his life at the first battle of Bull Run, Battery Bee, west of Fort Moultrie, was located as a flanking fort to the main work, Fort Moultrie. Under command of Lieutenant Colonel J. C. Simkins, it accommodated three companies of First South Carolina regulars, five ten-inch and one eight-inch Columbiads.

Confederate flag over the battered ramparts of Fort Sumter

By 1863 Fort Sumter was nothing but a pile of rubble. Pounded to pieces by the Federal monitors, the fort held out to the end of the war, even though breached by the Federal forts on Morris and Sullivan's islands. In the background the fleet of the Atlantic Blockading Squadron rides at anchor.

Battery Marshall, Sullivan's Island

Battery Marshall, located at the eastern extremity of Sullivan's Island, was the last of the chain of forts comprising Beauregard, Rutledge, and Moultrie. In the painting are barracks surrounded by parapets of sand, powder magazines, and two sea-coast Columbiads on field carriages.

Attack on Fort Fisher, North Carolina, December 24, 1864

The United States fleet, largest until then ever assembled by the Navy, attacked Fort Fisher. Under the command of Admiral David Dixon Porter, 60 warships of all types—monitors, ironclads, frigates—mounting a total of 316 heavy caliber naval rifles, plastered the powerful fort with 21,716 shells.

On Christmas Day an amphibious landing was attempted by the troops of General Benjamin Butler, but the fort proved to be still too strong and the troops were withdrawn. Finally, the fort was carried by assault with the forces of General Alfred H. Terry, January 15, 1865.

From a drawing by Lieutenant Allen C. Redwood. Courtesy The Century Company

Stampede of the 11th Corps on the plank road, Chancellorsville, 1863

From a painting by Captain Alexander Lawrie. Courtesy Victor D. Spark

"17th Pennsylvania Volunteers, Colonel Patterson, crossing the Monocassie River"

The Army of the Potomac on the march to Chancellorsville passing along the north bank
of the Rappahannock on the way to Kelly's Ford, April 30, 1863

Lieutenant Bayard Wilkeson holding his battery (G, 4th United States
Artillery) to its work in an exposed position at Gettysburg

Battle of Gettysburg, third day, July 3, 1863, 10 A.M.

The battle of Gettysburg, third day, July 3, 1863

One of the greatest battles of all time, Gettysburg was the turning point in the war for the Union. Over 23,000 men lost their lives in the holocaust. Here, depicted by the brush of Paul Philippoteaux, is the climax of General George E. Pickett's charge, the "high water mark" of the Confederacy.

The brigades of Pettigrew, Trimble, and Garnett dashed
themselves to pieces against the Union line of Major Alexander Webb's Philadelphia Brigade. It was Lee's last cast.
After that the war returned to Virginia, to end finally at
Appomattox. The painting is of heroic size, measuring 385
feet in length, 35 feet in height; about a quarter of it is re-
produced here.

173

The fight in the crater after the explosion of the Union mine under the Confederate fort, Jackson Road, Vicksburg, June 25, 1863

Union headquarters, July 3, at Vicksburg,
General Grant receiving General Pemberton's message

General Grant, in his *Personal Memoirs* wrote: "On leaving Bruinsburg for the front I left my son Frederick, who had joined me a few weeks before, on board one of the gunboats asleep, and hoped to get away without him until after Grand Gulf should fall into our hands; but on waking up he learned that I had gone, and being guided by the sound of the battle raging at Thompson's Hill—called the battle of Port Gibson—found his way to where I was. He had no horse to ride at the time, and I had no facilities for even preparing a meal. He, therefore, foraged around the best he could until we reached Grand Gulf. Mr. C. A. Dana, then an officer of the War Department, accompanied me on the Vicksburg campaign and through a portion of the siege."

Seated before the tent, under the flag, is General Grant. The young "soldier" with the pony is Master Frederick Dent Grant. Seated near him is Charles A. Dana, Assistant Secretary of War.

From a sketch made at the time by Theodore R. Davis. Courtesy The Century Company

First conference between Grant and Pemberton July 3, 1863

"Grant and Pemberton met near the tree and went aside to the earth-work, where they sat in conference. To their right is a group of four, including General John S. Bowen, C. S. A., General A. J. Smith, General James B. Mc-Pherson, and Colonel L. M. Montgomery. Under the tree are Chief-of-Staff John A. Rawlins, Assistant Secretary of War Charles A. Dana."

Standing with these officers is Theodore R. Davis, special artist who made this sketch.

From a drawing made at the time by Theodore R. Davis. Courtesy The Century Company

Arrival of General Grant at General Pemberton's Vicksburg house, July 4, 1863

The United States gunboats at Fort Donelson, February 14, 1862

The land attack in concert with the naval attack can be seen in the distance.

The ironclads *Carondelet* and *Pittsburg* capturing the batteries below New Madrid

176

The battle of Fort Pillow, May 10, 1862

U. S. gunboats *Mound City, Carondelet,* and *Cincinnati* are engaged with the Confederate river fleet: *Price, Bragg, Sumter,* and *Little Rebel.*

The battle of Memphis, Tennessee, June 6, 1862

In the foreground are the U. S. gunboats *Carondelet, Benton, St. Louis, Cairo, Louisville, Queen of the West,* and *Monarch.* In the distance can be seen the Confederate fleet advancing.

177

From a drawing by Rear Admiral Henry N. Walke. Courtesy The Century Company

The battle of Memphis, looking north, June 6, 1862

In the foreground is the remainder of the Confederate fleet, and the U. S. gunboats *Queen of the West* and *Monarch*. To the right of the drawing is the *Beauregard* sinking; the *Lovell* is already on the bottom.

From a drawing by Rear Admiral Henry N. Walke. Courtesy The Century Company

Close of the battle of Memphis, June 6, 1862

To the left of the drawing are the captured Confederate gunboats *Sumter*, *Bragg*, and *Thompson*, which can be seen blowing up. In line are the U. S. gunboats *Memphis*, *Louisville*, *Benton*, *St. Louis*, *Carondelet*, and *Cairo*.

A skirmish in the Wilderness

The most unusual of Civil War battles was Grant's battle in the Wilderness. In the campaign of 1864–1865, Grant and the Army of the Potomac aimed again at Richmond and Petersburg. This time there would be no turning back. Lee maneuvered Grant into fighting in an area known as the Wilderness, a dense forest of swamp, tangled thicket, scrub oak, and underbrush. From sketches made by Winslow Homer "on the spot" this painting was made.

Prisoners from the front

Homer's war painting won unstinted praise. The young Union officer is General Francis Barlow. "No picture has been painted in America in our day that made so deep an appeal to the feeling of the people . . ." said Clarence Cook.

179

Opening of the
spring campaign in Virginia

"Skirmishers forward!" "Feeling out" the enemy,
Confederate skirmishers advance over the bud-
ding countryside.

Company "Q" stragglers

Company "Q" was a mythical company and a designation
for unhorsed troopers who had lost their mounts in battle.
They belonged to Company "Q" until they either found
or stole another horse. Judging from the skillet in one
trooper's hand, they are begging a little food.

Reveille

The sharp notes of the bugle ring out
in the forest bivouac.

From water colors by Lieutenant William L. Sheppard, C. S. A.
Courtesy The Confederate Memorial Museum, Richmond

The battle of Spotsylvania Court House

Upton's Brigade at the "Bloody Angle"

Distributing ammunition under fire to Warren's 5th Corps
during the battle of the Wilderness, May 6, 1864

General Grant reconnoitering the Confederate position at Spotsylvania Court House

Charles H. Reed, the artist who made this sketch, was a soldier in Bigelow's 9th Massachusetts Battery, which, with a battery of the 5th U. S. Regular Artillery, was holding the Fredericksburg Road where General Grant made his observation. The troops in the background are the 9th Massachusetts Volunteers.

From a painting in oil by Winslow Homer. Courtesy The Detroit Institute of Arts

Defiance: inviting a shot before Petersburg, Virginia, 1864

From a drawing by Alfred R. Waud. Courtesy The Century Company

The battle of Resaca, Georgia, May 15, 1864

183

From a painting by James E. Taylor. Courtesy The Century Company

The battle of Atlanta, July 22, 1864

Fuller's division of the 16th Corps rallying to hold their ground after being forced back by the first charge of the Confederates in their flank attack.

From the Panorama of Atlanta. Courtesy The Century Company

Battle of Atlanta, July 22, 1864

The contest on Bald Hill, 4th Division, 15th Corps, in the foreground.

184

From a painting by James Walker. Courtesy of Victor D. Spark

Review of the Grand Army of the Republic

One of the proudest days of the nation's history is depicted in James Walker's painting of the last grand review of the Union armies before they disbanded. To the strains of popular music of the time they marched down Pennsylvania Avenue, bay- onets flashing in the sun. Walker's painting places the Capitol in the distant background, but according to Mathew Brady's photographs the troops marched within stone's throw of the Capitol. The war was won.

185

8

Light Cavalry Overture

Indian War

1876–1890

The long, bloody, and dramatic struggle with the red man in his own domain in the Great West is a story whose last episode begins soon after the Civil War. Many Union and Confederate soldiers and officers who had difficulty in rehabilitating themselves to the ways of peace made their way West and joined U. S. cavalry units fighting the Indians.

There is no question that the Indian was badly treated by the white man. The records show justification for the red man's claims. Government officials, many unscrupulous, made all sorts of treaties with the Indian, guaranteeing certain reservations of land to the red man, only to break them. The white man never kept his word. A deplorable string of broken promises and worthless treaties can be traced as far back as the days of Sir William Johnson. The Indian's lot was one of desperation. Being forced to migrate from one place to another, his natural instinct was to fight back with every means at his command. The result was the Indian wars.

An outstanding battle took place at the Little Big Horn in Montana in 1876, when Lieutenant Colonel George Armstrong Custer, sent on a scout with a small detachment of the U. S. 7th Cavalry, apparently disobeyed the orders of his commanding officer, General Alfred H. Terry, and foolishly brought on an engagement which cost him his life and the lives of his entire command. At least recorded evidence points in that direction. Colonel George Armstrong Custer was a rash officer, given to heroics. Custer's rise from lieutenant to brevet brigadier general was meteoric.

Somewhat of a dandy, he sported uniforms of his own special design and wore his blond hair in long flowing waves; he could have been called the American Murat. Colonel Newhall, author of *With Sheridan in Lee's Last Campaign,* describes him: "Custer of the golden locks, his broad sombrero turned up from his hard-bronzed face, the ends of his crimson cravat floating over his shoulders, gold galore spangling his jacket sleeves, a pistol in his boot, dangling spurs on his heels and a ponderous claymore swinging at his side, a wild dare-devil of a general, and a prince of advance guards, quick to see and act." Custer's love for fancy uniforms was no less flamboyant than his reckless attitude toward danger. He was daring and careless, not only of his own life but of the lives of his men as well. At the close of the Civil War Custer was appointed to the command of the United States 7th Cavalry at Fort Lincoln.

Colonel Gibbon's official report explains, as well as any, the action at the Little Big Horn as it had been planned: " . . . That evening the plan of operations was agreed upon. Lieutenant Colonel Custer, with the Seventh Cavalry, was to proceed up the Rosebud till he struck an Indian trail, discovered during Major Reno's scout. As my scouts had recently reported smoke on the Little Big Horn, the presence of an Indian camp some distance up that stream was inferred.

"Lieutenant Colonel Custer was instructed to keep constantly feeling toward his left, well up toward the mountains, so as to prevent the Indians escaping in that direction, and to strike the Little Big Horn, if possible above (south of) the supposed location of the camp, while my command was to march up the Yellowstone to the mouth of the Big Horn to the mouth of the Little Big Horn and up that stream, with the hope of getting the camp between the two forces . . .

"He got off with his regiment at 12 o'clock the next day [June 22]: three Gatling guns, under Lieutenant Low, Twentieth Infantry, being detached from his regiment and sent to join my command . . ."

The story of Custer's last stand, and of the massacre of his entire command, has been told and retold. For years controversy raged as to what actually happened. The only men who knew were Custer, and the sole survivor, Sergeant Edward Windolph. The only direct evidence was the battlefield strewn with the bodies of soldiers. Colonel Gibbon in his report wrote: " . . . We continued to move rapidly forward, still uncertain as to the fate of Custer's command, Captain Ball's company about a mile in advance. While passing through the Indian camp a report reached me from our scouts in the hills to the north of the river that a large number of bodies of white men had been discovered, and shortly afterward Lieutenant Bradley came in with the information that he had counted 194 bodies of dead soldiers. All doubt that a serious disaster had happened to Lieutenant Colonel Custer's command now vanished, and the march was continued under the uncertainty as to whether we were going to rescue the survivors or to battle with the enemy who had annihilated him . . ."

The life of a soldier or trooper in General Nelson A. Miles' command was no sinecure. The western frontier military service conducted by General Miles' troops on the southwestern border was a sort of police service. Small skirmishes could at any time break into open warfare over a large area. The marauding Indians had no homes, no base of operations, no supplies to cut off, no military code, no purpose or plan more definite than to wander about the mountains, to take their revenge, and to gratify their passion for cruelty. But while the Apaches could desist from fighting at any time, and retreat and renew their supplies by plunder, the soldiers had to always be on guard, subsist on scanty fare, and camp without tents.

If the individual U. S. Cavalry trooper that Frederic Remington sketched had had a biography, it would have contained nothing more notable than such notes as these:

"Jack Hayward, a tall young fellow, born in Connecticut, became bankrupt in New York; did not know what else to do, so he enlisted, and discovered that he was born with an uncommon capacity for Apache warfare. The grizzly veteran, who looks like a pirate, has enlisted five times. Of course he swore every time that he would never enlist again; but he was not happy out of the army. Another is a scarred soldier who got his military training in the Prussian military service; and another is an Irishman who kept going West without knowing why, and who tried to earn a living one way or another and then for the same reason, and without being able to explain it any more than he could foresee it, he found the soldier's life on the Frontier not only tolerable but an ideal life . . ."

Remington would probably have made an excellent soldier for he was vitally interested in the subject and loved soldier life. He was quite positive in his support of the Indian as a soldier, trained as a cavalryman. He wrote a very revealing article for *Harper's* which shows his aptitude not only as a military artist of distinction but as a discerning reporter as well.

"The Indian tribes are yet warriors; they have not lost their instincts or respect for the trade of war; but an Indian will do the most arduous and laborious work if he has a cavalry uniform on, when he would not lift his little finger to the task if dressed in his bright blanket and bead-work, both of which are emblematic of a thousand years of glorious deeds of arms. He sees the white soldiers work, and makes as great a distinction between the laboring soldier and his agricultural brother, as you would between a farmer and a gentleman cultivating orchids in his conservatory. I had become aware that the government was trying the experiment at Fort Keogh. When at that place I was driven out to the little village of Lieutenant E. W. Casey's Cheyenne scouts. I saw a long line of well-constructed log buildings, corrals, and stables, also a large garden fenced and cultivated. I entered the houses and saw comfort and cleanliness. I saw smiling faces and laughing children. I saw perfectly kept cavalry arms and accoutrements, and fine Indian soldiers, who stood like bronze statues, and saluted in the best possible form, while never a muscle of their stern faces twitched, and they looked a soldier, and felt a soldier, and were in fact the finest I had ever seen. I saw them mount and fall in and drill in admirable shape, all by a sign of Lieutenant Casey's right hand, because they do not understand English well enough. I admired the indomitable zeal of Lieutenant Casey, and hoped his work would lead to greater things. Indeed, if he were properly supported, why could not Fort Keogh be abandoned at some future day, and why could not Casey and his company of the First Irregular Cavalry do the work of the garrison, and let the Eighth Cavalry and the Twenty-second Infantry go to Fort Snelling, and there perfect themselves, so that when we call for the skeleton of our army organization in time of war, we will find it worthy to be built on to?

"Six months before, all these men were down at the Lame Deer Agency doing nothing, unless to go out gunning for a ranchman's cattle. Lieutenant Casey brought them up to the mouth of the Tongue River, uniformed and equipped them, and ploughed and made a garden after irrigating the land. He then took them up the Yellowstone, and—it is almost beyond belief—gave them axes, with which they mauled logs, and with the help of their ponies they tugged them out to the river, and drove them down to the fort. They then hewed the logs, and built cabins as good as any ranchman's in the country. Lieutenant Casey and his interpreter (an old Fifth Infantry soldier who has been in battle against Cheyennes) were the only white men along. Beyond doing all this work, they are well drilled, and all in six months. We keep army recruits four months at a depot before we forward them. I should not be surprised if Lieutenant Casey had his Indians herding sheep in course of time, and that is the particular thing that an Indian will not do.

"What did I see at the Lame Deer Agency? A lot of shrouded creatures lying about or darting over the hills, as purposeless and mysterious as creatures out of Dante's 'Inferno.' Later on in my travels a lot of dark-skinned soldiers were drawn up to escort a major-general. They were the Crow Scout Corps of Fort Custer, under command of Lieutenant S. C. Robertson, of the First Cavalry, another zealous young man with a fiery purpose to have the best scout corps on the crust of the earth. His methods are different from Casey's. He wastes no time on industrial affairs, but goes in for the purely military standard. He is a West-Pointer and a graduate of the French School of Cavalry, talks the sign language, and is rapidly mastering the Crow tongue. Lieutenant Casey is a West-Pointer, an old soldier who has fought with Indian scouts under him, and has seen much of their people. Here are young men as types. They are educated; they are brave; they are soldiers for life. They can have no success in life beyond what their military accomplishments bring them. They know that the least indiscretion on their part would cost them their commissions. This is the sort of man who should take the place of the ha'-penny politician who has been nurtured in the belief that to plunder the Indians is a natural reward for good service in his political district. As we rode along with these active warriors they would put their ponies at top speed down very steep hills; they were far ahead and on the flanks. It was the most perfect piece of escort duty that I ever saw. They wore leather leggins instead of cavalry boots, as did Casey's men, and they had no saddle pockets or rope lariats. Instead of this latter, they carried their own hair rope, lighter and stronger than the great piece of hemp of the cavalry. An Indian is the best possible light irreg-

ular cavalryman, and his methods cannot be improved by introducing ours, and he can learn little indeed from a white trooper."

On December 5, 1890, from South Dakota came ominous signs of trouble. Sitting Bull, old but still rebellious and full of fight, was believed to be planning another great Indian uprising. General Nelson Miles reported "that the seriousness of the situation has not been exaggerated . . ." and went so far as to say that 30,000 Indians were affected " . . . fully 6,000 of whom were fighting men . . ." and further stated that "Every Indian 'buck' has a Winchester and he knows how to use it."

Sitting Bull, determined to make one last strike against the white man's encroachment, gathered about him 5,000 fierce Sioux warriors in his camps, in the rocky hills of the Bad Lands, and prepared for war. General Nelson Miles received orders to pick up and arrest Sitting Bull, with specific orders to "avoid a battle at all costs." A detachment was sent out to locate and arrest the wily leader of the Sioux. The Indians, however, started a fight, and Sitting Bull and several of his braves were killed on December 15, 1890. The rest of his tribe scampered for the Bad Lands. Several U. S. scouting parties were sent to reconnoiter the Bad Lands, and Remington, with the help of General Miles, was assigned to Lieutenant E. W. Casey, Chief of Cheyenne Scouts and one of the best out-post officers in the army. After a short railroad trip the scouting party struck out into the Bad Lands in the dead of winter. Lieutenant Casey had strict orders to avoid warfare, orders that were not easily accepted by Casey's Cheyennes. When the little party reached Sioux territory, he halted his column at the base of the bluff, ordered his men to remain in column with the threat of being shot through the head if they disobeyed orders and broke ranks, turned, and rode on ahead for a powwow with some Sioux who had stopped nearby. Casey returned after a while, displeased and troubled with the results of his powwow. They then camped for the night. Remington's own story of the affair is interesting:

"The next morning I announced my intention of going to Pine Ridge Agency which is twenty-five miles away. Mr. Thompson, two scouts and a Swedish teamster are to go in for provisions and messages. Mr. Thompson ordered all guns put into the wagon and got in himself. 'If I can't talk them Injuns out of killing me,' he said, 'I reckon I'll have to go.'

"I trotted along with Red-Bear and Hairy-Arm, and a mile and a half ahead went the courier, Wells. Poor man! In two hours he lay bleeding in the road, with a bullet through the hips, and called two days for water before 'he struck the long trail to the kingdom-come.' After we had gone eight or ten miles and were just crossing a ravine we saw a Sioux buck on a little hill just ahead, out of pistol shot. Red-Bear turned his horse in the 'peace sign' and advanced. We drove over the ravine and halted. I dismounted. Six young Brule Sioux rose from the ground and rode up to Red-Bear, and the hills became full of pickets to the right and left. We waited to hear the result of Red-Bear's conversation. When he came back he spoke to Thompson in Cheyenne. I looked at him and knew that the situation was bad.

"'Red-Bear says we will have to go back,' explained Thompson, and turning to Red-Bear he requested that two might come closer and talk with us. 'This is a bad hole and I reckon our cake is dough right here,' said Thompson.

"Two young bucks came up and one asked Thompson for tobacco and he was handed a package of Durham, which was not returned. Another little buck slipped up behind me, whereat Mr. Thompson gave me a warning look. Turning, I advanced on him quickly (I wanted to be as near as possible, not being armed) and, holding out my hand, I said: 'how, *colah?*' He didn't like to take it, but he did, and I was saved the trouble of further action.

"'We'll never get this wagon turned around,' suggested Mr. Thompson, as our teamster whipped up; but we did. And as we commenced our movement on Casey's camp, Mr. Thompson said: 'Go slow now; don't run, or they'll sure shoot.'

"'Gemme gun,' said the little scout Red-Bear, and we all got our arms from the wagon.

"There was no suspense now. Things had begun to happen. A little faster, we go up the little banks of the *coulee*, and, ye gods! what!—five fully-armed, well-mounted cowboys—a regular rescue scene from Buffalo Bill's show.

"'Go back!' shouted Thompson.

"Bang! Bang! Bang! and the bullets whistle around and kick up the dust. Away we go.

"Four bucks start over the hills to our right to flank us. Red-Bear talked loudly in Cheyenne.

"Thompson repeated: 'If anyone is hit, get off in the grass and lie down. We must all hang together.' 'We will,' we all yelled.

"The cowboys, being well-mounted, could easily have gotten away, but they stuck like true blues. We deployed on the flanks of the wagon, so that the team horses might not be shot, which would have stopped the whole outfit and we did ten miles at a record-breaking gallop. We struck the scout camp in a blaze of excitement. The Cheyenne were in warpaint and the ponies' tails were tied up and full of feathers. Had the Sioux materialized at that time, Mr. Casey would have had his orders broken right there.

"After a lull in the proceeding, Mr. Thompson confided in me that 'the next time I go to war in a wagon it will put the drinks on me'; and he saddled Piegan and patted his neck in a way which showed his gratification at the change of transport.

"We pulled out again for the lower country and as our scouts had seen the dust of Colonel Sanford's command, we presently joined them.

"How we awoke the next morning with the sleet freezing in our faces and how we made camp in the blizzard, and borrowed Sibley stoves of the soldiers, and how we were at last comfortable, and spent New Year's Eve in the proper manner, is of little interest.

"I was awakened at a late hour by Captain Baldwin, of General Miles' staff, and told to saddle up for a night's ride to Pine Ridge. This was the end of my experience with Lieutenant Casey and his gallant corps. We shook hands cheerily in the dim candlelight of the tepee, and, agreeing to meet in New York at some not distant day, I stepped out of the Sibley, mounted and rode away in the night."

Within a few years the wars with the Indians were at an end. The Indian had been subjugated. The vast rolling plains and the mountains of the Great West that had once been his hunting grounds, for which he had fought so desperately, were now reduced to acres of land called "reservations" where he would spend his last days, neglected, despised by the white man who came to settle on the lands that were once his to roam. His battle was over.

Cavalry on the march

Lieutenant Casey, commandant of Cheyenne scouts

Cheyenne scout with led horse

Drawn by Frederic Remington. Courtesy Harper's Weekly

The supply train

Drawn by Frederic Remington. Courtesy Remington Art Memorial

Indian soldier in the Crow Scout Corps

Drawn by Frederic Remington. Courtesy Harper's Weekly

Lieutenant S. C. Robertson,
chief of Crow scouts

Fort Keogh scout

Ideal uniform
for Indian soldier

Indian soldier
in the Crow Scout Corps

Drawn by Frederic Remington. Courtesy Harper's Weekly

193

From a painting by Frederic Remington. Courtesy Harper's Weekly

The ambushed picket

Drawn by Frederic Remington. Courtesy Harper's Weekly

"Saddle up"

Drawn by Frederic Remington. Courtesy Harper's Weekly

Signaling the main command

The trooper's Thanatopsis

Drawn by Frederic Remington. Courtesy Harper's Weekly

Drawn by Frederic Remington. Courtesy Harper's Weekly

Troopers singing the Indian Medicine Song

196

Drawn by Frederic Remington. Courtesy Harper's Weekly

Skirmish line target practice

Drawn by Frederic Remington. Courtesy Harper's Weekly

A model squadron—over the hurdles in line

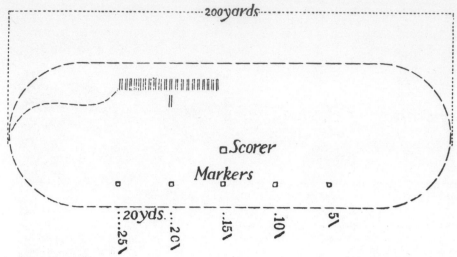

Diagram showing method used in pistol practice for cavalrymen

"Making a possible"

Mounted pistol practice

"He Won't Have It"

Concentrating United States Troops
on the Northern Indian Agencies

Soon after the Civil War, Indian uprisings broke out in the Western territories. It became so serious it was necessary to concentrate heavy bodies of troops at the northern agencies. Most of these troops, veterans of the disbanded Union and Confederate armies, re-enlisted in the Western forces simply for the adventure of it. These men were trained in Indian warfare, particularly the cavalrymen who fought in the major engagements with the Indians.

Drawn by Frederic Remington. Courtesy Harper's Weekly

Concentrating troops on the northern Indian agencies

Drawn by Frederic Remington. Courtesy Harold McCracken

General George Crook in Indian country

Drawn by Frederic Remington. Courtesy Harold McCracken

An old-time mountain man

"I Am Ready—I Will Go"

A trooper of the Tenth Horse

The scout

From a painting by Frederic Remington. Courtesy Harold McCracken

Drawn by Frederic Remington. Courtesy Harper's Weekly

Infantry on the march on the western plains

Drawn by Frederic Remington. Courtesy Harold McCracken

"A 'Government Six' Mired Down"

Courtesy Museum of Fine Arts, Houston, Texas

The battle of the Little Big Horn
—Custer's Last Stand against the Sioux under Sitting Bull

Water color (in color) by Frederic Remington from the Hogg Brothers collection of works by Frederic Remington

From a painting by Frederic Remington, Hogg Brothers Collection. Courtesy Museum of Fine Arts, Houston, Texas

The flight of Geronimo

From an oil on canvas by Frederic Remington. Courtesy Remington Art Memorial, Ogdensburg, New York

Cavalry charge on the southern plains

204

From a painting by Frederic Remington. Courtesy U. S. Army Signal Corps

The Lame Deer Fight, May 6, 1877

9

Cuban Interlude

The War with Spain

1898

"I am deeply sorry, Mr. President," Grover Cleveland is supposed to have said to William McKinley following the latter's inauguration, "to pass on to you a war with Spain. It will come within two years. Nothing can stop it."

Spain had been trying for years to quell a Cuban revolt that intermittently burst into violence. American public resentment, incited by newspapers alleging Spanish atrocities committed against Cubans, reached the point of wild talk of military intervention. That the United States was unprepared to fight a prolonged war never entered the minds of editors and politicians bent on involving the country in one. Despite unpreparedness, the newspapers, a few irresponsible individuals, and ex-Civil War officers who wanted a bit more of military glory, kept up the clamor.

Spain, no better prepared for war, boasted a navy of overage, leaky, thin-skinned warships and an army untrained and ill-equipped for anything except Old-World-style parades.

To arouse excitement for war, headlines continued to scream brazenly about Spanish "outrages" and "atrocities." Newspapers, particularly those of W. R. Hearst and Joseph Pulitzer, engaged in a reckless contest to see which could smear the blackest ink on the most bloodcurdling headline. Newspaper and public pressure on Congress, and the mysterious destruction of the battleship *Maine* in Havana Harbor on February 15, 1898, speedily settled the matter. War came in April.

With the outbreak of the war, William Glackens, assigned by *McClure's Magazine* under contract to make a portfolio of drawings of military operations, left for Tampa, Florida, muster-ground of the American army. Tampa, ordinarily a little seaport town, became overnight a warlike but decidedly unmilitary community. For several weeks contingents of the regular army and new volunteers had been pouring into the little town, swelling it beyond capacity. The huge and resplendent Tampa Bay Hotel became a rendezvous for hordes of hangers-on, foreign officials, adventurers, sightseers, and politicians.

Army conditions at Tampa were frightful. There were insufficient tents and little or no transportation. Tampa itself was badly situated for the accommodation of large bodies of troops. One single-track railroad connected the city with the camp nine miles away. Hundreds of freight cars, loaded with war supplies but unmarked as to contents, jammed the track. Bills of lading were lost. Officers, with no way of knowing what the cars contained, were obliged to break door seals and hunt from car to car for supplies for their men. One fifteen-car freight train, loaded with uniforms and shunted onto a siding 25 miles from Tampa, remained there for three weeks while officers and soldiers suffered for want of clothing. Officers hunted their commands; commands searched for their officers and supplies. Teamsters hunted for mules and harness. Cavalrymen did not know whether or not they had mounts and saddles.

To further confuse the situation, Major General William R. Shafter and Major General James F. Wade arrived, each under the impression he was to take command. Wade appeared to be Shafter's superior by a three-day priority in date of commission. Then Fitzhugh Lee, former Confederate Army officer, arrived, also in the uniform with a major general's stars. Embarrassed by this state of affairs the three generals retired to their respective hotel rooms and awaited clarification. The matter was finally settled by War Department orders which gave the command to Shafter.

Meanwhile the war had begun. Commodore George Dewey and the American fleet had left Hong Kong for the Philippines. On May Day, Dewey appeared at Manila Bay and destroyed the Spanish fleet in the bay to the last ship without loss to the Americans of a single man. Admiral William T. Sampson and Admiral Winfield S. Schley, with the remainder of the American fleet, were roaming the Caribbean, hunting the second Spanish fleet under Admiral Pascual Cervera y Topete, which, it was feared, would shell New York and other Atlantic seaboard cities. Cervera, surprisingly, brought his fleet into the harbor at Santiago de Cuba, where he was immediately bottled up. Sampson, on June 7, wired the Navy Department:

"Bombarded the forts at Santiago 7:30 A.M. to 10 A.M. today June 5. Have silenced works quickly without injury of any kind though stationary within 2,000 yards. If 10,000 were here, city and fleet would be ours within 48 hours. Every consideration demands immediate army movement. If delayed, city will be defended more strongly by guns taken from fleet."

Sampson, bringing his ships under the guns of the Santiago forts, observed the Spanish fleet riding at anchor. Investing the city meant that troops for the operation had to be sent from Tampa without delay. The effort promised much. The grand strategy—simple. Dewey controlled the Pacific. Sampson and Schley had Cervera's fleet bottled up in Santiago Harbor. The final trick now was to catch the Spanish army and navy at Santiago between the land and naval forces of the United States.

At this juncture the embarkation operation at Tampa was maddening. Many steamers were not fitted out for troop transportation service. Thousands of tons of military supplies congested the area and the wharves. Men, mules, army baggage became hopelessly entangled. Divisions and brigades, equally confused, waited for orders. Soon the Rough Riders arrived from Texas. Their officers, Colonel Leonard Wood and Lieutenant Colonel Theodore Roosevelt, after one look at the state of affairs, commandeered a train, loaded their regiment on board, arrived at the port, and seized the transport *Yucatan,* defying all and sundry to do anything about it.

At last, men and supplies were loaded aboard the transports and the trip to Cuba got under way. The tropical heat was unbearable. Men and animals alike, crowded in stuffy transports, suffered terribly. On board the transport carrying General Shafter went William Glackens—and probably Stephen Crane—and many other artists and correspondents.

Correspondents were not permitted to go ashore at Daiquiri, however, until the army had taken the blockhouses on the hills surrounding the landing place. Frederic Remington's account of the campaign and of his activities is as lively and spirited as Glackens' drawings.

"I sat on a hill," he wrote, "and down in the road below saw the long line of troops pressing up the valley toward Siboney. When our troops got on the beach, each soldier adjusted his roll, shouldered his rifle and started for Santiago, apparently by individual intuition. . . . I think our army would never have stopped until it cracked into the doomed city in column formation, if Shafter had not discovered this unlooked-for enterprise and sent his personal aide on a fast horse with positive orders to halt until the 'cracker line' could be fixed up behind them. . . .

"Sure enough, the road was jammed with troops; up El Paso Hill went the horses of Grimes' battery under whip and spur . . . and along the road stood the Rough Riders—Roosevelt's now, for Wood was a brigadier. Grimes fired a few shells toward Santiago, and directly came a screaming shrapnel from the Spanish lines. It burst over the Rough Riders, and the manoeuvre picture on the hill underwent a lively change. It was thoroughly evident the Spaniards had the range of everything in the country. For myself, I fled, dragging my horse up the hill. Some as gallant soldiers, and as daring correspondents as it is my pleasure to know, did their legs proud there. The tall form of Major John Jacob Astor moved in my front in jack-rabbit bounds. Directly came the warning scream of number 2, and we dropped and hugged the ground like starved fish. Bang! right over us it exploded. The next shell went into the battery, killing and doing damage. Following shells were going into the troops down in the road. . . .

"The column of troops was working it way into battle-line. I could hear noises such as you can make if you strike quickly with a small walking-stick at a very few green leaves. Some of them were very near and others more faint. They were the Mausers, and out in front through the jungle I could hear what sounded like Fourth of July morning. It struck me as new, strange, almost uncanny, because I wanted the roar of battle.

"Then came the light as I passed out of the jungle, and forded San Juan River. The clicking in the leaves continued, and the fire-crackers rattled out in front.

" 'Get down, old man; you'll catch one,' said an old alkali friend, and I got down sitting there with the officers of the cavalry brigade. Promptly some surgeons came along, saying it was the only safe place, and they began to dig the sand to level it. We, in consequence, moved out into the crackle, and I tied my horse with some others. 'Too bad, old fellow,' I thought; 'I should have you behind. Modern rifle fire is rough on horses. They can't get down. But, you dear old thing, you will have to take your chances.' And I then looked at the preparations for the field hospital. A man came, stooping over with his arms drawn up and hands flapping downward at the wrists—that's the way with all people when they are shot through the body.

"Then the oncoming troops poured through the hole in the jungle which led to San Juan Hill. As the troops came pouring across the ford they stooped as low as they anatomically could, and their faces were wild with excitement. The older officers stood up as straight as on parade. They must have done it through pride, or they may have known that it is better to be 'drilled clean' than to have a long-ranging wound. It was probably both. . . .

"The fire was now incessant. The horses lay down, one after another, as the Mausers found their billets. I tried to take mine to a place of safety, but a sharpshooter potted at me and I gave up. There was no place of safety.

"Now men came walking or were carried into the temporary hospital in a string. One boy was brought in by two tough, hairy old soldiers, his head hanging down behind. His shirt was off, and a big red spot shone brilliantly against his marble skin. They laid him tenderly down, and the surgeons stooped over him. The doctor folded his arms across his breast and turned to a man who held a wounded foot up to him, dumbly imploring aid as a dog might.

"I went down the creek, keeping under the bank and then out into the 'scrub,' hunting for our line. The bullets cut and clicked around, and a sharpshooter nearly did me. I ran quickly across a space. 'Wheet!' came a Mauser, and it was right next to my ear, and two more. I dropped in the tall guineagrass, and crawled to some soldiers, hidden under a mango tree. I think that episode cost me my sketchbook. I believe I lost it during that crawl, and the Spaniard shot so well I wouldn't trust him again.

"From the vantage of a little bank under a big tree I had my first glimpse of San Juan Hill—and the bullets whistled about. Our men out in front were firing. I had no idea that they were to assault that hill. I did not understand how our men could stay out there under the grueling fire. Directly I heard our line yelling and even then did not suppose it was an assault. Then the Mausers came in continuous whistle.

"I crawled along to a new place and finally got sight of the fort, and I could just see our blue soldiers on the hilltop—and I also noticed that the Mauser bullets rained no more. Then I started after.

"The country was alive with wounded men—some to die in the dreary jungle, some to get their happy home-draft, but all to be miserable. Only a handful of men got to the top, where they broke out a flag and cheered. 'Cheer' is the word for that sound. You have got to hear it once where it means so much, and ever after you will thrill when Americans make that noise.

"San Juan was taken by infantry and dismounted cavalry of the United States regular army without the aid of artillery. It was a most glorious feat of arms, considering every condition. It was done without grub, without reserves of either ammunition or men, and under tropical conditions. It was a storm of intrenched heights, held by veteran troops armed with modern guns, supported by artillery, and no other troops on the earth would have even thought that they could take San Juan heights let alone doing it."

The morning of July 17, 1898, broke warm and clear. Mounted orderlies rode along the lines at Santiago carrying an important message. General Orders No. 37:

"The Commanding General's compliments and the division and brigade commanders accompanied by their staffs are to assemble at corps headquarters to witness the surrender of the Spanish forces."

Orders had gone out to the men that there was to be no cheering. Soon generals, staff officers, and orderlies had assembled, some 200 in the procession, General William R. Shafter and Major General Joseph Wheeler in the forefront.

Midway between the lines the procession paused. In striking contrast to the plain blue campaign uniforms worn by Shafter and Wheeler, General Toral was dressed in a smart blue linen uniform, gaily decorated with a profusion of gold braid and medals. The atmosphere was friendly, smiles everywhere. The defeated Spaniards wore bright looks and seemed in a lighter mood than the American officers. Intense interest and curiosity were shown on both sides, for this was the first time the opposing forces had been afforded a good look at each other.

"General Toral rode forward and smilingly saluted General Shafter, who stretched forth his hand and heartily shook that of the Spanish general. He congratulated General Toral upon the bravery of his men and of their gallant defense of Santiago, and expressed satisfaction that the campaign had closed. . . . There was no giving up of General Toral's sword, as it had been previously arranged that the Spanish officers should retain their side arms."

Following formalities in the field, the procession

of American officers, now accompanied by two troops of United States cavalry, and the 9th United States Infantry, moved to the plaza in front of the palace. After a short welcome in the audience hall, the procession moved out into the plaza for the flag-raising ceremony. The troops lined up, two officers stood on the roof with the flag. The band made ready. Precisely at the stroke of noon by the cathedral clock, Captain William McKittrick hauled the flag to the top of the flag pole, while the band below played "The Star Spangled Banner." All the officers uncovered, the troops presented arms, and Santiago came into American hands.

After the surrender of Santiago, Spanish resistance collapsed. The conquest was easy. Stephen Crane, a newspaper correspondent, captured one town all by himself. He walked in, received the surrender, and then waited for the army to catch up with him. General Brooke had his detachment drawn up ready to attack Guayama on August 9, when he received a message from the president announcing that peace had been declared. The disappointed general, after reading the message, said "But three minutes and we should have fired." Now it was up to the occupation forces. The war was over.

Not long afterward, Glackens contracted a tropical sickness and became very ill. His drawings, arriving at *McClure's* too late to be of topical interest, were not seen publicly for almost thirty years. Nor did Glackens use them for transcription to oils. But as works of military art, his drawings take their rightful place among those of Redwood, Remington, and Homer.

Admiral Dewey on the navigating bridge
of the flagship U.S.S. *Olympia* at the battle of Manila

The *Olympia*'s magazines almost out of ammunition, Admiral Dewey, as the fog of battle
smoke cleared, saw that the Spanish fleet was out of action. The victory was complete.

From a painting by the Chinese artist, Pun Woo, Hong Kong. Courtesy U. S. Naval Academy Museum, Annapolis

The battle of Manila Bay, May 1, 1898

The decisiveness of this naval engagement has no precedent in naval history. In a little over thirty minutes, the United States Pacific Fleet under Admiral George Dewey, attacked the Spanish fleet and sank every ship without the loss of a single American seaman.

From a painting by R. F. Zogbaum. Courtesy U. S. Naval Academy Museum, Annapolis

The battle of Santiago de Cuba, July 3, 1898

In this battle the Spanish fleet, under Admiral Pascual Cervera y Topete, anchored in the harbor, was blockaded by the United States fleet under Admiral Sampson. Cervera made a desperate attempt to run the blockade and was completely destroyed by ships commanded by W. S. Schley, who carried out Sampson's plans.

Brigadier General William Ludlow,
U. S. Volunteers, chief of engineer forces
in the field

Major General William R. Shafter,
commanding 5th Army Corps, Tampa, Fla.

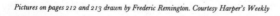

Pictures on pages 212 and 213 drawn by Frederic Remington. Courtesy Harper's Weekly

Brigadier General Guy U. Henry, U. S.
Volunteers, commanding 1st Brigade,
5th Corps, Tampa, Fla.

Brigadier General Adna R. Chaffee,
U. S. Volunteers, commanding 2nd Division,
5th Corps

Major General Joseph Wheeler,
U. S. Volunteers, commanding
Cavalry Division, Tampa

Lieutenant Colonel Wallace F. Randolph,
U. S. A., commanding Field Artillery
Brigade, Port Tampa, Fla.

Major General James F. Wade,
U. S. Volunteers, commanding 3rd Army
Corps, Chickamauga

213

The Battle Sketches of William Glackens

These remarkable sketches, executed on the spot by the artist, generally average 18 x 24 inches in size. The figures are sketched in black and sepia, some in crayon, others in ink, with the "filling in" done in dark blue water color, producing a striking over-all effect.

From a drawing by William Glackens. Courtesy The Kraushaar Galleries

Tampa, Florida, 1898

"A midday mess in the 6th Cavalry Regiment. Because of the heat they built for themselves a sort of arbor of branches which afforded protection of a sort from the sun and makes a picturesque mess tent."

From a drawing by William Glackens. Courtesy The Kraushaar Galleries

Arrival of Arizona cowboys,
Sunday evening, 31st

"They will be used as mule packers chiefly and
some as scouts."

Tampa, Florida, 1898

Embarkation of United States troops at Tampa,
Florida, 1898.

From a drawing by William Glackens. Courtesy The Kraushaar Galleries

Transports anchored in the bay, June 10

Shelling the woods before landing the troops at Daiquiri, Cuba, 1898

From a drawing by William Glackens. Courtesy The Kraushaar Galleries

Horses swimming ashore from the transports at Daiquiri, Cuba, 1898

From a drawing by William Glackens. Courtesy The Kraushaar Galleries

The beginning of debarkation of troops at Daiquiri, Cuba

From a drawing by William Glackens. Courtesy The Kraushaar Galleries

Just before the engagement, El Pozo, 1898

From a drawing by William Glackens. Courtesy The Kraushaar Galleries

Battle of El Pozo, Cuba, 1898

219

From a painting by Frederic Remington. Courtesy Yale University Art Gallery

The scream of shrapnel at San Juan Hill, July 1, 1898

The night after San Juan, Cuba, 1898

Mopping up operations on San Juan Hill immediately after the battle.

From a drawing by William Glackens. Courtesy The Kraushaar Galleries

The night after San Juan
—a field hospital

From a drawing by William Glackens. Courtesy The Kraushaar Galleries

The night after San Juan
—a field hospital

Bringing in the wounded the night after the battle of San Juan Hill.

From a drawing by William Glackens. Courtesy The Kraushaar Galleries

In the trenches during a truce

"The Spanish lines run right up in front of the city,
not five hundred yards from ours at this point."

From a drawing by William Glackens. Courtesy The Kraushaar Galleries

Santiago de Cuba, July 17, 1898

Showing the Spanish military officials (on the right) greeting the
American officers on their arrival to accept the surrender.

From a drawing in wash by William Glackens. Courtesy The Kraushaar Galleries

Surrender of the Spanish forces
to General William Shafter, Santiago de Cuba

Raising the United States flag
over the Governor's Palace, Santiago, Cuba

10

Armageddon

World War I

1917–1918

On November 14, 1918, General Peyton C. March, Chief of Staff, United States Army, wrote, "With the signing of the Armistice on November 11, 1918, the war has been practically brought to an end. The events of the past four years have been of such magnitude that the various steps, the numberless battles, and the growth of Allied power which led up to the final victory are not clearly defined even in the minds of many military men. . . ." It was, indeed, a complex war.

Never before in the history of the world were so many nations arrayed in battle against each other. Never before were such deadly weapons used for the achievement of military ends. Before the war ended, the belligerents were using poison gas, flame-throwers, machine guns, grenades, Mills bombs, submarine mines, depth charges, marine torpedoes, aerial bombs, aircraft, tanks, the heaviest of artillery, whippet tanks, antitank guns with armor-piercing shells, and nail-studded clubs.

The incident that started the hair-triggered guns of Europe shooting in all directions was provided by a Serbian patriot who, on June 28, 1914, shot and killed Archduke Francis Ferdinand of Austria at Sarajevo, Bosnia. Four weeks later, Austria declared war on Serbia. Germany, allied with Austria, had long planned how she would fight a general European war. Her army had been trained to the peak of perfection. Military storehouses bulged with army supplies. Her navy boasted a fleet of 380 U-boats in addition to ships of the German High Seas Fleet.

Germany, after an unanswerable ultimatum to the czar's government, declared war on Russia. The "Schlieffen Plan" an elaborate military stratagem, studied for 40 years by the German general staff, was quickly put into operation.

Allied mobilization was remarkably rapid. Three days after the declaration of war, British and French troops were fighting the Germans in Alsace-Lorraine. The overwhelming power of the German army forced the British and French to fall back after engagements at Morhange, Neufchateau, and Charleroi. Soon the entire Allied line was in retreat after the collapse of the British left wing at Mons. For two weeks the Belgians, fighting desperately, held the Germans at Liège. But the Germans brought up their biggest guns, pounded to pieces Liège's supposedly impregnable fortresses, and occupied Belgium.

The German advance into France seemed impossible to stop. Then came the "Miracle of the Marne." The decisive battle which the Germans had planned for four decades was not won, as is generally supposed, by a French army transported in Paris taxicabs. The French reserves arrived not to win the battle of the Marne, but just in time to win the battle of the Ourcq. The French army fought desperately for three days, recoiling under terrific pressure, suffering losses amounting to annihilation in some of the units, but General Foch broke the German thrust.

Oddly enough, the French believed they had won a

tremendous victory that drove the hated Hun out of France. Stranger yet, the Germans thought it a minor reverse. "They advanced seeking a second Sedan," wrote correspondent Frank Simonds, "and the French there won an Antietam."

The success at the Marne spurred the French into an attack against the German line along the Aisne River. Advancing on a 25 mile front, between Soissons and Reims, the French captured Craonne Ridge, while the British, attacking at Arras, carried Vimy Ridge and pierced the "unbreakable" Hindenburg line to the Argonne Forest. The war then went underground. Both sides dug trenches like moles, lived in water-filled dugouts, fired over muddy parapets, and stared across "No Man's Land" for three years.

When news of the sinking of the British liner *Lusitania* off the Irish coast by a German U-boat hit the front pages, the loss of 1,154 lives shocked the United States. Then Germany declared all the waters surrounding Great Britain, Ireland, and the English Channel were in the war zone. The United States, for the moment, did nothing except to demand reparations and damages; meanwhile, unrestricted U-boat warfare developed in intensity. Finally, on April 6, 1917, Congress declared war on imperial Germany. The American Expeditionary Forces were organized and placed under the command of General John J. Pershing. On June 26, the first troop convoy sailed secretly for France.

"It was in May, 1917," wrote Albert Eugene Gallatin, "that plans were set afoot to send artists to France to make a pictorial record of the various activities of our armies. Major Kendall Banning, who was at that time Director of the Division of Pictures of the Committee on Public Information, and who afterwards was attached to the War College Division of the War Department, was responsible for this recommendation. He at once consulted with representatives of Great Britain and France and learned what those countries had done in using their artists for portraying the history of their armies. Their advice was to commission capable artists and to assign them to duty within military zones, which would not be opened to civilians.

"In June, 1917, Major Banning got in touch with many artists who seemed to him to be available for duty as official artists; Major Banning also conferred with Charles Dana Gibson. Major Banning then submitted his recommendations to the Secretary of War. It was, however, not until late in January, 1918, that the Secretary of War took any action. Authority was obtained to commission eight men as official artists in the Engineer Reserve Corps. At Major Banning's suggestion, Mr. Charles Dana Gibson was chosen chairman of a group of artists to make recommendations. Mr. J. Andre Smith was the first of the group to be commissioned a Captain in the Engineer Reserve Corps and sent overseas. He was followed by Captains Ernest Peixotto, William J. Aylward, Harry Townsend, Wallace Morgan, George Harding, Walter J. Duncan and Harvey Dunn."

The port of St. Nazaire, Brest, France was the landing place of the first division of the American Expeditionary Forces. Seasoned and battle-hardened, having just taken part in the actions against Pancho Villa on the Mexican border, the first considerable number of troops landed in July, 1917, though high-ranking officers and staff men had arrived in June.

The great German offensive began on March 21, 1918. Ninety-five divisions of 22,000 men each, deployed over a 50 mile front, from Arras to La Fère, were thrown against the British northern flank. The British line held despite a terrific pounding. The Germans attacking the Allied southern flank were more successful, effecting a breakthrough to within four and one-half miles of the main railroad from Paris to Calais via Amiens.

The Germans, on April 9, opened a second and heavier attack north of Lens, gaining ten miles on a 30 mile front. The success of this attack was followed up on May 27 by an attack in Champagne which drove a salient to the Marne at Chateau-Thierry. Then all German action ceased until July 15, when, in a new and heavier offensive, launched south of Reims, they crossed the Marne.

Marine Captain John W. Thomason wrote his vivid impressions of the Marine action at Belleau Wood and Soissons:

"The Boche wanted Hill 142; he came, and rifles broke him, and he came again. All his batteries were in action, and always his machine guns scourged the place, but he could not make head against the rifles. Guns he could understand; he knew all about bombs and auto rifles and trench mortars, but aimed, sustained rifle fire, that comes from nowhere in particular and picks off men—it brought the war home to the individual and demoralized him."

With the organization of the 1st American Army on August 10, under the personal command of General Pershing, the history of the A.E.F. entered a new stage. The last two offensives—St. Mihiel (September 26–November 11) and the Meuse-Argonne (September 26–November 11)—were major operations planned and executed by American officers. "Through forty-seven days we were engaged in a persistent struggle with the enemy," wrote General Pershing, "to smash through his defenses. The attack started on a front of twenty-four miles, which gradually extended until the enemy was being assailed from the Argonne Forest to the Moselle River, a distance of ninety miles."

The terrain was composed of heavy densely

wooded ridges that ran between the almost impenetrable Argonne Forest on the western flank to the heights of the Meuse River on the eastern flank. Montfaucon was situated on high ground in the center of the line. Opened to artillery fire from three sides, the American troops, to attack it, had to run the gauntlet of this fire. The cost in men was great, but on September 27, Montfaucon was taken by American troops.

Meanwhile, the German salient, a great wedge in the French line at St. Mihiel, seriously threatened the supply route to the French zone. The Germans had held this sector for four long, bloody years. The American attack at St. Mihiel began at midnight, September 12, with a heavy artillery concentration. The devastating barrage continued all night, rolling from one end of the line to the other. At 5 A.M. the American army went "over the top" and struck both sides of this salient simultaneously. The American troops attacked in wave after wave, the Germans putting up fanatical resistance. For 24 hours the furious tide of battle swayed back and forth. Finally, the two wings of the American army met at Vigneulles, wiping out the salient. The cost of this action to the Americans was high. But the Germans' was higher: 40,000 men killed and wounded, and 27,000 taken prisoner. After the collapse of the St. Mihiel salient, so rapid was the German retreat that 30 villages were captured almost intact. In 24 hours American troops had taken more prisoners than had been taken on the French front during the entire war and had recovered a larger area of French territory than had been taken in any similar period.

After St. Mihiel, the German military effort gradually diminished. But the long road to the Rhineland was a series of desperate retreating actions fought by the Germans. In the end, reports told of victories all along the front. General Allenby, in a brilliant campaign, with Lawrence of Arabia, knocked Turkey out of the war, consolidated Arabia, and cleared Mesopotamia of German and Turkish troops. On November 11, 1918, the Armistice was signed and the war was over.

At the outset of the war the German navy engaged in unrestricted undersea warfare. The British navy, though listed first in naval tonnage, could not seem to cope with the U-boat situation. Then, on May 31, 1916, the greatest naval battle in history up to that time was fought between the German High Seas Fleet and the British Grand Fleet.

For 20 months battleships and cruisers of the German High Seas Fleet had been cooped up in Kiel Canal. Suddenly, the German fleet made a dash from the Jutland coast and steamed out 100 miles into the North Sea. Admirals von Hipper and von Scheer hoped to engage and destroy the British cruiser squadron of Admiral David Beatty in those waters before the Grand Fleet could come to its aid. Beatty caught the German fleet off guard, gave chase, cutting the Germans off from their home bases. Beatty's wireless gave a running account of the chase, meanwhile summoning aid from Jellicoe's Grand Fleet. Admiral Sir John Jellicoe, after receiving the urgent message, proceeded at full speed to join Beatty. The battle of Jutland was, perhaps, one of the first major naval engagements in which air reconnaissance was used. But the results of the battle were equivocal. British losses were much higher than German; tactically the Germans outfought the British. Nevertheless, the German High Seas Fleet did not escape, remained at its base for the rest of the war, did no raiding of Britain's supply lines. Like many another battle, "it was a famous victory"— but for whom depends on one's frame of reference.

Admiral William S. Sims arrived at Queenstown early in 1917 with the U.S. destroyer fleet amid cheers of an excited crowd of Britons waving small American flags. Not long after their arrival the U.S. destroyer fleet was assigned to convoy duty in the North Atlantic, hunting down and sinking U-boats. In these actions against the U-boats, aircraft came into play. In the meantime American shipbuilding production far exceeded tonnage lost to the German undersea raiders. That the United States Navy did its part in the war is evidenced by a note written by Archibald Hurd, the English naval expert.

"When the war is over," he wrote, "the nation will form some conception of the debt which we owe the American Navy for the manner in which it has cooperated, not only in connection with the convoy system, but in fighting submarines. If the naval position is improving today, as it is, it is due to the fact that the British and American fleets are working in closest accord, supported by an immense body of skilled workers on both sides of the Atlantic, who are turning out destroyers and other craft for dealing with the submarine, as well as mines and bombs. Some of the finest battleships of the United States Navy are now associated with the British Grand Fleet. They are not only splendid fighting ships but they are well officered and manned."

At the war's end General John J. Pershing, commander of the American Expeditionary Forces, closed his official report: "Finally, I pay the supreme tribute to our officers and soldiers of the line. When I think of their heroism, their patience under hardships, their unflinching spirit of offensive action, I am filled with emotion which I am unable to express. Their deeds are immortal, and they earned the eternal gratitude of our country."

From a drawing by Captain Harvey Dunn, Corps of Engineers, A.E.F. Courtesy The Smithsonian Institution

The machine gunner

The *Mauretania* at sea

One of the first Cunard luxury liners to be converted into a troop carrier, the *Mauretania* is seen here with a cargo of American troops bound for Brest, France. Her checkerboard camouflage, protection against submarines, was intended to break up the ship's silhouette against the horizon line and thus present a distracting target to the enemy.

American troops debarking at Brest, France, July 22, 1918

American troop supply train

Troops resting near Sanzey after a long march

From a drawing by Captain Ernest Peixotto, Corps of Engineers, A.E.F. Courtesy The Smithsonian Institution

German bomb shelters near Varennes, France

From a drawing by Captain Ernest Peixotto, Corps of Engineers, A.E.F. Courtesy The Smithsonian Institution

Mine crater on the road to Varennes, France

232

From a drawing by Captain George Harding, Corps of Engineers, A.E.F. Courtesy The Smithsonian Institution

Third Division passing through a village on the Marne

From a drawing by Captain Harry Townsend, Corps of Engineers, A.E.F. Courtesy The Smithsonian Institution

Contact with the enemy, France

233

From a drawing by Captain Harvey Dunn, Corps of Engineers, A.E.F. Courtesy The Smithsonian Institution

Morning on the Marne

From a painting in oil by Captain Harvey Dunn, Corps of Engineers, A.E.F. Courtesy The Smithsonian Institution

Machine-gun emplacement in a graveyard, Seicheprey

234

The tanks at Seicheprey, France, 1918

Ripping up the barbed wire, American tanks advance toward the German lines, straddling the enemy trenches.

On the wire

235

Valley of the Marne
at Mont St. Père, France

"Alive with military activity during
the American advance."

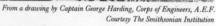

From a drawing by Captain George Harding, Corps of Engineers, A.E.F.
Courtesy The Smithsonian Institution

From a drawing by Captain George Harding, Corps of Engineers, A.E.F. Courtesy The Smithsonian Institution

American wounded making their way to a first aid station,
Chateau-Thierry, France, July, 1918

236

From a drawing by Captain Harvey Dunn, Corps of Engineers, A.E.F.
Courtesy The Smithsonian Institution

The sniper

From a drawing by Captain Harvey Dunn, Corps of Engineers, A.E.F.
Courtesy The Smithsonian Institution

The Boche looter

237

The air raid

A single-seater German plane strafes the streets of a French village, somewhere in France.

American soldiers billeted in an old Benedictine monastery, Toul sector

238

From a drawing by Captain Ernest Peixotto, Corps of Engineers, A.E.F. Courtesy The Smithsonian Institution

Neufmaison, France, 1918

"A typical village of the Lorraine front in which the American troops are billeted."

From an oil painting by John Singer Sargent. Courtesy The Museum of Fine Arts, Boston

The road, France, 1918

"The road near Arras."

Sketches from Captain John W. Thomason's notebook

Using any kind of paper he could get his hands on, Captain Thomason sketched his memorable scenes of Marines in action and "off duty" in the war against the "Boche," in the Argonne, Belleau Wood, Soissons, and the Rhine.

One of our aviators in his "Teddy Bear,"
France, 1918

The engineer

From a drawing by Captain Ernest Peixotto, Corps of Engineers, A.E.F. Courtesy The Smithsonian Institution

Rolling out a new plane for its first flight, Issoudun, France, 1918

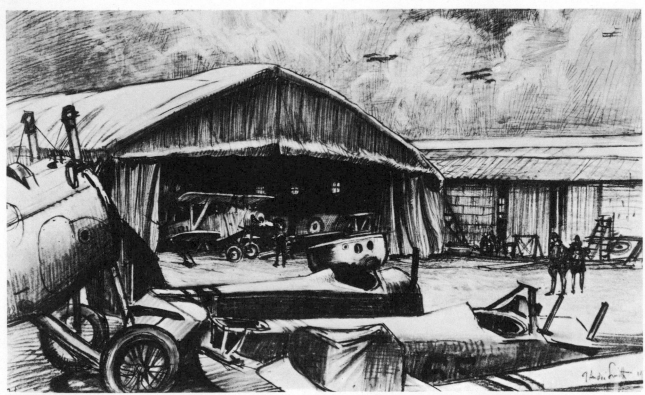

From a drawing by Captain J. Andre Smith, Corps of Engineers, A.E.F. Courtesy The Smithsonian Institution

Lame ducks

From a drawing by Captain Ernest Peixotto, Corps of Engineers, A.E.F. Courtesy The Smithsonian Institution

The test blocks at Issoudun, France, 1918

From a drawing by Captain Harry Townsend, Corps of Engineers, A.E.F. Courtesy The Smithsonian Institution

The alert Nieuports, France, 1918

"With the 147th Aero Squadron, First Pursuit Group."

From a drawing by Captain George Harding, Corps of Engineers, A.E.F. Courtesy The Smithsonian Institution

Vanquished by a Boche plane, Varennes, France, 1918

"September 26th, a Boche plane got two balloons in less than a minute."

From a drawing by Captain J. Andre Smith, Corps of Engineers, A.E.F. Courtesy The Smithsonian Institution

Air field No. I, at Issoudun, France, 1918

The morning wash-up, Neufmaison, France, 1918

From a drawing by Captain Wallace Morgan, Corps of Engineers, A.E.F. Courtesy The Smithsonian Institution

Supply train on the Paris-Metz road
during the battle of Belleau Wood, June 6, 1918

From a sketch by Captain John W. Thomason, U.S.M.C.
Courtesy Mrs. John W. Thomason and Charles Scribner's Sons, New York

"A Marine and His Rifle."

From a drawing by Captain John W. Thomason, U.S.M.C. Courtesy Mrs. John W. Thomason and Charles Scribner's Sons, New York

The Second Engineers

Off duty

From a drawing by Captain Harvey Dunn, Corps of Engineers, A.E.F. Courtesy The Smithsonian Institution

247

Listening post
in Belleau Wood, France, 1918

From a drawing by Captain J. Andre Smith, Corps of Engineers, A.E.F. Courtesy The Smithsonian Institution

From a painting by Captain Harvey Dunn, Corps of Engineers, A.E.F. Courtesy The Smithsonian Institution

Sunday morning at Cunel, France, 1918

248

"The fighting in the woods at Soissons was close and savage"

"Certain designated individuals watched," front line, France, 1918

His rifle resting on the parapet, "potato-mashers" and Mills bombs within easy reach, this sentry watches for signs of enemy activity.

Road to the front—northwest of Chateau-Thierry, 1918

American troops moving up through a war-damaged village
in France, 1918

From a painting by Captain Harvey Dunn, Corps of Engineers, A.E.F. Courtesy The Smithsonian Institution

The prisoner

Bringing in a German prisoner for interrogation, somewhere in France, 1918.

From a drawing by Captain Harvey Dunn, Corps of Engineers, A.E.F. Courtesy The Smithsonian Institution

The hand grenade

A group of German soldiers, hiding in a wrecked building, try to get out of the way of a hand grenade thrown through the doorway.

251

From a drawing by Captain George Harding, Corps of Engineers, A.E.F. Courtesy The Smithsonian Institution

Charging a German trench, Verdun offensive

"American troops following a barrage."

From a drawing by Captain Harvey Dunn, Corps of Engineers, A.E.F. Courtesy The Smithsonian Institution

Street fighting

From a drawing by Captain Wallace Morgan, Corps of Engineers, A.E.F. Courtesy The Smithsonian Institution

The pursuit

American forces crossing the old No Man's Land in pursuit of the retreating Germany army.

From a drawing by Captain George Harding, Corps of Engineers, A.E.F. Courtesy The Smithsonian Institution

Cleaning out a German machine-gun nest, St. Mihiel Drive, France, 1918

American troops waiting to advance at Hattonchatel, St. Mihiel drive

A fighting swirl of Senegalese

"Those sawed-off shotguns
they gave us at St. Mihiel"

The Senegalese

"With reason the Boche feared them
worse than anything living."

*Pictures on this page are from field sketches by Captain John W. Thomason,
U.S.M.C. Courtesy Mrs. John W. Thomason and Charles Scribner's Sons*

From a drawing by Captain Harvey Dunn, Corps of Engineers, A.E.F. Courtesy The Smithsonian Institution

Combat patrol

Street fighting in a town held by opposite forces, France, 1918.

From a drawing by Captain Harvey Dunn, Corps of Engineers, A.E.F. Courtesy The Smithsonian Institution

The flare, "No Man's Land," France, September, 1918

Bringing in the wounded, caught by a German flare.

256

From a drawing by Captain Harvey Dunn, Corps of Engineers, A.E.F. Courtesy The Smithsonian Institution

The harvest moon

From a drawing by Captain J. W. Aylward, Corps of Engineers, A.E.F. Courtesy The Smithsonian Institution

First Division headquarters kitchen, St. Mihiel drive, France, 1918

The St. Mihiel drive

"Troops leisurely advancing in St. Mihiel drive passing by the ruins of Seicheprey."

On the trail of the Hun, St. Mihiel drive, France, 1918

258

An American destroyer rescuing a British seaplane

From a painting by Burnell Poole. Courtesy U. S. Naval Academy Museum and Naval Historical Foundation, Annapolis

A fast convoy

An American destroyer escorting a camouflaged troopship bound for France, 1918.

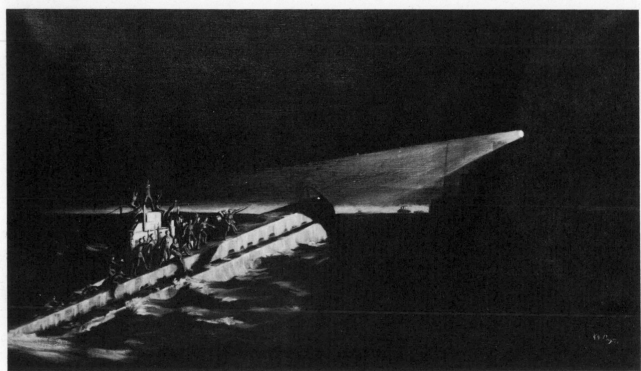

From a painting by K. K. Pointer. Courtesy U. S. Naval Academy Museum, Annapolis

Rescue of the crew of the German submarine M-103 by the United States destroyer *Davis*

From a painting by B. J. Gribble. Courtesy U.S. Naval Academy Museum, Annapolis

Arrival of the 6th Battle Squadron at Scapa Flow

From a painting by Burnell Poole. Courtesy U. S. Naval Academy Museum, Annapolis

Critical situation

An American destroyer-escort cutting across the bow of a troopship while on escort duty in a fog in the North Atlantic.

261

From a drawing by Captain Wallace Morgan, Corps of Engineers, A.E.F. Courtesy The Smithsonian Institution

The last long mile

From a drawing by Captain Wallace Morgan, Corps of Engineers, A.E.F. Courtesy The Smithsonian Institution

American troops marching through the Place de la Concorde, July 14, 1918

From a drawing by Captain Harvey Dunn, Corps of Engineers, A.E.F. Courtesy The Smithsonian Institution

Aftermath—No Man's Land—October, 1918

II

War Was Everywhere

World War II

1941–1945

The founding of the Combat Artists Program of the United States Navy in World War II was apparently conceived by the late Commander Griffith Baily Coale, distinguished mural painter of New York City. An expert on small boats and ship models, Griffith Baily Coale loved the sea. "You can't talk to Coale for half an hour," wrote the late Stephen Vincent Benét, "without realizing that his first love is, and remains, the sea, and that he has a wide and accurate knowledge of ships and sailormen, past and present, that he knows as much about salt water as he does about paint."

In a conversation with the late Mrs. Mary Minton, custodian of Naval Art Office of the Chief of Information, Navy Department, Rear Admiral Chester C. Wood, former Secretary of the Academic Board of the Naval Academy, discovered that there was apparently no record in existence which "described the inception and founding of the Combat Artists Program as it was carried out during World War II."

In a memorandum dated 11 August 1953, Admiral Wood wrote: "It so happens that I think I know something of this matter. Accordingly, as a matter of historical interest I have prepared and forward herewith some notes on the subject. These notes are written purely from memory inasmuch as I have no written records concerning the events. However, I can completely vouch for the authenticity of the statements made in the enclosure. On the other hand,

there may well be other factors and considerations which affect the authenticity of my statements and about which I have no knowledge.

"On the weekend of 15–17 March 1940, the late Mr. Griffith Baily Coale of New York City was a guest, with his wife, of mine at our quarters at the U. S. Naval Academy, Annapolis, Maryland. Mr. Coale was enroute to the official opening of the National [Mellon] Art Gallery in Washington on March 17. Mr. Coale was an old friend of my father's and a fellow painter in Baltimore, Maryland, prior to World War I. I had seen but little of him through the years but knew of his work in New York where he had achieved quite a reputation as a painter of murals and large-size decorations and portraits. His wife's father was the late Bishop Manning of New York.

"After a dinner party on the evening of March 16th, Mr. Coale informed me that he had a matter to discuss which he hoped would be of significant interest to me. The two of us retired to a small sitting room where Mr. Coale proceeded to unfold his ideas along lines which eventually developed into the entire Combat Artists Program.

"He specifically stated that he sensed that we would be shortly in the war; that he wanted an active part to play; that his long experience with ships and things maritime made him desire service within the Navy; but, his age (he was then about fifty) would prevent active duty in the line.

264

"He therefore proposed that he, and others similarly qualified be commissioned as line officers of appropriate rank, that they be actually sent to combat zones in naval ships; with no other directive than to produce a historical record of what they had seen in the form of paintings.

"He elaborated by stating that all should operate from one or principal bases where they would have studios and facilities for turning out the finished product. The artists would be sent to sea for varying periods of time—between three and six months, he felt was the optimum—and then would return to do the studio work. He insisted that they could only get the proper feeling for their work by being as much a part of the combat service as they could possibly be made. On this point he was adamant in his thinking.

"Quite naturally, I was very much impressed and continued to discuss the matter for several hours. As I think back on the conversation, there was hardly a detail which we missed. I found Mr. Coale had thought the entire program out with remarkable detail and clarity.

"The next morning from my office in the Administration Building I called two officers in the Bureau of Naval Personnel. (Note: I cannot with surety identify these officers in my memory. They were officers with whom I had had frequent contact in my capacity as Secretary of the Academic Board of the Naval Academy. I seem to remember that they were Captain Randall Jacobs and Commander Bidwell.)

"I informed these officers that a Mr. Coale would arrive before noon with an idea which I felt would interest them. Both officers expressed interest and promised to see Mr. Coale.

"Mr. Coale later informed me that he was most graciously received and generously treated.

"I suppose that it is a matter of record that his commissioning process was started that very day. In any event, he was the first of the combat artists to be commissioned.

"I happened to be in Mr. Coale's home in Stonington, Connecticut, in August 1941 just prior to his departure for Quonset, R. I., where he was to take a plane for Argentia and thence proceed across the Atlantic, by destroyer. This was the trip on which he gathered material for the book, *North Atlantic Patrol*.

"As a further footnote, Mr. Coale had no intention at any time of writing anything concerning his duty as a combat artist. However, while on the trip across the North Atlantic, he wrote some notes which he eventually showed to his neighbor in Stonington, the late Stephen Vincent Benét, the poet. Mr. Benét was so impressed with the notes that he urged Coale to put them into book form."

There soon followed other artists of reputation who entered the naval service, who would have as their "primary function the job of preserving for the public and for history the vivid scenes of modern war." Among these men were Lieutenant William Draper, Lieutenant (j.g.) Mitchell Jamieson, and Lieutenant Stanley Backus. All held commissions in the Naval Reserve. These combat artists went through the period of naval training, later being assigned to "combat battle stations along with everyone else in the ship or unit to which they are assigned." Following the convictions of Commander Coale, these Navy artists were to depend on their own eyesight and experience for subject matter, rather than on delayed reports sent to them at home. Soon these men would be traveling to every corner of the world theater of war to send back "an unequalled historical record of what they saw."

THE SOUTH PACIFIC

On December 7, 1941, the Naval Air Arm of the Imperial Japanese Fleet, in a surprise attack, struck the United States naval base at Pearl Harbor, Honolulu, Hawaii, almost crippling the U. S. Pacific Fleet. That same day, December 8, Far Eastern time, Japanese aerial bombs fell on Wake Island, Manila, Hong Kong, and Singapore. Within five months after Pearl Harbor the Japanese had possession of the Netherlands East Indies, Wake Island in the Central Pacific, Rabaul in New Britain, and the approaches to Australia.

In the Philippines, General Douglas MacArthur exacted a fearful price in Japanese lives in his stubborn defense of Bataan and Corregidor. General Jonathan Wainwright, his half-starved, malaria-ridden troops suffocating in the tunnels of Corregidor, was finally forced to capitulate on May 6, 1942, after five months of desperate resistance. General Wainwright and his men, gaunt, weary, and starved, emerged from the dark tunnels of the fortress as prisoners of war; their march to the Japanese internment camps was to become a symbol of horror.

That same month, May, 1942, saw the extension of Japanese military lines to Tulagi, off Florida Island in the Solomons. From their island airfield on Rabaul the Japanese began bombing Lae and Salamaua, New Guinea, off Huon Gulf. By July, 1942, Japanese military occupation extended more than halfway across the Pacific. Westward, Japanese penetration reached as far as the mountain fastnesses of India and Burma; while in the Northern Pacific the Japanese seized a firm foothold in the Aleutians. In Europe, France had fallen and Britain and Russia were battling for their very existence.

But the war in the Pacific for reasons of high strategy became secondary in importance to the war in Europe. Lacking the necessary equipment, American forces in the South Pacific performed miracles of defense, fighting with what they had, keeping a relentless pressure on the Japanese. It was an uncomfortable beginning, but there were no impossibilities to determined men.

"It had always been the concept of the United States Chiefs of Staff," wrote General Marshall, "that Japan could be defeated by a series of amphibious attacks across the far reaches of the Pacific. Oceans are formidable barriers, but for the nation enjoying naval superiority they become highroads of invasion." Before this operation could be executed, however, the Japanese Imperial Fleet, heretofore unchallenged and intact, had to be engaged and defeated. Despite the extensive damage sustained by the United States Pacific Fleet at Pearl Harbor, U.S. forces stopped the Japanese fleet early in May, 1942, in the Coral Sea attempting to break the supply lines to Australia. Then in June, for three days a fierce battle raged on the approaches to Midway Island, west of the Hawaiians. Every available ship and serviceable plane was thrown into the action against the ponderous Japanese naval force moving toward Midway.

Two hours before dawn on June 4 the Japanese were sighted. Marine dive bombers, Army B-26's armed with torpedoes, and Navy TBFs engaged the oncoming enemy carriers. Twenty-seven available fighting aircraft, heedless of their small numbers and outclassed planes, took on the enemy's big flying force.

As the Japanese planes and dive bombers approached the island, antiaircraft batteries opened up from redoubts in the sand on the suicidal attacks by the Jap pilots. The island soon became a raging inferno of exploding bombs, shells, and machine-gun fire.

Midway's small air force struck back with all its limited strength. Meanwhile, as the battle raged on the island, the Navy was attending to the job in hand at sea not too far away.

"For the next forty-eight hours," wrote Commander Coale, "American forces on Midway forestall the last Japanese landing attempt, while the Navy task force continues the pursuit. Once more the battle at sea rages as the fighting Naval task force engages the remaining Japanese ships. By midnight of June 7th the battle is over, but the gallant carrier Yorktown is mortally wounded after having received two torpedo hits. . . . the battle of Midway is over and won, with the Japanese Fleet in rout to the westward. The ships that came to save the Yorktown lie in a circle around the death-bed of the dying Amazon. She has come out patched from her last bold engagements, to add new laurels to the name of the

battle that she bears. The Yorktown helped tremendously to make this battle another salty Waterloo for our enemies. After slowly capsizing to port . . . the U.S.S. Yorktown sinks."

THE ALEUTIAN CAMPAIGN

The Aleutian campaign began six months after the attack on Pearl Harbor, when planes from the Japanese carriers Ryujo and Junyo, in a two-day attack, bombed Dutch Harbor in the Aleutians. The first activity was bitter. But the Japanese attack was not a full-scale invasion of Alaska. As a far-flung diversion to the main Japanese attack at Midway, to forestall an anticipated American advance via the Aleutians, the Japanese landed troops on Kiska and Attu.

Military, air, and naval operations in the Aleutians were complex and difficult because of the terrain and unpredictable weather, much of the fighting taking place on the little islands of the Aleutian chain. The few level spots, incapable of supporting a taxiway for heavy bombers, because of the soft tundra and layers of muskeg, had to be covered with steel matting.

Once the steel-matted landing fields were serviceable, B-24 bombers made sorties over the area searching out Japanese cruisers, carriers, and destroyers. When a "hole" or "break" in the overcast would occur, 11th Air Force planes dropped their bombs on the difficult moving targets. The Navy tried bombardment of Japanese installations in the Kiska area, but the risk of collision to the big warships in fog, and the inconclusive results, were too great a gamble to warrant continued actions of this kind. Once, happily, when an exceptionally good stretch of weather occurred, the 11th Air Force flew 1,175 sorties against Kiska.

The invasion of Attu developed into an infantry battle with a fanatical Japanese garrison force. Here the solution was different. By May 28, the Japanese had been pushed into a small area of ground around Chichagof Harbor. Major General Eugene Landrum, his larger force deployed on the surrounding heights, planned to finish the urgent work of clearing the Japanese from the peninsula. A surrender order was first sent through the lines to the Japanese commander, Colonel Yasuyo Yamasaki, who, instead of complying with the ultimatum, decided on a foolish and desperate counterattack. After two days of hand-to-hand fighting the Japanese garrison was wiped out. Heavy bombing missions in the months that followed finally put an end to the threat to the Aleutians.

GUADALCANAL

The first step on the long road to Tokyo was a large island, dark, jungle-covered, and forbidding, in the central Solomons, called Guadalcanal. Here began the battle to recapture the South Pacific. The very name, Guadalcanal, has blood on it. On this island the enemy had to be annihilated. Among the maze of coral atolls, reefs, lagoons, and islands that is the Solomons, the Americans and their allies fought the opening battles of the South Pacific. At the U. S. military and naval base at Noumea, on New Caledonia, was planned the simultaneous attack on Guadalcanal, Tulagi, Tanambogo, and Gavutu.

It was well known to American officers that the Japanese were building an airstrip on Guadalcanal. In fact, there was no movement the Japanese made that was not reported by the daring, resourceful coast-watchers. After a patient wait for the Japanese to complete the airstrip on Guadalcanal, on August 7, 1942, the 1st Marine Division, 10,000 strong, stormed ashore on the beach at Lunga Point in a surprise attack, took the Japanese off guard, and threw a defense perimeter around the airstrip. On that same day American forces and their allies landed at Tulagi, Tanambogo, and Gavutu.

For weeks the battle raged back and forth in jungle and swamp. At night gun flashes from American warships seared the night sky over Sealark Channel, forever afterward to be called "Iron Bottom Bay." At Guadalcanal the campaign developed into a series of small, personal, bitterly fought actions. Patrols, sweating mightily, fought desperately in the steaming jungle, taking one ridge after another in hand-to-hand fighting at night and during the day, while dogfights between the Jap Zeros and P-40's roared, screamed, and sputtered overhead.

The Japanese tried desperately to maintain their hold on Guadalcanal. The "Tokyo Express," Japanese troop transports supported by cruisers and destroyers, pushed down the seaway channel from Buin to Guadalcanal, which henceforth acquired the sobriquet of "The Slot," only to be beaten back by a Navy task force in the battle of Tassafaronga.

The Japanese, outwitted, tried every device they knew to retake Guadalcanal. Japanese bombers flew down from Rabaul with daily regularity. Sometimes at night a single plane would hover over American island installations and drop a flare, after which immediately followed heavy shell-fire from Japanese warships standing offshore.

Then, on November 12, 1942, was fought the great naval and air battle off Santa Cruz Island. During the enemy raid 16 bombers and 25 fighters met in furious battle with 24 Marine and Navy F4F Wildcats in which no less than 22 Japanese planes were shot out of the air, with not a single loss among U.S. Navy or Marine pilots.

On Guadalcanal attack after attack was repulsed by the Marines with great loss, but the baffled Japanese never got within one mile of the airstrip. From Truk, far to the northwest of Santa Cruz Island, a powerful Japanese naval task force staged the largest attack yet, and met American naval air and surface forces in a violent action in which three of the enemy's carriers were disabled and nearly a hundred Japanese planes destroyed. But the Japanese could brag that Vice Admiral Nagumo had sailed back to Truk, and that his planes had sunk the American aircraft carrier *Hornet.*

In another violent action off Savo Island, the United States Navy suffered one of its worst defeats. Admiral Mikawa, commander of the 8th Japanese Fleet, promptly gathered his warships for a fast strike at Allied invasion shipping. Fully aware that he was tackling superior naval forces, Admiral Mikawa planned a fast hit-and-run strike to clear Savo Sound for a convoy of troopships to reinforce the garrison cornered at the tip of Guadalcanal.

Radar failed to pick up the Japanese warships as they entered the seaway between Savo Island and Guadalcanal. Under cover of darkness the Japanese sailed confidently on, unchallenged, until they were sighted by the destroyer U.S.S. *Patterson* which radioed the alarm. Suddenly, the darkness was brilliantly broken by flares from the Japanese warships, silhouetting H.M.S. *Canberra* and U.S.S. *Chicago.* The flares were followed by a hail of shells which struck the *Canberra;* at the same instant two torpedoes slammed into her starboard side. The battle immediately took on a crazy black-and-white pattern, the night broken by gun flashes and blinding searchlights. Within minutes of the beginning of the wild, confusing action, three American cruisers took mortal hits: the *Astoria* exploded into a sheet of flame, the *Quincy* was shelled to pieces, the *Vincennes* became a disabled, burning wreck. The last was the U.S.S. *Ralph Talbot,* and to this day it is unknown whether friend or foe fired on her in the darkness. The Japanese withdrew, leaving four United States heavy cruisers on the floor of "Ironbottom Bay." For them, it was a tremendous victory; for the allies, a shocking defeat. But the Japanese did not get away altogether unscathed. Marine and Navy pilots systematically attacked the hapless Japanese transports, only three reaching Guadalcanal, where they were beached and destroyed by artillery and unrelenting air bombardment. The Japanese, in February, evacuated the island. The six months' campaign for Guadalcanal was ended.

United States forces then thrust their way up the Solomons chain from Guadalcanal, through the Russells to New Georgia, by-passing Kolombangara, on to Vella Lavella, and from there to Bougainville, posing a dangerous threat to the Japanese strong point at Rabaul. To keep their air strength effective in the northern Solomons, the Japanese, after suffering heavy losses, were forced to draw reinforcements from the Marshalls, Truk, the Marianas, and Celebes areas. The situation was critical, for if Bougainville fell, Rabaul would be virtually useless. The successful United States landing on Bougainville Island, November 1, 1943, convinced the Japanese High Command that "the threat in this section was greater than that of attack in the Central Pacific."

CAPE GLOUCESTER

New Britain

In the morning hours of December 26 (Christmas Day in the United States across the International Date Line), the first contingents of the Marine landing force headed in from the northwest toward Cape Gloucester, New Britain Island. The first streaks of dawn light were just breaking when, at 0600, cruisers and destroyers swung their batteries into position and opened fire, the guns thundering and flashing. Overhead at 0700 bombers of the 5th Air Force, escorted by fighters, roared over the target area and dropped their bombs, setting fire to and exploding ammunition dumps and fuel tanks. Strangely, to all this there was no reply from the Japanese except for a single round from a Japanese gun. As the convoy drew closer to the island, the keenest observers searched the shore line for a beach. Heavy smoke drifting offshore obscured the landing places; one battalion of Marines, missing its landing spot altogether, got mixed up in a short fight, the only opposition encountered.

The terrain was the worst encountered in any landing up to that time, and New Britain Island, to the men who fought there, will "remain one of the evil spots of this world." The onrushing assault waves, charging down the lowered ramps of their LCVPs, suddenly found themselves held up by a "wall of clotted jungle so dense as to be impenetrable even to the eye for more than a few feet." The men hacked and chopped their way through the jungle with machetes to where they found a system of shallow rifle pits and log-and-earth bunkers and a couple of abandoned 75-mm. guns.

The troops, moving through the swamp forest of Cape Gloucester, in places slogging through mud and water hip-deep, would plant their feet on what looked like firm ground only to have it give way, bringing them up to their waists in muck that held them helpless until their buddies could pull them out. Soon the column came within the sight of Japanese roadblocks on the way to the airstrip. A brisk little fight ensued which marked the strongest Japanese resistance of D-Day. The next day, December

27, a monsoon struck the island. "No one who has not endured it can have more than the faintest comprehension of what the northwest monsoon was like at Cape Gloucester," wrote Colonel Hough and Major Crown. "The first of the expected rains arrived on the afternoon of D-Day: what appeared a solid wall of water such as, seen rarely and briefly, in the U. S. is called a cloudburst. Only there is nothing brief or rare about this. It lasted for hours and recurred at least once every day for the next three months. The division had landed light, without tentage. Men in front line foxholes were soon up to their necks in water, those in jungle hammocks farther back were not much better off.

"This sort of thing became routine soon enough, but the storm previously mentioned was something of a special feature, though by no means unique. The wind roared in from the Bismarck Sea at hurricane velocity, bringing down giant trees with rendering, splintering crashes. Lightning, striking close by, blinded men, and deafening thunder drowned out the noise of gunfire where the Japanese were counter-attacking the center perimeter and Marine artillery fired over the defensive positions. In the midst of the elemental confusion, a Japanese plane dropped two flares into the area. Marines, recalling the Japanese signal for naval gunfire at Guadalcanal, promptly dove for their flooded foxholes. But no fire came from the sea, and foul weather precluded any further aerial activity, so the meaning of this futile gesture remains a mystery. All in all, it was quite a night."

Cape Gloucester was taken, and was followed by the battle of Arawe (Cape Merkus) and the Talasea operations, after which the Japanese withdrew from New Britain.

TARAWA

In the South Pacific, in the Gilberts, there is a triangular-shaped atoll called Tarawa. The atoll is about 18 miles long on the east side, 12 miles long on the south and west sides. Tarawa is more a continuous reef than an island, consisting of a thin string of coral sand islands, each about eight to ten feet above sea level. The atoll is L-shaped. Guarded by a barrier reef is the lagoon. The southernmost island is Betitu, or Betio.

On this island the 2nd Marine Division fought its bloodiest battle. Tarawa was strongly fortified. Running out into the water for a distance of about 100 yards was a barbed-wire apron which virtually encircled the island. The beaches were covered with log barricades bristling with machine guns. Inland, the defenses were of reinforced concrete and virtually defied reduction by naval shellfire and aerial bombs. These emplacements were armed with heavy naval rifles captured at Singapore. In the water were concrete tetrahedrons built to impale any landing ship.

On the morning of D-Day, November 20, 1943, the Japanese garrison fired a red star cluster, signaling the approach of U.S.S. *Colorado* and U.S.S. *Maryland*. Swinging their main batteries into action, the battleships began firing broadsides into the island stronghold. The shore batteries returned the fire but did no damage. The air strike, delayed because of the smoke and dust caused by the naval shelling, and from the danger of naval projectiles in flight, took over after the naval guns ceased fire for 30 minutes to allow the planes to do their bombing. But the aerial bombs had no material effect on the concrete buildings and installations. Salvo after salvo was poured into the smoking, burning island. Soon the entire island was enveloped in great clouds of black smoke and dust. The naval bombardment was then lifted. Amphibian tractors, loaded with the first wave of the 3rd Battalion, 2nd Marines, headed for the beach. Hard hit by the entrenched machine-gun fire, they nevertheless landed and made a rush for the log barricades which afforded only temporary protection.

Over the fire-swept water followed the men in the other assault waves, some drowning in the treacherous water covering the reef, pulled down by the weight of their packs, others killed by the intense machine-gun fire.

Tarawa was at last taken, but not until after 76 hours of bloody fighting. Over 3,300 Marines of the 2nd Division lay dead among the bunkers, palm stumps, barricades along the beach and in the waters of Betio. The Japanese garrison was wiped out almost to a man.

NORTH AFRICA

As early as April, 1942, plans were under way for the invasion of the European continent. Unprepared as the United States was at the time to undertake a full-scale invasion of Europe, the Pacific War notwithstanding, it was decided that the invasion of North Africa would lessen the terrific pressure of German military might on the Russian army, now fighting for its life. Field Marshal Erwin Rommel's Afrika Korps, having taken Tobruk, was now headed for Cairo, Egypt, with every chance for success. Rommel's advance was checked finally in a titanic battle at El Alamein by General Bernard L. Montgomery's 8th Army, which prevented the loss of the Suez Canal and the oil fields of Abadan. The Afrika Korps began a shore-line retreat to Tobruk.

The North African landings on November 8, given the code name "Torch," came as a complete surprise to the German High Command. No advance preparation to forestall such an attempt had been made, and all their efforts to halt it, wrote General Mark Clark, "suffered from hasty improvisation." First reports began to come in to General Clark's headquarters from General Patton at Casablanca to the effect that his forces were encountering stiff resistance. The Eastern Task Force assault at Algiers had been successful, landings being made at all three beaches; the heaviest resistance was met at Oran after the initial landing was made. Following the landings, the American army pushed on toward Bizerte and Tunis, but bad weather and torrential rains slowed down the American advance. The problem now was to cut off Rommel from joining his reinforcements in Tunis and Bizerte. Many weeks of hard fighting took place at Sfax, key point in the German lines along the African coast, before it was torn from Axis control. By May 12 the only Axis forces in Africa were those under guard in prison compounds.

SICILY

After the successful conclusion of the North African campaign came the amphibious assault on the island of Sicily. The attacking force was the 15th Army Group under the command of General Dwight D. Eisenhower.

The assault troops were embarked from Tunisia, following weeks of intensive aerial bombardment of rail lines, airfields, and fortifications on Sicily. On June 11, after a combined air and naval bombardment, the island of Pantelleria surrendered, soon to be followed by Lampedusa and Linosa.

On the night before D-Day, as the troop convoys slowly approached Sicily, a gale blew up that hampered operations, at the same time throwing the German and Italian defenders off guard. Nevertheless, "all the initial invasion moves were carried out smoothly," wrote General Eisenhower, "and an astonishing lack of resistance was encountered on the shore line."

The battle for Sicily lasted 38 days. Allied aircraft flew 1,200 sorties a day, blasting airdromes, rail lines, and German and Italian troop concentrations, while the infantry slugged it out on the ground. By July 16, the troops fighting in the rugged mountain passes had wrested from Axis forces all but the northeastern corner of the island. Despite the desperate fighting and concentrated attacks of the Allied armies, the Germans and Italians managed to extricate thousands of troops and panzer units across the Strait of Messina to fight again on the Italian mainland. The Sicilian campaign had been costly—31,-158 killed, wounded, and missing. But the Germans and Italians suffered 167,000 casualties and the loss of Sicily to the Axis was a major disaster.

269

SALERNO

At one minute past midnight, September 9, 1943, loudspeakers on the troop transports lying offshore broke the stillness of the night. Down the landing nets clambered the soldiers into the waiting landing craft alongside. Before long the calm sea was alive with LCMs, LCVPs, like busy water bugs, carrying the first assault waves toward the Salerno beaches.

Racing for the shore in landing boats, the spray-drenched men became seasick in the rolling surf. Three and a half hours later all the assault forces had left the transports. Behind them followed the craft carrying the heavy weapons, antiaircraft artillery, antitank guns loaded on DUKWs, and amphibian trucks. The 6th Corps attacked the beach at Paestum while the other beaches designated for landings received the other landing forces. It was a clean landing, the first waves hitting all four beaches exactly at H-Hour, 0330. The second and third assault waves followed at eight-minute intervals. Suddenly flares went up and enemy guns opened fire. During the first hour of the attack the beaches were torn with shells and machine-gun and small-arms fire. Resistance became very heavy. The Germans literally poured machine-gun fire down the irrigation ditches where the Allied soldiers had taken cover, causing many casualties.

The fighting was heavy and vicious, lasting six days, battles taking place at Ponte Sele, Altavilla, and the Tobacco Factory. The Germans fought with skill and stubbornness, but by nightfall of September 19, Salerno was in the hands of the 5th Army.

Then began the slugging campaign to the Volturno River, interspersed with enemy rear-guard actions in the rugged hillsides of the Italian terrain, blowing up bridges, laying mine fields, causing time-consuming problems for the engineers, and necessitating long, slow envelopment operations. Over the steep, narrow roads and slopes, through wind-swept passes, cliffs, and canyons the 5th Army forged ahead, crossing gorges, fighting an enemy in well-nigh impregnable positions. Meanwhile, General Montgomery's 8th Army, after turning the German left flank at Salerno, headed for Naples. All during the march heavy rains had bogged down operations, washing rocks and dirt down the mountainsides into the roads. But the herculean efforts of the Army engineers kept "the delay to a matter of days rather than of weeks." By October 2 Naples was occupied by the U. S. 5th and British 8th Armies.

OPERATION OVERLORD

By July, 1943, the Axis powers began to feel the crushing power of Allied war might, particularly in the air over Fortress Europe. Allied air assault forces pounded unmercifully at the German and Italian homelands, the over-all effect of the air raids nothing less than shattering.

Hermann Goering's Luftwaffe, with every plane it could get off the ground, concentrated the last ounce of effort to sweep the Allied air armadas from German skies. But American and British bombers spared nothing in day and night, around-the-clock bombings. Oil refineries, aircraft factories, ball-bearing plants, airdromes, and communication centers were literally smashed to rubble by the devastating explosions and were left burning, smoking wrecks. By the spring of 1944, overwhelming numbers of U. S. long-range bombers and fighters were hammering German industrial cities into a shambles. The R.A.F. laid waste the Ruhr and Rhineland industrial centers, leaving in its wake 900 locomotives, 16,000 freight cars, and miles of track destroyed, crippling rail centers, and throttling transportation. But, though victory in the air seemed certain, it was realized that to stab the heart of Germany a million men must take up where the bombers left off.

To supervise the labor of building an invasion army for the continent of Europe, General Dwight D. Eisenhower was selected as Supreme Commander at Cairo and directed to "enter the continent of Europe and in conjunction with other Allied Nations, undertake operations aimed at the heart of Germany and the destruction of her armed forces." Three weeks before the invasion, General Eisenhower was able to present a reassuring picture. "There is no question at all as to the readiness of the troops," he wrote, "they are well trained and fit, and impatient to get the job started and completed."

D-Day was set for June 5, 1944—unseasonal weather necessitated a one-day postponement to June 6—and the beaches of Normandy were selected for the initial landings, because of the apparent weaknesses of the enemy defenses there. The first invaders of the French coast were the 82nd and 101st American Airborne Divisions and British airborne troops; the dropping zone, behind the rear of the German coastal fortifications guarding Cherbourg, Caen, and Normandy. From air bases in England had come thousands of gliders laden with troops, towed by bombers across 100 miles of English Channel in one of the most hazardous air operations of the war.

At dawn, June 6, the sea lane to France was marked by the Allied invasion armada carrying 35 divisions for the assault. Overhead, the combined British and American air forces flew 5,000 sorties in support of the assault. Sections of "Utah" and "Omaha" beaches were code-worded "Charlie," "Easy Red," "Fox Green," "Dog Red," "Dog Green," "Fox Red," "Dog White," covering a distance of 50 miles.

The Germans brought up their heaviest artillery, including one of their largest railroad guns, with which to engage the Allied naval forces shelling the landing beaches before the arrival of the landing craft. Racing through heavy seas the landing craft and transports deployed ten miles offshore for the run to the beach, while the battleships, cruisers, and destroyers threw salvo after salvo into German positions. And then, a sudden wave burst upon the beaches into a hail of shells and spattering bullets from the enemy. The men, crouching behind the ramps of the LSTs and LCIs, the moment each landing barge hit the beach, rushed into the surf and struggled toward shore, shells and machine-gun bullets in a storm about them. The long rolls of thunder that was the German artillery, the bursts of raw flame and smoke, reached the heights of fury as the men struggled toward the designated landing areas, wading through the surf with heavy packs, many never reaching the beach.

Ten thousand yards of beach area, in the American sectors at "Omaha" and "Utah," were filled, 75 yards apart, with landing craft. Assault infantry pouring down the ramps fought their way through the water around steel underwater obstacles, designed to tear the bottoms out of landing craft and to break up their formations. As the men fought their way ashore past these obstacles, a steady stream of fire poured from concrete pillboxes and presighted gun emplacements.

But the beachheads were established, and the advance inland began. Soon a steady stream of ships and landing craft bearing men and supplies was crossing the Channel virtually unopposed, while on land the raucous voice of battle developed in intensity as the Germans sought to stall the advance. To accommodate the landing ships, a breakwater made of a million tons of concrete, floated in sections, was put into position offshore, while 54 ships were scuttled to form a breakwater. All this was interlaced with steel ramps capable of supporting military vehicles and heavy tanks. The Germans tried unsuccessfully to bomb this massive engineering achievement, but failed, and just when all seemed to be going well, one of the worst storms in 80 years broke over the Channel. In less time that it takes to tell it, the entire harbor installation was a mass of wreckage.

After 21 days of savage fighting the city of Cherbourg fell to General Lawton Collins' forces. Ten days later, other Allied forces blasted their way into Caen and St. Lô, where a particularly brittle, desperate battle with German armor took place in the hedgerows and marshes at the base of the Contentin Peninsula.

The weather now turned bad, rain and mud bogging down air and ground operations, all but stalling the advance. General Bradley's offensive at St. Lô and Avranches, preceded by one of the heaviest concentrated air assaults of the war, brought his forces as far as the Meuse River. Following the battle of Avranches, the inland advance developed rapidly.

General Patton's 3rd Army broke out of Avranches, cut off Brittany, and bottled up four German divisions, while Hodges' 1st Army and the British 2nd Army swept north and around from Le Mans circling the southern flank of the German position in Normandy toward Argentan. Meanwhile, the British, driving south from Caen toward Falaise, closed the pincers, killing thousands of German soldiers and capturing over 100,000 troops. The Germans, realizing that Normandy was lost, retreated toward the Seine River, the forces of the Allies in close pursuit.

The campaigns in the Mediterranean and Italy were progressing favorably, if slowly, pinning down enemy forces there, preventing their support in the defense of Normandy. The invasion of southern France included the port of Marseilles, the naval base at Toulon, the French Riviera, and the "Azure Coast." The colorful coves and bays of the lush resort area concealed heavy German gun emplacements, like cobras hidden in rose bushes. Big German Tiger tanks guarded all the roads along the shore while U-boats prowled shipping lanes off the coast. Through the Straits of Gibraltar, into the Mediterranean, sailed the convoys, Nazi U-boats taking a heavy toll of ships and men sailing through the Tunisian war channel.

After an air offensive and naval bombardment, the American 7th Army landed on the beaches at Cannes. After the capture of Toulon, Marseilles, and Nice, the German armies retreated up the Rhone Valley. Lyon fell to American troops on September 1, six days before the 2nd French Armored Division of the U.S. 1st Army entered Paris. The Germans pulled no punches and heavy losses were sustained on both sides. Meanwhile the Siegfried Line, long reputed impregnable to attack, was now being cautiously approached.

The reduction of the Siegfried Line was estimated to take the combined strength of the entire Allied forces. Consequently Field Marshal Montgomery, on September 17, struck the northern flank of the Westwall, while Lieutenant General Lewis H. Brereton's 1st Allied Airborne Army landed in Holland in the Arnhem region, in the largest airborne operation ever attempted.

To the south, the 1st Army fought its way to Aachen where the Hürtgen Forest concealed a strongpoint in the Siegfried Line. Squarely in the path of the 1st Army, which had fought its way from Normandy in the battles of the hedgerows, Hürtgen Forest had to be cleared of hidden mine fields and heavy gun emplacements before the advance to Berlin could continue. The attack advanced along old woodlot roads and trails where the troops suffered some of the heaviest artillery and mortar barrages of the whole war, barrages lasting 48 hours at a time.

The trails became muddy roads. The infantry advanced inch by inch behind the tanks, the troops jumping into shell holes every chance they got. Pillboxes and emplacements were taken at bayonet point, following the grenades and flame-throwers. During the fighting it rained constantly. Not until early December did the three divisions of the 1st Army break out of the tortured forest, reduced now to nothing more than a mass of charred stumps and churned-up mud. When this battle ended, 12,000 men failed to answer roll call. But the way to the Rhine was open.

At Bastogne, a little town in Belgium, there is a monument made of field stone. At its base is an American tank turret. On the column is a plaque mounting one word, "Nuts!" commemorating General Anthony McAuliffe's 101st Airborne Division, and his reply to a German surrender ultimatum. McAuliffe's men faced capture. On December 22, the Germans sent their surrender demand. McAuliffe replied. The Germans threw all their available strength in the "Battle of the Bulge" to take Bastogne. But on the day after Christmas, the American 3rd Army, coming up from the south, attacked and relieved McAuliffe's weary men.

The German armies had fought desperately to hold back the advancing wave of Allied forces up the Italian peninsula and in early 1944 mounted a powerful thrust against an Allied beachhead established at Anzio to outflank the Axis forces as a diversion for General Mark W. Clark's 5th Army. The American 6th Corps fought a terrific battle to hold Anzio, while the Germans threw everything they had in a herculean effort to push the American forces into the sea. The 5th Army, on the defensive for the first time, fought desperately in the worst weather the region had known in many years.

The lines of the 5th Army held and the Germans were gradually pushed back; the Allied march to Rome continued. The 5th Army's entry into Rome on June 4 climaxed months of bitter fighting all over the Italian peninsula. When Allied troops moved into the Eternal City they found little trace of the fast-retreating Germans. Operation Shingle was at long last capped with success.

In Germany, on March 7, 1945, the U. S. 3rd Army Corps reached Remagen Bridge on the Rhine River to find that German demolition crews were ready to blow it up. But an American platoon raced across, ripped up the demolition wires, and secured the bridgehead before the switch could be thrown. Before the bridge collapsed under heavy shellfire, five divisions got across safely, established a *tête-du-pont*, encircled the Ruhr, and stamped a foothold in what was left of the industrial heart of Germany.

The deadlock on the Rhine broken, the end of the war was in sight as the Allied armies converged on Berlin. After a terrible battle in the streets of the German capital, Admiral Carl Doenitz took over command of the remnants of the German forces and announced Hitler's death on May 1. In Italy, partisans had grabbed Mussolini and his mistress two days before and strung them up by their toes on poles in front of a gasoline station in the streets of Milan. Finally, surrounded on all sides, on May 7, Germany surrendered unconditionally to the Allies and the war in Europe was over.

"SHORE TO SHORE OVER WATER"

The early months of 1944 saw the slow crumbling of the Japanese Pacific defense system. Yet, Japanese difficulties were only beginning. The United States Pacific Fleet was spreading destruction far and wide among Japanese naval and merchant tonnage. Fast carriers with their fleets of planes pounded Japanese island bases unmercifully. Admiral Marc Mitscher's Task Force 58 struck at Truk atoll, largest Japanese Pacific naval base, rendering it useless and hastening withdrawal of Japanese naval aviation units from Rabaul. "At the turn of the year 1943," wrote General George C. Marshall, "Army forces in the South Pacific area were added to General MacArthur's strategic command . . . to maintain the initiative, advancing by amphibious flanking actions on the Philippines and the Japanese islands from the south and the east. The advance across the tremendous reaches of the Central Pacific was placed under the command of Admiral Chester W. Nimitz. It was General MacArthur's intention to proceed by a series of envelopments up the coast of New Guinea and into the Philippines."

After the final breakthrough of the Bismarck barrier, by June, 1943, General MacArthur and Admiral Nimitz landed two regimental combat teams on Woodlark and Kiriwina islands, off the western tip of New Guinea, and established airfields for effective operations against New Guinea itself, the now famous "shore to shore over water" operations along the northern shore of New Guinea from Hollandia to Vogelkop Peninsula. MacArthur and the Navy's fast carriers took Hollandia and leap-frogged to Biak, southern end of the Japanese defense perimeter, seizing airfields there and isolating thousands of Japanese in the almost impenetrable jungles.

"MARIANAS TURKEY SHOOT"

The Mariana Islands, discovered by Magellan in 1521 and named in 1668 for Queen Maria Anna of Spain, are an almost unbroken chain of small, rocky islands, 1,350 miles south of Japan. Saipan, Tinian, Rota, and Guam, the larger islands of the group, provided a string of bases for airfields which protected Japan's line of communications with her home islands. Saipan, approximately 14 miles long and 6 miles wide, and Tinian Island, three nautical miles northwest of Saipan, formed the key defense of the Marianas.

On June 11, 1944, Vice Admiral Marc Mitscher's Task Force 58 subjected Saipan, Tinian, Rota, Guam, and Pegun islands to an intense naval bombardment of three and a half days. Meanwhile, LSTs and transports, carrying assault troops, were rushing toward Saipan from Pearl Harbor. In a fast carrier strike and 225 "fighter-plane sweep" against Saipan, Admiral Mitscher's carrier planes surprised its Japanese defenders. Tons of bombs were dropped on airfields and other installations, the Japanese, under cover of night, replying with feeble, sporadic fire from shore batteries. The battleships plastered the island for seven hours, "turning the impact areas into scenes of desolation." Around-the-clock shelling gave the Japanese no rest. One Japanese officer reported that "scores of enemy Grumman fighters . . . ran amuck and finally left leisurely amidst unparalleledly inaccurate antiaircraft fire . . ." and gloomily added "the enemy holds us in utter contempt."

"H-Hour was set for 1830," wrote Major Carl Hoffman. "Aboard all ships everything was ready. A substantial breakfast had been nervously devoured; guns and winches were manned, boats being lowered, hatches cleared; troops were alert and keyed to the occasion. The day was clear—there would be no serious trouble with the weather."

The first wave, sent in with guns blazing, went surging through the surf at full speed in the 4,000 yard run to the beach, subjected to heavy Japanese artillery fire. "Terrifying, indeed, was the sound of the enemy shells bursting around the amtracs," wrote Major Hoffman, "particularly the high-angle shells which whistle ominously at the bobbing targets. And the Marines, clustered in these 'sitting ducks,' hoped and prayed that none of the shells would find its intended mark. Some, however, did."

While the battle for Saipan was going through its first phase, the Japanese Imperial Fleet was racing eastward from the Philippines. Admiral Mitscher's Task Force 58 met them in the waters off the Philippines. Task Force 58 and Admiral Ozawa and Japan's Mobile Fleet slugged it out in the Philippine Sea in what was perhaps the greatest of aircraft-carrier battles. The Japs lost 426 planes, "or all but 47 planes in Ozawa's Mobile Fleet." American submarines "scratched" two Jap carriers. The disastrous results to Admiral Ozawa's fleet earned for the battle the sobriquet the Marianas Turkey Shoot.

In less than a month Saipan was secured. All that remained now was to stalk and ferret out the remaining Japanese hidden about the island. With the Marianas captured, the Seabees and aviation engineers arrived and began construction of bases and airfields capable of handling the big B-29's for the bombing of Japan itself. From Saipan the B-29's began flying over Tokyo in a series of raids which began on March 10 and almost leveled Tokyo to the ground.

THE BATTLE OF LEYTE GULF

In a double-pronged attack with an Australian force and an American regimental combat team, General MacArthur knocked out Salamaua and Lae after some difficult fighting. "On 19th of October [1944] two assault forces, the 3rd commanded by Admiral Wilkinson and the 7th commanded by Rear Admiral Daniel E. Barbey, approached the east coast of Leyte with the Sixth Army under General Krueger aboard," wrote General Marshall. "It was an armada of combat and assault vessels that stretched across the vast Pacific horizon. In the covering naval forces were the battleships *California, Mississippi, Maryland, Pennsylvania, Tennessee,* and *West Virginia* with their screen of cruisers and destroyers. . . . The air cover was provided by planes from 18 escort carriers. . . . That day a Japanese search plane discovered this great amphibious force and reported its presence to Admiral Kurita's Singapore Fleet, which then constituted 60 per cent of Japan's major naval units. This report precipitated one of the decisive battles of history."

The Japanese committed their entire fleet to prevent the return of the United States forces to the Philippines. In a raging sea battle that lasted six days the U. S. 3rd and 7th Fleets virtually eliminated the Japanese Fleet. In the great naval action the United States lost the carrier *Princeton* to a single Jap "Judy" which broke through the air defense and unleashed a bomb that landed squarely amidships, in a hangar. Realizing it was impossible to save the great carrier, Admiral Sherman ordered the cruiser *Reno* and destroyer *Irwin* to torpedo the burning hulk.

General MacArthur's forces were now firmly planted on Leyte. Operations for the invasion of Luzon got under way the first week of 1945 when an American assault force slipped through the Strait of Surigao, passed into the Mindanao and Sulu Seas and through the Philippine Archipelago, and effected a landing in Lingayen Gulf. Final operations against the Japanese on Luzon began when General Krueger's forces drove northward from Balete Pass to the Cagayan Valley. They ran into stiff resistance north of Baguio from remnants of the Japanese army entrenched in the mountains, but with the capture of the Cagayan Valley the Luzon campaign was virtually over.

The fighting was very heavy in and around Manila, particularly around Clark Field where the invaders were strongly entrenched in hill positions. By January 29 the 11th Corps was ashore on the west coast of Luzon near Subic Bay where they met light opposition. Driving eastward they cut off the Bataan Peninsula, where General MacArthur had made his stand just three years before.

The battle for Manila raged, and as the troops of the 6th Army advanced on the city Japanese forces within fought furiously from street to street and house to house. After terrific Allied bombardment from the air and sea, Corregidor fell. Thus ended the Philippine campaign. "From California to the coast of China," wrote General Marshall, "the vast Pacific abounded with American power . . . the day of final reckoning for a treacherous enemy was at hand."

General MacArthur now massed his combined forces for the final assault on Japan itself.

IWO JIMA AND OKINAWA

Iwo Jima, one of the last most powerful Japanese strongholds in the Pacific, was attacked on February 19, 1945, by 60,000 Marines, who stormed across Iwo's beaches of volcanic sand. Formidable Mount Suribachi, tunneled with a mass of interlocked pillboxes and caves, was defended by 20,000 Japanese. A terrific naval barrage and aerial pounding failed to dislodge them and it was left to the Marines to take each pillbox and cave by brute force. After nearly a month of battle, Iwo Jima was taken and the famous photograph of the Marines raising the flag on Mount Suribachi is now part of the American tradition. Tokyo was now only 665 miles away.

On April 1, preceded by an intense naval bombardment, the 24th Army Corps and the 3rd Marine Corps landed on Okinawa and established beachheads on the west coast. The Japanese offered little resistance to the initial landing, but the army met the main Japanese army entrenched near Naha, principal city of the island. It took days, but soon Marine and Army combat teams were operating from Yontan Airfield.

The fighting was ferocious. The Japanese used every conceivable weapon at their command, including kamikaze attacks with a piloted version of the German V-1 rocket. When the campaign ended, American forces had suffered 49,000 casualties. But over 100,000 Japanese soldiers and airmen had been killed, over 7,000 captured.

Okinawa had fallen to the U. S. 10th Army in a slugging campaign that had taken three months to complete. On Okinawa, stretched across a line four miles in width, had advanced six divisions in drenching rains and red, soupy, clinging mud, to take Shuri Castle and Sawtooth Ridge. The island secured, now Japan itself could be invaded.

While plans for the invasion of Japan were being put into effect, the atomic bomb was fired on the sands of New Mexico. The report of the devastating results of the terrible explosion were rushed to President Truman at a meeting at Berlin, Germany, with Prime Minister Churchill and Generalissimo Stalin. The bomb, it was decided, would be immediately used and General Carl Spaatz received orders to drop the bomb on an industrial center of the Japanese mainland. The city of Hiroshima was one of the selected targets, and on August 6 the bomb was dropped with terrifying results. Then, on August 9, a second and more destructive bomb was dropped on Nagasaki. The blast wiped out a large section of the city, its smoke, rising 50,000 feet into the air, visible more than 175 miles. Their situation hopeless, the Japanese asked for terms. August 10, the unconditional surrender of the Japanese was accepted.

"What happens to all these drawings and paintings?" wrote Colonel Donald L. Dickson, U.S.M.C. "The Marine Corps Division of Public Information has sponsored exhibits from time to time in this country and abroad. These exhibits never fail to generate great interest wherever they are shown. Some originals are hung in Marine Clubs, recreation rooms, in Headquarters offices and class rooms throughout the Marine Corps. All of them are strictly accounted for by the Special Services Branch. Occasionally some disappear—but not without good reason.

"Near the end of World War II an exhibit of Marine Combat Art was sent to Australia, for display. As it was being flown back to the States, one of the plane's engines failed somewhere east of Fiji and the Captain radioed a picket boat to stand by for a crash water landing. The destroyer saved the crew and cargo manifest but the plane went down. Three of my drawings were in that shipment, including my own favorite 'Too many—too close—too long.'"

From a painting by William P. Welsh. Courtesy Department of the Air Force, Historical Properties Office

Pacific overture

275

From a painting by Fujita Tsuguji, Japanese war art in custody of U. S. Army of Occupation, Japan, Ueno Museum, Tokyo. Courtesy Department of the Air Force, Historical Properties Office

Pearl Harbor on 8 December 1941 (Japanese time)

From a drawing by Lieutenant Commander Griffith Baily Coale, U.S.N.R. Courtesy Combat Art Division, U S. Navy

Attack on the Japanese cruisers *Mogami* and *Mijuma* from the air

From an oil study by Lieutenant Commander Griffith Baily Coale. U.S.N.R. Courtesy Combat Art Division, U. S. Navy

Dive bombing Japanese carriers, battle of Midway, June 4, 1942

The Japanese aircraft carrier *Kaga* passes across the picture with the planes she sought to launch caught on her deck. At the left, columns of water geyser up and around the carrier *Akagi*. The carrier *Soryu* is burning fiercely from stem to stern.

In the center a light cruiser's stern rises as she makes her final plunge. On the horizon two battleships have been hit by 1000-pound bombs and are beginning to burn. A Zero, trailing smoke, dives into the sea.

From a water color by Captain Ogden Pleissner. Courtesy Department of the Air Force, Historical Properties Office

Clearing Weather in the Aleutians

From a painting in oil by Lieutenant Commander William F. Draper, U.S.N.R. Courtesy Combat Art Division, U. S. Navy

War and Peace—Amchitka, Alaska

The peace of an Aleut grave is broken by the bark of a machine gun.

From a charcoal drawing by Chief Boatswain's Mate Hunter Wood. Courtesy U. S. Coast Guard

Storming ashore to attack on a South Pacific atoll

Coast Guard-manned landing craft plow through a heavy surf to invade an unidentified
Japanese-held island in the South Pacific.

From a water color by Lieutenant Dwight Shepler, U.S.N.R. Courtesy Combat Air Division, U. S. Navy

Bombardment—Guadalcanal

Marine artillerymen using 155-mm. howitzers fire salvo after salvo into the Japanese positions in the jungle of Guadalcanal.

279

From a water color by Lieutenant Dwight Shepler, U.S.N.R. Courtesy Combat Air Division, U. S. Navy

Action on the river—Guadalcanal

The "point" of a Marine patrol secures the opposite bank of a sluggish river in Japanese territory. The first three riflemen fire at a Japanese patrol in the deep jungle. Other Marines follow, with more than one man in midstream as a target.

From a water color by Lieutenant Dwight Shepler, U.S.N.R. Courtesy Combat Air Division, U. S. Navy

Fighter scramble—Guadalcanal

After the initial landing of the Americans on Guadalcanal Japanese planes raided the U. S. positions almost continually. When they did come, Marine and Navy interceptor pilots would return to Fighter Strip One for fuel and ammunition. The pilots frequently took their Grummans off three abreast in clouds of dust as they returned to the fray. In the foreground stands a newly arrived Army P-38 being serviced by mechanics before taking off for battle.

Killer—Guadalcanal

" 'Doggie' going down as a barrage of 88's burst around us"

Private Melvin "Mike" Levine, Guadalcanal

Guadalcanal Marine

To the victor

From a water color by Lieutenant Commander Dwight C. Shepler, U.S.N.R. Courtesy Combat Art Division, U. S. Navy

Battle of Santa Cruz Islands

A U.S. task force undergoes prolonged attack by Japanese carrier-based planes, October 26, 1942. An American carrier (right, center) narrowly escapes two bombs. On the horizon on the left, another U. S. carrier is afire. In the left center, an American battleship is under attack. The artist was aboard the cruiser in the left foreground.

From a water color by Lieutenant Dwight C. Shepler, U.S.N.R. Courtesy Combat Art Division, U. S. Navy

Night action off Savo Island

On the calm night of November 14, 1942, American battleships open up with broadsides in the second phase of the battle against two strong Japanese naval forces. Japanese naval craft, hit during the first phase of the action, burn and sink behind Savo Island to the eastward, while salvos from the battleships attend to the force to the north.

282

From an oil painting by Lieutenant Commander William F. Draper, U.S.N.R. Courtesy Combat Art Division, U. S. Navy

Night attack—South Pacific

A U. S. task force is attacked by six Japanese torpedo planes. Two of the planes were shot down and the others retired. Here, a "Betty" burns fiercely on the water just beyond an *Independence*-class carrier. Five-inch shells explode in the sky and tracers weave through the dark, searching other attackers.

From an oil painting by Lieutenant Commander Griffith Baily Coale, U.S.N.R. Courtesy Combat Art Division, U. S. Navy

The U. S. cruiser *San Francisco* in the night action off Savo Island

283

From an oil painting by Lieutenant Commander William F. Draper, U.S.N.R. Courtesy Combat Art Division, U. S. Navy

The landing—invasion of Bougainville

Here are shown the first desperate moments of the landing. Two landing boats from the flagship are seen. Number five was unlucky, a direct hit from a Japanese mortar killing many Marines and crew members. Many other men were killed by Japanese rifle fire.

From a drawing by combat artist Kerr Eby. Courtesy The Abbott Laboratories, Chicago

"Long Tom" bellows

Perspiring and covered with grime, Marines labor at top speed on Cape Gloucester. The Japanese feared this artillery piece more than anything else, except perhaps the great naval guns on the battleships, or a flame-thrower.

From a drawing by combat artist Kerr Eby. Courtesy The Abbott Laboratories, Chicago

Wounded man at the front, Bougainville

At a station only a few hundred feet from the battle front, the wounded are prepared
for the grueling and hazardous trip back to base hospital.

By Master Sergeant Victor P. Donahue, U.S.M.C.R. Courtesy U. S. Marine Corps

Stinking Island

By Master Sergeant Victor P. Donahue, U.S.M.C.R. Courtesy U. S. Marine Corps

Stopped by snipers, Cape Gloucester

286

Marine wounded in Bougainville jungle

The Japs came in to strafe

"I was still running when the first Jap came in to strafe. I couldn't find a hole to jump in now. I had to get down fast. I heard the bullets singing over my head and smacking into the trees around me. My only cover was broken branches and limbs. The plane came in and this time I thought I was a goner for sure. Bullets missed me by inches, snapping off twigs and branches. The thought ran through my mind that I was going to get hit before I even had a chance to see anything. All of a sudden it became quiet. I raised my head and saw two planes going down in flames."

287

From a charcoal drawing by Chief Boatswain's Mate Hunter Wood. Courtesy U. S. Coast Guard

The first wave at Tarawa

One of the costliest engagements of the war in the South Pacific was the battle for Tarawa, an island in the Gilberts. Here the United States Marines fought perhaps the bloodiest action in all their history. The island was taken, but not before the beach was strewn with the bodies of the Marines' Second Division. Despite repeated bombings and heavy shelling, later called "woefully inadequate," the fortifications had to be taken by hand-to-hand fighting.

From a drawing by combat artist Kerr Eby. Courtesy The Abbott Laboratories, Chicago

The first assault

Their landing craft jarred to a sudden halt by a submerged reef, an assault contingent leaps into the water.

288

From a drawing by combat artist Kerr Eby. Courtesy The Abbott Laboratories, Chicago

D-Day on Tarawa

Wading through a leaden surf, under an overcast sky, U.S. Marines secure a beachhead on Tarawa November 20, 1943. Navy dive bombers and torpedo bombers scream down through a blanket of black smoke to blast the Japanese, entrenched in well-nigh invulnerable pillboxes.

From a drawing by combat artist Kerr Eby. Courtesy The Abbott Laboratories, Chicago

The last full ounce of devotion

Bullets and barbed wire: both constituted tremendous barriers to victory in the battle for Tarawa; but this Marine, rifle swung grimly in one hand, typifies the resurgent spirit of the conquerors of the Gilberts. Past the wire on which hang the bodies of his comrades the tattered Marine presses on toward the beach.

289

From a drawing by combat artist Kerr Eby. Courtesy The Abbott Laboratories, Chicago

The long, desperate road to victory

Marines, bodies angled forward as if against a wind, press forward on Tarawa. In the background an armored tractor lumbers ahead, shelling the enemy defenses.

From a painting by Howard Cook, U.S.A. Courtesy Department of the Army, Chief of Military History

Landing at Rendova, New Georgia, Solomons

From a water color by Lieutenant Dwight C. Shepler, U.S.N.R. Courtesy Combat Art Division, U. S. Navy

Building the base—Espiritu Santo

A dock of the Seabees, Navy construction battalions, in a rapidly growing New Hebrides outpost.

Hat Styles of the Fighting Marine in the South Pacific

What the well-dressed Marine wore while on fatigue duty

"The Park Avenue or I read Esquire type"

"The clerical or Robin Hood type"

"The Chicago or Oh Yea-a-ah type"

"The I don't give a damn type"

"The windswept or Pony Express type"

The facile brush of Master Sergeant Victor P. Donahue, U.S.M.C., captures
"Gyrene" styles in headgear as modeled by Marine combat veterans of the South Pacific.

"The Hollywood or I made
$300 a week type"

"The Harold Teen type"

"The Semper Fidelis or the hell
with you I got mine type"

"The intellectual or combat
correspondent type"

"Sergeant major type"

From a water color by Major Milton Marx, 9th U.S.A.A.F. Courtesy Historical Properties Branch, Department of the Air Force

A bomber gets a checkup somewhere in North Africa

A 9th U.S.A.A.F. bomber receives a checkup and re-arming on an airfield somewhere in North Africa while a squadron of bombers wings its way in the sky overhead. The 9th Air Force was organized in Egypt by Major General Lewis H. Brereton and saw service in the African and European campaigns.

From a drawing in sepia and wash by John Groth. Courtesy of the artist and The World Publishing Company

Close combat in North Africa

American troops fighting to halt a German attack somewhere in North Africa. The fighting has become close and savage at point-blank range.

From a painting by Chief Boatswain's Mate Hunter Wood. Courtesy U. S. Coast Guard

Hot moment off Sicily

American invasion craft fight off an attack. At the upper left is a Supermarine Spitfire; in the foreground is a Messerschmitt 109F.

From an oil painting by Coast Guard combat artist William Goadby Lawrence. Courtesy U. S. Coast Guard

Mountain guns blast shellfire at LCS at Salerno

While laying a smoke screen to cover a wave of landing barges in Salerno Bay, a Coast Guard-manned LCS is straddled by shells from German 88's in mountain emplacements.

Anzio harbor under German bombardment, Italy, 1944

"Purple Heart Valley," winter line, Italy, 1944

297

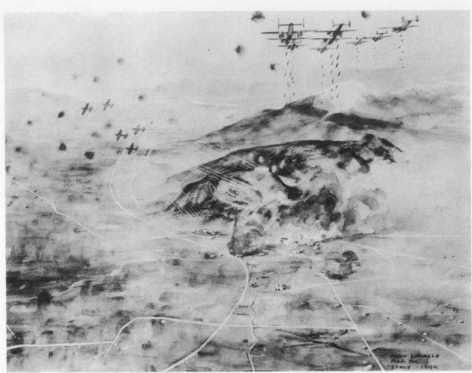

From a painting by Major John Lavalle, A.C. Courtesy Department of the Air Force, Historical Properties Office

Over Cassino, Italy, 1944

From a painting by Savo Radulovich. Courtesy Department of the Army, Office of the Chief of Military History

Battle for Cassino, Italy, 1944

Picture signed by (————) Duncan, U.S.A. Courtesy The War Department, Historical Properties Section

Monte Cassino, Italy, 1944

The ruins of the famous monastery were sketched shortly
after the Poles, who fought there, had removed their dead.

From a painting by Harry Davis, U.S.A. Courtesy Department of the Army, Office of the Chief of Military History

Retreating Germans destroying their equipment, Italy, 1944

299

The American Fifth Army reaches Rome

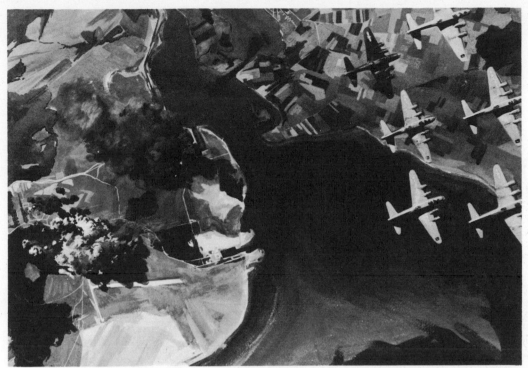

Mission to Peenemunde, Europe, 1944

Attack on Merseburg, Europe, 1944

Mission to Cologne, Europe, 1945

Train-busting, Europe, 1945

LCI flotilla under way for France

Moving across the English Channel, an LCI (Landing Craft, Infantry) flotilla heads toward the French invasion coast on D-Day. At the moment, their air cover is three curious sea gulls.

Normandy: D-Day breaks—opening the attack

Matriarch of the Fleet, the elderly U.S.S. *Arkansas* opens fire on the beachhead. To seaward, the French cruisers *Georges Laygues* and *Montcalm,* flying extremely large battle flags, send shells hurtling into their captive homeland. Assault waves stream in while attack transports fill the horizon.

From a painting by Coast Guardsman H. B. Vestal. Courtesy U. S. Coast Guard

Going in—Normandy

The first wave of Coast Guard and Navy-manned LCTs going into Normandy beach-head on D-Day. Coast Guard 83-footers and Navy sub-chasers escort the landing craft.

From a water color by Coast Guardsman H. B. Vestal. Courtesy U. S. Coast Guard

The first wave

Coast Guard LCI flotilla in European invasion waters, surrounded by landing barges loaded with troops, headed toward the coast of France at H-Hour.

From a wash drawing by Coast Guardsman H. B. Vestal. Courtesy U. S. Coast Guard

Hitting the beach under fire

A direct hit on a Coast Guard-manned LCI as it noses into the Normandy beach.

From a water color by Coast Guardsman H. B. Vestal. Courtesy U. S. Coast Guard

Pinned down by enemy shell fire

Coast Guard and Navy-manned LCTs (Landing Craft, Tanks), LCVPs (Landing Craft, Vehicle Personnel), and LCMs (Landing Craft, Mechanical Equipment) "hit the beach" at Normandy on D-Day. In the left foreground soldiers are pinned down behind a rock pile by enemy gunfire. A near miss by a mortar shell has overturned a barge at the water's edge.

305

The battle for "Fox Green Beach"—Normandy, June 6, 1944

"We fought all day for this stretch of 'Omaha' beachhead. Its benign green bluffs and valley entrance were a maze of crossfire from enfiladed 88's, mortars, and machine guns, which raked the beaches and pinned the infantry to the shingle before the fiendish mine fields. By mid-afternoon, disabled landing craft were clogging the few gaps in the beach obstacles, while long-range artillery fire pounded the beach. Support waves circled and jockeyed for an opening. Destroyers moved far into shoal water to pump salvos of five-inch shells into stubborn emplacements and mobile targets of opportunity. The house in the valley and the spire of Colleville-sur-Mer on the hill were landmarks of 'Fox Green Beach.' The spire was used as an artillery control tower by the Germans. Its lovely Renaissance architecture crumbled into sad rubble when a shore-fire-control party called on the destroyer *Emmons* to demolish it."

From a water color by Lieutenant Dwight C. Shepler, U.S.N.R. Courtesy Combat Art Division, U. S. Navy

The tough beach

A Coast Guard LCI, holed by 88's and mortars, is trapped in the retreating 21-foot tide
and the obstacles of "Fox Green Beach."

From a water color by Olin Dows, U.S.A. Courtesy Department of the Army, Chief of Military History

Roadblock—Normandy, 1944

From a drawing by Sergeant Howard Brodie. Courtesy Department of the Army, Chief of Military History

Moving up

From an oil painting by Lawrence Beall Smith, U.S.A. Courtesy Department of the Army, Chief of Military History

The quick and the dead

From a water color by Chief Boatswain's Mate Hunter Wood, U.S.C.G. Courtesy U. S. Coast Guard

Sinking of a German submarine in the North Atlantic by the U. S. Coast Guard cutter *Spencer*

The cutter bears down on a U-boat forced to the surface by the *Spencer's* depth charges.

From a drawing by Warrant Boatswain Hunter Wood. Courtesy U. S. Coast Guard

U. S. S. *Borie* ramming and strafing a German submarine

The *Borie's* encounter with the submarine in the Atlantic is highlighted by several dramatic incidents. Following the ramming of the submarine, a U. S. Navy gunner, in the heat of battle, hurls an empty shell case which strikes one of the German crewmen. Another crewman lies on the deck of the sub, struck by a knife thrown by one of the *Borie's* complement. The Navy gunner, when he can no longer depress his gun low enough to bear on the sub, fires through the spray-shield with a machine gun. The Navy machine gunner, up forward, is taking care of the German deck-gun crew with a Tommy gun.

309

From a painting by Lieutenant Commander Anton Otto Fischer, U.S.C.G.R. Courtesy U. S. Coast Guard

Convoy duty in the North Atlantic, winter, 1943

The U. S. Coast Guard had the hazardous duty of escorting troop transports, tankers, and supply ships to European base ports through the sea lanes of the North Atlantic waters infested with Nazi submarine "wolf packs" which preyed on the convoys.

Night action off the Italian Riviera

Destroyers and cruisers, lying off the French coast, giving fire support to our troops, are in turn supported by PT boats. Here, off Mentone, the enemy has fired several rounds and lighted the sky in a blaze of light with star shells. The PTs lay smoke and retire behind it to carry out their plans.

From a water color by Commander Albert K. Murray, U.S.N.R. Courtesy Combat Art Division, U. S. Navy

From a water color by Lieutenant Albert K. Murray, U.S.N.R. Courtesy Combat Art Division, U. S. Navy

Anthéor landing

The first of the 36th Division assault troops reach this small Riviera beach.

From a drawing in sepia and wash by John Groth. Courtesy of the artist and The World Publishing Company

The fall of Berlin, May 3, 1945

The last of the Wehrmacht as they are herded along the Unter den Linden in the last act of World War II in the E.T.O.
"I witnessed this day the fall of Berlin," wrote the artist.

Running battle off Leyte, December 7, 1944

Following the surprise landing at dawn of the 77th Division at Ormoc, the naval attack force ran a day-long gauntlet of kamikaze attack by scores of Jap planes as it returned to Surigao Strait and Leyte Gulf. The screening destroyers, "fishtailing" at thirty knots in the confined shallow waters, found their course unavoidably leading through flotillas of Filipino outriggers almost becalmed in the spotty air of an incongruously lovely day. The *Mahan*-class destroyer *Flusser* is firing at a dive bomber coming out of the sun, while machine guns have fallen silent after "flaming" the suicide plane about to hit the water near the *Fletcher*-class destroyer in the middle distance.

From a water color by Lieutenant Dwight C. Shepler, U.S.N.R. Courtesy Combat Art Division, U. S. Navy

From a water color by Lieutenant Jon Whitcomb, U.S.N.R. Courtesy Combat Art Division, U. S. Navy

Attack on D-Day—Peleliu

From a water color with crayon by Lieutenant Mitchell Jamieson, U.S.N.R. Courtesy Combat Art Division, U. S. Navy

Ack-ack at sunset

D-Day on Okinawa and the sky fills quickly with tracers and bursts of antiaircraft fire, as Jap planes attack the ship off shore. LSTs are having their small boats lay down a smoke screen about them with smoke pots.

From a water color by Lieutenant Edward Millman, U.S.N. Courtesy Combat Art Division, U. S. Navy

Burning beachhead—Pegun Island, Dutch New Guinea

Ducks (amphibious trucks) move up through a curtain of smoke and dying fires.

314

From a water color by Pfc. Stan Lacey, U.S.M.C. Courtesy U. S. Marine Corps

Combat engineers, Tinian, Central Pacific

From an oil painting by Lieutenant William F. Draper, U.S.N.R. Courtesy Combat Art Division, U. S. Navy

Aftermath of battle—Saipan

The twisted remains of Tojo's imperial troops lie in this once flourishing sugar-cane field. In this stench-filled scene an American tank, burnt and disabled, stands victorious. Far in the background an ammunition dump on Aslite Airfield burns fiercely.

From a water color by Lieutenant Mitchell Jamieson, U.S.N.R. Courtesy Combat Art Division, U. S. Navy

Into the valley—Okinawa

"Fox" company is committed and starts shuffling down the trail to reinforce "Easy" and "George." "This is looking back in a southeasterly direction towards Nago Wan in the distance, and gives some idea of the terraced slopes and pine-covered hills of Okinawa. Although the interior country was much denser in vegetation and forest, the mountains got progressively higher inland."

From a black-and-white drawing by Sergeant R. G. James, U.S.M.C. Courtesy U. S. Marine Corps

"Crapped out along the road after six nights on the line, Okinawa, 1945"

Flier down in the jungle,
Mindanao, Philippine Islands

By Tech Sergeant Paul Arlt, U.S.M.C.R. Courtesy U. S. Marine Corps

From a water color by Lieutenant Commander Edward Millman, U.S.N.R. Courtesy Combat Art Division, U. S. Navy

H-Hour minus three minutes, Leyte Gulf

For the landing at Ormoc, destroyers lay down an initial barrage on the beach with their five-inch guns. Then amphibious landing craft begin their shoreward course after a blanket of fire has been laid down for a number of minutes by LCIs carrying rocket launchers.

317

From a water color with crayon by Lieutenant Mitchell Jamieson, U.S.N.R. Courtesy Combat Art Division, U. S. Navy

Green Beach—Iwo Jima

Looking toward Mount Suribachi, scene of the heaviest fighting of the Pacific War.

From a water color with crayon by Lieutenant Mitchell Jamieson, U.S.N.R. Courtesy Combat Art Division, U. S. Navy

Night on Mount Suribachi

A spotlight is played on Mount Suribachi all night from an Army camp at the foot of the mountain. The enemy has been making last-ditch sorties. The sentries are "trigger-happy," naturally enough, and it is dangerous to move about at night, with or without the password.

Destination—Tokyo Bay

Steaming back and forth some 300 miles southeast of Honshu during the twelve days between August 15 and August 27, 1945, the Third Fleet waits to enter Japanese waters. The confident form of the battleship *Iowa* eases along with stable steadiness through squalls that threaten typhoon weather.

Over the crater of Fujiyama, Japan, 1945

Hiroshima showplace, Japan, 1945

"A very few buildings in this modern city have become famous overnight because they are only landmarks. This is a brick-and-stone structure situated about a mile east of the center of the blast. It has been dislodged and gutted, and white bones were strewn about outside among the ashes."

Fleet Admiral Chester W. Nimitz at the surrender ceremonies aboard the U. S. S. *Missouri*: Tokyo Bay, September 2, 1945

This painting represents perhaps the greatest moment in the lives of Fleet Admiral Chester W. Nimitz, General of the Army Douglas MacArthur, and Admiral William F. Halsey. Beside number two turret are, right to left, General LeClerc, France; Admiral Fraser, England; General Blamey, Australia; Lieutenant Admiral Helfrich, Netherlands; Air Vice Admiral Isitt, New Zealand, and several U. S. officers. At the left can be seen the Japanese delegation.

From a painting by William P. Welsh, U.S.A.A.F. Courtesy Department of the Air Force, Historical Properties Office

Business district, Tokyo, Japan, 1945

From a painting by R. Munsell Chambers, U.S.A.A.F. Courtesy Department of the Air Force, Historical Properties Office

Don Juan in Tokyo, Japan, 1945

12

Korean Interlude

The Korean War

1950-1953

In 1945 the American soldier came to Korea on the mission of liberating the Asiatic peninsula from the Japanese. During the American occupation of Korea, aside from routine duties, life for the GI was pleasant. The Korean countryside, rich in orchards and rice paddies, had not yet been touched by war. The Korean people, happy and hard-working, got their living from their tiny farms, employing farming methods ancient when Korea was young, handed down by their ancestors. Into this primitive scene burst the GI and his jeep. From that moment Korean road traffic became a strange and amusing mixture of ancient oxcarts, drawn by dreamy-eyed oxen, Army jeeps, and laughing GI's. If the Japanese had lifted the face of Korea by building modern roads and buildings, the GI made it laugh. With him had come a new, light-hearted spirit to Korea. To the GI, walking the crowded side streets, the Koreans were a friendly people, and the familiar greeting was always a warm "Hi Joe!"

During the intervening years Russia engaged in what was called, for want of a better name, the Cold War, in which her armies, instead of returning home and demobilizing, as had those of the other Allies, remained in the occupied countries to communize by threats of violence and enslavement, refuting the very concepts for which World War II was fought. To the people of the unfortunate occupied countries, Russian occupation meant nothing more than a

brand-name change. Totalitarianism was still with them.

Russian occupation forces set up a blockade of Berlin, Germany, cutting the corridor between Berlin and the occupation zones of the other powers, isolating the city in an attempt to force withdrawal of the Western powers. But the Russians had not counted on the air lift, nor on the resourcefulness of American military personnel under the command of General Lucius Clay. U. S. military planes carried everything from staple foods, coal, machinery, and clothing, to toys and candy, while the Russians watched. It was a new experience for the Air Force, and a great experiment successfully planned and executed. The Russians got a few lessons in determination and resourcefulness. Seeing that the blockade was hopeless, with world opinion mounting against them, they discontinued the blockade.

Korea had not been divided at Japan's surrender, but was set up as the free Republic of Korea. Russia, refusing to accept the majority vote taken at Paris, set up a puppet regime at Pyongyang, withdrew its troops beyond the 38th parallel, about halfway up the peninsula, and organized a powerful military force. The United States had withdrawn most of its troops from Korea. Then, without warning, on June 25, 1950, the North Korean Communists crossed the 38th parallel with Russian tanks, trucks, and artillery, determined to take all of Korea.

THE KOREAN WAR

The United Nations at once branded the Korean Reds aggressors and ordered them out of Korea, but the order was ignored and the headlong advance continued.

The United States threw all the available troops it could spare from Japan into Korea. The Reds, with the advantage of surprise, sweeping everything before them in their initial thrust against the unprepared American and South Korean troops, captured the capital city of Seoul, encircled American and South Korean troops in the area around Pusan at the southeastern end of the peninsula, thought they had won the war at one stroke. But supplies of tanks, troops, heavy guns, and aircraft completely reversed the situation.

General MacArthur conceived the landing at Inchon. Landing his troops behind the Reds, cutting them off and forcing their withdrawal from Pusan, General MacArthur drove them all the way back to the Yalu River, all but destroying their army. Then Communist China struck. Swarming from the mountains of north China, 200,000 Chinese, outnumbering the American and South Korean forces, compelled a withdrawal.

The Korean War became a bloody stalemate for three years, the line of battle weaving back and forth, through bitter cold winters and blazing hot summers, like a rope caught in a slow-moving stream. At last, in 1953, after talks that had dragged on—and had been called off—for months, a truce was agreed upon and a line of demarcation established. Outwardly, the "police action" had succeeded; actually the three years of fighting reached no conclusion. But history has recorded the great, flaming actions that took place in the mountains, valleys, and rice paddies. Old Baldy, Inchon, Seoul, Porkchop Hill, Outpost Berlin, and many bunkers where fighting became vicious, bloody, and personal, will take their places in American military history alongside the Wilderness, Cold Harbor, Bunker Hill, Saratoga, Gettysburg, the Argonne, Corregidor, Guadalcanal, and Tarawa.

Scenes during the American Occupation
of Korea in 1945

When the American soldiers came to Korea in 1945 they came as liberators of a country which had undergone thirty-five years of Japanese rule. The amusing and tranquil scenes recorded by John Pike and Sergeant Steven R. Kidd in fifty paintings would be soon transformed to scenes of war-ravaged ruins.

From a water color by John Pike. Courtesy Department of the Army, Chief of Military History

A rainy day in a Korean village

Korean children gape and stare at two American soldiers
as they thumb a ride from a passing jeep.

324

Street scene in Inchon, Korea, during the United States Army occupation

The Japanese have left, and the country has returned to peaceful pursuits. The street swarms with GI's and sailors and the populace makes way for an Army "6 by 6" truck.

Shopping—Korean style

American soldiers on a shopping tour in Korea. One American soldier bargains while his buddy and a young Korean lady watch with interest and no little amusement.

325

From a drawing in sepia and wash by John Groth. Courtesy of the artist and The World Publishing Company

"Figures in a fiery landscape"

"In a scene that might have been lifted from a Hieronymus Bosch landscape, burning villages
spouted flame and columns of smoke joined a skywide pall that hid the sun."

From a prismacolor painting by Herbert C. Hahn, U.S.N.R. Courtesy Combat Art Division, U. S. Navy

Into the wind—Korean coast

Carriers heel over in the wind as they make a high-speed turn to receive aircraft.

From a prismacolor painting by Herbert C. Hahn, U.S.N.R. Courtesy Combat Art Division, U. S. Navy

The fighting Corsair

The F4U fighter, work horse of the carriers, fires its rockets in close support to ground forces.

327

From a drawing in sepia and wash by John Groth. Courtesy of the artist and The World Publishing Company

The great crossing of the Han

A combat patrol splashes up the river bank of the Han River under fire. "There was action ahead of us somewhere," wrote the artist. "We could hear the staccato of small arms fire in the din of the barrage now shrouding the farther hills in smoke."

From a sepia drawing in wash by John Groth. Courtesy of the artist and The World Publishing Company

"The advance was slow and cautious"

"There was no live enemy on the next hilltop . . . progress on the next was slowed to a halt by small arms fire. We dug in and waited for our artillery to silence it."

From a drawing by John Groth. Courtesy of the artist and The World Publishing Company

Patrol on the road to Pyong-yang

"The Chinese held a row of hills two thousand yards north of Pyong-yang, a town five miles down the river. The mission of the company-size patrol was to seize the hills."

329

From a prismacolor painting by Hugh Cabot III, U.S.N. Courtesy Combat Art Division, U. S. Navy

A Navy Banshee hit and in trouble

The Banshee, one of the most powerful airplanes of modern times, loses its superiority
as it force-lands in the primitive mountains of North Korea. Its teammates will circle,
providing cover from attack on the ground, until help arrives or fuel runs low.

From a prismacolor painting by Herbert C. Hahn, U.S.N.R. Courtesy Combat Art Division, U. S. Navy

Scratch one!

Task Force 77 systematically destroyed hundreds of bridges in North Korea.

From a water color by Hugh Cabot III, U.S.N. Courtesy Combat Art Division, U. S. Navy

Dying Banshee

Score one for the enemy. Just off target, hit and flaming but striving skyward for altitude to parachute, the pilot of a burning Banshee is caught in the fleeting seconds between life and death.

From a water color by Hugh Cabot III, U.S.N. Courtesy Combat Art Division, U. S. Navy

Jet strike!

On the coast of North Korea, a Navy Panther Jet roars off the beaten target at 400 miles per hour and on to another.

From a drawing in pen and ink by Airman First Class Arthur C. Butts IV

Russian jet fighter, MIG-15, Korea, 1951

For the first few months of the Korean War this plane was the mysterious enemy air element. It was not long before American fighter pilots discovered its performance characteristics. The MIG fought well, but it met its match in the F86 Sabre.

From a prismacolor painting by Herbert C. Hahn, U.S.N.R. Courtesy Combat Art Division, U. S. Navy

Rocket run—North Korea

A Corsair from the U.S.S. *Boxer* finds a target for its rockets in North Korea.

From a prismacolor painting by Herbert C. Hahn, U.S.N. Courtesy Combat Art Division, U. S. Navy

The sitting duck

Mokpo during an attack in the early stages of the Korean War by planes from Task Force 77.

From a prismacolor painting by Herbert C. Hahn, U.S.N.R. Courtesy Combat Art Division, U. S. Navy

Victory pass

Jets returning to the aircraft carrier *Boxer* make a pass which denotes a successful mission.

General Douglas MacArthur

Supreme Commander for the Allied Powers, Tokyo, Japan,
Commander of the United Nations Forces in the Korean War.

From a sketch in pen and ink by John Groth. Courtesy of the artist and The World Publishing Company

From a prismacolor painting by Herbert C. Hahn, U.S.N.R. Courtesy Combat Art Division, U. S. Navy

The landing at Inchon, Korea

Amphibious landing of General MacArthur's forces at Inchon, September 15, 1950,
supported by Task Force 77.

335

From a water color by Hugh Cabot III, U.S.N. Courtesy Combat Art Division, U. S. Navy

The corpsmen

Two U. S. Marine Corps tanks, pinned down by artillery fire in the mountains
of North Korea, have suffered casualties and are coming under serious enemy fire.
Naval hospital corpsmen go in to evacuate the wounded and dead.

From a water color by Hugh Cabot III, U.S.N. Courtesy Combat Art Division, U. S. Navy

Forward operations

High ground for observation is a desirable position to hold. The topmost point of any one of the
many pock-marked Korean hills has probably been at some time an observation post. For the most
part, the hilltop is under constant enemy fire.

336

From a water color by Hugh Cabot III, U.S.N. Courtesy Combat Art Division, U. S. Navy

"76" Alley

From a water color by Hugh Cabot III, U.S.N. Courtesy Combat Art Division, U. S. Navy

Off the hill—Korea

In the mountainous regions of Korea, where the going was tough, many a combat Marine owed his life to the men who took him off the hill—the Korean Service Corps.

337

From a water color by Hugh Cabot III, U.S.N. Courtesy Combat Art Division, U. S. Navy

Evacuation under fire—Korea

The 'copter gets in and gets out in a hurry with the wounded man. Time, the difference between life and death in many wounds, is now an enemy of only hours, not days.

From a water color by Hugh Cabot III, U.S.N. Courtesy Combat Art Division, U. S. Navy

Incoming

"Under constant mortar and artillery fire, the Company CP has war at the bunker door. The shortest distances must be covered on the run. When it's incoming, there's no time to think, and barely enough time to duck. No home, no hole is more welcome than the inside of a bunker."

338

From a prismacolor painting by Herbert C. Hahn, U.S.N.R. Courtesy Combat Art Division, U. S. Navy

Windmills

Delegates to the truce talks leave the base camp for a meeting at Kaesong.

Acknowledgments

The preparation of this book called for specialized assistance. For that assistance I am greatly indebted to a large group of distinguished professional people in the military, naval, and air services of the United States military establishment, and to an equal number of distinguished scholars and archivists of the United States and Canada who so generously came forward and contributed their valuable time and knowledge toward the preparation of the materials contained in this book.

I am deeply grateful to my friend Professor Robert M. Langdon of the United States Naval Academy at Annapolis, for his personal assistance and tenfold courtesies in the selection of and search for the pictorial and manuscript materials contained in the naval sequences; to Louis H. Bolander, Librarian of the Naval Academy, for his kindness in locating the important Henry N. Walke paintings and bibliographical notes pertaining thereto; and to Rear Admiral John B. Heffernan, Director of Naval History, Department of the Navy, for his kindness and assistance in the selection of the Thomas Birch paintings; to the late Mrs. Mary Minton, Curator and Custodian of Naval Combat Art, Department of the Navy, for her untiring efforts in my behalf—a very gracious lady.

For the use of the extremely important drawings and paintings of the United States Marine Corps combat artists, I am deeply in debt to Colonel Donald Lester Dickson, a brilliant artist who contributed many of his own drawings and a portion of the text on the actions in the South Pacific in which he himself took part; and to Captain James S. Roberts, U.S.M.C., Special Services Branch, for his help in locating Marine Corps material, I extend my grateful appreciation.

Grateful acknowledgment is forthcoming to Major General A. C. Smith, Chief of Military History, and to members of his staff, Lieutenant Colonel Carl D. McFerren, Executive

Officer, Major Leonard O. Frieze, and Mrs. Marion McNaughton, Curator of Military Art, for their many kindnesses to me in the selection of important pictorial material and military drawings concerning the Army in the War with Mexico and in World Wars I and II. Their expert assistance simplified a job that would otherwise have taken many weeks to complete.

I am indeed greatly indebted to Colonel W. T. Morton, Librarian of the United States Military Academy at West Point, for his scholarly assistance in the early stages of this book; and to Milton H. Perry, Assistant Curator of the West Point Museum, for his friendly, valuable suggestions on American historical military matters. To Lieutenant Alvin Bailey of the United States Coast Guard, an old friend of World War II days, and to the Coast Guard Public Relations Staff, I give my grateful thanks. To John Groth, for his kindness in allowing me to use his fine drawings on World War II and Korea, my sincere appreciation is extended.

I am indeed under obligation to Lieutenant Colonel Arthur J. Larsen, Chief, Historical Branch, Office of the Secretary of the Air Staff, United States Air Force, for his valuable services and personal kindness to me in the search for and the use of the combat art of the Air Force.

Likewise, I am especially indebted to Mr. J. B. MacKenzie of the Canada Steamship Lines, for his untiring efforts in helping me locate the important military art covering the French and Indian War, and for allowing me use of the William H. Coverdale Collection at Manoir Richelieu, Murray Bay, Province of Quebec; to Major Pierre Brunet, Chief Administrative Assistant, Public Archives of Canada, and to Mr. H. O. Curry, Director of the National Gallery of Canada, and William K. Lamb, Dominion Archivist of the Public Archives of Canada.

My grateful appreciation I extend to Mr. Sylvestre Vig-

ACKNOWLEDGMENTS

ilante, formerly of the American History Department, New York Public Library, who spared no effort to locate for me many old volumes important to the early research for this book. To him and to his staff, I offer my thanks. To Mr. Ira Glackens of the National City Bank of Paris I offer my thanks and appreciation for permission to use the military drawings of the Spanish-American War executed by his famous father, William Glackens; and to Miss Antoinette Kraushaar of the Kraushaar Galleries, for the preparation of these paintings and drawings for publication.

Miss India W. Thomas, Regent of the Confederate Museum at Richmond, gave me valuable assistance in locating many important drawings and paintings of the soldier-artists of the Confederacy. To Mr. Harold McCracken, an old friend and colleague, for use of his Remington collection and for permission to quote from his scholarly book, *Frederic Remington,* go my gratitude and thanks.

Grateful acknowledgment is also extended to the following distinguished curators, archivists, and scholars:

To Dr. F. M. Setzler, Head Curator, Department of Anthropology, The Smithsonian Institution; Mr. M. L. Peterson, Curator of Military History, U. S. National Museum, and Mr. Russell Sirlouis, Assistant Curator of the same institution. Their kindness and assistance is greatly appreciated. To Dr. J. O. Brew, Director of the Peabody Museum of Archaeology, Harvard University; Mr. R. N. Williams, 2nd, Director of the Historical Society of Pennsylvania, and Miss Sarah Smith, Librarian of the Society; to Mr. W. G. Constable, Curator of Paintings, Museum of Fine Arts, Boston; Miss Katherine Newton Wray, Registrar of the Museum of Fine Arts, Houston, Texas; Miss Sarah M. Usher, Chief of Records, Public Library, City of Boston; Mr. Magill James, Assistant Director, National Gallery of Art, Washington, D. C.; Mr. Allan E. Kent, Research Associate, Wisconsin

Historical Society Museum; Mr. Calvin S. Hathaway, Director, Cooper Union Museum of Fine Arts; Mr. James D. Breckenridge, Keeper of the Clark Collection, The Corcoran Gallery of Art; Mr. James W. Foster, Director of the Maryland Historical Society; Mr. Victor D. Spark of New York, for his permission to use several fine paintings; Mr. J. W. Davidson of M. Knoedler Company, Inc., New York, for the use of one of their fine paintings; Mr. John Marshall Phillips, Director, Yale University Art Gallery; Mr. Burton W. Adkinson, Director of the Library of Congress; and to The Abbott Laboratories, Chicago, for permission to reproduce some of Kerr Eby's combat drawings.

My special thanks are due to Mrs. John W. Thomason of Texas, for her kind permission to use portions of the text from *Fix Bayonets,* a book written and illustrated by her husband, the late Colonel John W. Thomason, U.S.M.C., and for the use of his wonderful drawings of Marines in action in World War I. To Charles Scribner's Sons, his publishers, also go thanks for permission to reproduce some of this material. And to my friend and colleague, C. James Proud of the Advertising Federation of America, who lent his assistance, valued and appreciated during a trying period. I was fortunate, too, in having the services of my son Arthur, Airman, First Class, Special Artist attached to the staff of the Commanding General, 57th Air Division, Fairchild Air Force Base, for assistance in air research, and those of Anne Meredith and Jacqueline Andrew in typing and preparing the manuscript.

All possible care has been taken to make full acknowledgment for the use of every illustration included in this book. If any errors have accidentally occurred, they will be corrected in subsequent editions, provided notification is sent to the publisher.

ROY MEREDITH

Philadelphia, February, 1955

Contributing Institutions and Historical Societies

United States Military Academy Library, West Point, N. Y.
United States Military Academy Museum, West Point, N. Y.
United States Naval Academy Museum, Annapolis, Md.
United States Naval Institute, Annapolis, Md.
Department of the Navy, Office of the Chief of Naval Operations, Department of Naval History, Washington, D. C.
Department of the Army, Office of the Chief of Military History, Washington, D. C.
Department of the Air Force.
Library of Congress, Washington, D. C.
Canada Steamship Lines Limited, Montreal, Canada.
The National Gallery of Canada, Ottawa, Canada.
Public Archives of Canada, Ottawa, Canada.
The Smithsonian Institution, Washington, D. C.
The Museum of Fine Arts of Houston, Texas.
The Confederate Memorial Museum, Richmond, Va.
The Cooper Union Museum for the Arts of Decoration, New York.
Metropolitan Museum of Art, New York.

National Gallery of Art, Washington, D. C.
Wisconsin State Historical Society, Madison, Wisc.
The Peabody Museum of Archaeology, Harvard University, Cambridge, Mass.
The Historical Society of Pennsylvania, Philadelphia, Pa.
Cincinnati Art Museum, Cincinnati, Ohio.
Public Library of Boston, Mass.
New York Public Library, New York.
Museum of Fine Arts, Boston, Mass.
The Frick Art Reference Library of New York, N. Y.
Remington Art Memorial, Ogdensburg, N. Y.
Maryland Historical Society, Baltimore, Md.
Yale University Art Gallery, New Haven, Conn.
Corcoran Gallery of Art, Washington, D. C.
Charles M. Kraushaar Galleries, New York.
Victor D. Spark Galleries, New York.
M. Knoedler & Company Galleries, New York.
Canajoharie Art Gallery, Canajoharie, N. Y.

Military Artists of
The American Wars

AYLWARD, WILLIAM J. (*Chapter 10*) born in Milwaukee, Wisc., September 5, 1875. Aylward studied with Howard Pyle, and during World War I was assigned to the A.E.F. as an artist by the War Department. He is noted as an illustrator of marine and naval subjects.

BACKUS, STANDISH (*Chapter 11*) born in Detroit, Mich., April 5, 1910. He studied art and architecture at Princeton and later spent a year in Europe for further study. He was commissioned in the Naval Reserve in 1940 and in 1945 helped to establish a unit to work on special presentation of naval reports to the president. He was assigned to the Pacific as a combat artist for the invasion of Japan, but the end of the war in August made the projected operation unnecessary.

BEAUGUREAU, FRANCIS I. (*Chapter 11*) born in Chicago, April 5, 1920. He attended the Chicago Art Institute and the Frederick Mizen Art Academy in Chicago. In World War II he was consultant on art matters to the chief of staff of the U. S. Army Air Force and served as a combat artist during that war and the Korean War.

BIRCH, THOMAS (*Chapter 3*) born in London, July 26, 1779. He emigrated to the United States in 1793 and in 1800 established himself in Philadelphia as a portrait painter. His training as a topographical artist led to his famous "Views of Philadelphia," in which he collaborated with his father, the enamelist William Russell Birch. Though he was basically a landscape and not a marine painter, his historical series of the U. S. naval victories in the War of 1812 demonstrates his grasp of the technical problems and his drawing ability. Birch designed a num-

ber of coins for the Mint. He died in Philadelphia January 14, 1851.

BLODGET, SAMUEL (*Chapter 1*) born at Woburn, Mass., April 1, 1724. He fought in the French and Indian War, then briefly turned to farming before again joining the troops as a sutler to a New Hampshire regiment. Following the action at Fort William Henry, Blodget entered business and from his merchandising, manufacture of potash, and trade in lumber and furs became a comparatively rich man. Early in the Revolution he was again a sutler, to Sullivan's Brigade, but when the war shifted from Boston he returned to civilian pursuits. In 1794 Blodget began building a canal around Amoskeag Falls on the Merrimac River, but his money alone was not sufficient to complete the work, especially after a flood washed away most of what had been done. He managed to raise funds, however, and in May, 1807, the canal, an important link in New England communications for 35 years afterward, was opened. Blodget died at Derryfield, Mass., September 1, 1807.

BLYTHE, DAVID GILMOUR (*Chapter 7*) born at East Liverpool, Ohio, May 9, 1815. He learned the wood-carver's trade in Pittsburgh and at the age of 19 sailed as ship's carpenter in the Navy. He studied painting at the J. J. Gillespie Gallery, the oldest art establishment in America. During the Civil War he followed the 13th Pennsylvania Volunteers in the capacity of artist without rank. He died at Pittsburgh, Pa., May 15, 1865.

BRODIE, HOWARD J. (*Chapter 11*) born in San Francisco, Calif., November 28, 1916. After studying at the Califor-

342

nia School of Fine Arts, he became a member of the staff of the San Francisco *Chronicle*. During World War II he was a combat artist with the U. S. Army in the European Theater of Operations.

BUTTS, ARTHUR CLARKSON (*Chapter 12*) born in New York, January 28, 1930. He attended the Pennsylvania Academy of Fine Arts and the University of Pennsylvania. Attached to the staff of the commanding general, 57th Air Division, Spokane, Washington, Airman Butts drew one of the first accurate pictures of the Russian MIG-15 from aerial photographs taken during combat over Korea.

CABOT, HUGH (*Chapter 12*) born in Boston, Mass., March 22, 1930. He was a staff artist for the Boston Museum of Science, a free lance artist, and director of a summer art school in Massachusetts before he enlisted in the Navy shortly after the outbreak of the Korean War. He served aboard aircraft carriers off Korea, and then, as the only officially assigned combat artist in the Far East theater, was directed to the 1st Marine Division to record their winter campaign. Later he covered the truce talks and the Chinese Nationalist island of Formosa.

CAVADA, FREDERIC (*Chapter 7*) Lieutenant Cavada served with the 14th Pennsylvania Volunteers. His painting appears to derive from Waud's on-the-spot drawing, but whether Cavada worked from Waud's original or from a reproduction is not clear.

CHAPMAN, CONRAD WISE (*Chapter 7*) born at Rome, Italy, 1842. His father, the artist John Gadsby Chapman, gave Conrad his early training in art. At the outbreak of the Civil War, Chapman left Italy and, after landing in New York, made his way to the Confederate lines, where he joined the troops of A. S. Johnston. His father having made inquiries regarding the runaway's whereabouts, Conrad was located by General Henry H. Wise, who obtained a transfer for the youth to his own brigade. Wise's men were soon ordered to Charleston, where Chapman was put to work painting a series of pictures on the siege. A head wound received at Shiloh notwithstanding, at the end of the Civil War Chapman went to Mexico, where Maximilian's empire was coming to its bloody end. A few years later he was following the Franco-Prussian War at first hand. Chapman was an extremely prolific artist, but it has been noted that even his sketches are carefully done. He died at Hampton, Va., in 1917.

COALE, GRIFFITH BAILY (*Chapter 11*) born at Baltimore, Md., May 21, 1890. He studied in Germany, France, Italy, and Spain and subsequently became a professional painter in Baltimore. During World War I he served in a camouflage unit working on merchant ships. Many of his paintings of the period between 1922, when he came to New York, and 1939 appear in public buildings. Coale is credited with giving initial impetus to the Combat Artists Program of the Navy. In 1941 he was commissioned lieutenant commander in the Naval Reserve, and during the war observed action in the North Atlantic, Pacific, Southeast Asia, and other theaters of war. He wrote and illus-

trated two books on his experiences. He died soon after the war.

DAVIS, JEFFERSON (*Chapter 5*) born in Kentucky, June 3, 1808. After graduating from West Point in 1838, he was stationed at frontier posts. He resigned from the army in 1835 to manage his plantation in Mississippi. In 1845 he was elected to Congress. He fought with distinction in the Mexican War and later was a member of the Senate. Davis left the Senate to campaign for the governorship of Mississippi, but he was defeated. Franklin Pierce appointed him secretary of war and he occupied that cabinet post throughout Pierce's presidency. In 1857 Davis returned to the Senate, resigning in 1861 when Mississippi seceded, and was chosen president of the Confederacy, a decision confirmed when he was elected in October of that year. With the fall of the Confederacy he was captured and imprisoned for two years, finally to be released without being brought to trial. His remaining years were spent in writing, in semiretirement on his estate. He died at New Orleans, La., December 6, 1889.

DICKSON, DONALD LESTER (*Chapter 11*) born in Cambridge, Mass., January 28, 1906. He studied art at the Worcester Art Museum School and became a prominent commercial artist. In 1941 he joined the 1st Marine Division when it was formed in Cuba and remained with it after World War II, rising through the ranks from private first class to colonel. He is a staff member of *The Leatherneck*, the official magazine of the U. S. Marine Corps.

DONAHUE, VICTOR (*Chapter 11*) born in Philadelphia, August 28, 1918. He served with the 1st Marine Division from 1942 to 1945 in all their campaigns in the South Pacific.

DUNCAN, WALTER J. (*Chapter 10*) born in Indianapolis, Ind., January 1, 1881. He studied at the Art Students League in New York and became an illustrator for national magazines and for books, among them Booth Tarkington's works. During World War I he was appointed an official artist with the A.E.F. and served in the Army's major engagements in France making drawings for the official records. He died April 11, 1941.

DUNN, HARVEY T. (*Chapter 10*) born at Manchester, S.D., March 8, 1884. He studied at the Art Institute of Chicago. During World War I he served as an official artist with the A.E.F.

DU PORTAIL, LOUIS LE BECQUE (*Chapter 2*) A French military engineer, he came to America at about the same time as Lafayette. The Continental Congress voted that he should "take rank and command of all engineers previously appointed," and it was du Portail who laid out the defenses for the camp at Valley Forge. He remained with Washington, who greatly admired him, until the surrender of Cornwallis at Yorktown, in the siege of which he had charge of engineering operations. From November, 1790, to December, 1791, he was French minister of war. He died in 1802.

EASTMAN, SETH (*Chapter 4*) born at Brunswick, Maine, January 24, 1808. There is no evidence that Eastman, a graduate of West Point in 1828, had any formal art training, but a self-portrait done at about the time he graduated shows remarkable talent. His career after his graduation is outlined in the text of Chapter 4. He died at Washington, D.C., August 31, 1875.

EBY, KERR (*Chapters 10 and 11*) born in Tokyo, Japan, October 19, 1889. He was a prize student at the National Institute and became a book illustrator. He was Charles Dana Gibson's assistant with the A.E.F. during World War I as a combat artist. After the war he resumed his career as a commercial illustrator. In 1932 he was commissioned to do the Bi-Centennial Portfolio—*Life of Washington*. During World War II he was engaged by the Abbott Laboratories of Chicago to make a special series of drawings of the U. S. Marines in action. Eby was at Tarawa, New Britain, and other important Pacific campaigns with the 1st Marine Division. He died in Westport, Conn., November 18, 1946.

FULLER, LAWSON M. (*Chapter 5*) born in Wisconsin, March 5, 1866. A graduate of West Point in the class of 1891, he served with the cavalry during the Philippine insurrection and twice won the Silver Star for gallantry. In 1908 he was retired for disability, but in World War I he was recalled to active service as a colonel in the ordnance department. He died at Hamilton, Bermuda, September 17, 1929.

GLACKENS, WILLIAM JAMES (*Chapter 9*) born at Philadelphia, March 13, 1870. He studied at the Pennsylvania Academy of Fine Arts and after completing his courses became an illustrator for Philadelphia newspapers. In 1895 he went to Paris for a year's study and on his return became a member of the staff of the New York *Herald,* in which his illustrations attracted much notice. When war was declared against Spain, Glackens went to Cuba under contract to *McClure's Magazine* but yellow fever felled him and his drawings were finished long after the editors of *McClure's* could find any news interest in them. Glackens recovered and returned to New York, where he devoted himself to oil painting. He and a group of kindred artists organized the famous Armory Show in 1913 as a reaction against the formalism of the "salon" artists. In 1933 he was elected a member of the National Academy of Design. He died May 22, 1938.

GRANT, ULYSSES SIMPSON (*Chapter 5*) born Hiram Ulysses Grant at Point Pleasant, Ohio, April 27, 1822. In 1843 Grant graduated from West Point and, after service in Missouri and Louisiana and in the Mexican War, became a captain while stationed on the West Coast. He resigned from the Army in 1854, returned to service as colonel of Illinois volunteers soon after the outbreak of the Civil War, and was made a brigadier general in August, 1861. His victories in the West brought him national fame and, in March, 1864, he became commander of the Union armies. He brought the conflict to a successful conclusion and after the war became a full general, the first man in U. S. history to be appointed to this rank. He was

commander in the South during the early Reconstruction period and briefly served as secretary of war. In 1868 he was elected president and was re-elected in 1872. He died at Mount McGregor, N. Y., July 23, 1885.

GROTH, JOHN (*Chapters 11 and 12*) born in Chicago, February 26, 1908. He studied at the Chicago Art Institute and the Art Students League in New York. Groth became the first art director for *Esquire* magazine, traveling widely on writing and drawing assignments. During World War II he was sent overseas by the Chicago *Sun* syndicate and *Parade* magazine, from which came his book *Studio: Europe. Studio: Asia* resulted from his travels in the war-torn Far East.

HARDING, GEORGE (*Chapters 10 and 11*) born in Philadelphia, 1882. He studied at the Pennsylvania Academy of Fine Arts and later with Howard Pyle. After extensive travel, which resulted in several articles accompanied by his illustrations, he became an illustrator for magazine stories. In 1918 the War Department assigned him to the A.E.F. as an artist. His murals appear in a number of public buildings. Harding is a member of the National Academy of Design.

HOFF, WILLIAM BAINBRIDGE (*Chapter 3*) born at Philadelphia, 1846. While still a midshipman at Annapolis, Hoff for a time commanded the famous racing yacht *America*. He graduated from the Naval Academy in 1863 and in subsequent years rose through the ranks. He retired in 1897 as a captain. Hoff is known for his books on naval tactics. Inspired by Porter's drawings, Hoff made a series of his own of the *Essex*'s engagements. He died in 1903.

HOMER, WINSLOW (*Chapter 7*) born at Boston, February 24, 1836. While still a boy he manifested great talent in art and, at the age of 21, was serving his apprenticeship in a leading lithographic house in Boston. In 1859 he moved to New York, where he became a free-lance illustrator and attended evening classes at the National Academy of Design. He traveled with the army in the field for much of the Civil War, making sketches which were later used for some of his oil paintings or for illustrations in *Harper's Weekly*. In 1865 he was elected a member of the National Academy of Design. After some further study in Europe, he settled in Maine. His water colors and his marine paintings are among the finest American works of art. He died at Scarboro, Maine, September 28, 1910.

HOPE, JAMES (*Chapter 7*) born at Drygrange, Scotland, November 29, 1818. His father, who had brought him to Canada, died about 1831 and Hope moved to Vermont as a wagon-maker's apprentice. He established himself as a professional artist and as a teacher of painting and drawing. When the Civil War began, he was elected captain of a volunteer company he helped to recruit. He took part in 11 major battles; because of his artistic ability he was often called upon to serve as a topographical engineer. After the war he used battlefield sketches he had made to paint several large canvases notable as accurate depictions of the scenes they recorded. He died at New York, January 21, 1904.

JAMIESON, MITCHELL (*Chapter 11*) born at Kensington, Md., October 27, 1915. He studied at the Abbott School of Fine and Commercial Arts and at the Corcoran School of Art, Washington, D. C. Afterward he worked on several government projects, including a series of pictures for the National Defense program. Commissioned in the Navy in 1942, he served through the war in campaigns from North Africa to Okinawa.

LAWRIE, ALEXANDER (*Chapter 7*) born in New York, 1828. After attending classes at the Academy of Design, he went to Europe in 1854 to study in Germany, France, and Italy. He returned to New York, where he opened a studio in 1858, and when the studio failed went to Philadelphia. In 1861 he enlisted in a Pennsylvania volunteer regiment; in 1862, he re-enlisted as a captain of volunteers, but illness contracted apparently during "Burnside's Mud March" resulted in his discharge on a surgeon's certificate in June, 1863. In 1864, he again opened a studio in New York, this time maintaining it until 1878; he was elected an associate of the National Academy of Design, but barely managed to eke out a living. In 1895 he finally left New York to live with a brother in Indiana, but a disagreement caused him to enter a veterans' home in Hampton, Virginia. Finally, in 1902 he was admitted to the State Soldiers' Home at Lafayette, Indiana, where he spent his declining years painting a series of portraits of all the Civil War generals. He died at Lafayette in 1917.

LEE, ROBERT EDWARD (*Chapter 5*) born in Westmoreland County, Va., January 19, 1807. The son of General Henry Lee, he was second in his class at West Point when he graduated in 1829 and became a lieutenant of engineers. Service at seacoast forts and on the Mississippi led to an appointment to Winfield Scott's staff during the Mexican War. He returned to Army post life after the war, serving at Baltimore, on the frontier, and as superintendent, from 1852 to 1855, of the Military Academy at West Point. Lee was commander of the troops that put down John Brown's brief rebellion at Harper's Ferry and by the time the Civil War erupted had risen to colonel. He was offered supreme command of the Union field armies by President Lincoln but refused the appointment that would mean invading his native state. When Virginia joined the secession, Lee resigned his commission and assumed command of Virginia's forces. As commander of the Army of Northern Virginia he was the principal Confederate general in the East and in February, 1865, was named general in chief of the Confederate armies, but was forced to surrender two months later. After the war he became president of the college known today as Washington and Lee University, a position he held until his death at Lexington, Va., October 12, 1870.

LITTELL, ISAAC W. (*Chapter 5*) born at Elizabeth, N. J., December 5, 1857. A graduate of West Point in 1883, he served in the Philippines during the insurrection. In World War I, General Littell was in charge of all cantonment and national guard camp construction. He died at Washington, D. C., May 1, 1924.

MACKELLAR, PATRICK (*Chapter 1*) born 1717. An ordnance clerk, he became engineer in ordinary at Minorca in 1751, then came to America as one of Braddock's engineers. In 1756 he was appointed chief engineer for the forts along the frontier but was captured by the French and held in Canada until 1757. He was promoted to chief engineer during the siege of Louisbourg and was chief engineer on Wolfe's staff during the struggle for Quebec. He served in the campaigns against Martinique and Havana in 1761 and 1762, then returned to Minorca, where in 1777, the year before his death, he became a colonel.

MARCH, PEYTON CONWAY (*Chapter 5*) born at Easton, Pa., December 27, 1864. He graduated at West Point in 1888 and commanded a battery of artillery in the Philippines during the war with Spain, receiving the Distinguished Service Cross for heroism. During the Philippine insurrection March was five times decorated for gallantry. During the Russo-Japanese War he was a U. S. military observer with the Japanese forces. In 1917 he went to France as artillery commander but was recalled to serve as chief of staff of the army. He retired in 1921. General March died in 1955.

MEADE, GEORGE GORDON (*Chapter 5*) born at Cadiz, Spain, December 31, 1815. Following his graduation from West Point in 1835, he fought in the Seminole War, resigned from the army, worked for the Texas-U.S. border commission, and re-entered the army as lieutenant of topographical engineers. Meade served with distinction in the Mexican War and afterward performed such engineer's duties as building lighthouses along the Florida coast. At the start of the Civil War he became a brigadier general of volunteers and thereafter saw action in every battle fought by the Army of the Potomac. He received a severe wound in 1862, but soon was back in the field. In June, 1863, he became commander of the Army of the Potomac; within a week of his notification he had defeated Lee at Gettysburg, but his failure to follow up his victory caused severe criticism. In 1864 he became a major general in the regular army. He held several area commands during the Reconstruction period. He died at Philadelphia, November 6, 1872.

MILLMAN, EDWARD (*Chapter 11*) born in Chicago, January 1, 1907. He studied at the Art Institute of Chicago under Leon Kroll and John Norton. From 1929 to 1933 he was on the art staff of the Chicago *Evening American,* and in the latter year painted a series of murals for the Chicago World's Fair. After studying mural painting in Mexico, he returned to the United States as first state director of mural projects for the Federal Art Program. During World War II he was officer in charge of the Navy Training Aids Development Center at New York and later was assigned as a combat artist to the Philippines and Dutch New Guinea invasions.

MONTRESOR, JOHN (*Chapter 1*) born at Gibraltar, April 6, 1736. His father was chief engineer at Gibraltar when young Montresor entered the army as assistant engineer. When the elder Montresor became chief engineer to Braddock's expedition, John accompanied him. He was wounded in the Monongahela battle but recovered to take part in the campaign against the French in Canada, serving at various points in the line of British outposts and on Wolfe's headquarters staff before Quebec. In 1765 he was promoted to captain-lieutenant and in 1775, at the outbreak of the Revolutionary War, was chief engineer for the British forces in America. He built the defensive system around British-held Philadelphia. In 1779 he retired, having attained the rank of colonel. He died June 26, 1799.

MORGAN, WALLACE (*Chapter 10*) born in New York, 1873. After studying at the National Academy of Design, he worked as an illustrator for New York City newspapers. He was assigned by the War Department as an artist for the A.E.F. in 1918.

MURRAY, ALBERT KETCHAM. (*Chapter 11*) born at Emporia, Kansas, December 29, 1906. A graduate in fine arts from Syracuse University in 1930, he studied in London and Paris and later under Wayman Adams in New York and Mexico. During World War II, he was one of the artists originally assigned to the Combat Art Section and served in the Caribbean area, the South Atlantic, North Africa, the invasion of southern France, and the Italian sector.

PEALE, CHARLES WILLSON (*Chapter 2*) born at Chestertown, Md., April 16, 1741. A saddler's apprentice, he gave such evidence of talent in oil painting while studying under John Singleton Copley that a group of gentlemen subsidized his voyage to England to work under Benjamin West. Peale returned to America and settled near Annapolis, where he gained great success as a portrait painter, Washington and his family being among those who sat for the artist. During the Revolutionary War, Peale "fit and painted, and painted and fit," serving at Trenton, Valley Forge, and Princeton, and turning out propaganda pictures that he later discarded as worthless. At the war's end he returned to Philadelphia where he opened a natural history museum in which exhibits were arranged before painted backgrounds to resemble "the world in miniature." He was one of the founders in 1805 of the Pennsylvania Academy of Fine Arts. His declining years were spent as an inventor and the despair of his family, who were not unaccustomed to seeing the old man coasting down a hill on one of America's first bicycles. Energetic to the last, he died, February 22, 1827, as the result of over-exertion "while searching for a fourth wife in Philadelphia."

PEALE, JAMES (*Chapter 1*) born in Chestertown, Md., 1749. A brother of Charles Willson Peale, he is noted as a miniaturist, though his landscapes, historical compositions, and portraits have also drawn much interest. He died May 24, 1831.

PEIXOTTO, ERNEST CLIFFORD (*Chapter 10*) born in San Francisco, Calif., October 15, 1869. He studied in France. During World War I he was assigned to the A.E.F. by the War Department as an artist and in 1919 was director of painting at the training school established for American troops at Bellevue, France. An associate member of the National Academy of Design, he taught mural painting at the Beaux-Arts Institute, New York, and was a consultant in the planning of the World's Fair in New York. He died in New York, December 6, 1940.

PIKE, JOHN (*Chapter 12*) born in Boston, Mass., June 30, 1911. A student of Charles Hawthorne and Richard Miller, he was a commercial illustrator when the U. S. Army appointed him to make a record of the occupation of Korea after World War II.

PLEISSNER, OGDEN M. (*Chapter 11*) born in Brooklyn, N. Y., April 29, 1905. He was a pupil of George Bridgeman and a member of the Art Students League. In 1938 he was elected to the National Academy of Design. In World War II he enlisted and became a captain in the Air Force.

POCOCK, NICHOLAS (*Chapter 3*) born in Bristol, England, about 1741. A captain in the British merchant marine, he retired from active duty before he was 40 to devote himself to his own pursuits. A marine painting he submitted to the Royal Academy for exhibition in 1780 arrived too late, but Sir Joshua Reynolds recognized the great talent behind the painting and encouraged Pocock to continue with his marine work. In 1789 he settled at London as a painter of sea battles—the wars of the time furnished more than ample material—and he soon became the most noted of all British marine painters. In 1804 he was one of the founders of the Water-colour Society and he continued to exhibit his paintings there and at the Royal Academy to the end of his life. He died at Maidenhead, Berkshire, England, 1821.

PORTER, DAVID (*Chapter 3*) born at Boston, February 1, 1780. A merchant seaman, he was one of the victims of the British impressment, but he escaped in 1798 and joined the young United States Navy as a member of the crew of the *Constellation*. He fought in the Tripolitanian War, became a lieutenant aboard the *Philadelphia*, and was captured when that frigate ran aground off Tripoli. As commander of the *Essex*, he undertook one of the most colorful voyages in the Navy's history, around Cape Horn to the Pacific, where he disrupted British shipping. In 1823 he became involved in a quarrel with civilian authorities in Puerto Rico when one of his men was arrested; Porter's high-handed methods caused a diplomatic complaint to the U. S. government and he was suspended after a court-martial. He resigned from the Navy in 1826 and became head of the Mexican navy, directing it against the Spanish forces attempting to suppress the young republican government there. With the end of Spain's attempts at reconquest, Porter resigned. In 1831 he became U. S. chargé d'affaires at Constantinople, and in 1841 was appointed minister. He died at Constantinople, March 3, 1843.

REDWOOD, ALLEN CARTER (*Chapter 7*) born in Virginia, April, 1834. In his youth, he moved to Brooklyn, N. Y., where he lived until about 1852. With the outbreak of the

Civil War, he joined the Confederate Army, with which he served until the surrender at Appomattox, seeing service in all the major engagements as a member of the staffs of Lomax and Heth. He retired a major. After the war, Redwood became well known as a magazine and book illustrator and as a cartoonist, his minstrel cartoons being probably his most famous work. He died in October, 1922.

REMINGTON, FREDERIC (*Chapters 8 and 9*) born at Canton, N. Y., October 4, 1861. He studied at the Yale Art School and at the Art Students League in New York before being forced to move West because of his health. In the West he traveled with U. S. troops in their battles against the rebellious Indians and became noted as a delineator of horses and horsemen. He was a correspondent in the war with Spain, sketching Shafter's men in action in Cuba. His magazine illustrations, his books, and his sculpture place him in the forefront of the artists of the American West. He died at Ridgefield, Conn., December 26, 1909.

ROBINSON, WIRT (*Chapter 5*) born in Virginia, October 16, 1864. A graduate of West Point in 1887, Robinson became famous as a scientist. He was professor of chemistry at the Academy from 1911 to 1928. Besides his national reputation as a naturalist, he was recognized as a leading authority on explosives. His textbooks carried his own illustrations. He died at Washington, D. C., January 19, 1929.

RUSSO, ALEXANDER (*Chapter 11*) born in Atlantic City, N. J., June 11, 1922. He studied at Pratt Institute and at the same time worked as a free-lance illustrator. During World War II he served with naval intelligence making shoreline sketches for use by the assault forces in Sicily. His drawings of life aboard ship appeared in John Mason Brown's *To All Hands.* He volunteered for service in the Normandy invasion, and later served aboard the hospital ship *Tranquillity* in the Pacific.

SARGENT, JOHN SINGER (*Chapter 10*) born at Florence, Italy, 1856. He studied in Europe and opened a studio in London in 1885. Frequent visits to the United States resulted in his opening a studio in Boston as well in 1903. Elected to the Royal Academy in 1897, he refused, ten years later, a knighthood on the ground that he was an American citizen. He is best known as a portrait painter, some of his work in that field ranking with the world's best. As an artist with the A.E.F. in France, Sargent several times showed a bland disregard for military necessities, once completely ignoring the warning from the two captains assigned to watch him that the white umbrella he used to protect himself from the sun offered a prime target for enemy shellfire. He died April 15, 1925.

SCOTT, JULIAN (*Chapter 7*) born in Johnson, Vermont, February 14, 1846. He enlisted in the army at the outbreak of the Civil War and rose to become a colonel with the Union forces. He was awarded a medal of honor by Congress. After the war he studied at the National Academy of Design and worked as an illustrator. His principal work consists of pictures of army life and Western, especially Indian, scenes. He died in 1901.

SHEPLER, DWIGHT C. (*Chapter 11*) born at Everett, Mass., August 11, 1905. He taught water-color painting in Boston and did commercial art work after his graduation from college in 1928. During World War II he served as a Naval Reserve lieutenant in the Pacific, notably in the fighting around the Solomons, and in Europe during the invasion period. Later he returned to the Pacific for the Philippine invasion. Two of his murals were painted for the Academy at Annapolis.

SHEPPARD, WILLIAM LUDLOW (*Chapter 7*) born in Brooklyn, N. Y., 1830. A sergeant in the Confederate Army throughout the war, he spent a year in Italy studying when the war was ended. He was well known for his cartoons, many of which appeared in *Harper's Weekly,* and for a series of scenes published under the title *Picturesque America.* His ability as a sculptor may be seen in the Soldiers and Sailors Monument, the statue of A. P. Hill, and the Howitzer Memorial Hall in Richmond. He died in Richmond, Va., March 27, 1912.

SHERMAN, WILLIAM TECUMSEH (*Chapter 5*) born at Lancaster, Ohio, February 8, 1820. A graduate of West Point in 1840, Sherman fought in the Seminole War and was stationed at various posts in the South. During the Mexican War he was sent to California to administer the government there. He resigned his commission in 1853 to become California branch manager of a St. Louis bank and, after the bank closed the branch, entered the business world and practiced law. In 1859 he was appointed superintendent of the new Louisiana state military academy, left the post in 1861 just before the state seceded, and became colonel of an infantry regiment. By July, 1863, he had become a brigadier general in the regular army, and he was given command of the Army of the Tennessee when Grant went east. Sherman is best remembered for his march across Georgia, from Chattanooga to Atlanta and from Atlanta to Savannah, in 1864. In 1869 he became a full general. He retired in 1884, refusing in that same year the chance to become Republican nominee for the presidency of the United States. He died at New York, February 14, 1891.

SMITH, J. ANDRE (*Chapter 10*) born in New York, 1886. He traveled and studied in France and Spain. Smith was awarded the gold medal for etching at the Panama-Pacific Exposition.

SMYTH, HERVEY (*Chapter 1*) born at Ampton, England, May 30, 1734. In 1751 he entered the Royal Horse Guards as cornet; three years later he became a captain in the 15th Regiment of Foot. He took part in the siege of Louisbourg and was selected by Wolfe as an aide for the campaign against Quebec. Wolfe and Smyth became friends and in Wolfe's will Smyth was left 100 guineas to buy a remembrance token. He retired from the army May 12, 1769. At the death of his father he became baronet and spent his last years at Elswell, Suffolk, where he died in 1811.

THOMASON, JOHN WILLIAM, JR. (*Chapter 10*) born at Huntsville, Texas, 1893. He studied at the Art Students

League in New York. In 1917 he became a second lieutenant with the 2nd Marine Division in France, later served with the Marines in China, Central America, and the West Indies. He died at San Diego, Calif., March 12, 1944.

TOWNSEND, HARRY E. (*Chapter 10*) born at Wyoming, Ill., March 10, 1879. He studied at the Art Institute of Chicago and was a pupil of Howard Pyle. He was an official artist with the A.E.F. in World War I.

TRUMBULL, JOHN (*Chapter 2*) born at Lebanon, Conn., June 6, 1756. The son of Jonathan Trumbull, who served as Connecticut's governor from 1769 to 1783 and was the original of "Brother Jonathan," Trumbull early decided on a career in art. Soon after his graduation from Harvard in 1773 as the youngest member of his class, the outbreak of war interrupted his art studies and he enlisted as a private despite his uneasiness about the prevalent ideas of equality. His sketches of the works around Boston soon brought him appointment as an aide to Washington and later as deputy adjutant general to Gates. In 1777 he resigned his commission and traveled to London to study under Benjamin West. Trumbull spent some months in prison after being arrested in retaliation for the execution of John André, whose rank had been the same as Trumbull's. He was released and resumed his studies under West, later going to the Continent for further work. From 1794 to 1796 he was engaged in diplomatic work abroad, first as secretary to John Jay during the negotiations leading to Jay's Treaty and afterward as a commissioner to see to the working of the treaty. In 1804 he established himself as a portrait painter in New York and he served from 1816 to 1825 as president of the American Academy of Fine Arts. He died in New York November 10, 1843.

WALKE, HENRY N. (*Chapters 6 and 7*) born Dec. 24, 1808. As a lieutenant, he commanded a bomb-brig during the Mexican War, and was promoted to captain for his services. During the years that elapsed before the outbreak of the Civil War, he served in many capacities in the Navy. In 1861 he received a wartime commission as rear admiral and was placed in command of the ironclad *Carondelet* on the Mississippi. In the famous battle of Island No. 10 and at Memphis and Vicksburg, Walke covered himself with glory. In 1863 he was given command of the *Sacramento* and spent the remainder of the war chasing Confederate raiders. In 1870 he received a regular appointment as rear admiral. He died March 8, 1896.

WALKER, JAMES (*Chapter 6*) born in England, 1811. With his parents, he emigrated from England when a boy and was given his first training in New York City. His travels took him to New Orleans and later to Mexico City, where he was living when the Mexican War began. Despite an order expelling all Americans, he remained in the city for six weeks, finally escaping to the American lines at Matamoros. He became an interpreter at Army headquarters, his principal duty the interrogation of prisoners. He accompanied the troops through the campaign right up to the taking of Mexico City. After the war he returned to New York, where, after a trip to South America, he settled and established a studio. His paintings of the Mexican War, especially his "Battle of Chapultepec," brought him a number of commissions after the Civil War. Soon after the war ended he moved to Watsonville, California, where he died September 10, 1889.

WAUD, ALFRED R. (*Chapter 7*) born in London, October 2, 1828. He came to the United States in 1858 and worked as a magazine illustrator. His important Civil War drawings were made for *Harper's Weekly*; he is said to have covered every important campaign during the war. After the war Waud traveled on the Western frontier with charting and surveying expeditions. He died at Marietta, Ga., 1886.

WEIR, ROBERT WALTER (*Chapter 5*) born at New Rochelle, N. Y., June 18, 1803. He was elected to the National Academy in 1829. In 1834 he was appointed professor of drawing at West Point, a position he held until his resignation in 1879, when advancing years caused him to resign. He died at New York May 1, 1889.

WHISTLER, JAMES ABBOTT MCNEILL (*Chapter 7*) born at Lowell, Mass., July 10, 1834. He attended West Point from 1851 to 1853, but failed to keep up with his studies and was forced to leave. He studied art in London and Paris and in 1859 settled at London. Whistler is most famous for his etchings, but his oil paintings, water colors, lithographs, and pastels are notable for his understanding of the medium in which he worked. His sharp tongue and eccentricities often made him a storm center; his libel suit against John Ruskin, in which he was awarded one farthing's damages by the court after a long trial, is but one of the many incidents in a colorful career. He died at London July 17, 1903.

About the Author

ROY MEREDITH is an expert in presenting facts visually. Long experience in motion pictures (he is a member of the Society of Motion Picture Engineers) and television (in which he was a pioneer producer and is credited with many "firsts") have given him a "feel" for the picture that says more than words can possibly say. To this must be added his stature as a historian, notably of the Civil War period.

Mr. Meredith was born in New York and attended schools in New York City, among them the Juilliard School of Musical Art. With the coming of World War II, he left the National Broadcasting Company's television division to become camera department supervisor for the Fifth Air Force's combat film detachment, from 1941 to 1945. After the war he returned to television and to writing; two of his books, *Mr. Lincoln's Camera Man: Mathew B. Brady* and *Mr. Lincoln's Contemporaries,* have been best sellers. He is married and has one son.